MOSAICOS

MOSAICOS

Spanish as a World Language

Matilde Olivella de Castells
Emerita, California State University, Los Angeles

Elizabeth Guzmán
College of Saint Benedict, St. John's University

Paloma Lapuerta
Central Connecticut State University

Carmen García
Arizona State University

BRIEF EDITION

PEARSON
Prentice
Hall

Upper Saddle River, NJ 07458

Library of Congress Cataloging-in-Publication Data

Mosaicos : Spanish as a world language / Matilde Olivella de Castells . . . [et al.].— 4th ed.
    p. cm.
    Includes bibliographical references and index.
    ISBN 0-13-192324-2 (student ed. : alk. paper) — ISBN 0-13-154420-9
    (brief ed. : alk. paper) — ISBN 0-13-192325-0 (annotated instructor's ed. : alk. paper)
    1. Spanish language—Textbooks for foreign speakers—English. I.
Castells, Matilde Olivella de.

PC4129.E5M69 2005
468.2'421—dc22

2005002713

Executive Editor: *Bob Hemmer*
Sr. Director of Market Development: *Kristine Suárez*
Director of Editorial Development: *Julia Caballero*
Production Supervision: *Amy Rose of Interactive Composition Corporation*
Project Manager: *Claudia Dukeshire*
Asst. Director of Production: *Mary Rottino*
Supplements Editor: *Meriel Martínez Moctezuma*
Media Editor: *Samantha Alducin*
Media Production Manager: *Roberto Fernández*
Prepress and Manufacturing Buyer: *Brian Mackey*
Prepress and Manufacturing Assistant Manager: *Mary Ann Gloriande*
Interior Design: *Andrew Ogus*
Cover Design: *Ximena Tamvakopoulos*
Line Art Coordinator: *Maria Piper*

Illustrator: *Mari Isabel Rodriguez Martin*
Director, Image Resource Center: *Melinda Reo*
Manager, Rights and Permissions IRC: *Zina Arabia*
Manager, Visual Research: *Beth Boyd Brenzel*
Manager, Cover Visual Research & Permissions: *Karen Sanatar*
Image Permissions Coordinator: *Debbie Hewitson*
Photo Researcher: *Elaine Soares*
Cover image: Antonio Gaudi y Cornet. Mosaics in Park Guell, Barcelona, Spain. Date created: 1900-1914. Photographer: *Charles Lenars*
Sr. Marketing Manager: Jacquelyn Zautner
Marketing Assistant: *William J. Bliss*
Publisher: *Phil Miller*

This book was set in Sabon by *Interactive Composition Corporation* and was printed and bound by *Courier Kendallville*. The cover was printed by *Coral Graphics*.

Student Text, Regular Edition: ISBN 0-13-192324-2
Student Text, Brief Edition: ISBN 0-13-154420-9
Annotated Instructor's Edition: ISBN 0-13-192325-0

Pearson Education LTD., *London*
Pearson Education Australia PTY, Limited, *Sydney*
Pearson Education Singapore, Pte. Ltd.
Pearson Education North Asia Ltd., *Hong Kong*
Pearson Education Canada, Ltd., *Toronto*

Pearson Educación de México, S.A. de C.V.
Pearson Education–Japan, *Tokyo*
Pearson Education Malaysia, Pte. Ltd.
Pearson Education, Upper Saddle River, *New Jersey*

BRIEF CONTENTS

LECCIÓN	OBJETIVOS COMUNICATIVOS	A PRIMERA VISTA

LECCIÓN	OBJETIVOS COMUNICATIVOS	A PRIMERA VISTA
3 **Las actividades y los planes 92** 	Asking about and discussing leisure activities Communicating by phone Ordering food in a restaurant Making suggestions and future plans Accepting and rejecting invitations Using numbers 100 and above	Diversiones populares 94 La comida 97
4 **La familia 128** 	Identifying and describing family members Describing routine activities Expressing preferences, desires, and feelings Asking and giving permission Expressing when, where, or how an action is done Expressing how long events and states have been going on	Las familias 130 ¿Qué hacen los parientes? 133
5 **La casa y los muebles 164** 	Asking about and describing housing and household items Discussing daily activities in the home Asking about and discussing daily schedules Expressing ongoing actions Describing physical and emotional states Expressing obligation	En casa 166 Las tareas domésticas 169

EXPLICACIÓN Y EXPANSIÓN	MOSAICOS	ENFOQUE CULTURAL

About the Mosaicos Program

With each new edition, more and more instructors across North American are discovering that *Mosaicos* offers a distinct and better alternative for their elementary Spanish classes. Why? **Because Mosaicos enables instructors to emphasize communication while taking into account the realities of the classroom!** In most classrooms, the goal is communication, but the realities are . . . that students are taking the course because of a language requirement . . . . that students come to class with questions about grammar . . . . that students feel anxious about communicating in a second language . . . and that students need help developing their reading, writing, and listening skills. With Mosaicos' commonsense communicative approach, the beginning classroom becomes a setting for true communication and cultural exchange. *Mosaicos* combines the best elements of language instruction in a highly interactive approach. An emphasis on frequently used vocabulary, practical applications of grammar, illustrated language contexts, and engaging activities to help successfully develop good communication skills.

    Mosaicos is built on a foundation of interaction, communication, and culture. Its functional grammatical syllabus provides an understanding of the language in a clear, concise format. Structures are presented as a means to effective communication and valuable class time can be spent interacting as well as developing and improving language skills in Spanish.

Highlights of the Program

The fourth edition of Mosaicos continues the successful tradition of the first three editions, retaining and enhancing the core features, and integrating many new and exciting features.

Contextualized Vocabulary

The *Mosaicos* program features a lively and visual communicative format for presenting and practicing new language. Abundant activities in the *A primera vista* section of each chapter foster use of newly-acquired and previously-learned words and expressions in a variety of contexts. These contexts provide a natural environment for learning and practicing new vocabulary, as well as for recycling previously-taught language and previewing new structures.

WHAT'S NEW! Active vocabulary words are now highlighted in boldface type to help students quickly identify active vocabulary within each thematic unit and negotiate the meaning of the word as it is presented in the context of words they already know.

WHAT'S NEW! Recordings of the dialogues and language samples in *A primera vista* are now included in the *Mosaicos* audio program. The recordings give students opportunity to hear vocabulary pronounced in context, as well as giving them exposure to a variety of native speakers.

WHAT'S NEW! *En directo* boxes throughout the chapter introduce colloquial expressions and ideas and encourage students to use them in communicative activities such as Situaciones, A conversar, and others.

Integrated Grammar

Mosaicos presents grammar as a means to communicate effectively. The clear and concise bulleted explanations are easy to understand and are designed to be studied at home, yet their integration into the text enables students to use them for quick reference as they practice communication in class.

The carefully sequenced, communicative activities that practice the grammar in the *Explicación y expansión* section of each chapter have been a hallmark feature of *Mosaicos* since the first edition. They develop the ability to use linguistic structures for direct communicative purposes.

WHAT'S NEW! The first activity in each activity sequence in *A primera vista* and *Explicación y expansión* is now consistently an input-oriented comprehension check requiring minimal output from the student. This helps students recognize new forms and meanings based on language input before progressing to activities requiring guided output, then open-ended communication.

WHAT'S NEW! The open-ended *Situaciones* activities that culminate the activity sequence for each grammar point have been thoroughly revised to focus more on real-life situations. Direction lines for these activities are now consistently in English.

The grammatical scope and sequence in *Mosaicos* has always been dictated by the perceived communicative needs of beginning students. Based on reviewer suggestions we have retained the third edition scope and sequence of grammatical topics in *Mosaicos, Fourth Edition,* with one exception.

WHAT'S NEW! The indirect commands and the equivalents of English *let's* have been moved from chapters 10 and 11, respectively, to the *Expansión gramatical* section at the back of the text. Many instructors no longer consider these structures necessary to the elementary year language acquisition process, and we have responded accordingly. However, these structures, as well as others in the *Expansión gramatical* section, use the same format as the grammatical material throughout *Mosaicos* and may easily be incorporated, if desired.

Integrated Culture

The fourth edition of *Mosaicos* continues with the successful integration of culture and language of the third edition. Each chapter focuses on a country or region and numerous examples from that country or region are used consistently throughout the chapter in language samples, photos, maps, and realia. Related cultural content is interwoven throughout the text in activities and readings.

Mosaicos also includes a section called *Enfoque cultural* in each chapter that provides practical knowledge of specific cultural topics of the Spanish-speaking world as well as an orientation to the countries that make up that world.

WHAT'S NEW! **Enfoque cultural** sections of each chapter are now less textual and more visual; they feature several large, colorful photographs and an attractive topographical map highlighting the country or countries that forms the focus of the chapter. This section whets students' appetites and creates interest in cultural features without turning itself into a serious reading activity.

WHAT'S NEW! **Notas,** a new section within the *Enfoque cultural,* features a song corresponding to the Hispanic country or region of the chapter, along with pre-, during-, and post-listening activities. *Notas* uses music to motivate student interest in Hispanic culture.

A four-skills synthesis

Following the *A primera vista* and *Expansión grammatical* sections is the 4-skills section called *Mosaicos*. This section provides the student with a unique opportunity to bring all the pieces of the chapter together: vocabulary, grammar, and culture. The fourth edition of *Mosaicos* retains the core elements of skill-building, skill-using and skill chaining for listening, speaking, reading, and writing and adds new features to enhance and extend the effectiveness of this section.

WHAT'S NEW! The *process approach* is applied to the acquisition of all four skills. Pre-, during, and post-activities for listening, speaking, reading, and writing are included in each chapter.

WHAT'S NEW! In the *Mosaicos* section of each chapter, explicit strategies are provided for listening, reading and writing. In addition to skill-building activities, "strategies" for speaking are addressed in new *En directo* boxes.

Listening. In *Escuchar* in the *Mosaicos* skills section, students listen for different purposes, for example: to make inferences, to distinguish between facts and opinion, identify the speaker, listen for specific details, etc. In many cases, students are asked to fill in charts, comment on, or otherwise process the information they hear after completing the specific listening task, integrating listening with productive skills.

(WHAT'S NEW!) New scripts, audio recordings, and accompanying activities have been created for practically all listening sections. Scripts now simulate authentic discourse. Their short conversations, announcements, etc. all relate to the topics and content of each chapter.

Speaking. Open-ended activities in every chapter provide opportunities for individuals, pairs and groups of students to gather, process and share information in Spanish, stimulating real communication in the classroom. Conversation activities in the *Conversar* section of each chapter encourage interaction on a personal level combining newly acquired structures and vocabulary in discussions of chapter topics.

Reading. Pre- and post-reading activities provide opportunities and strategies for developing reading skills. Reading selections include a greater number of authentic texts and reflect a variety of discourse types and styles ranging from journalistic to literary.

(WHAT'S NEW!) **Visual Advance organizers** have been added to the pre-reading activities in every chapter to help students activate their background knowledge and prepare them to comprehend the reading passage that follows.

(WHAT'S NEW!) The last three chapters of the full version *Mosaicos* now have **literary readings.** (Chapters 1-12 offer cultural readings.) Chapters 13-15 expose students to Hispanic literature and serve as a transition to Intermediate Spanish while continuing to develop their abilities to read literature in Spanish.

(WHAT'S NEW!) Many **new readings** have been selected to reflect greater diversity of topics and appeal to a broader range of students.

(WHAT'S NEW!) Readings in early chapters are now shorter and simpler, with length and difficulty of readings increasing consistently from chapter to chapter. This allows students to develop confidence gradually in their ability to read materials in the target language.

Writing. Carefully-crafted process writing activities conclude each *Mosaicos* section. Pre- and post-writing activities are a guide through critical steps in the writing process. Throughout, extensive annotations guide instructors to teach writing as a recursive—rather than linear—process.

(WHAT'S NEW!) Writing tasks have been simplified and revised to relate more directly to chapter theme. The writing task is now more realistic—assignments are realistic in both scope and content, ensuring that students can complete the task with confidence.

(WHAT'S NEW!) Sample texts have been included in the pre-writing activity of each chapter and function as input for the writing process. The sample texts also give students a model so that they have clear guidelines to successfully complete the task.

Other features of the fourth edition are:

(WHAT'S NEW!) New *En directo* boxes highlight formulaic expressions that will help students sound more "adult-like," and more spontaneous in their speech. The *En directo* boxes are found throughout the text and are placed alongside the activity in which students can put them to immediate use. Learning these expressions will help students carry out their interpersonal or presentational exchanges more effectively.

The range of the *Cultura* boxes has been expanded in the third edition and they now appear in each chapter to ensure students gain an understanding and appreciation of people and cultures while building linguistic skills.

Acentos boxes are placed strategically throughout *Mosaicos*. The stress and accent rules in Spanish are presented on an as-needed basis. A complete presentation of accents is located in Appendix 1.

Lengua boxes, which inform learners of socio-linguistic distinctions in the Spanish language, appear at strategic intervals throughout the fourth edition, just as they did in the third edition.

Extensive, practical teachers' annotations provide instructors with lively ideas and pertinent information to facilitate their task in getting the most out of the *Mosaicos* Program.

(WHAT'S NEW!) *Vínculos* are a new type of annotation. Located in the Annotated Instructor's Edition, the *Vínculos* correlate appropriate sections of supplementary materials with the activities in the Student Text.

Organization of the Text

The full version of *Mosaicos* consists of a preliminary chapter (*Bienvenidos*) and fifteen regular chapters.

(WHAT'S NEW!) A brief version of *Mosaicos* is now available for those instructors who wish to cover less material during the first year of instruction. The brief edition contains the preliminary chapter and chapters 1-12 of the full edition.

Through a variety of visual stimuli, the *Bienvenidos* chapter allows instructors to conduct classes in Spanish from the very first day. Each regular chapter maintains the following consistent structure:

A primera vista.   This opening section of each chapter provides a richly contextualized, cultural framework for learning and practicing new language. New material is presented within two or three thematic groupings, which make use of photos, illustrations, and authentic documents. Comprehensible input is provided through a wide variety of language samples (dialogs, brief narratives, brochures, comic strips, captions, etc.). Within each thematic grouping, activities provide opportunities to practice the new vocabulary and in some cases preview grammar points which are formally presented later in the chapter. The last activity in this section is a listening activity that recycles vocabulary in an authentic conversational framework while providing practice of global listening skills. Previously-taught material is consistently recycled and reinforced.

Explicación y expansión.   The *Explicación y expansión* sections consist of concise grammar explanations focused on usage and followed by immediate practice of each new structural item within a contextualized framework. The exercises and activities in this section develop students' abilities to use linguistic structures for direct communicative purposes. Contextualized and personalized, the exercises focus student attention on a variety of useful tasks and provide practice for communicating effectively in pairs or small groups in a variety of real-life situations. These activities reinforce both vocabulary introduced in the *A primera vista* section of the chapter and vocabulary presented in previous chapters.

Mosaicos.   Students get an opportunity to "bring all the pieces together" in this process-oriented, strategy-focused section. Skills and topics are interwoven at the end of each chapter into a series of skill-building and skill-chaining activities that bring together the chapter vocabulary, structures, and cultural content:

Escuchar develops students' ability to listen to and understand spoken Spanish in a variety of authentic contexts: brief exchanges and longer conversations between two or more speakers, telephone messages, radio broadcasts, literary texts, etc.

Conversar includes open-ended speaking activities based on naturally-occurring discourse situations and authentic written texts. Students learn to express and discuss their own needs and interests. This section provides many opportunities for personalized expression.

Leer teaches students how to become independent readers by introducing basic strategies for understanding the general meaning of a text as well as for extracting specific information from it. The activities guide students to develop their ability to read a variety of high-interest, authentic Spanish texts, from simple documents such as advertisements to the extended discourse of brochures, newspaper and magazine articles, letters, literary texts, etc.

Escribir provides step-by-step activities in which students learn to compose messages and memos, postcards and letters, journals, simple expository paragraphs and brief essays. Activities guide students through critical steps in the writing process, including: brainstorming (to develop ideas for topics); defining one's purpose, means of communication, tone, and reader; making an outline; revising; and conferencing and peer editing. Additionally, useful tips in **Leer** provide students with specific lexicon, structures, and points of syntax relevant to the writing task at hand.

Enfoque cultural. This lively and informative section focuses on contemporary cultural issues related to the chapter theme. Each section of the *Enfoque cultural* includes activities that encourage students to explore the cultural topics and compare and contrast them with their own.

Temas introduces students to a broad variety of topics ranging from distinctive and changing aspects of daily life, such as family, housing, shopping, and travel, to broader social, political, and economic issues in Hispanic countries. Pre- and post-activities accompany the short illustrated reading.

Vistas employs a graphic layout, combining photos, maps, and captions to capture students' interest and expose them to key cultural information.

 Fortunas, a storyline video, is now integrated into the student texts with pre-, during–, and post-activities included in the text.

 Notas exposes beginning students to the various rhythms and topics of Hispanic music.

The Complete Program

Mosaicos is a complete learning and teaching program that includes the following components.

For the student

Mosaicos: Spanish as a World language (0-13-192324-2)
The full Student edition consists of a preliminary chapter followed by Chapters 1-15.

Mosaicos: Spanish as a World Language (0-13-154420-9)
The brief Student text consists of a preliminary chapter followed by Chapters 1-12 (the same content as the full edition).

Student Activities Manual (0-13-192326-9)
The new Student Activities Manual includes both workbook and lab manual materials in a single convenient volume, with all materials for a given chapter grouped together, saving students money and simplifying navigation. The *Mosaicos* Workbook parallels the organization of the text and provides more reading comprehension activities, sentence building and completion exercises, fill-ins, realia and art-based activities as well as composition exercises. Each chapter of the *Mosaicos* Lab Manual contains activities based on recordings of native speakers in situations thematically related to the corresponding chapters in the text. The listening material for the Lab Manual, the student audio for the in-text listening activities, and recordings of all the text's active vocabulary is provided for free on the *Mosaicos* Companion Website™.

Answer Key to Accompany Student Activities Manual (0-13-196985-4)
A separate Answer Key to the *Mosaicos* SAM is available, giving instructors the option of providing their students with answers to check their homework. The Answer Key now includes answers to both Workbook and Lab Manual activities.

Supplementary Activities Book (0-13-193045-1)
The Supplementary Activities Book consists of a range of fun, engaging activities that complement the vocabulary and grammar themes of each chapter and offers instructors additional in-class activities that serve to energize and enrich students' classroom experience.

Audio CDs to Accompany Text (0-13-196984-6)
These CDs correspond to the in-text listening activities and include recordings of the end-of-chapter vocabulary.

Audio CDs to Accompany Student Activities Manual (0-13-154642-2)
These CDs correspond to the Lab Manual portion of the Student Activities Manual.

Student Video CD-ROM (0-13-196979-X)
The Student Video CD-ROM contains the entire *Fortunas* video as well as the *Entrevistas* interview segments together with interactive comprehension activities. The *Fortunas* video will be accompanied by new comprehension activities and increased pedagogical support. The video is displayed using the Divace® media player developed by Sanako—the only media player on the market that was designed specifically for the language learner.

For the instructor
Annotated Instructor's Edition (0-13-192325-0)
The Annotated Instructor's Edition now includes *Vínculos* boxes with cross-references to related material in other components of the *Mosaicos* program. This enables instructors to see at a glance what material is available for homework assignments or additional practice, as well which specific materials are available for instructor use. Marginal annotations in the Annotated Instructor's Edition include warm-up and expansion exercises and activities, teaching tips and additional cultural information. The annotations are specifically designed for novice teaching assistants and adjunct faculty teaching from *Mosaicos* for the first time or who may have limited course preparation time. Answers to discrete point activities and the tapescript for the in-text listening activities are also provided for the instructor's convenience.

Instructor's Resource Manual (0-13-196982-X)
The Instructor's Resource Manual now contains complete lesson plans for all chapters as well as helpful suggestions for foreign and new instructors. Additionally, there are new video activities for the *Fortunas* video, and video activities will also be provided for the new *Entrevistas* and cultural videos. The Instructor's Resource Manual is a comprehensive source that contains everything from information on the philosophy behind the textbook to a complete Testing Program, Video Manual, and full, integrated syllabi and lesson plans.

Testing Audio CD (0-13-154643-0)
These CDs correspond to the listening comprehension portions of the Testing Program.

Image Resource CD (0-13-196983-8)
All illustrations from the textbook are provided on the CD. Instructors can use the images to create their own activities, implement in testing, create unique transparencies, etc.

Spanish Picture File (0-13-931313-3)
A beautifully crafted photo file of 50 full-color photographs mounted on cardboard and indexed by theme also accompanies *Mosaicos*. These can be used in the classroom in order to provide practice using the target vocabulary while discussing lesson themes and culture.

Instructor's Music CD (0-13-193419-8)
The Instructor's Music CD contains recorded versions of the songs found in the *Notas* section of each chapter, giving instructors convenient access to music for classroom use. The songs on this CD represent a variety of musical styles from a range of Spanish-speaking countries.

***Fortunas* VHS Video Cassette** (0-13-196980-3)
Written and filmed specifically for *Mosaicos*, the *Fortunas* video is an ongoing drama that features four contestants competing to locate three fortunes within Mexico. The three fortunes correspond with the three cultural periods of Mexican history (Pre-colonial, Colonial and Contemporary). Clues highlight and teach students about these cultural periods while the contest atmosphere provides students with a dynamic, interesting environment in which to learn the target grammar and vocabulary. New video activities are included in the IRM that include pre-, during–, and post-viewing exercises designed for in-class or lab use.

Online resources
  🔑 **Mosaicos OneKey** is available in CourseCompass, WebCT, and Blackboard.

Companion Website™ *www.prenhall.com/mosaicos*
The *Mosaicos* Web site contains a wealth of practice and expansion exercises for students. Each chapter of the web site complements a chapter in the text and contains automatically graded exercises that practice and reinforce the vocabulary and grammar in each chapter. The section *Para investigar* includes link-based activities that take the student to a wealth of Spanish-language websites for linguistic and cultural discovery. In addition, the complete audio program to accompany the text and the Student Activities Manual is available for free, as well as an interactive soccer game and flashcard module.

National Standards

The National Standards in Foreign Language Education Project published *Standards for Foreign Language Learning: Preparing for the 21st Century* which identified five goal areas for programs of foreign language instruction: Communication, Cultures, Connections, Comparisons, and Communities. These goal areas inform the pedagogy of the fourth edition of *Mosaicos*.

Communication. Throughout the text, students engage in meaningful conversations, providing and obtaining information, expressing their opinions and feelings, and sharing their experiences. Students also listen to, read, and interpret language on a variety of topics. Through *informes* as part of many activities and in compositions in **Escribir,** students present information and ideas in both written and oral communication.

Cultures. *Cultura* boxes and the *Enfoque cultural* sections of each chapter give students an understanding of the relationship between culture and language throughout the Spanish-speaking world.

Connections. Realia, readings, and conversation activities throughout the text provide opportunities for making connections with other discipline areas. Students gain information and insight into the distinctive viewpoints of Spanish speakers and their cultures.

Comparisons. *Lengua* boxes often provide students with points of comparison between English and Spanish. *Para pensar* activities in the *Enfoque cultural* sections encourage students to reflect on aspects of daily life in their own culture before reading about and investigating similar aspects of daily life in Spanish-speaking countries.

Communities. The text encourages students to go beyond the classroom through Internet activities, and the *Mosaicos* Website provides abundant opportunities for exploration, personal enjoyment, and enrichment. Instructors are reminded to encourage students to explore and become a part of Spanish-speaking communities in their areas.

Acknowledgments

The fourth edition of *Mosaicos* is the result of a collaborative effort between ourselves, our publisher, and you, our colleagues. We are sincerely appreciative of all the comments and suggestions from first, second, and third edition users, and we look forward to continuing the dialog and having your input on this edition. We are especially indebted to the many members of the Spanish teaching community whose reviews and comments at various stages throughout the preparation of the first, second, third, and fourth editions have made *Mosaicos* the solid program that it is. We especially acknowledge and thank:

Shannon Álvarez, Monmouth College
Jorge Arbujas, Louisiana State University
Antonio Baena, Louisiana State University
Cora Bauza, Louisiana State University
Heather Beal, Louisiana State University
Betty Becker-Theye, University of Maine Hutchinson Center
Dr. Joan Cammarata, Manhattan College
Olga Casanova-Burgess, Baruch College City University of New York
José J. Colín, University of Oklahoma
Michelle Connolly, Community College of Rhode Island
David Cruz de Jesús, Baruch College/CUNY
Mark Del Mastro, The Citadel
Claudia Díaz, Texas Tech University

Carmen Eblen, Oxnard College

José Antonio Fábres, College of Saint Benedict/ St. John's University

Sara Fernández-Medina, Texas Tech University

Wayne Finke, Baruch College (CUNY)

Jill Gauthier, Miami University—Hamilton

Jim Gregory, Texas Tech University

Janis Hanson, University of WI—La Crosse

María Hernández, Louisiana State University

Kelly Holmquist, Idaho State University

Hildegart Hoquee, San Jacinto College Central

Casilde Isabelli, University of Nevada, Reno

Kyra Kietrys, Davidson College

Nancy Laguna-Luque, Louisiana State University

Miguel Lechuga, Germanna Community College

Armanda Lewis, Columbia University

Nuria López Ortega, Miami University

Magdalena Maíz-Pena, Davidson College

Paola Marin, Gustavus Adolphus College

Rosa-María Moreno, Cincinnati State Technical & Comm. College

Jeanne Mullaney, Community College of Rhode Island

William O'Donnell, Canisius College

Carimer Ortiz Cuevas, Columbia University

María Pérez, Iowa Western Community College

Silvia Peart, Texas Tech University

Michelle Petersen, Arizona State University

Silvia T. Pulido, Brevard Community College

M. Mercedes Rahilly, Lansing Community College

Marilyn Reit, Shasta Tehama Junior College

Maria Rippon, The Citadel

Patricia Romero, Columbia University

Raúl Rosales, Columbia University

Linda Stewart, Idaho State University

Julie Sykes, Arizona State University

Andrew Tabor, Louisiana State University

Helen Tarp, Idaho State University

Glenn Thompson, Texas Tech University

Janos Welsch, Louisiana State University

Angela Willis, Davidson College

Hilma-Nelly Zamora, Valparaiso University

Sally Zengaro, University of Alabama

We would like to thank Blanca and César Gómez Villegas, Ana María and Juan Jorge Sanz, Gloria Toriello de Herrera, Johanna Herrera, Miguel Ordóñez, Benjamín Guzmán, and Raúl E. Salas for their help in obtaining authentic materials, and their advice regarding elements of current Spanish usage in their respective countries; Ninon Larché for her English language advising and technical support.

We would also like to thank all the editorial, production, and marketing staff at Prentice Hall who have contributed to the *Mosaicos* program. The authors of *Mosaicos, Fourth Edition* are deeply grateful to Bob Hemmer, Executive Editor, for his insightful guidance, invaluable support, and tireless work, particularly considering the special circumstances under which the fourth edition of *Mosaicos* was written. Many thanks to Julia Caballero, Director of Editorial Development, for her organization and continued encouragement.

We are also grateful to Mercedes Roffe, Development Editor, and Sarah Ramsey, for their dedication and meticulous work on the manuscript; Mary Rottino, Assistant Director of Production, who supervised all phases of the book's production; Claudia Dukeshire, Production Editor, for her careful and resourceful attention to every detail; Ximena de la Piedra Tamvakopoulos for the beautiful cover design; Meriel Martínez Moctezuma, Supplements Editor, for her calm efficiency and good humor in managing the print and audio supplements; Samantha Alducin, Media Editor, for her creativity, dedication, and many hours of hard work on the exciting online materials and videos; Roberto Fernández, Media Production Manager, for his commitment to the success of the Web site and CD-ROM projects; Kristine Suárez, Senior Director of Market Development, for her keen observations and market knowledge; and Jacquelyn Zautner, Senior Marketing Manager, for her many excellent ideas for the marketing campaign.

We are also grateful for the work of our talented colleagues at other institutions who have contributed to the supplementary materials for *Mosaicos, Fourth Edition.* Thanks to Mónica Prieto (Florida International University), Silvia Sobral (Brown University), JoAnne Flanders, Rebecca Williams and María Luisa Torres (all of Coastal Carolina University), Michelle Petersen (Arizona State University), Lina Lee (University of New Hampshire), James Crapotta (Barnard College), and Nurial López-Ortega (Miami University).

The coauthors of *Mosaicos* would like to express their thanks and admiration to Matilde Castells for her strength, love of life, and disposition to bringing *Mosaicos, Fourth Edition*, to a successful completion.

MOSAICOS

LECCIÓN PRELIMINAR
BIENVENIDOS

Objetivos comunicativos

- Introducing oneself and others
- Greetings and good-byes
- Expressions of courtesy
- Spelling in Spanish
- Identifying people and classroom objects
- Locating people and objects
- Using numbers from 0–99
- Expressing dates
- Telling time
- Using classroom expressions

Contenido

Un primer paso

- Las presentaciones
- Los saludos
- Las despedidas
- Expresiones de cortesía
- El alfabeto
- Identificación y descripción de personas
- Cognados
- ¿Qué hay en el salón de clase?
- ¿Dónde está?
- Los números 0–99
- Los meses del año y los días de la semana
- La hora
- Expresiones útiles en la clase

Las presentaciones

AUDIO ANTONIO: **Me llamo** Antonio Mendoza.
Y tú, ¿cómo te llamas?
BENITO: Benito Sánchez.
ANTONIO: **Mucho gusto.**
BENITO: **Igualmente.**

PROFESOR: **¿Cómo se llama usted?**
ISABEL: Me llamo Isabel Mendoza.
PROFESOR: Mucho gusto.
ISABEL: **Encantada.**

LAURA: María, **mi amigo** José.
MARÍA: Mucho gusto.
JOSÉ: **Encantado.**

- Spanish has more than one word meaning *you*. Use **tú** when talking to someone on a first-name basis (close friend, relative, child). Use **usted** when talking to someone you address in a respectful or formal manner; for example, **doctor, doctora, profesor, profesora, señor, señora,** and so on. Finally, use it to address individuals you do not know well.

- Young people normally use **tú** when speaking to each other.

- **Mucho gusto** is used by both men and women when they are meeting someone for the first time. A man may also say **encantado,** and a woman, **encantada.**

- When responding to **mucho gusto,** you may use either **encantado/a** or **igualmente.**

¿Qué dice usted?

P-1 Presentaciones. Complete the following conversation with the appropriate expressions from the box on the right. Then move around the classroom, introducing yourself to several classmates and introducing classmates to each other.

ALICIA: Me llamo Alicia. Y tú, ¿cómo te llamas?

ISABEL: Isabel Pérez. _____.

ALICIA: _____.

ALICIA: Isabel, _____.

ISABEL: Mucho gusto.

PEDRO: _____.

> | Igualmente |
> | Mucho gusto |

> | Encantado |
> | mi amigo Pedro |

Los saludos

AUDIO

SEÑOR: **Buenos días, señorita** Mena.

SEÑORITA: Buenos días. **¿Cómo está usted, señor** Gómez?

SEÑOR: **Bien, gracias.** ¿Y usted?

SEÑORITA: **Muy** bien, gracias.

MARTA: **¡Hola,** Inés! **¿Qué tal? ¿Cómo estás?**

INÉS: **Regular,** ¿y tú?

MARTA: **Bastante** bien, gracias.

SEÑORA: **Buenas tardes,** Felipe. **¿Cómo estás?**

FELIPE: Bien, gracias. Y usted, ¿cómo está, **señora**?

SEÑORA: **Mal,** Felipe, mal.

FELIPE: **Lo siento.**

- Use **buenos días** until lunch time.

- Use **buenas tardes** from noon until nightfall. After nightfall, use **buenas noches** (*good evening, good night*).

- **¿Qué tal?** is a more informal greeting. It is normally used with **tú**, but it may also be used with **usted.**

- Use **está** with **usted** and **estás** with **tú**.

¿Qué dice usted?

P-2 Saludos. You work as a receptionist in a hotel. Which greeting (**buenos días, buenas tardes, buenas noches**) is appropriate at the following times?

a. 9:00 a.m   c. 4:00 p.m.   e. 1:00 p.m.
b. 11:00 p.m.   d. 8:00 a.m   f. 10:00 p.m.

Las despedidas

AUDIO

adiós	*good-bye*
hasta luego	*see you later*
hasta mañana	*see you tomorrow*
hasta pronto	*see you soon*

■ **Adiós** is generally used when you do not expect to see the other person for a while. It is also used as a greeting when people pass each other but have no time to stop and talk.

■ **Chao** (also spelled **chau**) is an informal way of saying good-bye. It is very popular in South America.

Expresiones de cortesía

AUDIO

con permiso	*pardon me, excuse me*
de nada	*you're welcome*
gracias	*thanks, thank you*
lo siento	*I'm sorry*
perdón	*pardon me, excuse me*
por favor	*please*

Con permiso and **perdón** may be used "before the fact," as when asking a person to allow you to go by or when trying to get someone's attention. Only **perdón** is used "after the fact," as when you have stepped on someone's foot or have interrupted a conversation.

¿Qué dice usted?

P-3 ¿Perdón o con permiso? Would you use **perdón** or **con permiso** in these situations?

a.   b.   c.

d.   e.

P-4 Expresiones de cortesía, y despedidas. Which expression(s) would you use in the following situations?

gracias	de nada	por favor
adiós	hasta luego	lo siento

1. Someone thanks you.
2. You say good-bye to a friend you will see later this evening.
3. You are asking a classmate for his/her notes.
4. You hear that your friend is sick.
5. You receive a present from a friend.
6. Your friend is leaving for a vacation in Spain.

P-5 Encuentros. You meet the following people on the street. Greet them, ask them how they are, and then say good-bye. Switch roles.

1. su (*your*) amigo Miguel
2. su profesor/a
3. su amiga Isabel
4. su doctor/a

Distinguishing Registers

AUDIO When you talk to different people, you use different registers. For example, when you talk to a professor, you most likely use more formal language than when you talk to your classmates or friends. In Spanish, one way of marking this difference is by using **tú** (informal) and **usted** (formal).

Now you will hear four brief conversations in which people greet each other. But before you listen, complete the following chart with the pronoun you think you would use.

WHEN TALKING TO YOUR . . .	TÚ	USTED
1. brother or sister		
2. doctor		
3. coach		

Saludos. As you listen to the four brief conversations, mark the appropriate column to indicate whether the greetings are formal (with **usted**) or informal (with **tú**). Do not worry if you do not understand every word.

FORMAL   INFORMAL

1. _____   _____
2. _____   _____
3. _____   _____
4. _____   _____

AUDIO ## El alfabeto

a	a	**o**	o
b	be	**p**	pe
c	ce	**q**	cu
d	de	**r**	ere, erre
e	e	**s**	ese
f	efe	**t**	te
g	ge	**u**	u
h	hache	**v**	ve, uve
i	i	**w**	doble ve,
j	jota		doble uve
k	ka		uve doble
l	ele	**x**	equis
m	eme	**y**	i griega, ye
n	ene	**z**	zeta
ñ	eñe		

- The Spanish alphabet includes **ñ**, a letter that does not exist in English. Its sound is similar to the pronunciation of *ni* and *ny* in the English words *onion* and *canyon*.

- The letters **k** and **w** appear mainly in words of foreign origin.

¿Qué dice usted?

P-6 ¿Cómo se escribe? Ask your classmate how to spell these Spanish last names.

MODELO:　Zamora
　　　　　E1: ¿Cómo se escribe Zamora?
　　　　　E2: Con z.

1. Celaya
2. Montalvo
3. Salas

4. Bolaños
5. Henares
6. Velázquez

P-7 Los nombres. Ask three of your classmates their names. Write down their names as they spell them.

MODELO:　E1: ¿Cómo te llamas?
　　　　　E2: Me llamo David Robinson.
　　　　　E1: ¿Cómo se escribe Robinson?
　　　　　E2: R-o-b-i-n-s-o-n

Identificación y descripción de personas

AUDIO　CARLOS: ¿Quién es ese chico?
　　　　SANDRA: Es Julio.
　　　　CARLOS: ¿Cómo es Julio?
　　　　SANDRA: Es romántico y sentimental.

　　　　　　LUIS: ¿Quién es esa chica?
　　　　QUIQUE: Es Carmen.
　　　　　　LUIS: ¿Cómo es Carmen?
　　　　QUIQUE: Es activa y muy seria.

SER (to be)			
yo	soy	I	am
tú	eres	you	are
usted	es	you	are
él, ella	es	he, she	is

- Use **ser** to describe what someone is like.

    Es Carmen. Ella **es** activa y muy seria.

- To make a sentence negative, place the word **no** before the appropriate form of **ser**. When answering a question with a negative statement, say *no* twice.

Ella es inteligente.	→	Ella **no** es inteligente.
¿Es rebelde?	→	**No,** no es rebelde.

Cognados

Cognates are words from two languages that have the same origin and are similar in form and meaning. Since English shares many words with Spanish, you will discover that you already recognize many Spanish words. Here are some cognates that are used to describe people.

The following cognates use the same form to describe a man or a woman.

arrogante	importante	optimista	popular
eficiente	independiente	paciente	responsable
elegante	inteligente	perfeccionista	tradicional
idealista	interesante	pesimista	valiente

The following cognates have two forms. The **-o** form is used to describe a man, and the **-a** form to describe a woman.

ambicioso/a	creativo/a	impulsivo/a	religioso/a
atlético/a	dinámico/a	introvertido/a	sincero/a
atractivo/a	extrovertido/a	moderno/a	tímido/a
cómico/a	generoso/a	pasivo/a	tranquilo/a

There are also some words that appear to be cognates but do not have the same meaning in both languages. These are called false cognates. **Lectura** (*reading*) and **éxito** (*success*) are examples of this kind. You will find some examples in future lessons.

¿Qué dice usted?

P-8 Conversación. Ask each other about your classmates. Describe them by using cognates from the lists above.

MODELO: E1: ¿Cómo es... ?
         E2: Es...

2 **P-9 ¿Cómo es mi compañero/a?** Choose from the cognates list on page 10 to ask the person next to you about his/her personality traits.

MODELO: E1: ¿Eres pesimista?
          E2: No, no soy pesimista. *o* Sí, soy (muy) pesimista.

Then find out what he/she is really like.

MODELO: E1: ¿Cómo eres (tú)?
          E2: Soy activo, optimista y creativo.

SITUACIÓN

You are walking through campus, and you run into a friend from your hometown. Your friend is walking with a person you do not know. As your friend is doing the introductions, your Spanish professor walks by. Your friend asks you who she/he is. Describe your professor to your friend and his/her companion, using at least three cognates.

¿Qué hay en el salón de clase?

¿Qué dice usted?

P-10 Identificación. With a partner, identify the items on this table.

P-11 Para la clase de español. Write down a list of the things you need for this class. Compare your list with that of your partner.

¿Dónde está?

To ask about the location of a person or an object, use **dónde + está.**

¿Dónde está la profesora?   Está en la clase.
¿Dónde está el libro?   Está sobre el escritorio.

¿Qué dice usted?

P-12 ¿Sí o no? Primera fase. Indicate whether each of the following statements is true or false, based on the relative position of people or objects in the drawing.

	Sí	No
1. El televisor está detrás de la profesora.	_____	_____
2. Juan está al lado de la profesora.	_____	_____
3. El libro está sobre el escritorio.	_____	_____
4. María está entre Mercedes y Juan.	_____	_____
5. Mercedes está enfrente de la ventana.	_____	_____
6. El cesto está debajo de un pupitre.	_____	_____

Segunda fase. Now complete the following sentences, based on the relative position of people or objects in the drawing.

1. La pizarra está _____ la profesora.
2. María está _____ la profesora.
3. Mercedes está _____ Juan y María.
4. Juan está _____ Mercedes
5. El cesto está _____ Juan.
6. El televisor está _____ la pizarra y la puerta.

P-13 La clase de español. Look at the seating chart below, and then follow the instructions.

María	Juan	Ester	Susana	Pedro
Carlos	Cristina	Ángeles	Alberto	Anita
Mercedes	Victoria	Roberto	Rocío	Pablo
		Profesor Gallegos		

1. Tell where Juan, Ángeles, Rocío, and Pedro are seated.
2. Ask questions about the location of other students.

P-14 ¿Dónde está? Take turns asking where several items in your classroom are. Answer by giving their position in relation to a person or another object.

MODELO: E1: ¿Dónde está el libro?
              E2: Está sobre el escritorio.

P-15 ¿Quién es? Based on what your partner says regarding the location of another student, guess who he/she is.

MODELO: E1: Está al lado de Juan. ¿Quién es?
              E2: Es María.

AUDIO **Listening with Visuals**

When you are talking with someone, you can understand what is being said by paying attention to the pictures or objects that the people point or refer to. Sometimes these objects are around you, but other times they are not. You have only a mental representation of them. For example, when a friend describes his/her Spanish classroom, an image of a classroom comes to your mind from your experience of being a student.

In Spanish, make a list of the people and objects you expect to see in a regular classroom.

_____

_____

_____

Now look at the drawing of the classroom on page 12. As you hear the different statements about the location of several people and objects, mark the appropriate column to indicate whether each of the statements is true (**cierto**) or false (**falso**).

	CIERTO	FALSO		CIERTO	FALSO
1.	____	____	4.	____	____
2.	____	____	5.	____	____
3.	____	____	6.	____	____

Los números 0–99

AUDIO

¿Cuál es tu dirección?

Calle Colón, número 10

¿Y cuál es tu teléfono?

234-19-05

0	cero	11	once	21	veintiuno
1	uno	12	doce	22	veintidós
2	dos	13	trece	30	treinta
3	tres	14	catorce	31	treinta y uno
4	cuatro	15	quince	40	cuarenta
5	cinco	16	dieciséis	50	cincuenta
6	seis	17	diecisiete	60	sesenta
7	siete	18	dieciocho	70	setenta
8	ocho	19	diecinueve	80	ochenta
9	nueve	20	veinte	90	noventa
10	diez				

- Numbers from sixteen through twenty-nine are usually written as one word. Note the spelling changes and the written accent on some forms.

    18: **dieciocho**   22: **veintidós**

- Beginning with thirty-one, numbers are written as three words.

    31: **treinta y uno**   45: **cuarenta y cinco**

- The number *one* has three forms in Spanish: **uno, un,** and **una.** Use **uno** when counting: **uno, dos, tres...** Use **un** or **una** before nouns: **un borrador, una mochila, veintiún libros, veintiuna mochilas.**

- Use **hay** for both *there is* and *there are.*

    Hay un libro sobre la mesa.   *There is a book on the table.*
    Hay dos libros sobre la mesa.   *There are two books on the table.*

¿Qué dice usted?

P-16 ¿Qué número es? Your instructor will read a number from each group. Circle the number.

    a. 8   4   3   5
    b. 12   9   16   6
    c. 37   59   41   26
    d. 54   38   76   95
    e. 83   62   72   49
    f. 47   14   91   56

P-17 Una lista. This is a list of items you might need for your new office. Choose five items and tell your partner (the acquisitions manager) how many of each you want. Exchange roles.

MODELO: 4–7 mesas: Necesito cuatro mesas.

a. 6–10 teléfonos
b. 8–12 escritorios
c. 14–18 sillas
d. 6–12 calculadoras
e. 10–20 cestos
f. 24–48 bolígrafos
g. 9–15 computadoras
h. 1–2 computadora(s) portátiles
i. 1–3 reloj(es)
j. ...

P-18 Problemas. Take turns in solving the following problems. Use **y** (+), **menos** (−), and **son** (=).

MODELO: 2 + 4 =   12 − 5 =
           dos y cuatro son seis   doce menos cinco son siete

a. 11 + 4 =   d. 20 − 6 =   g. 50 − 25 =
b. 8 + 2 =   e. 39 + 50 =   h. 26 + 40 =
c. 13 + 3 =   f. 80 − 1 =   i. 90 − 12 =

ACENTOS

You may have noticed that the word **tú** (meaning *you*) has an accent, and that the word **tu** (meaning *your*) does not. Beginning with *Lección 1,* you will learn and practice the rules for accentuation step by step in the *Pronunciación* section of the Activities Manual. Additional practice is also presented in the manual. In your text, boxes similar to this will help you focus your attention on when to use accents. You will find a complete set of the rules for accentuation in the appendix.

P-19 Los números de teléfono y las direcciones. Ask each other the addresses and phone numbers of some of these people. Use the chart below.

MODELO: Castellanos Rey, Carlos   Colón 62   654-6416
  E1: ¿Cuál es la dirección de Carlos Castellanos Rey?
  E2: Calle Colón, número 62.
  E1: ¿Cuál es su teléfono?
  E2: (El) 6-54-64-16

● Cárdenas Alfaro, Joaquín	General Páez 40	423-4837
● Cárdenas Villanueva, Sara	Avenida Bolívar 7	956-1709
● Castelar Torres, Adelaida	Paseo del Prado 85	218-3642
● Castellanos Rey, Carlos	Colón 62	654-6416
● Castelli Rivero, Victoria	Chamberí 3	615-7359
● Castillo Montoya, Rafael	Santa Cruz 73	956-3382

Los meses del año y los días de la semana

enero	*January*	mayo	*May*	septiembre	*September*
febrero	*February*	junio	*June*	octubre	*October*
marzo	*March*	julio	*July*	noviembre	*November*
abril	*April*	agosto	*August*	diciembre	*December*

Days of the week and months of the year are not generally capitalized in Spanish, but sometimes they are capitalized in advertisements and invitations.

■ Monday (**lunes**) is normally presented as the first day of the week.

■ To ask what day it is, use **¿Qué día es hoy?** Answer with **Hoy es...**

■ To ask about the date, use **¿Qué fecha es?** or **¿Cuál es la fecha?** Respond with **Es el (14) de (octubre).**

■ Express *on + a day of the week* as follows:

el lunes	*on Monday*
los lunes	*on Mondays*
el domingo	*on Sunday*
los domingos	*on Sundays*

■ Cardinal numbers are used with dates (e.g., **el dos, el tres**) except for the first day of the month, which is **el primero**. In Spain the first day is also referred to as **el uno**.

¿Qué dice usted?

P-20 ¿Qué día de la semana es? Take turns asking and answering the following questions. Use the calendar on page 16.

1. ¿Qué día de la semana es el 2?
2. ¿Qué día de la semana es el 5?
3. ¿Qué día de la semana es el 22?
4. ¿Qué día de la semana es el 18?
5. ¿Qué día de la semana es el 10?
6. ¿Qué día de la semana es el 13?
7. ¿Qué día de la semana es el 28?
8. ¿Qué día de la semana es el... ?

P-21 Preguntas. Take turns asking and answering these questions.

1. ¿Qué día es hoy?
2. Hoy es... ¿Qué día es mañana?
3. Hoy es el... de... ¿Qué fecha es mañana?
4. ¿Hay clase de español los domingos? ¿Y los sábados?
5. ¿Qué días hay clase de español?

P-22 Fechas importantes. Tell each other the dates on which these events take place.

MODELO: la reunión de estudiantes (10/9)
          E1: ¿Cuándo es la reunión de estudiantes?
          E2: (Es) el 10 de septiembre.

1. el concierto de Cristina Aguilera (12/11)
2. el aniversario de Carlos y María (14/4)
3. el banquete (18/3)
4. la graduación (22/5)
5. la fiesta de bienvenida (24/8)

P-23 El cumpleaños. Find out when your classmates' birthdays are. Write your classmates' names and birthdays in the appropriate space in the chart.

MODELO: E1: ¿Cuándo es tu cumpleaños?
          E2: (Es) el 3 de mayo.

CUMPLEAÑOS			
enero	febrero	marzo	abril
mayo	junio	julio	agosto
septiembre	octubre	noviembre	diciembre

La hora

■ Use **¿Qué hora es?** to inquire about the hour. To tell time, use **es la...** from one o'clock to one thirty and **son las...** with the other hours.

Es la una.	*It is one o'clock.*
Son las tres.	*It is three o'clock.*

■ To express the quarter hour, use **y cuarto** or **y quince**. To express the half hour, use **y media** or **y treinta**.

Son las dos **y cuarto**.	*It is two fifteen.*
Son las dos **y quince**.	
Es la una **y media**.	*It is one thirty.*
Es la una **y treinta**.	

■ To express time after the half hour, subtract minutes from the next hour, using **menos**.

Son las cuatro **menos** diez.	*It is ten to four.*

■ Add **en punto** for the exact time and **más o menos** for approximate time.

Es la una **en punto**.	*It is one o'clock sharp.*
Son las cinco menos cuarto, **más o menos**.	*It is about quarter to five.*

■ For *a.m.* and *p.m.*, use the following:

de la mañana	(from midnight to noon)
de la tarde	(from noon to nightfall)
de la noche	(from nightfall to midnight)

¿Qué dice usted?

P-24 ¿Qué hora es en...? What time is it in the following cities?

Los Ángeles, A.M.

México, P.M.

San Juan, P.M.

Buenos Aires, P.M.

Madrid, P.M.

② **P-25 El horario de María.** Take turns to ask and answer questions about María's schedule.

MODELO: E1: ¿A qué hora es la clase de español?
          E2: Es a las nueve.

LUNES	
9:00	clase de español
10:15	receso
10:30	clase de matemáticas
11:45	laboratorio
1:00	almuerzo
2:00	clase de física
5:00	partido de tenis

LENGUA

To ask the hour at which an event takes place or something happens, use **¿A qué hora es...?** To answer, use **A la(s)...**
¿A qué hora es la clase?
At what time is (the) class?
(Es) **a las** nueve y media.
It is at 9:30.

② **P-26 Mi horario.** Write down your Monday schedule, omitting the time each class meets. Exchange schedules with your partner, and find out what time each of his/her classes starts.

Expresiones útiles en la clase

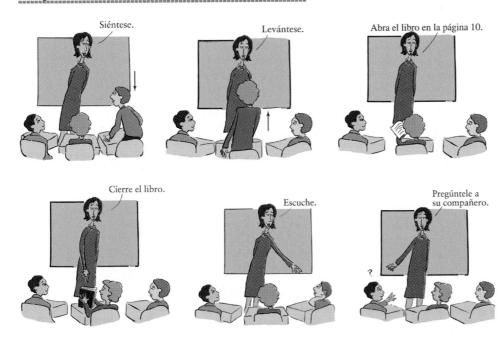

Siéntese.

Levántese.

Abra el libro en la página 10.

Cierre el libro.

Escuche.

Pregúntele a su compañero.

Vaya a la pizarra.

La tarea, por favor.

Conteste.

Repita.

Levante la mano.

Lea.

Escriba.

- When asking two or more people to do something, the verb form ends in -n: vaya → vayan, conteste → contesten, repita → repitan.

- Although you may not have to use all these expressions, you should be able to recognize them and respond accordingly. Other expressions that you may hear or say in the classroom include the following:

Más alto, por favor.	*Louder, please.*
Otra vez.	*Again.*
¿Comprende(n)?	*Do you understand?*
¿Tiene(n) alguna pregunta?	*Do you have any questions?*
No comprendo.	*I do not understand.*
No sé.	*I do not know.*
Tengo una pregunta.	*I have a question.*
Más despacio, por favor.	*More slowly, please.*
¿En qué página?	*On what page?*
¿Cómo se dice... en español?	*How do you say . . . in Spanish?*
¿Cómo se escribe...?	*How do you spell . . . ?*
Presente.	*Here (present).*

VOCABULARIO*

Presentaciones

¿Cómo se llama usted?	*What's your name?* (formal)
¿Cómo te llamas?	*What's your name?* (familiar)
encantado/a	*delighted*
igualmente	*likewise*
me llamo...	*my name is . . .*
mucho gusto	*pleased/nice to meet you*

En el salón de clase

el bolígrafo	*ballpoint pen*
el borrador	*eraser*
la calculadora	*calculator*
el cesto	*wastepaper basket*
la computadora	*computer*
el cuaderno	*notebook*
el escritorio	*desk*
la grabadora	*tape recorder, cassette player*
el lápiz	*pencil*
el libro	*book*
la mesa	*table*
la mochila	*backpack*
la pizarra	*chalkboard*
la puerta	*door*
el pupitre	*student's desk*
el reloj	*clock*
la silla	*chair*
el televisor	*television set*
la tiza	*chalk*
la ventana	*window*
la videocasetera	*VCR*

La dirección

la calle	*street*
el número	*number*

Personas*

el/la amigo/a	*friend*
la chica	*girl*
el chico	*boy*
él	*he*
ella	*she*
el/la estudiante	*student*
el/la profesor/a	*professor*
señor (Sr.)	*Mr.*
señora (Sra.)	*Mrs.*
señorita (Srta.)	*Miss*
tú	*you* (familiar)
usted	*you* (formal)
yo	*I*

Posición

al lado (de)	*next to*
debajo (de)	*under*
detrás (de)	*behind*
enfrente (de)	*in front of*
entre	*between, among*
sobre	*on, above*

Tiempo, hora y fecha**

el año	*year*
cuarto	*quarter*
el día	*day*
en punto	*sharp*
la fecha	*date*
la hora	*hour, time*
hoy	*today*
mañana	*tomorrow*
la mañana	*morning*
media	*half*
menos	*minus, to* (for telling time)
el mes	*month*
la semana	*week*

Verbos

eres	*you are* (familiar)
es	*you are* (formal), *he/she is*
está	*he/she is, you are* (formal)
estás	*you are* (familiar)
hay	*there is, there are*
son	*they, you* (plural) *are*
soy	*I am*

Palabras útiles

a	*at, to*
en	*in*
ese/a	*that* (adjective)
mi	*my*
sí	*yes*
tu	*your* (familiar)
un/una	*a, an*
y	*and*

Expresiones útiles

¿Cómo es?	*What is he/she/it like?*
¿Dónde está...?	*Where is . . . ?*
más o menos	*more or less*
¿Quién es...?	*Who is . . . ?*

*See page 10 for cognates.
**See pages 14 and 16 for numbers, days of the week, and months of the year.

LOS ESTUDIANTES Y LA UNIVERSIDAD

Objetivos comunicativos

- Asking for and providing information
- Expressing needs
- Asking for prices

- Talking about daily activities
- Asking about and expressing location

Contenido

A primera vista

- Los estudiantes y los cursos
- La vida estudiantil

- En la universidad

Explicación y expansión

- Subject pronouns
- Present tense of regular -*ar* verbs
- Articles and nouns: Gender and number

- Present tense of the verb *estar*
- Question words
- Algo Más: Some regular -*er* and -*ir* verbs

Mosaicos

- Escuchar: Listening for the gist
- Conversar: Summarizing the results of a poll

- Leer: Identifying the format and content of a text to guess meaning; identifying cognates to improve reading comprehension
- Escribir: Identifying basic aspects of writing; writing an email to a friend to talk about classes

Enfoque cultural

- Temas: Las universidades en España y en Hispanoamérica
- Vistas: España
  Para investigar en Internet

- Fortunas: Episodio 1
- Notas: Cuéntame alegrías, *Tachú*

Vocabulario

AUDIO *Los estudiantes y los cursos*

Me llamo Carmen Granados. **Estudio sociología** en la **Facultad** de **Humanidades** de la **Universidad** de Salamanca. **Llego** a la universidad a las ocho y media. Mis cursos este semestre son **economía, ciencias políticas, psicología, antropología** y **estadística.** La clase de **economía** es mi **favorita.** La clase de antropología es **difícil,** pero el profesor es muy bueno. La clase de psicología es **fácil** y muy interesante. Por las tardes **trabajo** en una **oficina.**

Este chico es mi amigo. Se llama David Thomas. Es **norteamericano** y estudia español en mi universidad. **También** estudia **literatura, historia** y **geografía.** David es un chico muy responsable y **estudioso.** Generalmente llega a la universidad a las diez. Habla español y **practica todos los días** con sus **compañeros** de clase, sus profesores y sus amigos de la universidad. Por la tarde, estudia con uno de sus compañeros y **escucha** música o programas en español.

¿Qué dice usted?

2 **1-1 ¿Qué sabe usted de Carmen?** First circle all of the classes above that Carmen is taking. Then match the courses in the right column with the information on the left.

1. _____ nombre completo
2. _____ universidad
3. _____ clase favorita
4. _____ clase difícil
5. _____ clase fácil

a. antropología
b. psicología
c. Salamanca
d. economía
e. Carmen Granados

1-2 ¿Y David? Indicate whether each statement is true (**Cierto**) or false (**Falso**).

1. David es norteamericano.
2. David habla español.
3. David estudia literatura, historia y geografía.
4. David llega a la universidad a las nueve.
5. David practica español con sus amigos.
6. David escucha música por la mañana.

AUDIO **David y Carmen hablan de sus clases**

DAVID: Hola, Carmen. ¿Cómo estás?

CARMEN: Hola, David. **¿Cómo te va?**

DAVID: Bueno... bastante bien, **pero** mi clase de historia es muy difícil.

CARMEN: ¿Quién es tu profesor?

DAVID: Se llama Pedro Hernández. Es inteligente, pero la clase es **aburrida.**

CARMEN: ¡Vaya! Lo siento. ¿Estudias bastante?

DAVID: Estudio mucho, pero **saco malas notas.**

CARMEN: **¡Qué lástima!** Mis cinco clases son excelentes. Y tú, **¿cuántas clases tienes?**

DAVID: **Tengo sólo** cuatro.

CARMEN: ¡Uy! Son las once. Tengo un **examen** de economía **ahora.** Hasta luego.

DAVID: Hasta pronto. **¡Buena suerte!**

¿Qué dice usted?

1-3 ¿En qué clase... ? Match the words on the left with the appropriate class on the right.

1. _____ casete y CD
2. _____ números
3. _____ mapa digital
4. _____ animales
5. _____ Freud
6. _____ Napoleón

a. geografía
b. biología
c. español
d. historia
e. matemáticas
f. psicología

Ⓖ **1-4 Mis clases.** Make a list of your classes. Next to each one, indicate the days and time it meets. Also say whether the class is easy, difficult, interesting or boring. You will find some subjects in the box below. Compare your list with those of your classmates.

ciencias	comunicaciones	historia contemporánea
bioquímica	geografía	historia del arte
física	cálculo	genética
artes plásticas	estadística	seminario
contabilidad	astronomía	filosofía

CLASE	DÍAS	HORA	¿CÓMO ES?

A INVESTIGAR

Look up Universidad de Salamanca on the Internet (www.usal.es).

1. Go to **Centros y Departamentos** and write down six of the departments listed.

2. Find the name of one professor in each department. Share your findings with those of other classmates.

3. Did you notice any differences between the last names used in the United States and those from Spain?

1-5 Las clases de mis compañeros/as. Primera fase. Use the following questions to interview one of your classmates. Take notes. Then switch roles.

1. ¿Qué estudias este semestre?
2. ¿Cuántas clases tienes?
3. ¿Cuál es tu clase favorita?
4. Tu clase de español, ¿es fácil, difícil, interesante o aburrida?
5. ¿Trabajas con computadoras/ordenadores?
6. ¿Escuchas casetes en el laboratorio?
7. ¿Sacas buenas notas?
8. ¿Tienes muchos exámenes?

G **Segunda fase.** First, introduce your new friend to another classmate and give him/her one piece of information about your new friend that you find interesting. Your classmate will ask your friend questions about his/her classes.

MODELO: Él es Pedro, estudia ciencias políticas y tiene cuatro clases este semestre.

La vida estudiantil

AUDIO **En la biblioteca**

Unos **alumnos** estudian en la **biblioteca.** No **conversan porque** está prohibido. Estudian, **toman apuntes** y trabajan en sus **tareas. A veces buscan** palabras en el **diccionario.**

¿Y qué hacen los fines de semana?

Los estudiantes **toman algo** en un **café**.

Miran televisión en **casa**.

Bailan en una **discoteca** con amigos.

Caminan en la **playa**.

Montan en bicicleta.

¿Qué dice usted?

1-6 Para escoger. Look at the illustrations above and on the previous page. Then choose the word or phrase that makes sense.

1. Los estudiantes _____ en la biblioteca.
   a. toman café
   b. estudian
   c. hablan

2. Buscan palabras en _____.
   a. el reloj
   b. el diccionario
   c. el laboratorio

3. Miran televisión en _____.
   a. la biblioteca
   b. la playa
   c. casa

4. Montan en bicicleta _____.
   a. los fines de semana
   b. en el café
   c. los jueves

AUDIO **En la librería**

ESTUDIANTE:	**Necesito comprar** un diccionario **para** mi clase de español.
DEPENDIENTE:	¿**Grande** o **pequeño**?
ESTUDIANTE:	Grande y todo en español.
DEPENDIENTE:	**Este** diccionario es muy bueno.
ESTUDIANTE:	¿**Cuánto cuesta**?
DEPENDIENTE:	Cuarenta y ocho euros.

¿Qué dice usted?

1-7 Para completar. Complete the following statements, based on the previous conversation.

1. El estudiante necesita _____.
2. Es un diccionario _____.
3. Es para su clase de _____.
4. El diccionario cuesta _____.

1-8 ¿Cuánto cuesta? You are at the university bookstore. Ask the salesclerk how much each of the following items costs.

MODELO:

ESTUDIANTE:
¿Cuánto cuesta la grabadora?

DEPENDIENTE/A:
Cuesta cincuenta euros.

En la universidad

Facultad de Arquitectura

Facultad de Medicina

Gimnasio

Cafetería

Plaza

Librería

Facultad de Informática

Facultad de Humanidades

Facultad de Ciencias

Biblioteca

¿Qué dice usted?

1-9 Entrevista (*Interview*). Ask a classmate where and when he/she does each of the following activities.

MODELO: practicar frisbi
          E1: ¿Dónde practicas frisbi?
          E2: Practico frisbi en la plaza.
          E1: ¿Cuándo practicas?
          E2: Practico por las tardes.

ACTIVIDAD	DÓNDE	CUÁNDO
1. estudiar para un examen difícil		
2. mirar televisión		
3. tomar café/chocolate		
4. bailar salsa		
5. escuchar música		
6. comprar un diccionario		

1-10 En la universidad. Tell your partner about your classes. Take turns completing the following sentences.

1. Llego a la universidad a la(s)...
2. Mi clase favorita es...
3. El/La profesor/a se llama...
4. La clase es muy...
5. Practico español en...
6. Para mi clase de composición en español, necesito...

1-11 Busco una escuela. With a classmate, read the following brochure and look for the following specific information: name of the school, classes offered, school's address, and school's telephone number.

Centro Audiovisual

MÉTODOS AUDIOVISUALES

Informática

Inglés

Contabilidad

Prácticas de oficina

Cálculo comercial

Secretariado y administración

Miguel Moya, 16 - 2.°, Valencia
Telf. (96) 329 58 48
(Junto al Mercado)

AUDIO **1-12 ¿Qué hacen estas personas?** You will hear three people talking about their activities during the week and on weekends, but before you listen, complete the following chart with your own activities.

MIS ACTIVIDADES DE TODOS LOS DÍAS	MIS ACTIVIDADES DEL FIN DE SEMANA
1.	
2.	
3.	

Now pay attention to the general idea of what is said. As you hear the three people talking about their activities, determine what they are talking about. Then write the number of the description next to the appropriate heading.

_____ los estudios
_____ el tiempo libre
_____ el trabajo

EXPLICACIÓN Y EXPANSIÓN

1. Subject pronouns

SINGULAR		PLURAL	
yo	*I*	nosotros, nosotras	*we*
tú	*you*	vosotros, vosotras	*you* (familiar)
usted	*you* (formal)	ustedes	*you* (formal/familiar)
él	*he*	ellos	*they* (masculine)
ella	*she*	ellas	*they* (feminine)

- In Spain, the plural of **tú** is **vosotros** or **vosotras.** In other Spanish-speaking countries, the plural of both **tú** and **usted** is **ustedes.**

- Except for **ustedes**, the plural pronouns have masculine and feminine endings. Use **-as** for a group composed only of females; use **-os** for a mixed group or one composed only of males.

- Because the endings of Spanish verbs indicate the subject (the doer of the action), subject pronouns are generally used only for emphasis, clarification, or contrast.

¿Qué dice usted?

1-13 ¿Qué pronombre usa usted? Primera fase. You are talking *about* the people in the left column. Match the pronouns on the right with the people on the left.

1. _____ Alfredo y Juana   a. él
2. _____ la Sra. Gómez   b. ella
3. _____ usted (*yourself*)   c. ellas
4. _____ el Sr. Martínez   d. ellos
5. _____ Ana y usted   e. yo
6. _____ Alicia y Susana   f. nosotros/as

Segunda fase. Now you are talking *with* the following people. Match the pronouns on the right with the people mentioned on the left.

1. _____ su profesor de historia   a. tú
2. _____ su amigo íntimo   b. usted
3. _____ dos doctores   c. ustedes
4. _____ una senadora
5. _____ dos compañeros
6. _____ un niño (*a child*)

G 1-14 Mis compañeros. Ask questions to find out what your classmates are like. Every student will take notes to share answers with the class.

MODELO:　　E1: ¿Quién es optimista?
　　　　　　　E2: Yo (o él, ella, nosotros, etc.).
COMENTARIO:　Hay tres estudiantes optimistas. o
　　　　　　　No hay estudiantes optimistas en el grupo.

	TOTAL	COMENTARIO
responsable	3	Hay 3 estudiantes responsables.
pesimista		
estudioso/a		
hiperactivo/a		
perfeccionista		
tolerante		
creativo/a		

2. Present tense of regular -ar verbs

HABLAR			
yo	hablo	nosotros/as	hablamos
tú	hablas	vosotros/as	habláis
él, ella, Ud.	habla	ellos, ellas, Uds.	hablan

■ Use the present tense to express what you and others generally or habitually do or do not do. You may also use the present tense to express an ongoing action. Context will tell you which meaning is intended.

Ana trabaja en la oficina.　*Ana works in the office.*
　　　　　　　　　　　　　　　Ana is working in the office.

■ Here are some expressions you may find useful when talking about what you and others habitually do or do not do.

siempre	*always*	**muchas veces**	*often*
todos los días/meses	*every day/month*	**a veces**	*sometimes*
todas las semanas	*every week*	**nunca**	*never*

■ Other common -ar verbs are **bailar, buscar, caminar, comprar, conversar, escuchar, estudiar, llegar, montar, practicar, tomar, trabajar.**

¿Qué dice usted?

1-15 Preferencias. Primera fase. Rank the following activities from 1 to 8, according to your preferences (1 = most interesting, 8 = least interesting).

_____ bailar en una discoteca
_____ mirar televisión en casa
_____ conversar con amigos en los cafés
_____ caminar en la playa
_____ montar en bicicleta los fines de semana
_____ escuchar música rock
_____ comprar casetes y videos
_____ hablar por teléfono con amigos

Segunda fase. Now compare your answers with those of a classmate according to the model.

MODELO:　E1: Para mí, caminar en la playa es número 1. ¿Y para ti?
　　　　　　E2: Para mí, conversar con amigos en los cafés es número 1.

1-16 Mis actividades. Primera fase. Indicate with a check mark the activities that are part of your routine at the university.

1. _____ Llego a la universidad a las nueve de la mañana.
2. _____ Tomo notas en todas las clases.
3. _____ Converso con mis amigos en la plaza.
4. _____ Hablo con mis compañeros en la cafetería.
5. _____ Estudio en la biblioteca por las mañanas.
6. _____ Practico español con el CD-ROM en el laboratorio de computadoras.
7. _____ Miro programas cómicos en la televisión.
8. _____ A veces camino en el parque con un amigo.

Segunda fase. Now compare your answers with those of a classmate. The expressions in the box will help you react to the information you hear as your classmate tells you about himself/herself. Report your findings to the class.

MODELO: Daniel y yo somos (muy) similares. Él y yo miramos programas cómicos en la televisión. *o* Daniel y yo somos (muy) diferentes. Yo estudio por las mañanas; él estudia por las tardes.

1-17 A preguntar. Find one classmate who does each of the following activities. Write his/her name in the corresponding column. The expressions in the box will help carry out a more spontaneous conversation.

MODELO: mirar televisión por la noche
E1: ¿Miras televisión por la noche?
E2: Sí, miro televisión por la noche.
No, miro televisión por la tarde.

PERSONA	ACTIVIDAD
_____	estudiar español los fines de semana
_____	llegar a la universidad a las 9:30 a.m.
_____	escuchar música clásica en casa por la noche
_____	trabajar en una oficina por la tarde

1-18 Unos estudiantes excelentes. Make a list of things that the excellent students in your class do. Then, compare your lists.

MODELO: Siempre toman apuntes.

1-19 Mis actividades. Primera fase. Place a check mark in the space that indicates the frequency with which you do the following activities.

ACTIVIDADES	A VECES	MUCHAS VECES	SIEMPRE	NUNCA
estudiar con amigos				
sacar buenas notas				
llegar a la facultad a las ocho				
mirar televisión por la noche				
bailar los sábados				
montar en bicicleta los fines de semana				

EN DIRECTO

To express disbelief:
¡Qué increíble!
To show surprise at a coincidence:
¡Qué coincidencia!
To express interest at a finding:
¡Qué interesante!

EN DIRECTO

To call the attention of someone or to interrupt to ask questions:
¡Oye! (*to someone around your age or younger*)
Oiga, por favor. (*to someone unknown to you*)
Perdón, tengo unas preguntas.
To agree to answer:
Con mucho gusto.

② Segunda fase. Now, take turns telling the frequency with which you do the previous activities. Then, find out where he/she does them.

MODELO: E1: Yo estudio con amigos a veces, ¿Y tú?
         E2: Yo siempre estudio con amigos.
         E1: ¿Dónde estudias/estudian?
         E2: Estudio/Estudiamos en la biblioteca.

② 1-20 Tengo mucha curiosidad. You are really curious about how busy or quiet Friday evenings/nights are for one of your classmates. Write down four questions and ask him/her. Be prepared to answer his/her questions as well.

MODELO: ¿Estudias los viernes por la noche?

Ⓖ Segunda fase. Determine what activities are common to both of you. Then share them with another couple.

② 1-21 Un día típico en la vida de Luisa. Primera fase. Describe what Luisa does on a typical day.

MODELO: Luisa llega a la oficina a las nueve menos diez.

1.

2.

3.

4.

5.

6.

Segunda fase. Now, based on a typical day in her life, say what Luisa is like. Then explain what you normally do on a regular workday.

Use the expressions you have learned to sound more natural and spontaneous.

1. Your friend tells you that he/she works in the afternoons and you would like to know more about his/her job. Ask him/her a) where he/she works, b) the days of the week and the hours that he/she works, and c) how interesting/boring/difficult/easy the job is.

2. Greet your partner and ask a) how he/she is, b) what subjects he/she is studying this semester, c) the time of his/her first class **(primera clase)**, and d) what the professor is like.

3. Greet a new friend on campus and ask what he/she and his/her friends normally do on weekends (**¿Qué hacen...?**). Explain to him/her what you and your friends normally do on weekends.

4. You need to buy some school supplies at the university bookstore. Ask the salesperson for at least three items. Be specific and ask for prices. He/She will give you some choices and inform you of the prices.

3. Articles and nouns: Gender and number

Nouns are words that name a person, place, or thing. In English all nouns use the same definite article, *the,* and the indefinite articles *a* and *an*. In Spanish, masculine nouns use **el** or **un** and feminine nouns use **la** or **una**. The terms masculine and feminine are used in a grammatical sense and have nothing to do with biological gender.

Gender

	MASCULINE	FEMININE	
SINGULAR DEFINITE ARTICLES	el	la	*the*
SINGULAR INDEFINITE ARTICLES	un	una	*a/an*

- Generally, nouns that end in **-o** are masculine and require **el** or **un**, and those that end in **-a** are feminine and require **la** or **una**.

    el/un libro   el/un cuaderno   el/un diccionario
    la/una mesa   la/una silla   la/una ventana

- Nouns that end in **-dad, -ción, -sión** are feminine and require **la** or **una**.

    la/una universidad   la/una lección   la/una televisión

- Some nouns that end in **-a** and **-ma** are masculine.

    el/un día   el/un mapa
    el/un programa   el/un problema

- In general, nouns that refer to males are masculine and require **el/un,** whereas nouns that refer to females are feminine and require **la/una**. Masculine nouns ending in **-o** change the **-o** to **-a** for the feminine; those ending in a consonant add **-a** for the feminine.

    el/un amigo   la/una amiga
    el/un profesor   la/una profesora

- Nouns ending in **-ante** and **-ente** normally share the same form (**el/la estudiante**), but sometimes they have a feminine form ending in **-a** (**el dependiente, la dependienta**).

- Use definite articles with titles (except **don** and **doña**) when you are talking about someone. Do not use definite articles when addressing someone directly.

La señorita Andrade trabaja en el Departamento de Lenguas. Cuando **el** profesor Jones llega por la mañana, ella dice: "Buenos días, profesor Jones", y él contesta: "Buenos días, señorita Andrade".	*Miss Andrade works in the Department of Languages. When Professor Jones arrives in the morning, she says, "Good morning, Professor Jones," and he answers, "Good morning, Miss Andrade."*

Number

	MASCULINE	FEMININE	
PLURAL DEFINITE ARTICLES	los	las	*the*
PLURAL INDEFINITE ARTICLES	unos	unas	*some*

- Add **-s** to form the plural of nouns that end in a vowel. Add **-es** to nouns ending in a consonant.

la sil**la**	→	las sil**las**	el cuaderno	→	los cuadernos
la actividad	→	las actividad**es**	el señor	→	los señor**es**

- Nouns that end in **-z** change the **z** to **c** before **-es**.

    el lápi**z** → los lápi**ces**

- To refer to a mixed group, use masculine plural forms.

    los chicos   *the boys and girls*

¿Qué dice usted?

1-22 Conversaciones incompletas. Complete the following dialogs with the appropriate articles.

A. Supply the appropriate definite articles (**el, la, los, las**).

E1: ¿Dónde está María?
E2: Está en _____ clase de _____ profesora Sánchez.
E1: ¡Qué lástima! Necesito hablar con ella. Es urgente.
E2: Bueno, ella está en _____ salón de clase hasta _____ una, y por _____ tarde trabaja en _____ laboratorio.
E1: ¿Y a qué hora llega?
E2: Llega a _____ dos, más o menos.

B. Supply the appropriate indefinite articles (**un, una, unos, unas**).

E1: Necesito comprar _____ grabadora y _____ lápices.
E2: Y yo necesito _____ bolígrafo y _____ diccionario, pero no sé qué diccionario comprar.
E1: Para el primer curso, _____ profesores usan _____ diccionario pequeño y otros usan _____ diccionario grande. Habla con tu profesor.

C. Supply the appropriate definite or indefinite articles.

> **E1:** Tengo _____ examen de matemáticas mañana y necesito sacar _____ buena nota en esa clase.
>
> **E2:** ¿Quién es _____ profesor?
>
> **E1:** Es _____ doctora Solís.
>
> **E2:** ¡Ah! Es _____ profesora excelente.
>
> **E1:** Sí, pero _____ clase es muy difícil. Estudio y reviso _____ tareas todos _____ días, pero no saco buenas notas.
>
> **E2:** ¡Vaya! Lo siento mucho.

1-23 ¿Qué necesitan? Take turns saying what these classmates need.

MODELO: Alicia tiene que escuchar unos casetes.
           Necesita una grabadora.

1. Mónica tiene que tomar apuntes en la clase de historia.
2. Carlos y Ana tienen que hacer (*to do*) la tarea de matemáticas.
3. Alfredo tiene que estudiar para el examen de geografía.
4. Isabel tiene que escribir una composición para su clase de inglés.
5. Blanca y Lucía tienen que encontrar (*find*) dónde está Salamanca.
6. David tiene que copiar un programa de su computadora para un compañero.

SITUACIONES

To sound more natural and spontaneous In your conversation use the expressions you have learned.

1. **Role A.** You have missed the first day of class. Ask one of your classmates a) at what time the class is, b) who the professor is, and c) what you need for the class.

   Role B. Tell your classmate a) the time of the class, and if the class is in the morning, afternoon, or evening; b) the name of the professor and what he/she is like; and c) at least three items that your classmate will need for the class.

2. **Role A.** You work for the student newspaper at your college and you have been asked to interview students to find out what they typically do on weekends. After introducing yourself, find out from your interviewee a) if he/she works, and where; b) what he/she studies; and c) what he/she does on Saturdays and Sundays.

   Role B. Tell the interviewer a) if you work, and where you work; b) the classes you take; and c) the things you do on weekends, where you do them, and with whom you do them.

4. Present tense of the verb *estar*

ESTAR			
yo	estoy	I	am
tú	estás	you	are
Ud., él, ella	está	you are, he/she	is
nosotros/as	estamos	we	are
vosotros/as	estáis	you	are
Uds., ellos, ellas	están	you, they	are

■ Use **estar** to express the location of persons or objects.

¿Dónde **está** el gimnasio?   *Where is the gym?*
Está al lado de la cafetería.   *It is next to the cafeteria.*

■ Use **estar** to talk about states of health.

¿Cómo **está** el señor Mora?   *How is Mr. Mora?*
Está muy bien.   *He is very well.*

¿Qué dice usted?

1-24 En la cafetería. In the cafeteria, you run across a former classmate whom you have not seen for some time. Complete the following conversation, using the correct forms of **estar.**

estoy	estás	está	estamos	están

ROBERTO: Hola, Carlos. ¿Qué tal? ¿Cómo _____?
CARLOS: _____ muy bien. ¿Y tú?
ROBERTO: Muy bien, muy bien. ¿Y cómo _____ tu hermana *(sister)* Ana?
CARLOS: Ella y mamá _____ en España ahora.
ROBERTO: ¡Qué suerte! Y nosotros _____ en la universidad, ¡y en la semana de exámenes!

1-25 Lugares en el campus. Primera fase. Determine four places on campus that in your view are frequently visited by students in your university.

Segunda fase. You run across a classmate in the hallway. Tell him/her what you need from two of the buildings mentioned in **Primera fase,** and then ask where these buildings are located. He/She will answer as specifically as possible. Do not forget to address him/her appropriately as you approach him/her and ask for help. Also, thank him/her for the information.

MODELO: E1: Necesito un mapa. ¿Dónde está la biblioteca?
                      E2: Está _____.

1-26 Horas y lugares. Primera fase. Ask where your classmate usually is at the following times and days.

MODELO: 8:00 a.m. / los lunes
                      E1: ¿Dónde estás a las ocho de la mañana los lunes?
                      E2: Estoy en la clase de física. ¿Y tú?
                      E1: Estoy en casa.

a. 9:00 a.m. / los martes
b. 11:00 a.m. / los miércoles.
c. 1:00 p.m. / los viernes

d. 3:00 p.m. / los domingos
e. 9:00 p.m. / los lunes
f. ...

G **Segunda fase.** Ask two classmates where they usually are a) in the morning, b) in the afternoon, and c) in the evening on weekends. Then share this information with the class.

2 **1-27 Conversación.** Look at the following drawings. Ask a classmate where these people are, how they feel, and what they are doing.

MODELO: E1: ¿Dónde está María Luisa?
E2: Está en la biblioteca.
E1: ¿Cómo está?
E2: Está regular.
E1: ¿Qué hace?
E2: Estudia.

María Luisa

1. Berta Lorena

2. Carlos el Dr. Núñez

3. Marcelo Eduardo

SITUACIONES

1. **Role A.** You are the university representative who has to give directions to a graphic designer for the new student handbook. Explain to him/her the location of the various buildings below.

   la cafetería   la biblioteca   la Facultad de Humanidades
   la Facultad de Ciencias la librería   el gimnasio

   Role B. You are the graphic designer for the campus map. Ask questions about the location of these buildings as you draw the new map. When you have finished, show the map to the university representative to check if you have understood his/her explanations.

2. **Role A.** You are a new student at the university and you do not know where the bookstore is. Introduce yourself to one of your classmates. Then, a) tell him/her that you need to buy some books and b) ask where the bookstore is. Thank him/her for the help **(Gracias por la ayuda).**

   Role B. A new student will greet you and ask questions. Make your answers as complete and specific as possible.

ACENTOS

All question words have a written accent over the stressed syllable: **cómo**, **dónde**.

LENGUA

To request repetition or clarification, use **¿Cómo?** or **¿Perdón?** The use of **¿Qué?**, the equivalent of English *What?* is generally considered rude by some native speakers.

5. Question words

cómo	*how/what*	cuál(es)	*which*
dónde	*where*	quién(es)	*who*
qué	*what*	cuánto/a	*how much*
cuándo	*when*	cuántos/as	*how many*

■ If a subject is used in a question, it normally follows the verb.

¿Dónde **trabaja Elsa**?   *Where does Elsa work?*

■ Use **por qué** to ask *why* and **porque** to answer *because*.

¿**Por qué** está Pepe en la biblioteca?   *Why is Pepe at the library?*
Porque necesita estudiar.   *Because he needs to study.*

■ Use **qué + ser** when you want to ask for a definition or an explanation.

¿**Qué es** la sardana?   *What is the sardana?*
Es un baile típico de Cataluña.   *It is a typical dance of Catalonia.*

■ Use **cuál (es) + ser** when you want to ask which one(s).

¿**Cuál es** tu mochila?   *Which (one) is your backpack?*
¿**Cuáles son** tus papeles?   *Which (ones) are your papers?*

■ Questions that may be answered with **sí** or **no** do not use a question word.

¿Trabajan ustedes los sábados?   *Do you work on Saturdays?*
No, no trabajamos.   *No, we do not.*

■ Another way to ask a question is to place an interrogative tag after a declarative statement.

Tú hablas inglés, ¿**verdad**?   *You speak English, don't you?*
David es norteamericano, ¿**no**?   *David is an American, isn't he?*

¿Qué dice usted?

1-28 Entrevista. Look at the cues in the right column before completing the questions using **quién, cuándo, cuántos/as, cuál, por qué**, as needed. Then walk around the room to interview two classmates.

1. ¿_____ clases tomas?   Tomo...
2. ¿_____ son tus clases?   Por la...
3. ¿_____ es tu clase favorita?   La clase de...
4. ¿_____ es tu profesor favorito?   El/La profesor/a...
5. ¿_____ estudias español?   Porque...
6. ¿_____ estudiantes hay en tu clase de español?   Hay...

1-29 Entrevista. Ask appropriate questions to find out the following information. Use the appropriate expressions to show: disbelief, coincidence, how interesting the answers you hear are, etc.

1. número de clases que toma este semestre
2. su clase favorita y por qué
3. número de alumnos en la clase favorita
4. nombre del/de la profesor/a favorito/a
5. lugar donde estudia y cuántas horas
6. lugar donde trabaja

1-30 Entrevista. You are conducting a survey for a Spanish television station. Ask appropriate questions to find out the information requested below.

1. Dirección	_____
2. Teléfono	_____
3. Número de personas en la casa/el apartamento	_____
4. Número de televisores en la casa/el apartamento	_____
5. Programas favoritos	_____
6. Número de horas que miran televisión durante la semana	_____
7. Número de horas que miran televisión los fines de semana	_____

SITUACIONES

1. You have just run across a Spanish-speaking friend that you have not seen for a long time. Tell him/her about a) your university (location and size), b) your courses, and c) your activities. Ask him/her questions to get the same information.

2. **Role A:** It is the beginning of the term, and you missed yesterday's class. As usual, you expect some minor changes in the course schedule and syllabus. Ask your partner a) if there is homework, b) if there is an exam soon **(pronto)**, and c) when the exam is.

   Role B: Answer your classmate's questions being as specific as possible. You may add that the exam will take place in a different classroom and give him/her the classroom location.

ALGO MÁS

Some regular -er and -ir verbs

The verb form found in dictionaries and in most vocabulary lists is the infinitive: **hablar, estudiar,** etc. Its equivalent in English is the verb preceded by *to: to speak, to study.* In Spanish, most infinitives end in **-ar;** other infinitives end in **-er** and **-ir.**

So far you have practiced the present tense of regular **-ar** verbs. Now you will practice the **yo, tú,** and **usted/él/ella** forms of some **-er** and **-ir** verbs: **leer,** *to read;* **comer,** *to eat;* **aprender,** *to learn;* **escribir,** *to write;* **vivir,** *to live;* **asistir,** *to attend.*

- As you did with **-ar** verbs, use the ending **-o** when talking about your daily activities.

Leo y **escribo** en la clase todos los días.	*I read and I write in class every day.*

- For the **tú** form, use the ending **-es.**

¿**Comes** en la cafetería o en tu casa?	*Do you eat in the cafeteria or at home?*
Vives en una casa, ¿verdad?	*You live in a house, right?*

- For the **usted/él/ella** form, delete the final **-s** of the **tú** form.

Ella **vive** en la calle Salud.	*She lives on Salud Street.*

¿Qué dice usted?

1-31 Las actividades de su profesor. Try to guess whether the following information about your instructor is true (**cierto**) or false (**falso**). Then ask your instructor to verify the information.

1. _____ Escribe poemas.
2. _____ Come en restaurantes los fines de semana.
3. _____ Tiene cuatro clases todos los días.
4. _____ Vive en un condominio.
5. _____ Toma mucho café.
6. _____ Consulta Internet para sus clases.

1-32 ¿Con qué frecuencia? Decide who is going to be **Estudiante 1** and who will be **Estudiante 2.** After filling out the chart corresponding to your role, ask your classmate when he/she does each activity listed under his/her column.

MODELO: comer pizza
E1: Yo como pizza los domingos. Y tú, ¿cuándo comes pizza?
E2: Yo nunca como pizza.

ACTIVIDAD	TODOS LOS DÍAS	A VECES	LOS DOMINGOS	NUNCA
ESTUDIANTE 1				
comer hamburguesas				
mirar televisión por la noche				
leer novelas de detectives				
escribir composiciones				
ESTUDIANTE 2				
comer pasta				
asistir a conciertos de rock				
leer libros de ciencia				
aprender palabras en español				

M O S A I C O S

 Escuchar

Listening for the gist

When you are involved in a conversation or when you hear somebody else talking you may get the gist of the conversation without understanding every word or paying attention to every detail. You do this based on your experience, knowledge of the situation, etc.

Antes de escuchar

1-33 ¿Cierto o falso? You will hear two students talking about their classes. Before listening to the recording, think about the kinds of things they may say and make a list of what you might expect to hear based on your experience.

_____

_____

_____

A escuchar

AUDIO **1-34 Dos estudiantes.** First read the following statements. Then listen to the conversation between Ana and Mario and indicate whether each statement is **Cierto** or **Falso.**

	CIERTO	FALSO
1. Mario y Ana son buenos estudiantes.		
2. Mario toma clases de ciencias y de humanidades.		
3. Ana toma sólo clases de ciencias.		
4. Todas las clases de Ana son muy fáciles.		
5. La clase favorita de Mario es historia.		

Después de escuchar

1-35 ¿Y usted? Answer the following questions.

1. ¿Toma usted clases de humanidades y ciencias?
2. ¿Cuál es su clase más fácil?

Antes de escuchar

1-36 ¿Qué clases toman? You will listen to the class schedule of three students. Before you listen, list the classes you take on Mondays, Wednesdays, and Fridays. Then list the classes you take on Tuesdays and Thursdays.

LUNES, MIÉRCOLES Y VIERNES	MARTES Y JUEVES

A escuchar

1-37 Horarios. Now you will listen to Cristina's, Ester's, and Jorge's schedule. As you listen, complete the following chart based on the information that you hear.

NOMBRE DEL ESTUDIANTE	LUNES, MIÉRCOLES Y VIERNES	MARTES Y JUEVES
	economía	biología
	química	psicología
	contabilidad	
	matemáticas	biología
	química	física
		portugués
	portugués	psicología
	geografía	informática

Después de escuchar

1-38 ¿Y usted? In the following chart, write down your schedule and compare it with that of a classmate.

HORA	LUNES	MARTES	MIÉRCOLES	JUEVES	VIERNES

Conversar

Antes de conversar

1-39 El arte de preguntar. In column A, write the questions to the answers provided in column B.

      A   **B**

1. _____ La dirección de la librería es Calle Mayor, número 50.
2. _____ Si, tengo libros de historia de España en español.
3. _____ Sí, tengo diccionarios en español.
4. _____ Los estudiantes compran más el diccionario que cuesta 40 euros.

A conversar

1-40 Un favor. You live in Málaga, Spain. Your American friend would like to send his girlfriend some gifts from Spain: a fancy pen, a history book, a Spanish dictionary, and a map of Spain. Read the following ad and call the bookstore to find out if it has what your friend needs. Your classmate will play the role of the bookstore clerk. Remember to follow the formalities of phone conversations with someone you do not know. Switch roles.

EN DIRECTO

To answer the phone in Spain:
¿Diga?

To greet someone formally:
Buenos días/Buenas tardes.

To ask if they have what you need:
Necesito/Busco un/una...
(*name what you are looking for*).

Después de conversar

1-41 Favor hecho (*done*). Write an e-mail to your American friend informing him whether the bookstore has each item he needs and the price.

Antes de conversar

1-42 ¿Qué clases tomas este semestre? Make a list of the classes you are taking this term.

A conversar

G **1-43 Entrevista.** Ask all members of your group what courses they are taking and what their classes are like. Complete the chart with the results of your poll.

MODELO: E1: ¿Estudias estadística?
                     E2: Sí, estudio estadística./No, no estudio estadística. Estudio...
                     E1: ¿Es una clase difícil?
                     E2: No, es (una clase) fácil.
                     E1: ¿Es una clase obligatoria?
                     E2: Sí, (es obligatoria). / No, (es optativa).

MATERIAS	ESTUDIANTE	DIFÍCIL	FÁCIL	OBLIGATORIA	OPTATIVA
ciencias políticas					
economía					
español					
literatura inglesa					
matemáticas					

Después de conversar

G **1-44 Resultados de la entrevista.** Now summarize the results of your poll and share them with the class.

1. ¿Cuántos/as compañeros/as estudian economía, física, etc.?
2. Según la opinión del grupo, ¿qué clases son fáciles? ¿Qué clases son difíciles?
3. ¿Qué clases son obligatorias? ¿Y qué clases son optativas?

 ## Leer

Introduction to reading

Reading is an important skill that you will develop as you study Spanish. You should not expect to be able to read proficiently at first; however, it is important to begin developing this ability early in the language learning process.

In each chapter of *Mosaicos,* you will be focusing on one or two reading strategies to improve your reading skills in Spanish. As the term unfolds, you will also review previously learned strategies that are necessary to face more complex texts.

In *Lección 1,* you will do the following:

- Draw on your experience and knowledge of the world to comprehend an unfamiliar text. Use what you know about the topic as you read; this will help you predict and/or discover new meanings.

- Pay attention to cognates; that is, words that are spelled similarly in Spanish and English and that bear the same meaning. Such words will help tremendously with comprehension of the text. Beware that there are also false cognates (words with the same or almost the same spelling), which may hinder your interpretation of meaning.

- Pay close attention to visual cues like photographs, illustrations, and charts that may accompany the reading, or to the size of type used for headings, and so on. These visual cues will help you make educated guesses about the content and meaning of the text.

- Get used to reading every text at least twice. First read the text to get the general sense and main ideas. When you read the second time, underline or jot down unfamiliar expressions that block your comprehension of the text. Make hypotheses about possible meanings and read the text a third time. This last reading should serve as a confirmation of your guesses.

Guía de prelectura

1. As you take a quick look at the text in 1-46, rely on your previous knowledge to answer these questions:

   A. Does the following text appear in a newspaper? Yes No

   B. What information led you to answer the way you did?
      1. the format of the text Yes No
      2. some cognates in the text Yes No
      3. the illustrations Yes No

2. Use your knowledge of the English language for comprehension.
   If cognates helped you figure out the kind of text this is, can you write at least three of the cognates that facilitated your work?

   a. _____   b. _____   c. _____

Antes de leer

1-45 Preparación. Which of the classes below should be mandatory for students majoring in the following careers? Write the classes under the corresponding career.

fisiología	muralistas mexicanos
diseño gráfico	anatomía
drogas tóxicas	medicinas alternativas
conflictos sociales contemporáneos	historia de las lenguas modernas
la estructura del español	la depresión

MEDICINA	BELLAS ARTES	FARMACIA	PSICOLOGÍA	FILOLOGÍA

A leer

1-46 Primera mirada. Underline the correct response in each statement taken from the Web page of a Spanish educational institution.

1. Esta página web es de una escuela secundaria/de una universidad/del gobierno español.
2. El logo indica que esta institución es muy nueva/muy antigua.
3. Esta página web presenta una lista de clases/una lista de carreras.
4. La información de esta página web es muy específica/muy general.
5. Esta institución tiene un campus/más de un campus.
6. Es posible/No es posible escribir un correo electrónico (*e-mail*) para obtener información sobre las carreras.

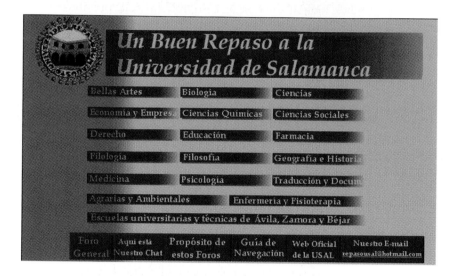

1-47 Segunda mirada. According to the information on the Web page, answer the following questions.

1. ¿Qué palabras de esta página Web son probablemente nombres de ciudades?
2. Al final (*the bottom*) de esta página Web hay varias teclas (*keys*). ¿Qué tecla usan los estudiantes para conversar con personas que trabajan en la Universidad de Salamanca?
3. Imagínese que usted necesita información sobre su especialidad en la Universidad de Salamanca. ¿Qué facultad tiene la información que usted necesita?

Después de leer

1-48 Ampliación. In general, most of the words ending in **-ía, -cia, -ción** are feminine in Spanish. Find the names of some careers that have a feminine ending. Write them below.

-ÍA	-CIA	-CIÓN

Escribir

Identifying basic aspects of writing

Writing is an act of communication in every language. In order for your writing to be effective, you need to consider the following questions before you begin:

1. **Purpose:** Why are you writing? To communicate with a friend? To request something in a business situation? To complain? To inform?
2. **Medium of communication:** What medium of communication are you using? Is it a letter, a postcard, an essay? Are you filling out a form, writing a report?
3. **Reader:** Are you writing to a friend, a business person, a young or an old person?
4. **Topic:** What is the content of your writing? Are you writing about your personal experience or about a broader, more general topic?
5. **Language:** What vocabulary and structures will you potentially need to develop your topic? When writing in a language other than your own, you will find it helpful to list these before you begin. For example, if you are interviewing a classmate about his or her background, you will find it useful to make a list of the questions for requesting personal information: *¿Dónde vives? ¿Qué estudias?*, and so on.

In this chapter, you have talked about your life at school, outside school, and your daily routine. Now, you will have the opportunity to do it in writing.

Antes de escribir

1-49 Preparación. Primera fase. Imagine that this is your first year in college and you would like to write your Spanish-speaking pen pal an e-mail about your new life as a university student. To show your pen pal that your Spanish skills have improved greatly, think about the following information and complete what's missing.

1. Specify the purpose of your message/writing.
2. Determine your reader.
3. Determine the topic of your message.

Segunda fase. Now plan the language you will probably use.

1. Think of two ways to tell your friend how things are going for you. Write them down.
2. Make a list in Spanish of the classes you are taking this term.
3. Write some expressions that you would use to describe what your professors and your classes are like.
4. Make a list of the activities that you routinely do . . .
    a. during the week: When and where do you do them? Do you do them in the morning, in the afternoon, or at night? Do you do them with a friend or with a classmate?
    b. on weekends: How different is your weekend from the rest of the week? Do you break up your routine? How?

A escribir

1-50 Manos a la obra. Now write your Spanish-speaking pen pal an e-mail telling him/her about your new life at the university. You may use the information you gathered in Activity 1-49. Do not forget to tell him/her . . .

- how things are going for you.

- about your university or college, the number and names of your classes, when you are taking them, how interesting (or not) your classes and professors are.

- what your daily routine at school is like, what you do after (*después de*) class and on weekends, where and with whom you do these activities, and so on.

Para: _____

Asunto: _____

Querido/a....,

Hasta pronto.....

Después de escribir

1-51 Revisión. After writing your e-mail, discuss it with a classmate. Then make any necessary changes.

- Make sure you have provided all the information requested in 1-50 or any other you may deem necessary.

- Revise any possible inaccuracies you may find regarding language use, spelling, punctuation, accentuation, and so on.

- Finally, make any necessary changes that will make your text clear and comprehensible to your e-mail pen pal.

ENFOQUE CULTURAL

TEMAS: LAS UNIVERSIDADES

Para pensar

¿Cómo se llama su universidad? ¿Es grande o pequeña? ¿Nueva o antigua? ¿Privada o pública? ¿Es difícil ingresar (*be admitted*) a la universidad en los Estados Unidos? ¿Qué examen toman los estudiantes de secundaria para entrar a la universidad?

Algunas universidades españolas son modernas, pero también hay otras que son muy antiguas. Entre las universidades más antiguas está la Universidad de Salamanca, fundada en el siglo XIII.

En Hispanoamérica, las primeras universidades se fundan en el siglo XVI: la Universidad de Santo Tomás de Aquinas (en la foto), en Santo Domingo, República Dominicana; la Universidad de San Marcos, en Lima, Perú; y la Universidad de México.

Para contestar

A. Las universidades. Responda a las siguientes preguntas:

1. ¿Cómo son las universidades en el mundo hispano? Explique.
2. ¿Hay muchas universidades antiguas en los países hispanos? Dé un ejemplo.

G **B. Riqueza cultural.** Mencionen dos cosas similares y alguna diferencia entre las universidades de los Estados Unidos y las de España o Hispanoamérica.

Algunas universidades son muy grandes, como, por ejemplo, la Universidad Complutense de Madrid, donde estudian más de 120.000 estudiantes. Otras son mucho más pequeñas y tienen menos estudiantes.

Para pensar

¿Sabe usted dónde está España? ¿Qué ciudades importantes hay? ¿Qué museos y parques importantes hay? ¿Conoce usted (*do you know*) alguna actividad típica española? ¿Cuál es?

Café al aire libre en la Plaza Mayor de Madrid.

El Museo del Prado en Madrid.

Madrid, la capital de España, es una ciudad de gran vitalidad y energía. Durante el día los madrileños se reúnen en los cafés y terrazas y en la noche, hasta la madrugada, en los bares y discotecas.

Expresiones españolas:

ir de tapas	¡Vamos de tapas!	*Let's go have some tapas!*
catear	¡Me han **cateado**!	*They've flunked me!*
majo/a	Ella es muy **maja**.	*She's a very nice person.*
vale	Te llamo luego, ¿**vale**?	*I'll call you later, OK?*
chaval	¿Dónde está ese **chaval**?	*Where's that kid?*

Para contestar

En el mapa

1. Busque tres ciudades importantes de España. Indique dónde están.
2. Diga qué ciudad está más cerca de (*near*) Portugal. ¿Y de Francia?

Ahora diga...

1. ¿Por qué es famosa Sevilla?
2. ¿Qué lugar de Madrid le gustaría (*would you like*) visitar?

Los madrileños también disfrutan de los muchos museos, palacios, iglesias, y de las impresionantes plazas, fuentes y parques de su ciudad.

En el sur de España está Sevilla, ciudad de un encanto sin par. Sevilla es famosa por sus históricos edificios y también por sus celebraciones de Semana Santa con sus procesiones religiosas. En la Feria de abril, las sevillanas, que son los bailes típicos, y las corridas de toros llenan de alegría la ciudad. Visitar España es una experiencia cultural muy importante.

¿Qué dice Ud...

1. para describir a una persona agradable?
2. si quiere comer algo con sus amigos?
3. si saca una nota muy mala en un examen?

Para investigar en Internet

Busque información en *www.prenhall.com/mosaicos* sobre elementos importantes en la vida universitaria en España y en Hispanoamérica (eventos deportivos, bibliotecas, cafés, exposiciones de arte, conferencias, etc.). Informe a sus compañeros de alguna actividad interesante.

¡Prepárese!

1-52 Cognados. Before watching the first episode of *Fortunas*, look at the following list of cognates. Can you guess the meaning of these words?

a. la fortuna   _____

b. el misterio   _____

c. la competencia   _____

d. el/la participante   _____

e. el público   _____

1-53 Diccionario. Now use a bilingual dictionary or the glossary at the back of the book to learn the meanings of the following words, which will also be helpful as you participate in *Fortunas*.

a. la pista   _____

b. el premio   _____

c. el concurso   _____

d. la regla   _____

e. la encuesta   _____

Ángela y Manolo trabajan en la producción del video.

Tito anuncia que el concurso es en México.

Sabrina es de España.

Carlos es de Colombia.

Efraín es de Argentina.

Katie es de los Estados Unidos.

¡Responda!

1-54 Participantes. After watching the first episode of *Fortunas*, answer the following questions in Spanish, based on what you saw.

1. ¿Cómo es Manolo?
2. ¿Cómo es Ángela?
3. ¿De qué habla Tito?
4. ¿Cuántos participantes hay?
5. ¿Cuál es su participante favorito y por qué?

The rhythms and singing style of this song (*canción*) reflect the influence of Spanish flamenco music, which originated in southern Spain.

¡Prepárese!

G **1-55 Estilos musicales.** What other styles of music besides flamenco do you know that are popular in Spain and other countries of the Spanish-speaking world? Work in groups to generate a list and then compare your list to those of other groups. Which group has the longest list?

¡Escuche!

1-56 Parejas. Primera fase. Look at each of the following words you will hear in *Cuéntame alegrías*. Then, match them to the English equivalents.

1. corazón _____   a. *flower*
2. flor _____   b. *heart*
3. amor _____   c. *happiness*
4. luz _____   d. *love*
5. alegría _____   e. *light*

Segunda fase. Thinking of the words in the **Primera fase,** what will the song that you will hear probably refer to? Mark your answer.

a. love _____   b. nature _____   c. sorrow _____

Cuéntame alegrías, mi "vía",
y dame tu amor.
Hazme una caricia, sonrisa,
dame el corazón.
Tienes mi alma, caramba,
hay para ti un rincón
y siempre presente en mi mente
Ahí te mantengo yo.

No quiero que llegue el día
¡Ay! que me digas que en la vida
todo tiene que acabar.
Que me digas que el cariño
igual que viene se va,

que ese amor que compartimos
lo arrastra una tempestad,
que ese amor tú lo compartas
con una persona más.

Eres luz del día, mi "vía",
flor de mi jardín
donde guardo flores y olores
sólo para ti.
Entre tierra y cielo, te quiero.
¡Ay! Nunca podrá haber
amor más sincero, espero
que nuestro querer

¡Responda!

1-57 Cantar, escuchar... After listening to the song, write sentences in Spanish, using the words of the two columns provided and adding some further information.

MODELO: Los chicos escuchan *Cuéntame alegrías* en la radio.

SUBJECTS	VERBS
yo	escuchar
la cantante (*singer*)	bailar
la canción (*song*)	cantar (*to sing*)
la música española	hablar
el flamenco	ser
mis compañeros y yo	estar

VOCABULARIO

AUDIO En la clase

el diccionario	*dictionary*
el examen	*test, examination*
el mapa	*map*
la nota	*note, grade*
la tarea	*homework*

Materias o asignaturas

la antropología	*anthropology*
las ciencias políticas	*political science*
la economía	*economics*
el español	*Spanish*
la geografía	*geography*
la historia	*history*
la literatura	*literature*
la (p)sicología	*psychology*
la sociología	*sociology*

Lugares

la biblioteca	*library*
el café	*coffee house*
la cafetería	*cafeteria*
la casa	*house, home*
la discoteca	*dance club*
el gimnasio	*gymnasium*
el laboratorio	*laboratory*
el laboratorio de lenguas	*language lab*
la librería	*bookstore*
la oficina	*office*
la playa	*beach*
la universidad	*university*

Facultades

arquitectura	*architecture*
ciencias	*sciences*
humanidades	*humanities*
informática	*computer science*
medicina	*medicine*

Personas

el/la alumno/a	*student*
el/la compañero/a	*partner, classmate*
el/la dependiente/a	*salesperson*
ellos/ellas	*they*
nosotros/nosotras	*we*
ustedes	*you* (plural)

Descripciones

aburrido/a	*boring*
difícil	*difficult*
estudioso/a	*studious*
excelente	*excellent*
fácil	*easy*
grande	*big*
malo/a	*bad*
norteamericano/a	*American*
pequeño/a	*small*

Verbos*

bailar	*to dance*
buscar	*to look for*
caminar	*to walk*
comprar	*to buy*
conversar	*to talk, to converse*
escuchar	*to listen (to)*
estar	*to be*
estudiar	*to study*
hablar	*to speak*
llegar	*to arrive*
mirar	*to look (at)*
montar	*to ride*
montar en bicicleta	*to ride a bicycle*
necesitar	*to need*
practicar	*to practice*
sacar	*to get, to take (out)*
tomar	*to take, to drink*
tomar apuntes	*to take notes*
trabajar	*to work*

Palabras y expresiones útiles**

algo	*something*
buena suerte	*good luck*
¿Cómo te va?	*How is it going?*
con	*with*
¿Cuánto cuesta?	*How much is it?*
este/a	*this*
el fin de semana	*weekend*
para	*for, to*
pero	*but*
¡Qué lástima!	*What a pity!*
su	*his, her, their, your* (formal)
también	*also*
tengo/tienes	*I/you have*
¿Verdad?	*Right?*

*See page 32 for expressions of frequency.
**See page 41 for some *-er* and *-ir* verb forms.
***See page 40 for question words.

LOS HISPANOS EN LOS ESTADOS UNIDOS

Objetivos comunicativos

- Asking about and describing persons, animals, places, and things
- Expressing nationality and place of origin

- Expressing where and when events take place
- Expressing possession
- Expressing likes and dislikes

Contenido

A primera vista

- Mis amigos y yo
- ¿Cómo son...?

- ¿De qué color son...?
- ¿De dónde son...?

Explicación y expansión

- Adjectives
- Present tense and some uses of the verb *ser*
- *Ser* and *estar* with adjectives

- Possessive adjectives
- Algo Más: Expressions with *gustar*

Mosaicos

- Escuchar: Listening for specific information
- Conversar: Describing appearance and personality

- Leer: Scanning a text; inferring meaning
- Escribir: Responding to an ad; addressing an unknown reader

Enfoque cultural

- Temas: Los hispanos en los Estados Unidos
- Vistas: La influencia hispana en los Estados Unidos
  Para investigar en Internet

- Fortunas: Episodio 2
- Notas: Oh Naná, *Millo Torres y el Tercer Planeta*

Vocabulario

A PRIMERA VISTA

AUDIO *Mis amigos y yo*

Me llamo Mario Quintana. Soy de Puerto Rico, y tengo veintidós años. **Me gusta** escuchar música y mirar televisión. Estudio en una universidad americana y **deseo ser** profesor de historia. Los **chicos** en estas fotografías son **mis amigos. Ellos también** son **hispanos** y estudian en la universidad. **Todos** somos **bilingües.**

Esta chica es Amanda Martone. Es **alta, delgada,** tiene los **ojos de color café** y el **pelo castaño** y muy **largo.** Amanda es una chica muy **agradable.** Estudia mucho y desea ser economista. Su familia es argentina, pero vive en los Estados Unidos.

Este chico se llama Ernesto Fernández. Ernesto es **moreno, bajo, fuerte,** muy **conversador** y **simpático.** Le gusta **usar** la computadora para conversar con sus amigos de aquí y de México.

Esta amiga se llama Ana Villegas. No es alta ni baja, es **mediana** y usa **lentes de contacto.** Es **pelirroja,** tiene pelo **corto** y ojos **negros.** Ana es **callada, trabajadora** y muy inteligente. Sus padres son cubanos.

Esta chica es Marta Chávez Conde. Es española y tiene veintiún años. Es **rubia,** tiene los ojos **azules,** y es muy **divertida.** Este año está en los Estados Unidos con su familia.

CULTURA

The results of the year 2000 census indicate that one of every nine people in the United States is of Hispanic origin. With a population of 32,800,000, Hispanics account for 12 percent of the country's inhabitants. The Foundation of the Americas predicts that by the year 2015, this group will be the largest minority in the United States, with a population of around 62.7 million. Although Hispanics can be found everywhere in the United States, most live in Los Angeles, New York, Miami, San Francisco, and Chicago. Mexicans constitute the largest group, followed by Puerto Ricans, Cubans, and citizens of other Latin American countries.

¿Qué dice usted?

2-1 Asociaciones. To whom do the descriptions on the left refer?

1. _____ Tiene el pelo largo.
2. _____ Tiene veintidós años.
3. _____ Es de España.
4. _____ Es bajo y fuerte.
5. _____ Es callada y muy inteligente.
6. _____ Habla mucho.
7. _____ Tiene los ojos de color café.
8. _____ Es rubia.
9. _____ Tiene los ojos azules y es muy divertida.
10. _____ Desea ser profesor de historia.

a. Mario Quintana
b. Amanda Martone
c. Ernesto Fernández
d. Ana Villegas
e. Marta Chávez

2-2 ¿Quién es? Primera fase. Read again the texts on pages 60–61 and write a list of at least eight expressions that you may use to describe people in regards to: a) their physical appearance and b) their personality traits.

G **Segunda fase.** Now, without mentioning his/her name, describe a classmate in at least three sentences, using the vocabulary from **Primera fase,** or any other that you may need. The rest of the group will guess who this person is. If they cannot guess his/her identity, they should ask Yes/No questions to the student who made the description. He/She will answer using **Sí** or **No.**

MODELO: E1: Es alto y delgado. Tiene pelo negro. Es fuerte y callado.
          E2: Es...

2-3 ¿Qué (no) me gusta? Indicate whether you like or dislike each of the following activities. Then ask a classmate, and compare your answers.

MODELO: estar en casa por las noches
          E1: ¿Te gusta estar en casa por las noches?
          E2: Sí, me gusta. /No, no me gusta.

ACTIVIDADES	USTED		COMPAÑERO/A	
	Sí	No	Sí	No
1. mirar televisión por la tarde				
2. estudiar español				
3. practicar tenis/fútbol/béisbol				
4. escribir en la computadora				
5. trabajar los fines de semana				
6. tomar café por la noche				
7. bailar los sábados por la noche				
8. hablar con los amigos en los cafés				

¿Cómo son...

estas personas?

fuerte   débil   joven   vieja/mayor

lista

tonto   trabajador   perezoso

        antipático

alegre

simpático   triste

rica

pobre

casado   soltero

estos animales?

el hipopótamo   **la gata**   **la serpiente**   **el oso**

Es feo.   Es muy bonita.   Es delgada.   Es gordo.

¿De qué color son...

estos autos?

Es rojo.   Es amarillo.

LENGUA

There are several Spanish words, depending on the country, to express the color brown: **café, marrón, carmelita, castaño,** and **pardo/a.** The words **naranja** and **rosa** are also used instead of **anaranjado** and **rosado.**

Otros colores

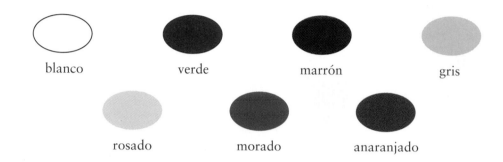

blanco   verde   marrón   gris

rosado   morado   anaranjado

2-4 Opuestos. Complete the following statements.

MODELO: Shakira no es vieja, es joven.

1. ____ Penélope Cruz no es gorda, es...   a. trabajador
2. ____ El presidente no es perezoso, es...   b. lista
3. ____ Jennifer López no es antipática, es...   c. delgada
4. ____ Madonna no es tonta, es...   d. rico
5. ____ Bill Gates no es pobre, es...   e. guapo
6. ____ Enrique Iglesias no es feo, es...   f. simpática

2-5 Autodescripción. Primera fase. You are appearing on the TV program **Cita a ciegas** (*Blind Date*). Describe yourself to make a good first impression. Your partner should take notes.

1. Me llamo...
2. Soy... No soy...
3. Tengo...
4. Estudio...
5. Trabajo...
6. Me gusta...

Segunda fase. Use your notes to describe your partner to the rest of the class.

1. Se llama...
2. Es... No es...
3. Tiene...
4. Estudia...
5. Trabaja...
6. Le gusta...

2-6 Vamos a describir. Look at the following photos and describe the people in them.

Alberto

Nicolás

Marisol

Mirta

2-7 ¿Quién soy? Write down a brief description of yourself (physical and personality wise). **Do not** include your name. Give the piece of paper to your instructor. He/She will ask each of you to pick a description, read it, and match the description with the name of your classmate who wrote it.

MODELO: Soy alta y morena; llevo lentes, tengo el pelo corto; soy muy trabajadora.

¿De dónde son...?

¿Qué dice usted?

2-8 ¿Quiénes son? Primera fase. Identify the following people (map pg. 65).

1. jugador (*player*) de béisbol dominicano
2. diseñadora (*designer*) famosa de Venezuela
3. escritor de Perú; autor de *La ciudad y los perros*
4. actriz mexicana, protagonista de *Frida*
5. activista guatemalteca, Premio Nobel de la Paz, 1992
6. bailarín argentino
7. cofundador de Microsoft
8. ex-presidenta de Nicaragua
9. escritor colombiano, autor de *Cien años de soledad*, Premio Nobel, 1982
10. novelista chilena, autora de *La casa de los espíritus*

a. Bill Gates
b. Mario Vargas Llosa
c. Isabel Allende
d. Rigoberta Menchú
e. Gabriel García Márquez
f. Sammy Sosa
g. Carolina Herrera
h. Julio Bocca
i. Salma Hayek
j. Violeta Chamorro

Segunda fase. Which of the public personalities in **Primera fase** is interesting to you? Why?

MODELO: Para mí, ... es interesante. Es un/a actor/actriz famoso/a.

2-9 Adivinanzas. Think of a well-known person. A classmate will try to guess his or her identity by asking you questions.

MODELO: E1: ¿De dónde es?
            E2: Es española.
            E1: ¿Cómo es?
            E2: Es bonita, morena y muy inteligente.
            E1: ¿En qué trabaja?
            E2: Es actriz.
            E1: ¿Es Penélope Cruz?
            E2: ¡Sí!

AUDIO **2-10 ¿Quiénes son?** Before you listen to a student describing himself, mark in the appropriate **Antes de Escuchar** column the information you think he will provide.

	ANTES DE ESCUCHAR		DESPUÉS DE ESCUCHAR	
	Sí	No	Sí	No
1. name				
2. age				
3. his parents' names				
4. physical description				
5. country where he was born				
6. place where he will work in the future				

Now, pay attention to the general idea of what is said. Then, in the **Después de escuchar** column in the chart, indicate if the information was or was not provided.

EXPLICACIÓN Y EXPANSIÓN

1. Adjectives

Adjectives are words that describe people, places, and things. Like articles (**el, la, un, una**) and nouns (**chico, chica**), they generally have more than one form. In Spanish an adjective must agree in gender (masculine or feminine) and number (singular or plural) with the noun or pronoun it describes. Adjectives that describe characteristics usually follow the noun.

■ Most masculine adjectives end in **-o,** and most feminine adjectives end in **-a** when used with feminine words. To form the plural, these adjectives add **-s.**

	MASCULINE	FEMININE
SINGULAR	el chico alto	la chica alta
PLURAL	los chicos altos	las chicas altas

■ Adjectives that end in **-e** and some adjectives that end in a consonant are both masculine and feminine. To form the plural, adjectives that end in **-e** add **-s;** adjectives that end in a consonant add **-es.**

	MASCULINE	FEMININE
SINGULAR	un amigo interesante	una amiga interesante
	un chico popular	una chica popular
PLURAL	unos amigos interesantes	unas amigas interesantes
	unos chicos populares	unas chicas populares

■ Other adjectives that end in a consonant add **-a** to form the feminine and **-es** and **-as** to form the plurals.

	MASCULINE	FEMININE
SINGULAR	el alumno español	la alumna española
	el alumno trabajador	la alumna trabajadora
PLURAL	los alumnos españoles	los alumnas españolas
	los alumnos trabajadores	las alumnas trabajadoras

■ Adjectives that end in **-ista** are both masculine and feminine. To form the plurals, add **-s.**

Pedro es muy optim**ista,**	*Pedro is very optimistic,*
pero Alicia es pesim**ista.**	*but Alicia is pessimistic.*
Ellos no son material**istas.**	*They are not materialistic.*

¿Qué dice usted?

2-11 ¿Cómo son estas personas? Choose the correct completion to describe the following people. In some cases, there is more than one possible answer.

1. Muchos de los alumnos de mi universidad son...
   - a. alto
   - b. hispanos
   - c. norteamericanas
   - d. mexicanos

2. Mi profesora favorita es muy...
   - a. joven
   - b. perezosas
   - c. atractiva
   - d. delgado

3. En mi clase de español, los estudiantes son...
   - a. trabajadora
   - b. calladas
   - c. agradables
   - d. simpáticos

4. Mi amigo Nicolás es muy...
   - a. tonta
   - b. fuerte
   - c. callado
   - d. antipática

5. Mi amiga Isabel es...
   - a. rubio y guapo
   - b. simpática y divertida
   - c. joven y soltero
   - d. baja y pelirroja

6. Las dos chicas más populares de la clase son...
   - a. activos y trabajadores
   - b. inteligentes y estudiosas
   - c. altos y morenos
   - d. anaranjadas y verdes

2-12 Descripciones. You are the personnel manager of a Hispanic company in California and you have just hired some staff. Mark the qualities that you think these people have and then describe them to a partner, making all the necessary changes. Answer the questions he/she may have.

1. La directora de relaciones públicas

   _____ activo   _____ competente   _____ pasivo   _____ agradable
   _____ bilingüe   _____ callado   _____ antipático   _____ trabajador
   _____ extrovertido   _____ atractivo   _____ casado   ...

2. Dos empleados para la oficina de ventas (*sales*)

   _____ perezoso   _____ inteligente   _____ débil   _____ hablador
   _____ tímido   _____ perfeccionista   _____ tonto   _____ simpático
   _____ imparcial   _____ eficiente   _____ joven   ...

2-13 Personas importantes. Primera fase. Take turns describing the people below, using at least three of the following adjectives or expressions for each one. Compare your description with those of other classmates.

serio	trabajador	cómico
inteligente	simpático	atlético
guapo	extrovertido	liberal
tiene ojos...	tiene pelo...	...

1. Christina Aguilera
2. Toni Morrison
3. Alex Rodríguez

4. Shakira
5. Antonio Banderas
6. Tiger Woods

Segunda fase. Now, take turns describing someone important in your life. Your partner will ask questions to get more information about the person you describe and to find out why he/she is important to you.

SITUACIONES

1. **Role A.** You have just rented a two bedroom apartment near campus and are looking for a roommate (**compañero de cuarto**). You receive a call from a student who is interested. Verify his name and ask him a) where he is from, b) what his personality traits are, c) if he currently works; if so, where, and d) what he likes to do in his free time (**tiempo libre**).

   Role B. Through an ad (**anuncio**) on a campus bulletin board, you found out that someone is looking for a roommate (**compañero de cuarto**) to share an apartment. You call the person in the ad. Answer your potential roommate's questions in detail and ask any questions you may have.

2. **Role A.** Your best friend has called to tell you that she has a new boyfriend (**novio**). Ask a) where your best friend's boyfriend is from, b) what he is like, c) what he studies, d) if he has a car, and e) what car he has.

   Role B. You call your best friend to tell him about your new boyfriend. Your friend wants to know more about him. Answer all of your friend's questions in as much detail as possible.

2. Present tense and some uses of the verb *ser*

SER (*to be*)			
yo	soy	nosotros/as	somos
tú	eres	vosotros/as	sois
Ud., él, ella	es	Uds., ellos/as	son

You have practiced some forms of the verb **ser** and have used them for identification (**Ese señor es el dependiente**) and to tell time (**Son las cuatro**). Below you will learn other uses of the verb **ser**.

■ **Ser** is used with adjectives to describe what a person, a place, or a thing is like.

¿Cómo **es** ella?	*What is she like?*
Es inteligente y simpática.	*She is intelligent and nice.*
¿Cómo **es** la casa?	*What is the house like?*
La casa **es** grande y muy bonita.	*The house is big and very beautiful.*

■ **Ser** is used to express the nationality of a person; **ser + de** is used to express the origin of a person.

NATIONALITY

Luis **es** chileno.	*Luis is Chilean.*
Ana **es** mexicana.	*Ana is Mexican.*

ORIGIN

Luis **es** de Chile.	*Luis is from Chile.*
Ana **es** de México.	*Ana is from Mexico.*

- **Ser + de** is also used to express possession. The equivalent of the English word *whose* is **¿de quién?**

¿De quién es la casa?	*Whose house is it?*
La casa **es de** Marta.	*The house is **Marta's**.*

- **Ser** is also used to express the location or time of an event.

El baile **es** en la universidad.	*The dance is (takes place) at the university.*
El examen **es** a las tres.	*The test is (takes place) at three.*

3. *Ser* and *estar* with adjectives

- **Ser** and **estar** are often used with the same adjectives. However, the choice of verb determines the meaning of the sentence.

- **Ser** + *adjective* states the norm—what someone or something is like.

Manolo **es** delgado.	*Manolo is thin. (He is a thin boy.)*
Sara **es** muy nerviosa.	*Sara is very nervous. (She is a nervous person.)*
El libro **es** nuevo.	*The book is new. (It is a new book.)*

- **Estar** + *adjective* expresses a change from the norm, a condition, or how one feels about the person or object being discussed.

Manolo **está** delgado.	*Manolo is thin. (He lost weight recently.)*
Sara **está** muy nerviosa.	*Sara is very nervous. (She has been nervous lately.)*
El libro **está** nuevo.	*The book is/looks new. (It seems like a brand new book.)*

- The adjectives **contento/a, cansado/a, enojado/a** are always used with **estar.**

Ella **está contenta** ahora.	*She is happy now.*
El niño **está cansado.**	*The boy is tired.*
Carlos **está enojado.**	*Carlos is angry.*

- Some adjectives have one meaning with **ser** and another with **estar.**

Ese señor **es** malo.	*That man is bad/evil.*
Ese señor **está** malo.	*That man is ill.*
El chico **es** listo.	*The boy is clever.*
El chico **está** listo.	*The boy is ready.*
La manzana **es** verde.	*The apple is green.*
La manzana **está** verde.	*The apple is not ripe.*
Ella **es** aburrida.	*She is boring.*
Ella **está** aburrida.	*She is bored.*

¿Qué dice usted?

2-14 ¿Cómo somos? Primera fase. Look at the following descriptions and write an X under the appropriate heading.

	Sí	No
1. Soy muy estudioso/a y trabajador/a.	____	____
2. A veces soy callado/a.	____	____
3. Mi familia es muy religiosa y tradicional.	____	____
4. Mi mejor amigo es muy simpático y conversador.	____	____
5. Él y yo somos agradables.	____	____
6. Mis clases de este semestre son interesantes.	____	____

Segunda fase. Now compare your answers with those of a classmate. Ask questions to get additional information about your classmate.

2-15 Descripciones. Ask what the following people and places are like.

MODELO: tu profesor/a de inglés
E1: ¿Cómo es tu profesor de inglés?
E2: Es alto, moreno y muy simpático.

1. la oficina del Departamento de Lenguas
2. tu cuarto (*bedroom*)
3. tu compañero/a de cuarto
4. tu auto/bicicleta
5. los chicos/las chicas de la clase
6. el laboratorio de lenguas

2-16 ¿De quién es/son...? You walk into your room and find several objects that do not belong to you. Ask your classmate (roommate) whose they are. He/She will ask you at least two questions to help you identify the owner.

MODELO: computadora portátil (*laptop*)
E1: ¿De quién es la computadora?
E2: No sé. ¿De qué color es?
E1: Es negra.
E2: ¿Es grande o pequeña?
E1: Es pequeña.
E2: Entonces es la computadora portátil de Luis.

1.

2.

3.

4.

5.

6.

2-17 Una persona diferente. One of you will use the adjectives in the following list to describe several people you both know. The other, who knows those people have changed, tells him/her what they are like now.

MODELO: Arturo/gordo
                E1: Arturo es gordo.
                E2: Pero ahora está muy delgado.

1. Ramón/optimista
2. Ana y Gustavo/conversadores
3. Catalina/tranquila
4. Julián/fuerte
5. Berta y Luisa/trabajadoras
6. Carmen/alegre

2-18 ¿Quiénes son estas personas? You are at a gathering where there are several foreign students. Ask a friend about the following people. Follow the model.

MODELO: Olga Mendoza/Bolivia
                E1: ¿Quién es esa chica?
                E2: ¿Qué chica?/¿Cuál de ellas?
                E1: La chica alta y rubia.
                E2: ¡Ah! Es Olga Mendoza.
                E1: ¿De dónde es?
                E2: Es boliviana. Es de La Paz.

1. Elda Capetillo/México
2. Fernando y Eduardo Arenas/Argentina
3. María Juana Herrera/Nicaragua
4. Ernesto Gutiérrez/Colombia
5. Alberto Díaz/Puerto Rico
6. Carmen Cisneros/Venezuela

2-19 Termómetro emocional. Primera fase. Write an *X* under the words that describe how you feel in the corresponding places and situations. Then write two more words, one under **yo** and the other under **compañero/a**, showing how you feel and how you guess your classmate feels.

LUGARES	ABURRIDO/A	CONTENTO/A	TRANQUILO/A	NERVIOSO/A	YO	COMPAÑERO/A
en la cafetería con mis compañeros						
en los exámenes finales						
en la oficina de un/a profesor/a						
en el parque con mis amigos						
en una fiesta formal						
en mi casa por la noche						

Segunda fase. Now compare your responses and write down one similarity and one difference between you and your classmate. Report to the class.

MODELO: en la clase de español
E1: En la clase de español, yo estoy contento/a. Tú también estás contento/a (en la clase de español).
E2: Sí, yo estoy contento/a. *o* No, yo estoy aburrido/a.

2-20 Eventos y lugares. You are working at the university's information booth, and a visitor (your classmate) stops by. Answer his/her questions. Then switch roles.

MODELO: la exposición del club de fotografía

VISITANTE: Perdón/Disculpe, ¿dónde es la exposición del club de fotografía?
EMPLEADO/A: Es en la biblioteca.
VISITANTE: ¿Dónde está la biblioteca?
EMPLEADO/A: Está al lado de la cafetería.

1. el concierto
2. la conferencia
3. el banquete
4. la reunión de profesores
5. la fiesta del club de español
6. la ceremonia de graduación

SITUACIONES

1. **Role A.** A new student from a Spanish-speaking country has joined your math class. Introduce yourself and find out the following information from him/her: a) name; b) country and city (**ciudad**) of origin; and c) characteristics of people from his/her country (what they are like).

   Role B. You are a foreign student from a Spanish-speaking country who has recently joined a class. Answer your classmate's questions with as much detail as possible. Then ask him/her questions in order to get the same information he/she obtained from you.

2. **Role A.** You are trying to set up your classmate on a blind date with a friend. Answer your classmate's questions trying to tailor your answers to what you think he/she would like in a person since you want them to meet.

   Role B. Your classmate is trying to set you up on a blind date. Ask as many questions as possible to get the information you would like to know before deciding what to do.

ACENTOS

All words that are stressed on the third syllable from the end must have a written accent:

examen → e xá me nes.
　　　　　 3　2　1

joven → jóvenes
　　　　　3 2　1

4. Possessive adjectives

POSSESSIVE ADJECTIVES	
mi(s)	*my*
tu(s)	*your* (familiar)
su(s)	*your, his, her, its, their*
nuestro(s), nuestra(s)	*our*
vuestro(s), vuestra(s)	*your* (familiar plural)

■ These possessive adjectives always precede the noun they modify.

  mi casa   **tu** bicicleta

■ Possessive adjectives change number to agree with the thing possessed, not with the possessor.

  mi casa, **mis** casas

■ The **nosotros** and **vosotros** forms must agree also in gender.

  nuestro profesor, **nuestros** amigos; **nuestra** profesora, **nuestras** amigas

■ **Su** and **sus** have multiple meanings. To ensure clarity, you may use **de** + the name of the possessor or the appropriate pronoun.

$$\text{\textbf{su} compañera = la compañera +} \begin{cases} \textbf{de ella} \text{ (la compañera de Elena)} \\ \textbf{de él} \text{ (la compañera de Jorge)} \\ \textbf{de usted} \\ \textbf{de ustedes} \\ \textbf{de ellos} \text{ (la compañera de Elena y Jorge)} \\ \textbf{de ellas} \text{ (la compañera de Elena y Olga)} \end{cases}$$

¿Qué dice usted?

2-21 Mi mundo. Primera fase. Write down two things that you own and two different people that you value very much.

POSESIONES   PERSONAS

1. _____   1. _____
2. _____   2. _____

Segunda fase. Take turns describing the two objects and the people you value.

Posesiones

  E1: Mi bicicleta es nueva y muy bonita. ¿Y cómo es tu bicicleta?
  E2: Mi bicicleta es azul y bastante vieja.

Personas

  E1: Mi madre es muy alegre y activa. ¿Y tu mamá, cómo es?
  E2: Es tranquila y muy inteligente.

2-22 Mi familia. First, mark your answers in the appropriate column. Then interview each other and compare your answers.

	YO		MI COMPAÑERO/A	
	Sí	No	Sí	No
1. Mi familia es grande.	_____	_____	_____	_____
2. Otros miembros de la familia viven en nuestro barrio (*neighborhood*).	_____	_____	_____	_____
3. A veces pasamos las vacaciones con mis abuelos (*grandparents*).	_____	_____	_____	_____
4. Siempre conversamos sobre temas políticos.	_____	_____	_____	_____
5. A veces no estamos de acuerdo y discutimos.	_____	_____	_____	_____
6. Nuestros amigos visitan la casa frecuentemente.	_____	_____	_____	_____

2-23 Nuestra universidad. Primera fase. In preparation for **Segunda fase**, write down some words that describe in general the following at your university.

1. profesores: _____
2. clases: _____
3. estudiantes: _____
4. equipo (*team*) de béisbol/basquetbol/fútbol: _____

Segunda fase. Now, prepare a short oral presentation—to a group of students from another college/university—about your university, using the correct form of **nuestro.**

SITUACIONES

1. **Role A.** You are looking for a new apartment. One of your classmates is trying to talk you into moving in with him/her into his/her apartment. Before making a decision, ask questions regarding a) size, b) location c) cost, and d) color.

   Role B. You would like your classmate to move in with you. Answer his/her questions regarding your apartment trying to make it look as spacious and desirable as possible.

2. **Role A.** You are planning to give your best friend a surprise birthday party at your house and would like to invite one of your classmates. Tell your classmate a) that your friend's birthday is on Sunday, and b) where the party will take place.

   Role B. You've been invited to a party. Find out a) the exact address, b) the time of the party, c) who the other guests (**otros invitados**) are, and d) thank your classmate for the invitation (**por la invitación**).

EN DIRECTO

To emphasize a characteristic, use the adverb **muy.**
El apartamento es **muy** grande.
Está **muy** cerca (*near*) de la Universidad, etc. . .

To initiate the conversation:
Mira, el domingo es el cumpleaños de...
¿Sabes? (*You know?*) El domingo es el cumpleaños de, ...

To acknowledge information by showing surprise:
Ah, ¿sí?
¡No me digas! (*Oh, really?*)

ALGO MÁS

Expressions with gustar

- To express what you like to do, use **me gusta** + *infinitive*. To express what you don't like to do, say **no me gusta** + *infinitive*.

Me gusta bailar.	*I like to dance.*
No me gusta mirar la televisión.	*I don't like to watch television.*

- To express that you like something, use **me gusta** + *singular noun* or **me gustan** + *plural noun*.

Me gusta la música clásica.	*I like classical music.*
Me gustan las fiestas.	*I like parties.*

- To ask a classmate what he/she likes, use **¿Te gusta/n... ?** To ask your instructor, use **¿Le gusta/n... ?**

¿Te gusta/Le gusta tomar café?	*Do you like to drink coffee?*
¿Te gustan/Le gustan los chocolates?	*Do you like chocolates?*

A INVESTIGAR

The number of Hispanics has increased tremendously in the last few years. Find out the percentage of Hispanics in the population of your state according to the last census and the one before. Has it increased? Can you give some examples of the Hispanic presence in this country?

¿Qué dice usted?

 2-24 Mis preferencias. Fill in the following chart, based on your preferences. Compare your answers with those of a classmate.

ACTIVIDAD	ME GUSTA MUCHO	ME GUSTA	NO ME GUSTA
escribir correos electrónicos			
hablar por teléfono			
bailar salsa			
leer libros sobre Hispanoamérica			

2-25 ¿Te gusta...? Ask a classmate if he/she likes the following things. Do not forget to ask follow-up questions as appropriate.

1. el gimnasio de la universidad
2. las discotecas
3. la informática
4. los autos de este año
5. los animales
6. los conciertos de música pop

G 2-26 ¿Qué te gusta hacer? Primera fase. Write down some questions that you would ask a classmate to find out the following:

1. What he/she likes to do during the week: in the morning, afternoon, night.
2. What he/she likes to do over the weekend: Saturdays and Sundays.

Segunda fase. Interview two classmates and ask each of them the questions you prepared in **Primera fase.** Compare their responses and be prepared to share your conclusions regarding how your classmates spend their time with the rest of the class or with another group. The expressions in the box may help you express your conclusions.

EN DIRECTO

To compare:
M y N son semejantes.
Los/Las dos hablan mucho por teléfono.
M y N son diferentes.
M estudia mucho toda la semana. N estudia de lunes a viernes.

Escuchar

Listening for specific information

When you are asking specific questions, you need to understand only the answer to the question you have asked; that is, you need to understand the specific information you have requested. For example, if you want to know the name or place of origin of a new friend, you might want to focus only on his/her name or the place he/she is from. Although you might understand everything else, you just need to understand what you are interested in.

Antes de escuchar

2-27 ¿Quiénes son? You will listen to a conversation between two Hispanic students, Rafael and Laura. First write down the names of four Spanish-speaking countries and the nationality of the people born in each of them.

Countries: _____

Nationalities: _____

A escuchar

AUDIO **2-28.** Now, listen to the conversation and complete the following chart.

NOMBRE	NACIONALIDAD	FACULTAD	UNIVERSIDAD
Rafael			
Laura			

Después de escuchar

2-29 ¿Y usted? Answer the following questions.

1. ¿Cómo se llama usted? _____
2. ¿De dónde es? _____
3. ¿Dónde estudia? _____

Antes de escuchar

2-30 ¿Cómo son? In **2-31**, you will listen to a conversation between a student and her mother. The student is talking about how different her roommates are. Before listening to their conversation, write your roommate(s)' name(s) and a sentence that describes her/him/them.

_____

_____

A escuchar

AUDIO 2-31 Dos personas diferentes. Now, listen to the conversation between a student and her mother. Mark the appropriate column(s) to indicate whether the following statements describe Rita, Marcela, or both.

	RITA	MARCELA
1. Estudia economía.		
2. Le gusta bailar.		
3. Es baja, morena y tiene los ojos negros.		
4. Es alta, delgada y es muy seria.		
5. Estudia arte moderno.		

Después de escuchar

2-32 ¿Semejantes o diferentes? Complete the following ideas, according to your experience.

1. (No) Me gusta(n) mi(s) compañero/a(s) de cuarto porque _____

_____

2. Es/Son semejantes/diferentes porque _____

_____

Conversar

▪▪

Antes de conversar

G 2-33 ¿Descripción física o de personalidad? Classify the following expressions under the appropriate column in the chart below.

Es inteligente.   Es guapa.
Tiene buen humor.   Es listo.
Tiene los ojos marrones. Es pelirroja.
Es simpático.   Es muy delgada.
Le gusta bailar.   Tiene el pelo largo.

CARACTERÍSTICAS FÍSICAS	CARACTERÍSTICAS DE PERSONALIDAD

A conversar

2-34 Adivinen quién es. Describe a student in the class or a public figure that everyone knows. The class will guess who this person is.

Después de conversar

2-35 Descripción. Choose one of the persons described and write a complete paragraph about him/her. Describe the person physically as well as his/her personality. Also indicate whether or not you like the person and why.

Antes de conversar

www **2-36 Condorito y sus amigos.** *Condorito* is a comic strip magazine named after its central character. *Condorito* is very popular among children and adults in many Spanish-speaking countries. Go to www.prenhall.com/mosaicos, choose one of the characters shown in the picture below, and read the description about him/her.

World Editors®

A conversar

2-37 Mi personaje (*character*) favorito. Describe physically and in personality terms the *Condorito* character you read about in **2-36.** Your classmate will ask questions or make comments when appropriate.

Después de conversar

2-38 Mi visión de un personaje cómico. Find out about another popular comic character, like those mentioned in the *Cultura* box, page 80, and make a small information poster that includes a description of the character.

Leer

Accurate, fluent reading is an important skill that must be developed to become proficient in another language. It is important to develop this skill from the earliest stages of learning a new language.

Reading proficiently means more than just knowing words. It represents an active process in which linguistic and non-linguistic variables intervene while you are trying to make sense of a written text.

Before proceeding with the following activities, review some of the reading tips you practiced on pp. 46–47 of *Lección 1*. Then, in *Lección 2*, you will skim a text and infer meaning from context clues.

Guía de prelectura

Skim the texts in activity 2-40 and answer the questions, based on what you know from your own experience.

1. What type of texts are the following?
   a. e-mail messages
   b. for sale ads
   c. personal ads

2. What helped you identify the type of text?
   a. the format
   b. some expressions used
   c. the length

3. What do the people in the texts probably need?
   a. to find a lost relative
   b. to find someone to marry
   c. to make friends

4. Now, use your knowledge of the English language to comprehend what you read.

What cognates helped you figure out the answer to question 3 in the previous section?

   a. _____   b. _____   c. _____

Antes de leer

2-39 Preparación. Primera fase. Read the following list and mark with an X those aspects that you find desirable in a friend.

1. _____ las características físicas
2. _____ el dinero (*money*)
3. _____ la ideas políticas
4. _____ el lugar de origen
5. _____ la educación
6. _____ la raza (*race*)
7. _____ la personalidad
8. _____ la fidelidad

② Segunda fase. Now interview each other to find out the qualities that your best friends have. Mark your choices with an X. Then, determine which aspects in **Primera fase** are important for both of you. Do both of you value the same characteristics in a friend?

MODELO: E1: Tu mejor amigo/a, ¿es generoso/a?
          E2: Sí, es generoso/a. *o* No, no es generoso/a. Es tacaño (*stingy*).

1. _____ moreno/a
2. _____ rubio/a
3. _____ simpático/a
4. _____ conservador/a
5. _____ liberal
6. _____ rico/a
7. _____ alegre
8. _____ extranjero/a
9. _____ trabajador/a
10. _____ ...

A leer

2-40 Primera mirada. Read the ads below and find one person you would like as your friend or as a friend of someone you know. Fill in the form below. In some cases, it may not be possible to provide all the information requested.

	SU CANDIDATO/A	CANDIDATO/A PARA OTRA PERSONA
Nombre		
Edad		
Forma de comunicación		
Estado civil		
¿Por qué?		

LENGUA

Y changes to **e** when it precedes a word beginning with **i** or **h**.

inglés y español, but **español e inglés**

inteligente y agradable, but **agradable e inteligente**

hipócrita y ambicioso, but **ambicioso e hipócrita**

Amigos sin fronteras

Soltera, sin hijos y sin compromiso. Me llamo Susana y tengo 24 años. Busco amigos extranjeros, solteros, separados o divorciados, jóvenes o mayores. Soy amable, cariñosa y muy trabajadora. Por mi trabajo, viajo mucho, pero me gusta la compañía de otras personas. Soy bilingüe. Hablo español e inglés. Escriban a sincompromiso@comcast.net.

Soy Ricardo Brown. 21 años, sincero, dedicado. Me gustan las fiestas. Deseo conocer a una chica de unos 23 años. Prefiero una mujer activa e independiente. Me gusta practicar deportes y explorar lugares nuevos. Escríbanme a amigosincero@msn.com.

Me llamo Pablo Sosa, tengo 31 años, y soy chileno. Soy agradable y muy trabajador. Me gusta hacer mi trabajo a la perfección, pero soy tolerante. Mi pasión son los autos convertibles. Deseo mantener correspondencia por correo electrónico con jóvenes del extranjero para intercambiar información sobre los convertibles europeos o americanos. Mi dirección electrónica es locoporlosautos@yahoo.com.

Soy Xiomara Stravinsky, decoradora y fotógrafa. Soy joven, dinámica, agradable y generosa, pero tengo pocos amigos porque tengo dos trabajos y paso muchas horas con mis clientes. Necesito un cambio en mi vida. ¿Deseas ser mi amigo/a? Por favor, escríbeme a xiomarastravinsky@hotmail.com.

Después de leer

 2-41 Ampliación. What qualities do you associate with Susana (**S**), Ricardo (**R**), Pablo (**P**), and Xiomara (**X**)? Why? With a classmate, write the initial(s) next to each quality, and support your opinions.

1. _____ sociable
2. _____ simpático/a
3. _____ divertido/a
4. _____ perfeccionista

5. _____ mayor
6. _____ flexible
7. _____ trabajador/a
8. _____ ocupado/a

▦ *Escribir*

Writing a Description

Writing a description is similar to painting a picture, except we use words instead of paint. There are many ways to write a description, but in general a good written description . . .

- presents enough information about the object so the reader may visualize the characteristics of what is described: colors, physical characteristics, personality traits, etc.

- places the object described in a particular space and time: an empty classroom after classes are over looks and feels different from a crowded one during class time. The physical or psychological description of an individual helps the reader visualize what is described. Through the use of adjectives, the writer may cause the reader to like, dislike, enjoy, remember, etc.

- requires organization of information, and a good selection of vocabulary and structures (nouns, adjectives, verbs, adverbs, etc.).

- is always made with the reader in mind: What does the reader need to know? How much information should be provided? Why will he/she read our description?

As you gain more experience with the language, you will start focusing on ways to approach the writing task more effectively with your peers and your instructor. The following will be very useful in discussing your writing:

- to state the purpose (**propósito**) of your writing: **describir, narrar, explicar,** etc.

- to describe the means of communication (**medio de comunicación**): **carta** (*letter*), **anuncio** (*ad*), **correo electrónico,** etc.

- to determine the reader (*lector/a*)*:* **amigo/a, conocido/a** (*acquaintance*), **familiar,** etc.

Antes de escribir

2-42 Enfoque (*Focus*). Primera fase. A male movie fan writes the following ad
in the local newspaper to meet other people with whom he can share his passion
and with whom he can have fun outdoors. First, read the ad and the response
he got from a female reader of the ad. Then, follow the instructions.

> Fanático del cine necesita amigos para discutir películas los fines de semana.
> Tengo 24 años y estudio cinematografía. Me fascinan las películas de acción
> y también las románticas. Soy fuerte, activo, atlético y aventurero. Me gusta
> practicar deportes, especialmente el tenis y el esquí. Siempre estoy muy
> ocupado, pero tengo unas horas todas las semanas para conversar sobre
> películas y hacer deportes. Interesados, favor de enviar correo electrónico a
> fanaticodelcine@yahoo.com.

```
Para: fanaticodelcine@yahoo.com
De: Marta20@chat.com
Asunto: anuncio

Estimado fanaticodelcine,

Me llamo Marta y me gustan mucho las películas y los deportes. Tengo
20 años y estudio en la universidad. Tú y yo somos similares. Yo soy
atlética, aventurera, pero muy responsable. Me gusta tener muchos
amigos y explorar lugares con ellos.

Este semestre tomo seis clases y tengo mucho trabajo, pero siempre
miro películas o practico deportes. Los fines de semana tengo un poco
de tiempo para hacer actividades interesantes. Vivo cerca de la
universidad y me gusta mucho mi apartamento. No necesito tomar el
bus para asistir a clase. También me gusta mucho caminar. Por favor,
responde a mi dirección de correo electrónico: marta20@chat.com

Hasta pronto.
```

Segunda fase. Answer the following questions based on Marta's response.

1. Does Marta describe herself appropriately in her response to *fanaticodelcine?*
       Yes   No
2. Mark with an X the reason for your response or write your own response:
   _____ Marta describes herself as a physically attractive young woman.
   _____ Marta provides *fanaticodelcine* with a description of the potential
           friend he is looking for.
   _____ Marta addresses the needs of *fanaticodelcine* by telling him how
           compatible their free time activities are.
   _____ Marta plans her ideas carefully. She specifies her free time activities
           and hobbies, talks about her personality features, etc. to match the
           person *fanaticodelcine* is looking for.

   _____ . . .

2-43 Preparación. Reread the ads in **Amigos sin fronteras**, page 81, and choose one ad you would like to respond to. Then, make a list of words that will help you describe yourself (or someone you'd like to be) to become friends with the person who wrote the ad.

1. one way to tell your age
2. indicate your place of origin
3. some words (adjectives) that describe you physically
4. some expressions (adjectives) that describe your personality
5. some activities (verbs) that you like to do that match the needs of the person in the ad

A escribir

2-44 Manos a la obra. Now answer the ad using the information you prepared in the previous activity.

```
Para: _____

De: _____

Asunto: Anuncio

Hola _____,

Respondo a tu anuncio del periódico. Me llamo _____.

Primero, aquí tienes alguna información personal: _____

_____

_____

En segundo lugar, éstas son algunas de las actividades similares a
tus actividades que me gustan en mi tiempo libre: _____

_____

En tercer lugar, por las tardes/noches, o los fines de semana, me gusta
_____

_____

Finalmente, deseo ser tu amigo/a. Por favor, escríbeme un correo
electrónico a mi dirección: _____

Hasta pronto.
```

Después de escribir

2-45 Revisión. After completing your letter or e-mail, read it at least twice. Check the following:

■ The content of the letter or e-mail: Did you include all the information your reader needs?

■ The form of the text: Did you use punctuation correctly? Did you verify that there are no spelling or grammatical mistakes?

Finally, discuss your letter or e-mail with a classmate.

TEMAS: LOS HISPANOS EN LOS ESTADOS UNIDOS

Para pensar

¿Tiene usted amigos hispanos? ¿De qué países son? ¿Hay estudiantes hispanos en su universidad? ¿Sabe usted el nombre de una comida hispana?

Las personas de origen hispano viven en muchos estados de los Estados Unidos: Arizona, California, Colorado, Illinois, Nueva York, Nueva Jersey, Nuevo México, Texas, etcétera.

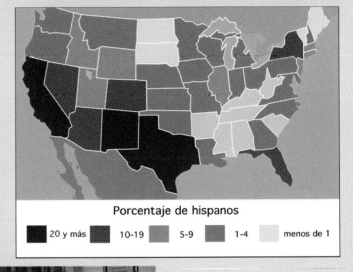

Porcentaje de hispanos

| 20 y más | 10-19 | 5-9 | 1-4 | menos de 1 |

Algunos hispanos abandonan sus países por razones políticas o económicas. Otros buscan mejores oportunidades de trabajo o una educación especializada.

Los hispanos en los Estados Unidos vienen de todos los países de Hispanoamérica, pero no todos son inmigrantes; los chicanos (personas de ascendencia mexicana) son ciudadanos desde que la región del suroeste pasó a ser territorio norteamericano en 1848. Los puertorriqueños son ciudadanos norteamericanos desde 1917.

Los hispanos traen su rica y valiosa cultura, su voluntad de trabajo y deseo de superación, y contribuyen a la vida cultural, política, artística y deportiva de los Estados Unidos.

Para contestar

2 **Los amigos hispanos.** Respondan a las siguientes preguntas:

1. ¿De qué países vienen los hispanos que viven en los Estados Unidos?
2. ¿Cómo contribuyen los hispanos a la vida de los Estados Unidos?

G **Riqueza cultural.** Mencionen las ventajas y desventajas (*advantages and disadvantages*) que tiene un país con muchos inmigrantes.

Para pensar

¿Conoce usted alguna ciudad en los Estados Unidos con una gran influencia hispana? ¿Cómo se refleja esa influencia?

Al lado del Viejo San Juan está el San Juan moderno, una ciudad con una intensa vida nocturna y hermosas playas.

El Viejo San Juan es una parte muy hermosa de la capital de Puerto Rico. En esta zona hay muchas tiendas, cafés al aire libre y museos.

La influencia de la población cubana en Miami es inmensa. Hay muchos festivales donde la gente baila, come y disfruta de muchas tradiciones de su país de origen.

Expresiones puertorriqueñas:

cabuya	No le des **cabuya**.	*Don't give him/her ammunition to bother you.*
macacoa	Yo no compro la lotería porque tengo una **macacoa** terrible.	*I don't buy the lottery because I have horrible bad luck.*
majarete	Dejó su cuarto hecho un **majarete**.	*He/she left his/her room a complete mess.*
babada	No hagas caso. Es una **babada**.	*Don't pay attention. It is something foolish.*

Expresiones chicanas:

Ando brujo.	*I have no money.*
¡Ándale, güero!	*Let's go, blondey (male).*

En San Diego, California, y San Antonio, Texas, la población y la arquitectura de origen mexicano son partes integrales de estas ciudades.

Para contestar

En el mapa

1. Busque una ciudad en los Estados Unidos con una alta población hispana. Indique dónde está.
2. Diga qué ciudad con una alta población hispana está más cerca de su ciudad.

Ahora diga...

1. qué ciudad de los Estados Unidos con una alta población hispana quiere visitar y por qué.
2. una actividad de los cubanos en Miami.

¿Qué dice usted si...

1. no tiene dinero?
2. su compañero/a de cuarto no limpia (*clean*) su cuarto?

WWW Para investigar en Internet

Busque el nombre de diez personas importantes de origen hispano en el gobierno, en la empresa privada, en los deportes, en el arte o en el mundo de la moda de los Estados Unidos. Seleccione una persona y después informe a la clase sobre esta persona.

¡Prepárese!

2-46 Misterios y pistas. Before watching the second episode of *Fortunas*, read the first mystery (*misterio*) and the four clues (*pistas*). In groups of three, discuss the meanings of the *misterio* and the *pistas* and possible relationships between them. Use the following questions as a guide for your discussion. Remember that the first mystery is related to the history of the Aztecs.

Misterio No. 1: Cinco es suficiente.

Pistas:

a. Destrucción de los gigantes por el viento (monos)
b. Destrucción por la lluvia (pájaros)
c. Destrucción por el diluvio (peces)
d. Destrucción por el jaguar

1. ¿El número cinco tiene un significado especial en la cultura o en la sociedad?
2. ¿Qué importancia tiene el número cinco, u otros números, para usted personalmente?
3. ¿Qué tienen en común el viento, la lluvia y el diluvio?
4. ¿Es importante la idea de la destrucción en la historia de los aztecas?
5. ¿Qué tipo de animal es el jaguar?

Manolo y Ángela hablan del comienzo del concurso.

Tito habla con Sabrina y Efraín sobre el concurso.

Sabrina y Efraín están en Xochimilco.

A Sabrina le gustan mucho los misterios pero a Efraín no.

Efraín no es mucha competencia para Sabrina.

Sabrina desea ganar el concurso, pero su plan es un secreto.

¡Responda!

2-47 Ser o estar. Primera fase. After watching the second episode of *Fortunas*, complete the following sentences with the correct form of **ser** or **estar**.

1. Manolo y Ángela _____ contentos con el concurso.
2. Tito _____ en Xochimilco para hablar con los participantes.
3. Efraín _____ de Argentina, y Sabrina _____ española.
4. Efraín _____ músico.
5. Sabrina _____ una persona inteligente y agresiva.

Segunda fase. Now, write complete sentences in Spanish to describe the following people and things related to the *Fortunas* contest. Use adjectives from the list or any others that you can think of.

MODELO: E1: concurso
             E2: El concurso es muy interesante.

alegre	listo/a	joven
simpático/a	divertido/a	tonto/a
interesante	nervioso/a	misterioso/a
contento/a	hablador/a	ridículo/a

1. Ángela y Manolo
2. Xochimilco
3. Tito

4. misterio número 1
5. Efraín y Sabrina
6. la entrevista de Sabrina

The music of this Puerto Rican group combines several musical styles like rock, reggae, ska, and Afro-Caribbean rhythms. Their songs frequently comment on social problems.

2-48 ¡Prepárese! Try to match the following themes from *Oh Naná* with their Spanish equivalents. Use a bilingual dictionary if necessary.

1. sadness
2. the enjoyment of life
3. happiness

a. _____ respira alegría
b. _____ ríe también, vive, goza
c. _____ la pena

What things do you associate with these themes? Do you know any songs in your own language with the same themes?

> Hoy desperté con la pena
> de mi corazón, que entre latidos me
> decía no pierdas la razón.
> Me dijo, mira el cielo brillando está
> y si llueve no temas, ya el sol vendrá,
> que yo te digo, canta conmigo
> Oh Naná, Oh Nanananá.
> Y luego en la noche un viejo amigo que
> me visitó. Y aunque vestía su sonrisa,
> su rostro demostró, entró y lloró.
> Yo le dije, oye, mira, escucha bien
> respira alegría y luego ven
> que yo te digo, canta conmigo
> Oh Naná, Oh Nanananá.
> No sé por qué desperté con tanta
> tristeza, me lastimé el corazón,
> perdí la cabeza, pero alguien dijo así.
> Si sufres llora, ríe también, vive, goza,
> tiene que ser, y yo te digo,
> canta conmigo...
> Oh Naná, Oh Nanananá.

2-49 ¡Escuche! As you listen to *Oh Naná,* indicate with an X which adjectives from the list below you would use to describe the song.

_____ agradable   _____ bonita   _____ aburrida
_____ interesante   _____ corta   _____ divertida
_____ feliz   _____ fuerte   _____ enojada
_____ tranquila   _____ triste   _____ seria
_____ alegre   _____ simpática   _____ lenta

2-50 ¡Responda! Now, using the adjectives you have chosen and the verb **ser,** write five questions to ask your partner to find out how he/she would characterize the song (*la canción*), the lyrics (*la letra*), and/or the rhythm (*el ritmo*). Then answer the questions your partner has written.

MODELO: E1: ¿Es bonita la canción?
         E2: Sí, es bonita./No, no es bonita.

VOCABULARIO

AUDIO **Descripciones**

agradable	nice
alegre	happy, glad
alto/a	tall
antipático/a	unpleasant
bajo/a	short (in stature)
bilingüe	bilingual
bonito/a	pretty
callado/a	quiet
cansado/a	tired
casado/a	married
contento/a	happy, glad
conversador/a	talkative
corto/a	short (in length)
débil	weak
delgado/a	thin
divertido/a	funny, amusing
enojado/a	angry
feliz	happy
feo/a	ugly
fuerte	strong
gordo/a	fat
guapo/a	good-looking, handsome
joven	young
largo/a	long
listo/a	smart, ready
mayor	old
mediano/a	average, medium (height)
moreno/a	brunet, brunette
nervioso/a	nervous
nuevo/a	new
pelirrojo/a	redhead
perezoso/a	lazy
pobre	poor
rico/a	rich, wealthy
rubio/a	blond
simpático/a	nice, charming
soltero/a	single
tonto/a	silly, foolish
trabajador/a	hardworking
tranquilo/a	calm, tranquil
triste	sad
viejo/a	old

Verbos

desear	to wish, to want
ser	to be
usar	to use

El cuerpo

los ojos	eyes
ojos azules	blue eyes
ojos verdes	green eyes
ojos (de color) café	brown eyes
el pelo	hair
pelo castaño	brown hair
pelo negro	black hair

Nacionalidades*

argentino/a	Argentinean
chileno/a	Chilean
colombiano/a	Colombian
cubano/a	Cuban
dominicano/a	Dominican
español/a	Spanish
guatemalteco/a	Guatemalan
mexicano/a	Mexican
nicaragüense	Nicaraguan
peruano/a	Peruvian
puertorriqueño/a	Puerto Rican
venezolano/a	Venezuelan

Palabras y expresiones útiles

ahora	now
de	of, from
¿de quién?	whose?
del	of the (contraction of de + el)
le gusta(n)	you (formal) like
los lentes de contacto	contact lenses
me gusta(n)	I like
mucho/a	much, a lot
no (ni)... ni	neither . . . nor
pero	but
que	that
te gusta(n)	you (familiar) like
Tengo... años.	I am . . . years old
tiene	he/she has, you (formal) have

*Other adjectives of nationality can be found in the English-Spanish and Spanish-English glossaries at the end of the book.
See pages 63–64 for animals and additional colors.
See pages 74 for possessive adjectives.

LAS ACTIVIDADES Y LOS PLANES

Objetivos comunicativos

- Asking about and discussing leisure activities
- Communicating by phone
- Ordering food in a restaurant
- Making suggestions and future plans
- Accepting and rejecting invitations
- Using numbers 100 and above

Contenido

A primera vista

- Diversiones populares
- La comida

Explicación y expansión

- Present tense of regular *-er* and *-ir* verbs
- Present tense of the verb *ir*
- *Ir* + *a* + infinitive to express future action
- The present tense to express future action
- Numbers 100 to 2,000,000
- Algo Más: Some uses of *por* and *para*

Mosaicos

- Escuchar: Using background information
- Conversar: Discussing menus and events
- Leer: Identifying key words to comprehend
- Escribir: Writing a letter to a friend
  Using appropriate form of address

Enfoque cultural

- Temas: El cine, el teatro, las peñas
- Vistas: El Perú
  Para investigar en Internet
- Fortunas: Episodio 3
- Notas: Camino de la montaña, *Los kjarkas*

Vocabulario

AUDIO *Diversiones populares*

En las **fiestas** y **reuniones**, los jóvenes bailan, escuchan **música** o conversan. A veces **tocan** la **guitarra** y **cantan canciones** populares.

Estas chicas **van** a la playa en su **tiempo libre** y también **durante** las **vacaciones**. Allí, caminan y conversan mientras otras personas **toman el sol**, **nadan** en **el mar**, **corren** o **descansan**.

Este señor **lee** el **periódico al aire libre.** Y usted, ¿lee el periódico? ¿Qué periódicos o **revistas** lee?

*Muchos jóvenes van al **cine**, especialmente los fines de semana. También es común **alquilar películas** para **ver** en casa.*

AUDIO Una conversación por teléfono

TERESA: ¿Aló?

JAVIER: Hola, Teresa, ¿qué te parece si **vamos** al cine esta tarde y **después** vamos a **cenar** a un restaurante de **comida** peruana para **celebrar** tu **cumpleaños**?

TERESA: ¡Ay, Javier, qué bien! ¿Y qué vamos a ver?

JAVIER: Tú decides, mi amor; es tu **cumpleaños.**

TERESA: Pues, la película nueva de Alfonso Cuarón.

JAVIER: **Fabuloso.** Voy para la casa ahora. Hasta pronto.

TERESA: Chao.

¿Qué dice usted?

3-1 Asociaciones. What activities do you associate with the following places?

1. _____ la playa
2. _____ la fiesta
3. _____ el cine
4. _____ la biblioteca
5. _____ la casa

a. ver una película
b. leer el periódico
c. tomar el sol
d. mirar televisión
e. bailar y conversar

3-2 Mis actividades. What do you do in the following places? Take turns asking each other questions.

MODELO: las fiestas
E1: ¿Qué haces en las fiestas?
E2: En las fiestas bailo mucho. ¿Y tú?
E1: Bailo y hablo con mis amigos.
E2: Y tú, ¿qué haces en... ?

1. la universidad por las mañanas
2. la biblioteca pública de tu ciudad
3. casa el fin de semana
4. un parque de tu ciudad
5. la playa durante las vacaciones
6. la discoteca con tus amigos

3-3 ¿Adónde vamos? Primera fase. Look at the cultural section of a Peruvian newspaper below. Underline three activities that you would like to do on the weekend. Then fill in the information in the following chart, including the day and the time that you are planning to do them.

EL Diario de Trujillo

Muestras y Exposiciones

Exposición del séptimo concurso de artes visuales. *Pasaporte para un artista*, que este jueves, a las 7:30 p.m., se inaugura en la Casona Orbegoso.

Los monstruos de Salid. Muestra del pintor Sadid Luján. Lugar: Casa de la Emancipación. Horario al público: De 9 a.m. a 1 p.m. y de 4 a 7 p.m.

Presencia colombiana en nuestro país. Cuadros de los pintores colombianos Félix Ángel y Jenaro Mejía. Lugar: Sexto piso de El cultural.

Sarita & Co. Muestra colectiva con motivo del Día Internacional de la Mujer. Lugar: Casa de la Emancipación.

Música y Teatro

Orquesta Sinfónica de Trujillo. (OST), Dirigida por el maestro Teófilo Álvarez: Suite No. 1 de la ópera Carmen de Bizet y Obertura de Rossini. Teatro Municipal de Trujillo a las 10:30 de la mañana.

Compañía Regional del Ballet. Escenas de la ópera rock, *Jesucristo Superstar*. La coreografía pertenece a Stella Puga, la música a Andrew Lloyd Webber y la letra a Timothy Rice.

Cine

La prueba (*The Recruit*). Un thriller que nos muestra los secretos de la CIA: cómo se recluta a los agentes, cómo se entregan para el espionaje y cómo aprenden las reglas de la supervivencia. Con Colin Farrell y Al Pacino. V.O.S. A las 5 p.m., 8 p.m. y 10 p.m. En los Minicines Trujillo.

Las horas (*The Hours*). Tres mujeres que viven en épocas y lugares diferentes, pero están vinculadas entre sí porque las tres buscan el sentido de sus vidas. Con Nicole Kidman, Julianne Moore y Meryl Streep. V.O.S. A las 12 p.m, 4 p.m. y 7 p.m. En los Minicines Trujillo.

Mi vida sin mí de la directora catalana Isabel Coixet. Sobre una mujer que decide vivir a fondo los pocos meses que le quedan de vida. Con Sarah Polley y Mark Ruffalo. A las 2 p.m. 8 p.m. y 10 p.m. En los Minicines Trujillo.

¿ADÓNDE VAMOS?	¿QUÉ VAMOS A VER/ HACER/ ESCUCHAR?	¿CUÁNDO?

Segunda fase. Phone a classmate and invite him/her to one of the events you chose in *Primera fase*. He or she will give you an excuse as in the model.

MODELO: E1: ¿Aló?

E2: Hola, Pedro. Soy María. ¿Vamos el viernes por la tarde a la exposición "Los monstruos de Salid"?

E1: Lo siento, María, el viernes Carlos y yo vamos al cine a las cuatro. Vamos a ver *Las horas*.

La comida

ESPECIALIDADES DE LA CASA

ENTRADAS

Ceviche de pescado S/.15
Papa a la huancaína S/.10
Causa a la limeña S/.12

PLATO PRINCIPAL

Chupe de camarones S/.25
Ají de gallina S/.18
Lomo saltado S/.17

POSTRES

Suspiro de limeña S/.8
Alfajor S/.8
Mazamorra morada S/.6

BEBIDAS

Chicha morada S/.4
Jugo de maracuyá S/.4
Inca Kola S/.3

AUDIO **En el restaurante.** Ahora Javier y Teresa están en el restaurante *El jardín limeño* para **celebrar** el **cumpleaños** de Teresa.

CAMARERO: Buenas noches. ¿Qué desean los señores?

JAVIER: Teresa, ¿qué vas a comer?

TERESA: Para mí, una **ensalada** primero y después **pollo** con **verduras.**

JAVIER: Yo, para empezar, **ceviche** de camarones. Y luego un **bistec** con **papas.**

CAMARERO: ¿Y para **beber**?

JAVIER: Vamos a beber **vino.** Y también **agua** con gas, por favor.

A INVESTIGAR

"S/." is the abbreviation for the monetary unit in Peru. What is the name of the monetary unit? What is the current rate of exchange?

CULTURA

Peruvian cooking uses mainly regional ingredients and follows the traditional ways of preparing them inherited from various indigenous cultures. A very typical dish of Peru and other countries in Latin America is *ceviche*. It is generally made with seafood that is not cooked, but cured in lime and spices. For more information about this dish and its variations, see www.prenhall.com/mosaicos

Tap water is generally not brought to the table in restaurants in the Spanish-speaking world as it is in the United States. Most restaurant-goers order bottled mineral water (*agua mineral*) to drink with their meal, in either its carbonated (*con gas*) or noncarbonated (*sin gas*) form.

La comida rápida

La comida rápida es muy popular entre la gente joven. Las "hamburgueserías" de tipo norteamericano existen en muchas **ciudades** del mundo hispano. Los restaurantes de comida rápida en los **países** hispanos frecuentemente combinan comida de los Estados Unidos con comidas **típicas** de cada país. Por ejemplo, usted puede comer una **hamburguesa** con **papas fritas** o con **arroz** y frijoles negros. En muchos países, usted puede tomar vino o **cerveza** en estos restaurantes.

Ají de gallina

Papas a la huancaína

Ceviche de pescado

Más comidas y bebidas

el desayuno

el cereal
la leche
el jugo de naranja
el café caliente
el pan tostado/las tostadas
los huevos fritos

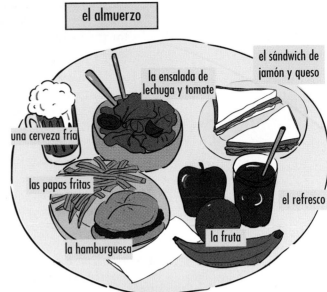

el almuerzo

el sándwich de jamón y queso
la ensalada de lechuga y tomate
una cerveza fría
las papas fritas
el refresco
la fruta
la hamburguesa

¿Qué dice usted?

3-4 La dieta. Primera fase. Which of the following contains more calories? Underline your response.

1. la sopa de tomate, las hamburguesas, la sopa de pollo
2. el pollo frito, el pescado, la ensalada
3. los vegetales, la fruta, las papas fritas
4. la cerveza, la leche, el café
5. el helado de chocolate, el cereal, el arroz

Segunda fase. Mention one food item or drink in *Primera fase* that you eat or drink frequently. Do you and your classmate like to eat and drink the same foods?

MODELO: E1: Frecuentemente como ensaladas y bebo
                cerveza. ¿Y tú?
          E2: Yo frecuentemente como papas fritas y bebo
                refrescos.

la comida/la cena

el pescado
el arroz
el helado
el pollo
el agua
los vegetales/las verduras
los espaguetis
la sopa

3-5 Las comidas. Tell a classmate what you have for breakfast, lunch, and dinner. Then find out what he/she has.

MODELO: En el desayuno, como tostadas y bebo café. ¿Y tú?

3-6 Dietas especiales. Look at the menu below and decide which would be the best option for the following people.

SOPAS	
Sopa de pollo	S/. 12
Sopa de tomate	S/. 10
Sopa de vegetales	S/. 10
Sopa de pescado	S/. 14
ENSALADAS	
Ensalada de lechuga y tomate	S/. 8
Ensalada de pollo	S/. 14
Ensalada de atún	S/. 12
PLATOS PRINCIPALES	
Bistec con papas y vegetales	S/. 20
Hamburguesa con papas fritas	S/. 16
Pescado con papas fritas	S/. 18
Arroz con vegetales	S/. 15

1. Su padre y usted son un poco delgados y desean subir de peso (*gain weight*) ¿Qué van a comer de este menú?
2. Su mamá es alérgica a los productos del mar. ¿Cuál de las ensaladas va a comer?
3. Su mejor amigo/a está un poco gordo/a y quiere bajar de peso (*lose weight*). ¿Cuál de los platos principales no debe comer?
4. El/La profesor/a de español está enfermo/a (*sick*) hoy. ¿Qué debe comer?

3-7 ¿Qué te gusta más? Using the words below, ask a classmate what he/she prefers to drink **por las mañanas, a la hora del almuerzo, por las noches.** Alternate asking questions and taking notes. Then in small groups decide which are the most popular drinks.

MODELO: E1: ¿Qué te gusta más por las mañanas, el té o el café?
E2: Me gusta más el café.

el té	un vaso (*a glass*) de leche	una cerveza	un chocolate caliente
el café	el agua mineral con gas	un refresco	un batido (*shake*) de fruta
el jugo de naranja	el agua mineral sin gas	una copa de vino	un té de hierbas

3-8 En el café. It is 8:00 Saturday morning, and a friend and you are in your favorite café. Ask your friend what he or she would like to order. Then say what you would like to order.

MODELO: E1: El desayuno es muy bueno aquí. ¿Qué deseas comer?
E2: _____ ¿Y tú?
E1: _____ ¿Y qué vas a tomar?
E2: _____

café	S/.4
té	S/.4
café con leche	S/.6
jugo de naranja	S/.5
chocolate	S/.7
tostadas	S/.5
pan con mantequilla	S/.5
pan dulce	S/.6
cereal	S/.8
huevos fritos	S/.10

G **3-9 Una excursión.** You are spending a few days in Peru, and you are planning a day trip to Machu Picchu. Make arrangements to take some food and beverages for a picnic.

a. Make a list of the food and beverages that you need to take.
b. Talk about the things that you are going to see.

La ciudad de Machu Picchu en los Andes

2 **3-10 Nuestro menú.** Your roommate and you want to have guests for dinner tonight. First decide whom each of you is going to invite; then ask each other the guests' phone numbers so one of you can make the calls later. Decide what you are going to serve. Finally, compare your menu with that of another pair of classmates.

AUDIO **3-11 ¿Qué hacen estos estudiantes?** You will listen to two students, Rafael and Miguel, talking about their daily and leisure activities. Before you listen, write down three activities you do in your leisure time, and three activities other students you know do.

Mis actividades: _____

_____

Las actividades de otros estudiantes: _____

_____

Now, listen to the audio and pay attention to the general idea of what is said. Then, in the chart below, mark **Sí** next to the activities they mention they will do during the weekend and **No** next to those ones they will not do.

	Sí	No
1. leer el periódico al aire libre	___	___
2. estudiar para los exámenes	___	___
3. ir a la playa y nadar	___	___
4. descansar y conversar	___	___
5. trabajar en la librería	___	___

EXPLICACIÓN Y EXPANSIÓN

1. Present tense of regular -er and -ir verbs

COMER (to eat)			
yo	como	nosotros/as	comemos
tú	comes	vosotros/as	coméis
Ud., él, ella	come	Uds., ellos/as	comen

VIVIR (to live)			
yo	vivo	nosotros/as	vivimos
tú	vives	vosotros/as	vivís
Ud., él, ella	vive	Uds., ellos/as	viven

■ The endings for **-er** and **-ir** verbs are the same, except for the **nosotros** and **vosotros** forms.

■ The verb **ver** has an irregular **yo** form.

　　ver: **veo**, ves, ve, vemos, veis, ven

■ Use **deber** + *infinitive* to express what you *should* or *ought to* do.

　　Debes beber mucha agua.　　　*You should (must) drink lots of water.*

■ Other common -er and -ir verbs are **aprender, correr, leer, asistir,** and **escribir.**

¿Qué dice usted?

3-12 Mi profesor/a modelo. Primera fase. Indicate which of the following activities are or are not part of an ideal instructor's routine.

	Sí	No
1. Lee el periódico en la clase.	_____	_____
2. Nunca está en su oficina.	_____	_____
3. Siempre prepara sus clases.	_____	_____
4. Saca libros de la biblioteca y lee mucho.	_____	_____
5. Comprende los problemas de los estudiantes.	_____	_____
6. Bebe café en la clase todo el tiempo.	_____	_____
7. Escribe ejemplos muy buenos en la pizarra.	_____	_____
8. Come papas fritas en la clase.	_____	_____

Segunda fase. Compare your answers with those of a classmate. Do both of you agree? Finally, write down two more features of an ideal instructor's academic life and ask your instructor if they are part of his/her real routine.

3-13 Para pasarlo bien *(To have a good time)*. **Primera fase.** Indicate which of the following activities your classmates do to have a good time.

1. _____ Estudian español hasta las dos de la mañana.
2. _____ Escriben y leen correos electrónicos.
3. _____ Van de vacaciones con sus amigos.
4. _____ Asisten a conferencias y exposiciones de arte.
5. _____ Corren en el gimnasio o en el parque.
6. _____ Leen el periódico y revistas para jóvenes.
7. _____ Alquilan películas para ver en casa.
8. _____ Comen en restaurantes donde la comida es buena.
9. . . .
10. . . .

②Segunda fase. Compare your answers with those of a classmate. Then get together with another pair and exchange information about the activities that all of you do to have a good time. Use the expressions in *En directo* to help you react more naturally to your classmates' responses.

MODELO: PAREJA 1: Nosotros bailamos en discotecas los sábados por la
                              noche. ¿Y ustedes?

                   PAREJA 2: Bebemos cerveza y conversamos con amigos en
                              un café.

②3-14 Lugares y actividades. Ask a classmate what he/she does in the following places. He/She will respond with one of the activities listed. Then ask your classmate what he/she does not do in each place.

MODELO: en la clase/ver videos
                   E1: ¿Qué haces en la clase?
                   E2: Veo videos en español.
                   E1: ¿Y qué no haces en la clase?
                   E2: No hablo inglés (ni leo el periódico).

LUGARES	ACTIVIDADES
en la playa	beber cerveza
en un café	tomar el sol y descansar
en una discoteca	bailar salsa
en una fiesta	mirar televisión
en el cine	leer el periódico
en la casa	comer un sándwich y tomar algo
en un restaurante	ver películas españolas y argentinas
en la biblioteca	escuchar música clásica

Ⓖ 3-15 Las diversiones estudiantiles. Primera fase. Working in a small group, appoint a secretary to tally responses. Then find out which of you do the following things in your free time. Next get together with another group, compare your findings, and tally responses once again.

EN DIRECTO

To react to what someone said:
¡Qué interesante!
¡Qué divertido! *(How funny!)*
¡Qué aburrido!

MODELO: nadar en la playa
E1: ¿Nadas en la playa los fines de semana?
E2: Sí, nado (en la playa) los fines de semana.

	Sí	No
1. beber café y conversar con amigos	_____	_____
2. tocar la guitarra	_____	_____
3. comer en restaurantes peruanos	_____	_____
4. ver programas cómicos en la televisión	_____	_____
5. tomar cerveza con amigos	_____	_____
6. leer libros de misterio	_____	_____

Segunda fase. Finally, as a class, discuss the following:

1. ¿Cuál es la actividad favorita de la clase?
2. ¿Cuál es la actividad que le gusta menos a la clase?

3-16 ¿Qué deben hacer? Read the situations in the column on the left and select the appropriate advice for each person(s) from the column on the right.

1. _____ Mariela desea estar delgada.
2. _____ Los turistas están en Lima y desean visitar Machu Picchu.
3. _____ Mónica estudia música y canta muy bien.
4. _____ Mis amigos están aburridos.
5. _____ Emilia y yo siempre estamos cansados.
6. _____ Yo tengo problemas de estómago porque bebo mucho café.

a. Debes beber té o café sin cafeína.
b. Deben ir al cine o alquilar una película cómica.
c. Deben tomar vitaminas y descansar más.
d. Deben ir a Cuzco primero.
e. Debe caminar todos los días y beber mucha agua.
f. Debe aprender canciones en español.

3-17 Sugerencias. What should or should not the following people do?

MODELO: Luis está muy cansado.
E1: ¿Qué debe hacer Luis?
E2: Debe descansar o No debe trabajar hoy.

1. Juan tiene un examen el lunes.
2. Francisco está débil y muy delgado.
3. Manuel y Victoria no tienen trabajo.
4. Marta ve televisión todos los días y saca malas notas.
5. Luis y Emilia desean aprender español.
6. Isabel y Lucía desean visitar Perú.

3-18 Un/a compañero/a nuevo/a. Get together with a classmate you do not know very well and ask him/her questions to find out more about him/her.

1. lugar donde vive
2. si ese lugar le gusta o no le gusta
3. lugar donde come fuera de casa
4. si le gusta o no le gusta la comida de ese lugar
5. comida favorita
6. bebida favorita
7. ...
8. ...

ACENTOS

You have probably noticed that the words **examen, casas, fruta** do not have a written accent, whereas **débil, sándwich, López** do. In Spanish, words stressed on the next-to-last syllable do not have a written accent if they end in **n, s,** or a vowel (**examen, casas, fruta**). If they end in any other letter, they carry an accent mark (**débil, sándwich, López**).

SITUACIONES

1. You meet one of your classmates at the library. After greeting him/her, find out (a) if your partner likes to read, (b) when he/she reads, (c) what newspapers and magazines he/she reads, and (d) if he/she reads newspapers or magazines in Spanish. If the answer is yes, find out the names of the newspapers or magazines.

2. You are a waiter/waitress at a café. Two of your classmates will play the part of the customers. Greet your customers and ask them what they would like to eat and drink. Be prepared to answer any questions they may have.

2. Present tense of the verb *ir*

IR (*to go*)			
yo	**voy**	nosotros/as	**vamos**
tú	**vas**	vosotros/as	**vais**
Ud., él, ella	**va**	Uds., ellos/as	**van**

■ Use **a** to introduce a noun after the verb **ir.** When **a** is followed by the article **el**, the two words contract to form **al.**

Voy **a la** fiesta de María.   *I am going to María's party.*
Vamos **al** gimnasio.   *We are going to the gymnasium.*

■ Use **adónde** when asking *where to* with the verb **ir.**

¿**Adónde** vas ahora?   *Where are you going now?*

3. *Ir + a +* infinitive to express future action

■ To express future action, use the present tense of **ir** + **a** + the infinitive form of the verb.

Ellos **van a nadar** después.   *They are going to swim later.*
¿**Vas a ir** a la fiesta?   *Are you going to go to the party?*

4. The present tense to express future action

■ You may also express future action with the present tense of the verb. The context shows whether you are referring to the present or the future.

Mañana **tengo** un examen.   *I have a test tomorrow.*
¿**Vas** al cine esta noche?   *Are you going to the party tonight?*

■ The following expressions denote future time:

después	*afterwards, later*
más tarde	*later*
esta noche	*tonight*
mañana	*tomorrow*
pasado mañana	*the day after tomorrow*
la próxima semana	*next week*
el próximo mes/año	*next month/year*

¿Qué dice usted?

3-19 Lugares y actividades. Match where the following people are going with the activities that they are probably going to do there.

1. _____ Victoria va a su casa.
2. _____ Elena y Alberto van a la biblioteca.
3. _____ Rodrigo y Berta van a la playa.
4. _____ Alina va a una librería hispana.
5. _____ Nosotros vamos al cine.
6. _____ Estela va a un café.

a. Va a comprar un libro sobre Perú.
b. Van a tomar el sol y a nadar.
c. Vamos a ver una película española.
d. Va a descansar y a mirar televisión.
e. Va a tomar un refresco.
f. Van a estudiar para un examen.

(G) 3-20 Mi agenda para la semana. Primera fase. Invite six classmates individually to do the following activities with you. Each will accept or reject your invitation according to his/her agenda for the week. Write down your plans in the chart, indicating the activity and the name of the classmate who accepted your invitation.

MODELO: estudiar en la biblioteca el lunes
E1: ¿Vamos a estudiar en la biblioteca el lunes?
E2: Lo siento, Miguel, el lunes voy a ir al cine con David. Pero, ¿por qué no comemos en un restaurante peruano el martes?
E3: Buena idea. Hablamos después.

1. ir al cine
2. mirar televisión en casa
3. tomar algo en un café
4. estudiar para la clase de español
5. bailar en la discoteca
6. correr una milla

DÍA	¿QUÉ VA A HACER?	¿CON QUIÉN?
martes	comer en un restaurante peruano	Miguel

EN DIRECTO

To accept an invitation:
¡Estupendo! ¿Dónde quedamos? (*Where do we meet?*)
Sí, gracias, ¡qué bien!

To turn down an invitation politely:
Lo siento, pero no tengo tiempo/tengo mucho trabajo, etcétera.
Ese día no puedo (*I can't*); debo estudiar para un examen.

Segunda fase. Prepare your own agenda for the upcoming week. Take turns asking questions to find out what your partner is going to do.

3-21 Vamos a comer fuera. A friend and you are planning to eat out tonight. Each one should suggest a restaurant and mention the dishes they prepare, the prices (*precios*), and so on. Decide on the time and where you will go. Finally, tell other classmates about your plans.

3-22 Los planes de Maribel. Primera fase. Take turns to tell what Maribel is going to do. Ask questions to get additional information from your partner regarding Maribel.

Segunda fase. Tell your classmate what you are going to do on Friday. Are your plans similar or different from Maribel's?

3-23 Este fin de semana. With a classmate, discuss what each of you is going to do this weekend. Expand the conversation by asking questions of each other to get more details, if necessary. Take notes about each other's plans. Then share your findings about your partner with another classmate.

3-24 ¡Vivan los feriados! Choose a new classmate with whom you would like to share information about your plans for the next holiday; for example **Navidad** *(Christmas)*, **Januká, Ramadán, el Año Nuevo, el Día de la Independencia**. Get as much information as possible about each other's plans. Make sure to address the following points.

1. lugar adonde va a ir
2. con quién(es) va a ir

3. cuánto tiempo va a estar allí
4. qué va a hacer

 SITUACIONES

1. Your friend is planning to go to a concert **(un concierto).** Call him/her to find out a) where and when the concert is going to be, b) who is going to sing, c) who is going to play an instrument, and d) how much the ticket **(el boleto/billete, la entrada)** costs.

2. A friend calls you on the phone. Tell him/her about your plans for tonight. Tell him/her a) what you are planning to do, b) with whom, and c) how much money **(dinero)** you are going to need. Inquire about his/her plans too.

5. Numbers 100 to 2.000.000

100	cien/ciento	1.000	mil
200	doscientos/as	1.100	mil cien
300	trescientos/as	2.000	dos mil
400	cuatrocientos/as	10.000	diez mil
500	quinientos/as	100.000	cien mil
600	seiscientos/as	150.000	ciento cincuenta mil
700	setecientos/as	500.000	quinientos mil
800	ochocientos/as	1.000.000	un millón (de)
900	novecientos/as	2.000.000	dos millones (de)

■ Use **cien** to say 100 used alone or followed by a noun, and use **ciento** for numbers from 101 to 199.

100	**cien**
100 chicos	**cien** chicos
120 profesoras	**ciento** veinte profesoras

■ Multiples of 100 agree in gender with the noun they modify.

200 periódicos	**doscientos** periódicos
1.400 revistas	**mil cuatrocientas** revistas

■ Use **mil** for *one thousand.*

1.000	**mil alumnos, mil alumnas**

■ Use **un millón** to say *one million*. Use **un millón de** when a noun follows.

| 1.000.000 | **un millón** |
| 1.000.000 (personas) | **un millón de personas** |

■ In many Spanish-speaking countries, a period is used to separate thousands, and a comma to separate decimals.

| $1.000 | $19,50 |

¿Qué dice usted?

3-25 Para identificar. Your instructor will say a number from each of the following series. Identify each one.

a. 114	360	850	524
b. 213	330	490	919
c. 818	625	723	513
d. 667	777	984	534
e. 1.310	1.420	3.640	6.860
f. 10.467	50.312	100.000	2.000.000

② 3-26 ¿Cuándo va a ocurrir? Exchange opinions with a classmate about when each of the following events will occur.

MODELO: Todos los libros van a ser electrónicos.
E1: En el año 2010.
E2: Estoy de acuerdo. *o* No estoy de acuerdo. Va a ser en el 2020.

1. Las personas van a trabajar sólo 20 horas a la semana.
2. Los estudiantes no van a ir a clases. Van a estudiar en universidades virtuales.
3. Todos los autos van a ser eléctricos y muy rápidos.
4. Los turistas van a ir de un país a otro sin pasaporte.
5. La contaminación va a ser muy grande, y las personas van a usar máscaras (*masks*) en los parques y en las calles.
6. Los robots, y no los camareros, van a servir la comida en los restaurantes.
7. Las personas van a comunicarse por telepatía.

② 3-27 Unas vacaciones. Primera fase. Your classmate has chosen one of the destinations in the ad on page 111 for his/her next vacation. To find out where he/she is going, ask him/her the following questions. Switch roles.

1. ¿Adónde vas?
2. ¿Con quién vas?
3. ¿Qué lugares vas a ver?
4. ¿Cuándo vas?
5. ¿Cuántos días vas a estar allí?
6. ¿Por qué vas a ir a ese lugar?
7. ¿Cuánto cuesta la excursión?
8. …

Segunda fase. Based on your classmate's answers, fill in the information requested and share it with the rest of the class.

1. Su compañero/a necesita…
   a. _____ sacar un pasaporte.
   b. _____ obtener una visa.
   c. _____ hacer reservaciones.

2. Lugar(es) que va a visitar: _____
3. Tiempo que va a estar allí: _____
4. Costo de la excursión: _____
5. Dinero extra que usted cree que su compañero va a necesitar: _____

AGENCIA MUNDIAL

A SU SERVICIO SIEMPRE 20 años de experiencia, responsabilidad y profesionalismo.

TODOS LOS PRECIOS INCLUYEN PASAJES AÉREOS Y SERVICIOS TERRESTRES POR PERSONA

PERÚ Y BOLIVIA

LIMA, AREQUIPA, CUZCO, MACHU PICCHU, PUNO, LA PAZ, 15 días. La Ruta del Inca. Hoteles de 3 y 4 estrellas. Desayuno incluido.
$1.960

PERÚ

LIMA, CUZCO, MACHU PICCHU, NAZCA, 12 días. Visite fortalezas incas. Vea las misteriosas líneas de Nazca desde el aire. Hoteles de primera. Desayuno y cena incluidos.
$2.250

LIMA, NAZCA, AREQUIPA, LAGO TITICACA, 10 días. Admire la arquitectura colonial de Lima y Arequipa. Vea las líneas de Nazca desde el aire. Navegue en el lago más alto del mundo. Hoteles de primera.
$1.650

ARGENTINA

BUENOS AIRES, BARILOCHE, MENDOZA, 12 días. Disfrute de una gran metrópoli. Esquíe en uno de los lugares más bellos del mundo. Hoteles de 4 y 5 estrellas. Desayuno y cena.
$2.990

CHILE Y ARGENTINA

SANTIAGO, PUERTO MONTT, BARILOCHE, BUENOS AIRES, 12 días. Excursión a Viña del Mar y Valparaíso. Cruce de los Andes en minibús y barco. Hoteles de 3 y 4 estrellas.
$3.190

CARIBE

JAMAICA, 7 días. Happy Inn, todo incluido. Exclusivo para parejas.
$1.750

PUERTO RICO

SAN JUAN, 5 días. Hotel de 5 estrellas. Excursión a Ponce. Visita con guía al Viejo San Juan. Desayuno incluido.
$1.250

MÉXICO

MÉXICO, TAXCO, ACAPULCO, 7 días. Hoteles de 3 y 4 estrellas. Excursión a Teotihuacán. Desayuno bufet incluido.
$1.450

CANCÚN, 5 días. Hotel de 4 estrellas. Excursión a Cozumel. Visita a ruinas mayas. Las mejores playas.
$1.150

Solicite los programas detallados con variantes de hoteles e itinerarios a su agente de viajes.

Tel: 312-785-4455   Fax: 312-785-4456

EN DIRECTO

To call the attention to an unusual fact:
¡Fíjate qué noticia! (*Imagine the news!*)
¡Imagínate!

To express happiness upon hearing good news:
¡Qué suerte!
¡Qué maravilla!
¡Qué bien!

To convince someone:
¡Ven/Anda, anímate! (*Come on!/Come along, cheer up!*)
Lo vamos a pasar muy bien. (*We are going to have a good time.*)

SITUACIONES

1. **Role A:** You are going to receive a very generous check from your rich aunt (*tía*) to take the trip of your dreams. Call your best friend to explain to him/her (a) where you plan to go, (b) when, and (c) what you plan to do.

   Role B: Your classmate is going to receive a large sum of money from his/her wealthy aunt (*tía*) to take a trip. Ask him/her (a) with whom he/she is planning to go, (b) what places he/she is going to visit, and (c) what he/she is planning to buy.

2. **Role A:** A friend and you are making plans for Saturday. Your friend is going to tell you what he/she plans to do. Tell your friend that you need to rest and want to spend (*pasar*) the day at the beach. He/She will try to convince you to change your mind. Inquire about specifics of his/her plan, such as: where he/she is going, with whom, and so on. Politely, be firm about your original plans.

   Role B: Your friend and you are making plans for Saturday. Tell him/her that you want to go to a fancy restaurant and to a discotheque afterward. Try to convince your friend to change plans. Answer his/her questions. Finally, tell him/her that you are going to go along with his/her plans.

ALGO MÁS

Some uses of por and para

In previous activities, you used **para** as an equivalent of *for*, with the meaning *intended* or *to be used for*:

Necesito un diccionario **para** la clase.	*I need a dictionary for the class.*

You used **por** in expressions such as **por favor, por teléfono,** and **por la mañana/tarde/noche.** Other fixed expressions with **por** that you will find useful when communicating in Spanish are:

por ejemplo	*for example*	por lo menos	*at least*
por eso	*that is why*	por supuesto	*of course*
por fin	*finally, at last*	por ciento	*percent*

Por and **para** can also be used to express movement in space and time.

- Use **para** to indicate movement toward a destination.

Caminan **para** la playa.	*They walk toward the beach.*
Vamos **para** el túnel.	*We are going toward the tunnel.*

- Use **por** to indicate movement through or by a place.

Caminan **por** la playa.	*They walk along the beach.*
Vamos **por** el túnel.	*We are going through the tunnel.*

- You may also use **por** to indicate length of time or duration of an action. Many Spanish speakers omit **por** in this case, or they use **durante.**

Necesito el auto (**por**) tres días.	*I need the car for three days.*

¿Qué dice usted?

3-28 ¿Para dónde van? Read the following, guess where these people are going, and compare your guess with that of your classmate. Are the guesses similar? Then find out where a classmate is going after class, and why.

MODELO: *Jorge busca su uniforme de fútbol.*
Va para el estadio.

1. Es la una de la tarde, y Pedro desea comer.
2. Sebastián lleva una mochila con sus libros de química y una calculadora.
3. Magdalena y Roberto van a consultar unos libros porque tienen un examen.
4. Gregorio va a comprar un libro para su clase de español.
5. Ana María va a ver una película de su actor favorito.
6. Amanda y Clara están muy elegantes y contentas. En este momento llegan Arturo y Felipe en su auto.

3-29 Caminante. Your classmate likes to walk. Ask him/her the following questions. Then, switch roles.

1. ¿Por dónde caminas?
2. ¿Te gusta caminar por la playa o por un parque?
3. ¿Caminas por la mañana?
4. ¿Caminas con amigos o solo/a (*by yourself*)?
5. ¿Caminas durante media hora o más?

M O S A I C O S

 Escuchar

Using background information

When you are listening to a conversation, you use your background knowledge of the situation to understand what is happening or what is being said. For example, it is probably much easier for you to understand what your roommate tells you about his/her daily activities than to understand a neurosurgeon talking about his/her day in the operating room. This is because you have much more experience with the activities of a college student than with the activities of a neurosurgeon.

Antes de escuchar

3-30 Las grabaciones telefónicas. In **3-31,** you will be calling several museums in Lima to find out their days and hours of operation, addresses, and phone numbers. Use your knowledge of museum hours to write down what days and hours you think the museums you are calling will be open.

Horario: _____

A escuchar

3-31 Exhibiciones y horarios. Now listen to the automated recorded messages and fill in the following chart with the missing information.

	DÍAS	HORAS	DIRECCIÓN	TELÉFONO
Museo de Arte			Avenida Ponce de León 1782	423-.......
Museo de Historia		9:00–...........	San Martín	
Museo de Antropología	los lunes, ... y	desde las .... hasta las	Mercaderes	
Museo de Ciencias Naturales	.... y sábado		..........Bolívar 840	

Después de escuchar

3-32 ¿Y usted? Answer the following questions.

1. ¿Qué museo desea visitar? _____

2. ¿Qué museo tiene un horario conveniente para usted? _____

Antes de escuchar

3-33 Diferentes precios. In **3-34,** you will listen to a recorded announcement of ViajaMás, a travel agency. The recording will provide the name of the destination cities in Latin America, the flight numbers, the days of the flights, and the price of the ticket from Miami. Before you listen, using your knowledge of Latin American countries and your knowledge of traveling costs, write down the names of three large cities you think the recording may mention and the probable cost of the ticket.

Ciudad: _____   Precio del pasaje: _____
Ciudad: _____   Precio del pasaje: _____
Ciudad: _____   Precio del pasaje: _____

A escuchar

3-34 Días y vuelos. Now listen to the recording and complete the following chart with the information provided.

CIUDAD	VUELO #	DÍAS	PRECIO DEL PASAJE
		sábados y domingos	
Buenos Aires	479		
			$250
Bogotá			

Después de escuchar

3-35 ¡Ahora usted! Your best friend, who is studying Spanish, would like to visit a large capital city in Latin America, but he/she is unsure where to go. After listening to the ad in **3-34,** you would like to suggest a city to him/her. Complete the following e-mail for your best friend.

```
De: ........................
A:..........................
Asunto: Una ciudad interesante en América Latina
Hola.......,
¡Tengo una información excelente para ti! Hay tarifas fantásticas para
visitar ................... Los vuelos salen .............. y los
boletos cuestan .............. Hablamos por teléfono este fin de semana,
¿OK?
............................
```

Conversar

Antes de conversar

3-36 ¿Qué comen sus compañeros? A new cafeteria is going to open on campus. You have been hired to do a random survey on the most popular foods so the cafeteria may include them on the menu. First find out what your classmates like to eat and drink at different meals on campus. Write down the names of students who answer **Sí** or **No** in the appropriate column.

MODELO: E1: Susana, ¿comes cereal en el desayuno?
E2: Sí, como cereal en el desayuno./No, no como cereal.

	DESAYUNO		ALMUERZO		CENA	
	SÍ	NO	SÍ	NO	SÍ	NO
cereal con leche						
café/chocolate caliente						
jugo de naranja/tomate/manzana						
hamburguesas						
ensalada de frutas						
vino						
pan						
...						

A conversar

A la cafetería. Analyze the information you collected in *Primera fase* and go to see the new cafeteria supervisor (your classmate). Explain what most students eat and drink. Discuss with him/her a possible menu for breakfast, lunch, and dinner. Write down your menu.

Después de conversar

3-37 ¿Cuál es el menú más saludable (*the healthiest*)? Compare your menu with those of other classmates. Then vote on which menu is the healthiest and the most complete. Explain why.

Antes de conversar

 3-38 ¿Cómo pasarlo bien? Go to www.prenhall.com/mosaicos and find out how to have fun in any of the countries whose websites have been provided, or in another of your choice. Take notes on at least the following information.

1. Nombre del lugar o evento: _____
2. Dirección: _____
3. Teléfono: _____
4. Actividad(es) que las personas hacen allí: ¿Son actividades culturales, deportivas (*sports*), etcétera? _____

A conversar

3-39 ¡Vamos a pasarlo bien! Invite a classmate to the event or place you researched in activity **3-38**. Explain to him/her (a) what type of event or place it is, (b) where it is, (c) how you are planning to get there. He/She may accept or reject the invitation. Make sure to review expressions on pages 106 and 110.

Después de conversar

3-40 Planes excepcionales. Write a postcard to a friend, explaining what you are planning to do, with whom, where, how you are going to get there, and so on. Include as much information as possible.

Leer

In *Lección 1* and *Lección 2* you used some basic reading strategies to help you comprehend a text better: a) drawing on your knowledge of the world to anticipate the content of a text; b) identifying cognates; and c) determining the kind of text and the text format. It is important to remember that successful second-language readers systematically use these strategies as they face the reading of a variety of texts. Therefore, as you gain insights and experience with other reading strategies, keep in mind the ones you have practiced before and utilize them.

In this chapter, you will practice identifying key words to comprehend the message of the text. Do not worry if you do not answer correctly the first time. Over time, practice will help you improve this crucial reading skill in Spanish.

Guía de pre-lectura. Skim the texts in activity **3-42** and answer the questions, based on your knowledge of the world.

1. What type of texts are included in **3-42?**
   a. brochures
   b. ads advertising services
   c. entertainment ads

2. In what section of the newspaper would you find these texts?
   a. in the sports section
   b. in the business section
   c. in the recreations section

3. What is the purpose of the ads? Use an X to mark all that apply.
   a. _____ to get the attention of adults with children
   b. _____ to catch the attention of ethnic food restaurant goers
   c. _____ to entice potential actors
   d. _____ to advertise a play in Spanish

4. Now, use your knowledge of the English language for comprehension. What words *in each text* helped you figure out the answer to question 3 above?
   Text 1. _____ Text 3. _____
   Text 2. _____ Text 4. _____

Antes de leer

3-41 Preparación. Primera fase. Look at the picture and follow the instructions.

1. La fotografía muestra (*shows*) una ciudad importante de Perú. ¿Qué ciudad peruana es probablemente?
2. Marque con una X los lugares de diversión (*entertainment*) que probablemente hay en esta ciudad.
   a. _____ museos para los aficionados (*fans*) al arte
   b. _____ discotecas para bailar y pasar el tiempo libre
   c. _____ hospitales modernos
   d. _____ teatros que presentan dramas y comedias nacionales e internacionales
   e. _____ cines que pasan películas nacionales y extranjeras
   f. _____ parques de diversión para los niños
   g. _____ restaurantes de comida étnica
   h. _____ universidades excelentes

Segunda fase. Take turns answering the following questions.

1. En la opinión de usted, ¿cuál es la mejor hora para divertirse (*to have fun*)?
2. ¿Qué hace usted para divertirse?

A leer

3-42 Primera mirada. Read these ads from a Peruvian newspaper, and offer a solution for each of the problems.

NIÑOS

CORPORACIÓN CULTURAL DE LIMA. Santa María y Gálvez. 2209451. A las 12 y 16 horas. Bagdhadas. S/. 12.

TEATRO INFANTIL A DOMICILIO. 2390176. El patito feo. Adaptación del cuento de Andersen. Compañía Arcoiris.

CENTRO LIMA. Av. Grau y Velásquez. A las 12, show especial de Navidad.

FANTASÍA DISNEY. Desde las 15. Niños, S/. 8; adultos, S/. 14. Parque de entretenimientos.

EL MUNDO FANTÁSTICO DE MAFALDA. Desde las 10. Entrada general a todos los juegos. Niños, S/. 12. Calle Domingo Sarmiento 358.

PLANETARIO DEL MORRO SOLAR. A las 12, 17 y 19. Gratis para niños; adultos, S/. 15. Circunvalación, Nuevo Perú. Tel. 5620841.

PARQUE DE LAS LEYENDAS (ZOO). De 9 a 19 hrs. Niños y 3ra edad, S/. 5; S/. 10, otro público. Cerro Tongoy, 3701725.

Costa Verde

Sabrosa comida tradicional peruana
Menú especial los fines de semana

- Aperitivo
- Entrada
- Segundo
- Postre
- Café y plus café (crema de café, crema de menta, anisado)

Valor: S/. 75

Carnes, pescados y mariscos preparados por los mejores cocineros del país

Avenida Arequipa 357
Reservas: 428 9654
Fax: 428 9655

TEATRO MUNICIPAL
CORPORACIÓN CULTURAL DE LA
ILUSTRE MUNICIPALIDAD DE LIMA

Directores: ALBERTO ISOLA, OSWALDO CATTON

Presenta

EL HOMBRE DE LA MANCHA

Con DAVID Y ETTY ELKIN

| Lunes 20 Dic., 7:00 p.m. | Martes 21 Dic., 6:00 p.m. |
| Miércoles 22 Dic., 8:00 p.m. | Jueves 23 Dic., 7:00 p.m. |

ENTRADAS EN VENTA DESDE S/.20–40

Boleterías en Teatro Municipal
Fonoventas: 7624901 (con tarjetas de crédito)

El Chifa Lungfung

La más exquisita, variada y exótica carta de comida cantonesa-peruana: finas carnes, pescados y todo tipo de mariscos.

SÁBADOS Y DOMINGOS:

Almuerzos y cenas familiares

...los esperamos

AIRE ACONDICIONADO
MÚSICA AMBIENTAL
CAMAREROS PROFESIONALES
AV. REPÚBLICA DE PANAMÁ 8720
RESERVAS 3817543, 3816532, 3814241

PROBLEMAS

1. El señor y la señora Molina tienen cuatro hijos entre tres y ocho años. A los niños les fascinan los animales, en particular las especies que no existen en Perú. Toda la familia desea salir este fin de semana, pero tiene poco dinero. ¿Adónde van a ir ellos probablemente? ¿Por qué?

2. El señor Liskin, un turista norteamericano, visita Lima por primera vez. Él desea ver todo lo típico de Perú. Este fin de semana va a poder hacer sus actividades favoritas. Al señor Liskin le gusta mucho escuchar música clásica, ir al teatro y comer bien. ¿Qué debe hacer durante el fin de semana?

3. Hoy es el cumpleaños de Carlitos, el hijo de Paloma. ¡Ya tiene ocho años! A diferencia de otros años en esta fecha, hoy el niño está en casa. El doctor dice que no debe caminar porque se fracturó una pierna. Carlitos está muy triste porque no va a celebrar su fiesta de cumpleaños con sus amigos, pero su mamá tiene una sorpresa para él. ¿Qué va a hacer Paloma?

4. Cuatro médicos alemanes visitan el Centro de Investigaciones del Cáncer del Hospital Central. El Dr. Moreira, director del Centro, desea invitar a sus colegas a un buen lugar esta noche para comer productos del mar peruanos. Él desea un restaurante cómodo, con buena comida y excelente atención. ¿A qué restaurante va a invitarlos? ¿Por qué?

3-43 Segunda mirada. Go back and read the ads (3-42) again to answer the following questions.

1. ¿Cuál de los anuncios es básicamente para menores (*minors*)? Indique algunas palabras que indican esta idea.

2. En la sección de niños, Parque de las Leyendas, ¿qué significa 3ra edad? ¿Cuántos años tiene como mínimo una persona de la 3ra edad?

3. En el anuncio del restaurante Costa Verde, identifique la expresión que indica que este restaurante prepara comida nacional.

4. Chifa Lungfung es probablemente un restaurante de excelente calidad (*quality*). ¿Qué expresiones en el anuncio se refieren a la buena calidad del restaurante?

5. En el anuncio de Chifa Lungfung, ¿qué palabra significa *reservation*?

Después de leer

3-44 Expansión. With a classmate, answer the following questions on the ads in activity **3-42**.

1. ¿Cuál de las siguientes actividades desean hacer ustedes en Lima: ir a un parque de entretenimiento (*entertainment park*), comer comida tradicional peruana, ver teatro o comer comida china? ¿Por qué?

2. ¿Cuál de los dos restaurantes sirve comida que a ustedes les gusta, Costa Verde o Chifa Lungfung?

Escribir

The writing process

The series of steps you follow to produce a clear and effective piece of writing is the same in any language. First you organize your thoughts, perhaps by writing an outline. Then you write a first draft. As you write, or once you finish, you may revise to find better ways of expressing your ideas. For example, you may change the organization, rewrite sentences, or choose better words. Finally, you correct any content inaccuracies or errors in spelling, punctuation, accent marks, and so on.

In *Lección 3* you will have the opportunity to write a letter to a friend. Although correspondence to friends tends to be less formal, well-written messages always follow writing conventions such as including the date, a salutation, an introduction, a body, a closing line, and so on. What follows is an example of a letter to a friend.

Antes de escribir

3-45 Enfoque. Primera fase. Juanita recently took a trip to Peru with her family. She wrote the following letter to a friend about her trip. Read Juanita's letter and do as indicated.

Cuzco, 8 de enero de 2005

Querida María Fernanda,

¿Cómo están tú y tu familia? ¿Cómo van tus clases? Espero que fantástico.

¡Sorpresa! En estos momentos, mi familia y yo estamos en Perú, un país increíble. Esta semana visitamos Cuzco y Machu Picchu, lugares con una historia muy interesante.

Muchos turistas visitan Cuzco y Machu Picchu para aprender sobre la cultura de los incas. En Cuzco, algunos visitan los mercados artesanales, compran productos indígenas y caminan por las antiguas calles de la ciudad. Otros montan en bicicleta y hacen excursiones por las montañas. Por las noches, muchos comen en restaurantes de comida típica de Perú. Los cuzqueños son muy amables y simpáticos. Muchos hablan español y quechua, su lengua nativa. En Machu Picchu, algunos escalan los Andes y escuchan a los expertos que hablan sobre la historia del lugar.

Tengo muchas fotografías de los Andes, de los mercados artesanales, de algunos restaurantes peruanos, etcétera. María Fernanda, debes visitar Perú. Te va a gustar. Es un lugar ideal para vacaciones, con mucha historia y tradiciones antiguas.

Bueno, ahora vamos a una excursión a Tambopata, una reserva natural con muchos animales autóctonos. Te llamo pronto. Chao.

Tu amiga,
Juanita

Segunda fase. Answer the following questions about Juanita's letter.

1. Mark with an X the purposes of Juanita's letter to María Fernanda.
   _____ To describe her vacation activities.
   _____ To describe a vacation spot that she likes.
   _____ To inform her friend of fun leisure activities people can do in Cuzco and Machu Picchu.
   _____ To suggest that her friend visit Peru.
   _____ To provide a profile of Peruvian people.

2. Based on its purpose, is Juanita's letter effective? _____ Yes _____ No
   Mark some possible reasons for your response.
   _____ Juanita organizes the information clearly.
   _____ The letter is poorly organized.
   _____ Juanita describes Cuzco and Machu Picchu very well.
   _____ The tone of the letter is friendly.
   _____ Juanita informs María Fernanda of the way her days are spent in Peru.
   _____ Juanita presents a positive portrait of Cuzco and Machu Picchu so María Fernanda may visit them in the future.

3. What salutation did María Fernanda use with her friend? How would you write the salutation to a male friend? Do you know any other way to say hello to a friend in Spanish? What is it?

4. How does María Fernanda say good-bye to her friend in the letter? Do you know any other way to say good-bye to a friend in Spanish? What is it?

3-46 Preparación. Choose a vacation spot or any other fun place you know well. Pretend that you are visiting the place. To prepare to write a letter to a friend informing him/her of your vacation, do the following:

1. Identify the place: Is it a beach, a park, a city, a historical landmark?
2. Make a list of words (adjectives) that describe the place: Is it small, big, beautiful, comfortable?
3. Write down some fun activities (verbs) that people do there: Are they outdoor activities, sports, culturally oriented (museums, explorations, fairs)?
4. Indicate some of the activities in #3 that you personally like.
5. Write down possible salutations and closings you may use.

A escribir

3-47 Manos a la obra. Now write a brief letter to your best friend, informing him/her of your vacation. Use the information you prepared in **activity 3-46.** Do not forget to date your letter and write the salutation and closing.

Después de escribir

3-48 Revisión. After completing your letter, read it at least twice with your reader in mind. Check the following:

- The content of the letter: Did you include information your friend would like to read about? Is there any new information for your friend?
- The form of the text: Did you use punctuation correctly? Did you verify that there are no spelling or grammatical mistakes?

Finally, discuss your letter with one of your peers.

ENFOQUE CULTURAL

Para pensar

¿Qué hace usted cuando quiere pasar un rato agradable? ¿Adónde va—A la playa, al cine, al teatro, a la discoteca, al parque? ¿Con quién va a estos lugares?

Muchas familias peruanas pasan los meses de verano en las playas cerca de sus ciudades.

En los países hispanos, una costumbre muy popular entre los jóvenes y los adultos es ir al cine con amigos. Generalmente después del cine las personas van a un café a conversar y disfrutar del ambiente.

En Perú, unos lugares muy atractivos para jóvenes y adultos son las peñas, donde se presentan cantantes de música criolla y conjuntos de bailes folclóricos (marinera, huayno, tondero, por ejemplo), y donde las personas escuchan música, cantan, bailan y comen comida criolla. Si prefieren conversar con sus amigos y disfrutar al mismo tiempo de una obra de teatro, van a los café-teatros donde se presentan comedias cortas y se puede comer y tomar un café o una copa.

Para contestar

Los amigos hispanos. Responda a las siguientes preguntas:

1. Si uds. son personas muy activas y visitan Perú, ¿a qué lugares les gustaría ir?
2. Si prefieren actividades más tranquilas, ¿qué pueden hacer en un país hispano?

Riqueza cultural. Hablen sobre las actividades que pueden hacer en los países hispanos y que no pueden hacer en los Estados Unidos.

Para pensar

¿Conoce usted a alguna persona del Perú? ¿Sabe dónde está el Perú? ¿Qué lugares le gustaría visitar en el Perú?

El Perú es un país de geografía muy variada. Tiene una larga costa, una zona andina y una selva amazónica.

Lima, la capital del Perú, tiene zonas antiguas de gran belleza y valor histórico, y también tiene zonas modernas. Hay muchos museos importantes. El Museo de Oro tiene una excelente colección de joyería (jewelry) y objetos precolombinos; el Museo de la Nación exhibe joyería, artesanía y gran variedad de objetos de las civilizaciones que se desarrollaron en el Perú.

Otro lugar de gran interés en la costa del Perú es Nazca, al sur de Lima, muy conocida por sus famosas líneas de origen desconocido en el desierto.

Una de las ciudades más importantes del Perú es Cuzco, la antigua capital del imperio de los incas. Cerca de Cuzco se encuentran las ruinas de la ciudad inca de Machu Picchu y la fortaleza de Sacsayhuamán.

Expresiones peruanas

chamba	Me conseguí una chamba.	*I got myself a job.*
maldita	¡La película estuvo maldita!	*The movie was great!*
bacán	¡Ella es bacán!	*She is great / a lot of fun!*
chancón	¡Él es un chancón!	*He studies all the time.*

Para contestar

En el mapa

1. Busque tres ciudades del Perú: una en la costa, otra en la zona andina y otra en la selva amazónica.
2. Diga qué países están al norte, al sur y al este del Perú.

Ahora diga...

1. si le gustaría visitar las líneas de Nazca o las ruinas de Machu Picchu, y por qué.
2. qué ciudad del Perú le gustaría visitar, y por qué.

¿Qué dice usted si...?

1. le gusta mucho su nuevo auto
2. su compañero/a de cuarto es muy estudioso

Para investigar en Internet

Busque información *www.prenhall.com/mosaicos* sobre los espectáculos que hay en una peña en Lima esta semana. Averigüe el nombre de la peña, dónde está, a qué hora abre, qué artistas se presentan, cuánto cuesta el espectáculo, etcétera. Traiga a clase la información e informe a la clase.

¡Prepárese!

3-49 Los personajes. Before watching the *Fortunas* video segment for *Lección 3*, conjugate the verbs in parenthesis for the following sentences that go with the video images below.

1. A Ángela no le _____ (gustar) la reacción del público.
2. Carlos y Katie _____ (caminar) por Coyoacán.
3. Katie _____ (deber) decidir colaborar o no colaborar con Carlos.
4. Ellos _____ (ir) a investigar la mitología para solucionar el misterio.
5. Carlos _____ (leer) un libro sobre la mitología de los aztecas.
6. Los padres de Efraín _____ (vivir) en diferentes países.

Ángela está preocupada sobre la reacción del público.

Carlos y Katie están en Coyoacán.

Hay una posible colaboración entre Carlos y Katie.

Las pistas tienen una posible relación con la mitología.

Carlos sabe bastante sobre la mitología azteca.

Efraín habla sobre sus padres y sus problemas familiares.

¡Responda!

3-50 Katie y Carlos. Keeping in mind the concept of collaboration discussed by Katie and Carlos, after watching the *Fortunas* video segment for *Lección 3*, work together in groups of three on the following word association activity.

Asociación de palabras:
Take turns saying the following words. After each word the members of your group should say aloud any words or phrases that come to mind. Record your answers.

> destrucción / gigantes / viento / monos / global / jaguar

Look at your lists. Discuss possible connections and relations to see if you can form an idea of what the first *misterio* means. Share your ideas with the class.

In your opinion, what are the advantages and disadvantages of collaborating with your classmates?

The title of *Camino de la montaña*, which means "mountain journey," is a metaphor for the journey we take in life. The country and people of Peru are closely associated with the Andes mountains; thus, the symbolic mountain of the song is related to Peruvian culture and tradition.

¡Prepárese!

3-51 Metáforas. Before listening to *Camino de la montaña* think about the idea of metaphor and what it means to you. The mountain journey is a metaphor for life's journey. Based on your personal experience, what are some possible metaphors for the following concepts from the song? Refer to the lyrics if necessary.

1. *la libertad* / freedom
2. *la verdad* / truth
3. *el peregrino* / pilgrim
4. *el destino* / destiny

> Camino de la montaña, camino de libertad
> Yo quiero subir por ella en busca de mi verdad
> Ser el santo y peregrino en busca de mi destino
> Y unos ojos soñadores que mi vida me alumbran
> Camino de la montaña, camino de libertad
> Yo quiero subir por ella en busca de mi verdad
> Ser el santo y peregrino en busca de mi destino
> Y unos ojos soñadores que mi vida me alumbran
> Hay amores en la vida que se buscan locamente
> Que andan perdidos sin rumbo por los caminos del mundo
> Más buscarán sus destinos, quizás por otros caminos
> Porque la vida misma es un camino por andar
> Más buscarán sus destinos, quizás por otros caminos
> Porque la vida misma es un camino por andar

¡Escuche!

3-52 Los instrumentos. Indicate with an X the instruments you hear as you listen to the song.

_____ el piano	_____ la quena*	_____ la guitarra
_____ el clarinete	_____ la trompeta	_____ las maracas
_____ el tambor		

Which instrument do you like most, and why? Describe it in your own words in Spanish, using adjectives you have learned.

¡Responda!

3-53 La entrevista. Imagine that you are a journalist who has been assigned to interview the artists of Los Kjarkas. Use the **ir + a** + *infinitive* construction with the verbs from the list to find out what their plans are. Present your questions and answers to the class.

MODELO: ¿Van Uds. a cantar en un concierto en EE.UU.?

cantar / escribir / ir / tocar / vivir / celebrar

*an Andean flute prominent in Peruvian music

VOCABULARIO*

Comunicación

el periódico	newspaper
la revista	magazine
el teléfono	telephone

Diversiones

la canción	song
el cumpleaños	birthday
la fiesta	party
la guitarra	guitar
la música	music
la película	film
la reunión	meeting, gathering
las vacaciones	vacation

Personas

| e/la camarero/a | waiter/waitress |
| el/la joven | young man/woman |

En un café o restaurante

el agua	water
el almuerzo	lunch
el arroz	rice
la bebida	drink
el bistec	steak
el café	coffee
la cena	dinner, supper
la cerveza	beer
el ceviche	raw fish dish
la comida	dinner, supper
el desayuno	breakfast
la ensalada	salad
la fruta	fruit
la hamburguesa	hamburger
el helado	ice cream
el huevo	egg
el jugo	juice
la leche	milk
la lechuga	lettuce
la naranja	orange
el pan	bread
la papa	potato
las papas fritas	French fries
el pescado	fish
el pollo	chicken
el refresco	soda
la sopa	soup
el tomate	tomato
la tostada	toast

| el vegetal/la verdura | vegetable |
| el vino | wine |

Lugares

el cine	movies
la ciudad	city
el mar	sea
el país	country, nation

Descripciones

caliente	hot
fabuloso/a	fabulous, great
frío/a	cold
frito/a	fried
rápido/a	fast
típico/a	typical

Verbos

alquilar	to rent
beber	to drink
cantar	to sing
celebrar	to celebrate
cenar	to have dinner
comer	to eat
correr	to run
deber	ought to, should
descansar	to rest
escribir	to write
ir	to go
leer	to read
nadar	to swim
tocar	to touch
tocar (un instrumento)	to play (an instrument)
tomar el sol	to sunbathe
ver	to see
vivir	to live

Palabras y expresiones útiles

¿Aló?	Hello
¿Adónde?	Where (to)?
al	to the (contraction of a + el)
al aire libre	outdoors
otro/a	other, another
si	if
tiempo libre	free time

*See page 105 for expressions that denote future time.
**See page 111 for expressions with *por*.

LA FAMILIA

Objetivos comunicativos

- Identifying and describing family members
- Describing routine activities
- Expressing preferences, desires, and feelings
- Asking and giving permission
- Expressing when, where, or how an action is done
- Expressing how long events and states have been going on

Contenido

A primera vista

- Las familias
- ¿Qué hacen los parientes?

Explicación y expansión

- Present tense of stem-changing verbs: $e \rightarrow ie$, $o \rightarrow ue, e \rightarrow i$
- Adverbs
- Present tense of *hacer, poner, salir, traer,* and *oír*
- Hace with expressions of time
- Algo Más: Some reflexive verbs and pronouns

Mosaicos

- Escuchar: Listening for specific information to fill in a chart or form
- Conversar: Discussing family; expressing agreement and disagreement about generalizations about the family
- Leer: Anticipating and inferring topic; guessing meaning of new words through context clues and identifying suffixes
- Escribir: Corresponding with family members

Enfoque cultural

- Temas: La familia hispana
- Vistas: Colombia
  Para investigar en Internet
- Fortunas: Episodio 4
- Notas: Tu ausencia, *Los Tupamaros*

Vocabulario

AUDIO Las familias

Una foto familiar de tres generaciones: **abuelos, hijos** y **nietos**. ¿Cuántos **niños** hay? ¿Hay muchos niños en la familia de usted? ¿Es el **perro** parte de la familia?

Una familia colombiana celebra el **bautizo** de su hija. En estas ceremonias participan los **padres,** los **padrinos** y los **ahijados.** Para muchas familias hispanas, el bautizo es un día muy especial.

La familia de Pablo

AUDIO Pablo habla de su familia

Me llamo Pablo Méndez Sánchez y vivo con mis padres, mi **hermana** y mis **abuelos** en un apartamento en Bogotá, la capital de Colombia.

Mi **madre** tiene un hermano, mi **tío** Jorge. Su **esposa** es mi tía María. Tienen tres hijos y viven también en Bogotá. Mi **primo** Jorgito es el **menor**. Mis primas Elenita y Ana son **gemelas**. Mis primos son muy simpáticos y **pasamos** mucho tiempo **juntos**.

Mis tíos tienen sólo dos **sobrinos** en Bogotá, mi hermana Inés y yo. Su otra **sobrina**, la hija de mi tía Lola, vive en Cartagena, al norte del país.

La **nieta** favorita de mis abuelos es mi hermanita Inés. Tiene sólo tres años y es la **menor** de todos sus nietos.

> **LENGUA**
>
> The equivalent of the English word *apartment* varies depending on the country: *piso* in Spain and **apartamento** or *departamento* in Latin America.

¿Qué dice usted?

4-1 Asociación. Asocie la descripción a la izquierda con la expresión correcta.

1. _____ la esposa de mi papá
2. _____ el hermano de mi prima
3. _____ los padres de mi papá
4. _____ el hijo de mi hijo
5. _____ el hermano de mi mamá

a. mi primo
b. mi nieto
c. mi madre
d. mis abuelos
e. mi tío

4-2 La familia de Pablo. Complete las siguientes oraciones de acuerdo con el árbol genealógico (*family tree*) de Pablo.

1. La hermana de Pablo se llama _Inés_.
2. Don José y doña Olga son los _____ de Pablo. Ellos tienen _____ hijas y _____ hijo.
3. Pablo es el _____ de Jaime.
4. Jaime es el _____ de Pablo, y Elena es su _____.
5. Inés y Ana son _primos_. Elenita y Ana son _hermanas_.
6. Don José y doña Olga tienen _dos_ nietos y _cuatro_ nietas en Bogotá.
7. Elena es la _tía_ de Jorgito, Elenita y Ana.
8. Lola es la _____ de Jorge y Elena.
   hermana

> **CULTURA**
>
> The ending **-ito/a** (**Jorge** → **Jorgito**) is very common in Hispanic countries; it is particularly used to differentiate parents from children of the same name. The ending **ito/a** also expresses smallness (**hermanito/a, sillita**) or affection (**mi abuelita**).
>
> Hispanics are often given more than one name (**Carlos Alberto, María del Carmen**). These names are often combined (**Mariví**, from **María Victoria**). The name **María** may also be used as part of a man's name: **José María**.

4-3 ¿Quién es y cómo es? Escoja (*Choose*) a un miembro de la familia de Pablo. Su compañero/a debe decir cuál es su relación familiar con Pablo y usar su imaginación para dar información adicional.

MODELO: E1: ¿Quién es Elenita?
             E2: Es la prima de Pablo. Tiene dieciocho años y estudia psicología. Es muy simpática y tiene muchos amigos.

Otros miembros de la familia de Pablo

Paula　Sergio　Lola　Osvaldo

Roberto　Sofía

AUDIO La única hermana de mi mamá es mi tía Lola. Lola y Sergio están **divorciados** pero tienen una hija, mi prima Sofía. Ahora tía Lola está casada con Osvaldo, el **padrastro** de Sofía. Sergio está **casado** con Paula y tienen un hijo, Roberto. Paula es la **madrastra** de Sofía, y Roberto es su **medio hermano**.

¿Qué dice usted?

4-4 ¿Cierto o falso? Marque la columna adecuada de acuerdo con la información sobre la familia de Lola.

	CIERTO	FALSO
1. La tía Lola está casada con Sergio.		✓
2. Osvaldo es el papá de Roberto.		✓
3. Paula es la madrastra de Roberto.		✓
4. Lola es la madre de Sofía.	✓	
5. Sofía tiene un medio hermano.	✓	

4-5 El arte de preguntar. Primera fase. Preparen las preguntas necesarias para obtener la siguiente información.

1. Tengo cuatro abuelos vivos (*alive*). *cuantos abuelos vivos tienes*
2. No, no soy hija única. *eres hija única*
3. Tengo dos hermanos. *cuantos hermanos tienes*
4. Vivo con mi madre y mi padrastro.
5. Mis abuelos no viven con nosotros. *abuelos vivo con son?*
6. Tengo muchos primos. *tienes muchos primos*
7. Tengo una media hermana, pero no vive con nosotros.
8. Mi media hermana vive con su madre.

② **Segunda fase** Ahora intercambien preguntas para obtener información sobre sus propias familias. Después, compartan (*share*) esta información con la clase.

4-6 Mi familia. Preparen un árbol genealógico individualmente. Luego, deben intercambiar su árbol. Finalmente, cada uno/a debe hacerle preguntas a su compañero/a sobre su familia para obtener la siguiente información.

1. nombre de los abuelos vivos
2. nombre de los padres (padrastro/madrastra)
3. número y nombre de los hermanos o medios hermanos
4. número y nombre de los primos
5. descripción de dos familiares

AUDIO ¿Qué hacen los parientes?

Mis abuelos viven en una casa al lado del parque. Normalmente, ellos **pasean** por las mañanas y **almuerzan** muy temprano. Después, **duermen** una siesta, y por la tarde **visitan** a sus **parientes.**

Jorgito es mi primo favorito. Es **un poco** menor que yo, pero corremos y **jugamos** mucho **juntos.** También nos gusta ver el fútbol en la televisión y montar en bicicleta los domingos.

Hace dos años que mi prima Ana tiene **novio,** y **frecuentemente** dice que **quiere casarse** muy pronto. Elena, su hermana gemela, **piensa** que Ana no debe casarse porque es muy joven.

Mi tío Jorge es un hombre muy **ocupado. Sale** de casa muy **temprano** y **vuelve tarde** todos los días. Mi tía María, su esposa, dice que él **prefiere** el trabajo a su familia. Pienso que en todas las familias hay problemas. En la mía también, pero me gusta mi familia.

¿Qué dice usted?

4-7 ¿Cierto o falso? Conteste de acuerdo a la información adicional sobre la familia de Pablo.

	CIERTO	FALSO
1. Normalmente los abuelos están muy ocupados.		✓
2. El tío Jorge cree que Elenita tiene problemas.	✓	✓
3. Elenita piensa que su hermana es muy joven para casarse.	✓	✓
4. Jorgito y Pablo montan en bicicleta frecuentemente.	✓	✓
5. El tío Jorge trabaja mucho.	✓	
6. El tío Jorge llega temprano a su casa.	✓	✓

4-8 ¿Y qué hace su familia? Hágale preguntas a su compañero/a para obtener más información sobre su familia, basándose en los siguientes puntos:

1. *Cuntas* número de personas en la casa, edad y relación
2. ocupación y descripción (física y de personalidad) de algunos miembros de la familia
3. actividades de estas personas en su tiempo libre
4. nombre del pariente favorito, relación familiar y razón de su preferencia

4-9 Familias de famosos. Primera fase. Va a hacer el árbol genealógico de una familia famosa. Vaya a **www.prenhall.com/mosaicos** para obtener la información necesaria. Haga el árbol genealógico. Incluya toda la información posible.

Segunda fase. Túrnese (*Take turns*) con su compañero/a para describir la familia que escogieron (*chose*).

AUDIO **4-10 Algunas familias hispanas.** You will listen to descriptions of four Hispanic families. Before you listen, answer the following questions: Is your family large or small? How many brothers and sisters, cousins, aunts, and uncles do you have?

_____

_____

_____

Now pay attention to the general idea of what is said. As you hear each description, write a check mark in the corresponding column.

	TIENE UNA FAMILIA GRANDE	TIENE HERMANOS	TIENE MUCHOS TÍOS	TIENE PRIMOS
Pedro				
Alicia				
Magdalena				
Alberto				

1. Present tense of stem-changing verbs: *e → ie*, *o → ue, e → i*

PENSAR (e → ie) (*to think*)			
yo	pienso	nosotros/as	pensamos
tú	piensas	vosotros/as	pensáis
Ud., él, ella	piensa	Uds., ellos/as	piensan

VOLVER (o → ue) (*to return*)			
yo	vuelvo	nosotros/as	volvemos
tú	vuelves	vosotros/as	volvéis
Ud., él, ella	vuelve	Uds., ellos/as	vuelven

PEDIR (e → i) (*to ask for, to order*)			
yo	pido	nosotros/as	pedimos
tú	pides	vosotros/as	pedís
Ud., él, ella	pide	Uds., ellos/as	piden

- These verbs change the stem vowel **e** to **ie**, **o** to **ue**, and **e** to **i** except in the **nosotros** and **vosotros** forms.[1]

- Other common verbs and their vowel changes are:

e → ie	o → ue	e → i
cerrar (*to close*)	**almorzar** (*to have lunch*)	**servir** (*to serve*)
empezar (*to begin*)	**costar** (*to cost*)	**repetir** (*to repeat*)
entender (*to understand*)	**dormir** (*to sleep*)	
preferir (*to prefer*)	**poder** (*to be able to, can*)	
querer (*to want, to love*)		

- Use **pensar** + *infinitive* to express what you or someone else is planning to do.

Pienso estudiar esta noche.	*I plan to study tonight.*
Pensamos comer a las ocho.	*We are planning to eat at 8:00.*

- Note the irregular **yo** form in the following **e → ie** and **e → i** stem-changing verbs.

tener (*to have*)	**tengo**, tienes, tiene, tenemos, tenéis, tienen
venir (*to come*)	**vengo**, vienes, viene, venimos, venís, vienen
decir (*to say, tell*)	**digo**, dices, dice, decimos, decís, dicen
seguir (*to follow*)	**sigo**, sigues, sigue, seguimos, seguís, siguen

- The verb *jugar* (*to play* a game or a sport) changes **u** to **ue**.

  Mario **juega** muy bien al tenis, pero nosotros **jugamos** regular.

[1]Stem-changing verbs are identified in vocabulary lists as follows: **pensar** (ie); **volver** (ue); **pedir** (i).

LENGUA

■ The Spanish equivalent for *to think of/about* someone or something is **pensar en.**
¿**Piensas en** tu familia cuando estás fuera de casa?
Do you think of your family when you are away from home?
Sí, **pienso** mucho **en** ellos. Y también **pienso en** mi casa
Yes, I think about them a lot. And I also think of my home.

■ **Pensar de** is used to inquire for an opinion about someone or something. **Pensar que** is normally used to answer these questions.
¿Qué **piensas de** los planes de ayuda familiar?
What do you think of the plans to help families?
Pienso que son excelentes.
I think they are excellent.

¿Qué dice usted?

4-11 Preferencias de la familia. Primera fase. En la casilla (*box*) adecuada, escriba una **Y** para indicar lo que usted prefiere beber y comer, y una **F** para lo que prefiere otro miembro de su familia.

¿QUÉ PREFIERO BEBER YO Y QUÉ PREFIERE...?			
EN EL ALMUERZO	leche	chocolate caliente	café
DESPUÉS DE CORRER	jugo	refresco	agua
PARA CELEBRAR UN CUMPLEAÑOS	vino	cerveza	champaña

¿QUÉ PREFIERO COMER YO Y QUÉ PREFIERE...?			
EN EL DESAYUNO	cereal	tostadas	huevos
LOS DOMINGOS	comida mexicana	comida italiana	comida española
EN UN RESTAURANTE	pollo	pescado	espaguetis

Segunda fase. Túrnense para decirle a su compañero/a qué prefieren beber y comer usted y otro miembro de su familia en cada situación. Después pregúntele a su compañero/a cuáles son sus preferencias.

MODELO: Por la mañana: jugo, café, té
E1: Por la mañana, yo prefiero tomar té, pero mi hermano prefiere tomar café. ¿Y tú?
E2: Pues yo prefiero té.

4-12 ¿Qué piensan hacer estas personas? Túrnense para decir qué piensa hacer cada persona en las situaciones siguientes. Cada uno debe dar una respuesta diferente.

MODELO: Mi hermano desea estar delgado.
E1: Piensa correr mucho.
E2: Piensa empezar una dieta.

1. Mi hermana tiene un examen de matemáticas mañana.
2. Mi hermana estudia bastante, pero no entiende muchos de los problemas.
3. Mi tía está muy débil y cansada.
4. Mis abuelos están de vacaciones en Colombia.
5. Mis primos quieren ir a Cartagena para visitar a los abuelos.

4-13 Comidas y bebidas. Túrnense para preguntarle a su compañero/a qué pide para comer y beber en estos lugares. Él/Ella debe contestarle y además decir lo que pide algún miembro de la familia que tiene gustos diferentes.

MODELO: en un partido de béisbol
　　　　E1: ¿Qué pides en un partido de béisbol?
　　　　E2: Pido un perro caliente y un refresco, pero mi hermano pide una hamburguesa.

1. en un restaurante español muy elegante
2. en un McDonald's si quieres estar delgado/a
3. en un bar con tus amigos
4. en un restaurante en una playa
5. en una pizzería

4-14 Entrevista. Túrnense para entrevistarse entre ustedes (*each other*). Deben cubrir los siguientes puntos en su entrevista y después compartir la información con otro/a compañero/a.

1. hora del desayuno y qué prefiere beber y dónde
2. lugar donde almuerza y qué prefiere comer
3. bebida que prefiere a la hora del almuerzo   *cuantas horas .*
4. sus actividades después del almuerzo
5. hora de la cena, dónde y con quién
6. número de horas que duerme por la noche

4-15 ¿Cuándo y con quién? Primera fase. Háganse preguntas entre ustedes para obtener la siguiente información sobre lo que cada uno hace con sus amigos.

1. lo que hacen juntos durante el año académico durante la semana y los fines de semana
2. si practican algún deporte (*sport*), qué días y dónde
3. actividades preferidas del fin de semana

Segunda fase. Comparen sus actividades. ¿Cuáles son semejantes o diferentes? Compártanlas con otra pareja.

MODELO: Durante la semana, nosotros almorzamos en la cafetería de la universidad.

4-16 Una reunión. Imagínense que todos son miembros de una misma familia y determinen cuál es la relación entre ustedes (hermanos, primos, tíos, etc.). Ahora, organicen una reunión familiar para celebrar el aniversario de los abuelos y decidan lo siguiente:

1. lugar y hora de la reunión
2. número de niños y adultos que participan (especifiquen la relación familiar)
3. obligaciones de los adultos antes de la reunión
4. comida y bebida que van a servir
5. actividades y diversiones para los niños y para los adultos

SITUACIONES

1. You and a/some member(s) of your family are planning to take a trip abroad. Your partner should find out a) when you are planning to go, b) with whom you are going, c) what country and cities you prefer to visit, d) why, and e) if the other family member(s) prefer(s) to go to other places.

2. **Role A:** Your grandparents are celebrating their 50th wedding anniversary and the entire family has gathered for a party. You encounter an old aunt who is very curious about your life in college. After commenting on the party and several family members, answer her questions politely.

   Role B: You are very happy to see your young nephew/niece who is studying in college. After commenting on the party and several family members, ask him/her the following questions about college life: a) the classes he/she is taking; b) which one(s) he/she prefers; c) the type of job he/she wants to do in the future; d) where he/she normally eats; e) when vacations start; f) what he/she is planing to do; and g) when he/she is coming back.

2. Adverbs

■ Adverbs are used to describe when, where, and, how an action/event takes place. You have used Spanish adverbs when expressing time (**mañana, siempre, después**) and place (**detrás, debajo**). You have also used adverbs when expressing how you feel (**bien, muy mal, regular**). These same adverbs can be used when expressing how things are done.

> Rafael nada **bien**.　　　　*Rafael swims well.*

■ Spanish also uses adverbs ending in **-mente**, which corresponds to the English *-ly*, to qualify how things are done. To form these adverbs, add **-mente** to the feminine form of the adjective. With adjectives that do not have a special feminine form, simply add **-mente**.

> María lee **lentamente**.　　　*María reads slowly.*
> Cantan **alegremente**.　　　*They sing happily.*

■ Some commonly used adverbs ending in **-mente** are:

básicamente	normalmente	relativamente
frecuentemente	perfectamente	simplemente
generalmente	realmente	tradicionalmente
lógicamente	regularmente	tranquilamente

¿Qué dice usted?

4-17 ¿Está de acuerdo o no? Primera fase. Indique si está de acuerdo (**Sí**) o no (**No**) con las siguientes afirmaciones.

1. _____ Los padres deben hablar frecuentemente con sus hijos adolescentes.
2. _____ Los nietos deben visitar regularmente a sus abuelos.
3. _____ Normalmente los hijos solteros viven con sus padres.
4. _____ Los padres siempre hablan lentamente cuando están enojados con sus hijos.
5. _____ Generalmente las familias grandes son más felices que las familias pequeñas.
6. _____ Los padres deben tener reuniones con los profesores de sus hijos regularmente.

Segunda fase. Compare sus respuestas con las de su compañero/a y diga por qué están o no están de acuerdo.

4-18 ¿Lenta o rápidamente? Primera fase. Escriba tres actividades que usted hace rápidamente y tres que hace lentamente.

RÁPIDAMENTE	LENTAMENTE
1. _bailar_	1. _____
2. _____	2. _____
3. _____	3. _____

Segunda fase. Compare sus actividades con las de su compañero/a. Puede usar las actividades de la **Primera fase** o usar los verbos que aparecen más abajo.

MODELO: Nado lentamente.
   E1: Yo nado lentamente cuando estoy cansado/a.
   E2: Pues, yo siempre nado rápidamente.
   E1: ¡Qué impresionante!

almorzar	beber	estudiar
bailar	caminar	nadar
hablar español	tomar apuntes	leer el periódico
escribir composiciones	pasear	...

EN DIRECTO

To express surprise at what you hear:
¡Qué increíble! *Incredible!*
¡Qué impresionante! *How impressive!*

4-19 Entrevista. Primera fase. Hágale estas preguntas a su compañero/a. Después él/ella le debe hacer las mismas preguntas a usted.

1. ¿Qué haces normalmente por la tarde?
2. ¿A qué lugares vas regularmente y con quién?
3. Generalmente, ¿adónde vas por la noche?
4. ¿Adónde vas para conversar tranquilamente con tus amigos?
5. ¿A quiénes llamas por teléfono más frecuentemente, a tus amigos o a tu familia?

Segunda fase. Ahora escriba una breve comparación entre usted y su compañero/a con respecto a cada pregunta en la **Primera fase**. ¿Hacen ustedes actividades semejantes (*similar*) o diferentes? ¿Van ustedes a los mismos (*same*) lugares? ¿Quién de ustedes es más sociable: usted o su compañero/a? ¿Por qué?

SITUACIONES

1. Your class is conducting a survey regarding students' movie habits. Ask a classmate a) when he/she goes to the movies, b) with whom he/she generally goes, c) the type of movies he/she normally prefers (romantic, dramas, science fiction, etc.), d) what he/she eats or drinks at the movies, and e) the name of his/her favorite movie theater.

2. You are conducting a survey regarding family customs and activities for your Sociology class. Ask a classmate a) if the members of his/her immediate family generally eat together, b) if they visit other family members frequently (grandparents, aunts, uncles, cousins), c) who is the family member that normally organizes family reunions, and d) if there are traditions in his/her family and what they are.

3. Present tense of *hacer, poner, salir, traer,* and *oír*

El padre pone la mesa.

La madre oye música y también las noticias.

La hija trae las tostadas a la mesa.

El hijo hace la cama.

El abuelo pone la televisión.

La familia desayuna y sale.

HACER (*to make, to do*)			
yo	hago	nosotros/as	hacemos
tú	haces	vosotros/as	hacéis
Ud., él, ella	hace	Uds., ellos/as	hacen

PONER (*to put*)			
yo	pongo	nosotros/as	ponemos
tú	pones	vosotros/as	ponéis
Ud., él, ella	pone	Uds., ellos/as	ponen

■ **Poner** normally means *to put*. However, with some electrical appliances, **poner** means *to turn on*.

Yo **pongo** los platos en la mesa a la hora de la cena.

I put the plates on the table at dinner time.

Mi abuelo siempre **pone** la televisión después de la cena.

My grandfather always turns on the T.V. after dinner.

SALIR (*to leave*)			
yo	salgo	nosotros/as	salimos
tú	sales	vosotros/as	salís
Ud., él, ella	sale	Uds., ellos/as	salen

■ **Salir** can be used with several different prepositions: to express that you are leaving a place, use **salir de**; to express the place of your destination, use **salir para**; to express with whom you go out or the person you date, use **salir con**; to express what you are going to do, use **salir a**.

Yo **salgo de** mi cuarto ahora.
Salgo para la librería.
Mi hermana **sale con** Mauricio.
Ellos **salen** a bailar los sábados.

I am leaving my room now.
I am leaving for the bookstore.
My sister goes out with Mauricio.
They go out dancing on Saturdays.

TRAER (*to bring*)			
yo	traigo	nosotros/as	traemos
tú	traes	vosotros/as	traéis
Ud., él, ella	trae	Uds., ellos/as	traen

OÍR (*to hear*)			
yo	oigo	nosotros/as	oímos
tú	oyes	vosotros/as	oís
Ud., él, ella	oye	Uds., ellos/as	oyen

¿Qué dice usted?

4-20 El rey (*king*) de la organización. Primera fase. Alberto es una persona muy organizada, considerada, estudiosa y puntual. Marque con una X las afirmaciones que Alberto probablemente hace sobre sí mismo (*about himself*).

1. _____ Yo no **hago** mi cama.
2. __X__ Yo **hago** mi cama temprano por la mañana.
3. __X__ Para concentrarme en mis estudios, yo no **pongo** música.
4. _____ Siempre **pongo** música rock cuando estudio.
5. __X__ Para ayudar (*help*) a mi madre, **pongo** la mesa para el desayuno.
6. _____ No **pongo** la mesa porque no me gusta trabajar en casa.
7. __X__ Generalmente, **traigo** el periódico a la mesa porque me gusta leer las noticias mientras desayuno.
8. __X__ En general, no **traigo** el periódico a la mesa mientras desayuno porque prefiero conversar con mi familia.
9. _____ Después de desayunar **salgo** rápidamente para la universidad porque no me gusta llegar tarde.
10. __X__ Desayuno lentamente y luego **salgo** para la universidad porque tengo suficiente tiempo para llegar a la hora que la clase empieza.

② Segunda fase. Túrnense para comparar las actividades de Alberto con las actividades de ustedes. ¿Son ustedes organizados/as, considerados/as, estudiosos/as y puntuales como Alberto?

MODELO: E1: Yo también... ¿Y tú?
          E2: Pues yo también... o No, yo no...

4-21 ¿Familias tradicionales o modernas? Primera fase. Indique quiénes hacen estas actividades en su familia: los hombres (H), las mujeres (M) o ambos (*both*) (A).

1. _____ comprar la comida
2. _____ poner la mesa
3. _____ hacer el desayuno
4. _____ salir solo/a porque no le gusta la compañía de otras personas
5. _____ hacer las camas
6. _____ oír los chismes (*gossip*) más recientes sobre los famosos en la radio
7. _____ traer el periódico a la casa
8. _____ poner la televisión para ver las noticias

② Segunda fase. Comparen sus respuestas. Determinen cuál de las familias es más tradicional y cuál es más moderna. ¿Por qué?

② 4-22 Intercambio. Primera fase. Hoy la familia de su compañero/a está muy ocupada. Hágale preguntas a su compañero/a para saber a qué hora salen y para dónde van las personas que aparecen en la tabla.

MODELO: E1: ¿A qué hora sale Juan?
         E2: (Sale) a las 8 de la mañana.
         E1: ¿Para dónde va Juan?
         E2: Va para el gimnasio.

NOMBRE	HORA	LUGAR
Juan	8:00 a.m.	gimnasio
Alicia	9:30 a.m.	laboratorio de computadoras
tu sobrino	2:00 p.m.	café
Cristina	8:30 p.m.	oficina
tú	...	...

Segunda fase. Respondan a las siguientes preguntas sobre las personas de la **Primera fase.**

1. ¿Quién hace ejercicio (*exercise*)? ¿Por qué?
2. ¿A quién le gusta socializar?
3. ¿Quién es fanático/a del trabajo? ¿Por qué?
4. ¿A quién le gusta usar las computadoras?

❷ 4-23 Las clases de español de mi hermano. Hable sobre las actividades escolares de su hermano, y después pregúntele a su compañero/a sobre sus actividades.

MODELO: tener la clase de español por la mañana
         E1: Mi hermano tiene la clase de español por la mañana. ¿Y tú?
         E2: Yo tengo la clase (de español) por la tarde. *o* Yo también tengo la clase (de español) por la mañana.

1. hacer la tarea por la noche
2. salir para la universidad a las nueve frecuentemente
3. poner la tarea sobre el escritorio del profesor generalmente
4. traer los libros a la casa
5. salir de la clase a las diez normalmente

❷ 4-24 Entrevista. Usted quiere saber qué hace su compañero/a en su tiempo libre y él/ella quiere saber qué hace usted. Háganse preguntas para averiguar (*to find out*) lo siguiente:

1. hora de salida de la universidad
2. lugares para donde va
3. actividades en esos lugares
4. actividades en su casa por las noches
5. programas de televisión favoritos
6. ...

4-25 ¿De dónde salen, con quién y para dónde? Mire el dibujo y complete el siguiente párrafo (*paragraph*) con la forma correcta de **salir + de, salir + para** o **salir + con.**

1. Javier y Marcelo son amigos. Ellos _____ la casa de Javier. _____ el cine. Javier siempre _____ Marcelo los domingos por la tarde.

Ahora complete el siguiente párrafo de acuerdo con sus propias actividades y su propio horario. Compare sus respuestas con las de su compañero/a.

2. Yo _____ casa a las _____ de la mañana. _____ la universidad. Llego a la universidad a las _____. Las clases terminan a las _____. A esa hora _____ casa. Por las noches _____ mi novio/a.

SITUACIONES

1. Find out the following information about your partner's family: a) who sets the table, b) who prepares breakfast, c) who makes the beds, and d) what time each family member leaves the house in the morning.

2. **Role A.** You are participating in a school play in which you act out the part of a character who has many family problems. In this scene, you are telling your counselor: a) that you have a stepsister/brother that is very lazy and unpleasant, b) that you work a lot in the house, c) that your stepmother is not nice to you and explain why, and d) that you talk with your father about these problems, but he thinks you exaggerate (*exagerar*). Then ask your counselor what you should do in this situation.

   Role B. You play the part of the family counselor. After listening to your client, you ask for the following information: a) the number of family members, b) what they are like, and c) the things he/she does at home. Then, tell your client to be nice to his/her step sister/brother for two weeks, to write down the work her sister/brother should do in the house and to note whether he/she does it or not.

4. *Hace* with expressions of time

- To say that an action/state began in the past and continues into the present, use **hace** + *length of time* + **que** + present tense.

   Hace dos horas que juegan.   *They've been playing for two hours.*

- If you begin the sentence with the present tense of the verb, do not use **que.**

   Juegan hace dos horas.   *They've been playing for two hours.*

- To find out how long an action/state has been taking place, use **cuánto tiempo + hace que** + *present tense.*

   ¿Cuánto tiempo hace que juegan?   *How long have they been playing?*

¿Qué dice usted?

4-26 Éste soy yo. Primera fase. Lea la siguiente descripción y contesta las preguntas.

Me llamo Jaime Caicedo. Soy de Cali, Colombia, pero mis padres viven ahora en Bogotá. Hablo español, pero deseo aprender inglés para poder hablar con personas de los Estados Unidos. Estudio inglés **hace** dos años, pero debo estudiar más para hablar, leer y escribir inglés correctamente. Para aprender más, siempre miro programas de televisión en inglés en los canales del cable. Mi programa favorito es *Friends*. **Hace** dos años **que** miro el programa y me gusta mucho. En mi tiempo libre, voy al cine y a fiestas. Tengo un auto un poco viejo **hace** un año, pero salgo en él con mis amigos y también con mi novia. **Hace** cuatro meses **que** somos novios. Somos muy felices.

1. Jaime Caicedo es de...
   a. los Estados Unidos   b. Bogotá   c. *Friends*

2. Hace dos años que Jaime...
   a. tiene novia   b. va al cine   c. mira *Friends*

3. En su tiempo libre, jaime...
   a. va a fiestas   b. estudia inglés   c. estudia español

Segunda fase. Ahora escriba su propia descripción, siguiendo el modelo. Luego, comparta su descripción con un/a compañero/a.

Me llamo _____. Soy de _____, _____ (ciudad y país). Hablo _____ (su lengua materna), pero deseo aprender _____ (lengua extranjera) para _____ (razón). Estudio _____ **hace** _____ (lengua extranjera y período de tiempo), pero debo estudiar más para hablar, leer y escribir en la lengua correctamente. Para aprender más, siempre miro _____ (programa que usted escucha o mira para aprender más). Mi programa favorito es _____. **Hace** dos años **que** _____ el programa y me gusta mucho. En mi tiempo libre, _____ Tengo _____ (vehículo/objeto o animal) **hace** _____. También **hace** _____ (período de tiempo) **que** tengo _____ (novio/a o nuevo amigo/a). _____ (Describa sus sentimientos sobre esta relación).

4-27 Entrevista. Túrnense para hacerse las siguientes preguntas. Después compartan la información con otra pareja.

1. ¿Dónde vives? ¿Cuánto tiempo hace que vives allí?
2. ¿Dónde trabaja tu padre/madre? ¿Cuánto tiempo hace que trabaja allí?
3. ¿Cuánto tiempo hace que estudias en esta universidad?
   ¿Y por qué estudias español?
4. ¿Practicas algún deporte? ¿Cuánto tiempo hace que juegas al...?
   ¿Juegas bien?

SITUACIONES

1. You are a new student at the university, and a cousin from Colombia is coming to visit you. Since you are not familiar with the area, ask your friend about the good Colombian restaurant where he/she usually goes. Ask a) how long he/she has been going to this restaurant, b) what Colombian dishes they serve (e.g., **ajiaco de pollo, papas chorreadas, arroz con coco**) and how much they cost, and c) thank him/her for the information. Your friend will answer giving as much information as possible.

ALGO MÁS

Some reflexive verbs and pronouns

LAVARSE		
yo	**me lavo**	*I wash myself*
tú	**te lavas**	*you wash yourself*
Ud.	**se lava**	*you wash yourself*
él/ella	**se lava**	*he/she washes himself/herself*

■ Reflexive verbs are those that express what people do to or for themselves.

REFLEXIVE
Mi hermana **se lava**.   *My sister washes herself.*
                                 (She is the doer and the receiver.)

NONREFLEXIVE
Mi hermana **lava** el auto.   *My sister washes the car.*
                                 (She is the doer and the car is the receiver.)

■ A reflexive pronoun refers back to the subject of the sentence. In English this may be expressed by pronouns ending in -*self* or -*selves*; in many cases, Spanish uses reflexives where English does not.

Yo **me levanto, me baño, me**   *I get up, take a shower, dry myself,*
seco y **me visto** rápidamente.   *and get dressed quickly.*

■ Place reflexive pronouns after the word **no** in negative constructions.

Tú **no te peinas** por la   *You don't comb your hair in the*
mañana.   *morning.*

■ The pronoun **se** attached to the end of an infinitive shows that the verb is reflexive.

lavar   *to wash*
lavarse   *to wash oneself*

¿Qué dice usted?

4-28 La rutina diaria de mi compañero/a. Primera fase. Indique con un número (1, 2, 3, . . .) el orden en que, según usted, su compañero/a hace lo siguiente.

_____ desayuna   _____ sale
_____ se peina   _____ se baña
_____ se seca   _____ se viste
_____ se levanta

Segunda fase. Ahora hágale preguntas a su compañero/a para verificar el orden.

4-29 ¿Qué hace? Escoja a un miembro de su familia de quién va a hablar en esta actividad. Intercambie preguntas con su compañero/a sobre las actividades de este pariente y llene la tabla.

Miembro de la familia _____

	7:00 A.M.	8:00 A.M.	?
Se levanta			
Desayuna	hora	comida	bebida
Se baña	mañana	tarde	noche
Actividades	lavar el auto	hacer la cama	poner la mesa
Sale para	trabajo	universidad	?

Escuchar

Filling in charts or forms

Listening for specific information is a much-needed skill in many settings and contexts such as special events (sports, academic, religious), traveling, shopping, and so on. Once you have determined what information you are interested in, you listen to it, screen it, and select only those bits and pieces that you need. You let go what is irrelevant or unnecessary.

In an academic setting (your chemistry class, for example), you may listen to your professor's lecture and fill in a chart or a form in order to solve a problem later.

Antes de escuchar

4-30 Un bautizo. In **4-31**, you will listen to a conversation between two friends talking about the christening of one of their relatives. Before you listen, and using your knowledge of this or a similar type of ceremony, state who participates and where the event takes place.

Participantes: _____

Lugar: _____

A escuchar

AUDIO **4-31** Now, listen to the recording and circle the correct information in the following chart.

Nombre del niño	a. Rafael José	b. Álvaro Mejía
Fecha de nacimiento	a. 12 de agosto	b. 11 de octubre
Lugar de nacimiento	a. Bogotá	b. Santa Clara
Nombre de la madre	a. Mónica	b. Ana María
Nombre del padre	a. Miguel	b. Rafael
Nombre de la madrina	a. María Elena	b. Rosa
Nombre del padrino	a. Álvaro	b. José

Después de escuchar

4-32 ¿Y usted? With a classmate, share your answers to the following questions.

1. ¿Tiene usted sobrinos? ¿Cuántos?
2. ¿Tiene usted una madrina o un padrino? ¿Cómo se llama(n)?
3. ¿Qué ocasión es más importante para usted: un bautizo o un cumpleaños? ¿Por qué?

Antes de escuchar

4-33 El mensaje telefónico. In **4-34,** you will listen to a message Pedro left on Julio's answering about a surprise party he is organizing. Before you listen, write down the arrangements that would generally be made for such a party.

_____

_____

_____

A escuchar

4-34 Now, complete the chart below with the correct information as you listen to the message. Do not worry if you do not understand every word.

La fiesta va a ser en la casa de:	pedro
La dirección es:	
El día de la fiesta es:	domingo
José debe llegar a la casa a las:	
Julio debe llevar (*take*):	CD's refrescos

Después de escuchar

4-35 ¿Y usted? You are going to give a surprise party for one of your friends in your Spanish class, and you would like to invite your Spanish professor. Complete the following note you will leave in your professor's campus mailbox.

Estimado/a profesor/a ... _____ :

Este fin de semana, pienso dar una fiesta sorpresa para ___Pedro___ .

¿Le gustaría venir? Vamos a comer __papis frutas__ y __pollo__ . Vamos a tener refrescos para todos.

La fiesta va a ser el ___lunes___ en mi casa/apartamento a la(s) ___ocho___ de la mañana/~~tarde~~/noche. Mi dirección es ___veinticinco treinta tres___

Lo/La espero el ___ocho___ . de noviembre

Hasta pronto.

___Andrés___

Conversar

Antes de conversar

4-36 ¿Quién de mi familia? En cada espacio en blanco, escriba el nombre de un familiar, incluyendo el parentesco (*family relationship*) y la actividad que hace.

MODELO: _____ en restaurantes los fines de semana.
Mi primo David come en restaurantes los fines de semana.

1. _____ cerveza frecuentemente cuando mira(n) fútbol en la televisión.
2. _____ mucho y con frecuencia está(n) cansado/a(s).
3. _____ a conciertos de música popular.
4. _____ en casa los fines de semana. Descansan, leen, escuchan música, etc.
5. _____ ejercicio físico tres o cuatro veces por semana.
6. _____ con amigos o con la familia en casa el día de su cumpleaños.
7. _____ música romántica a todas horas.
8. _____ por el teléfono celular.

A conversar

Ⓖ 4-37 ¿Cómo es familia? Respondan a las siguientes preguntas.

1. ¿Quiénes son más activos en su familia: las mujeres o los hombres?
2. ¿Qué miembros de la familia pasan más tiempo en casa: los jóvenes o los mayores?
3. ¿Quiénes son más sociables: las mujeres o los hombres, los jóvenes o los mayores? ¿Por qué?

Después de conversar

Ⓖ 4-38 Nuestras familias. Completen un pequeño informe con la información que obtuvieron (*got*) en la actividad **4-37** y compártanlo con el resto de la clase.

- En nuestras familias (los hombres/las mujeres) _____ son más activos/as porque _____.

- (Los jóvenes/los mayores) _____ pasan más tiempo en casa porque _____.

- Las mujeres/los hombres/los jóvenes/los mayores) _____ son más sociables porque _____.

Antes de conversar

4-39 Generalizaciones. A continuación hay algunas generalizaciones sobre la familia hispana. Léanlas y luego escriban algunas generalizaciones sobre las familias de su comunidad.

LA FAMILIA HISPANA	LAS FAMILIAS DE MI COMUNIDAD
1. La religión es una parte importante de la vida.	1. _____
2. Para los padres, la educación de sus hijos es vital.	2. _____
3. Los jóvenes respetan mucho a los mayores. Cuando los padres hablan, los hijos escuchan.	3. _____ _____
4. Los hijos viven en casa con los padres mientras estudian.	4. _____
5. Muchas madres trabajan doble, en casa y fuera de ella.	5. _____
6. Los miembros de las familias celebran ocasiones especiales juntos como cumpleaños, bautizos, etc.	6. _____ _____
7. Las hijas colaboran con la madre en el trabajo de la casa. Los hijos reparan cosas (*things*) con el padre.	7. _____ _____
8. Los padres que son mayores viven frecuentemente con sus hijos.	8. _____

A conversar

4-40 ¿De acuerdo o no? Ahora compartan con otro grupo sus ideas sobre la familia de su comunidad (actividad **4-39**). ¿Están de acuerdo en sus generalizaciones? ¿En qué están de acuerdo? ¿En qué no están de acuerdo?

Después de conversar

4-41 ¿Son las familias semejantes o diferentes? Escriba un breve informe sobre las diferencias y semejanzas de las familias hispanas y las familias de su comunidad.

EN DIRECTO

To agree or disagree with someone:
(No) Estoy de acuerdo.
Tiene(s) razón. (*You are right*)
Está(s) equivocado/a. (*You are wrong.*)

 Leer

In *Lecciones 1* through *3* you used a variety of basic reading strategies to become a more proficient reader in Spanish such as 1) relying on your knowledge of the world to anticipate the content of a text, 2) identifying cognates, 3) determining the kind of text and the text format, 4) using visuals to comprehend better, and 5) skimming and scanning. Remember to use these strategies as the need arises.

Guía de prelectura

Read the title of the article in activities **4-45** and **4-46** and answer the following questions, based on your previous knowledge.

1. Thinking of the theme of *Lección 4* and after reading the title of the article, can you guess what the theme of the article will be?
   a. communication between friends
   b. communication among family members
   c. communication with peers at work

2. Can you anticipate some ideas that the article probably contains? Circle all that may apply. Do not worry if you miss some answers. You may come back and verify your responses after reading the article.
   a. Today, adults and children communicate better than in the past.
   b. Children do not talk about their problems with their parents because the latter are busy all the time.
   c. Modern life has affected communication between parents and children.
   d. There is lack of communication between family members today, although communication is very important.

3. Now, use your knowledge of the English language to comprehend the text. What words in the title helped you figure out the answers to question 2? Write them down.

   _____

   Are they cognates?   Yes   No

4. Judging from the title, in what kind of printed media can an article on this topic be found?
   a. _____ in a family magazine
   b. _____ in a journal of medicine
   c. _____ in a sports magazine

Antes de leer

2 **4-42 Preparación.** Mire esta fotografía con su compañero/a. Luego respondan a las preguntas.

1. Este niño y su padre, ¿tienen una buena o mala relación? ¿Por qué?
2. ¿Cuántos años tienen los padres del niño probablemente? En su opinión, ¿es más fácil para los padres jóvenes comprender a sus hijos?
3. Generalmente, ¿cuándo conversan los hijos con sus padres?
4. Probablemente, ¿de qué temas conversan? ¿De problemas familiares o de problemas escolares? ¿De otros temas?
5. ¿A qué edad es más difícil la comunicación entre padres e hijos? ¿Por qué?

2 **4-43 Asociación.** Marque con una X las actividades que usted asocia con una buena relación entre padres e hijos. Luego, compare sus respuestas con las de un/a compañero/a.

1. _____ conversar
2. _____ pasar tiempo juntos
3. _____ hablar por teléfono
4. _____ pelear (*argue*)
5. _____ escribir correos electrónicos a un miembro de la familia que vive lejos (*far*)
6. _____ comprar regalos (*presents*)
7. _____ expresar amor
8. _____ estar conectados a Internet por muchas horas

A leer

4-44 Primera etapa. El siguiente artículo es de una revista que se dedica a los temas de familia. Lea los dos primeros párrafos y siga las instrucciones.

Subraye (*Underline*) ...

1. las palabras en el título que probablemente indican el tema del artículo
2. una palabra que describe la condición de la familia de hoy
3. una palabra que indica la importancia de la comunicación dentro de la familia

Escriba...

4. una causa de los problemas de comunicación en la familia
5. tres necesidades de los hijos que tienen padres que trabajan fuera
6. dos efectos de la ausencia de los padres de la casa

La importancia de la comunicación familiar

(1) Los expertos afirman que la familia de nuestros días está en crisis por la falta[1] de comunicación entre sus miembros o por la mala comunicación que existe entre ellos. También coinciden en que la comunicación es vital en todas las relaciones, especialmente en la familiar.

(2) Pero, ¿por qué existen problemas de comunicación en las familias? Las razones son varias. Una es que la madre y el padre trabajan largas horas fuera de casa y los hijos están solos mucho tiempo, sin la compañía, la orientación y la supervisión de sus mayores. La ausencia casi diaria de los padres puede crear cierta independencia en los hijos y una distancia emocional que dificulta la comunicación entre padres e hijos.

[1]*lack*

4-45 Segunda etapa. Ahora lea el resto del artículo y siga las indicaciones. En el párrafo número tres, el artículo presenta otra razón de la mala comunicación entre padres e hijos.

Indique...

1 una palabra asociada con los problemas de comunicación familiares.
2 por qué la tecnología probablemente afecta las relaciones de la familia.
3 dos ejemplos de cómo la tecnología causa problemas cuando no se usa bien.
4 dos palabras que indican la calidad (*quality*) de la comunicación cuando usamos el correo electrónico.

En el párrafo número cuatro, el artículo indica algunas formas de usar la tecnología en beneficio de la relación familiar.

5 ¿Cómo es posible usar la tecnología positivamente en la comunicación con la familia?

---

(3) Un segundo factor es la tecnología. Nuestro mundo está controlado por la tecnología, en casa, en el trabajo, etc. Evidentemente la tecnología facilita mucho la vida, pero su uso excesivo puede complicar nuestra existencia. En las sociedades donde el uso de la tecnología tiene un costo bajo, un gran número de hogares[2] están conectado a Internet. Así, muchos jóvenes tienen acceso ilimitado a la Red y al correo electrónico. Idealmente, el bajo costo de conexión debería afectar positivamente la comunicación en la familia, pero la realidad indica que, en general, la comunicación por correo electrónico, por ejemplo, tiende a ser más breve y más superficial. Los hijos prefieren no discutir por correo electrónico su depresión o sus malas notas en la universidad. Prefieren hablar directamente con sus padres, si es que estos tienen el tiempo. Lo mismo ocurre con el teléfono celular. La comunicación es casi instantánea. Es cierto que muchos jóvenes usan celulares para llamar a sus padres, pero, ¿cuántos de ellos hablan 15 minutos sobre temas importantes como sus problemas, alegrías, éxitos, etc.? ¡Muy pocos!

(4) En conclusión, el tiempo limitado que los padres pueden dar a sus hijos y la naturaleza impersonal de la comunicación electrónica pueden afectar negativamente las relaciones familiares. Por eso es importante crear oportunidades para una comunicación real y profunda dentro de la familia. Use la tecnología de manera positiva para expresar el amor y el cariño que siente por sus padres, hijos, abuelos, tíos. Su familia va a ser más fuerte y unida.

[2]*homes*

4-46 Identificación. Primera fase. La terminación (*ending*) de las palabras revela información importante sobre ellas: si la palabra es un nombre, un adjetivo, un verbo o un adverbio, por ejemplo. Observe las siguientes palabras del artículo y, luego, clasifíquelas en la columna correspondiente.

facili**ta**   orienta**ción**   imperson**al**   electrón**ico**
supervi**sión**   ausen**cia**   afec**tar**   ilimit**ado**
dificul**ta**   negativa**mente**   socie**dades**   positiva**mente**

NOMBRES	ADJETIVOS	FORMAS VERBALES	ADVERBIOS

Segunda fase. Las siguientes terminaciones indican que las palabras son nombres femeninos en español: **-sión, -ción, -cia, -ía, -dad.** Escriba abajo otros nombres con estas terminaciones que aparicen en el artículo.

_____

_____

_____

Después de leer

4-47 Expansión. Lea el siguiente texto incompleto sobre las relaciones familiares y, luego, seleccione la palabra que corresponde lógicamente en cada espacio en blanco.

supervisión	ausencia	electrónico	trabajo
trabajan	facilita	compañía	positivamente

Mi familia es como una pequeña sociedad. Todos los miembros colaboran a la felicidad del grupo. Mis padres (1) _____ mucho fuera de casa cada día, y nosotros necesitamos su (2) _____. Pero su (3) _____ es solamente de lunes a viernes. Cuando ellos están en su (4) _____, ellos realizan la (5) _____ de sus hijos por teléfono. Siempre llaman por teléfono para verificar nuestro trabajo en casa y nuestras tareas. El teléfono celular (6) _____ mucho nuestra comunicación. Mi padre, en particular, se comunica con nosotros por correo (7) _____. Cuando hay pequeños problemas entre nosotros, nuestros padres siempre reaccionan (8) _____. Hablan pacientemente con nosotros para resolver nuestros conflictos.

 ## Escribir

In _Lección 3_, you practiced writing a letter to a friend. Any correspondence with friends usually lacks formality. However, writing to elders in your family, such as your parents, older aunts and uncles, may be more formal. To show love and respect, you choose your language more carefully, you may talk about different issues more seriously, and you address your elders differently from the way you address your friends.

Although there is no standard manner of addressing your elders in Spanish, since family relationships are unique to each home, the expressions in _En directo_ constitute some common address forms to elders with whom you maintain a close relationship.

In letter writing, closings are also important. Again, as is the case with salutations, closings also reflect a certain degree of formality and closeness to the person to whom you are writing. _En directo_ has some common closing lines you may wish to use when writing to elders in your family or close older friends.

EN DIRECTO

Querido abuelo/ tío: _Dear …_
Querida abuela/ mamá:

EN DIRECTO

Con cariño,
Affectionately,
Con mucho cariño,
With much love,
Abrazos y besos,
Hugs and kisses,
Te recuerdo con cariño,
_I remember you (familiar),
with affection._

Antes de escribir

4-48 Preparación. Primera fase. La madre de Julián, un alumno universitario colombiano, escribe la siguiente carta a su hijo. La madre está triste y preocupada porque su hijo estudia en la Universidad de Los Andes y vive lejos de casa. Lea la carta y siga las instrucciones.

Querido Julián:

¿Qué tal estás? ¿Cómo van tus clases? Hace un mes que no tenemos información sobre ti. ¡No escribes correos electrónicos, no llamas por teléfono! ¿Qué ocurre?

Bueno, es el fin del semestre y debes tener mucho trabajo. ¿Estás muy estresado? ¿Duermes suficiente? ¿Comes bien en la universidad? Un estudiante necesita una buena dieta. En tu próxima visita, voy a preparar tus platos favoritos. Tu hermana Mariela, tus abuelos y tíos van a estar con nosotros y vamos a conversar largas horas.

Tengo una sorpresa para ti. Tu hermano Marcos tiene novia; se llama Alicia. Es una chica fascinante. Pasan mucho tiempo juntos; van al cine, pasean por el parque de la universidad, salen a comer por las noches, etc. A Marcos le gusta mucho Alicia. La semana próxima Marcos y Alicia tienen vacaciones y, para conocerla un poco más, Marcos piensa ir a Cartagena con ella por unos días. Las temperaturas allí están perfectas para nadar y descansar un poco.

Debo confesarte que tu padre y yo pensamos mucho en ti. ¿Por qué no escribes? ¿Tienes problemas en tus clases? ¿Sacas buenas notas en tus exámenes? ¿Trabajas mucho y no tienes tiempo para estudiar? ¿Estás desconectado de Internet? Por favor, escribe o llama pronto.

Un beso de papá, Mariela y toda la familia.

Abrazos,

Tu madre

Segunda fase. Imagínese que usted es Julián. Después de leer la carta de su madre, usted está muy triste. Prepárese para responder a la carta. Haga lo siguiente:

1. Identifique las preguntas de su madre a las que usted va a responder y escriba algunas ideas o información para la respuesta.
2. Escriba algunas preguntas que usted quiere hacerle a su madre: sobre su padre, sus hermanos, sus abuelos, su perro o gato, etc.

A escribir

4-49 Manos a la obra. Ahora en una hoja de papel responda a la carta de su madre. Use la información de la **Segunda fase** de la **Actividad 4-48**. Incluya la fecha, un saludo y una despedida (*closing*) apropiados.

Después de escribir

4-50 Revisión. Antes de darle su carta a su compañero/a editor/a, revise:

- primero, la coherencia de sus ideas y la cantidad de información que su madre necesita.
- luego, la precisión gramatical (el vocabulario apropiado al contexto, la estructura de las oraciones, la concordancia, etc.).
- finalmente, la ortografía y la acentuación.

ENFOQUE CULTURAL

TEMAS: LA FAMILIA HISPANA

Para pensar

¿Tiene usted una familia grande o pequeña? ¿Quiénes forman parte de su familia? ¿Dónde viven? ¿Con qué frecuencia ve usted a los miembros de su familia? ¿Quiénes trabajan fuera de la casa? ¿Quiénes se ocupan de las tareas domésticas?

La familia es una de las instituciones sociales más importantes del mundo hispano. En general, las familias pasan bastante tiempo juntas y es común verlas en almuerzos, paseos, fiestas y otras actividades.

La familia hispana incluye a los padres e hijos, pero también a abuelos, primos, tíos y padrinos. La familia hispana tiene una larga tradición de ser numerosa y unida.

En la familia tradicional los hombres trabajan fuera de la casa, y las mujeres hacen las tareas domésticas y crían (raise) a los niños.

Para contestar

2 **4-51 La familia hispana.** Responda a las siguientes preguntas:

1. Compare la familia hispana tradicional y la moderna con respecto al tamaño, la persona que hace las tareas domésticas, etc.
2. Compare la familia hispana moderna y la familia americana con respecto al tamaño, la persona que hace las tareas domésticas, etc.
3. Además de los padres y los hijos, ¿qué otras personas forman parte de la familia hispana?

G **Riqueza cultural.** Hablen de las ventajas y desventajas para los padres y para los hijos de vivir con los abuelos, tíos y primos en una misma casa.

En la actualidad muchas mujeres tienen menos hijos y trabajan fuera de la casa, pero también se ocupan de las tareas domésticas.

Para pensar

¿Qué sabe usted acerca de (*about*) Colombia? ¿Hay colombianos en el área donde usted vive?

Colombia está en el norte de América del Sur y tiene costas en el Océano Pacífico y en el Océano Atlántico.

Bogotá, la capital de Colombia, es una hermosa ciudad de muchos contrastes: tiene zonas muy ricas y otras muy pobres, zonas muy modernas y zonas antiguas como el barrio colonial de la Candelaria.

En Bogotá está el famoso Museo del Oro, que tiene la colección más grande del mundo de objetos de oro de la época precolombina.

La ciudad de Cartagena, fundada en 1533, está en la costa del Atlántico. Los jóvenes y adultos pueden disfrutar aquí de hermosas playas y fiestas muy divertidas. La música típica de la costa Atlántica es la cumbia, género musical que se asocia con Colombia.

Expresiones colombianas:

soplar y hacer botellas	Sacar una A en español es difícil. Eso no es **soplar y hacer botellas**.	*To get an A in Spanish is hard. It is not as easy as it looks.*
camello	No puedo ir al cine. Tengo mucho **camello**.	*I cannot go to the movies. I have a lot of work.*
afán	Él no tiene afán (no está de **afán**).	*He is in no hurry.*
pereque	Te voy a poner un **pereque**.	*I am going to ask you a favor.*

Para contestar

En el mapa

1. En el mapa de la página 158, busque una ciudad de Colombia en la costa del Pacífico y otra en la costa del Atlántico.
2. Indique qué países están cerca de Colombia.

Ahora diga...

1. si le gustaría ir al Museo del Oro y por qué.
2. dónde se puede escuchar música colombiana como la cumbia o el vallenato.

¿Qué dice usted si...

1. tiene un examen muy difícil mañana.
2. su compañero/a de cuarto tiene clase en diez minutos pero camina muy lentamente.

Para investigar en Internet

Vaya a **www.prenhall.com/mosaicos** y busque anuncios de bautizos, matrimonios, avisos de defunción, etc. en un periódico colombiano. Haga una lista de los miembros de la familia que se mencionan.

¡Prepárese!

4-52 Adivinen. Antes de mirar el video, formen grupos de tres para hablar sobre las imágenes y el texto. Luego completen juntos/as las oraciones siguientes de acuerdo a lo que dijeron en su conversación.

1. Ángela dice que el público está aburrido porque...
2. La solución que tienen Carlos y Katie es...
3. Tres cosas que sabemos sobre la civilización azteca son...
4. Sabrina y Efraín miran la cámara de video de Tito porque...
5. A Carlos le gusta Katie porque...

Al mirar el video comparen sus respuestas con lo que observan. ¿Están correctas?

Ángela dice que el público está aburrido.

Carlos y Katie tienen la solución.

Las nuevas pistas están relacionadas con la civilización azteca.

Katie explica lo que es el "peregrinaje".

Sabrina y Efraín miran la cámara de video de Tito.

A Carlos le gusta Katie.

¡Responda!

G **4-53 Significados.** Después de mirar el video, consulten un diccionario bilingüe para ver el significado de las siguientes palabras y expresiones del segundo misterio.

la cuna	el peregrinaje	el éxodo
de nuevo	el águila	la serpiente

Katie dice que ella y Carlos deben ir al Zócalo. Con sus compañeros/as, investigue, en su libro o en la Red qué es el "Zócalo". ¿Por qué deben Katie y Carlos ir allí?

Esta canción colombiana, en la cual un hombre se pregunta por qué lo abandona su novia, trata del tema del amor perdido. Es un ejemplo de **cumbia**, un ritmo bailable de Colombia, que es muy popular.

¡Prepárese!

4-54 La ausencia. Antes de escuchar *Tu ausencia* mire la letra de la canción para saber más sobre el tema. Después complete los espacios en blanco de las oraciones siguientes con la forma correcta del verbo apropiado, según la letra de la canción.

decir	empezar	querer
repetir	entender	hacer

1. El cantante _____ que no soporta la ausencia de su novia.
2. La canción _____ con un ritmo rápido y alegre.
3. Él no _____ por qué su novia lo abandona.
4. El ritmo de la canción me _____ bailar.
5. El coro se _____ dos veces.
6. El cantante _____ ver a su novia otra vez.

¡Escuche!

4-55 Parejas. Mientras escucha la canción, asocie la palabra de la columna izquierda con la palabra lógica de la columna derecha, según la letra.

1. _____ los recuerdos   a. pasan
2. _____ los días   b. tu ausencia
3. _____ lloro   c. mi adoración
4. _____ los ojos   d. tu partida
5. _____ me duele   e. lindos

No soporto ya tu ausencia   ¿Por qué se marchó?   Y era todo para mí
Me destroza el corazón   Dímelo, Dios mío   Vuelve ya mi vida
Son tan lindos tus recuerdos   Ya no están los ojos   Calma mi dolor
Me hacen perder la razón   Que fueron mi adoración   Me duele tu ausencia
Pasan y pasan los días   ¿Por qué se marchó?   Me duele tu amor.
Y no sé nada de ti   Dímelo, Dios mío
Lloro y lloro tu partida   No me quites todo
Siento que voy a morir

¡Responda!

4-56 Una encuesta. Pregúnteles a sus compañeros/as su opinión sobre *Tu ausencia*. Indique con una **T** cuando la respuesta se refiere al tema y con una **R** si se refiere al ritmo.

_____ interesante	_____ seria	_____ bonita
_____ sentimental	_____ aburrida	_____ rápida
_____ positiva	_____ buena	_____ mala
_____ dinámica	_____ lenta	_____ triste
_____ romántica	_____ alegre	_____ bailable
_____ divertida	_____ creativa	_____ negativa

Según los resultados de la encuesta, ¿son compatibles el tema y el ritmo de la canción? ¿Por qué? ¿Les gusta la canción a sus compañeros/as? ¿Y a usted?

VOCABULARIO

AUDIO La familia

la abuela	grandmother
el abuelo	grandfather
el/la ahijado/a	godchild
la esposa	wife
el esposo	husband
la hermana	sister
el hermano	brother
la hija	daughter
el hijo	son
hijo/a único/a	only child
la madrastra	stepmother
la madre	mother
la madrina	godmother
la mamá	mom
la media hermana	half sister
el medio hermano	half brother
la nieta	granddaughter
el nieto	grandson
el/la niño/a	child
la novia	fiancée, girlfriend
el novio	fiancé, boyfriend
el padrastro	stepfather
el padre	father
los padres	parents
el padrino	godfather
el papá	dad
los parientes	relatives
el/la primo/a	cousin
la sobrina	niece
el sobrino	nephew
la tía	aunt
el tío	uncle

Verbos

almorzar (ue)	to have lunch
bañar(se)	to take a bath, to bathe
casarse	to get married
costar (ue)	to cost
decir (g, i)	to say, tell
desayunar	to have breakfast
dormir (ue)	to sleep
dormir la siesta	to take a nap
empezar (ie)	to begin, to start
entender (ie)	to understand

hacer (g)	to do, to make
hacer la cama	to make the bed
jugar (ue)	to play (game, sport)
lavar(se)	to wash (oneself)
levantarse	to get up
oír (g)	to hear
pasar	to spend (time)
pasear	to take a walk, to stroll
pedir (i)	to ask for
peinar(se)	to comb
pensar (ie)	to think
pensar + inf.	to plan to + verb
poder (ue)	to be able to, can
poner (g)	to put, to turn on
poner la mesa	to set the table
preferir (ie)	to prefer
querer (ie)	to want
salir (g)	to leave
secar(se)	to dry (oneself)
seguir (i)	to follow, to go on
servir (i)	to serve
tener (g, ie)	to have
traer (g)	to bring
venir (g, ie)	to come
vestir(se) (i)	to dress, to get dressed
visitar	to visit
volver (ue)	to return

Descripciones

divorciado/a	divorced
gemelo/a	twin
ocupado/a	busy

Palabras y expresiones útiles

el bautizo	baptism, christening
la foto (grafía)	photo
juntos/as	together
el/la mayor	the oldest
el/la menor	the youngest
la noticia	news
tarde	late
temprano	early
un poco	a little

*A list of adverbs can be found on p. 138.

LA CASA Y LOS MUEBLES

Objetivos comunicativos

- Asking about and describing housing and household items
- Discussing daily activities in the home
- Asking about and discussing daily schedules
- Expressing ongoing actions
- Describing physical and emotional states
- Expressing obligation

Contenido

A primera vista

- En casa
- Las tareas domésticas

Explicación y expansión

- Present progressive
- Expressions with *tener*
- Direct object nouns and pronouns
- Demonstrative adjectives and pronouns
- *Saber* and *conocer*
- Algo Más: More on adjectives

Mosaicos

- Escuchar: Matching descriptions with pictures
- Conversar: Looking for housing
- Leer: Looking at visuals; getting informed about a topic
- Escribir: Describing an imaginary house to an expert audience

Enfoque cultural

- Temas: Las casas y la arquitectura
- Vistas: Nicaragua, El Salvador y Honduras
  Para investigar en Internet
- Fortunas: Episodio 5
- Notas: Marimba con Punta, *Los Profesionales*

Vocabulario

AUDIO *En casa*

Una casa de estilo colonial en Granada, Nicaragua. Algunas personas prefieren vivir **cerca** del **centro**, generalmente en **edificios** de apartamentos. Creen que los **barrios** de las **afueras** están muy **lejos** del **trabajo** y de los centros de **diversión**.

Bienes Raíces Su Casa

En Altos de Castaños,
moderna residencia
con piscina, vista, jardín y terraza con bar,
sala, comedor, estudio, baño visitas,
3 habitaciones, 3 baños,
cocina completa,
garaje para 2 autos,
400 mts. de construcción,
$300.000.00 o su equivalente
en lempiras.

☎ TEL. 232-3277, 232-5551 • FAX 232-5154

décimo: Rodríguez
noveno: Peralta
octavo: Elizondo
séptimo: Díaz
sexto: Gómez
quinto: Lizaur
cuarto: Sánchez
tercero: Carreras
segundo: Iglesias
primero: Olmos
planta Baja

CULTURA

Notice that the first floor is normally called **la planta baja** in most Hispanic countries. The second floor is called **el primer piso.**

Alquilo

Apartamento Edificio Venecia, Lomas de Miraflores Sur, sala-comedor, cocina con muebles, dos **dormitorios**, dos baños, dormitorio y baño para empleada, portón eléctrico, **estacionamiento**, TV cable, L. 6.500.00. Tel. 239-3367

AUDIO Ordenando la casa

RICARDO: ¿Aló?

CATALINA: Hola, Ricardo, ¿qué estás haciendo?

RICARDO: ¡Ay, Catalina! Estoy trabajando en la casa, **limpiando** todo, el baño, la cocina, un clóset y mi **cuarto.**

CATALINA: Pero, ¿no tienes que estudiar para el examen de matemáticas?

RICARDO: ¡**Claro** que tengo que estudiar! Pero mañana mis padres **regresan** de sus vacaciones, y tengo que tener la casa **limpia** y **ordenada** porque todo está **sucio.** Tú **sabes** que mi madre es muy maniática con la limpieza.

CATALINA: Sí, ya lo sé, pero es muy tarde. ¿No tienes **sueño**?

RICARDO: Sí, pero **todavía** tengo que **ordenar** la cocina, pasear al perro, y **regar** las plantas... ¡Uf, para qué hablar!

¿Qué dice usted?

5-1 ¿En qué parte de la casa están? Primera fase. Marque con una X el lugar donde generalmente están los siguientes objetos.

	TERRAZA	COCINA	BAÑO	SALA	DORMITORIO	COMEDOR	JARDÍN
la estufa y el lavaplatos		X					
la barbacoa	X						
el sofá y las butacas				X			
la mesa de comer						X	
las toallas y el jabón (*soap*)			X				
la cama y la cómoda					X		
el televisor				X			
las almohadas y las sábanas					X		

② Segunda fase. Ahora describan qué actividades ocurren normalmente en cada cuarto de la casa. ¿Qué parte de la casa prefieren ustedes? ¿Por qué?

5-2 ¿Aparatos eléctricos, muebles o accesorios? Primera fase. Escriba cada una de las siguientes palabras en la columna apropiada.

el cuadro	el armario	las cortinas
la cómoda	la silla	la alfombra
el refrigerador	el radio	el horno

APARATOS ELÉCTRICOS	MUEBLES	ACCESORIOS
el horno	la silla	el cuadro
el radio	la cómoda	las cortinas
el refrigerador	el armario	la alfombra

② Segunda fase. Con su compañero/a responda a las siguientes preguntas relacionadas con la **Primera fase.**

1. ¿Qué aparato eléctrico cuesta más dinero?
2. ¿Qué muebles necesita un estudiante que estudia cada día?
3. ¿Qué accesorios tienen ustedes en su cuarto?

② 5-3 El curioso. Intercambien preguntas para describir los cuartos de la casa/apartamento de cada uno/a. Traten de obtener la mayor información posible.

MODELO: E1: ¿Cómo es la sala de tu casa?
E2: Es pequeña. La alfombra es verde, y hay un sofá grande, dos sillas modernas y una mesa con una lámpara. ¿Y tu dormitorio?

5-4 La casa ideal. Primera fase. Dibujen un plano de su casa/apartamento ideal. Hablen para ponerse de acuerdo sobre los siguientes puntos:

1. número de habitaciones
2. número de baños
3. distribución de los cuartos
4. localización de los muebles
5. color de las paredes

6. otras características (garaje, jardín, sótano (*basement*), ático, etc.)
7. localización de la casa en relación a la universidad

Segunda fase. El alquiler de la casa cuesta mucho dinero y ustedes deben compartir los gastos con otro/a compañero/a. Escriban un anuncio—similar a los de la página 166—para encontrar (*find*) a una persona. Expliquen las condiciones del alquiler.

5-5 Ventajas y desventajas (*Advantages/disadvantages*). Discutan los aspectos positivos y negativos de las siguientes opciones. Escriban una o dos frases en la tabla. Después compartan sus opiniones con el resto de la clase.

	VENTAJAS	DESVENTAJAS
1. vivir en un apartamento		
2. vivir en una casa		
3. tener una piscina		
4. vivir con un/a compañero/a de cuarto/casa		

AUDIO *Las tareas domésticas*

Gustavo **lava** los platos.

Beatriz **seca** los platos.

el (horno) microooondas

el lavaplatos

Beatriz **cocina.** Ella usa mucho los **electrodomésticos.**

Gustavo **limpia** el baño y **pasa** la **aspiradora.**

Gustavo **saca** la **basura.**

Gustavo **barre** la terraza.

Beatriz **tiende** la **ropa.**

la lavadora   la secadora

Después la **dobla** cuando está seca.

Beatriz **plancha** la ropa.

¿Qué dice usted?

5-6 Por la mañana. ¿En qué orden hace usted estas cosas según los debujos en la página 169? Compare sus respuestas con las de su compañero/a.

_4_ lavar los platos   _3_ desayunar
_2_ preparar el café   _5_ secar los platos
_6_ salir para la universidad   _1_ hacer la cama

5-7 Actividades en la casa. Pregúntele a su compañero/a dónde hace estas cosas normalmente.

MODELO: E1: ¿Dónde ves televisión?
          E2: Veo televisión en mi cuarto. ¿Y tú? o No veo televisión. ¿Y tú?

1. dormir la siesta
2. escuchar música
3. planchar
4. estudiar para un examen
5. almorzar durante la semana
6. desayunar el fin de semana
7. vestirse
8. hablar por teléfono con amigos/as

5-8 Preparativos. Primera fase. Usted va a casarse pronto y tiene que comprar muchos muebles, accesorios y electrodomésticos para su nueva casa. Póngalos en los lugares adecuados de la tabla.

	MUEBLES	ACCESORIOS	ELECTRODOMÉSTICOS
para el dormitorio	la cama	la fombra	el ...do
para la sala	él sofa	el euredo	el cuadro
para el comedor	la mesa	la cortinas	
para la cocina	él fregadero	la toalla	la estufa

Segunda fase. Comparta la lista con su compañero/a. Él/Ella le va recordar otras cosas que probablemente va a necesitar.

MODELO: E1: Tengo que comprar una cama nueva para el dormitorio.
          E2: ¿Y no tienes que comprar sábanas y mantas?

5-9 De compras (*Shopping*). Ahora usted va a una mueblería para comprar algunas cosas de su lista. Pregúntele al/a la dependiente/a dónde están los muebles, los accesorios y los electrodomésticos que necesita comprar. Él/Ella le va a contestar de acuerdo con el directorio de la tienda a continuación.

MODELO: E1: Perdón, ¿en qué piso están las lámparas?
E2: Están en el primer piso.

BIENVENIDOS A LA MEJOR

4º	• Muebles para: salitas, dormitorios juveniles de estilo clásico y moderno, muebles convertibles, sofás-cama.
3º	• Salones, comedores, dormitorios de matrimonio, muebles auxiliares de estilo moderno. Alta calidad.
2º	• Mobiliario de estilo chino, muebles auxiliares de estilo clásico y provenzal.
1º	• Electrodomésticos, televisiones y equipos musicales, lámparas, muebles de cocina, galería de cuadros. Muebles para entradas de estilo clásico y moderno. Artículos de regalo. Accesorios de baño.
Planta Baja	• Salones, comedores y dormitorios de estilo clásico y moderno. Muebles para oficina y despacho.
SÓTANO	• Terraza y jardín. Muebles rústicos y coloniales, sofás-cama, muebles de caña y mimbre. Comedores ECONÓMICOS.

AUDIO **5-10 El agente de bienes raíces.** You will listen to a conversation between a couple and a real estate agent in El Salvador. Before you listen, write down some of the questions the couple might be interested in asking.

_____

_____

_____

Now, as you listen to the conversation, circle the letter next to the correct information.

1. Los señores Mena quieren comprar...
   a. una casa.
   b. un apartamento.

2. El señor y la señora Mena prefieren vivir...
   a. en una buena zona.
   b. lejos de un parque.

3. El agente de bienes raíces...
   a. no sabe cómo ayudarlos.
   b. tiene una casa buena para ellos.

4. El agente dice que la casa del barrio La Mascota...
   a. cuesta mucho.
   b. tiene un buen precio.

1. Present progressive

	ESTAR (*to be*)	PRESENT PARTICIPLE (*-ando/-iendo*)
yo	estoy	
tú	estás	hablando
Ud., él, ella	está	comiendo
nosotros/as	estamos	escribiendo
vosotros/as	estáis	
Uds., ellos/as	están	

■ Use the present progressive to emphasize an action in progress at the moment of speaking, as opposed to a habitual action.

> Marcela **está limpiando** la casa.   *Marcela is cleaning the house.* (at this moment)
>
> Marcela **limpia** la casa.   *Marcela cleans the house.* (normally)

■ Spanish does not use the present progressive to express future time, as English does; Spanish uses the present tense instead.

> **Salgo** mañana.   *I am leaving tomorrow.*

■ Form the present progressive with the present of **estar** + *the present participle*. To form the present participle, add **-ando** to the stem of **-ar** verbs and **-iendo** to the stem of **-er** and **-ir** verbs.

> hablar → **hablando**
> comer → **comiendo**
> escribir → **escribiendo**

■ When the verb stem of an **-er** or an **-ir** verb ends in a vowel, add **-yendo**.

> leer → **leyendo**
> oír → **oyendo**

■ Stem-changing **-ir** verbs (o → ue, e → ie, e → i) change o → u and e → i in the present participle.

> dormir (duermo) → **durmiendo**
> sentir (siento) → **sintiendo**
> pedir (pido) → **pidiendo**

¿Qué dice usted?

5-11 ¿Qué están haciendo y por qué? Primera fase. Asocie las acciones de la columna de la izquierda con las explicaciones de la columna de la derecha.

1. __d__ La Sra. Villa está preparando una cena deliciosa.
2. __e__ Su hijo Marcelo está barriendo la terraza.
3. __b__ Su hija Ana está lavando los platos en el fregadero.
4. __c__ Alicia está regando las plantas.
5. __a__ Pedro está estudiando en su cuarto.

a. Tiene un examen mañana.
b. El lavaplatos no está funcionando.
c. Están muy secas.
d. Es el cumpleaños de su esposo.
e. Está muy sucia y vienen unos amigos esta tarde.

Segunda fase. Piense en dos actividades que uno o dos miembros de su familia está(n) probablemente haciendo en este momento. Comparta estas ideas con su compañero/a. ¿Están las personas en las que ustedes piensan haciendo actividades semejantes?

MODELO: Probablemente mi padre está lavando el auto en este momento y mi madre está mirando televisión.

5-12 La vida activa. Túrnense para decir qué están haciendo las personas en los dibujos y lo que ustedes piensan que van a hacer después.

MODELO: E1: Ellos están cantando en una fiesta.
E2: Después van a bailar y a conversar con sus amigos.

Efraín   Madela   Memo

Oscar   Felipe

5-13 Lugares y actividades. Primera fase. Piense en un lugar de su país, de España o de Hispanoamérica, y haga lo siguiente:

■ Escriba dos o tres palabras que describen el lugar.

■ Escriba dos o tres actividades que típicamente se asocian con este lugar.

Segunda fase. Descríbale el lugar a su compañero/a y diga dos o tres actividades que las personas probablemente **están haciendo** en este lugar en este momento. Su compañero/a debe adivinar el nombre del lugar.

MODELO: E1: Ésta es una ciudad muy antigua que está en América del Sur. Es muy popular entre los turistas. Está en los Andes, y en este momento muchos turistas están visitando la ciudad.

E2: ¡Ah! Es Machu Picchu./ Es Cuzco.

SITUACIONES

1. **Role A.** Your best friend calls you to find out what you are doing. Respond that you are doing a major cleaning of the apartment that you share with other friends. Explain to her/him the chores that each one of you is doing.

   Role B. Call your best friend to find out what she/he is doing. Inquire about who is doing what and tell your friend to remind the others what they should do in case they are not doing it.

2. You cannot attend a big reunion that your family is having and you feel homesick. You call home; your partner is the family member who answers the phone. a) Greet him/her, b) excuse yourself for not being there, c) find out who is at the reunion and how everyone is, and d) ask what each family member is doing right now.

2. Expressions with *tener*

■ You have already seen the expression **tener... años:** *Eduardo tiene veinte años.* Spanish uses **tener** + *noun* in many cases where English uses *to be* + *adjective*.

TENER + NOUN			
	hambre		*hungry*
	sed		*thirsty*
	sueño		*sleepy*
	miedo		*afraid*
tener	calor	*to be*	*hot*
	frío		*cold*
	suerte		*lucky*
	cuidado		*careful*
	prisa		*in a hurry/rush*
	razón		*right, correct*

■ With these expressions use **mucho(a)** to indicate *very*.

Tengo **mucho** calor (frío, miedo, sueño, cuidado).	*I am very hot (cold, afraid, sleepy, careful).*
Tienen **mucha** hambre (sed, suerte).	*They are very hungry (thirsty, lucky).*

■ Use **tener** + **que** + *infinitive* to express obligation.

Tengo que regresar hoy.   *I have to return today.*

¿Qué dice usted?

5-14 Asociaciones. Asocie las oraciones de la izquierda con las expresiones de la derecha.

1. ___f___ Mi hermano va a comer mucho.
2. ___d___ Mi hermana siempre duerme diez horas.
3. ___e___ Mis primos están en el Polo Norte.
4. ___a___ Mis abuelos toman mucha agua cada día.
5. ___c___ Mi mamá siempre gana (*wins*) cuando juega a la lotería.
6. ___b___ Son las 8:00 y tengo que estar en casa a las 8:10.

a. Tienen sed.
b. Tengo prisa.
c. Tiene mucha suerte.
d. Tiene sueño.
e. Tienen mucho frío.
f. Tiene hambre.

5-15 ¿Cómo están estas personas? Primera fase. Use una expresión con el verbo **tener** para decir cómo están estas personas.

MODELO: Pablo tiene frío.

Pablo

Sixto y Daniel

Lázaro

Josefina

Julio

Aida

Segunda fase. Dígale a su compañero/a cómo se siente (*feel*) usted en este momento y qué va a hacer para sentirse mejor (*better*).

MODELO: Tengo sueño. Voy a caminar un poco.

5-16 Agenda. Haga una lista de todas las cosas que tiene que hacer cada día de la semana próxima. Después intercambie información con un/a compañero/a.

MODELO: E1: ¿Qué tienes que hacer el lunes?
E2: Tengo que estudiar para el examen de matemáticas. ¿Y tú?

SITUACIONES

Role A: You share an apartment with a messy friend. Complain to him/her about the fact that a) his/her books, backpack, etc. are always all over the living room, b) that he/she uses dishes, but does not wash them, c) that his/her dirty clothes are always in the washer, etc., and c) that you have to do that extra work.

Role B: The friend with whom you share an apartment has some complaints about you. a) Apologize to him/her by saying that you will be more careful in the future and explain how, b) suggest to your friend making a list of house chores, and c) say for which chores you will be responsible.

3. Direct object nouns and pronouns

¿Qué hacen estas personas?

¿Quién lava **el auto**?
Juan **lo** lava.

¿Quién saca **la basura**?
Alicia **la** saca.

Miguel corta **el césped** y su hija recoge las hojas.
¿Quien ayuda **a Miguel**?
Su hija **lo** ayuda.

■ Direct object nouns and pronouns answer the question **what?** or **whom?** in relation to the verb.

| ¿Qué lava Pedro? | *What does Pedro wash?* |
| (Pedro lava) **los platos.** | *(Pedro washes) the dishes.* |

■ When direct object nouns refer to a specific person, a group of persons, or to a pet, the word **a** precedes the direct object. This **a** is called the personal **a** and has no equivalent in English. The personal **a** followed by **el** contracts to **al.**

Amanda seca **los platos.**	*Amanda dries the dishes.*
Amanda seca **a la niña.**	*Amanda dries off the girl.*
¿Ves la piscina?	*Do you see the swimming pool?*
¿Ves **al** niño en la piscina?	*Do you see the child in the swimming pool?*

■ Direct object pronouns replace direct object nouns. These pronouns refer to people, animals, or things already mentioned, and they are used to avoid repeating the noun.

DIRECT OBJECT PRONOUNS

me	*me*	nos	*us*
te	*you* (familiar, singular)	os	*you* (familiar plural, Spain)
lo	*you* (formal, singular), *him, it* (masculine)	los	*you* (formal and familiar, plural), *them* (masculine)
la	*you* (formal, singular), *her, it* (feminine)	las	*you* (formal and familiar, plural), *them* (feminine)

■ Place the direct object pronoun before the conjugated verb form.

¿Limpia Mirta **el baño?**	*Does Mirta clean the bathroom?*
No, no **lo** limpia.	*No, she does not clean it.*
¿Quieres mucho **a tu perro?**	*Do you love your dog a lot?*
Sí, **lo** quiero mucho.	*Yes, I love him a lot.*

■ With compound verb forms (a conjugated verb and an infinitive or present participle), a direct object pronoun may be placed before the conjugated verb, or be attached to the accompanying infinitive or present participle.

¿Vas a ver **a Rafael?**	*Are you going to see Rafael?*
Sí, **lo** voy a ver./Sí, voy a ver**lo.**	*Yes, I am going to see him.*
¿Están limpiando **la casa?**	*Are they cleaning the house?*
Sí, **la** están limpiando.⎫	*Yes, they are cleaning it.*
Sí, están limpián**dola.** ⎭	

■ Since the question word **quién(es)** refers to people, use the personal **a** when **quién(es)** is used as a direct object.

| **¿A quién(es)** vas a ver? | *Whom are you going to see?* |
| Voy a ver a Pedro. | *I am going to see Pedro.* |

ACENTOS

You have learned that words that stress the next-to-the-last syllable do not have a written accent if they end in a vowel: **lav*an*do.** If we attach a direct object pronoun, the stress falls on the third syllable from the end and a written accent is needed: **lav*án*do*lo.***

¿Qué dice usted?

5-17 La división del trabajo. Tres de sus compañeros comparten un apartamento y usted les hace las siguientes preguntas para saber cómo dividen las tareas domésticas entre ellos. Escriba la letra de la respuesta correcta.

1. ¿Quién lava los platos?
   a. Yo lo lavo.   b. Pedro los lava.   c. Julio y yo las lavamos.

2. ¿Quién prepara las comidas?
   a. Pedro la prepara.   b. Yo los preparo.   c. Martín las prepara.

3. ¿Quién limpia el baño?
   a. Los tres lo limpiamos.   b. Pedro los limpia.   c. Martín la limpia.

4. ¿Quién saca la basura?
   a. Martín lo saca.   b. Pedro las saca.   c. Julio la saca.

5. ¿Quién pasa la aspiradora?
   a. Martín y yo las pasamos.   b. Julio la pasa.   c. Yo lo paso.

5-18 ¿Qué es lógico hacer? Primera fase. Las afirmaciones de la columna de la izquierda describen algunas situaciones domésticas. Léalas y, luego, asocie cada una de ellas con una acción lógica para resolverlas.

1. __b__ Las camas están sin hacer.
2. __d__ La ropa está seca.
3. __a__ Los dormitorios están desordenados.
4. __f__ El aire acondicionado no funciona.
5. __c__ Las ventanas están sucias.
6. __e__ No pueden poner el auto en el garaje porque hay muchos muebles viejos y cajas (boxes) con libros.

a. Los hijos los van a ordenar.
b. La madre las hace después de leer el periódico.
c. El padre las va a limpiar.
d. Hay que plancharla.
e. Los hijos lo van a limpiar.
f. El hijo mayor lo va a reparar.

Segunda fase. Dígale a su compañero/a cuál(es) de las afirmaciones de la **Primera fase** describe(n) mejor su apartamento o casa en este momento. Luego, explíquele qué va a hacer usted y cuándo.

5-19 Mis responsabilidades en casa. Primera fase. Averigüe si su compañero/a es responsable de las siguientes tareas domésticas en su casa.

MODELO: sacar la basura
          E1: ¿Sacas la basura?
          E2: Sí, la saco./No, no la saco. ¿Y tú?

1. limpiar la cocina
2. lavar los platos
3. secar los platos
4. tender las camas
5. lavar la ropa
6. cortar el césped

G Segunda fase. Ahora, comparen sus respuestas. Después díganle a otra pareja cuáles son las tareas domésticas que ustedes dos hacen y averigüen si ellos las hacen también.

MODELO: E1: Nosotros no lavamos los platos en casa porque tenemos lavaplatos. ¿Y ustedes los lavan?
          E2: Sí, nosotros los lavamos y hacemos las camas también.

5-20 El apartamento de mi compañero/a. Usted va a cuidar el apartamento de su compañero/a por una semana, y quiere saber cuáles son sus responsabilidades y lo que puede o no puede hacer allí.

MODELO: E1: ¿Debo sacar la basura?
E2: Sí, la debes sacar/debes sacarla todos los días.
E1: ¿Puedo usar tu estéreo?
E2: Claro que lo puedes usar.

¿DEBO O NO DEBO?	SÍ	NO	¿PUEDO O NO PUEDO?	SÍ	NO
regar las plantas	____	____	leer los libros	____	____
pasear al perro	____	____	usar los electrodomésticos	____	____
limpiar el apartamento	____	____	invitar a un/a amigo/a	____	____
poner la alarma	____	____	hacer la tarea en la computadora	____	____
...	____	____	...	____	____

5-21 Los preparativos para la visita. La familia Granados está muy ocupada porque espera la visita de unos parientes. Conteste las preguntas de su compañero/a sobre lo que está haciendo cada miembro de la familia.

MODELO: E1: ¿Quién está preparando la comida?
E2: La abuela la está preparando/está preparándola.

5-22 Una mano amiga. Primera fase. Conteste las preguntas de su compañero/a sobre sus relaciones con otras personas y lo que ellas hacen por usted.

MODELO: ayudar económicamente   mis padres
        E1: ¿Quién te ayuda económicamente?
        E2: Mis padres me ayudan económicamente.

1. querer mucho
2. escuchar en todo momento
3. llamar por teléfono con frecuencia
4. ayudar con los problemas
5. aconsejar (*advise*) cuando estás indeciso/a
6. entender siempre

a. mi padre
b. mi madre
c. mi mejor amigo/a
d. mi novio/a
e. ...

Segunda fase. Dígale a su compañero/a lo que usted hace por las siguientes personas. Indique en qué circunstancias lo hace.

MODELO: su esposo/a
        E1: Lo/La ayudo cuando está cansado/a.
        E2: Y yo lo/la escucho cuando tiene problemas en el trabajo.

1. su papá
2. su mamá
3. su mejor amigo/a
4. su novio/a
5. sus vecinos (*neighbors*)

 SITUACIONES

Role A. You are at a furniture store buying a sofa. Tell the salesperson which sofa you want and ask him/her when they can deliver (**entregar**) it. Tell the salesperson you are not going to be home at that time, but that you can be home in the afternoon. Agree to the time and thank the salesperson.

Role B. You are a salesperson at a furniture store. Tell the customer that the sofa he/she wants is a very good one and that you can deliver it next Monday morning. Since the convenient time for the customer is the afternoon, tell him/her that you can deliver it between three and five o'clock.

4. Demonstrative adjectives and pronouns

Demonstrative adjectives

Esta silla tiene que estar aquí y esa mesa allí.

Los otros muebles están allá, en aquel edificio.

- Demonstrative adjectives agree in gender and number with the noun they modify. English has two sets of demonstratives (*this, these* and *that, those*), but Spanish has three sets.

this	{ **este** cuadro **esta** butaca	*these*	{ **estos** cuadros **estas** butacas
that	{ **ese** horno **esa** casa	*those*	{ **esos** hornos **esas** casas
that (over there)	{ **aquel** edificio **aquella** casa	*those* (over there)	{ **aquellos** edificios **aquellas** casas

- Use **este, esta, estos,** and **estas** when referring to people or things that are close to you in space or time.

Este escritorio es nuevo.   *This desk is new.*
Traen el sofá **esta** semana.   *They will bring the sofa this week.*

- Use **ese, esa, esos,** and **esas** when referring to people or things that are not relatively close to you. Sometimes they are close to the person you are addressing.

    Esa lámpara es muy bonita.   *That lamp is very pretty.*

- Use **aquel, aquella, aquellos,** and **aquellas** when referring to people or things that are more distant.

    Aquel edificio es muy alto.   *That building (over there) is very tall.*

Demonstrative pronouns

- Demonstratives can be used as pronouns. A written accent mark may be placed on the stressed vowel to distinguish demonstrative pronouns from demonstrative adjectives.

    Compran este espejo y **ése**.   *They are buying this mirror and that one.*

- To refer to a general idea or concept, or to ask for the identification of an object, use *esto, eso,* or *aquello.* These pronouns do not take an accent.

    Trabajan mucho y **eso** es muy bueno.   *They work a lot and that is very good.*
    ¿Qué es **esto**?   *What is this?*
    Es un espejo.   *It is a mirror.*

¿Qué dice usted?

5-23 Cerca, relativamente cerca o lejos. Decida qué adjetivo demostrativo debe usar de acuerdo con el lugar donde se encuentran los siguientes objetos.

Cerca de usted

1. _____ mesa es de Honduras.   a. Esta b. Esa c. Aquella
2. _____ cuadros también son de Honduras. a. Estos b. Esos c. Aquellos

Relativamente cerca de usted

3. _____ sofá es muy cómodo (*comfortable*). a. Este b. Ese c. Aquel
4. _____ alfombra tiene unos colores muy alegres. a. Esta b. Esa c. Aquella

Lejos de usted

5. _____ espejo es nuevo.   a. Este b. Ese c. Aquel
6. _____ lámparas son antiguas.   a. Estas b. Esas c. Aquellas

5-24 En una mueblería en Managua. Usted y su compañero/a van a hacer los papeles de cliente/a y dependiente/a. El/La cliente/a pregunta los precios de algunos muebles y accesorios (usando los demostrativos correctos). El/La dependiente/a le hace preguntas para saber específicamente a qué se refiere.

MODELO: CLIENTE/A: ¿Cuánto cuesta esa mesa?

          DEPENDIENTE/A: ¿Cuál? ¿La mesa que está al lado de la silla?

           CLIENTE/A: No, la mesa que está entre la butaca y la silla pequeña. *o* Sí, ésa.

          DEPENDIENTE/A: Cuesta 750 córdobas. *o* Cuesta 2.150 córdobas.

A INVESTIGAR

¿Managua es la capital de qué país? ¿Cuál es la unidad monetaria de ese país? ¿A cuánto está el cambio (*rate of exchange*) en estos momentos?

5-25 ¿De quién es? En su tiempo libre, usted y un/a compañero/a están trabajando de asistentes en una escuela primaria. Al final del día ustedes revisan el salón de clase y notan que los niños dejaron (*left*) varios objetos en diferentes lugares. Pregúntense (*ask each other*) de quién es cada objeto.

MODELO: E1: ¿De quién es este/ese/aquel bolígrafo?

              E2: Éste/ése/aquél es de David. *o* Es de Miguel.

un cuaderno	unos lentes	una mochila azul	una grabadora
un libro	unos apuntes	una calculadora	unos lápices

5-26 Descripciones. Piense en un objeto o mueble y diga en qué parte de la casa está. Su compañero/a va a hacerle preguntas para adivinar qué es. Cada uno/a debe pensar en tres objetos.

MODELO: E1: Este mueble está generalmente en el comedor.
E2: ¿Es grande?
E1: Puede ser grande o pequeño.
E2: ¿Lo usamos para comer?
E1: Sí.
E2: Es la mesa.

SITUACIONES

Role A. You are planning to buy a larger home. A real estate agent has already shown you pictures of one house and is now showing you pictures of a second one. Discuss with him/her a) the price, b) the number of rooms, and c) facilities such as laundry room **(lavandería)**, garage, and pool, of both houses. Tell him/her which of the two houses you want to see and say why.

Role B. You are a real estate agent. You already showed your client pictures of one house and now are showing him/her pictures of a second house. Answer his/her questions by saying a) that the first house is $145,000 dollars and the second one is $150,000, b) that both houses have three bedrooms, and c) that the first house has a one-car garage while this one has a two-car garage. Also tell him/her the advantages of each of the two houses.

5. *Saber* and *conocer*

Both *saber* and *conocer* mean *to know*, but they are not used interchangeably.

	SABER	CONOCER
yo	sé	conozco
tú	sabes	conoces
Ud., él, ella	sabe	conoce
nosotros/as	sabemos	conocemos
vosotros/as	sabéis	conocéis
Uds., ellos/as	saben	conocen

■ Use **saber** to express knowledge of facts or pieces of information.

Él **sabe** dónde está el edificio. *He knows where the building is.*

■ Use **saber** + *infinitive* to express that you know how to do something.

Yo **sé** reparar electrodomésticos. *I know how to repair appliances.*

■ Use **conocer** to express acquaintance with someone or something. **Conocer** also means *to meet.* Remember to use the personal **a** when referring to people.

Conozco a mis vecinos. *I know my neighbors.*
Conozco bien ese libro. *I am very familiar with that book.*
Ella quiere **conocer a** Luis. *She wants to meet Luis.*

¿Qué dice usted?

5-27 Un encuentro en un pasillo. Raúl, un estudiante nuevo en la universidad, necesita información, y le hace preguntas a Sergio, otro estudiante. Escoja la respuesta correcta para completar la conversación.

RAÚL: Soy un estudiante nuevo y no _____ donde está la librería.
     a. sé   b. conozco

SERGIO: Es muy fácil. Tú _____ dónde está la cafetería, ¿no? Pues está al lado.
     a. sabes   b. conoces

RAÚL: Gracias. ¿Y _____ si hay un club de español?
     a. sabes   b. conoces

SERGIO: Sí, claro, y _____ que esta noche tiene una reunión.
     a. sé   b. conozco

RAÚL: Magnífico. Sólo _____ a dos o tres compañeros de clase.
     a. sé   b. conozco

SERGIO: Pues allí vas a _____ a muchos estudiantes.
     a. saber   b. conocer

5-28 ¿Sabes quién es...? Túrnense para preguntarle a su compañero/a si sabe quién es la persona mencionada y si la conoce.

MODELO: el actor principal de *Troya*
     E1: ¿Sabes quién es el actor principal de *Troya?*
     E2: Sí, sé quién es. Es Brad Pitt.
     E1: ¿Lo conoces?
     E2: No, no lo conozco. *o* Sí, lo conozco.

1. tu representante en el congreso
2. el/la decano/a de la facultad
3. el/la jefe/a (*boss*) de tu papá o de tu mamá
4. el rey de España
5. el/la presidente/a de Nicaragua
6. ...

5-29 Adivina, adivinador. En grupos pequeños, túrnense para leer las siguientes descripciones y adivinar de quién se habla.

MODELO: E1: Es una chica muy pobre que va a un baile. Allí conoce a un príncipe, pero a las 12:00 de la noche ella debe volver a su casa.
     E2: Sí, sé quién es. Es Cenicienta (*Cinderella*).

1. Es un gorila gigante con sentimientos (*feelings*) humanos. En una película aparece en el edificio Empire State de Nueva York.
2. Es una actriz y cantante puertorriqueña. Es joven, bonita y canta en inglés y español. En 2003, actuó con el actor Ben Affleck en la película *Una relación peligrosa.*
3. Es una diseñadora de ropa y joyas, hija de un famoso pintor español. Su perfume más famoso lleva su nombre.
4. Es un hombre de otro planeta con doble personalidad. Trabaja en un periódico, pero cuando se pone una ropa azul especial, puede volar (*fly*).
5. Es un hombre joven y fuerte, educado por los gorilas en la jungla. Nada muy bien y su compañera se llama Jane.
6. Fue (*She was*) una mujer muy importante en Argentina. Su esposo gobernó ese país por varios años. Hay un musical con su nombre y también una película donde Madonna la representa.

5-30 ¿Qué sabes hacer? Pregúntele a su compañero/a si sabe hacer las siguientes cosas. Si responde que sí, hágale más preguntas para obtener (*get*) más información.

MODELO:　bailar música rock
　　　　　　E1: ¿Sabes bailar música rock?
　　　　　　E2: Sí, sé bailar música rock. *o* No, no sé bailar música rock. ¿Y tú?

1. tocar la guitarra
2. jugar al tenis
3. nadar
4. preparar tacos

5. cocinar platos muy elaborados
6. trabajar con computadoras
7. usar el microondas
8. ...

5-31 Bingo. Para ganar el Bingo, usted debe llenar vertical, horizontal o diagonalmente tres casilleros (*boxes*) con los nombres de los/las compañeros/as que contestan afirmativamente las preguntas y dan la respuesta correcta.

¿Sabes dónde está la ciudad de Tegucigalpa?	¿Sabes cuál es la capital de El Salvador?	¿Sabes dónde está la ciudad de Managua?
¿Conoces a los padres de tu mejor amigo/a?	¿Sabes cuál es la unidad monetaria de Nicaragua?	¿Sabes el nombre de un lago importante que está en Nicaragua?
¿Sabes preparar platos centroamericanos?	¿Conoces algún país hispanoamericano?	¿Sabes dónde están las ruinas mayas de Copán?

5-32 Saber y conocer. Complete con su compañero/a el siguiente diálogo con las formas correctas de **saber** y **conocer.**

　　　E1: ¿＿＿＿＿＿＿ a esa chica?
　　　E2: Sí, yo ＿＿＿＿＿＿ a todas las chicas aquí.
　　　E1: Entonces, ¿＿＿＿＿＿ dónde vive?
　　　E2: No, no lo ＿＿＿＿＿＿.
　　　E1: Pero ＿＿＿＿＿＿ su número de teléfono, ¿verdad?
　　　E2: No, tampoco lo ＿＿＿＿＿＿.
　　　E1: Y... ¿＿＿＿＿＿ cómo se llama?
　　　E2: Pues, la verdad es que no lo ＿＿＿＿＿＿.
　　　E1: ¿Cómo dices que la ＿＿＿＿＿＿? Tú no ＿＿＿＿＿＿ dónde vive,
　　　　　tú no ＿＿＿＿＿＿ su nombre.
　　　E2: Es que tengo muy mala memoria.

SITUACIONES

Your partner wants to set a blind date for you with his/her friend from Honduras but you want to have some information about the person before agreeing to a date. Using **saber** or **conocer**, ask your partner if he/she knows: a) the person's family, b) how old the person is, and c) how long he/she has known this person, d) from what part of Honduras he/she comes, and e) if he/she speaks English. Also, find out if the person knows how to play tennis, and if he/she likes to dance.

ALGO MÁS

More on adjectives

- Ordinal numbers are adjectives and agree in gender and number with the noun they modify (e.g., **la segunda casa, el cuarto edificio**). **Primero** and **tercero** drop the final **o** when used before a masculine singular noun.

  el **primer** cuarto   el **tercer** piso

- When **bueno** and **malo** precede masculine singular nouns, they are shortened to **buen** and **mal**.

  Es un **buen** edificio.   *It is a good building.*
  Es un **mal** momento para comprar.   *It is a bad time to buy.*

- **Grande** shortens to **gran** when it precedes any singular noun. Note the meaning associated with each position.

  Es una casa **grande**.   *It is a big house.*
  Es una **gran** casa.   *It is a great house.*

¿Qué dice usted?

5-33 ¿En qué piso viven? Pregúntele a su compañero/a dónde viven las diferentes personas. Su compañero/a debe contestarle de acuerdo con el dibujo.

MODELO: E1: ¿Dónde viven los Girondo?
          E2: Viven en el cuarto piso, en el apartamento 4-A.

5-34 Opiniones. Túrnense para explicar qué o quiénes son las siguientes personas y lugares. Después, den su opinión sobre cada uno. Usen algunas de las siguientes palabras.

| buen | bueno/a | gran | grande | mal | malo/a | primer | primero/a |

MODELO: el Parque El Imposible
          Es una gran reserva natural donde hay muchos animales en peligro de extinción. El Parque El Imposible está en El Salvador. Es muy grande y es una reserva natural muy importante de América Central.

1. el Parque Central
2. Antonio Banderas
3. la Casa Blanca
4. Daniel Ortega
5. el lago Nicaragua
6. ...

MOSAICOS

Escuchar

Matching descriptions with pictures

You have already learned that you can understand what is being said by paying attention to the pictures or objects that people point or refer to. Sometimes these objects are around you, but sometimes they are not. For example, when you hear a description of somebody's house, an image of a house comes to your mind from your experience.

Antes de escuchar

5-35 La casa de los Esquivel. In 5-36, you will listen to a description of a house. Before you listen, and using your knowledge of what houses look like, make a list of **four** rooms and **three objects** (furniture, appliances, accessories) you expect to hear about **in each** room.

PARTE DE LA CASA	OBJETOS
_____	_____
_____	_____
_____	_____
_____	_____

A escuchar

AUDIO 5-36 Now, look at the following drawing, and as you hear the different statements about the location of several pieces of furniture and objects, mark the appropriate column to indicate whether each of the statements is true (**Sí**) or false (**No**).

	Sí	No
1.	_____	_____
2.	_____	_____
3.	_____	_____
4.	_____	_____
5.	_____	_____
6.	_____	_____
7.	_____	_____
8.	_____	_____

Después de escuchar

5-37 ¿Y tu casa? Ask each other these questions and compare your answers.

1. ¿Cómo es tu casa/apartamento? ¿Cuántos dormitorios tiene?
2. ¿Qué muebles hay en tu dormitorio?
3. ¿Qué electrodomésticos hay en tu casa/apartamento?

Antes de escuchar

5-38 Un apartamento cómodo. In **5-39**, you will listen to some descriptions of an apartment. Before you listen, look at the picture and in the lines below write down the number of bedrooms, bathrooms and closets this apartment has.

dormitorios _____   baños _____   armarios _____

A escuchar

AUDIO **5-39 El apartamento.** Now, you will listen to four different descriptions of this apartment. As you listen, mark the appropriate column to indicate whether the description is true (**Sí**) or false (**No**).

	Sí	No
1.	_____	_____
2.	_____	_____
3.	_____	_____
4.	_____	_____

Después de escuchar

5-40 ¿Y usted? Imagine you buy the apartment of your dreams. Discuss where this apartment is located, how many bedrooms it has, and what furniture, appliances and conveniences the apartment has.

Conversar

Antes de conversar

5-41 Busco apartamento. Usted necesita alquilar un apartamento. En cada columna, escriba algunas características esenciales y algunas secundarias del apartamento que usted necesita.

CARACTERÍSTICAS ESENCIALES	CARACTERÍSTICAS SECUNDARIAS
_____	_____
_____	_____
_____	_____
_____	_____

A conversar

5-42 Buscando vivienda (housing). Su mejor amigo/a (su compañero/a) siempre lee los anuncios de los periódicos. Llámelo/la por teléfono y hágale preguntas para obtener información sobre las características esenciales y secundarias del apartamento que usted busca. Puede usar las siguientes ideas. Su mejor amigo/a va a responder con información sobre **dos** apartamentos de los siguientes anuncios. Luego, cambien de papel.

- alquiler
- localización del apartamento
- piso en el edificio
- número de habitaciones y baños
- con muebles o sin muebles
- aire acondicionado/calefacción
- otras características esenciales para usted
- número de teléfono o dirección de contacto
- ¿?

ALQUILERES

Se alquila apartamento en zona céntrica, cuarto piso: amueblado, 2 habitaciones, 2 baños, 5.000 colones mensuales. Tfno. 2 33 14 78

Se arrienda apartamento espacioso para familia: quinto piso, ascensor, excelente ubicación, cerca de centros comerciales, sin muebles, 3 dormitorios, dos baños, aire acondicionado, jardín, garaje para dos autos. 6.500 colones. Tfno. 2 54 22 83

Alquilo apartamento cerca de centro comercial. Transporte público a la puerta. Ideal para profesionales. 1 dormitorio, 1 baño con jacuzzi, con muebles y electrodomésticos, terraza, sistema de seguridad, garaje doble. 7.500 colones. Tfno. 2 65 16 92

Se alquila habitación en casa particular. Amplia, cómoda, iluminada, enorme clóset, cable gratis. Se comparten cocina, baño y garaje. Muebles finos. Preferible mujer soltera. Tfno. 2 38 84 29

Después de conversar

5-43 ¡Éste me gusta! Escríbale una breve nota a su mejor amigo/a para informarle sobre el apartamento que usted piensa alquilar. Explíquele por qué. Déle las gracias (Thank him/her) por su ayuda.

Fecha: _____, 200____
De: _____
A: _____

Asunto: Mi nuevo apartamento

_____
_____
_____
_____
_____

Adiós,

_____

Antes de conversar

5-44 La casa o apartamento ideal. Ustedes son un grupo de buenos amigos que piensan vivir juntos durante sus estudios universitarios. Piensen en su casa ideal y descríbanla. Incluyan la siguiente información en su descripción:

- la ciudad o pueblo (town) donde va a estar la casa
- los cuartos y comodidades (comforts) que la casa va a tener
- los muebles, los electrodomésticos, etc.
- la(s) persona(s) que va(n) a vivir en ella

A conversar

5-45 Mi casa ideal en imágenes. Ahora hagan un dibujo (o un collage) de su casa ideal para compartirlo con la clase. Indiquen el número de cuartos, garajes, y para quién es cada cuarto. Especifiquen cómo va a ser la sala, el comedor, la cocina, etc.

Después de conversar

5-46 Ésta es mi casa ideal. Preséntenle su casa ideal a la clase y respondan a sus preguntas.

 # Leer

In this chapter, you will practice the following strategies to aid your reading comprehension in Spanish: 1. looking at visuals, and 2. informing yourself about a topic.

Looking at visuals in a written text enables foreign language readers to anticipate and comprehend the text message. Pictures, signs, schedules, charts, arrows, and color may provide you with essential information at a department store where you are doing shopping, a train station or an airport when traveling, etc.

Besides visuals, getting acquainted with a topic may greatly facilitate your comprehension. Imagine that you are planning to study in a Spanish-speaking country. Since, as you may know, most students usually do not live on campus, you are faced with the task of finding housing for yourself. Where do you start? How do you go about renting an apartment or a room? Should you seek help from a housing office on campus? What if there isn't one? Also, what commodities or basic needs should you expect when you rent an apartment or a room, for example: a private bathroom, a phone in your room, or one to share with someone else? The most efficient manner to accomplish this task is by informing yourself, by asking people, by reading about the topic in your own language, etc. Keep in mind the importance of visuals and of informing yourself as you read or before you read a text.

Guía de prelectura

Read the title of the article in activity **5-49** and answer the questions, using your knowledge of the topic.

1. Thinking of the theme of *Lección 5* and looking at the picture that accompanies the article, can you anticipate its content?
   a. The wide use of computers by women at home
   b. Technology at the service of humans at home
   c. Houses that communicate with human beings

2. The article contains some of the following ideas. Circle all that may apply, in your opinion. In case you miss some answers, you will be able to verify your responses later.
   a. Today's homes have nothing in common with those of the future.
   b. Future homes will be much more automated than those of today.
   c. Human beings will have much more free time due to the abundance of technology at home.
   d. Electrical appliances and electronic devices will duplicate their functions in the house of the future.

3. Now, use your background knowledge to comprehend the text. On what did you base your answers to question 2?
   a. The cognates in the title
   b. The photo that accompanies the article
   c. Your knowledge of technology

Antes de leer

5-47 Preparación. Muchas casas modernas tienen aparatos eléctricos y electrónicos. Clasifiquen los siguientes aparatos en la columna correspondiente.

sensor de temperatura	microondas	teléfono inalámbrico	ventilador (*fan*)
aire acondicionado	computadora	televisor	fotocopiadora
lámpara	aparato de DVD	aspiradora	cafetera

FUNCIÓN	APARATOS ELÉCTRICOS	APARATOS ELECTRÓNICOS
1. para trabajar desde (*from*) casa	_____	_____
2. para hacer trabajos domésticos	_____	_____
3. para controlar la temperatura de la casa	_____	_____
4. para comunicarse con otras personas	_____	_____
5. para entretenerse (*have fun*) en casa	_____	_____

5-48 Anticipación. Primera fase. Indique con una *X* las características que, según usted, va a tener la casa del futuro.

1. _____ múltiples dispositivos (mecanismos) para controlar la energía
2. _____ puertas automáticas
3. _____ sensores de temperatura y humedad
4. _____ sensores de voz (*voice*)
5. _____ sistema de seguridad activado por la voz
6. _____ música ambiental en todos los cuartos

Segunda fase. Ahora, comparen sus respuestas. ¿Están de acuerdo o no?

A leer

5-49 Primera fase. El siguiente artículo describe la casa del futuro. Léalo y siga las instrucciones.

1. Pase un marcador (*highlighter*) por las palabras que se asocian con tecnología en cada párrafo.
2. Escriba **AC** si una palabra se refiere a un aparato eléctrico y **EL** si indica un aparato electrónico.

La casa inteligente del futuro

Las casas inteligentes o automatizadas ya existen en el presente. Los expertos las describen con un gran número de aparatos eléctricos y electrónicos —controlados por una computadora— que se comunican entre ellos. Pero, muchos se preguntan, ¿cuáles son las diferencias entre una casa tradicional y una inteligente?

Básicamente, la casa inteligente incorpora los últimos avances tecnológicos en beneficio de las personas que viven en ella. A través de complejos dispositivos y sensores, estas casas facilitan el trabajo doméstico de sus dueños: abren y cierran cortinas y puertas, hacen funcionar electrodomésticos (cafeteras, microondas, ventiladores, etc.), el aire acondicionado y la calefacción, por ejemplo.

Además, la casa inteligente ofrece un uso más eficiente y múltiple de los aparatos eléctricos y electrónicos en su interior. Un microondas se puede usar para calentar comida y también para ver televisión. De la misma manera, un refrigerador puede conectarse a Internet y permitir a una persona navegar por la red o enviar mensajes electrónicos.

Si a la familia le gusta escuchar música mientras descansa o mirar películas en su tiempo libre, basta conectar dispositivos de red a servidores con suficiente ancho de banda y capacidad de almacenamiento[1] como para distribuir música y películas a cada habitación de la casa.

En resumen, la casa del futuro es una versión técnicamente más sofisticada de la casa del presente. Es difícil predecir con exactitud cómo vamos a vivir en 50 años más. Sin embargo, muchos se preguntan si esta abundancia de tecnología va a afectar nuestra vida positiva o negativamente.

[1]*storage space*

Segunda fase. Lea el artículo otra vez y haga lo siguiente.

1. En el primer párrafo, el autor del artículo da una definición de una casa inteligente. Escriba la definición.

2. El segundo párrafo contrasta la casa inteligente con la casa tradicional. ¿Cuál es la diferencia? Escríbala.

3. El párrafo dos también indica algunas formas en que la casa inteligente ayuda a las personas que viven en ella. Indique una función útil para una persona de su familia. ¿Por qué es útil?

4. En el tercer párrafo, se mencionan algunas de las funciones múltiples de los aparatos eléctricos y electrónicos. ¿Cuál de estas funciones múltiples es más beneficiosa para un estudiante? ¿Por qué?

5. En el cuarto párrafo, el autor presenta un ejemplo que indica la superioridad del ser humano sobre la tecnología. Subraye el ejemplo.

5-50 Búsqueda (*Search*). Busquen en el artículo algunas palabras con las siguientes terminaciones y, luego, clasifíquenlas en la tabla: **-ado/a, -cia, -ción/-sión, -ar, -al, -ico, -dad, -mente.**

SUSTANTIVOS	ADJETIVOS	FORMAS VERBALES RELACIONADAS CON LA TECNOLOGÍA	ADVERBIOS

Después de leer

5-51 Expansión. Lea la siguiente nota que el arquitecto de una casa inteligente le escribe a uno de sus colegas. Complete los espacios en blanco con la palabra adecuada.

urgentemente	funcionar	inteligente	ventanas	tecnológicos
ideal	construir	sensores	funciones	

Manolo,

¡Te tengo una gran sorpresa! Oscar de la Renta necesita (1) ___urgentemente___ una casa (2) ___inteligente___ en Managua. Como sabes, de la Renta es muy rico y quiere los últimos avances (3) ___tecnológicos___ en ella. Desea una casa con dispositivos para abrir y cerrar puertas y (4) ___ventanas___. También quiere incorporar electrodomésticos con (5) ___funciones___ múltiples. Quiere calefacción controlada por (6) ___sensores___. Tú sabes mucho de sistemas automatizados y yo de construcción, y pienso que eres la persona (7) ___ideal___ para ayudarme en este proyecto. Vamos a (8) ___construir___ una casa espectacular. Todo va a (9) ___funcionar___ perfectamente.

Debemos responder pronto. Llámame.

Ricardo

Escribir

In *Lección 4,* you practiced writing a letter to a family member older than you. You also paid attention to ways of addressing a family member and appropriate closings. Writing to the public at large is somewhat similar to writing to elders in your family. When you do not know your audience personally, you can do the following:

- Anticipate what your audience knows or may not know about the topic you are writing. Provide as much detail as necessary.

- Accommodate the language of your text to your audience. Use less technical language with an audience who is not an expert on the topic; be more technical with an expert audience.

- Use a more formal tone. In Spanish, a formal tone may be signaled, among others, by the use of the pronoun **Ud.**

In this chapter, you will write a descriptive pamphlet for a general, unknown audience. As you plan and write your pamphlet, keep in mind the amount of information and degree of formality of your text.

Antes de escribir

5-52 Preparación. Primera fase. En el siguiente panfleto, la Facultad de Arquitectura de la Universidad Católica de Honduras, en Tegucigalpa, invita a los alumnos a participar en el concurso (*contest*) **La casa automatizada del futuro.** Lea los requisitos del concurso.

Departamento de Arquitectura
Universidad Católica de Honduras
Campus Tegucigalpa

Concurso: **La casa automatizada del futuro**

Bases del concurso:

Los participantes deben enviar la siguiente información por fax (233-2210) a la Facultad de Arquitectura, Campus Tegucigalpa:

1. una ficha con información personal: nombre completo, dirección, teléfono, facultad donde estudia y dirección de correo electrónico
2. una descripción de la casa automatizada con la siguiente información:
   a. tamaño de la casa (pies [feet] o metros cuadrados [square meters])
   b. número y nombre de las habitaciones
   c. aparatos eléctricos y electrónicos de la casa y sus funciones
   d. dispositivos y sensores y su(s) función(es)

3. si es posible, un dibujo o foto digital de la casa automatizada

Fecha límite: el 30 de marzo
Premio: Un semestre de estudios gratis en la Facultad de Arquitectura de la Universidad de Milán, Italia

---

Segunda fase. Usted decide participar en el concurso con un proyecto excepcional. Para preparar su proyecto, haga lo siguiente:

1. Imagine la casa automatizada que usted desea construir.
   a. ¿Qué tamaño (*size*) tiene? Indíquelo en pies (*feet*) o metros cuadrados (*square meters*) ¿Qué cuartos va a tener esta casa? ¿Cuántas habitaciones, salas, terrazas, etc.? ¿Cuántos garajes, áticos, etc.?
   b. ¿Qué aparatos eléctricos y electrónicos va a tener? ¿Dónde va a estar cada uno de ellos?
   c. ¿Qué función(es) va a tener cada aparato eléctrico y electrónico? (Por ejemplo: Una aspiradora que limpia las alfombras y seca platos también.)
   d. Esta casa automatizada, ¿va a tener dispositivos y sensores? ¿Qué función(es) va a tener cada dispositivo y sensor? (Por ejemplo: ¿Un dispositivo para encender y apagar el televisor? ¿Un sensor que determina la calidad del aire dentro de la casa?)

2. ¿Sabe usted dibujar? Dibuje con lápiz o digitalmente su casa automatizada.

A escribir

5-53 Manos a la obra. Ahora prepare su descripción de *La casa automatizada del futuro* para el comité que selecciona a los ganadores (*winners*). Use sus ideas de la **Segunda fase** de la actividad **5-48**. Recuerde incluir toda la información que pide el concurso.

Después de escribir

5-54 Revisión. Antes de presentar su proyecto, revise:

- primero, la claridad de sus ideas y la cantidad de información dada

- luego, la precisión gramatical (el vocabulario común y corriente y el vocabulario más técnico, la estructuras que utiliza para describir, la concordancia, etc.)

- finalmente, la ortografía y la acentuación

TEMAS: LAS CASAS Y LA ARQUITECTURA

Para pensar

¿Vive Ud. en un apartamento o en una casa? ¿Cómo es, grande o pequeño/a? ¿Moderno/a o antiguo/a? ¿Hay apartamentos/casas semejantes al/a la suyo/a en su vecindario? ¿Dónde está su casa o apartamento, cerca del centro de la ciudad o en las afueras?

Hay mucha variedad de viviendas en los países hispanoamericanos. En esta foto se ve la influencia de la época colonial. Se puede admirar una casa con hermosos balcones de madera, grandes patios interiores, azulejos (tiles) en los pisos y paredes y bellas rejas (iron work) exteriores.

En algunos lugares se puede ver la influencia de la cultura española y las culturas precolombinas en la arquitectura.

Para contestar

2 Las casas. Con su compañero/a responda a las siguientes preguntas:

Generalmente no hay gran variedad de electrodomésticos en las casas, debido principalmente a su alto costo pero también a la posibilidad de tener empleados que ayudan con las tareas domésticas.

1. ¿Cómo son las casas coloniales? ¿Hay casas de estilo colonial en su vecindario?
2. ¿Qué electrodomésticos hay en su casa? ¿Cuáles probablemente se pueden encontrar en la mayoría de las casas hispanoamericanas, según ustedes? ¿Por qué?
3. En España e Hispanoamérica, ¿en qué lugares de la casa pasa más tiempo conversando o tomando algo la familia?

G Riqueza cultural. En grupos de tres, describan cómo es su casa ideal, usando la información de **Las casas y la arquitectura.**

En España e Hispanoamérica, la familia pasa mucho tiempo conversando, tomando un refresco en el patio o jardín o viendo televisión en la sala de su casa.

Para pensar

¿Qué sabe usted acerca de América Central? ¿Sabe usted qué países están en América Central? ¿Conoce usted a alguna persona de Nicaragua, Honduras o El Salvador?

Nicaragua, llamada la tierra de los lagos y volcanes, es un hermoso país. Managua, su capital, está en la costa sur del Lago Managua y es el principal centro administrativo y comercial del país.

Expresiones nicaragüenses:

ñeque	Él es **ñeque**.	He is strong/vigorous.
jalar	Ella está **jalando** con Luis.	She is Luis' girlfriend.
chavalo/a	Ese **chavalo** es terrible.	That kid is terrible.

Cerca de Managua está Granada, conocida por su arquitectura colonial.

El Salvador está en la costa del Océano Pacífico. En El Salvador usted puede visitar hermosas playas, lagos, interesantes ruinas mayas y bosques tropicales como el Parque El Imposible.

Expresiones salvadoreñas:

chinear	María **chinea** a su hijo continuamente.	*María holds her child in her arms continuously.*
cipote	Sólo es un **cipote**.	*He is only a child.*
primero	—¿Vas a la playa mañana? —**Primero** Dios.	*—Are you going to the beach tomorrow? —God willing.*

La Catedral de Tegucigalpa es un edificio importante del siglo XVI.

Expresiones hondureñas:

| agarrar a uno de ojo de gallo | Parece que José me **agarró de ojo de gallo**. | *It looks like Jose has ill will towards me.* |
| güirro | ¿Qué está haciendo ese **güirro**? | *What is that child doing?* |

Si le interesan las culturas precolombinas, debe visitar las ruinas de Copán, una de las ciudades más importantes de la civilización maya.

Para contestar

En el mapa

1. Busque una ciudad de Nicaragua en la costa del Atlántico y otra en la costa del Pacífico.
2. Diga qué país está al sur de Nicaragua.

Ahora diga...

1. a cuál de los tres países le gustaría ir y por qué.
2. qué lugar de interés le gustaría visitar en cada uno de los tres países y por qué.

¿Qué dice usted si...

1. su hermano hace mucha gimnasia y es muy fuerte?
2. su compañero/a de cuarto no le habla y no quiere ayudarlo/a en nada?

Para investigar en Internet

Busque información (**www.prenhall.com/mosaicos**) acerca de viviendas de estilo colonial en diferentes ciudades hispanoamericanas (descripción, localización), estado en el que se encuentran— bien conservadas/necesitan reparaciones, etc.). Traiga algunas ilustraciones, si es posible, y compártalas con sus compañeros/as. Describan entre todos las diferentes viviendas y escojan su favorita.

¡Prepárese!

5-55 Competencia y romance. Antes de mirar el Episodio 5 de *Fortunas* mire las imágenes y los títulos que siguen. Es evidente que la competencia entre los participantes se está poniendo más seria y que está comenzando un romance entre dos de ellos. Complete la tabla para indicar sus ideas y opiniones sobre estos temas.

	Sí/No	Por qué
■ Soy una persona competitiva.	_____	_____
■ Es posible trabajar con una persona que me interesa románticamente.	_____	_____
■ El romance es más importante que la competencia.	_____	_____
■ Las personas competetivas tienen más éxito (*success*) en la vida.	_____	_____

¿Romance o misterio? Ángela y Manolo tienen opiniones diferentes.

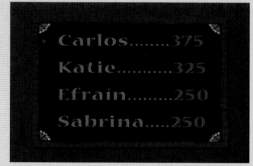

Carlos tiene el número máximo de puntos en la encuesta.

Entre Carlos y Katie está comenzando un romance.

Carlos y Katie ven a Sabrina y a Efraín.

Carlos y Katie están preocupados por la competencia.

Sabrina y Efraín dicen que ganaron por ser inteligentes y serios.

¡Responda!

5-56 Informe. Imagínese que su amigo no puede mirar el Episodio 5 de *Fortunas* porque su disquete está roto (*broken*). Escriba un informe breve sobre este episodio para ponerlo al día (*up to date*). Use verbos de la lista en la página 203 y otros. La primera oración ya está escrita.

INFORME: En el Episodio 5 de *Fortunas* sabemos que Sabrina y Efraín
           solucionan el segundo misterio. También...

Esta canción es un ejemplo de "punta rock", una música regional bailable de Centroamérica en la cual se toca la marimba, un instrumento típico del oeste de África.

¡Prepárese!

5-57 Música regional. ¿Qué ejemplos de música "regional" de su país o de otros conoce? ¿Por qué se considera regional?

¡Escuche!

5-58 La canción. Mientras escucha *Marimba con punta* complete las siguientes estrofas de la canción con las palabras de la lista.

chicas	discotecas	ritmo	gorditos	rico	verano
ricos	sabroso	cocineros	casa	muchachos	

Este es un _____ _____
que el mundo lo baila ya.
[...]
Que el mundo entero lo baila ya.
Lo bailan los _____
_____ y pobres, ¡Qué _____ está!
Bailamos flacos, _____
altos, bajitos, ¡Oye mamá!

Todos en este _____
Se apresuran a bailar.
Todos en este verano
se apresuran a bailar.

Las _____ que hay en la playa
con los _____ la gozarán
otros lo bailan en _____,
en _____ en cualquier lugar.

5-59 La letra. Ahora conteste en español las siguientes preguntas, según la letra de la canción.

1. ¿Cómo es el ritmo de esta canción?
2. ¿Quién baila "punta rock"?
3. ¿Cuándo lo baila(n)?
4. ¿Dónde lo baila(n)?

¡Responda!

5-60 Expresiones con tener. Imagínese que usted y sus amigos están en una fiesta donde están tocando y bailando "punta rock" hasta muy tarde en la noche. Indique con una cruz (X) qué expresiones con **tener** pueden usar Uds. para describir cómo se sienten al final de la fiesta.

_____ tener hambre   _____ tener prisa
_____ tener sed   _____ tener cuidado
_____ tener frío   _____ tener sueño
_____ tener calor   _____ tener suerte
_____ tener miedo   _____ tener razón

5-61 Nosotros tenemos... Ahora escriba cinco oraciones completas y lógicas en español usando algunas de las expresiones de arriba y los sujetos siguientes.

1. mis amigos
2. yo
3. mis amigos y yo
4. los músicos
5. todo el mundo (*Everybody*)

VOCABULARIO*

En una casa

el aire acondicionado	air conditioning
el armario	closet, armoire
el baño	bathroom
la barbacoa	barbecue
la basura	garbage, trash
la calefacción	heating
el césped	lawn
la chimenea	fireplace
la cocina	kitchen
el comedor	dining room
el cuarto/dormitorio	bedroom
el garaje	garage
el jardín	backyard, garden
la piscina	swimming pool
el piso	floor
la planta baja	first floor
la sala	living room
la terraza	terrace

Muebles y accesorios

la alfombra	carpet, rug
la butaca	armchair
la cama	bed
la cómoda	dresser
la cortina	curtain
el cuadro	picture
el espejo	mirror
la lámpara	lamp
la mesa de noche	night stand
el sofá	sofa

Electrodomésticos

la aspiradora	vacuum cleaner
la lavadora	washer
el lavaplatos	dishwasher
el (horno) microondas	microwave oven
el/la radio	radio
el refrigerador	refrigerator
la secadora	dryer

Para la cama

la almohada	pillow
la manta	blanket
la sábana	sheet

En el baño

la bañadera	tub
la ducha	shower
el inodoro	toilet
el lavabo	washbowl, bathroom sink
la toalla	towel

En la cocina

la estufa	stove
el fregadero	kitchen sink
el plato	dish, plate

Lugares

las afueras	outskirts
allá	over there
allí	there
el apartamento	apartment
aquí	here
el barrio	neighborhood
el centro	downtown, center
cerca (de)	near (close to)
el edificio	building
lejos (de)	far (from)

Descripciones

limpio/a	clean
ordenado/a	tidy
seco/a	dry
sucio/a	dirty

Verbos

ayudar	to help
barrer	to sweep
cocinar	to cook
conocer (zc)	to know, to meet
cortar	to cut
creer	to believe
doblar	to fold
limpiar	to clean
ordenar	to tidy up
pasar la aspiradora	to vacuum
planchar	to iron
preparar	to prepare
recoger (j)	to pick up
regar (ie)	to water
regresar	to come back
saber	to know
secar	to dry
sentir (ie, i)	to feel
tender (ie)	to hang (clothes); to make (a bed)

Palabras útiles

¡Claro!	of course
el perro	dog

*For expressions with **tener**, see page 174
**For direct object pronouns, see page 176
***For demonstrative adjectives and pronouns, see pages 181–2
****For ordinal numbers, see page 187

LA ROPA Y LAS TIENDAS

Objetivos comunicativos

- Talking about clothing and shopping
- Asking for and telling prices
- Expressing measurements

- Expressing likes and dislikes
- Expressing satisfaction and dissatisfaction
- Expressing opinions

Contenido

A primera vista

- La ropa
- De compras

Explicación y expansión

- Preterit tense of regular verbs
- Preterit of *ir* and *ser*
- Indirect object nouns and pronouns

- The verb *dar*
- *Gustar* and similar verbs
- Algo Más: More uses of *por* and *para*

Mosaicos

- Escuchar: Taking notes to recall important information
- Conversar: Haggling; determining what clothing is appropriate in a particular context

- Leer: Finding specific information to accomplish a task; identifying word endings that indicate places where certain products are sold or services rendered
- Escribir: Writing a letter of complaint to a store; narrating chronologically

Enfoque cultural

- Temas: De compras en el mundo hispano
- Vistas: Venezuela
  Para investigar en Internet

- Fortunas: Episodio 6
- Notas: Caminito de Guarenas, *Orquesta Billo's Caracas Boys*

Vocabulario

La ropa

... de mujer

el vestido

el traje pantalón

la falda

el camisón

los pantalones

la sudadera

el collar

los aretes

la blusa

la pulsera

el anillo

el sostén

los zapatos

los zapatos (de) tenis

las pantimedias

... de hombre

la corbata

el saco

el pañuelo

el traje

la camisa

el impermeable

la bata

el cinturón

los vaqueros/ los jeans

los calcetines/ las medias

los calzoncillos

la camiseta

el paraguas

las zapatillas

Las estaciones y la ropa

En el **invierno hace frío.** ¿Qué ropa **llevamos?**

el suéter
los guantes
la chaqueta
las botas
el abrigo
la bufanda

Y cuando **hace calor** en el **verano,** ¿qué **nos ponemos** para ir a la playa?

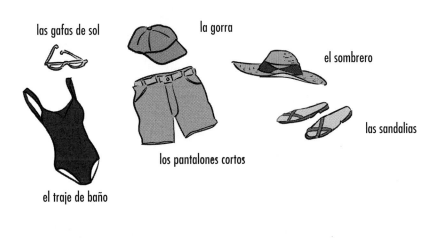

las gafas de sol
la gorra
el sombrero
las sandalias
el traje de baño
los pantalones cortos

el paraguas
el impermeable

En la **primavera** y el **otoño llueve mucho.**

¿Qué dice usted?

6-1 ¿Cuándo se usa? Asocie cada prenda de vestir de la columna de la izquierda con una situación o un lugar de la columna de la derecha.

1. _____ los guantes
2. _____ las gafas de sol
3. _____ el piyama
4. _____ la bata
5. _____ el impermeable
6. _____ el traje de baño

a. después de bañarse y antes de vestirse
b. para ir a dormir
c. para ver cuando hace mucho sol
d. en la piscina o en la playa
e. en los lugares fríos durante el invierno
f. cuando llueve

6-2 ¿Qué deben llevar estas personas? Primera fase. Escriban el nombre de dos prendas de vestir y un accesorio que se asocian con las siguientes ocasiones.

1. una graduación: _____
2. un partido de tenis: _____
3. un día de reparaciones en casa: _____
4. una reunión con el decano de la facultad: _____

Segunda fase. Ahora, digan (*say*) qué deben llevar estas personas, de acuerdo con las situaciones.

MODELO: Raúl y Rosa van a ir a una fiesta en casa del rector de la universidad.
E1: Raúl debe llevar pantalones, una camisa y una corbata.
E2: Rosa debe llevar un vestido o un traje pantalón y una blusa.

1. Dos estudiantes van a ir a un picnic.
2. Una chica y un chico tienen una entrevista para un trabajo en una oficina.
3. Dos mujeres van a un desfile de modas de la diseñadora Carolina Herrera.
4. Pedro va a jugar tenis con unos amigos, y Carmen va a visitar a sus parientes.
5. Los Sres. Montes van a ir a un té muy elegante en la Embajada de Venezuela.
6. El Sr. Jiménez y su esposa van a trabajar en el jardín de su casa.

6-3 Vacaciones en Venezuela. Primera fase. Usted y su amigo/a van a pasar sus vacaciones en Venezuela. Primero escojan el plan que más les interesa de las siguientes opciones.

1. Quince días en la isla Margarita. Por el día: ir a la playa; por la noche: ir a las discotecas.
2. Tomar un curso de verano en la Universidad de Caracas. Por la mañana: clases de español; por las tardes: lugares de interés turístico.
3. Explorar la fauna y flora de la región de Canaima. Por el día: caminar mucho; por las noches: estar en un campamento.

Segunda fase. Ahora, preparen una lista de la ropa y/o accesorios que van a necesitar de acuerdo con el plan que seleccionaron en la **Primera fase.**

PLAN #_____	YO	MI COMPAÑERO/A
por la mañana		
por la tarde		
por la noche		

Tercera fase. Informen al resto de la clase sobre sus **planes** y la ropa y accesorios que van a necesitar.

MODELO: Mi compañero/a y yo vamos a ir a la ciudad venezolana de Mérida. Yo necesito unos zapatos de tenis para caminar por la ciudad. Mi compañero/a necesita unos pantalones cortos. También necesitamos un traje para salir por las noches.

EN DIRECTO

To suggest something different:

¿Y qué te parece(n) un suéter/ zapatos de tenis? (*And how about . . .*)

To praise someone for a good suggestion:

¡Buena/Excelente/Fabulosa idea!

De compras

AUDIO **... a lo moderno**

Un **centro comercial** moderno donde **venden de todo.** Hay ropa para la familia, **muebles,** accesorios y **electrodomésticos** para la casa, **juguetes** para los niños y, en algunos **almacenes,** a veces también hay hasta un **supermercado.**

DEPENDIENTA: **¿En qué puedo servirle?**

CLIENTE: Quisiera comprar un **regalo** para una muchacha joven. Un **bolso** o una **billetera,** por ejemplo.

DEPENDIENTA: Hay unos bolsos **de cuero** preciosos y no son muy **caros.** Enseguida le muestro los que tenemos.

(La dependienta trae unos bolsos.)

CLIENTE: Me gustaría comprar éste, pero no puedo **gastar** mucho. ¿Cuánto cuesta?

DEPENDIENTA: Sólo vale 45.000 bolívares. El precio es muy bueno.

CLIENTE: Sí, no es mucho dinero.

DEPENDIENTA: Y están muy **de moda.** Las chicas jóvenes los llevan mucho.

CLIENTE: Bueno, lo voy a comprar.

DEPENDIENTA: Muy bien, señor. ¿Va a pagar con **tarjeta de crédito** o en **efectivo?**

CLIENTE: En efectivo.

A INVESTIGAR

¿Sabe usted en qué país el bolívar es la moneda oficial? Averigüe cuál es el equivalente de 90.000 bolívares en dólares.

LENGUA

To soften requests, Spanish uses the forms **me gustaría** (instead of **me gusta**) and **quisiera** (instead of **quiero**). English does this by adding *would.*
Me gustaría/Quisiera ir a esa tienda. *I would like to go to that store.*

AUDIO ... a lo tradicional

Muchas personas prefieren ir de compras a los **mercados** al aire libre. En estos mercados venden productos como comida, ropa, aparatos electrónicos, etc. Otras personas prefieren ir a los **centros comerciales** o a las **megatiendas.**

Telas y diseño

AUDIO

MARTA: Las **rebajas** son magníficas. Mira esa chaqueta. Está **rebajada** de 120.000 bolívares a 90.000. ¿Por qué no vemos si tienen tu **talla?**

ANA: Sí, y **me pruebo** la chaqueta para ver si **me queda** bien. Uso la talla 38 y a veces es difícil encontrarla. Esta chaqueta está **muy barata** y es **preciosa.**

MARTA: O te pruebas la chaqueta en casa y si te queda mal, la **cambias.** (Entran en la tienda.)

ANA: Buenos días; señorita, **quisiera** probarme esa chaqueta en la talla 38.

DEPENDIENTA: Lo siento, pero las únicas tallas que **nos quedan** son más grandes, la 42 y la 44.

ANA: ¡Qué lástima! Gracias.

Le queda estrecha.

Le queda ancha.

¿Qué dice usted?

6-4 ¡Lo mejor (*The best*)! Asocie las afirmaciones de la columna de la izquierda con una terminación lógica de la columna de la derecha.

1. ___c___ Elisa necesita una falda en la talla 12. La tienda tiene la talla 10.
2. ___a___ Raúl quiere regalarle un suéter de buena calidad a su mejor amigo.
3. ___e___ Mamá prefiere las telas naturales. No va a comprar esa blusa.
4. ___f___ Nos gustaría ver zapatos finos.
5. ___b___ Quisiera una camisa elegante para mi graduación.
6. ___d___ Necesito unos vaqueros a la moda.

a. Quisiera uno de lana fina.
b. Una de un solo color, por favor.
c. No la va a comprar porque le queda estrecha.
d. Los prefiero azules y anchos.
e. Es de nilón.
f. Solamente de cuero.

② 6-5 El cumpleaños de Nuria. Ustedes van a una tienda para comprarle un regalo a una buena amiga, pero cada artículo que ven presenta un problema. Analicen cada problema y piensen en la solución.

ARTÍCULO	PROBLEMA	SOLUCIÓN
collar	es muy caro	Debemos buscar uno rebajado/más barato.
impermeable	le queda ancho	
vaqueros	son de poliéster	
sudadera	es pequeña	
blusa	las rayas son muy anchas	
bolso	no es de cuero	
falda	le queda estrecha	

6-6 ¿Cuánto cuesta/n... ? Su compañero/a le va a preguntar el precio de algunos de los artículos que aparecen en el siguiente dibujo. Contéstele que usted tiene el mismo artículo y dígale cuánto pagó. Dé una breve descripción y diga cuándo lo usa. Después cambien de papel.

MODELO: E1: ¿Cuánto cuesta/vale la bufanda?
  E2: Cuesta/Vale 6.000 bolívares.
  E1: ¡Qué cara!
  E2: Sí, está cara. Yo tengo una igual y pagué 5.000. Es de seda y la uso mucho en el invierno.
  E1: ¿Dónde la compraste?
  E2: En... ¿Por qué no vamos allí?

EN DIRECTO

To express discontent with the price of an item:
¡Qué caro(s)/a(s)!

To show surprise at a bargain:
¡Qué barato(s)/a(s)!
¡Qué ganga! *What a bargain!*

6-7 Unos regalos. Cada uno de ustedes debe hacer unos regalos. Primero, escojan A o B. Lean los anuncios de abajo. Luego explíquele a su compañero/a para quiénes son los regalos. Su compañero/a le va a dar algunas ideas de qué comprar y el lugar donde puede comprar, según la información de los anuncios.

A. REGALOS PARA	B. REGALOS PARA
1. un sobrino que tiene cinco años	1. un hermano que va a pasar unos días en el Caribe
2. su mamá para el Día de la Madre	2. su padre para su cumpleaños
3. un/a amigo/a que necesita ropa informal	3. su novio/a para el Día de los enamorados

LA ELEGANTE

Todo lo que está de moda este verano

Ave. Andrés Bello con 3ª Transversal, Local B, 576 38 21

BARCELÓ

Las mejores camisas y guayaberas a los mejores precios

Segunda Avenida, Nº 40 271.88.20

LOS REYES MAGOS

Grandes rebajas

Ropa infantil de calidad

Plaza de las Américas Local Q-15 985 13 31

ALMACENES CARRASCO

Llévate tus jeans ahora a los mejores precios del año

30% menos

Ave. Teresa de la Parra Edificio Codazzi al lado del Banco Federal 661.45.81

EL CENTRO DE LAS TELAS

Entre la estación del Metro de Sabana Grande y Chacaíto Horario corrido de 9:00a.m. a 7:30p.m. Abrimos los domingos

985 50 43

6-8 Vestuario apropiado. Primera fase. Imagínese que usted es un/a experto/a en moda. Usted les da recomendaciones a sus clientes sobre la ropa apropiada para las diferentes ocasiones. Escriba algunas preguntas que usted les hace normalmente a sus clientes para ayudarlos.

MODELO: ¿Dónde va a ser la recepción? *o* ¿La recepción va a ser en un club elegante o en una casa de familia?

Para saber...

1. la hora del evento/ de la actividad
2. el tipo de personas que van a asistir al evento/ a la actividad
3. la ropa que la persona piensa/va a llevar
4. los accesorios que la persona tiene
5. cómo va a llegar la persona al lugar del evento/ de la actividad
6. ¿...?

Segunda fase. Uno/a de ustedes va a hacer el papel de cliente/a, y va a describir la ropa que piensa llevar para una ocasión especial. El/la experto/a le hace preguntas y recomendaciones sobre qué ropa es más apropiada para el evento/la ocasión.

MODELO: Una recepción a las 8:00 en un hotel
E1: El sábado próximo tengo que ir con mi esposo a una recepción en un hotel. Tengo un vestido negro corto muy bonito. ¿Es apropiado para la ocasión?
E2: Un vestido negro siempre es apropiado para una recepción, especialmente en el invierno. ¿Tiene un collar y unos aretes bonitos?
E1: Sí, tengo un collar y una pulsera muy bonitos.
E2: Va a necesitar un bolso pequeño y zapatos del mismo color del bolso.
E1: ¡Excelente idea! Mil gracias.

1. una invitación a un picnic con varias celebridades del mundo de la política
2. una cena de gala con el cónsul/embajador de Venezuela
3. la graduación de su mejor amigo/a
4. un crucero por el Mediterráneo
5. la primera cita (*date*) con un/a chico/a que a usted le gusta

6-9 Ropa para cada ocasión. You will listen to a brief conversation regarding the clothes people will wear for an event. Before you listen, list what you would wear on the following occasions.

Fiesta elegante _____

Fiesta informal _____

AUDIO Now as you listen to the conversation, write a check mark next to the appropriate clothes and to the event mentioned.

ROPA	EVENTO
_____ ropa elegante	_____ entrevista de trabajo
_____ falda y chaqueta	_____ reunión de jóvenes
_____ traje pantalón y blusa	_____ excursión de fin de semana
_____ pantalones cortos y camiseta	_____ fiesta formal

1. Preterit tense of regular verbs

Spanish has two simple tenses to express the past: the preterit and the imperfect (**el pretérito y el imperfecto**). Use the preterit to talk about past events, actions, and conditions that are viewed as completed or ended.

	HABLAR	COMER	VIVIR
yo	hablé	comí	viví
tú	hablaste	comiste	viviste
Ud., él, ella	habló	comió	vivió
nosotros/as	hablamos	comimos	vivimos
vosotros/as	hablasteis	comisteis	vivisteis
Uds., ellos/as	hablaron	comieron	vivieron

■ Note that the **nosotros** form of the preterit of **-ar** and **-ir** verbs is the same as the present **nosotros** form. Context will help you determine if it is present or past.

Llegamos a la tienda a las tres.   *We arrive at the store at three.*
We arrived at the store at three.

■ Stem-changing **-ar** and **-er** verbs in the present do not change in the preterit.

pensar: pensé, pensaste, pensó, pensamos, pensasteis, pensaron
volver: volví, volviste, volvió, volvimos, volvisteis, volvieron

■ Verbs ending in **-car** and **-gar** have a spelling change in the **yo** form to show how the word is pronounced. The spelling change of verbs ending in **-zar** (**empecé**) shows that Spanish rarely uses a **z** before **e** or **i**.

sacar: saqué, sacaste, sacó...
llegar: llegué, llegaste, llegó...
empezar: empecé, empezaste, empezó...

■ Some expressions that you can use with the preterit to denote past time are:

anoche	*last night*
anteayer	*day before yesterday*
ante(a)noche	*night before last*
ayer	*yesterday*
el año/mes pasado	*last year/month*
la semana pasada	*last week*

ACENTOS

The **yo** and the **Ud., él/ella** preterit verb forms are stressed on the last syllable and end in a vowel. Therefore, they carry a written accent; **hablé, comí, viví, habló, comió, vivió.**

2. Preterit of *ir* and *ser*

IR AND SER			
yo	**fui**	nosotros/as	**fuimos**
tú	**fuiste**	vosotros/as	**fuisteis**
Ud., él, ella	**fue**	Uds., ellos/as	**fueron**

Ir and **ser** have identical forms in the preterit. Context will help determine the meaning.

Ernesto **fue** a la tienda.	*Ernesto went to the store.*
Fue vendedor en esa tienda.	*He was a salesman at that store* (for some time).

¿Qué dice usted?

6-10 Ayer yo... Primera fase. Marque cuáles fueron sus actividades ayer y añada una actividad en cada grupo.

1. POR LA MAÑANA	2. POR LA TARDE	3. POR LA NOCHE
_____ Desayuné.	_____ Almorcé en la cafetería.	_____ Preparé la cena.
_____ Escribí una composición.	_____ Saqué libros de la biblioteca.	_____ Miré televisión.
_____ Tomé el sol en la playa.	_____ Lavé unas camisas.	_____ Planché unos pantalones.
_____ Estudié español.	_____ Fui al cine.	_____ Salí con mis amigos.

2 **Segunda fase.** Comparen sus respuestas. ¿Fueron sus actividades semejantes o diferentes? Expliquen.

2 **6-11 ¡Visita inesperada (*unexpected*)! Primera fase.** El gerente (*manager*) general de la cadena *La última moda* visitó una de sus tiendas y encontró muchas irregularidades. En la columna A están los problemas que encontró. Expliquen qué hicieron, probablemente, los empleados para tratar de resolver cada problema.

MODELO: uno de los dependientes ausente
E1: Probablemente los otros dependientes lo llamaron por teléfono a su casa.
E2: Sí, pero el dependiente probablemente no contestó el teléfono. *o* El dependiente contestó el teléfono y explicó todo.

indicar	limpiar	lavar	marcar
depositar	ordenar	sacar	llamar

A   PROBLEMAS

1. la ropa rebajada sin los nuevos precios
2. la ropa de niños muy desordenada
3. el baño público sucio
4. unos cheques en el mostrador (*counter*)
5. uno de los dependientes en el teléfono con un amigo
6. los probadores (*fitting rooms*) con ropa

B   ¿QUÉ HICIERON?

1. _____
2. _____
3. _____
4. _____
5. _____
6. _____

2 **Segunda fase.** Ahora digan qué hizo el gerente general con las siguientes personas. Pueden usar los siguientes verbos u otros.

conversar	hablar	explicar
ayudar	decidir	cambiar

1. la persona que limpia los baños
2. el empleado en el teléfono
3. la persona responsable de la ropa de niños

2 **6-12 El sábado pasado. Primera fase.** Yolanda y Pedro son una pareja moderna y muy activa. Mire los dibujos con su compañero/a y describan cómo pasaron Yolanda y Pedro el fin de semana.

1. _pasó_
2. _____
3. _bilò_
4. _miró_

5. _Schubho_
   Studiaste
6. _tomaron el sol_
   tomaste
7. _hablaron_
   comiaron

2 **Segunda fase.** Ahora hablen sobre el fin de semana de ustedes. ¿Fue un fin de semana igual o diferente al de Yolanda y Pedro?

1. ¿Qué actividades hizo cada uno de ustedes el fin de semana pasado?
2. ¿Quién pasó un mejor fin de semana, ustedes o Yolanda y Pedro? ¿Por qué?

2 **6-13 Un día de compras. Primera fase.** Usted y su compañero/a fueron de compras el sábado. Para recordar sus actividades ese día, deben hacer lo siguiente:

■ Escribir una lista de todas las cosas que hicieron durante su día de compras

■ Anotar qué compraron, dónde, cuánto gastaron, etc.

G **Segunda fase.** En grupos de cuatro estudiantes intercambien información.

■ Comparen sus actividades y contesten las preguntas de sus compañeros sobre sus compras y actividades.

■ Explíquenle a la clase si hicieron cosas similares o diferentes y qué grupo gastó más.

SITUACIONES

1. You went to a party last Saturday. Your friend would like to know a) where the party was, b) what time the party started, c) with whom you went, d) what clothes you wore, d) what time the party ended, and f) where you went after the party. Answer his/her questions in as much detail as possible.

2. **Role A.** You are at the store trying to get your best friend the same kind of sweat suit you wear for your exercise class, but you don't see it among the sports clothes. Explain to the salesperson a) when you bought your sweat suit, b) what it looks like, and c) give him/her the brand name **(marca)** and size of the product.

   Role B. After listening to the customer, explain that a) you don't have that brand name any more, b) that you received a similar one that costs less, c) that you have all sizes and colors, and d) ask if he/she would like to try it on.

3. Indirect object nouns and pronouns

Ana María le da un regalo a su amigo.
¿Qué le dice su amigo?
¿Qué le contesta Ana María?

INDIRECT OBJECT PRONOUNS	
me *to/for me*	**nos** *to/for us*
te *to/for you* (familiar)	**os** *to/for you* (familiar)
le *to/for you* (formal), *him, her, it*	**les** *to/for you* (formal), *them*

■ Indirect object nouns and pronouns tell *to whom* or *for whom* an action is done.

Mi madre **me** compró ropa la semana pasada.

My mother bought me clothes last week.

Yo **te** presto mis zapatos para la fiesta.

I will lend you my shoes for the party.

- Indirect object pronouns have the same form as direct object pronouns except in the third person: **le** and **les.**

¿El dependiente? Ella **lo** ve por la mañana. (direct object)	*She sees him in the morning.*
¿El dependiente? Ella **le** da los recibos por la mañana. (indirect object)	*She gives him the receipts in the morning.*

- Place the indirect object pronoun before the conjugated verb form. It may be attached to an infinitive or to a present participle.

Te voy a comprar un regalo.	
Voy a compra**rte** un regalo.	*I am going to buy you a present.*
Juan **nos** está preparando la cena.	
Juan está preparándo**nos** la cena.	*Juan is preparing dinner for us.*

- Use indirect object pronouns even when the indirect object noun is stated explicitly.

Yo **le** compré un regalo a **Victoria.**	*I bought Victoria a present.*

- To eliminate ambiguity, **le** and **les** are often used with the preposition **a** + *pronoun.*

Le hablo **a usted.**	*I am talking to you. (not to him)*
Siempre **les** compro algo **a ellos.**	*I always buy them something. (not you)*

- For emphasis, use **a mí, a ti, a nosotros/as,** and **a vosotros/as** with indirect object pronouns.

Pedro **te** habla a **ti.**	*Pedro is talking to you (not to someone else).*

4. The verb *dar*

DAR (*to give*)		
	PRESENT	PRETERIT
yo	doy	di
tú	das	diste
Ud., él, ella	da	dio
nosotros/as	damos	dimos
vosotros/as	dais	disteis
Uds., ellos, ellas	dan	dieron

- **Dar** is almost always used with indirect object pronouns. Notice the difference in meaning between **dar** (*to give*) and **regalar** (*to give as a gift*).

Ella le **da** la camisa a Pedro.	*She gives (hands) Pedro the shirt.*
Ella le **regala** la camisa a Pedro.	*She gives Pedro the shirt (as a gift).*

- In the preterit, **dar** uses the endings of **-er** and **-ir** verbs.

¿Qué dice usted?

6-14 Una clase optativa (*elective*). Imagínense que están tomando la clase optativa *Elegancia con poco dinero*. Marquen las sugerencias que les da su instructor a usted y a sus compañeros/as.

1. __✓__ Nos da nombres de tiendas de ropa buena y barata.
2. __✓__ A mí me recomienda artículos sobre la moda actual.
3. __✓__ Nos dice los secretos para ser elegantes y gastar poco.
4. __✓__ Nos muestra telas que son elegantes y baratas.
5. __✓__ A mí me da ejemplos de cómo combinar ropa y accesorios.
6. __✓__ A mí me explica cómo comprar ropa por Internet.

6-15 Expertos en moda. Primera fase. Imagínense que ustedes tienen un/a experto/a que siempre les da recomendaciones para estar a la moda. En la siguiente lista, marquen las cosas que esta persona hace por ustedes. Después deben añadir una actividad más y compartir sus ideas con otros/as compañeros/as.

MODELO: hacer preguntas sobre la ropa que necesitamos
           Nos hace preguntas sobre la ropa que necesitamos.

1. _____ dar nombres de tiendas famosas en los países hispanos
2. _____ hablar sobre las cosas que venden en los mercados al aire libre
3. _____ comprar ropa
4. _____ dar ideas sobre accesorios
5. _____ decir las telas que debemos comprar
6. _____ mostrar fotos de almacenes y tiendas en varios países hispanos
7. _____ regalar libros sobre la moda
8. ...

Segunda fase. Ahora, ustedes desean recompensar (*compensate*) a este/a experto/a. Indiquen qué es lo que van a hacer por él/ella.

1. ordenar su oficina
2. preguntar cómo está
3. lavar su auto
4. hacer pequeños favores
5. comprar regalos por su cumpleaños
6. contestar el teléfono de su oficina
7. comprar revistas de moda en español
8. mandar correos electrónicos

6-16 Para estar a la última moda. Primera fase. Imagínense que cada uno de ustedes tiene los deseos o necesidades de la lista de abajo. Explíquense entre ustedes la situación. Después pidan y den una recomendación.

MODELO: E1: Quiero llevar ropa a la última moda. ¿Qué me recomiendas?
           E2: Te recomiendo comprar ropa de colores claros.
           E1: ¿Me recomiendas alguna marca en especial?
           E2: Te recomiendo comprar ropa de diseñadores venezolanos.

1. Quiero llevar pantalones a la moda.
2. Necesito zapatos cómodos y modernos.
3. Deseo protegerme del sol.
4. Quiero ropa buena y barata
5. Quiero estar más delgado/a.
6. Me gustaría llevar ropa elegante y fina a la entrevista de trabajo.

Segunda fase. Comparta con otro/a compañero/a tres buenas recomendaciones que recibió en la **Primera fase.**

6-17 Afortunados. Primera fase. Ustedes acaban de (*have just*) ganar la lotería y quieren compartir su fortuna con su familia y sus compañeros de clase.

- Hagan una lista de los miembros de su familia a quienes desean regalarles algo.

- Indiquen el regalo que piensan hacerle a cada uno.

MODELO: E1: A nuestros padres les vamos a regalar/vamos a regalarles un
                crucero por el Caribe.
           E2: A Sara le vamos a comprar/vamos a comprarle una mochila.

Segunda fase. Ahora, hagan una lista de cuatro compañeros/as a quienes ustedes les quieren dar algo. Indiquen en la siguiente lista el regalo que piensan hacerle a cada uno. Compartan la información con otra pareja.

1. una invitación para un desfile de moda (*fashion show*)
2. la revista de moda *En voga*
3. una entrada para ver el concurso Señorita Venezuela
4. 150.000 bolívares para gastar en el Centro Sambil en Caracas
5. un perfume de Óscar de la Renta o Carolina Herrera

6-18 Entrevista. Basándose en la siguiente lista, háganse preguntas sobre sus hábitos de compras y los regalos que hacen y reciben de otras personas. Después comparen sus respuestas.

1. Ir de compras: ¿adónde? ¿cuándo?
2. Tienda(s) favorita(s): ¿cuál(es)?
3. Comprar regalos caros: ¿a quién(es)?
4. Le compran regalos a usted: ¿quién(es)?

SITUACIONES

1. **Role A.** You are a customer at a department store. Tell the salesperson that a) you are looking for a present for a young man/lady, b) you are not sure what you should buy, and c) the amount that you can spend.

   Role B. You are a salesperson. A customer comes into the store to ask for your advice: a) inquire about the young man's/lady's age, taste, size, favorite color, or any other pertinent information; b) make reasonable suggestions to your customer; and c) give him/her information about the quality of the products, prices, sales, etc.

2. **Role A.** You are starting a new job and you go to the store to get some new clothes. Tell the salesperson a) that you saw a suit/dress at the shop window **(escaparate)** and b) inquire if he/she has your size. Answer all the salesperson's questions and decide which suits/dresses you would like to try on.

   Role B. You are a salesperson. First, a) ask the client for more details to identify the suit/dress the customer is referring to, b) tell him/her that you have it in brown, blue, gray, and black, c) that you also have some new suits/dresses that you can show him/her (describe the styles), and d) ask him/her if she would like to see them.

5. *Gustar* and similar verbs

¿Le gusta esta camisa?   Me gustan éstas. ¿Y a usted?
No, no me gusta.   Me gustan mucho.

■ In previous lessons you have used the verb **gustar** to express likes and dislikes. As you have noticed, **gustar** is not used the same way as the English verb *to like*. **Gustar** is similar to the expression *to be pleasing (to someone)*.

Me gusta ese vestido.   *I like that dress.*
(That dress is pleasing to me.)

■ In this construction, the subject is the person or thing that is liked. The indirect object pronoun shows to whom something is pleasing.

me		*I*	
te		*you* (familiar)	
le	gusta el traje.	*you* (formal), *he/she*	*like/s the suit.*
nos		*we*	
os		*you* (familiar)	
les		*they, you*	
		(formal and familiar)	

■ The most frequently used forms of **gustar** in the present are **gusta** and **gustan** and for the preterit **gustó** and **gustaron**. If one person or thing is liked, use **gusta/gustó**. If two or more persons or things are liked, use **gustan/gustaron**. To express what people like or do not like to do, use **gusta** followed by infinitives.

Me **gusta** ese **collar.**	*I like that necklace.*
No me **gustaron** los **anillos.**	*I did not like the rings.*
Nos **gusta caminar** por la mañana.	*We like to walk in the morning.*
¿No te **gusta correr** y **nadar?**	*Do not you like to run and swim?*

■ Some other Spanish verbs that follow the pattern of **gustar** are **encantar** (*to delight, to love*), **interesar** (*to interest, to matter*), **parecer** (*to seem*), and **quedar** (*to fit, to have something left*).

■ To express that you like or dislike a person, you may also use **caer bien** or **caer mal,** which follow the pattern of **gustar.**

Les cae bien Miriam.	*They like Miriam.*
La dependienta **me cae mal.**	*I do not like the salesclerk.*

■ To emphasize or clarify to whom something is pleasing, use **a + mí, a + ti, a + él/ella,** etc. or **a +** *noun.*

A mí me gustaron mucho los zapatos, pero **a Pedro** no le gustaron.	*I liked the shoes a lot, but Pedro did not like them.*

¿Qué dice usted?

6-19 Mis preferencias en la ropa. Primera fase. Complete la siguiente tabla según sus preferencias.

ROPA	ME ENCANTA/N	ME GUSTA/N	NO ME GUSTA/N
la ropa deportiva			
los aretes			
las chaquetas de cuero			
los suéteres de lana			
las blusas/camisas de seda			
los vaqueros			
los pantalones cortos			

G **Segunda fase.** Comparen sus preferencias, y luego, explíquenle al resto de la clase si ustedes coinciden en sus gustos.

MODELO: E1: A dos de nosotros nos gustan los colores fuertes.
E2: Y también nos encanta la ropa deportiva. *o* A todos nos encantan los vaqueros.

2 **6-20 Problemas.** Lean estos problemas y busquen la solución.

MODELO: Pilar tiene 50.000 bolívares. Paga 25.000 bolívares por una blusa y 10.000 por unos aretes. ¿Cuánto dinero le queda? 15.000 bolívares.

1. Ernesto tiene 75.000 bolívares. Le da 15.000 a su hermano. ¿Cuánto dinero le queda?
2. Érica tiene 25.000 bolívares. Va al cine y a cenar con una amiga. El cine cuesta 5.000 bolívares y la cena 12.000. ¿Cuántos bolívares le quedan?
3. Gilberto tiene 40.000 bolívares. Compra un suéter por 39.000 bolívares. ¿Cuánto dinero le queda?
4. Mis amigos tienen 30.000 bolívares. Van a la playa y almuerzan en un restaurante por 25.000 bolívares. ¿Cuántos bolívares les quedan?

EN DIRECTO

To ask for someone's opinion:

¿Qué opinión tiene(s) sobre...?

¿Qué opina(s) sobre/de...?

¿Qué te/le parece(n)...?

¿Qué piensa(s)/cree(s) de...?

To give an opinion:

Opino que...

Me parece que...

Creo/Pienso que...

G 6-21 ¿Qué opinan ustedes? Primero, pregúntense y den su opinión sobre los siguientes temas. Luego, intercambien sus opiniones en grupos pequeños.

MODELO: el uso de uniformes en las escuelas

E1: ¿Qué piensas del uso de uniformes en las escuelas?

E2: Me parece que es una idea excelente. Y tú, ¿qué opinas?

E1: Pues yo creo que cada estudiante debe llevar la ropa que le gusta.

1. los almacenes de descuento
2. la ropa que llevan los artistas a la ceremonia de los Óscares
3. los precios de la ropa de los diseñadores famosos
4. los desfiles de moda en la televisión
5. los chicos que llevan aretes
6. las personas que se pintan el pelo de colores fuertes

6-22 ¿Qué planes tienes? Ustedes van a ir a una recepción muy elegante el sábado próximo. Averigüe qué ropa piensa llevar o comprar su compañero/a y qué le gustaría hacer después de la recepción. Después él/ella debe hacerle a usted las mismas preguntas.

SITUACIONES

1. One of you is shopping at a clothing store, the other is the clerk. Tell the clerk a) what you need (e.g., pants, shoes, and so on), b) ask the price of each item, c) say whether or not you like each item, and d) decide if you will buy it/them. He/She will ask you pertinent questions.

2. **Role A:** You are at the store where you bought a pair of jeans last week. Tell the clerk that a) you tried them on at home and they didn't fit, and b) that you would like to exchange them. Listen to the clerk and respond accordingly.

   Role B: You are the clerk at a store. A customer comes to you to exchange a piece of clothing. Listen to his/her case and tell the customer that you don't have any other sizes in that style. Try to interest the customer in another style.

ALGO MÁS

More uses of por and para

- Use **por** to indicate the reason or motivation for an action.

No le compra el collar **por** el precio.	*He is not buying her the necklace because it is too expensive (because of the price).*

- If you use a verb to express the reason or motivation, you must use **porque**.

No le compra el collar **porque** es muy caro.	*He is not buying her the necklace because it is very expensive.*

- Use **para** to indicate for whom something is intended or done.

Compró otro collar **para** su novia.	*He bought another necklace for his girlfriend.*

¿Qué dice usted?

6-23 ¿Cuál es el motivo? Usen **por** o **porque** para terminar las oraciones de la columna de la izquierda con un motivo lógico de la columna de la derecha.

MODELO:　Pedro compró un traje　　　　　　lo invitaron a una fiesta
　　　　　　Pasamos el fin de semana preocupados　el examen del lunes

　　　　　　Pedro compró un traje porque lo invitaron a una fiesta.
　　　　　　Pasamos el fin de semana preocupados por el examen del lunes.

1. Pepito quiere una bicicleta　　　　　　　a. le queda grande
2. No va a comprar los pantalones　　　　　b. sus buenas notas
3. Rebeca va a cambiar el vestido　　　　　c. el tráfico
4. Ellos llegaron tarde　　　　　　　　　　d. la ropa es más barata
5. Voy a ir de compras hoy　　　　　　　　e. son muy cortos
6. Isabel prefiere comprar en un mercado　　f. las rebajas

6-24 Unos regalos. Usted fue a Caracas la semana pasada y su compañero/a quiere saber para quién son los regalos que usted compró.

MODELO:　una pulsera
　　　　　　　E1: ¿Para quién es la pulsera?
　　　　　　　E2: Es para mi hermana.

1. los libros de español
2. la billetera
3. las camisetas
4. el collar
5. los discos compactos del Puma
6. ...

MOSAICOS

 ## *Escuchar*

Taking notes to recall important information

Sometimes when you want to remember something that somebody tells you, you benefit from taking notes. For example, when you ask for directions to go somewhere, you might remember better what you hear if you take notes.

Antes de escuchar

6-25 En el Centro Comercial Sambil. In **6-26,** Irma—a working mother who takes good care of her clothes and accessories—is at a big department store in Caracas. She is asking one the employees where to find different items. Before you listen, make a list of the different items of clothing and accessories that she might be interested in buying.

accesorios ___anillo, los aretes, los bolsas___

ropa ___el vestido, los zapatos___

A escuchar

AUDIO **6-26** Now, listen to Irma asking an employee at Centro Comercial Sambil where she can find different items she needs. As you listen to the conversation, look at her incomplete notes and complete them stating what items are on each floor. You do not have to remember all the items mentioned!

Primer piso ___Camisas, pants, shorts, suits, bluses___

Segundo piso ___lana por Sombra___

Tercer piso ___bolsas, zaptos, chaetas, sombreros___

Después de escuchar

6-27 ¿Y usted? Conversen sobre la última vez que cada uno de ustedes fue a un centro comercial.

1. ¿Cuándo fue la última vez que usted fue a un centro comercial?
2. ¿Qué compró? ¿Compró regalos? ¿Para quién?
3. ¿Qué le gustó pero no pudo comprar?

Antes de escuchar

6-28 De compras. In **6-29** you will listen to a conversation between Andrea and her parents in which Andrea talks about her needs for school. Before you listen, make a list of things you had to buy before you came to school this semester.

_____

_____

_____

A escuchar

AUDIO **6-29** Now, you will listen to the conversation between Andrea and her parents. As you listen, complete the notes her parents are taking. You don't have to remember all the items Andrea mentions!

Para ir a clases Andrea necesita ___botas chaqueta fonda___

Para practicar deportes Andrea tiene que comprar ___pnts medias___

Para salir con sus amigos Andrea quiere ___bluses , pals , vaqueros___

Después de escuchar

 6-30 ¿Y usted? Converse con su compañero/a sobre sus compras antes de venir a la universidad.

1. ¿Qué compró usted antes de venir a la universidad este semestre: ropa, muebles para su cuarto, aparatos electrónicos?
2. ¿Compró accesorios? ¿Qué accesorios compró usted? ¿Dónde los compró?
3. ¿Fue usted a unas rebajas? ¿Gastó mucho dinero? ¿Cuánto gastó?

Conversar

Antes de conversar

6-31 En un mercado. Usted tiene que comprar un regalo, algo para su apartamento/casa, etc. en un mercado al aire libre. Complete la tabla con la información de los productos que desea comprar.

¿QUÉ DEBE COMPRAR?	¿PARA QUIÉN(ES)?	DESCRIPCIÓN DEL PRODUCTO

A conversar

6-32 ¡A ahorrar! (*Let's save*). Usted ya está en un mercado al aire libre. Pregúntele al/ a la vendedor/a (su compañero/a) el precio de los productos que usted desea comprar. Regatee (*Haggle*) para obtener el mejor precio posible. Use las expresiones más apropiadas. Luego, cambien del papel.

Después de conversar

6-33 ¡Qué experiencia! Conversen sobre su experiencia de regateo en el mercado al aire libre de la actividad **6-32**. Cuéntense lo siguiente:

1. qué productos pudo comprar y para quién los compró.
2. cuánto le pidió el/la vendedor/a por cada producto.
3. cuánto dinero le ofreció usted.
4. cuánto pagó finalmente.

Antes de conversar

6-34 ¿Apropiado o inapropiado? Elimine la ropa y los accesorios que, según usted, son inapropiados en las siguientes ocasiones. Luego, compare sus respuestas con las de su compañero/a.

1. Un chico fue a escalar montañas en sus vacaciones de verano con botas, pantalones cortos, un sombrero, un cinturón, una chaqueta de lana.
2. Unas chicas fueron de picnic al lago Sinamaica en Venezuela. Todas se pusieron minifalda de color entero, zapatos de tenis, un collar de perlas, una blusa de algodón a rayas.
3. La semana pasada, el presidente de una corporación tuvo una reunión importante con los ejecutivos de la filial (*branch office*) en Caracas. Se puso un impermeable verde, zapatos negros, vaqueros azules, una guayabera, un sombrero mexicano.

A conversar

6-35 Inspector/a de la moda. Lean las siguientes descripciones y comenten si las personas llevan la ropa y los accesorios apropiados (A) o inapropiados (I) para la ocasión. Indiquen cuál(es) es/son inapropiado(s) para cada situación y digan por qué.

1. _____ Una actriz famosa fue a la ceremonia de los premios Óscar en traje de baño, gafas de sol y sandalias.
2. _____ El presidente de los Estados Unidos invitó a unos estudiantes a visitar la Casa Blanca. Los estudiantes se pusieron traje, corbata y zapatos de tenis.
3. _____ Usted y sus hermanos/as prepararon una gran fiesta para celebrar las bodas de plata (25 aniversario) de sus padres. Su padre llevó vaqueros, una camiseta blanca y botas tejanas; su madre se puso un vestido negro largo, un collar de perlas y unos aretes finos.
4. _____ A su primera entrevista de trabajo, su mejor amiga llevó una falda y una chaqueta azul, unos aretes pequeños, unas pantimedias oscuras, zapatos negros y una bolsa pequeña del color de los zapatos.

Después de conversar

6-36 ¿Elegante o de mal gusto? Usted trabaja en la revista *A la moda* y debe escribir un artículo para la sección **Inspector de la moda** de este mes. Seleccione una de las situaciones de la actividad **6-35** y escriba un breve informe sobre la situación para los lectores de su revista. Incluya como mínimo la siguiente información.

1. ¿Sobre qué persona(s) es la noticia?
2. ¿Cuál fue el evento/la situación y dónde fue?
3. ¿Qué ropa y accesorios usó/usaron la(s) persona(s)?
4. Según usted, ¿fueron apropiados los accesorios y la ropa? ¿Por qué?

 ## *Leer*

In this chapter, you will practice finding specific information to accomplish a task, and identifying word endings that indicate places where certain products are sold or services rendered.

As the need arises, remember to apply all the strategies you have learned so far.

Guía de prelectura

Skim the text in activity **6-38** and answer the questions, using your previous knowledge and experiences.

1. Thinking of the theme of *Lección 6* and looking at the text format and illustrations, can you anticipate the type of text it is?
   a. Guidelines to buy on online
   b. Online advertising for one store
   c. A listing of stores that sell online

2. Now, use your background knowledge to comprehend the text. On what did you base your answers to question 1?
   a. The cognates in the title
   b. Visuals in the text
   c. The use of key words for online shopping

3. The text probably contains the following information for shoppers. Circle all that may apply. You will be able to verify your responses later.
   a. Products and prices
   b. Method of payment for online purchases
   c. Bargains
   d. Alphabetically arranged list of online stores

Antes de leer

6-37 Megatiendas. Primera fase. ¿Qué productos o servicios se pueden obtener en una megatienda de su ciudad? Escriba **Sí** o **No** al lado del producto o servicio.

1. _____ ropa de mujer/hombre
2. _____ electrodomésticos
3. _____ camisetas para niños
4. _____ máquinas fotográficas
5. _____ seguros (*insurance*) de auto
6. _____ frutas y verduras
7. _____ ropa de fiesta
8. _____ muebles
9. _____ juguetes para niños
10. _____ acceso a Internet

Segunda fase. Converse con su compañero/a sobre lo siguiente:

1. ¿Les gusta comprar en las megatiendas o prefieren las tiendas más pequeñas? ¿Por qué?
2. En su ciudad o país, ¿hay megatiendas en internet? ¿Cuál(es) es/son?
3. ¿Cuáles son algunas ventajas de comprar en las megatiendas?

A leer

6-38 Primera mirada. Lea la siguiente página de Internet y, luego, siga las instrucciones.

Bienvenido a CompreenInternet.net

Menú	Nuestro Proceso	Beneficios
• Nuestra compañía • Nuestros Servicios • Cómo puede comprar • Recomendaciones prácticas • Preguntas frecuentes • Regulaciones de compras • Nuestras filiales	1. Hágase miembro 2. Busque su producto 3. Calcule los gastos de su envío 4. Pague con tarjeta de crédito 5. Espere su envío y disfrútelo	• Excelentes precios • Pagos en bolívares • Entrega en todo el país • Nuestras filiales de Nueva York o Miami hacen los envíos

Compra de una gran variedad de productos en Internet:

• Aparatos eléctricos/electrónicos
• Muebles accesorios, ropa, juguetes, software, etc.
• Asistencia de expertos mientras y después de su compra
• Envío gratis en Venezuela
• Descuentos por recomendarnos a otras personas
• Lista de las mejores tiendas en Internet
• Ofertas y gangas de la semana

Dirección en EE.UU.
1438 Flagger St.
Miami, Florida (Fl)
Código Zip: 33166
Tel: 305-328-6289
Utilice esta dirección para su envío (shipping)

• Asistencia para afiliados
• Actualizar datos personales
• Modificación de clave
• Salida

Indique si las siguientes afirmaciones son correctas (C) o incorrectas (I), según el contenido de la página Web. Si son incorrectas (I), corrija la información.

1. _____ Los productos y servicios que **CompreenInternet.com** ofrece son básicamente para personas que viven fuera de Venezuela.
2. _____ La sección **Nuestro proceso** de la página de Web les indica a los clientes las diversas fases de una compra en Internet.
3. _____ Las tiendas que promociona (*advertises*) **CompreenInternet.com** sólo incluyen tiendas que están en Venezuela.
4. _____ **CompreenInternet.com** tiene su oficina central en Venezuela.
5. _____ Los clientes de **CompreenInternet.com** solamente pueden comprar ropa.
6. _____ Los clientes ahorran dinero si compran en internet.

6-39 Segunda mirada. Lea otra vez la página de **CompreenInternet.com** y seleccione la alternativa correcta.

1. Los clientes que compran en **CompreenInternet.com** pagan solamente en...
   a. dólares   b. bolívares   c. dólares y bolívares

2. En el **Menú** de **CompreenInternet.com**, la palabra **búsqueda** probablemente es un nombre derivado del verbo...
   a. bañar   b. buscar   c. barrer

3. La expresión **envío gratis** significa que los clientes...
   a. pagan por recibir los productos en su casa.
   b. no pagan por recibir los productos en su casa.
   c. pagan sólo un 10% del costo por recibir sus productos en casa.

4. La expresión **Hágase miembro** en la sección **Nuestro proceso** probablemente significa que para comprar, las personas deben...
   a. subscribirse a una lista de clientes de la tienda en Internet.
   b. tener a un miembro de la familia en la tienda.
   c. comprar un mínimo al año.

2 **6-40 Tercera mirada.** Lean una vez más el menú de la página de **CompreenInternet.com** y completen la tabla con las categorías de tiendas que, según ustedes, las chicas, los chicos o ambos visitan con más frecuencia. Compartan sus respuestas con las de otra pareja.

LAS CHICAS	LOS CHICOS	AMBOS

Después de leer

6-41 Ampliación. Adivinen a qué tipo de tienda van a ir estas personas. Completen la tabla.

PERSONA QUE BUSCA UN PRODUCTO O SERVICIO	TIPO DE TIENDA
Modelo: El constructor civil necesita una herramienta (*tool*).	ferretería
1. El señor Fonseca desea comprar un **mueble** nuevo para su casa.	
2. La señora Méndez debe comprarle un **juguete** a su nuevo sobrino.	
3. Mauricio necesita comprar una **joya** (*jewel*) para su novia.	
4. Ustedes desean comprar **pescado** para la cena.	
5. Doña Sara quiere comprarle a su esposo unos **zapatos** elegantes.	
6. Ustedes quieren comprar **fruta** para su madre.	

 # Escribir

In *Lección 5*, you practiced writing for a general, unknown audience. However, writing for a specific reader, particularly one with whom you have done business, to fulfill a specific need requires attention to the following, among others:

■ The use of a formal, business tone. In Spanish, a business tone is signaled by the use of **Señores**, and the pronoun **usted/ustedes**, for example.

■ The length of the message to be communicated. Most business correspondence tends to be brief and straight to the point.

■ Clear descriptions and/or explanations. To meet their needs, customers must describe accurately and clearly the product/service they need or explain precisely what is wrong with a product they bought that did not meet their expectations.

In this chapter, you will write a letter of complaint to a store, agency, etc. As you plan and write your letter of complaint, keep in mind the degree of formality of business correspondence, and the accuracy and amount of information you will provide.

Antes de escribir

6-42 Enfoque. Primera fase. Hace dos semanas el señor Contreras compró un traje en Internet. Cuando lo recibió, él se dio cuenta de (*realized*) algunos problemas. Él le escribió una carta al Departamento de Ventas de la tienda en línea. Lea la carta y siga las instrucciones.

Avenida Simón Bolívar 1439, Apt. B
Maracaibo VENEZUELA
28 de enero de 2005

Alamoda.com
Departamento de ventas
Bulevar Las Américas # 392, Oficina 801
Caracas VENEZUELA

Estimados señores:
Les escribo para informarles sobre un problema con el traje que compré en la página Web de su tienda el 13 de enero de este año. Después de mirar la gran variedad de trajes que ustedes tienen, escogí uno con esta descripción:

Estilo: 7635; talla: 48, color: azul marino, material: lana inglesa, detalles del saco: doble abotonadura[1], bolsillos[2] pequeños, detalles del pantalón: pliegues[3], bolsillos sin botón.

Desafortunadamente, el 27 de enero recibí un traje que no corresponde a la descripción que ustedes me dieron en Internet. El traje que me mandaron tiene los siguientes problemas: Primero, es de poliéster, no de lana como yo lo pedí. Segundo, los pantalones no tienen bolsillos. Tercero, yo pedí un traje azul marino, pero recibí uno gris de rayas.

Yo necesito con urgencia el traje que les pedí. Les envío una copia del recibo por la cantidad de 190.000 bolívares que pagué con mi tarjeta VISA.

Por favor, mándenmelo a la dirección que incluí arriba.

Espero una solución rápida a este problema.

Muy agradecido por su pronta respuesta, los saluda muy atentamente,

Alberto Contreras

P.S.: Por favor, confirmen el envío a mi dirección electrónica: ras81@ter.com

[1]double-breasted   [2]pockets   [3]pleats

Segunda fase. Answer the following questions based on Mr. Contreras' letter.

1. Mark with an X the intended purpose of Mr. Contreras' letter to the Sales Department of **Alamoda.com:**

   _____ to describe the clothes he would like to order
   _____ to complain about a discrepancy between the description of the product online and the actual product they shipped to him
   _____ to request that **Alamoda.com** ship the right product to him
   _____ to inform **Alamoda.com** of a forthcoming lawsuit

2. Based on its purpose, is Mr. Contreras' letter effective?

Yes   No

Mark some possible reasons for your response.

_____ He narrates his shopping experience chronologically, starting with the present and moving toward the past.

_____ He provides the sales department with the exact online description of the product.

_____ He pinpoints the differences between the online description of the product and the actual product he received.

_____ The tone of his letter is businesslike.

_____ He writes to **Alamoda.com** as a friend.

_____ His letter of complaint is brief and straight to the point.

3. What salutation did Mr. Contreras use in his letter? _____

4. How does he close the letter? What does this sentence probably mean in English? _____

5. How does he say good-bye in the letter? Do you know any other way to say good-bye in a business letter in Spanish? What is it? _____

6-43 Preparación. Como Alberto Contreras, usted compró un producto en Internet (ropa, un mueble, un accesorio, etc.), pero el producto resultó ser diferente de sus expectativas. Usted decide escribir una carta de queja al Departamento de Ventas de la tienda en línea. Haga lo siguiente:

1. Escriba el nombre de la tienda donde usted compró los producto(s).

2. Indique el producto que compró en línea: ¿Qué compró? ¿Cuánto(s)/(as) compró?

3. Prepare una lista de expresiones (nombres y adjetivos) para describir cada producto que usted compró: ¿Un vestido negro largo? ¿Una camisa blanca ancha? ¿Un plato decorativo de cerámica?

4. Narre los hechos (*facts*) en orden cronológico: ¿Cuándo hizo la compra en internet? ¿Cómo describe los productos la tienda en internet? ¿Cuánto costó/costaron el/los producto(s)? ¿Cómo pagó usted? ¿Usó una tarjeta de crédito o llamó a un número gratis para pagar?

5. Escriba la(s) razón(es) de su insatisfacción con el/los producto(s).

A escribir

6-44 Manos a la obra. Ahora escríbale una carta de queja a la persona encargada del Departamento de Ventas de la tienda en línea. Use la información que preparó en la actividad **6-43.** Incluya la fecha, el saludo, el cierre de la carta y la despedida.

Después de escribir

6-45 Revisión. Ahora lea su carta por lo menos dos veces. Piense en la persona que la va a leer. Verifique lo siguiente:

■ El contenido: ¿Incluyó usted toda la información necesaria?

■ El tono de la carta: ¿Escribió su carta formalmente?

■ La forma de la carta de queja:

a. ¿Revisó la gramática de su texto: el vocabulario correcto, algunas expresiones que indican cronología en la narración, la concordancia (*agreement*), el tiempo (presente, pasado, futuro), etc.?

b. ¿Usó la puntuación y ortografía correctas?

Finalmente, comente su carta con un/a compañero/a.

ENFOQUE CULTURAL

TEMAS: DE COMPRAS EN EL MUNDO HISPANO

Para pensar

¿Cuáles son los lugares más populares para ir de compras en los Estados Unidos? ¿Qué puede usted comprar allí? ¿Cómo paga usted sus compras? ¿Pide rebajas?

En las metrópolis de los países hispanos hay grandes y lujosos centros comerciales donde se pueden comprar muchos productos nacionales o importados. Frecuentemente venden artículos de muy buena calidad y a precios muy altos. Se puede pagar en efectivo o con tarjeta de crédito.

En todas las ciudades hispanas, a lo largo de las avenidas del centro, hay innumerables tiendas pequeñas que se especializan en determinados productos. En las tiendas del Bulevar de Sabana Grande en Caracas, uno puede comprar muchas cosas.

Para contestar

2 **Las tiendas.** Hagan lo siguiente.

1. Comparen los centros comerciales, las tiendas pequeñas y los mercados al aire libre de los países hispanos con respecto a productos que se pueden comprar, localización de las tiendas, costo de los productos, forma de pago. Mencionen cuáles son las ventajas y las desventajas de cada lugar.
2. ¿En qué lugares se puede pedir rebaja en los países hispanos? Y en los Estados Unidos, ¿se puede pedir rebaja? ¿Dónde?

G **Riqueza cultural.** Comparen los lugares donde uno puede ir de compras en los Estados Unidos y en los países hispanos. Hablen de lo que se puede comprar en esos lugares y la forma de pago.

En estos mercados al aire libre se ofrece una gran variedad de productos: ropa, juguetes, perfumes, artículos de ferretería (hardware), artesanías, comida, etc. Los precios son más bajos y es posible regatear, pero por lo general sólo aceptan el pago en efectivo.

Para pensar

¿Qué sabe usted acerca de Venezuela? ¿Sabe usted dónde está? ¿Sabe usted cuál es su principal producto de exportación?

Venezuela está en la parte norte de América del Sur. Es un país que tiene hermosas playas caribeñas, tranquilos pueblos andinos, selvas amazónicas y grandes ciudades cosmopolitas.

En la parte oriental del país se encuentra el Parque Nacional Canaima, donde están las cataratas del Salto del Ángel, las más altas del mundo, con una caída de 807 metros (16 veces más altas que las cataratas del Niágara).

En la zona de los Andes está Mérida, llamada "la Ciudad de los Caballeros", una ciudad colonial, tranquila y muy agradable.

Maracaibo es el centro de la industria petrolera. Venezuela es un país de enormes recursos económicos; además del petróleo, hay oro, piedras preciosas, minerales, etc.

Expresiones venezolanas:

cónchale	**¡Cónchale!**	*Darn!*
la cara amarrada	Amaneció con la cara **amarrada**.	*He woke up in a bad mood.*
corotos	¿Dónde están mis **corotos**?	*Where are my things?*

Para contestar

En el mapa

1. Busque una isla de Venezuela que está en el Mar Caribe.
2. Diga qué países están al sur, al este y al oeste de Venezuela.

Ahora diga...

1. por qué se dice que Venezuela es un país privilegiado.
2. qué lugar de interés le gustaría visitar en Venezuela y por qué.

¿Qué dice usted si...

1. no encuentra sus cosas.
2. su amigo/a está de mal humor.

Para investigar en Internet

Busque ofertas de ropa o productos para el hogar en los periódicos de Caracas. Haga una copia de los anuncios para presentarlos en clase y comentar los precios. Describa el anuncio y diga en qué se parece o se diferencia de los anuncios que se publican en los periódicos de los Estados Unidos.

¡Prepárese!

6-46 Impresiones. En este episodio va a ver que los jefes de Ángela quieren cambios en el concurso porque desean algo impresionante, con más impacto. ¡Son muy exigentes (*demanding*)! Imagínese que es uno/a de los jefes de Ángela y exprese sus impresiones sobre el programa hasta este momento. Use los verbos **gustar, interesar, parecer, caer bien/mal** y el complemento indirecto.

MODELO: **Me parece** difícil el Misterio 3.

1. _____
2. _____
3. _____
4. _____
5. _____

Manolo y Ángela tienen que hacer cambios en el programa.

¿Es Katie simpática o agresiva?

En el Parque Chapultepec...

Sabrina y Efraín no están de acuerdo.

Efraín piensa que la solución no puede ser muy obvia.

Si no van a las pirámides de Teotihuacán, ¿adónde van?

¡Responda!

6-47 ¿Qué pasó? En las oraciones siguientes sobre el Episodio 6, use la forma correcta del pretérito del verbo apropriado.

hablar	ir	entrevistar
salir	mencionar	enseñar

1. Los jefes de Ángela le _____ de cambios en el concurso.
2. Manolo le _____ a Angela el video del Episodio 6.
3. En el video, Tito _____ a Katie.
4. Sabrina y Efraín _____ al Parque Chapultepec.
5. Sabrina _____ las tres pistas y la Pirámide del Sol en Teotihuacán.
6. Los dos _____ del Parque Chapultepec.

Esta canción de los años 50 en la cual el cantautor lamenta la ausencia de su novia, María Luisa, se refiere a un amor perdido.

¡Prepárese!

6-48 Los diminutivos. En el capítulo 4 vimos como la terminación "**-ito/-ita**" (el diminutivo) puede usarse para indicar afecto o tamaño o edad. En el título de esta canción hay un diminutivo. ¿Cuál es? Escriba los diminutivos de los siguientes nombres y palabras de la letra de *Caminito de Guarenas*.

PALABRA:	DIMINUTIVO:
María Luisa	_____
la morena	_____
una rosa	_____
solo (*alone*)	_____

¡Escuche!

6-49 ¿Qué pasó? Escuche la canción y después complete los espacios en blanco con la forma correcta del pretérito de los verbos que faltan.

jurar   perder   abandonar   olvidar   encontrar

Caminito de Guarenas
donde (1) _____ la novia mía,
María Luisa la morena,
la que (2) _____ que me quería,
y yo recuerdo aquella tarde
cuando una rosa deshojaba
pregúntandole al camino
si era verdad que yo la amaba.
Caminito de Guarenas
que yo encontré,
Caminito de Guarenas
que se me fue.

Caminito de Guarenas,
ya no te acuerdas de nosotros.
María Luisa la morena
me (3) _____ y se fue con otro.
Ha pasado mucho tiempo
de aquella flor no queda nada,
y en el alma sólo siento,
que tú solito te quedabas.

Ay! caminito que se (4) _____,
Caminito que me (5) _____.

¡Responda!

6-50 Un club. Imagínese que usted fue a un club a escuchar la música de la orquesta Billo's Caracas Boys. Complete los espacios en blanco con la forma correcta del pretérito de los verbos entre paréntesis.

El sábado pasado mis amigos y yo (ir) _____ a un club para escuchar la música de la Billo. (Bailar) _____ mucho y también (tomar) _____ algo. Allí yo (bailar) _____ con Julia, una muchacha bonita y simpática. Julia me (dar) _____ su número de teléfono. Yo la (llamar) _____. Nosotros (conversar) _____ mucho y (decidir) _____ volver al club el sábado siguiente.

VOCABULARIO*

AUDIO ## Los accesorios

el anillo	ring
el arete	earring
la billetera	wallet
la bolsa	purse
la bufanda	scarf
el cinturón	belt
el collar	necklace
las gafas de sol	sunglasses
la gorra	cap
el guante	glove
el pañuelo	handkerchief
el paraguas	umbrella
la pulsera	bracelet
el sombrero	hat

Las compras

el almacén	department store
el centro comercial	shopping center
el mercado al aire libre	open-air market
el precio	price
la rebaja	sale
el regalo	present
la talla	size
la tarjeta de crédito	credit card
la tienda	store

Telas y diseño

el algodón	cotton
de color entero	solid color
de cuadros	plaid
de cuero	leather
la lana	wool
de lunares	polka-dotted
el poliéster	polyester
de rayas	striped
la seda	silk

La ropa

el abrigo	coat
la bata	robe
la blusa	blouse
la bota	boot
el calcetín	sock
el calzoncillo	boxer shorts
la camisa	shirt
la camiseta	T-shirt
el camisón	nightgown
la chaqueta	jacket
la corbata	tie
la falda	skirt
el impermeable	raincoat
las medias	stockings, socks
los pantalones	pants
los pantalones cortos	shorts

las pantimedias	pantyhose
el saco	blazer
la sandalia	sandal
el sostén	bra
la sudadera	jogging suit, sweatshirt
el suéter	sweater
el traje	suit
el traje de baño	bathing suit
el traje pantalón	pantsuit
los vaqueros/jeans	jeans
el vestido	dress
la zapatilla	slipper
el zapato	shoe

Verbos

cambiar	to change, to exchange
contestar	to answer
dar	to give, to hand
encantar	to delight, to love
encontrar (ue)	to find
entrar	to go in, to enter
gastar	to spend
gustar	to be pleasing to, to like
interesar	to interest
llevar	to wear, to take
mostrar (ue)	to show
pagar	to pay
parecer (zc)	to seem
ponerse	to put on
probarse (ue)	to try on
quedar	to fit, to be left over
regalar	to give (a present)
valer	to be worth
vender	to sell

Descripciones

ancho/a	wide
barato/a	inexpensive, cheap
caro/a	expensive
estrecho/a	narrow, tight
magnífico/a	great
precioso/a	beautiful
rebajado/a	marked down

Palabras y expresiones útiles

así	this way
el dinero	money
en efectivo	cash
¿En qué puedo servirle(s)?	How may I help you?
enseguida	immediately
estar de moda	to be fashionable
ir de compras	to go shopping
Me gustaría...	I would like . . .
Quisiera...	I would like . . .

*A list of expressions denoting past time can be found on page 215.

EL TIEMPO Y LOS DEPORTES

Objetivos comunicativos

- Expressing and describing physical activities
- Asking and answering questions about weather conditions
- Expressing more measurements
- Talking about past events
- Expressing how long ago events and states occurred

Contenido

AUDIO *Los deportes*

El **fútbol** es el **deporte** número uno en los países hispanos.

Hay excelentes equipos de fútbol en España, Argentina, Uruguay, Colombia, México y otros países latinoamericanos. Los mejores **jugadores** de los equipos locales forman un **equipo** nacional. Esta selección representa al país en **campeonatos** internacionales y participa, cada cuatro años, en la Copa Mundial.

En la zona del Caribe, el béisbol es el deporte más popular, y muchos de sus jugadores, como Sammy Sosa y Pedro Martínez, forman parte de los mejores equipos de los Estados Unidos.

El **esquí** es un deporte que practican muchas personas en Argentina, Chile y España. Aquí vemos a unos jóvenes que van a **esquiar** en las **pistas** de Bariloche, Argentina, uno de los centros de esquí más importantes de la América del Sur.

El **ciclismo**, el tenis y el golf son otros deportes que cuentan con figuras renombradas en Hispanoamérica y España. Los españoles Aitor González y Roberto Heras son algunos de los líderes del Tour de France. En esta **carrera**, que dura más de 20 días, los ciclistas recorren a veces unos 200 kilómetros, el equivalente de 120 millas, en un solo día.

En cuanto al tenis, Juan Ignacio Chela, argentino, y Fernando González, chileno, son dos de los tenistas más conocidos del Cono Sur.

Sergio García, conocido como "El niño", es la promesa más joven del golf español.

Deportes y equipos necesarios

el béisbol

el bate

los jugadores

el guante

el golf

los palos de golf

el cesto/
la cesta

la raqueta

la cancha

el tenis

el basquetbol / el baloncesto

la pelota

la red

el vóleibol

¿Qué dice usted?

7-1 Deportes: ¿Quién es? Primera fase. Asocie los deportes de la columna de la izquierda con los jugadores hispanos de la columna de la derecha.

1. _____ ciclismo
2. _____ tenis
3. _____ béisbol
4. _____ golf

a. Sergio García
b. Pedro Martínez
c. Fernando González
d. Aitor González
e. Juan Ignacio Chela

Segunda fase. Ahora elijan dos deportes e intercambien datos sobre sus jugadores favoritos del deporte. Luego descríbale a la clase los jugadores favoritos de su compañero/a.

7-2 ¿Qué necesitamos para jugar? Primera fase. Además de una pelota, necesitamos ciertas cosas para practicar estos deportes. Indíquelo al lado de cada deporte en la siguiente tabla.

DEPORTE	EQUIPO
béisbol	
golf	
vóleibol	
baloncesto	
tenis	

Segunda fase. Entreviste a su compañero/a sobre los deportes que él/ella practica.

1. ¿Qué deporte(s) practicas?
2. ¿Dónde compras el equipo y la ropa que necesitas para practicarlo(s)?
3. ¿Por qué compras tu equipo allí?

7-3 ¿Qué deporte es? Túrnense para identificar los siguientes deportes.

1. Hay nueve jugadores en cada equipo y usan un bate y una pelota.
2. Es un juego para dos o cuatro personas; necesitamos raquetas y una pelota.
3. En este deporte los jugadores no pueden usar las manos.
4. Para practicar este deporte necesitamos tener una bicicleta.
5. En cada equipo hay cinco jugadores que pueden lanzar (*throw*) la pelota a un cesto.
6. Para este deporte necesitamos una red y una pelota; mucha gente lo juega en la playa.

7-4 Su deporte favorito. Háganse las preguntas necesarias para averiguar lo siguiente.

1. deporte favorito
2. lugar donde lo practica, con quién y cuándo
3. otros deportes que practica
4. nombres de sus jugadores/as favoritos/as

G **7-5 Encuesta.** En grupos de tres o cuatro, intercambien preguntas para completar la siguiente encuesta. Después, comparen los resultados de su grupo con los de otros.

1. deporte favorito
2. jugador/a favorito/a
3. equipo favorito
4. asistencia a los partidos
   a. todos   b. pocos   c. ninguno (*none*)
5. ver los partidos por televisión
   a. todos   b. pocos   c. ninguno
6. saber jugarlo bien
   a. Sí   b. No

El tiempo y las estaciones

AUDIO Verano

¿Qué tiempo hace? **Hace buen tiempo** y **hace calor.** Es un día perfecto para jugar al vóleibol en la playa. El cielo **está despejado** y **hace mucho sol.**

Otoño

Hace fresco y mucho **viento.** No es fácil jugar al golf cuando hace viento. Pero el otoño es muy bonito porque muchos **árboles** cambian de color antes de perder las **hojas.**

Invierno

Hace mal tiempo. Anoche **nevó** y hoy **hace frío.** Hay mucha **nieve** y **hielo** en las calles. Los **lagos** también **se congelaron** y algunas personas aprovechan para **patinar** en el hielo.

A INVESTIGAR

¿En qué estación son los campeonatos de béisbol en el Caribe? ¿Por qué cree usted que se realizan en esa estación?

Primavera

Hoy **está nublado** y **está lloviendo;** por eso estos chicos no pueden jugar al fútbol y están jugando a los **bolos.** Pero **la lluvia** es muy buena para las plantas y las **flores,** y además limpia la atmósfera contaminada.

¿Qué dice usted?

7-6 Asociación. Asocie la situación de la columna de la izquierda con el estado del tiempo de la columna de la derecha.

1. _____ Todo el césped está blanco.
2. _____ Las personas llevan impermeable y paraguas.
3. _____ La casa es un horno y vamos a ir a la playa.
4. _____ Está lloviendo, pero es imposible abrir el paraguas.
5. _____ Vamos a celebrar mi cumpleaños en el parque porque el clima está perfecto.
6. _____ El cielo está muy oscuro. No vamos a jugar al golf hoy.

a. Hace muy buen tiempo.
b. Hace mucho viento.
c. Está lloviendo.
d. Hace mucho calor.
e. Está nevando.
f. Está nublado.

EN DIRECTO

To express happiness and gratitude for someone's call:
Mil gracias por llamar. ¡Fue un gusto escucharte!
Gracias por llamar. ¡Qué placer escucharte!

7-7 ¿Qué tiempo hace? Uno/a de sus amigo/as lo/la llama por teléfono desde otra ciudad o país. Pregúntele qué tiempo hace donde él/ella está y averigüe cuáles son sus planes. Su amigo/a debe hacerle preguntas a usted.

MODELO: E1: ¡Qué sorpresa! ¿Dónde estás?
         E2: _____
         E1: ¿Qué tiempo hace allí?
         E2: _____
         E1: ¿Y qué piensas hacer esta tarde/noche/este fin de semana?
         E2: _____
         E1: Mil gracias por llamar.

7-8 Las estaciones y los deportes en mi ciudad. Primera fase. Háganse preguntas sobre las estaciones del año en su ciudad de origen y los deportes que practican en cada estación. Después, cambien de papel.

MODELO: E1: ¿De dónde eres?
         E2: _____.
         E1: ¿Y qué tiempo hace allí en _____?
         E2: _____.
         E1: ¿Qué deportes practicas?
         E2: _____.

G **Segunda fase.** Sin mencionar el nombre de su compañero/a, escriba un resumen de la información que obtuvo en la **Primera fase.** El resto de la clase va a adivinar sobre quién escribió. Siga el modelo.

MODELO: Es una persona de... En su ciudad/país, ... en invierno. En primavera, ... y... En otoño, ... y... En el invierno, el clima es... ¿Con quién conversé?

7-9 Las temperaturas. Escojan una ciudad del mapa y completen la siguiente conversación.

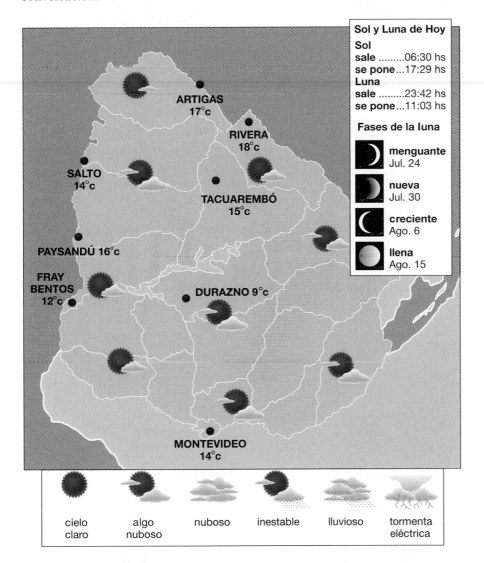

Sol y Luna de Hoy

Sol
sale ....06:30 hs
se pone...17:29 hs
Luna
sale ....23:42 hs
se pone...11:03 hs

Fases de la luna

🌙 **menguante** Jul. 24

🌑 **nueva** Jul. 30

🌓 **creciente** Ago. 6

🌕 **llena** Ago. 15

ARTIGAS 17°c
RIVERA 18°c
SALTO 14°c
TACUAREMBÓ 15°c
PAYSANDÚ 16°c
FRAY BENTOS 12°c
DURAZNO 9°c
MONTEVIDEO 14°c

cielo claro   algo nuboso   nuboso   inestable   lluvioso   tormenta eléctrica

E1: ¿Qué temperatura hace en _____?
E2: _____ grados, más o menos.
E1: ¿Por el día o por la noche?
E2: Por _____.
E1: ¿Cuál es el equivalente en Fahrenheit?
E2: _____.
E1: ¿Y qué tiempo hace allí?
E2: _____.

Las actividades diarias

AUDIO **Un partido importante**

Hoy es el juego decisivo del campeonato de fútbol.

Rigoberto **se despierta** temprano.

Se levanta.

Se lava los dientes.

Se afeita.

Se viste.

Se sienta a desayunar. Después se va para el campo de fútbol.

CULTURA

Hispanic sports fans generally do not boo opposing teams or particular players. Instead they whistle when they want to show their displeasure. This kind of behavior may occur at a soccer game, a boxing match, or other popular sports events.

El partido está terminando y el equipo de Rigoberto gana. Los aficionados aplauden porque están muy emocionados. Un jugador del equipo contrario está discutiendo con el **árbitro** porque no **está de acuerdo** con su decisión.

Rigoberto **se quita** el uniforme.

Se baña.

Se seca.

Se peina.

Se **pone** la ropa.

Va a una fiesta para celebrar el triunfo.

Vuelve a casa muy tarde.
Está muy cansado y **se acuesta.**

¿Qué dice usted?

7-10 ¿Qué significa? Lean estas palabras relacionadas con los deportes con su compañero/a. Asocien cada palabra con su significado.

1. _____ ganar	a.	jugador/a número 1 en un deporte
2. _____ equipo	b.	persona que mantiene el orden en un partido
3. _____ decisión	c.	tener más puntos al terminar un juego
4. _____ partido	d.	juego entre dos equipos o individuos
5. _____ árbitro	e.	la palabra final del árbitro
6. _____ campeón/campeona	f.	un grupo de jugadores

7-11 Las actividades de Rigoberto. Primera fase. Contesten las preguntas sobre las actividades de Rigoberto el día del partido.

1. ¿Qué es lo primero que hace Rigoberto?
2. Después de levantarse, ¿se lava los dientes o se viste?
3. ¿Se afeita por la mañana o por la noche?
4. ¿Qué usa para secarse?
5. ¿Adónde va después de bañarse y vestirse?
6. ¿Cuándo se acuesta?

G **Segunda fase.** Indiquen qué actividad(es) de Rigoberto muestra(n) que es una persona...

1. limpia
2. puntual
3. responsable
4. que cuida su salud (*health*)

¿Hacen ustedes lo mismo?

7-12 Mi rutina diaria. Primera fase. Intercambien información sobre lo que hace cada uno/a de ustedes todos los días desde que se levanta hasta que se acuesta. Háganse preguntas sobre lo siguiente:

1. hora de despertarse y de levantarse
2. actividades que hace por la mañana y por la tarde
3. número de horas de estudio
4. deporte(s) que practica y frecuencia con que lo(s) practica
5. actividades que hace con otras personas y frecuencia con que las hace

Segunda fase. Después, comparen su rutina diaria, contestando las siguientes preguntas:

1. ¿Quién de ustedes está más ocupado/a durante el día? ¿Por qué?
2. Normalmente, ¿quién se levanta más temprano? ¿Quién se acuesta más tarde?
3. ¿Quién estudia más? ¿Quién practica más deportes?
4. ¿Quién es más sociable? ¿Por qué?

AUDIO **7-13 El clima en América Latina.** You will listen to the weather forecast for four Latin American cities. Before you listen, write down the phrases that you might hear in a weather forecast in the following seasons:

primavera _____
verano _____
otoño _____
invierno _____

Now, pay attention to the general idea of what is said. Then, as you listen to the weather forecast, use a check mark to indicate whether each forecast predicts good or bad weather.

	BUEN TIEMPO	MAL TIEMPO
Lima		
Buenos Aires		
Caracas		
Madrid		

1. Preterit of *-er* and *-ir* verbs whose stem ends in a vowel

LEER			
yo	leí	nosotros/as	leímos
tú	leíste	vosotros/as	leísteis
Ud., él, ella	leyó	Uds., ellos/as	leyeron

OÍR			
yo	oí	nosotros/as	oímos
tú	oíste	vosotros/as	oísteis
Ud., él, ella	oyó	Uds., ellos/as	oyeron

The preterit endings of verbs whose stem ends in a vowel are the same as those of regular **-er** and **-ir** verbs, except for the **usted, él, ella** form and the **ustedes, ellos, ellas** form, which end in **-yó** and **-yeron**.

2. Preterit of stem-changing *-ir* verbs (e → i) (o → u)

PREFERIR			
yo	preferí	nosotros/as	preferimos
tú	preferiste	vosotros/as	preferisteis
Ud., él, ella	prefirió	Uds., ellos/as	prefirieron

DORMIR			
yo	dormí	nosotros/as	dormimos
tú	dormiste	vosotros/as	dormisteis
Ud., él, ella	durmió	Uds., ellos/as	durmieron

- The preterit endings of stem-changing **-ir** verbs are the same as those for regular **-ir** verbs.

- Stem-changing -ir verbs (e → ie, e → i, o → ue) change e → i and o → u in the **usted, él, ella** and **ustedes, ellos, ellas** preterit forms.

Marta prefirió salir temprano.	*Marta preferred to leave early.*
José durmió tranquilamente.	*José slept calmly.*

¿Qué dice usted?

G **7-14 Encuesta. Primera fase.** En grupos pequeños, hagan la siguiente encuesta. Anoten los datos.

¿QUIÉNES EN EL GRUPO...?	TOTAL DEL GRUPO
1. ... leyeron el periódico ayer	_____
2. ... oyeron las noticias esta mañana	_____
3. ... fueron a un partido de tenis o béisbol recientemente	_____
4. ... practicaron un deporte esta semana	_____
5. ... durmieron siete horas o más anoche	_____
6. ... durmieron menos de seis horas anoche	_____

G **Segunda fase.** Ahora, calculen y comenten lo siguiente. Luego, compartan sus datos con el resto de la clase.

1. ¿Qué porcentaje de ustedes practicó un deporte esta semama o fue a un partido recientemente?
2. ¿Qué porcentaje oyó las noticias esta mañana?
3. ¿Qué porcentaje durmió la siesta?
4. Según ustedes, ¿usaron bien el tiempo ayer? ¿Por qué?

G **7-15 El domingo pasado.** Hagan una lista de las actividades que todos los miembros del grupo hicieron el domingo pasado. Después, comparen su lista con la de otro grupo. ¿En qué actividades coinciden?

7-16 Celebrando la victoria. Primera fase. Uno de los equipos de su universidad ganó un campeonato importante y ustedes decidieron organizar una fiesta en su honor. Explíquenle a otra pareja los siguientes detalles de la fiesta.

1. deporte y nombre del equipo que representó a la universidad
2. hora y lugar de la fiesta
3. número de personas que invitaron y cuántas asistieron
4. dinero que le pidieron a cada persona para los gastos de la fiesta
5. comida y bebida que sirvieron, y tipo de música que escucharon en la fiesta
6. regalos que les dieron a los jugadores

SITUACIONES

1. **Role A.** You had to work late last night and missed a very important basketball game at your college/university. Call a friend who went to the game and after greeting him/her a) explain why you did not go, b) ask as many questions as possible about the game, c) answer your friend's questions, and d) accept his/her invitation to go to another game next Saturday.

   Role B. A friend calls you to find out about last night's basketball game. Answer his/her questions giving as many details as possible. Then a) tell him/her that there is another game on Saturday, b) find out if he/she is free that evening, and d) if free, invite him/her to go with you.

2. One of you read in today's newspaper that a famous football player is going to be interviewed on TV tonight. The other should find out a) in which newspaper you read about the interview, b) the time of the interview, c) the channel (**el canal**), and d) who will do the interview.

3. Reflexive verbs and pronouns

REFLEXIVES		
yo	**me lavo**	*I wash myself*
tú	**te lavas**	*you wash yourself*
Ud.	**se lava**	*you wash yourself*
él/ella	**se lava**	*he/she washes himself/herself*
nosotros/as	**nos lavamos**	*we wash ourselves*
vosotros/as	**os laváis**	*you wash yourselves*
Uds.	**se lavan**	*you wash yourselves*
ellos/ellas	**se lavan**	*they wash themselves*

■ In *Lección 4*, you learned that true reflexive verbs express what people do *to* or *for* themselves. You also practiced the **yo, tú,** and **usted, él, ella** forms of some reflexive verbs, placing the reflexive pronouns before the conjugated verb. Now you will learn more about reflexives and practice other verb forms.

Alicia **se levanta** a las siete y media. *Alicia gets up at seven thirty.*
Nosotros **nos vestimos** rápidamente. *We get dressed quickly.*

■ With verbs followed by an infinitive, place reflexive pronouns before the conjugated verb or attach them to the infinitive.

Yo **me** voy a acostar a las diez.⎫
Yo voy a acostar**me** a las diez. ⎬ *I am going to go to bed at ten.*

■ With the present progressive (**estar** + **-ndo**), place reflexive pronouns before the conjugated form of **estar** or attach them to the present participle. When attaching a pronoun, add a written accent mark to the stressed vowel (the vowel preceding **-ndo**) of the present participle.

Amelia **se** está maquillando ahora.⎫
Amelia está maquillándo**se** ahora. ⎬ *Amelia is putting on makeup now.*

■ When referring to parts of the body and articles of clothing, use definite articles rather than possessives with reflexive verbs.

Me lavo **los** dientes. *I brush my teeth.*
Me pongo **la** sudadera. *I put on my sweatshirt.*

■ There are other Spanish verbs that use reflexive pronouns, but they do not necessarily convey the idea of doing something to or for oneself. These verbs normally convey the idea of mental or physical states.

María **se enfermó** la semana pasada, *María **got sick** last week and that*
y eso **nos preocupó** mucho. ***worried us** a lot.*

■ Some verbs change meaning when used reflexively.

acostar	*to put to bed*	**acostarse**	*to go to bed, to lie down*
dormir	*to sleep*	**dormirse**	*to fall asleep*
ir	*to go*	**irse**	*to go away, to leave (for)*
levantar	*to raise, to lift*	**levantarse**	*to get up*
llamar	*to call*	**llamarse**	*to be called*
quitar	*to take away*	**quitarse**	*to take off*

ACENTOS

The verb form **maquillándose** has an accent mark. Do you know why?

¿Qué dice usted?

7-17 ¿Qué hacemos todos los días? Ponga estas actividades en el orden más lógico.

a _____ me duermo
b. _____ me levanto
c. _____ me voy a la universidad

d. _____ me acuesto
e. _____ me lavo la cara
f. _____ me siento a desayunar

7-18 ¿Qué hacemos? Primera fase. Hablen sobre sus actividades diarias. ¿Sus horarios son similares o diferentes?

MODELO:　E1: Yo me despierto a las siete.
　　　　　　E2: Y yo (me despierto) a las ocho.

1. Yo me levanto....
2. Después me lavo....
3. Me visto....
4. Me siento a desayunar....

5. Me voy a la universidad....
6. Yo me baño....
7. Me acuesto....
8. Me duermo....

Segunda fase. Cambien de pareja y hablen sobre su propio horario y el de su compañero/a anterior. Comenten cuáles son sus horarios los fines de semana y compárenlos.

MODELO:　E1: Juan y yo nos levantamos a las ocho. También nos bañamos por la tarde. ¿Y tú?
　　　　　　E2: Yo me levanto a las siete.

7-19 Mis actividades de ayer. Haga una lista de todo lo que hizo ayer para cuidar de su salud. Después, compárela con la de su compañero/a.

7-20 Los horarios. Túrnense para hablar del horario de estos atletas. Háganse preguntas para compararlo con el horario de ustedes.

MODELO:　acostarse / 11:00 / 10:30
　　　　　　E1: Arturo se acuesta a las once.
　　　　　　E2: Y Alicia y Berta se acuestan a las diez y media. ¿Y tú?
　　　　　　E1: Yo me acuesto a _____.

	ARTURO	ALICIA Y BERTA	YO
despertarse	8:00	7:00	
levantarse	8:15	7:05	
bañarse	8:20	7:10	
vestirse	8:30	7:20	

7-21 ¿Qué hacen estas personas? Lean las siguientes situaciones y túrnense para hablar de lo que hacen y lo que van a hacer estas personas. Usen los verbos de la lista. Después, comparen sus opiniones con las de otros/as compañeros/as.

acostarse	afeitarse	bañarse	dormirse	irse	lavarse
levantarse	maquillarse	ponerse	quitarse	secarse	vestirse

MODELO: Bernardo está durmiendo y suena el despertador.
    E1:   Bernardo se despierta cuando oye el despertador. En tu opinión, ¿qué va a hacer después?
    E2:   Va a levantarse enseguida y después va a bañarse.

1. Teresa está enfrente del espejo y se prepara para ir a una fiesta muy elegante.
2. Juan y Tomás entran en el vestuario (*dressing room*) del gimnasio porque van a jugar al baloncesto con unos amigos.
3. Marisa y Sarita están en una playa de Punta del Este, en Uruguay.
4. Rogelio sale de la ducha y toma una toalla.
5. Son las once de la noche. Marta está en su cuarto y tiene mucho sueño.

7-22 Nuestra preparación para el campeonato. El mes pasado ustedes representaron a su universidad en un campeonato de tenis en Montevideo, Uruguay. Digan lo que hicieron...

■ para prepararse físicamente.

■ para prepararse mentalmente.

■ para cumplir (*to fulfill*) con las responsabilidades académicas.

SITUACIONES

1. **Role A.** You are a well-known sportsperson, highly admired by youngsters in your country. The reporter of a TV network is going to interview you to prepare a special about your life. Answer the reporter's questions as completely as possible. Remember that you are considered a role model by young people.

   Role B. You are a reporter for a major TV network. Today you are interviewing a well-respected and admired sports figure. After introducing yourself and greeting him/her, find out a) when he/she started to play, b) what school he/she went to, c) what his/her daily routine is, and d) the things he/she does daily to keep in shape (**estar en forma**).

2. **Role A.** You would like your younger brother to attend a summer camp. Ask the camp director questions to find out a) how many children there are per counselor (**consejero/a**), b) what time the children get up, c) what sports they play, d) what they eat, e) what they do in the evenings, and f) what time they go to bed.

   Role B. You are the director of the summer camp. Answer your prospective client's questions and add more information regarding the variety of activities.

4. Pronouns after prepositions

Voy a la reunión del equipo ahora. ¿Quieres ir conmigo?

Sí, voy contigo.

- In *Lección 6*, you used **a + mí, ti,** and so on to clarify or emphasize the indirect object pronoun: **Le di el suéter a él.** These same pronouns are used after other prepositions, such as **de, para,** and **sin.**

Siempre habla **de ti.**	*He is always talking about you.*
El boleto es **para mí.**	*The ticket is for me.*
No quieren ir **sin nosotros.**	*They do not want to go without us.*

- In a few cases, Spanish does not use **mí** and **ti.** After **con,** use **conmigo** and **contigo.** After **entre,** use **tú y yo.**

¿Vas al partido **conmigo?**	*Are you going to the game with me?*
Sí, voy **contigo.**	*Yes, I am going with you.*
Pedro va a sentarse **entre tú y yo.**	*Pedro is going to sit between you and me.*

¿Qué dice usted?

7-23 Un amigo preguntón. Rosario habla con un amigo que hace muchas preguntas. Lea las preguntas en la columna de la izquierda y conéctelas con una respuesta o un comentario lógico de Rosario en la columna de la derecha.

1. ¿Con quién vas a ir al partido de tenis, Rosario?
2. ¿Por qué no vemos las finales del campeonato con Sofía?
3. Rosario, ¿para quién es esta raqueta de tenis?
4. ¿Pueden mis amigos ir a la cancha con nosotros?
5. En el partido de ayer hubo un accidente. ¿A quién le informaron primero del accidente?
6. ¿De quién van a recibir el trofeo los ganadores?

a. La compré para ti. ¿Te gusta?
b. Imposible. No podemos ir con ellos. Tengo sólo dos billetes (*tickets*).
c. Contigo, ¡por supuesto!
d. A la policía. Hay que informarles rápidamente.
e. De nosotros. De ti y de mí. ¡Qué emocionante!
f. Prefiero verlas sin ella. Habla mucho y no puedo concentrarme.

③ 7-24 Las prácticas de tenis. Identifíquense cada uno/a con un número y hagan preguntas para saber quién va a practicar tenis con quién. Contesten según la tabla.

MODELO: E1: ¿Con quién practica Jorge el sábado?
E3: Practica conmigo. (*o* E2: Practica con él/ella.)

LUNES	MARTES	MIÉRCOLES	JUEVES	VIERNES	SÁBADO
Pedro	Alicia	Carmen	Jorge	Carmen	Jorge
E1	E2	E3	E1	E2	E3

② 7-25 ¿Con quién va? Completen el siguiente diálogo, usando pronombres.

E1: Yo salgo ahora. ¿Vienes conmigo?
E2: No, no puedo ir _____. Tengo que trabajar media hora más en la tienda.
E1: ¡Cuánto lo siento! Entonces, ¿vas a ir con Roberto?
E2: Sí, voy a ir con _____.
E1: Seguro que él no quiere ir sin _____. Tú eres su mejor amigo/a.
E2: Sí, somos muy buenos amigos. ¿Y tú sabes dónde te vas a sentar?
E1: Sí, voy a sentarme entre _____ y _____.

SITUACIONES

Role A. Your friend, the coach, gave you two tickets for today's football game, but you have no transportation. Call a friend and after greeting him/her, a) explain how you got the tickets for the game, b) invite him/her to go with you, and c) explain that you have no transportation.

Role B. A friend calls you to invite you to a football game. After exchanging greetings, a) thank him/her for the invitation, b) say that you would be delighted to go with him/her, c) that you can pick him/her up in your car, and d) agree on a time and place.

5. Some irregular preterits

Some irregular verbs do not stress the last syllable in the **yo,** and **usted, él, ella** preterit forms.

■ The verbs **hacer, querer,** and **venir** have an **i** in the preterit stem.

INFINITIVE	NEW STEM	PRETERIT FORMS
hacer	**hic**	hice, hiciste, hizo, hicimos, hicisteis, hicieron
querer[1]	**quis**	quise, quisiste, quiso, quisimos, quisisteis, quisieron
venir	**vin**	vine, viniste, vino, vinimos, vinisteis, vinieron

---

[1]The verb **querer** in the preterit followed by an infinitive normally means *to try (but fail) to do something.*

Quise hacerlo ayer.   *I tried to do it yesterday.*

■ The verbs **decir**, **traer**, and all verbs ending in **-ducir** (e.g., **traducir**–*to translate*) have a **j** in the stem and use the ending **-eron** instead of **-ieron**. *Decir* also has an **i** in the stem.

INFINITIVE	NEW STEM	PRETERIT FORMS
decir	**dij**	dije, dijiste, dijo, dijimos, dijisteis, dijeron
traer	**traj**	traje, trajiste, trajo, trajimos, trajisteis, trajeron
traducir	**traduj**	traduje, tradujiste, tradujo, tradujimos, tradujisteis, tradujeron

■ The verbs **estar**, **tener**, **poder**, **poner**, and **saber** have a **u** in the preterit stem.

INFINITIVE	NEW STEM	PRETERIT FORMS
estar	**estuv**	estuve, estuviste, estuvo, estuvimos, estuvisteis, estuvieron
tener	**tuv**	tuve, tuviste, tuvo, tuvimos, tuvisteis, tuvieron
poder[1]	**pud**	pude, pudiste, pudo, pudimos, pudisteis, pudieron
poner	**pus**	puse, pusiste, puso, pusimos, pusisteis, pusieron
saber[2]	**sup**	supe, supiste, supo, supimos, supisteis, supieron

¿Qué dice usted?

7-26 Un equipo indisciplinado. Después de las irregularidades en la práctica de ayer, el entrenador de la selección uruguaya de vóleibol se prepara para escribir un informe. Como el entrenador es de Inglaterra y su español no es perfecto, él revisa su texto. Para ayudarlo, haga un círculo alrededor de la expresión que corresponda en cada caso y escríbala en el espacio apropiado.

Les informo que durante la práctica de ayer, ocurrieron varios incidentes que me preocupan. Al comienzo, yo les (1) _____ (digo, dije, dijimos) a los jugadores que íbamos a practicar un poco más de tiempo. Ellos me (2) _____ (dijo, dijeron, dicen) que no podían quedarse más tiempo. Yo (3) _____ (hago, hice, hicieron) un gran esfuerzo para convencerlos de la importancia de prolongar un rato más la práctica, pero ellos no (4) _____ (quisieron, quieren, quiso) comprenderlo, y empezaron a protestar. Como no me escuchaban, mi asistente y el físicoterapeuta (5) _____ (tuvieron, tenemos, tuvimos) que llamar al director de deportes de la universidad. Solamente él (6) _____ (pudo, puede, pudieron) tranquilizarlos. El subdirector que (7) _____ (viene, vino, vinieron) con él les habló sobre sus obligaciones con la universidad, y todos juntos (8) _____ (pusieron, puso, pusimos) fin al problema. Después de unas horas, yo (9) _____ (sé, supe, supimos) que los jugadores escribieron una carta para pedir perdón.

---

[1]**Poder** used in the preterit usually means *to manage to do something.*

      Pude hacerlo esta mañana.   *I managed to do it this morning.*

[2]**Saber** in the preterit normally means *to learn* or *to find out.*

      Supe que llegaron anoche.   *I learned that you arrived last night.*

7-27 ¿Qué hizo Ud. ayer? Imagínese que ayer usted hizo una lista de cosas que tenía que hacer, pero sólo pudo hacer dos o tres. Marque lo que hizo y lo que no pudo hacer, y después conteste las preguntas de su compañero/a.

MODELO: comprar el trofeo para el campeonato
        E1: ¿Compraste el trofeo para el campeonato?
        E2: Quise comprarlo, pero no pude. o
            Sí, pude comprarlo.
        E1: ¿Por qué no pudiste comprarlo?
            Porque tuve que regresar a una práctica en el laboratorio.

	Sí	No
1. cambiar la chaqueta	_____	_____
2. comprar los zapatos de tenis	_____	_____
3. probarse el uniforme nuevo	_____	_____
4. conocer al nuevo entrenador	_____	_____
5. ver el video del último partido	_____	_____
6. comentar las estrategias del próximo partido	_____	_____

7-28 ¿Qué ocurrió? Expliquen qué le ocurrió a Javier el día de su cumpleaños. Den la mayor cantidad de información posible.

1.   2.   3.

4.   5.   6.

7-29 Unos días de descanso. Su compañero/a estuvo unos días en Argentina. Hágale preguntas sobre los siguientes puntos para saber más de su viaje.

1. lugares adonde fue
2. tiempo que estuvo fuera
3. cosas interesantes que hizo
4. los lugares que le gustaron más
5. si pudo hablar español y con quién(es)

SITUACIONES

1. **Role A.** You won a contest **(concurso)** to attend the soccer World Cup **(la Copa Mundial)**. Tell your friend that a) you won the contest and b) you went to the World Cup. Answer all his/her questions, giving as many details as possible.

   Role B. A friend tells you about the prize he/she won. Ask your friend a) how he/she found about the contest, b) how long he/she was away, c) how many games he/she attended, d) with whom he/she went, and e) details about the last game.

2. **Role A.** Imagine that yesterday you went to a sports event and had the opportunity to see and talk with your favorite sports star. Explain to a friend a) where you went, b) what happened and where, c) what you did when you saw this famous sports star, d) what he/she literally told you, and d) what happened finally.

   Role B. Your friend tells you that he/she saw a very famous sports star yesterday and that he/she had the opportunity to talk to him/her. Ask him/her questions about what happened and their conversation.

EN DIRECTO

To express interest and to ask for details:

¡No me digas! ¿Qué pasó? *You don't say! What happened?*

¡Cuenta, cuenta! *Tell me more!*

¿Y qué más pasó? *And what else happened?*

 ALGO MÁS

Hace, meaning *ago*

■ To indicate the time that has passed since an action was completed, use **hace** + *length of time* + **que** + *preterit tense*. If you begin the sentence with the preterit tense of the verb, do not use **que**.

Hace dos horas que llegaron.
Llegaron **hace** dos horas. } *They arrived two hours ago.*

Hace una hora **que** empezó el partido.
El partido empezó **hace** una hora. } *The game started an hour ago.*

¿Qué dice usted?

7-30 ¿Cuánto tiempo hace...? Seleccione la pregunta más lógica para cada situación. Más de una respuesta correcta puede ser posible.

1. Usted observa que Jorge López, su entrenador, corre dos horas sin parar (*nonstop*) y no se cansa. Usted le pregunta:
   a. Sr. López, ¿cuánto tiempo hace que usted empezó a correr?
   b. ¿Cuánto tiempo hace que usted puede correr tanto (*so much*), Sr. López?
   c. ¿Cuánto tiempo hace que no corre, Sr. López?

2. La semana pasada, usted vio un gran cambio en su ex compañero/a de cuarto. A diferencia del año pasado, ahora está más delgado/a y atlético/a, y parece más fuerte. Usted le pregunta:
   a. ¿Cuánto hace que comenzaste a practicar deportes?
   b. ¿Cuánto tiempo hace que no haces actividades físicas?
   c. ¿Cuánto tiempo hace que estás enfermo?

3. Isabel, una de las jugadoras de su equipo de baloncesto, hace un tiempo que no asiste a las prácticas. La entrenadora les pregunta a los miembros del equipo:
   a. ¿Cuándo fue la última vez que ustedes vieron a Isabel?
   b. ¿Cuánto tiempo hace que Isabel practicó por última vez?
   c. ¿Cuándo fue la última vez que nuestro equipo se reunió para practicar?

4. La persona que limpia el gimnasio desea limpiar los baños, pero no puede porque los jugadores todavía se están duchando. La persona le pregunta al primer jugador que sale del baño:
   a. ¿Cuánto tiempo hace que usted se duchó?
   b. ¿Cuánto tiempo hace que los jugadores empezaron a ducharse?
   c. ¿Cuánto tiempo hace que terminó el partido?

7-31 ¡A conocernos mejor! Para conocerlo/la mejor, su compañero/a quiere saber cuánto tiempo hace que usted hizo estas cosas. Responda con todos los detalles posibles.

MODELO: ganar el campeonato de tenis
E1: ¿Cuánto tiempo hace que ganaste el campeonato de tenis?
E2: Hace dos años. Fue un día extraordinario. Todos mis amigos me felicitaron, y después fuimos a un café a celebrar.

1. conocer a tu novio/a (esposo/a)
2. jugar al tenis, golf, etc. por primera vez
3. leer una buena revista de deportes
4. jugar vóleibol en la playa
5. ir a un estadio muy moderno
6. ver un partido de la Copa Mundial

7-32 Figuras del mundo de los deportes. Uno/a de ustedes va a hacer de reportero/a de una revista deportiva y otro/a va a escoger a uno/a de los deportistas de abajo. El/La reportero/a debe hacer por lo menos tres preguntas usando **hace.** El/La deportista debe contestar con los datos del/de la deportista que escogió. Después, cambien de papel.

SANDRA ORDÓÑEZ

NACIONALIDAD: chilena
FECHA DE NACIMIENTO: 22 de febrero de 1979
RÉCORD DEPORTIVO:
1. Copa Nacional de Tenis, 1997 (cuarto lugar)
2. Copa Davis, 1998 (ganadora de la copa)
3. Torneo femenino de tenis en Chile, 1998 (segundo lugar)
4. Copa Davis, 1999 (tercer lugar)

JORGE PEDRERO

NACIONALIDAD: uruguayo
FECHA DE NACIMIENTO: 18 de abril de 1965
RÉCORD DEPORTIVO:
1. Capitán del equipo en el Torneo Nacional de Vóleibol de 1990 a 1995
2. Marcó 14 puntos en el partido entre la selección de vóleibol uruguaya y la argentina, 1994
3. Premio al deportista del año en Uruguay, 1993
4. Entrenador del equipo juvenil de vóleibol de Montevideo, 1988–1990

MÓNICA BERNINI

NACIONALIDAD: argentina
FECHA DE NACIMIENTO: 20 de diciembre de 1976
RÉCORD DEPORTIVO:
1. Primer lugar en las competencias de esquí de Bariloche, 1992
2. Segundo lugar en la Competencia de Esquí Chile-Argentina, 1995
3. Finalista del equipo argentino de las Olimpiadas de Invierno, 1996
4. Ganadora de la Competencia Nacional de Esquí, 2001

FELIPE JIMÉNEZ

NACIONALIDAD: boliviano
FECHA DE NACIMIENTO: 18 de junio de 1972
RÉCORD DEPORTIVO:
1. Jugador del Año, 1994
2. Representante de la Comisión Deportiva de Bolivia, 1996
3. Segundo lugar en el Campeonato Interamericano de Golf, 1998
4. Primer lugar en el Campeonato Nacional de Golf, 2001

MOSAICOS

Escuchar

Differentiating facts from opinions

When you talk to a person or watch a television report, you have to differentiate between factual information and personal opinion. You may hear someone say, "Today temperatures will rise to 40° Celsius, so avoid exercising outside." Facts indicate that the temperature will rise to 40° Celsius. The rest of the statement is a personal opinion.

Antes de escuchar

7-33 Los deportes. In activity **7-34,** you will listen to a conversation between Armando and Pablo, two soccer players, discussing the results of the game they just played. Before you listen, write down in Spanish one statement of factual information you think they will make and one opinion they will provide.

Información concreta: _____

Opinión personal: _____

A escuchar

AUDIO **7-34** Now, listen to the conversation between Armando and Pablo and write down in Spanish three facts and three opinions the soccer players provided.

Información concreta: _____

_____

_____

Opinión personal: _____

_____

_____

Después de escuchar

7-35 ¿Y usted? Take turns asking and answering the following questions.

1. ¿Qué deportes practica la gente en su ciudad o región en el invierno? ¿Y en la primavera?
2. ¿Qué deportes practica usted en el invierno o la primavera? ¿Qué hace o no usted antes de practicar deportes? ¿Y después?
3. En su opinión, ¿cuál es el mejor equipo de fútbol americano? ¿Es su equipo favorito realmente un buen equipo?

Antes de escuchar

7-36 El atleta. In activity **7-37**, you will listen to a TV reporter interviewing Nicolás, an Argentinean skier, who discusses his recent stay in Bariloche. Before you listen, write down in Spanish one statement of factual information you think he will make about the slopes where the ski resort is located and one opinion about the people he may meet there.

Información concreta _____

Opinión personal _____

A escuchar

AUDIO **7-37** Now listen to Nicolás' interview and write down in Spanish three statements of factual information and three opinions Nicolás offered about the place and/or the people.

Información concreta: _____

_____

Opinión personal: _____

_____

Después de escuchar

7-38 ¿Y usted? Ask your partner questions to find out the following information.

1. deporte que practica y dónde lo practica
2. tiempo que hace que lo practica
3. atleta favorito/a en ese deporte y por qué

Conversar

Antes de conversar

7-39 ¿Fanáticos del deporte? Primero averigüen cuáles son los dos deportes favoritos de su grupo y, luego, completen la tabla con la información pertinente.

DEPORTE	INDIVIDUAL	EN GRUPO	LUGAR DONDE SE PRACTICA	CLIMA IDEAL PARA PRACTICARLO

A conversar

G **7-40 Canal "Deportes para todos".** Imagínense que ustedes son reporteros de "Deportes para todos", una estación de televisión dedicada a los deportes. Con la información que aparece en el mapa, hagan lo siguiente:

■ Preparen un informe del tiempo para la televisión en el que describen las condiciones del clima de hoy en cuatro ciudades hispanas en regiones diferentes: 1. en la costa del Atlántico, 2. en una zona de montañas, 3. en una región de clima muy frío, 4. en unas islas del Átlantico o del Pacífico. Indiquen para qué deportistas o aficionados es útil este informe del tiempo.

■ Incluyan el pronóstico del tiempo (*weather forecast*) para mañana.

■ Preséntenlo a la clase y contesten las preguntas de sus compañeros/as.

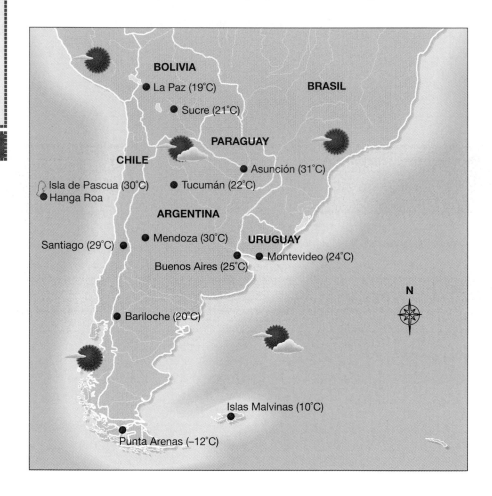

MODELO: Ahora canal "Deportes para todos" presenta el informe del tiempo para los aficionados al tenis. En este momento, en la ciudad de Tucumán, el cielo está un poco nublado y hace fresco. Los termómetros marcan 22 grados centígrados. Mañana va a estar despejado durante el día, con temperaturas entre los 24 y los 27 grados centígrados.

Después de conversar

(G) 7-41 Informe del tiempo en Internet. Ahora escriban el informe del tiempo que presentaron en la actividad **7-40** para los aficionados que consultan la página de Internet de "Deportes para todos". Pueden añadir imágenes si desean.

Antes de conversar

(G) 7-42 Historia de los deportes. En www.prenhall.com/mosaicos, busquen la siguiente información sobre uno de los deportes que se practican en Argentina, y tomen apuntes.

1. El nombre del deporte
2. Dos o tres datos históricos básicos sobre el deporte: a. cuándo empezó a practicarse, b. dónde empezó, c. algo interesante sobre los comienzos (*beginnings*) del deporte.
3. Un/a deportista argentino/a famoso/a en la historia de este deporte: a. nombre, fecha y lugar de nacimiento, b. datos sobre su carrera deportiva.

A conversar

(G) 7-43 Deportes y deportistas famosos. Hagan una presentación sobre el deporte que investigaron en la actividad **7-42** Usen la información que ya tienen u otra que deseen. Para hacer su presentación más interesante, pueden usar Internet o *Power Point*.

Después de conversar

7-44 Un/a deportista estrella (*star*). La revista *Deportes*, con la participación del público, va a seleccionar al deportista del año. Usted debe escribir la ficha (*personal history*) de uno de los deportistas nominados. Use la información de la actividad **7-42** y complete la ficha de este/a deportista famoso/a. Si quiere, puede incluir una foto.

> **EN DIRECTO**
>
> **To maintain the interest of listeners:**
> Hay hechos/ datos interesantes sobre...
> La información que tengo/ tenemos sobre... es increíble.
> ¡Imagínense! Ganó el primer puesto en...
> Este/a deportista juega (al...) como nadie.

Nombre: _____

Fecha de nacimiento: _____

Lugar de nacimiento: _____

Torneos/campeonatos en que participó:

_____

_____

Torneos/copas/campeonatos que ganó:

_____

_____

Dos razones para ser el/la deportista del año:

_____

_____

📖 *Leer*

In this chapter, you will read a text in Spanish and differentiate facts from opinions. Remember to apply any other specific reading strategies you have learned so far to accomplish your goals.

Guía de prelectura

Look at the visuals, skim the text in activity **7-45**, and answer the questions.

1. Looking at the visuals, using your knowledge of the Spanish language, and keeping in mind the theme of this lesson, can you anticipate the main theme of this text?
   a. places where sports can be practiced in Uruguay
   b. sports people admired in Uruguay
   c. Uruguayans love sports

2. Now, use your background knowledge and your knowledge of Spanish to comprehend the text. On what did you base your answers to question 1?
   a. cognates in the title   b. visuals in the text c. format of the text

3. Mark with a circle all the ideas that you anticipate will be covered in the text.
   a. sports frequently practiced in Uruguay
   b. sports originated in Uruguay
   c. places where sports may be practiced
   d. Uruguayan sports stars

Antes de leer

7-45 ¿Qué se necesita para practicarlo? Primera fase. Clasifiquen cada palabra en la columna correspondiente.

fútbol	pelota	guantes	esquí
esquiar	montañas	correr	jugar
botas	pista	dunas	bicicleta
surf en la arena	cancha	ciclismo	saltar

DEPORTE	MATERIAL DEPORTIVO	LUGAR DE PRÁCTICA	VERBO

Segunda fase. Ahora, respondan a estas preguntas.

1. ¿Les gustan los deportes individuales o prefieren los de equipo? ¿Por qué?
2. ¿Saben esquiar? ¿Esquían en la nieve o en el agua? ¿Esquían bien o regular?
3. ¿Hay buenos lugares donde se puede practicar surf acuático o en la arena en su país? ¿Dónde?

A leer

7-46 Primera mirada. Lea el siguiente artículo y, luego, siga las instrucciones.

LOS DEPORTES: UNA PASIÓN URUGUAYA

El Uruguay es un país pequeño donde los deportes forman una parte integral de la vida de la mayor parte de sus habitantes.

Entre las grandes pasiones nacionales, desde luego, está el fútbol. Desde su infancia, muchos uruguayos acompañan fielmente a sus
5 equipos predilectos. En varias ocasiones, la selección nacional uruguaya ganó títulos y campeonatos importantes.

Pero los uruguayos son un pueblo inquieto, de una personalidad versátil que no limita su interés a un solo deporte. El basquetbol, el ciclismo, el fútbol de salón, el rugby, el boxeo y la pelota de
10 mano son otros deportes que tienen muchos aficionados.

Las hermosas y privilegiadas playas del Uruguay también favorecen los deportes acuáticos, como el surf, que, según los expertos, cuenta hoy con un gran número de aficionados. En 1993 en Uruguay se formó la Unión de Surf del Uruguay (USU). Ese
15 mismo año, el país envió a sus representantes a competir internacionalmente en el Primer Campeonato Panamericano de Surf en Isla Margarita, Venezuela. Hoy en día la USU promueve el surf, arbitra las competencias clasificatorias a nivel nacional, apoya a los competidores nacionales, representa a Uruguay en
20 competencias internacionales y compite en los Juegos Olímpicos con la Selección Uruguaya de Surf.

Sin duda, uno de los lugares predilectos de los uruguayos y turistas extranjeros para practicar el surf es Punta del Este. Ubicada al sureste del Uruguay, a 140 kilómetros de Montevideo, Punta del
25 Este es una hermosa península de enormes playas, con arenas finas y gruesas, rocas y un entorno de bosques y médanos[1].

Precisamente en estos médanos nació, en el siglo pasado, una variante del surf que está despertando grandes polémicas en el país: el surf en la arena o sandsurf. Los brasileños inventaron este deporte
30 en los años ochenta para no aburrirse cuando no había olas. La agradable temperatura de las playas uruguayas, la escasez de olas que a veces impide practicar el surf en el agua y la formación arenosa de algunas playas aumentaron considerablemente el número de personas que practican el surf en la arena. Por ejemplo, los médanos
35 de Valizas son los más grandes de Sudamérica y los terceros más grandes del mundo, algunos con 30 metros de altura y una longitud de bajada[2] de aproximadamente 125 metros. Sin embargo, las autoridades uruguayas están controlando e incluso prohibiendo la práctica de este deporte por el posible deterioro ecológico que
40 ocasiona. No hay duda de que la prohibición del surf en la arena no va a detener el espíritu activo de los uruguayos. Su creatividad los incentivará a buscar o inventar otras opciones para entretenerse.

[1]*dunes* [2]*slope*

7-47 Opinión? Diga si las siguientes citas textuales (*quotations*) representan información concreta (C) o una opinión (O) del autor.

1. _____ "Desde su infancia, muchos uruguayos acompañan fielmente a sus equipos predilectos."

2. _____ "Pero los uruguayos son un pueblo inquieto, de una personalidad versátil que no limita su interés a un solo deporte."

3. _____ "En 1993 se formó la Unión de Surf del Uruguay (USU)."

4. _____ "Punta del Este es una hermosa península de enormes playas, con arenas finas y gruesas, rocas y un entorno de bosques y médanos."

5. _____ "La agradable temperatura de las playas uruguayas, la escasez de olas que a veces impide practicar el surf sobre el agua y la formación arenosa de algunas playas aumentaron considerablemente el número de adeptos al surf en la arena."

6. _____ "No hay duda de que la prohibición del surf en la arena no va a detener el espíritu activo de los uruguayos."

7-48 Segunda mirada. Lea el artículo otra vez y, según la información que aparece en él, haga lo siguiente:

1. Indique dos razones que explican la popularidad del fútbol en Uruguay.
2. Diga por qué los uruguayos tienen un carácter inquieto.
3. Nombre tres deportes que se juegan en equipo, dos que son principalmente deportes individuales, y uno que no requiere una pelota.
4. Dé dos razones para explicar por qué Punta del Este le ofrece al/a la surfista acuático/a un lugar ideal para practicar su deporte.
5. Explique dos hechos que provocaron el nacimiento del surf en la arena.
6. En su opinión, ¿deben prohibir el surf en la arena? ¿Por qué?

Después de leer

G **7-49 ¡Adivinen cuál es el deporte!** Preparen una hoja descriptiva sobre el deporte favorito del grupo sin mencionar el nombre del deporte. Den la siguiente información e intercambien su hoja con otro grupo que debe adivinar cuál es el deporte.

1. Lugar donde se practica
2. Deporte individual o en grupo (número de personas en el equipo)
3. Clima ideal para practicarlo: Se practica en invierno/en... /cuando hace..., etc.
4. Un/a jugador/a famoso de este deporte
5. Su opinión sobre el/la jugador/a

 Escribir

Writing for a broader, impersonal audience about a specific subject requires special attention to the content about which you write, the amount of information you include, the use or avoidance of technical language, and the degree of objectivity and subjectivity of your text.

Readers of sports magazines are generally sports-oriented and knowledgeable about one or more sports. To write for such an audience of 'experts,' you should:

- Anticipate the kind of information your readers may know or may need.
- Use words specific to the sport.
- Use agile language that reflects the vitality of sports activities: action verbs, brief sentences, words that show intensity (adverbs), etc.
- Differentiate sports facts from people's opinions

7-50 Enfoque. Primera fase. Lea el siguiente informe deportivo y siga las instrucciones.

13 de abril

Copa América: Argentina vence a Uruguay 4-2

Argentina derrotó a Uruguay por 4-2 y se clasificó en la Copa América como segunda del Grupo B.

Fabián Estoyanoff marcó sorpresivamente un gol para Uruguay a los 7 minutos. Pero a los 19 minutos, Cristián González, del cuadro argentino, marcó un gol de penal y luego, Luciano Figueroa marcó otro gol magistral a los 20 minutos. Vicente Sánchez igualó a los 37 minutos para el equipo uruguayo. Argentina definió el partido con los goles de Roberto Ayala, a los 80 minutos, y otra vez Figueroa, a los 89 minutos.

El árbitro expulsó a un jugador uruguayo por mala conducta.

El partido fue desordenado y rudo, pero muy emocionante. Unos 23.000 espectadores llegaron muy temprano al estadio "Miguel Grau" para acompañar a sus equipos. Rubén Selman arbitró impecablemente el partido.

Segunda fase. Answer the following questions, based on the sports report.

1. Mark with an X the main idea of the report.
   _____ Uruguay and Argentina were finalists in the World Soccer Cup.
   _____ Argentina beat Uruguay in the Cup America.
   _____ Uruguay defeated Argentina in the Cup America.

2. Is this sports report effective?   Yes   No

3. Mark some possible reasons for your response to question 2.
   _____ Reporter narrates the sports event chronologically.
   _____ There is no chronology in the report.
   _____ Reporter provides a detailed description of what went on during the game.
   _____ Reporter uses words specific to soccer.
   _____ The report uses action verbs, brief sentences, words that show intensity.
   _____ The report is objective, that is, it informs the reader about facts of the game.

Antes de escribir

7-51 Preparación. Primera fase. En www.prenhall.com/mosaicos busque una noticia sobre un evento deportivo. Léala y anote lo siguiente:

1. el tipo de evento: un partido, un torneo, una competencia entre instituciones, un campeonato, una copa, etc.
2. dónde y cuándo ocurrió.
3. nombres de los/las deportistas, equipos, árbitros que participaron.
4. información concreta sobre el evento: ¿Quién ganó? ¿Cuál fue el puntaje (*score*)? ¿Batieron (*break*) un récord? ¿Quiénes fueron los deportistas sobresalientes (*outstanding*) en el evento?

Segunda fase. Prepárese para escribir un informe deportivo. Haga lo siguiente:

1. Haga una lista de palabras clave para su informe: nombres, verbos, adjetivos, adverbios, etc. Recuerde que debe usar palabras específicas del deporte.
2. Ordene cronológicamente los hechos del evento de la **Primera fase.**
3. Imagínese que usted fue uno de los espectadores. Escriba su opinión sobre el evento: ¿Le gustó el partido? ¿Le pareció sorprendente el puntaje? ¿Le gustó el árbitro? ¿Y los jugadores? ¿Cómo reaccionaron los aficionados?

A escribir

7-52 Manos a la obra. Usted es un/a periodista deportivo/a para la revista *Deportes del milenio.* Esta revista va a tener una página en la red, y usted va a ser la persona responsable de informar a los lectores sobre las noticias deportivas. Usando la información que recogió en **7-51, Segunda fase,** escriba su primer informe. Incluya lo siguiente:

1. información concreta sobre un evento deportivo en un país hispano
2. la reacción de los espectadores durante y después del evento
3. la opinión de los expertos o su opinión sobre el evento deportivo

Después de escribir

7-53 Revisión. Antes de presentar su proyecto, revise:

■ la claridad y cantidad de información presentada. Recuerde que los informes deportivos por lo general son breves

■ el vocabulario general y vocabulario especializado, la estructuras que utilizó para narrar cronológicamente el evento y la concordancia

■ las expresiones para introducir su opinión o la de otras personas

■ la ortografía y la acentuación

EN DIRECTO

To report factual information about a past sports event:

Los/las jugadores/as hicieron/ marcaron/corrieron, etc.

En realidad, el árbitro, el/la entrenador/a, el/la jugador/a número... , etc.

Asistieron... personas.

To express an opinion about an event:

Según...

En mi opinión, ...

Me parece que...

Sin duda, ...

ENFOQUE CULTURAL

TEMAS: EL FÚTBOL Y LOS DEPORTES

Para pensar

¿Cuáles son algunos de los deportes favoritos en los Estados Unidos? ¿Qué deportes practica usted? ¿Y sus amigos/as? Piense en dos o tres deportes que se practican en su universidad.

El béisbol es uno de los deportes más populares del área del Caribe, especialmente en Cuba, Venezuela, la República Dominicana y Puerto Rico. Sammy Sosa es un famoso beisbolista dominicano.

El deporte más popular de Latinoamérica es el fútbol. Los partidos de fútbol tienen siempre muchos aficionados que animan a sus equipos favoritos.

El polo es otro deporte muy popular en Argentina y en Uruguay. El equipo nacional argentino ganó varios campeonatos mundiales. Uno de los jugadores de polo más conocidos es Nicolás Scortichini.

Para contestar

Los deportes. Conteste las siguientes preguntas.

1. ¿Qué deportes se practican más en España e Hispanoamérica? ¿Qué deportes piensa usted que no se practican? ¿Por qué?
2. ¿Cuáles son los deportes favoritos de los países hispanohablantes? ¿Dónde los practican?

Riqueza cultural. Mencionen a dos famosos/as futbolistas, tenistas y beisbolistas españoles o hispanoamericanos. Digan de qué país son y, si es posible, en qué equipo(s) juegan.

Los españoles y los hispanoamericanos también disfrutan del ciclismo. Además de importantes competencias, hay muchas excursiones a lugares de interés turístico y ecológico organizadas para los aficionados de este deporte.

Para pensar

¿Qué sabe usted acerca de Argentina y Uruguay? ¿Sabe usted dónde están? ¿Qué lugares de interés hay en estos países?

Argentina y Uruguay están en la costa oriental de América del Sur. Ambos países tienen una intensa vida intelectual y cultural.

Montevideo, la capital de Uruguay, es una ciudad moderna con un centro histórico que data de la época colonial. Precisamente, una de las ciudades más importantes del Uruguay se llama Colonia, y es famosa por su diseño y arquitectura. Montevideo, en cambio, está rodeada de hermosas playas.

En Montevideo se puede disfrutar de tiendas, museos, cafés, mercados y ferias. Por ejemplo, se puede visitar el Mercado del Puerto y la Avenida 18 de julio, donde hay muchas tiendas, teatros, museos y galerías de arte. De especial interés es el Museo del Gaucho, donde se puede apreciar todo lo relacionado con los gauchos, es decir, los vaqueros (cowboys) típicos de Uruguay y Argentina.

Expresiones uruguayas:

fenómeno	¡La pasé **fenómeno**!	*I had a great time!*
chiquilín/a	¡Mi **chiquilín** es muy tranquilo!	*My kid is very quiet!*
irse embalado	¡Se fue **embalado**!	*He/she left in a hurry!*
salvar/perder el examen	Mario **salvó el examen** de español, pero José lo **perdió**.	*Mario passed his Spanish exam, but José flunked it.*

Buenos Aires, la capital de Argentina, tiene un aire muy europeo, con amplios parques, anchas avenidas y altos edificios.

La amistad tiene gran importancia en la vida de los porteños, que es como se llama a las personas que nacieron en Buenos Aires. Por eso, los numerosos cafés de la ciudad están siempre llenos de personas que se reúnen a conversar mientras toman un delicioso cortado (café con crema) acompañado de una medialuna (un croissant pequeño).

Bariloche, a las orillas del lago Nahuel Huapi, es el lugar ideal para las personas a las que les gusta esquiar.

Expresiones argentinas:

ché	Ché, Martita, ¿dónde está mi camisa?	Hey, Martita, where is my shirt?
mandarse la parte	¡No te mandes la parte!	Don't brag!
laburo	Siempre salgo temprano para el laburo.	I always leave early to go to my job.
morocho/a	Isabel es morocha.	Isabel is brunnette.

Una de las características geográficas más distintivas de Argentina es la pampa. Estas enormes extensiones de tierra (land) llana y fértil constituyen una de las bases de la economía argentina.

Para contestar

En el mapa

1. Busque tres ciudades de Argentina y tres ciudades de Uruguay y diga dónde están situadas.
2. Diga qué países están al oeste, norte y este de Argentina.
3. Diga qué países están al este y norte de Uruguay.

Ahora diga...

1. por qué puede ser interesante ir a Montevideo o a Punta del Este.
2. qué lugar de interés le gustaría visitar en Argentina y por qué.

¿Qué dice Ud. si...

1. su amigo uruguayo sacó una mala nota en el examen final de biología.
2. Ud. no quiere ir a su trabajo hoy.
3. pasó momentos muy divertidos en una fiesta con sus compañeros/as.

Para investigar en Internet

Busque el nombre de dos equipos de fútbol de Uruguay y dos equipos de Argentina. Traiga esta información a clase y hable con sus compañeros/as sobre el último partido que jugaron, dónde jugaron, contra quién jugaron, quién ganó y cuál fue el puntaje.

¡Prepárese!

7-54 La honestidad. En el Episodio 7 aparece el tema de la honestidad o, mejor dicho, la falta de ella. Carlos está muy molesto por las acciones de Katie y empieza a dudar de su honestidad. La lista siguiente contiene algunas palabras importantes de este episodio. Indique sus equivalentes en inglés.

a. decepcionar
b. la mentira
c. la integridad
d. competitivo/a
e. el/la traidor/a

_____ *traitor*
_____ *competitive*
_____ *to deceive, cheat*
_____ *lie*
_____ *integrity*

Ángela no quiere perder su trabajo.

Katie y Carlos van al Museo Nacional de Antropología.

¡Sabrina y Efraín ganaron la primera fortuna!

Carlos tiene dudas sobre la honestidad de Katie.

Carlos no quiere entrevistarse con Tito.

Ahora Ángela está muy contenta.

¡Responda!

7-55 Comparaciones. Usando las palabras de la lista en ejercicio 7-54, escriba oraciones completas en español, comparándose con los personajes de *Fortunas*. ¿Es usted como ellos o diferente?

MODELO: Katie dice mentiras y yo también. *o*
                Katie dice mentiras pero yo digo la verdad.

Esta canción moderna combina estilos musicales españoles y latinoamericanos como el flamenco, la salsa y la música tropical en un ritmo alegre y positivo.

¡Prepárese!

7-56 El título. ¿Puede adivinar lo que significa "Huracán", el título de la canción? En su opinión, ¿cuáles pueden ser algunos temas?

¡Escuche!

7-57 La letra. Mientras escucha la canción lea las palabras siguientes e indique sus equivalentes en inglés. Use un diccionario bilingüe si es necesario.

a. sentimiento _____ *kisses*
b. alma _____ *heaven*
c. fuego _____ *feeling*
d. besos _____ *fire*
e. cielo _____ *soul*

Ahora que conoce mejor la canción, ¿cuáles son sus ideas sobre el tema?

"Huracán"

Aunque digan lo que digan

No me importa el qué dirán
Sólo basta una mirada

Y desato un huracán

[...]

No me importa qué murmuren
Porque soy un huracán

¡Responda!

7-58 Las expresiones. Muchos países tienen expresiones populares que se usan coloquialmente y que pueden variar de país a país y de región a región. En "Huracán" la cantante dice que no le importa "el qué dirán", lo que dice la gente o el chisme (*gossip*). La lista siguiente contiene otras expresiones en español, léalas e indique sus equivalentes en inglés.

a. tener mala cara _____ *to keep one's word*
b. ser tal para cual _____ *to be sophisticated*
c. tener palabra _____ *two of a kind*
d. en un dos por tres _____ *to look bad*
e. tener mundo _____ *in a second/right away*

7-59 Más expresiones. Ahora indique los equivalentes en inglés de las siguientes expresiones en español.

a. ¡Salud! _____ *First rate!*
b. ¡Del uno! _____ *Nonsense!*
c. ¡Venga ya! _____ *All right!*
d. ¡Qué va! _____ *Cheers!*
e. ¡Vaya! _____ *Come off it!*

7-60 Ahora usted. Escriba una lista de expresiones populares de su país o región y luego intercambie su lista con la de un/a compañero/a. ¿Hay semejanzas? ¿Hay diferencias?

VOCABULARIO

AUDIO Deportes

el baloncesto/basquetbol	*basketball*
el béisbol	*baseball*
los bolos	*bowling*
el ciclismo	*cycling*
el esquí	*skiing, ski*
el fútbol	*soccer*
el tenis	*tennis*
el voleibol	*volleyball*

Equipo deportivo

el bate	*bat*
el/la cesto/a	*basket, hoop*
los palos	*golf clubs*
la pelota	*ball*
la raqueta	*racket*
la red	*net*

Eventos

el campeonato	*championship*
la carrera	*race*
el juego/partido	*game*
el torneo	*tournament*

Lugares

la cancha	*court, golf course*
el campo	*field*
la pista	*slope, court, track*

Personas

el/la aficionado/a	*fan*
el árbitro	*umpire, referee*
el campeón/la campeona	*champion*
el/la ciclista	*cyclist*
el/la entrenador/a	*coach*
el equipo	*team*
el/la jugador/a	*player*
el/la tenista	*tennis player*

Naturaleza

el árbol	*tree*
la atmósfera	*atmosphere*
la flor	*flower*
el lago	*lake*

Tiempo

despejado/a	*clear*
fresco/a	*cool*
el hielo	*ice*
la lluvia	*rain*
la nieve	*snow*
nublado/a	*cloudy*
el sol	*sun*
el viento	*wind*

Descripciones

contaminado/a	*polluted, contaminated*
contrario/a	*opposite, contrary*
emocionado/a	*excited*
mejor	*best*
mundial	*worldwide*

Verbos

acostar (ue)	*to put to bed*
acostar(se)	*to go to bed, to lie down*
afeitar(se)	*to shave*
aplaudir	*to applaud*
aprovechar	*to take advantage*
competir (i)	*to compete*
congelar(se)	*to freeze*
despertar(se) (ie)	*to wake up*
discutir	*to argue*
dormirse (ue)	*to fall asleep*
durar	*to last*
esquiar	*to ski*
ganar	*to win*
ir(se)	*to go away, to leave*
jugar a los bolos	*to bowl*
lavar(se) los dientes	*to brush one's teeth*
levantar	*to raise*
llover (ue)	*to rain*
maquillar(se)	*to put on makeup*
nevar (ie)	*to snow*
participar	*to participate*
patinar	*to skate*
perder (ie)	*to lose*
quitar	*to take away, to remove*
quitar(se)	*to take off*
representar	*to represent*
sentar(se) (ie)	*to sit down*
traducir (zc)	*to translate*

Palabras y expresiones útiles

cada	*each*
conmigo	*with me*
contigo	*with you* (familiar)
estar de acuerdo	*to agree*
el fin	*end*
Hace calor.	*It's hot.*
¿Qué tiempo hace?	*What's the weather like?*
sin	*without*

FIESTAS Y TRADICIONES

Objetivos comunicativos

- ❖ Talking about holiday activities
- ❖ Expressing ongoing actions in the past
- ❖ Extending, accepting, and declining invitations
- ❖ Making comparisons

Contenido

A primera vista

- Fiestas y tradiciones
- Otras celebraciones

Explicación y expansión

- The imperfect
- Imperfect of regular and irregular verbs
- The preterit and the imperfect
- Comparisons of inequality
- Comparisons of equality
- The superlative

Mosaicos

- Escuchar: Making inferences
- Conversar: Comparing experiences; narrating
- Leer: Identifying information stated in a text; making inferences
- Escribir: Narrating a real or an imaginary experience or event

Enfoque cultural

- Temas: La religión
- Vistas: México y Guatemala
  Para investigar en Internet
- Fortunas: Episodio 8
- Notas: El Chapo, *Los Originales de San Juan*

Vocabulario

Fiestas y tradiciones

AUDIO Estas **carretas** adornadas "**hicieron el camino**" para llegar a El Rocío, un pequeño **pueblo** de la provincia de Huelva, en España, donde está la Ermita de la Virgen del Rocío. En el pueblo **se reúnen** cada año cerca de un millón de personas para celebrar la fiesta de la Virgen del Rocío.

El Día de los **Muertos**, también conocido como el Día de los Difuntos, se conmemora el 2 de noviembre y muchas familias van al **cementerio** ese día o el día anterior para recordar y llevarles **flores** a sus familiares o amigos **difuntos**. Especialmente en México, los preparativos para el día de los muertos **comienzan** con mucha anterioridad y hay familias que pasan la noche del primero al 2 de noviembre acompañando a sus muertos en el cementerio, como se ve en esta foto tomada en Pátzcuaro.

Las fiestas y los bailes que se celebran ayudan a mantener las **costumbres** de los **antepasados**. La diablada es uno de los festivales folclóricos con más colorido en Hispanoamérica. Se celebra durante el carnaval de Oruro en Bolivia y también en el norte de Chile y otros países, entre ellos, Perú.

La música, el baile y la **alegría** reinan en los **carnavales.** Hay **carrozas** y **comparsas** que bailan en las calles, muchas personas **se disfrazan** y todo el mundo **se divierte.** El último día de Carnaval es el martes **antes** del **comienzo** de la Cuaresma.

Ésta es una de las procesiones de Semana Santa en la Antigua Guatemala. Esta ciudad fue la **antigua** capital de Guatemala y es famosa por su arquitectura colonial y las **maravillosas** alfombras que se hacen con flores, semillas y aserrín para el paso de las procesiones.

El día de **San Fermín,** el 7 de julio, se inicia la celebración de los **sanfermines** en Pamplona. Esta celebración, que dura del 7 al 14 de julio, es famosa mundialmente por **los** "encierros". Los jóvenes corren por las calles seguidos de los **toros,** hasta llegar a la **plaza** donde encierran a los toros y más tarde tienen lugar las corridas.

CULTURA

Los hispanos y los norteamericanos tienen muchas fiestas y celebraciones diferentes. Por ejemplo, el Día de Acción de Gracias (*Thanksgiving*) no se celebra en los países hispanos y tampoco es tradicional el Día de las Brujas (*Halloween*), aunque se está comenzando a celebrar en algunas ciudades de Hispanoamérica. Por otro lado, debido a la importancia e influencia de la religión católica en los países hispanos, algunas fiestas religiosas se consideran también fiestas oficiales. Pero lo más importante es la gran diversidad de fiestas locales. Muchas personas trabajan todo el año para garantizar el éxito de estas celebraciones, en las que la gente baila y se divierte durante días enteros.

AUDIO Días y fechas importantes

la Nochebuena

la Navidad

la Nochevieja

el Año Nuevo

el Día de la Independencia

la Pascua

el Día de la Madre

el Día del Padre

el Día de Acción de Gracias

el Día de las Brujas

el Día de los Enamorados/del Amor y la Amistad

¿Qué dice usted?

8-1 Asociaciones. Primera fase. Asocien las fechas de la izquierda con los días festivos de la derecha.

1. _____ el 25 de diciembre
2. _____ el 2 de noviembre
3. _____ el 6 de enero
4. _____ el 4 de julio
5. _____ el 24 de diciembre
6. _____ el 31 de diciembre
7. _____ el 14 de febrero
8. _____ el 31 de octubre

a. el Día de la Independencia de los Estados Unidos
b. el Día de las Brujas
c. la Nochebuena
d. la Nochevieja, el fin de año
e. el Día de los Enamorados, del Amor y la Amistad
f. el Día de los Reyes Magos
g. el Día de los Muertos
h. la Navidad

Segunda fase. En grupos pequeños, comenten:

■ cuál(es) de estas fiestas celebra cada uno de ustedes.

■ cuál es la predilecta de la mayoría de las personas del grupo, y por qué.

8-2 Festivales o desfiles. Piense en algunos festivales o desfiles (*parades*) importantes y complete el cuadro. Su compañero/a va a hacerle preguntas sobre ellos.

MODELO: E1: ¿En qué fiesta o desfile importante estás pensando?
E2: En el Cinco de Mayo
E1: ¿Dónde lo celebran?
E2: En México y en algunas ciudades de los Estados Unidos, como Austin, Texas.

FESTIVAL	FECHA	LUGAR	DESCRIPCIÓN	OPINIÓN

8-3 Unos días festivos. Hablen sobre cómo celebran ustedes estas fechas.

MODELO: E1: ¿Cómo celebras tu cumpleaños?
E2: Lo celebro con mi familia y mis amigos. Recibo regalos, y mi madre prepara mi comida favorita con pastel de chocolate de postre. Después escuchamos música, conversamos, y a veces bailamos.

1. la Nochevieja, el Fin de Año
2. la Navidad
3. el Día de Acción de Gracias
4. el Día de la Independencia
5. el Año Nuevo
6. el Día de la Madre

8-4 Una celebración importante. Primera fase. Con su compañero/a escojan una celebración importante del mundo hispano (Carnaval, Semana Santa, Año Nuevo, La Diablada, Día de la Independencia, etc.) y busquen información en Internet sobre:

1. lugar
2. época del año
3. forma en que se celebra

G **Segunda fase.** Imagínense que usted y su compañero/a estuvieron en un país hispano durante la celebración sobre la que investigaron en la **Primera fase.** Explíquenles a otros/as dos compañeros/as dónde estuvieron, qué fiesta celebraron y qué hicieron. Sus compañeros les van a hacer preguntas para obtener más información o aclarar algo que no comprendieron.

Otras celebraciones

AUDIO Una invitación a cenar

SRA. MENA: Pedro, tenemos que **invitar** a los Sosa a cenar.

SR. MENA: Es verdad. Ellos nos invitaron el mes pasado. ¿Por qué no los llamas ahora? Podemos reunirnos este fin de semana o el próximo.

(Unos minutos más tarde, las dos señoras hablan por teléfono.)

SRA. MENA: ¿Pueden cenar con nosotros el sábado?

SRA. SOSA: ¡Ay, María! Lo siento muchísimo, pero este sábado tenemos entradas para el **teatro.**

SRA. MENA: Ah, **¡qué lástima!** ¿Y el sábado 15?

SRA. SOSA: **Encantados.** Tenemos muchos deseos de verlos.

SRA. MENA: Y nosotros también.

EN DIRECTO

To accept an invitation:
Gracias. Me encanta la idea.
Con mucho gusto.
Encantado/a.
Será un placer.

To apologize:
Me gustaría ir, pero...
¡Qué lástima/pena! Ese día tengo que...
No puedo, tengo un compromiso.

8-5 Una invitación. Primera fase. Completen el siguiente cuadro según la conversación de la señora Mena y la señora Sosa.

FECHAS DE LAS INVITACIONES	EXPRESIONES QUE USA LA SRA. SOSA
primera invitación:	para disculparse por no aceptar:
segunda invitación:	para aceptar la invitación:

Segunda fase. Ahora invite a su compañero/a a cenar, o a ir al teatro o a un partido importante. Después, su compañero/a va a invitarlo/la a usted. Además de las expresiones del diálogo, pueden usar las de la tabla.

Celebraciones personales

La boda del príncipe Felipe, en mayo de 2004, fue un gran acontecimiento histórico y social que millones de hispanos pudieron ver por televisión. En los países hispanos, el padrino de la boda es la persona que acompaña a la novia al altar y generalmente es su padre. La madrina está en el altar con el novio y normalmente es su madre.

8-6 Una invitación de boda. Lean la invitación de boda y la de la recepción, y contesten las preguntas. Luego preparen una lista con las diferencias que encuentran ustedes entre estas invitaciones y las de este país.

Pedro Martín Salda
Juana Montoya de Martín

Eduardo Calderón Solís
Elisa Noriega de Calderón

participan el matrimonio de sus hijos

Estelita
y
Alberto

y tienen el honor de invitarle a la ceremonia religiosa que se celebrará el viernes 9 de febrero, a las diecinueve treinta horas en el Convento de San Joaquín, Santa Cruz Cocalco N° 15, Legaria, dignándose impartir la bendición nupcial el R.P. José Ortuño S.J.
Ciudad de México, 2001

Agradecemos su presencia después de la ceremonia religiosa en el Club de Golf Chapultepec Av. Conscripto N° 425, Lomas Hipódromo

R.S.V.P.
529-99-43
520-16-85

Personal

1. ¿Cómo se llaman los padres de la novia? ¿Y los del novio?
2. ¿Cómo se llaman los novios?
3. ¿Qué día es la boda?
4. ¿A qué hora es?
5. ¿En qué país se celebra esta boda?
6. ¿Adónde van a ir los invitados después de la ceremonia?

CULTURA

La monarquía constitucional española es una de las más antiguas de Europa. Hoy en día la familia real es muy popular en el mundo hispano. El rey Juan Carlos I y la reina Sofía tienen tres hijos: Elena, Cristina y Felipe, Príncipe de Asturias y heredero del trono. Recientemente, el príncipe Felipe se casó con la periodista Letizia Ortiz.

Para obtener más información sobre los reyes de España vaya a www.prenhall.com/mosaicos.

CULTURA

Los mariachis son grupos musicales de México que cantan y tocan violines, guitarras, guitarrones, trompetas y vihuelas. Muchos creen que la palabra "mariachi" viene del francés *mariage*, que significa "boda". En la época colonial, el novio contrataba estas bandas para festejar a la novia la noche de la boda. Otros opinan que "mariachi" proviene de una palabra indígena que designa la plataforma donde se paraban los músicos para tocar.

2 **8-7 Un día especial.** Lean la invitación y contesten las preguntas.

Nuestro querido hijo

David

será llamado a la lectura de la Tora
con motivo de su Bar Mitzvah
el jueves 18 de noviembre de 2004
a las ocho de la mañana en la Sinagoga
Centro Hebreo, Avenida 13-15 Zona 9.

Nos sentiremos muy honrados en compartir
con ustedes tan memorable ocasión
y será un placer recibirles en el desayuno
que seguidamente ofreceremos en el
salón de fiestas de la sinagoga.

David y Ruth Bauman

Fax: (502) 238-2042
Ciudad de Guatemala, Guatemala

1. ¿Cuál es el motivo de la celebración?
2. ¿Qué día es la celebración? ¿A qué hora?
3. ¿Hay algo, además de la celebración religiosa?
4. ¿Quiénes son David y Ruth Bauman?
5. ¿En qué país tiene lugar esta celebración?

2 **8-8 Una fiesta especial.** Individualmente piensen en una celebración o fiesta en la que cada uno participó recientemente. Luego, explíquense cómo fue esa fiesta. Incluyan detalles sobre el número de invitados, el lugar, el menú, la música, cuánto costó todo, etc.

AUDIO **8-9 Fiestas y tradiciones.** You will listen to four short dialogues about different holidays celebrated in the Hispanic world. Before you listen, write down the names of two holidays that you have studied or read about in this chapter.

_____

_____

Now, pay attention to the general idea of what is said. Then, as you listen, identify the holiday each conversation refers to by writing the appropriate conversation number next to it.

_____ el día del amor y la amistad, día de los enamorados
_____ el día de los muertos
_____ el día de los reyes magos
_____ el día de las brujas

1. The imperfect

Antes la música **era** más suave y romántica. **Tenía** más **melodía** y las **orquestas eran** magníficas.

Hoy en día no hay música; hay sólo **ruido,** y la gente se mueve mucho para bailar.

Antes las familias **hablaban** y **había** más **seguridad** en las calles.

Y seguro que tu abuela decía lo mismo de los niños.

Ahora es horrible. Hay mucha **violencia,** mucha **droga,** mucho **sexo,** y los niños no **respetan** a las personas mayores.

■ So far you have seen two ways of talking about the past in Spanish: the preterit and the imperfect. In the preceding monolog, the grandmother used the imperfect because she was focusing on what used to happen when she was young. If she had been focusing on the fact that an action was completed, like something she did yesterday, she would have used the preterit. Generally, the imperfect is used to:

1. express habitual or repeated actions in the past.

> Nosotros **íbamos** a la playa todos los días.
>
> *We used to go to the beach every day.*

2. express an action or state that was in progress in the past.

> Agustín **estaba** muy contento y **hablaba** de sus planes con su hermana.
>
> *Agustín was very happy and was talking about his plans with his sister.*

3. describe characteristics and conditions in the past.

La casa **era** blanca y **tenía** dos dormitorios.	*The house was white and it had two bedrooms.*

4. tell time in the past.

Era la una de la tarde; no **eran** las dos.	*It was one in the afternoon; it was not two.*

5. tell age in the past.

Ella **tenía** quince años entonces.	*She was fifteen years old then.*

■ Some time expressions that often accompany the imperfect to express ongoing or repeated actions or states in the past are **mientras, a veces, siempre, generalmente,** and **frecuentemente.**

2. Imperfect of regular and irregular verbs

REGULAR IMPERFECT			
	HABLAR	COMER	VIVIR
yo	hablaba	comía	vivía
tú	hablabas	comías	vivías
Ud., él, ella	hablaba	comía	vivía
nosotros/as	hablábamos	comíamos	vivíamos
vosotros/as	hablabais	comíais	vivíais
Uds., ellos/as	hablaban	comían	vivían

■ Note that the endings for **-er** and **-ir** verbs are the same. All these forms have a written accent over the **í** of the ending: comía, vivías.

■ The Spanish imperfect has several English equivalents.

Mis amigos bailaban mucho.
$\left\{\begin{array}{l}\textit{My friends danced a lot.}\\ \textit{My friends were dancing a lot.}\\ \textit{My friends used to dance a lot.}\\ \textit{My friends would dance a lot.}\\ \text{(implying a repeated action)}\end{array}\right.$

■ There are no stem changes in the imperfect.

Ella no d**ue**rme bien ahora, pero antes d**o**rmía muy bien.
She does not sleep well now, but she used to sleep very well before.

■ Only three verbs are irregular in the imperfect.

ir	iba, ibas, iba, íbamos, ibais, iban
ser	era, eras, era, éramos, erais, eran
ver	veía, veías, veía, veíamos, veíais, veían

■ The imperfect form of **hay** is **había** (*there was, there were, there used to be*). Both forms remain invariable.

Había una invitación en el correo.	*There was an invitation in the mail.*
Había muchas personas en la fiesta.	*There were many people at the party.*

¿Qué dice usted?

8-10 Cuando tenía cinco años. Primera fase. Marque cuáles eran sus actividades cuando usted tenía cinco años.

1. _____ Jugaba en el parque con mi perro.
2. _____ Ayudaba a mi mamá en la casa.
3. _____ Salía con mis padres los fines de semana.
4. _____ Iba a la playa en el verano.
5. _____ Miraba televisión hasta muy tarde.
6. _____ Celebraba el año nuevo con mis amigos.
7. _____ Asistía a las fiestas de la familia.
8. _____ ...

Segunda fase. Comparen sus respuestas y, luego, respondan a estas preguntas.

1. ¿Quién de ustedes miraba más televisión?
2. ¿Quién de ustedes tenía una vida más activa? ¿Por qué?

8-11 En la escuela secundaria. Primera fase. Marque en el cuadro la frecuencia con que usted y sus amigos/as hacían estas cosas. Después compare sus respuestas con las de su compañero/a.

MODELO: leer muchos libros
Siempre (frecuentemente/a veces/nunca) leíamos muchos libros.

ACTIVIDADES	SIEMPRE	FRECUENTEMENTE	A VECES	NUNCA
practicar deportes				
bailar mucho en las fiestas				
ir a los partidos de fútbol				
asistir a conciertos				
reunirse con amigos en el cine				

Segunda fase. Formen pequeños grupos para hablar de lo siguiente:

1. ¿Cuál era la actividad que realizaban con menos frecuencia o nunca? ¿Por qué?
2. ¿Cuáles eran las dos actividades que realizaban con más frecuencia? ¿Por qué?

8-12 Entrevista. Háganse las siguientes preguntas para saber cómo era la vida de cada uno/a cuando era pequeño/a.

1. ¿Dónde vivías, y con quién?
2. ¿A qué escuela ibas?
3. ¿Quién era tu mejor amigo/a? ¿Cómo era?
4. ¿Qué deportes practicabas?
5. ¿Qué programas de televisión veías?
6. ¿Qué te gustaba hacer en tu tiempo libre?

8-13 Mi casa. Descríbale a su compañero/a cómo era la casa o apartamento donde usted vivía cuando era niño/a. Después, su compañero/a debe hacer lo mismo.

8-14 Las fiestas infantiles. Comenten cómo eran las fiestas de cumpleaños y el día de las brujas cuando eran pequeños/as. Incluyan los siguientes puntos:

- lugar de la celebración
- horas (comienzo y final)
- actividades
- personas que participaban
- comida y bebida que servían
- ropa que llevaban

8-15 Antes y ahora. En pequeños grupos, expliquen cómo era la vida antes y cómo es ahora con respecto a los siguientes temas:

- la familia (tamaño, grado de movilidad, porcentaje de divorcios)
- la mujer en la sociedad (participación en el mundo del trabajo/de la política, su independencia económica)
- las ciudades (tamaño, los problemas ambientales (*environment*) como la contaminación, la delincuencia, el crimen)

SITUACIONES

1. **Role A.** You are a very famous public figure (a singer, a professor, a scientist, a sports person, etc.) who is going to be interviewed by a reporter from a major television station. The public is interested in knowing about your background. Give your interviewer as many details as possible as you talk about your past.

   Role B. You are interviewing a very famous person for a major television station. Ask your interviewee the following questions about his/her background: a) what the place he/she was born was like, b) how his/her family life and school days were, c) the type of music he/she used to listen to, d) the books he/she used to read, e) the holidays/ festivities he/she celebrated most and how he/she celebrated them, etc.

2. **Role A.** You are an exchange student and would like to find out about your host's weekend and holiday activities when he/she was in high school. Ask a) what he/she did on Saturday evenings, b) with whom, c) the time, and d) if the activities were the same during the summertime.

   Role B. You are the host of an exchange student. Answer his/her questions about your activities when you were in high school. Then explain that during a summer you went to a friend's house in Guadalajara, Mexico, and that while you were there you used to a) speak Spanish every day, b) go to the outdoor markets, c) listen to the mariachis, and d) eat excellent Mexican food everywhere (**en todas partes**).

EN DIRECTO

To talk about how things used to be:
Entonces...
Por aquel entonces...
En aquellos tiempos...

3. The preterit and the imperfect

■ The preterit and the imperfect are not interchangeable.

■ Use the preterit:

1. to talk about the beginning or end of an event, action, or condition.

Pepito **leyó** a los cinco años.	*Pepito read* (began reading) *at age five.*
El niño **se enfermó** el sábado.	*The child got sick* (began feeling sick) *on Saturday.*
Pepito **leyó** el cuento.	*Pepito read* (finished) *the story.*
El niño **estuvo** enfermo ayer.	*The child was sick* (he is no longer sick) *yesterday.*

2. to talk about an event, action, or condition that occurred over a period of time with a definite beginning and end.

Vivieron en México por diez años.	*They lived in Mexico for ten years.*

3. to narrate a sequence of completed actions in the past (note that there is a forward movement of narrative time).

Oyeron un ruido, se **levantaron,** y **bajaron** las escaleras.	*They heard a noise, got up, and went downstairs.*

■ Use the imperfect:

1. to talk about customary or habitual actions, events, or conditions in the past.

Todos los días **llovía,** y por eso **leíamos** mucho.	*It used to rain every day and that's why we read a lot.*

2. to talk about an ongoing part of an event, action, or condition.

En ese momento **llovía** mucho y los niños **estaban** muy tristes.	*At that moment it was raining a lot, and the children were very sad.*

■ In a story, the imperfect provides the background information, whereas the preterit tells what happened. Note that an ongoing action expressed with the imperfect is often interrupted by a completed action expressed with the preterit.

Era navidad. Todos **dormíamos** cuando los niños **oyeron** un ruido en el techo.	*It was Christmas. All of us were sleeping when the children heard a noise on the roof.*

¿Qué dice usted?

2 **8-16 ¡Qué día!** Ayer iba a ser un día especial para Pedro, pero todos sus planes terminaron mal. Marque con un círculo las tres cosas que, en su opinión, probablemente le ocurrieron mientras trataba de realizar sus planes.

1. Mientras se bañaba temprano por la mañana, se cayó en el baño.
2. Mientras desayunaba tranquilamente, el teléfono sonó y no pudo terminar de comer.
3. Iba a la tienda para comprarle un anillo a su novia cuando alguien le robó el dinero.

4. Mientras llamaba por teléfono a un restaurante para reservar una mesa, el restaurante se incendió.
5. Iba a proponerle matrimonio a su novia cuando su ex-novia lo llamó por teléfono.
6. Mientras preparaba una cena deliciosa para celebrar el cumpleaños de su novia, el perro se comió el pastel.

8-17 La última vez. Túrnense para preguntarse cuándo fue la última vez que cada uno de ustedes hizo estas cosas y cómo se sentía mientras las hacía.

MODELO: correr en los sanfermines
       E1: ¿Cuándo fue la última vez que corriste en los sanfermines?
       E2: Corrí el año pasado.
       E1: ¿Y cómo te sentías mientras corrías?
       E2: Tenía mucho miedo.

1. participar en un campeonato
2. ganar un premio
3. estar en un desfile
4. disfrazarse
5. bailar en un carnaval
6. ...

8-18 ¿Pretérito o imperfecto? Completen esta narración usando el pretérito o el imperfecto.

En el mes de abril del año pasado mi familia y yo (1) _____ (ir) a Guatemala de vacaciones. Primero nosotros (2) _____ (estar) en la ciudad de Guatemala, la capital. Allí (3) _____ (ver) a unos parientes y (4) _____ (visitar) lugares muy interesantes, como el Museo Nacional de Arqueología y Etnología, donde (5) _____ (poder) admirar una excelente colección de objetos de la cultura maya, y el Mercado Central, donde mi mamá (6) _____ (comprar) unas blusas con unos diseños mayas preciosos.

En la mañana del tercer día, nosotros (7) _____ (irse) a Antigua, que está bastante cerca de la capital. (8) _____ (Hacer) un tiempo fabuloso. Como (9) _____ (ser) primavera, muchos árboles y plantas (10) _____ (tener) flores, y todo (11) _____ (estar) muy verde. Nosotros (12) _____ (salir) del hotel cerca de las cinco de la tarde y poco después (13) _____ (llegar) a una plaza donde había mucha gente. Allí (14) _____ (ver) las procesiones de semana santa. El ambiente (15) _____ (ser) impresionante; las personas (16) _____ (llevar) túnicas largas y (17) _____ (caminar) lentamente por la calle. ¡Nunca vamos a olvidar esa experiencia!

8-19 Un evento inolvidable. Cuéntele a su compañero/a con todos los detalles algo inesperado (sorprendente) que le ocurrió durante una celebración, día festivo o evento especial el año pasado. Indique qué pasó, dónde, cuándo, etc. Describa la escena y los personajes. Su compañero/a debe hacerle preguntas para obtener más información.

SITUACIONES

1. **Role A.** Tell your friend about a festival, celebration or ceremony in which you participated recently. Answer his/her questions with as many details as you can.

   Role B. Your friend is going to tell you about an important event in which he/she participated. Ask him/her questions about where the event/festivity took place, the way people were dressed, how the place was decorated, etc. React appropriately to what you hear.

2. **Role A.** You have just come back from a Spanish-speaking country where you visited a town or city that was having a local festival. Explain to your friend what you saw and answer his/her questions.

   Role B. Your friend went to a festival in a Spanish-speaking country. Ask him/her: a) what the people were doing, b) what they were wearing, c) what they were eating, d) if there were open air markets, e) what people sold there, f) if he/she bought something etc.

4. Comparisons of inequality

En esta fiesta hay **más** personas **que** en la otra. Es **más** divertida **que** la otra. Las personas bailan **más**.

En esta fiesta hay **menos** personas **que** en la otra. Esta fiesta es **menos** alegre **que** la otra. Las personas se divierten **menos**.

■ Use **más... que** or **menos... que** to express comparisons of inequality with nouns, adjectives, and adverbs.

COMPARISONS OF INEQUALITY	
Cuando Alina era joven tenía { **más** / **menos** } amigos que Pepe.	When Alina was young she had { *more* / *fewer* } friends than Pepe.
Ella era { **más** / **menos** } activa que él.	She was { *more* / *less* } active than he.
Salía { **más** / **menos** } frecuentemente que él.	She went out { *more* / *less* } frequently than he.

■ Use **de** instead of **que** before numbers.

Había **más de** diez carrozas en el desfile. — *There were more than ten floats in the parade.*

El año pasado vimos **menos de** diez. — *Last year we saw fewer than ten.*

■ The following adjectives have regular and irregular comparative forms.

bueno	más bueno *o* mejor	*better*
malo	más malo *o* peor[1]	*worse*
pequeño	más pequeño *o* menor	*smaller*
joven	más joven *o* menor	*younger*
grande	más grande *o* mayor	*bigger*
viejo	más viejo *o* mayor[2]	*older*

Esta banda es $\left\{ \begin{array}{c} \textbf{mejor} \\ \textbf{peor} \end{array} \right\}$ que aquélla.   *This band is* $\left\{ \begin{array}{c} better \\ worse \end{array} \right\}$ *than that one.*

■ When **bien** and **mal** function as adverbs, they have the same irregular comparative forms as **bueno** and **malo**.

bien → mejor	Yo canto **mejor** que Héctor.	*I sing better than Héctor.*
mal → peor	Héctor canta **peor** que yo.	*Héctor sings worse than I.*

¿Qué dice usted?

8-20 Comparación de dos desfiles. Primera fase. Lea la siguiente información sobre los desfiles de Veracruz y de Mérida en México. Después diga si las siguientes oraciones son correctas de acuerdo con la información de la tabla.

A INVESTIGAR

Busque la siguiente información antes de hacer la actividad **8-20:**

¿Quién fundó la ciudad de Veracruz?

¿Por qué es importante esta ciudad?

¿Qué ciudades mayas están cerca de Mérida?

	VERACRUZ	MÉRIDA
Habitantes	320.000	750.000
Público	8.000 personas	12.000 personas
Número de bandas	4	5

	Sí	No
1. Mérida tiene más habitantes que Veracruz.	____	____
2. Menos personas asisten al desfile de Veracruz que al de Mérida.	____	____
3. Hay más bandas en el desfile de Veracruz que en el de Mérida.	____	____
4. Hay más público en el desfile de Veracruz que en el de Mérida.	____	____
5. Veracruz tiene menos habitantes que Mérida.	____	____

Segunda fase. Debido a los costos, la banda de su universidad sólo puede participar en uno de estos dos desfiles. Con la información que tienen de la Primera fase y la que aparece más abajo, decidan a cuál debe asistir y expliquen por qué.

	DESFILE DE VERACRUZ	DESFILE DE MÉRIDA
Transporte	30.000 pesos	30.500 pesos
Hotel	12.000 pesos	10.000 pesos
Comidas	2.000 pesos	3.000 pesos

[1]**Más bueno** and **más malo** are not used interchangeably with **mejor** and **peor**. **Más bueno** and **más malo** refer to a person's moral qualities.

[2]Use **mayor** to refer to a person's age. **Más viejo** is generally used with nouns other than people.

8-21 Personas famosas. Compare a las siguientes personas considerando su aspecto físico, su edad, el tipo de trabajo, dinero o popularidad.

1. Brad Pitt y Antonio Banderas
2. Penélope Cruz y Jennifer López
3. Tiger Woods y Sammy Sosa
4. el presidente y el vicepresidente

5. Comparisons of equality

COMPARISONS OF EQUALITY	
tan... como	*as . . . as*
tanto/a... como	*as much . . . as*
tantos/as... como	*as many . . . as*
tanto como	*as much as*

- Use **tan... como** to express comparisons of equality with adjectives and adverbs.

| La boda fue **tan** elegante **como** la fiesta. | *The wedding was as elegant at the party.* |
| El padre bailó **tan** bien **como** su hija. | *The father danced as well as his daughter.* |

- Use **tanto(s)/tanta(s)... como** to express comparisons of equality with nouns.

Había **tanto** ruido **como** en el carnaval.	*There was as much noise as a Mardi Gras.*
Había **tanta** alegría **como** en el carnaval.	*There was as much joy as at Mardi Gras.*
Había **tantos** desfiles **como** en el carnaval.	*There were as many parades as at Mardi Gras.*
Había **tantas** orquestas **como** en el carnaval.	*There were as many orchestras as at Mardi Gras.*

- Use **tanto como** to express comparisons of equality with verbs.

| Ellos bailaron **tanto como** nosotros. | *They danced as much as we did.* |

¿Qué dice usted?

8-22 Cuatro estudiantes guatemaltecos. Comparen a estos cuatro estudiantes.

MODELO: E1: Vilma tiene tantos hermanos como Marta.
E2: Sí, pero tiene más hermanos que Ricardo.

	PEDRO	VILMA	MARTA	RICARDO
Hermanos	2	3	3	2
Clases	5	5	4	6
Dinero	50 quetzales	80 quetzales	50 quetzales	80 quetzales
Discos	200	180	180	215
Videos	40	32	40	32

8-23 Opiniones. Primero, den dos nombres de personas, desfiles, etc. Luego, expresen su opinión para compararlos. Pueden usar las palabras que aparecen entre paréntesis u otras de su elección.

MODELO: dos actores (bueno)
　　　　　　E1: Tom Cruise es tan buen actor como Johnny Depp.
　　　　　　E2: Sí, estoy de acuerdo/tienes razón. *o*
　　　　　　　　 No, Johnny Depp es mejor actor que Tom Cruise.

1. dos actrices norteamericanas
   (atractiva, alta, famosa, buena actriz...)
2. dos desfiles o celebraciones locales o nacionales
   (número de personas, carrozas, divertido...)
3. dos películas nominadas para el Óscar
   (actores, fotografía, acción, ...)
4. dos programas cómicos de la televisión
   (cómico, malo, loco...)

8-24 Las diversiones. Primera fase. Comparen las películas o los programas de televisión de antes con los de hoy en día, basándose en lo siguiente: los temas, los personajes, el uso de la tecnología, la violencia y el sexo.

Segunda fase. Ahora contesten las siguientes preguntas e intercambien opiniones con otros grupos.

1. ¿Creen ustedes que hoy en día hay más sexo y violencia en las películas y los programas de televisión que antes?
2. ¿Piensan ustedes que hoy hay más violencia social porque se ve más televisión, o porque los medios de comunicación tienen más influencia en los jóvenes que sus padres y la escuela?
3. ¿Piensan que el gobierno debe tener más control sobre los medios de comunicación y el arte?

SITUACIONES

1. One of you is in favor of small weddings and the other prefers big weddings. Compare both in regard to
   a) expenses (*gastos*), b) stress (*estrés*) for the bride and groom, c) work involved, and d) problems.

2. **Role A.** You are a student representative in charge of making a presentation before the Faculty Senate. You are to compare the graduation ceremony at your own university with the graduation ceremony at University X. Convince the faculty that the graduation ceremony at University X is better because it is: smaller, better organized, less expensive, there is better music and there are better speeches (*discursos*), etc.

   Role B. The rest of the class will represent the faculty senate and will ask questions to get a clear idea of the advantages of one type of ceremony over the other.

6. The superlative

■ Use superlatives to express *most* and *least* as degrees of comparison. To form the superlative, use *definite article + noun +* **más/menos** *+ adjective.* To express *in* or *at* with the superlative, use **de.**

Es **el** disfraz **más/menos** caro (de la fiesta).	*It is the most/least expensive costume (at the party).*

■ Do not use **más** or **menos** with **mejor, peor, mayor,** and **menor.**

Son **los mejores** vinos del país.	*They are the best wines in the country.*

■ You may delete the noun when it is clear to whom or to what you refer.

Son **los mejores** del país.	*They are the best (ones) in the country.*

Superlative with *-ísimo*

■ To express the idea of *extremely*, add the ending **-ísimo** (**-a, -os, -as**) to the adjective. If the adjective ends in a consonant, add **-ísimo** directly to the singular form of the adjective. If it ends in a vowel, drop the vowel before adding **-ísimo.**

fácil	Este baile es **facilísimo.**	*This dance is extremely easy.*
grande	La carroza es **grandísima.**	*The float is extremely big.*
bueno	Las bandas son **buenísimas.**	*The bands are extremely good.*

¿Qué dice usted?

8-25 Encuesta. Después de contestar individualmente estas preguntas sobre su universidad y su pueblo/ciudad, comparen sus respuestas.

PUEBLO/CIUDAD	UNIVERSIDAD
¿Dónde sirven...?	¿Cuál es...?
la mejor pizza	la clase más fácil
la mejor hamburguesa	el/la profesor/a más interesante
la peor comida	el deporte más popular
el peor café	el mejor equipo
los mejores helados	la fiesta más importante para los alumnos

8-26 Mis compañeros/as. En pequeños grupos decidan cuáles son los compañeros/as que tienen estas características. Después, contesten las preguntas de otros grupos.

MODELO: simpático/a
　　　　　E1: ¿Quién es el/la más simpático/a de la clase?
　　　　　E2: ... es el/la más simpático/a (de la clase).

1. popular
2. serio/a
3. trabajador/a
4. elegante
5. optimista
6. hablador/a

LENGUA

Spanish and English often use adjectives as nouns. Whereas English frequently uses *one* or *ones* after the adjective, Spanish simply drops the noun.

El **traje rojo** es más bonito.
El rojo es más bonito.
The red one is prettier.

ACENTOS

Spanish words can have only one written accent. Therefore, adjectives with written accents lose the accent when *-ísimo* is added.

fácil → facilísimo
rápido → rapidísimo

8-27 Preguntas personales. Háganse las siguientes preguntas.

1. ¿Quién es tu mejor amigo? ¿Y tu mejor amiga?
2. ¿Hablas con tu mejor amigo/a cuando tienes un problema?
3. ¿Cuál es el peor día de la semana para ti? ¿Por qué?
4. ¿Y cuál es el mejor día? ¿Por qué?
5. ¿Cuál es la fecha más importante para ti? ¿Por qué?

8-28 Premios al talento. En pequeños grupos, decidan qué personas excepcionales (figuras famosas o alguien en su clase) son las ganadoras de estos premios. Dos de ustedes van a anunciar los premios principales, y después van a mencionar algunos de los logros (*accomplishments*) de los ganadores. Piensen en otras categorías posibles y anuncien a los ganadores.

MODELO: mejor diseñador/a
La mejor diseñadora es nuestra compañera Asunción Benítez. El año pasado ganó el Premio de la Moda por sus diseños y vestidos clásicos. La ropa de Asunción Benítez es siempre elegantísima.

1. mejor cantante
2. mejor actor/actriz
3. mejor bailarín/bailarina
4. mejor pianista/violinista
5. mejor escritor/a
6. la persona más creativa

SITUACIONES

Role A. You are talking to a well-known film critic. Since you have to write an article on the best American movies of the year, ask him/her a) which is the best American film, b) why, c) who is the best actor/actress, d) which is the worst film of the year, and e) what he/she thinks of Hispanic films.

Role B. You are a well-known film critic. Answer your friend's questions according to your own opinions regarding the best/worst American films and actors, and explain that: a) there are some excellent Mexican, Argentinean, and Spanish films, and b) several of them won Oscars in the last ten years.

MOSAICOS

 ## Escuchar

Making inferences

Sometimes when you talk to a friend or overhear a conversation you understand what the person means or feels without him/her actually saying it. For example, if you are driving with a friend and cannot find your way around, you might say, "There is a gas station up the road." Your friend might understand (infer) that you want to ask for directions.

Antes de escuchar

8-29 Costumbres diferentes. The end of the year is approaching and two friends are talking about a coming holiday. Before you listen to their conversation in 8-30, write down the name of the holiday that you think they are talking about.

A escuchar

AUDIO **8-30 Feriados.** Now, read the statements that follow and then listen as two friends talk about a Mexican holiday. Mark those statements that provide information you can infer from what you heard.

_____ Daniel es mexicano.
_____ Sandra es una persona muy tímida.
_____ Sandra no es americana.
_____ Daniel está muy preocupado.
_____ Sandra tiene una familia grande.
_____ Daniel no conoce las costumbres mexicanas.

Después de escuchar

8-31 ¿Y usted? With a classmate, share your answers to the following questions.

1. ¿Qué fiesta o tradición religiosa le gustaría celebrar en un país hispano? ¿Por qué?
2. ¿Celebran esa fiesta en su ciudad? ¿Cómo la celebran?
3. ¿Qué fiesta o tradición celebra usted solamente con sus amigos?

Antes de escuchar

8-32 El aniversario. In 8-33, you will listen to a couple talking about their upcoming wedding anniversary. Before you listen, write down what you know about how most couples celebrate their anniversaries: places they go, presents they buy for each other, things they do for each other, etc.

_____

_____

_____

A escuchar

AUDIO **8-33 ¿Un aniversario más?** Now, listen to the conversation. Read the statements that follow and mark those statements that provide information you can infer from what you heard.

_____ Eduardo no es mentiroso. Él siempre dice la verdad.

_____ Mariela está enojada con Eduardo.

_____ A Eduardo no le interesa su trabajo.

_____ Mariela es muy sentimental y romántica.

_____ Eduardo y Mariela son muy pobres.

_____ Eduardo y Mariela tienen una relación muy buena.

Después de escuchar

8-34 ¿Y usted? Now share your answers to the following questions.

1. En su familia, ¿se celebran los aniversarios de bodas? ¿Cómo se celebran?
2. ¿Le gustan a usted estas celebraciones? ¿Por qué?
3. ¿Qué reunión familiar es la más divertida o la mejor? ¿Y la más aburrida o la peor? ¿Por qué?

Conversar

Antes de conversar

8-35 Mi niñez y adolescencia. Usted tiene curiosidad por saber si usted y uno/a de sus compañeros/as tuvieron una infancia y adolescencia semejantes. Escriba preguntas que lo/la ayuden a obtener información en las siguientes áreas, u otras áreas de interés para usted.

- Deportes que su compañero/a practicaba y miraba en la televisión entre los siete y los doce años de edad

- La(s) fiesta(s) más importantes para la familia de su compañero/a y cómo la(s) celebraba

- Una o dos costumbres de la familia que a él/ella le gustaban y otras que no le gustaban y por qué

- ¿...?

A conversar

8-36 ¿Semejantes o diferentes? Entreviste a su compañero/a usando las preguntas de **8-35** y tome notas de sus respuestas.

Después de conversar

8-37 Almas gemelas (*Identical souls*) **o mundos apartes** (*worlds apart*). Anónimamente, escriban un breve informe comparativo de su infancia y adolescencia. Otra pareja va a leer su informe y va a tratar de averigüar quiénes son ustedes. Sigan los siguientes modelos o combínenlos, de acuerdo a sus experiencias. Mantengan su identidad en secreto.

MODELOS:

ALMAS GEMELAS	MUNDOS APARTES
Somos dos almas gemelas. Tanto mi compañero/a como yo nacimos en...	Somos dos mundos apartes. Uno/a de nosotros/as nació en..., el/la otro/a nació en...

Con respecto a los deportes...

La(s) fiesta(s) más importante(s)...

Durante/ Para... (nombre de la/s fiesta/s)...

Durante nuestra infancia/adolescencia...

Nuestras familias también tenían una/dos costumbre(s)

Mi compañero/a y yo tuvimos una niñez/adolescencia semejante/diferente.

Antes de conversar

8-38 Mi cumpleaños. Las siguientes palabras se relacionan con una fiesta de cumpleaños. Escríbalas en la columna apropiada.

pastel	comer	amigos	recibir regalos
bailar	auto	felicitar (*congratulate*)	familiares
ropa	joyas	divertirse	pasarlo bien
novio/a	colegas	sentirse contento/a	dinero

PERSONAS INVITADAS	ACTIVIDADES TÍPICAS	REGALOS	DESEOS DEL/DE LA CUMPLEAÑERO/A

A conversar

8-39 Recuerdos de mi mejor/peor cumpleaños. Conversen sobre su mejor/peor cumpleaños. Averigüen lo siguiente.

1. Cómo lo quería celebrar cada uno/a y cómo lo celebró realmente
2. Quiénes lo/la llamaron o visitaron
3. Cómo lo pasó cada uno/a
4. Qué quería recibir de regalo cada uno/a y qué recibió realmente

Después de conversar

8-40 Querido diario (*diary*). Imagínese que usted tuvo un cumpleaños fabuloso o uno muy malo. Narre en su diario lo que le ocurrió.

> *Querido diario:*
>
> *El día _____* (date) *fue mi cumpleaños. Cumplí _____*
> *años. _____ un día _____.* (Say how the day was.)
>
> *Yo quería hacer lo siguiente el día de mi cumpleaños: _____, _____*
> *y _____.*
>
> *Afortunadamente/Desafortunadamente*
> _____
>
> (Say what you could actually do or you couldn't do because something happened. Explain what happened then describe how you felt about what you were able/unable to do. Explain why.)
> _____
> _____
>
> *En general, mi cumpleaños fue _____.*

📖 Leer

In *Lección 8*, you will have the opportunity to further practice some strategies learned previously as well as focus on identifying information stated in a text and making inferences based on the information presented.

Guía de prelectura

Relying on the visuals, the text title, and cognates in activity **8-43,** answer these questions.

1. Thinking of the traditions and holidays celebrated in the Spanish-speaking world and of the ethnic diversity represented in the Hispanic cultures, what content areas do you expect the text will cover?
   a. The influence of the Spanish conquest on the indigenous cultures of America
   b. Some beliefs and customs of the indigenous people in America
   c. Cultures in contact in Spanish-speaking America

2. On what did you base your answers to question 1?
   a. The cognates in the title
   b. The photos in the text
   c. My personal knowledge of the topic

3. After reading the title, guess some of the information the reader will probably find in the text. Mark with an X all that may apply. You may verify your responses at a later time.
   a. _____ The geographic areas where the Maya empire settled and flourished
   b. _____ Some Mayans beliefs regarding life and death
   c. _____ Some rituals and practices of the Mayans
   d. _____ Some Mayan beliefs and practices that were affected by the Spanish Conquest

Antes de leer

8-41 Preparación. Las creencias (*beliefs*) sobre la muerte y las costumbres relacionadas con ella varían de una cultura a otra. Según sus conocimientos sobre el tema, indiquen si las siguientes prácticas se asocian con la cultura egipcia (**CE**), con alguna cultura indígena americana (**CI**), o con ambas (**A**).

1. _____ Creían que había vida después de la muerte.
2. _____ Construían pirámides para honrar a los muertos.
3. _____ Embalsamaban el cadáver para preservarlo.
4. _____ Rociaban (*Sprayed*) el cuerpo con perfumes.
5. _____ Vestían a los muertos con ropa funeraria especial.
6. _____ Preparaban comidas típicas de la región, y las ponían en las tumbas.
7. _____ Ponían una máscara sobre la cara del muerto.
8. _____ Enterraban (*buried*) al muerto en las pirámides, en tumbas o sepulcros, de acuerdo al estatus social de la persona muerta.
9. _____ La familia de la persona muerta depositaba joyas y objetos de valor en la tumba o pirámide.
10. _____ Rociaban el cadáver con un polvo de color rojo para simbolizar el renacimiento (*rebirth*).

8-42 Clasificación. Escriba cada palabra en la columna correspondiente.

anillo	carne	aretes
fruta	pulseras	copa
vegetales	cinturón	cuchillo de hueso

JOYAS	OTROS OBJETOS DE VALOR	COMIDA

A leer

8-43 Primera mirada. Lea el siguiente texto y, luego, siga las instrucciones.

Creencias y costumbres mayas sobre la muerte

El origen de los mayas es incierto. Sin embargo, se sabe que esta civilización ocupó y se desarrolló en los actuales territorios de Guatemala, México, Belice, Honduras y El Salvador. Durante su período de mayor esplendor, los mayas

construyeron ciudades y pirámides, donde enterraban a sus gobernantes y los veneraban después de muertos.

Los mayas compartían con otras culturas mesoamericanas algunas creencias y costumbres. Entre otras cosas, creían en la vida después de la muerte y en la interacción entre el mundo humano y el mundo espiritual. Creían que el destino de una persona después de la muerte dependía de la forma en que moría y no de su conducta mientras vivía. Los enterramientos[1] y los vestuarios funerarios confirman que los mayas creían que el espíritu se prolongaba más allá de la muerte. La mayoría de los

muertos iba a Xibalbá, un lugar en el mundo de abajo.

Para llegar al inframundo había que superar numerosos peligros. El espíritu debía comer bien y cuidarse. Por eso, los mayas dejaban en la tumba un ajuar o vestimenta funeraria. También colocaban comida, agua y amuletos[2] protectores, de acuerdo con el estatus social del muerto.

Los mayas rociaban el cadáver con un polvo rojo que simbolizaba el

renacimiento. También lo adornaban con joyas, collares, pulseras y anillos de jade, hueso o concha[3] y un cinturón ceremonial. En muchos enterramientos ponían una máscara sobre la cara del muerto para ocultar su identidad. En la boca le ponían una cuenta[4] de jade, símbolo de lo precioso y lo perenne, para preservar su espíritu inmortal.

Algunas de estas creencias y costumbres todavía se conservan, con ciertas variaciones, en algunas comunidades de Guatemala, México y El Salvador.

[1]*graves* [2]*amulets, charms* [3]*shell* [4]*bead*

Determine si las siguientes afirmaciones representan información explícita (**E**) en el texto o son inferencias (**I**) basadas en el contenido. Si es una inferencia, indique la(s) frase(s) en que se basa.

1. _____ Los expertos no saben de dónde vinieron los mayas.
2. _____ Los mayas crearon una gran civilización.
3. _____ Las comunidades mayas tenían autoridades que los gobernaban.
4. _____ Como los egipcios, los mayas construyeron edificios magníficos para honrar la memoria de personas de alto estatus en su comunidad.
5. _____ Los mayas, como otros grupos indígenas, pensaban que la vida continuaba después de la muerte.
6. _____ Para los mayas, el tipo de muerte determinaba el destino de una persona.
7. _____ No todos los mayas iban al mismo destino después de la muerte.
8. _____ La comida, el agua y los amuletos ayudaban al espíritu del muerto a llegar a su destino final.

8-44 Segunda mirada. Complete las siguientes ideas con información explícita en el texto.

1. Los mayas, como otras culturas indígenas de Mesoamérica, creían en...
   a. _____
   b. _____

2. Estas dos costumbres demuestran que los mayas tenían estas creencias...
   a. _____ b. _____

3. Para llegar a su destino final, el espíritu de los muertos tenía que...
   _____ y _____

4. Para indicar que el espíritu del muerto nacía otra vez, los mayas...
   _____

5. Para simbolizar la importancia y la inmortalidad del espíritu, los mayas...
   _____

Después de leer

8-45 Inferencias. Con un/a compañero/a, mencionen qué objetos probablemente ponían los mayas en la tumba o pirámide de un gobernante con las siguientes características:

1. era físicamente activo
2. le gustaba mucho el arte
3. estudiaba astronomía
4. le fascinaba la guerra

Escribir

In *this chapter* you will have the opportunity to review writing descriptions in the context of a narrative text.

In simple words, narrating is telling, recounting, reporting an event that may be real or imaginary following a sequence or order (from present to past, from past to present, or a combination of both). Furthermore, narration may serve a variety of purposes: to inform, to teach, to explain past or present actions or experiences, etc. However, how can we write narrative texts effectively?

The following tips will help you be a successful narrator:

1. Keep in mind the characters involved (their feelings, their physical and personality characteristics), the pace of action, the setting of your story (rural, cosmopolitan, mysterious, etc.), the time frame (present, past), the order (chronological, retrospective, etc.) in which the events unfold.
2. Determine the right perspective for your narration. Did you (and someone else) live the experience (protagonist/s)? Did you see how an event unfolded (eyewitness)?
3. Structure your narration as follows:

   - First introduce the character(s), describe the setting, and begin the action.

   - Then, present the unfolding of the action and describe the characters and the tensions caused by their actions or by the events around them.

   - Finally, present a closure to the tensions between/among characters or let the reader of your story imagine the end.

Antes de escribir

8-46 Enfoque. Primera fase. Lea la siguiente narración y siga las instrucciones.

Eran alrededor de las siete de la tarde del 24 de mayo cuando ocurrió lo que cambió nuestra vida por completo. Era una noche de otoño, y hacía viento. Empezaba a oscurecer. Era el cumpleaños de nuestra gran amiga Guadalupe Martínez.

Aunque tenía sólo viente años, Guadalupe era una chica excepcional. Estudiaba y también trabajaba para ayudar a su familia de ocho hermanos. Todos sus amigos la admirábamos por su generosidad, optimismo y alegría. Guadalupe era la hija, hermana y amiga que todos soñábamos tener.

El día de su cumpleaños por la mañana, Francisco y yo no la llamamos como de costumbre. Planeábamos darle una sorpresa para su cumpleaños. Después de todo, ¡sólo se cumplen veintiún años una vez en la vida! Primero, fuimos a un centro comercial y le buscamos un regalo especial. Caminamos varias horas hasta que encontramos un plato decorativo guatemalteco y un CD de su música favorita. Francisco también le compró un perfume, y yo agregué un buen libro al cesto de regalos. Finalmente, cerca de las cuatro de la tarde, volvimos a casa y envolvimos los regalos.

Después de un día muy ocupado, a las seis de la tarde Francisco y yo caminábamos a casa de Guadalupe. Estábamos a sólo unos 80 metros de su casa, cuando la ambulancia pasó a toda velocidad por la avenida en que caminábamos. Francisco y yo intuitivamente nos miramos y empezamos a caminar con más rapidez, pero en silencio. A sólo unos metros de su casa, supimos que algo pasaba en casa de Guadalupe. Francisco y yo corrimos. Cuando llegamos a la puerta de su cuarto, uno de los enfermeros nos dijo: "La señorita Martínez tuvo un accidente. Se quebró una pierna".

Francisco y yo sin decir una palabra llamamos al resto de nuestros amigos.

Les dimos suficiente tiempo a los médicos y a las enfermeras para hacer su trabajo, pero a las 9:00 de la noche, todos los amigos de Guadalupe le celebramos su cumpleaños en el hospital. Fue un cumpleaños diferente a todos los anteriores, pero lo pasamos al lado de la cama de nuestra gran amiga.

Segunda fase. Answer the following questions, based on the story you just read.

1. Mark with an *X* the intended purpose of the story.
   _____ To describe the life of a special person
   _____ To entertain readers
   _____ To inform the reader about a sad experience
   _____ To teach a lesson

2. Based on its purpose, is the narration effective?   Yes   No

3. Mark some possible reasons for your response to question 2.
   _____ The main character is described in an interesting manner to the reader.
   _____ The pace of the story is good: the action moves quickly, and the amount of description is about right.
   _____ There is too much description, and the pace of the story is slow.
   _____ There is enough information about the setting of the story.
   _____ The experience is told in a chronological order.
   _____ The narration has a clear organization: an introduction, a development, and a closure.
   _____ The perspective (narrator) of the story makes it interesting and realistic to the reader.

8-47 Preparación. En la actividad 8-48, usted va a narrar una historia o experiencia personal, real o imaginaria. Primero, haga lo siguiente:

- Decida la base de su narración: ¿va a contar una experiencia real o una que es producto de su imaginación?

- Determine el objetivo de su narración: ¿va a escribir usted para informar, relatar, entretener, enseñar?

- Haga una lista del/de los protagonista(s) de su historia: ¿Cómo se llaman? ¿Cuántos hay? ¿Qué características físicas y de personalidad tienen los protagonistas?

- Determine el tiempo y orden de su narración: ¿Va a relatar lo que ocurrió en el pasado o en el presente? ¿Va a narrar los hechos en orden cronológico (desde el pasado al presente o desde el presente al pasado)?

- Escriba una lista de verbos que lo/la ayuden a describir el ambiente, y otros que cuenten la acción.

- Organice la información de su narración: ¿Qué va a presentar en la introducción? ¿Cuál va a ser el conflicto? ¿Va a presentar la solución del problema o conflicto, o el lector va a imaginar el final?

EN DIRECTO

To indicate chronological order:

Primero, ...

Después, ...

Después de (un tiempo, unos minutos/días), ...

Luego, ...

Más tarde, ...

Finalmente, ...

Por fin, ...

To indicate something happened all of a sudden:

De repente, ...

A escribir

8-48 Manos a la obra. Usando la información de la actividad anterior, escriba la narración. Las siguientes expresiones en *En directo* pueden resultarle muy útiles.

Después de escribir

8-49 Revisión. Ahora lea su narración, pensando en el lector. Verifique lo siguiente:

- El contenido: ¿Incluyó usted toda la información necesaria o el lector todavía tiene preguntas? ¿Es interesante el contenido para el lector?

- La organización: ¿Tiene su narración un orden que ayude al lector a seguir el flujo (*flow*) de la historia? ¿Presentó usted el conflicto o problema en la introducción? Desarrolló el conflicto en el cuerpo (*body*) del texto? ¿Hay una conclusión o resolución del conflicto al final de la historia o el lector debe imaginar el final?

- La forma de su narración:

  a. ¿Revisó la gramática de su narración? ¿Usó el vocabulario correcto, expresiones para indicar el orden cronológico, concordancia de tiempos (presente, pasado), etc.?
  b. ¿Usó la puntuación y ortografía correctas?

Finalmente, comparta su narración con un/a compañero/a. Esto va a ayudar a mejorar algunas áreas débiles.

ENFOQUE CULTURAL

TEMAS: LA RELIGIÓN

Para pensar

¿Hay una religión oficial en los Estados Unidos? ¿Qué religiones hay en este país? ¿Qué fiestas religiosas se celebran aquí? ¿Cómo se celebran? ¿Participa usted en estas fiestas? ¿Qué hace?

La religión católica es la religión oficial en muchos países hispanos. Por eso hay muchas celebraciones de carácter religioso; por ejemplo, la procesión del día de la Virgen de Guadalupe en México.

En Guatemala, durante toda una semana a fines de noviembre, los hombres se preparan para celebrar la quema del diablo. Se visten de diablos y juegan a perseguir a los niños por las calles. Finalmente, el 7 de diciembre queman la figura de un diablo.

En Caracas, Venezuela, la fiesta religiosa más importante se celebra en la pascua de resurrección. Empieza con la bajada de palmeras el viernes antes del domingo de ramos, sigue con las procesiones el Jueves Santo y el Viernes Santo, y termina con la quema de Judas el domingo de pascua.

En la noche del 5 al 6 de enero, los Reyes Magos, montados en sus camellos, distribuyen regalos entre los niños. El día 6 hay una serie de procesiones de carrozas, orquestas y bailarines que recorren los pueblos y ciudades.

Para contestar

2 **Los feriados.** Contesten las siguientes preguntas.

1. Mencionen dos feriados religiosos que se celebran en el mundo hispano. ¿En qué países se celebran? ¿Cuándo se celebran?
2. Comenten cuándo y cómo se celebra una de las festividades mencionadas en el número 1.

G **Riqueza cultural.** En grupos de tres, escojan una fiesta religiosa y comparen cómo se celebra en los Estados Unidos y en el mundo hispano.

Para pensar

¿Conoce usted a alguien de México o de Guatemala? ¿Sabe usted qué civilizaciones importantes se desarrollaron en esos países?

México y Guatemala son países vecinos que tienen una historia común.

La Ciudad de México es una de las ciudades más pobladas del planeta. Tiene hermosos parques, museos, galerías, iglesias, maravillosos restaurantes y una intensa vida nocturna.

En la península de Yucatán hay ruinas precolombinas extraordinarias, como la ciudad maya de Chichén Itza.

Guadalajara, la segunda ciudad de México en importancia, es conocida como la ciudad de los festivales. Tiene un encanto colonial, y es el lugar de origen de los mariachis y el tequila. En octubre, Guadalajara celebra el festival de los mariachis, con desfiles, misas cantadas por mariachis y bailes folclóricos.

Expresiones mexicanas:

cuate	¿Cómo está, **mi cuate**?	*How are you, my friend?*
se me hace	**Se me hace** que ese hombre es malo.	*It seems to me that that man is bad.*
qué tanto	¿**Qué tanto** te gusta él?	*How much do you like him?*
chaparra, güera	Ella es **chaparra y güera**.	*She is short and blond.*

Hay muchos lugares de interés en Guatemala. Por ejemplo, Santiago de Atitlán es famoso por sus maravillosos tejidos (weavings) y su hermosa iglesia construida en el siglo XVI.

Guatemala es un país de atractivos diversos que ofrece la posibilidad de explorar selvas tropicales, subir a la cima de volcanes, disfrutar de hermosas playas y también visitar innumerables restos arqueológicos.

Otro lugar fascinante es Chichicastenango, un auténtico pueblo indígena, donde todos los jueves y domingos se realiza el mercado de artesanías más famoso de América Latina.

Expresiones guatemaltecas:

baboso/a	No seas **baboso/a**.	Don't be silly (a fool).
patojo	Los **patojos** están jugando.	The children are playing.
pisto	Tengo poco **pisto**.	I have little money.

Para contestar

En el mapa

1. Diga qué ciudades mexicanas están cerca de la frontera de los Estados Unidos.
2. ¿Qué países están cerca de Guatemala?
3. Mencione dos diferencias geográficas entre México y Guatemala.

Ahora diga...

1. qué ciudades le gustaría visitar en México y en Guatemala.
2. en qué celebraciones de México y Guatemala le gustaría participar y por qué.

¿Qué dice Ud. si...

1. su amigo mexicano hace algo tonto.
2. su novio/a mexicano/a es bajo/a y rubio/a.
3. usted quiere decirle a un/una amigo/a de Guatemala que usted no tiene mucho dinero.

Para investigar en Internet

Busque información sobre la celebración de una de las siguientes fiestas religiosas, y presente un informe al resto de la clase. Explique cómo se celebra, quiénes participan, qué usa la gente que participa, qué comidas especiales se preparan, y cualquier otro detalle que le parezca interesante. Si es posible, traiga fotografías.

- La semana santa en Sevilla, España, y en Antigua, Guatemala
- La procesión del Señor de los Milagros en el Perú
- El día de la Virgen del Carmen y el día de Corpus Christi en México.
- El día de San Agustín en Puebla, México

Para los amantes de la cultura maya, Tikal es el lugar indicado.

¡Prepárese!

8-50 Mentiras. Aunque Katie está ganando la competencia, tanto los otros participantes como el público, tienen una opinión negativa de ella, especialmente Carlos, porque Katie le mintió. En su opinión, ¿cuándo es aceptable mentir y cuando no es aceptable? Escriba una lista de ocasiones aceptables y no aceptables, y después compare su lista con las de sus compañeros/as.

MODELO: Es aceptable mentir para proteger a otra persona.

8-51 Una mentirita (piadosa). Un equivalente en español de la expresión inglesa *white lie* es "una mentirita (piadosa)". Cuando usted era niño/a, ¿decía mentiras o "mentiritas piadosas"? ¿Conocía a alguien que lo hacía? Escriba oraciones en español usando el imperfecto o el pretérito para contar su experiencia. Use las palabras que aparecen en las tres columnas.

MODELO: Yo decía mentiras frecuentemente cuando era joven.
    Una vez yo le dije una mentirita (piadosa) a mi maestra.

Yo	decir	una mentira
Mi mejor amigo/a		una mentirita (piadosa)
Mis hermanos		
Mi mamá		

El concurso es popular pero el público detesta a Katie.

¿Es posible el amor entre Katie y Carlos?

Carlos ya no tiene confianza en Katie.

Katie cree que es posible separar la relación y la competencia.

Según Carlos, no hay nada entre él y Katie.

Sabrina no está ganando pero está contenta; no le gusta lo que hizo Katie.

¡Responda!

8-52 Comparaciones. Imagínese que Tito, el periodista de *Fortunas,* quiere entrevistarlo/la para saber lo que piensa de los personajes del video. Compare a las siguientes personas para reflejar su opinión sobre ellas.

MODELO: Katie es más inteligente que Sabrina.

1. Katie y Carlos
2. Carlos y Efraín
3. Katie y Sabrina
4. Sabrina y Efraín
5. Angela y Manolo
6. Tito y Manolo

Esta canción es un ejemplo de corrido, una balada folclórica que expresa aspectos de la vida mexicana, sea en forma lírica, épica o narrativa. Este corrido es sobre la vida de El Chapo, un personaje, de fama local, originario de Michoacán.

¡Prepárese!

8-53 Comparaciones. En este curso usted ha tenido la oportunidad de escuchar varias canciones hispanas con estilos, influencias, instrumentos y temas diferentes. Escriba comparaciones de igualdad y de desigualdad con las palabras de la actividad para indicar sus opiniones personales sobre la música presentada.

MODELO: el piano / la trompeta
El piano es más difícil de tocar que la trompeta.

1. la música flamenca / la salsa
2. la quena andina / la marimba africana
3. la letra de "Cuéntame alegrías" / la letra de "Tu ausencia"
4. el rock español / el rock americano
5. bailar cumbia / bailar punta

¡Escuche!

8-54 Geografía. Los nombres de muchos lugares de México tienen origen indígena. Se mencionan algunos de éstos en "El Chapo". Mientras escucha la canción, llene los espacios en blanco con los nombres de la lista (uno de ellos se usa dos veces).

Apatzingán	Jalisco	Michoacán	Antúnez

Nació y creció entre los montes
Nunca lo podrá olvidar
El es de mérito _____
Muy cerca de _____
Por su apodo conocido
El Chapo de _____
...

Desciende de gente brava
De los famosos Arriola
Su hermano, el manchado es gallo
Que sabe usar la pistola
...

El Chapo sí que merece
Que le cante su corrido
El Chapo nació en _____
Pero se crió en _____

8-55 Sus orígenes. Ahora, conteste las siguientes preguntas personales.

1. ¿Dónde nació usted?
2. ¿Dónde se crió (raised)?
3. ¿Tenía algún apodo (nickname) cuando era niño/a?

¡Responda!

8-56 En México. Lea el relato de un viaje a México y llene los espacios en blanco con la forma correcta del pretérito o del imperfecto, según el caso.

Cuando mi mejor amigo, José, y yo (1) _____ (hacer) un viaje a México y a Guatemala, lo (2) _____ (pasar) muy bien. El viaje no (3) _____ (ir) sólo para diversión; también (4) _____ (aprender) mucho sobre la cultura de estos dos países.

En México nosotros (5) _____ (quedarse) en la capital por tres días. (6) _____ (visitar) muchos museos e iglesias que (7) _____ (ser) muy interesantes. Un día yo (8) _____ (ver) unas ruinas, y José (9) _____ (andar) por la ciudad. ¡(10) _____ (ser) unos días magníficos!

VOCABULARIO*

AUDIO Las fiestas

la alegría	joy
la boda	wedding
el carnaval	carnival, Mardi Gras
la carreta	cart, wagon
la carroza	float
la celebración	celebration
la comparsa	costumed group
la corrida (de toros)	bullfight
la costumbre	custom
el desfile	parade
la entrada	ticket for admission
la invitación	invitation
el preparativo	preparation
la procesión	procession
la tradición	tradition

Las personas

el antepasado	ancestor
la gente	people
el rey/la reina	king/queen

En el mundo moderno

la droga	drug
el ruido	noise
la seguridad	safety, security
el sexo	sex
la violencia	violence

La música

la melodía	melody
la orquesta	orchestra

Lugares

el camino	road, way
el cementerio	cemetery
la iglesia	church
la plaza (de toros)	bullring
el pueblo	town
el teatro	theater

Tiempo

antes	before
el comienzo	beginning
entonces	then
hoy en día	nowadays
mientras	while

Descripciones

antiguo/a	former, old
difunto/a, muerto/a	dead
maravilloso/a	marvelous
peor	worse, worst
suave	soft
último/a	last

Verbos

acompañar	to accompany
comenzar (ie)	to begin
disfrazarse	to wear a costume
divertirse (ie, i)	to have a good time
encerrar (ie)	to lock up
invitar	to invite
mantener (g, ie)	maintain
mover (ue)	to move
recordar (ue)	to remember
respetar	to respect
reunirse	to get together

Palabras y expresiones útiles

había	there was, there were
más... que	more . . . than, . . . -er than (e.g., shorter than)
menos... que	less than, fewer than
¡Qué pena!	What a pity!
tan... como	as . . . as
tanto/a como	as much . . . as
tantos/as como	as many as
tener deseos de + infinitivo	to feel like, to want

*See page 284 for holidays.

9

EL TRABAJO

Objetivos comunicativos

- Talking about the workplace and professions
- Discussing job skills and abilities
- Giving formal orders and instructions
- Expressing intention
- Avoiding repetition

Contenido

A primera vista
- Las profesiones
- La entrevista

Explicación y expansión
- *Se* + verb constructions
- More on the preterit and the imperfect
- Direct and indirect object pronouns
- Formal commands

Mosaicos
- Escuchar: Contextual guessing
- Conversar: Asking and answering job-related questions
- Leer: Identifying categories; making inferences
- Escribir: Answering a want ad

Enfoque cultural
- Temas: La economía
- Vistas: Chile
  - Para investigar en Internet
- Fortunas: Episodio 9
- Notas: "Gracias a la vida", *Violeta Parra*

Vocabulario

Las profesiones

AUDIO Carmen González, una **chef** de Coral Gables, FL muestra algunas de sus **especialidades.**

Una **médica** examina a un bebé en su **consultorio** en Santiago de Chile.

Dra. Alicia Gonica de Pérez

C A R D I Ó L O G A

Consultorio
La Concepción 81
Metro Pedro de Valdivia, Santiago
Teléfonos 264-2992 / 363-0690

Unos **bomberos apagan** un **incendio** en Ciudad de México.

Una **ejecutiva** atiende la **llamada** telefónica de un cliente.

Una **locutora** espera la **señal** para **comenzar** un programa de noticias en una estación de radio.

Un **técnico** revisa los controles de una **compañía** petrolera.

Una **peluquera** le **corta** el pelo y peina a una de sus clientas.

Eduardo Salas González
Ingeniero de Fabricación

Orrego Luco 161
Providencia
Santiago, Chile

Tel. (56-2) 3346622
Fax (56-2) 3344919

CULTURA

Uno de los hechos sociales más importantes de los países hispanos en los últimos años es el ingreso masivo de las mujeres al mercado laboral. Sin embargo, aún existen desigualdades evidentes. Por ejemplo, el desempleo entre las mujeres es mayor, y su representación en las empresas de alta productividad es mucho menor. Además, estudios recientes demuestran que, en general, los salarios de las mujeres son más bajos que los que reciben los hombres por el mismo tipo de trabajo.

Aunque se perciben algunos cambios, el trabajo doméstico no remunerado se continúa considerando una obligación que permanece asociada a las mujeres y niñas. No obstante, en muchos países hispanos ya se ofrecen programas educativos para combatir la discriminación.

Otras profesiones, oficios y ocupaciones

la juez

el abogado

el actor

el ama de casa

el policía

la bibliotecaria

la cajera

el chofer

la científica

el contador

la electricista

la enfermera

la mujer de negocios

el ingeniero

el intérprete

el obrero

el psicólogo

la arquitecta

la periodista

el plomero

¿Qué dice usted?

9-1 ¿Qué profesión debe tener? Lean las siguientes descripciones y digan qué profesión u oficio de la lista deben tener las personas con estas características. ¡Ojo! A veces, más de una respuesta es posible.

científico/a	ingeniero/a	artista
sicólogo/a	mecánico/a	médico/a
abogado/a	actor/actriz	plomero/a

1. A Pablo le gusta observar y analizar el comportamiento (*behavior*) de las personas.
2. Los hermanos Pedraza siempre resuelven los problemas del auto de su padre. Lo examinan y lo reparan a la perfección.
3. Eva y Ana son lógicas y tienen facilidad para encontrar las causas de un problema y resolverlo. También pueden explicar la solución sin dificultad.
4. Al pequeño Jaimito le fascina desarmar (*disassemble*) aparatos electrónicos para estudiar cómo funcionan.
5. Daniela es una chica muy sensible y una gran observadora. Le fascina expresar sus sentimientos y experiencias de manera artística.
6. Adela siempre lee libros sobre anatomía. Ella puede nombrar cada parte del cuerpo (*body*) humano.

9-2 Las profesiones y las características personales. Primera fase. Digan cómo deben ser estos/as profesionales.

MODELO: un piloto
inteligente / serio / perezoso(a) /...
Debe ser inteligente, serio y responsable. No debe ser perezoso.

1. un/a psiquiatra
valiente / romántico(a) / irónico(a) / antipático(a) / inteligente /...
2. un actor/una actriz
guapo(a) / atractivo(a) / simpático(a) / delgado(a) / alto(a)/...
3. un hombre/una mujer de negocios
autoritario(a) / serio(a) / perezoso(a) / viejo(a) / responsable /...
4. un/a recepcionista...
5. un/a astronauta...
6. un ama de casa...

Segunda fase. Intercambien ideas sobre lo siguiente.

1. ¿Conoce a algún/a... (*profesión*)? ¿Cómo se llama? ¿Dónde trabaja?
2. ¿Qué características personales o especiales, en su opinión, lo/la ayudan en su profesión?

9-3 Asociaciones. Asocien una o más profesiones con los siguientes lugares de trabajo, y digan lo que hacen estas personas.

LUGAR	PROFESIÓN	¿QUÉ HACE?
el hospital		
el restaurante		
la clase		
la estación de radio		
la tienda de ropa		
el consultorio médico		
la peluquería		
el banco		

9-4 ¿Cuál es la profesión? Primero identifiquen la ocupación o profesión, según la descripción. Luego, digan dos ventajas y dos desventajas de esta ocupación o profesión.

MODELO: Trabaja en la casa, limpia y lava los platos.
E1: Es un ama de casa.
E2: Una ventaja de ser ama de casa es que la mujer puede estar con los niños. Otra ventaja es que tiene un horario más flexible.
E3: Una desventaja es que no gana dinero. Otra desventaja es que todos los días el ama de casa trabaja mucho.

1. Escribe artículos para el periódico.
2. Presenta programas de televisión y a veces habla con el público.
3. Traduce simultáneamente del inglés al español.
4. Mantiene el orden público.
5. Apaga incendios.
6. Defiende o acusa a personas delante de un/a juez/a.

9-5 Mi ocupación ideal para el futuro. Primera fase. Piensen en su ocupación/
profesión ideal. Luego, sin mencionarla, pregúntele a su compañero/a lo que
hacen las personas en esa profesión para averiguar cuál es.

Segunda fase. Haga una lista de tres requisitos de su trabajo ideal y compruebe
si usted los tiene. Intercambie esta información con su compañero/a.

MODELO: Me gustaría ser actor/actriz. Un/a actor/actriz debe leer mucho;
           debe saber representar emociones y sentimientos y debe ser flexible
           para trabajar muchas horas. A mí me gusta leer y soy flexible, pero
           no puedo representar muy bien las emociones.

La entrevista

AUDIO La entrevista de trabajo

SRA. ARCE: Buenos días, Sr.
           Solano. Soy Marcela
           Arce, presidenta de la
           compañía.

SR. SOLANO: Mucho gusto, señora.

SRA. ARCE: Siéntese, por favor.
           Usted **solicitó** el
           puesto de **gerente de
           ventas**, ¿verdad?

SR. SOLANO: Sí, señora. Leí en *El Mercurio* que había una **vacante**. Después
            pedí y llené una **solicitud**.

SRA. ARCE: Sí, aquí la tengo, y también su **currículum**. **Por cierto**, es excelente.

SR. SOLANO: Muchas gracias.

SRA. ARCE: **Actualmente** usted trabaja en la empresa Badosa. ¿Por qué quiere
           dejar su **puesto**?

SR. SOLANO: Bueno, **en realidad** yo estoy muy contento allí, pero a mí me
            gustaría trabajar en una compañía internacional y poder usar
            otras lenguas. Como usted ve en mi currículum, yo hablo español,
            inglés y francés.

SRA. ARCE: En su solicitud, usted **indica** que desea un **sueldo** de dos millones
           de pesos al mes. **Sin embargo**, en el puesto que tenemos, el sueldo
           que se **ofrece** es de un millón ochocientos mil pesos.

SR. SOLANO: Sí, lo sé, pero la diferencia no es tan importante. **Lo importante** es
            que aquí puedo tener la **oportunidad** de **comunicarme** con los
            clientes en su **propia** lengua. Yo creo que esto puede mejorar las
            ventas de Computel notablemente.

SRA. ARCE: Pues si le parece bien el sueldo, ¿por qué no pasamos a la oficina
           del director general para seguir hablando?

SR. SOLANO: **¡Cómo no!**

¿Qué dice usted?

9-6 Buscando información. Busquen la siguiente información en el diálogo anterior.

1. nombre de la presidenta de la compañía
2. puesto que solicita el Sr. Solano
3. nombre de la compañía donde trabaja el Sr. Solano
4. nombre de la compañía donde desea trabajar
5. lenguas que habla
6. sueldo que desea el Sr. Solano
7. sueldo que se ofrece en el nuevo puesto
8. motivo para cambiar de puesto

9-7 Buscando trabajo. Imagínese que usted está buscando trabajo. Diga en qué orden haría (*would do*) estas cosas.

_____ Me llaman de la Compañía Rosell para una entrevista.
_____ Les contesto que no, que se cerró el almacén.
_____ Leo los anuncios del periódico.
_____ Envío la solicitud al apartado postal de la Compañía Rosell.
_____ Voy a la compañía para la entrevista.
_____ Me preguntan si me despidieron (*fired*) del trabajo anterior.
_____ Preparo mi currículum y lleno la solicitud para la Compañía Rosell.
_____ Me ofrecen el puesto de vendedor/a.

9-8 ¿Comportamiento apropiado o inapropiado? Preparen una lista de cuatro cosas que **se deben** o **no se deben hacer** antes de una entrevista y cuatro que se deben o no se deben hacer durante una entrevista. Después comparen su lista con la de otros/as compañeros/as.

(NO) SE DEBE HACER ANTES DE LA ENTREVISTA	(NO) SE DEBE HACER DURANTE LA ENTREVISTA

9-9 Entrevista para un trabajo. Ustedes están buscando trabajo y leen los siguientes anuncios en el periódico *La Tercera*. Cada uno/a debe escoger uno de los anuncios. Luego, como práctica para la entrevista, su compañero/a va a hacer el papel de jefe/a de personal de la empresa para obtener la siguiente información. Luego cambien de papel.

1. nombre de la persona que solicita el puesto
2. estudios que tiene
3. lenguas que habla
4. lugar donde trabaja y responsabilidades
5. experiencia anterior
6. razones para querer trabajar en esta compañía

INSTITUTO DE CIRUGÍA PLÁSTICA: CLÍNICA CÁRDENAS
Necesita Enfermera

Prótesis:
implantes faciales (Gorotex, silicona)
liposucción papada,
abdomen,
muslos

Informes:
Clinicasa, Apoquindo 4.100
Tel: 2062223/ 2129212

Llamar a secretaria: Marta

Hotel Galería Imperio

Necesita

RECEPCIONISTA
• Buena presencia
• Bilingüe español-inglés

CAMARERA
• Mín. 2 años experiencia
• Disponible trabajar por las mañanas y tardes

DIRIGIRSE AL HOTEL IMPERIO
Jefe de Personal
Alameda 237   ☎ **Tel.: 2376419**

EMPRESA EXPORTADORA DE FRUTAS
requiere
CONTADOR

Requisitos:
• Experiencia mínima de 5 años
• Graduado del Colegio de Contadores Públicos
• Para cita llamar a Curicó al 71-367801

EMPRESA MINERA

requiere
3 Ingenieros de Sistemas

REQUISITOS:
1. Mayor de 25 años
2. Experiencia en minas de cobre
3. Flexibilidad horaria
(incluidos fines de semana)

OFRECEMOS:
1. Ingreso superior a 2.000.000
2. Capacitación profesional
3. Bonos de participación

Interesados enviar currículum a:
Minería El Teniente

Oficina de Personal
Agustinas 1892, Santiago

AUDIO **9-10 Mi profesión.** You will listen to Julieta Odriozola talking about her profession. Before you listen, write down the names of four professions that you associate with women.

_____

_____

Now, pay attention to the general idea of what is said. Then, as you listen mark the appropriate ending to each statement.

1. Julieta Odriozola es...
   _____ artista
   _____ política
   _____ periodista

2. Julia tiene un horario...
   _____ de 9 a 5
   _____ variable
   _____ de lunes a sábado

3. Julieta hace casi todo su trabajo en...
   _____ su auto
   _____ su casa
   _____ diferentes lugares

4. Julieta trabaja básicamente con...
   _____ artistas jóvenes
   _____ personas importantes
   _____ empleados de la comunidad

1. *Se* + verb constructions

- Spanish uses the **se** + *verb* construction to emphasize the occurrence of an action rather than the person(s) responsible for that action. The noun (what is needed, sold, offered, etc.) usually follows the verb. The person(s) who sell(s), offer(s), etc. is not mentioned. This is normally done in English with the passive voice (is/are + *past participle*).

Se habla español aquí.	*Spanish is spoken here.*

- Use a singular verb with singular nouns and a plural verb with plural nouns.

Se necesita un auto para ese trabajo.	*A car is needed for that job.*
Se venden flores allí.	*Flowers are sold there.*

- When the **se** + *verb* construction is followed not by a noun, but rather by an adverb, an infinitive, or a clause, use a singular verb. This is done in English with indefinite subjects such as *they, you, one, people.*

Se trabaja mucho en esa oficina.	*They work a lot in that office.*
Se podía hablar con el jefe a cualquier hora.	*You could talk to the boss any time.*
Se dice que recibió un aumento.	*People say he/she/you got a raise.*

¿Qué dice usted?

9-11 Asociaciones. Primera fase. Asocie las actividades con los lugares donde ocurren.

1. _____ Se cambian cheques en...   a. un almacén
2. _____ Se vende ropa en...   b. un restaurante
3. _____ Se toma el sol y se nada en...   c. un periódico
4. _____ Se sirven comidas en...   d. una playa
5. _____ Se dan noticias en...   e. un teatro
6. _____ Se presentan comedias en...   f. un banco

Segunda fase. Piense en un edificio o lugar público que le gusta mucho. Luego dígale a su compañero/a qué se hace en ese lugar.

MODELO: Me gusta mucho la playa Reñaca, en Viña del Mar. Allí se camina por la playa, se participa en concursos durante el verano y se habla con chicos interesantes.

9-12 Organizando la oficina. Una compañía de limpieza sacó los muebles y otras cosas de su oficina para limpiar la alfombra. Para poner todo en su lugar, conteste las preguntas que le hacen los encargados de limpieza, de acuerdo con el dibujo.

MODELO: el sofá
E1: ¿Dónde se pone el sofá?
E2: Se pone entre las dos mesas pequeñas.

1. la mesa más larga
2. las revistas
3. la lámpara
4. las dos sillas
5. la computadora
6. la butaca grande
7. las plantas
8. el cesto

9-13 La oficina de antes y la de ahora. Primera fase. Decida qué cosas y/o servicios se necesitaban en una oficina hace treinta años y qué se necesita ahora. Compare sus respuestas con las de su compañero/a.

EQUIPO DE OFICINA	ANTES	AHORA
escritorio		
fotocopiadora		
computadora		
correo electrónico		
máquina de escribir		
teléfono		
calculadora		
fax		
escáner		

Segunda fase. Conversen sobre la oficina más moderna que cada uno/a de ustedes conoce. Expliquen cómo es.

9-14 Anuncios locos. Lean estos anuncios "locos". Luego, intercambien opiniones sobre cuáles les parecen más simpáticos. Finalmente, preparen juntos un anuncio "loco" para compartir con la clase.

1. Se necesitan ingenieros para diseñar y construir un puente desde Chile hasta China. Los interesados deben enviar su currículum en portugués.
2. Se necesita urgentemente un robot bilingüe para hacer todas las tareas de español.
3. Se busca un/a secretario/a para un ejecutivo muy desorganizado. Debe saber hablar y escribir en 40 lenguas.
4. Se compran monstruos para aterrorizar a los clientes de la compañía que nos hace la competencia. Se aceptan Dráculas o Frankensteins.
5. ¿?

EN DIRECTO

To express an idea in a convincing way:

Estoy seguro/a (de) que...

Sería magnífico... + *infinitive.*

Los expertos opinan que...

Sin duda es bueno/mejor + *infinitive.*

To agree with someone's idea:

Me parece perfecto.

Suena muy bien.

¡Qué buena idea!

SITUACIONES

1. **Role A.** You are an advertising manager (*gerente de publicidad*) who is presenting a new campaign (*campaña*) to the president of a company. After showing the president two ads, a) ask him/her if he/she likes them, b) mention the magazines where the ads will appear, and c) explain the reasons why you chose those magazines. Then answer his/her questions.

   Role B. You are the president of an important company who has to decide about a new advertising campaign. After telling the ad manager that you like the ads and listening to his/her explanations, inquire a) about the cost of the campaign, and b) when it will begin.

2. One of you is conducting interviews for your company; the other is a prospective employee. The interviewer asks the candidate a) where he/she read the ad for the job, b) where he/she worked before, c) what he/she used to do there, d) where he/she is working now, and e) why he/she wants to change jobs and work for your company.

2. More on the preterit and the imperfect

■ In *Lección 7* you practiced the preterit of **saber** with the meaning of finding out about something. You also practiced the preterit of **querer** with the meaning of wanting or trying to do something, but failing to accomplish it.

> **Supe** que llegaron anoche.   *I found out that they arrived last night.*
>
> **Quise** ir al aeropuerto, pero   *I wanted (and tried) to go to the*
> fue imposible.   *airport, but it was impossible.*

In the negative, the preterit of **querer** conveys the meaning of refusing to do something.

> **No quise** ir.   *I refused to go.*

■ Other verbs that convey a different meaning in English when the Spanish preterit is used follow:

IMPERFECT		PRETERIT	
Yo **conocía** a Ana.	*I knew Ana.*	**Conocí** a Ana.	*I met Ana.*
Podía hacerlo.	*I could do it. (was able)*	**Pude** hacerlo.	*I accomplished it. (managed to)*
No podía hacerlo.	*I couldn't do it. (wasn't able)*	**No pude** hacerlo.	*I couldn't do it. (tried and failed)*

■ To express intentions in the past, use the imperfect of **ir + a** + *infinitive.*

> **Iba a salir,** pero era muy tarde.   *I was going to go out, but it was very late.*

■ You have used the imperfect to express an action or event that was in progress in the past. You may also use the imperfect progressive when you want to emphasize the ongoing nature of the activity. Form the imperfect progressive with the imperfect of **estar** and the present participle (**-ndo**).

Pepe **estaba hablando** con el cajero cuando llegó el policía.

Pepe was talking to the cashier when the policeman arrived.

¿Qué dice usted?

9-15 ¿Tiene usted buena memoria? Anoche, el director del Hospital Providencia hizo una visita sorpresiva a la sala de emergencia. Desafortunadamente, cuando entró encontró muchas irregularidades, y se puso furioso. Marque las actividades que provocaron esta reacción del director del hospital.

1. _____ Las enfermeras estaban haciendo vida social entre ellas.
2. _____ Algunos médicos estaban mirando béisbol por televisión.
3. _____ Todos los asistentes de la sala de emergencia estaban trabajando.
4. _____ Una de las recepcionistas estaba hablando por teléfono con una paciente.
5. _____ Una empleada estaba hablando por teléfono con su esposo.
6. _____ Dos choferes estaban fumando en la recepción.
7. _____ Un chofer estaba saliendo del hospital para recoger a un paciente.
8. _____ El guardia estaba leyendo el periódico.

9-16 Una oficina muy ocupada. Ustedes visitaron la oficina que aparece en el dibujo. Túrnense para preguntar qué estaban haciendo las personas cuando cada uno/a de ustedes llegó.

MODELO: E1: ¿Qué estaba haciendo Alicia cuando tú llegaste a la oficina?
          E2: Estaba conversando con un cliente.

9-17 A usar la imaginación. Estas descripciones indican lo que estaban haciendo varias personas ayer. Identifiquen cuál era el oficio o profesión de estas personas y qué iban a hacer después.

MODELO: Un señor miraba los planos de un edificio y decía que ciertas cosas no estaban bien.
              E1: Era el arquitecto del edificio.
              E2: Iba a hacer unos cambios en los planos.

1. Un señor tenía un secador en la mano y le tocaba el pelo a una señora que estaba sentada enfrente de él.
2. Unos señores iban en un camión (*truck*) rojo con una sirena. El camión iba muy rápido y los autos y autobuses paraban al lado derecho de la calle.
3. Una joven que llevaba un vestido similar a los que se llevaban en la época de Cleopatra hablaba frente a una cámara. Estaba muy maquillada y tenía una línea negra alrededor de los ojos.
4. Esta persona llevaba un traje espacial, guantes, botas muy grandes y un plástico transparente frente a los ojos para poder ver.

9-18 Una explicación lógica. Ayer ustedes tuvieron una reunión muy importante en su compañía para mostrarles unos productos nuevos a unas empresas extranjeras. Pero varias cosas salieron mal. Busquen una explicación lógica para lo que sucedió.

MODELO: La secretaria no contestaba el teléfono.
              E1: Estaba buscando un intérprete para la reunión.
              E2: No, estaba buscando un salón más grande.

1. Varios empleados llegaron tarde.
2. El técnico no pudo arreglar una computadora que se necesitaba para la presentación.
3. Los periodistas no podían comprender lo que decía un director extranjero.
4. No les sirvieron café ni refrescos a los invitados.
5. Uno de los vendedores no quiso mostrar los productos nuevos.
6. No se pusieron anuncios en los periódicos.

SITUACIONES

Role A. One of your employees did not come to an important meeting at the office, so you call him/her to your office. Greet him/her and ask him/her why he was not at the meeting. After listening to his/her explanation, tell him/her a) that this is the second time this happens, and b) that you will not accept any more excuses in the future.

Role B. You are an employee who was supposed to attend an important meeting at the office, but could not make it. After greeting your boss, apologize and explain a) that your spouse got sick (*enfermarse*) and you had to take him/her to the hospital, and b) that you wanted to take a taxi to go to work, but all the taxis were occupied. Then, say that this will not happen again (*otra vez*).

3. Direct and indirect object pronouns

■ When direct and indirect object pronouns are used in the same sentence, the indirect object pronoun precedes the direct object pronoun. Place double object pronouns before conjugated verbs.

Ella me dio la solicitud.	*She gave me the application.*
Ella **me la** dio.	*She gave it to me.*

■ In compound verb constructions, you may place double object pronouns before the conjugated verb or attach them to the accompanying infinitive or present participle.

Él quiere darme el contrato.	*He wants to give me the contract.*
Él quiere dár**melo**.	*He wants to give it to me.*
Él **me lo** quiere dar.	
Te está diciendo la verdad.	*She is telling you the truth.*
Te la está diciendo.	*She is telling it to you.*
Está diciéndo**tela**.	

■ **Le** and **les** cannot be used with **lo, los, la,** or **las.** Change **le** or **les** to **se.**

Le dio el puesto a Berta.	*He gave the job to Berta.*
Se lo dio.	*He gave it to her.*
Les va a mostrar el anuncio.	*She is going to show them the ad.*
Se lo va a mostrar.	*She is going to show it to them.*

■ When a direct object pronoun and a reflexive pronoun are used together, the reflexive pronoun precedes the direct object pronoun.

Siempre me envío correos electrónicos para recordar lo que debo hacer.	*I always send myself e-mails to remember what I have to do.*
Siempre **me los** envío.	*I always send them to myself.*

¿Qué dice usted?

2 **9-19 ¿Qué hace usted?** La imparcialidad, la amabilidad y la confidencialidad son fundamentales en el trabajo. Lea las siguientes situaciones y seleccione lo que usted haría (*would do*) en cada una. Puede ser posible más de una respuesta correcta.

1. Un cliente le pide a usted el número de teléfono de la oficina del presidente de la compañía.
   a. _____ Usted se lo da.   b. _____ Usted no se lo da.

2. Alguien le pide a usted que le permita leer un documento confidencial.
   a. _____ Usted se lo muestra.   b. _____ Usted no se lo muestra.

3. La nueva jefa de personal le pide que le presente a todos los empleados de su oficina.
   a. _____ Usted se los presenta.   b. _____ Usted no se los presenta.

4. Una empleada nueva le dice a usted que quiere vacaciones después de trabajar sólo tres meses.
   a. _____ Usted se las da.   b. _____ Usted se las niega (*refuse*).

5. Un cliente bueno y uno malo le piden a usted una cita con el presidente de la compañía a la misma hora.
   a. _____ Usted se la concede al buen cliente.
   b. _____ Usted le pregunta al cliente malo si puede venir a otra hora.

ACENTOS

You have learned that when the stress falls on the third syllable from the end, a written accent is required; therefore, you need to add one on the verb when double object pronouns are attached to an infinitive.

¿Va a darme la solicitud?
→ ¿Va a dármela?

When double object pronouns are attached to a present participle, the stress falls on the fourth syllable from the end, and a written accent is also required:

Se la está dando. →
Está dán do se la.
  4   3   2   1

9-20 En ausencia del jefe. En su función de gerente de la compañía, usted tuvo que viajar. Pero antes de salir, usted responsabilizó al jefe de publicidad de tratar con un empleado nuevo en la compañía. De regreso, usted conversa con el/la empleado/a nuevo/a para saber qué hizo el jefe de publicidad.

MODELO: darle el contrato (a usted)
E1: ¿Le dio el contrato?
E2: Sí, me lo dio.

1. explicar la campaña de publicidad
2. mostrar los anuncios
3. traer las revistas
4. pedir el cheque
5. dejar las fotos
6. describir a los/las modelos que se necesitan

9-21 ¡El cliente siempre tiene la razón! Primera fase. Dos de ustedes son clientes que cenaron en el restaurante de un hotel muy elegante y el tercero es el encargado del servicio del hotel. Este último les va a hacer preguntas y tomar notas para saber la opinión de ustedes sobre el servicio que recibieron.

1. ¿Cuándo les sirvieron el agua?
2. ¿Les mostraron la carta (*list*) de vinos enseguida?
3. ¿Les trajeron pan caliente a la mesa?
4. ¿Les dijo el camarero cuáles eran los platos especiales del día?
5. ¿Se los describió?
6. Después de que ustedes empezaron a comer, ¿les preguntó el camarero si la comida estaba bien?
7. ¿Les ofreció el camarero postres y café?
8. ¿Cómo fue el servicio en general?

Segunda fase. Los encargados del servicio del restaurante deben comparar sus notas para decidir qué áreas necesitan mejorar. Los clientes deben reunirse para comentar sus experiencias y compartir sus opiniones sobre el servicio del restaurante.

A INVESTIGAR

¿Cuáles son los principales productos de exportación de Chile? ¿Cuáles son los países que compran más productos chilenos?

SITUACIONES

1. **Role A.** You are a reporter for *La Tercera*, a Santiago newspaper, and you have traveled to Valparaíso to cover a story. Since you left Santiago in a rush, you forgot your taperecorder and camera (*cámara*) in the taxi. Call a fellow reporter and a) tell him/her what happened, b) ask if he/she can lend you his/her car, taperecorder and camera, and c) explain that you need everything right away.

   Role B. You are a reporter for "Canal 5 de Playa Ancha" in Valparaíso. A colleague calls you to tell you about his/her ordeal. Ask him/her a) where it happened, and b) if he/she called the taxi company. Then say that he/she can come to your house to pick up what he/she needs.

2. One of you is an employee who has just returned from delivering a letter, the other is the boss. The boss will ask the employee questions to find out a) if he/she delivered the letter, b) to whom he/she gave the letter, c) when, and d) if the person signed a receipt (*recibo*).

4. Formal commands

Por favor, llene la solicitud y mándela por correo.

- Commands (**los mandatos**) are the verb forms used to tell others to do something. Use formal commands with people you address as **usted** or **ustedes.** To form these commands, drop the final **-o** of the **yo** form of the present tense and add **-e(n)** for **-ar** verbs and **-a(n)** for **-er** and **-ir** verbs.

		USTED	USTEDES	
hablar	→	hable	hable	hablen	*speak*
comer	→	come	coma	coman	*eat*
escribir	→	escribe	escriba	escriban	*write*

- Verbs that are irregular in the **yo** form of the present tense maintain the same irregularity in the command form.

		USTED	USTEDES	
pensar	→	pienso	piense	piensen	*think*
dormir	→	duermo	duerma	duerman	*sleep*
repetir	→	repito	repita	repitan	*repeat*
poner	→	pongo	ponga	pongan	*put*

- The use of *usted* and *ustedes* with command forms is optional. When used, they normally follow the command.

  Pase/Pase **usted.**   *Come in.*

- To make a formal command negative, place **no** before the affirmative command.

  No salga ahora.   *Do not leave now.*

■ Object and reflexive pronouns are attached to the end of affirmative commands (note the written accent over the stressed vowel). Object and reflexive pronouns precede negative commands and are not attached.

Cómprela.	*Buy it.*
No **la** compre.	*Do not buy it.*
Háblenle.	*Talk to him/her.*
No **le** hablen.	*Do not talk to him/her.*
Siéntese.	*Sit down.*
No **se** siente.	*Do not sit down.*

■ The verbs **ir, ser,** and **saber** have irregular command forms.

ir: **vaya, vayan**   ser: **sea, sean**   saber: **sepa, sepan**

■ Verbs ending in **-car, -gar, -zar, -ger,** and **-guir** have spelling changes in command forms.

sacar	sac**o**	→	sa**que**, sa**quen**
jugar	jue**go**	→	jue**gue**, jue**guen**
almorzar	almuer**zo**	→	almuer**ce**, almuer**cen**
recoger	reco**jo**	→	reco**ja**, reco**jan**
seguir	si**go**	→	si**ga**, si**gan**

¿Qué dice usted?

9-22 ¿Dónde se dicen estas cosas? Identifiquen el lugar donde se pueden escuchar o leer estas órdenes: en la sala de emergencia de un hospital (**E**), en un almacén (**A**), o en un estudio de televisión (**T**).

1. _____ Mande su solicitud para recibir la tarjeta de crédito por correo.
2. _____ No interrumpa a los médicos cuando hablan con los pacientes.
3. _____ Compren sus regalos de cumpleaños aquí.
4. _____ Pague en la caja.
5. _____ No haga visitas después de las nueve de la noche.
6. _____ Mueva el micrófono a la derecha.
7. _____ No traiga medicinas.
8. _____ Si hay luz roja, guarde silencio.

9-23 Preguntas de un/a estudiante. Usted estuvo ausente en clase durante la semana dedicada a Chile y quiere saber qué tiene que hacer para ponerse al día. Su compañero/a, en el papel de profesor/a, contesta afirmativamente a sus preguntas. Después, cambien de papel.

MODELO: estudiar la Lección 9
            E1: ¿Estudio la Lección 9?
            E2: Sí, estúdiela.

1. contestar las preguntas sobre el desierto de Atacama
2. escuchar los discos del pianista chileno Claudio Arrau
3. escribir algunas expresiones chilenas
4. leer el Enfoque cultural sobre Chile
5. hacer la tarea sobre las culturas indígenas de Chile

2 **9-24 En el hospital.** Un/a enfermero/a entra en la habitación y le hace las siguientes preguntas al/a la paciente. Túrnense para hacer los papeles de enfermero/a y paciente.

MODELO: E1: ¿Le abro las cortinas?
             E2: Sí, ábramelas, por favor. Quisiera leer.
                No, no me las abra. Voy a dormir.

1. ¿Le pongo la televisión?
2. ¿Le traigo un jugo?
3. ¿Le pongo otra almohada?
4. ¿Me llevo estas flores?
5. ¿Le traigo el teléfono?
6. ...

2 **9-25 Mandatos del entrenador de un equipo.** Preparen una lista de sugerencias que el/la entrenador/a puede darles a los miembros de su equipo para lograr los objetivos siguientes. Comparen su lista con la de otros estudiantes.

MODELO: para mantenerse en buen estado físico
             Practiquen todos los días. No se acuesten tarde.

1. para tener mejor rendimiento (*performance*)
2. para prepararse mentalmente para un partido difícil
3. para evitar problemas con el árbitro

2 **9-26 ¿Qué deben hacer estas personas?** Busquen una solución a los siguientes problemas y díganle a cada persona lo que debe hacer.

MODELO: El Sr. Álvarez no está contento en su trabajo.
             E1: Busque otro trabajo inmediatamente.
             E2: Hable con su jefe y explíquele la situación.

1. La Sra. Jiménez necesita más vendedores en su compañía.
2. El Sr. Jiménez es contador y tiene que terminar un informe, pero su computadora no funciona.
3. Unos hombres de negocios van a ir a Chile y no saben hablar español.
4. La Sra. Peña tuvo un accidente serio con su auto, y el otro chofer le dijo que iba a llamar a la policía.
5. La Sra. Hurtado entra en su apartamento y ve que hay agua en el piso de la cocina.
6. La cantante Mirta del Valle va a cantar en el Festival Internacional de la Canción en Viña del Mar, pero se siente bastante mal.

SITUACIONES

1. **Role A.** You are going to be away for a series of job interviews. Tell your neighbor a) how long you will be away and b) ask him/her if he/she could do a few things for you while you are away. After he/she agrees, tell him/her to a) feed the cat every day, b) water the plants every (*cada*) three days, c) pick up the mail (*correspondencia*), and d) any other things that you may think of. Thank him/her for his/her help.

   Role B. Your neighbor tells you that he/she is going to be away and you agree to help him/her out. After he/she tells you what you will have to do, ask him/her a) whom should you call in case of an emergency (*emergencia*), and b) the telephone number of the veterinary.

2. **Role A.** You have moved to Concepción, Chile, and have opened a checking account (*cuenta corriente*) at Banco del Estado. Since you are not familiar with their system, ask an employee to help you. After he/she gives you all the details, a) thank him/her, and b) say that you are very happy with the service the bank provides the customers.

   Role B. You are an employee at the Banco del Estado. Using the check below, explain to the customer where a) to put the date, b) to write the payee's name, c) to write the amount (*cantidad*) in numbers, d) to write the amount in words, and e) sign (**firmar**) the check.

Serie AD　　6703690　　　　　　　　$ _____

012-0587
446

PARRAL
Balmaceda 429

_____ - ___ DE _____ AÑO _ _ _ _ _

PÁGUESE A
LA ORDEN DE _____

O AL PORTADOR

LA CANTIDAD DE _____

_____ PESOS M/L

BANCO DEL ESTADO DE CHILE _____

06703690　　0190587446004 2102　　　01

Escuchar

Contextual guessing

Sometimes in the course of a conversation you might not understand a word or a phrase that you hear, but you can understand the message by using contextual cues, that is, by paying attention to the topic or to a part of the word that you don't understand. Also paying attention to the words that precede or follow what you did not understand will help.

Antes de escuchar

9-27. Profesiones diferentes. In activity **9-28,** you will listen to a conversation between two friends talking about their professions, what they do, and the advantages and disadvantages of their jobs. Before you listen, write down the name of two professions and an advantage and a disadvantage for each one.

PROFESIÓN	VENTAJA	DESVENTAJA
_____	_____	_____
_____	_____	_____

A escuchar

AUDIO **9-28.** First, read the words in the left column and listen to the conversation between Estela and Susana. Then, state the probable meaning of each word based on the contextual cues you heard in the conversation. Finally, write down the cue words that helped you understand.

ESCUCHÉ...	POSIBLE SIGNIFICADO	ADIVINÉ EL SIGNIFICADO PORQUE...
neuróloga		
primordial		
guardias		

Después de escuchar

9-29 ¿Y usted? With a classmate, share your answers to the following questions.

1. ¿Cuáles son las ventajas y desventajas de ser médico, abogado o plomero?
2. En general, ¿qué profesión u ocupación le parece a usted que produce menos estrés?
3. ¿Qué profesión u ocupación, según usted, da más satisfacciones personales? ¿Por qué?

Antes de escuchar

9-30 El plomero y el electricista. In **9-31,** you will listen to a plumber and an electrician talking about their jobs. Before you listen, write down what you know about what they do, where they work, etc.

plomero _____
electricista _____

A escuchar

9-31. First, read the words in the left column and listen to the conversation. Then, state the probable meaning of each word, based on the contextual cues you heard in the conversation. Finally, write down the cue words that facilitated your comprehension.

ESCUCHÉ...	POSIBLE SIGNIFICADO	ADIVINÉ EL SIGNIFICADO PORQUE...
inundó		
tubería		
ferretería		

Después de escuchar

9-32 ¿Y usted? With a classmate, share your answers to the following questions.

1. En su casa, ¿alguna vez tuvo que llamar a un plomero o a un electricista? ¿Por qué?
2. ¿Sabe usted hacer una instalación eléctrica? ¿Quién le enseñó?
3. ¿Cree usted que es importante saber arreglar las cosas en la casa? ¿Por qué?

Conversar

Antes de conversar

9-33 ¿Qué requisitos se piden? Completen la tabla con algunos requisitos que las compañías por lo general piden para los siguientes puestos.

PUESTOS	SE REQUIERE...	SE OFRECE(N)...
secretario/a	experiencia previa, capacidad de organización	sueldo compatible con experiencia, vacaciones pagadas
vendedor/a		
contador/a		
director/a de un instituto de idiomas extranjeros		

9-34 Se ofrece y se busca trabajo. Lea los siguientes anuncios con ofertas de trabajo, escoja un anuncio para un puesto que a usted le interese y prepare una lista de requisitos que, en su opinión, usted cumple (*meet*). Comparta su lista con su compañero/a.

INSTITUTO PRIVADO

necesita

DIRECTOR/A

Lugar de residencia, Región de los Lagos

Requisitos:
- Titulación adecuada al puesto
- Experiencia de 5 años en cargo similar
- Responsabilidad y constancia
- Capacidad de organización, coordinación y trabajo
- Relaciones públicas

Sueldo compatible con calificaciones

Interesados, enviar CV, con fotografía reciente a Casilla 934, Osorno, Chile   Se responderá por escrito

---

JEFE DE SERVICIO

necesita importante empresa

MANUFACTURERA DE PLÁSTICOS

Se requiere: Experiencia de 4 años en empresa del sector en puesto de similar responsabilidad. *Se ofrece:* Buenas perspectivas de avance profesional. Integración en empresa en expansión hacia el extranjero.

Interesados, enviar currículum y fotografía reciente, especificando pretensiones de sueldo, a Casilla 2568, Correo Santiago Centro, Santiago

---

BANCO O'HIGGINS

necesita

10 CONTADORES AUDITORES

Lugar de trabajo ideal: Viña del Mar

- Título universitario
- Mínimo 2 años de experiencia
- Flexibilidad horaria
- Deseo de viajar a otras regiones del país
- Capacidad de organización y trabajo

Sueldo atractivo

Interesados, enviar currículum, con fotografía a: Bco. O'Higgins, Casilla 1902-D, Viña del Mar

---

EMPRESA DE EXPORTACIONES
necesita para Chile y el extranjero

VENDEDORES/AS REPRESENTANTES

Sueldo inicial 1,000.000
Comisión de ventas

Se requiere: Experiencia en ventas y representación. Buena presencia y deseos de superación. Mayor de 25 años. Buen dominio del inglés y/o francés; japonés y árabe deseables.

Se ofrece: Trabajo inmediato. Entrenamiento en la empresa. Promoción rápida. Sueldo negociable más comisión después del período de prueba.

Interesados, llamar a los teléfonos
2218765, 2169036
Lunes a viernes de 8:30 a 15:00 hrs.

A conversar

9-35 Ahora escojan un papel: el de jefe de personal de las compañías representadas en los anuncios o el de una persona que busca un trabajo. Sigan las instrucciones para cada rol.

Jefe de personal: Entreviste separadamente a dos personas que están interesadas en el puesto que ofrece su compañía. Pregúnteles sobre: a) su experiencia, b) sus estudios, c) sus preferencias de sueldo, etc. y decida cuál es la persona indicada para el puesto.

Persona que busca trabajo: Escoja el anuncio con el trabajo que usted necesita. Responda a las preguntas del/de la jefe/a de personal de la manera más completa posible y haga preguntas si lo considera necesario.

Después de conversar

9-36 Expectativas y decisiones. Los jefes de personal y las personas que buscaban trabajo deben informar a la clase sobre lo siguiente:

Informe de las personas que buscaban trabajo:

1. ¿Qué puesto buscaba usted? ¿Qué requisitos para el puesto cumple usted?
2. ¿Qué aspecto de la oferta de trabajo le pareció más atractivo?
3. ¿Cree usted que va a recibir la oferta de trabajo? ¿Por qué?

Informe de los jefes de personal:

1. ¿Qué puesto ofrecía su compañía en el anuncio?
2. ¿Qué requisitos debía tener el/la candidato/a que buscaba su compañía?
3. ¿A qué candidato/a(s) va usted a contratar? ¿Por qué?

Antes de conversar

9-37 Conflictos profesionales. Lean las siguientes situaciones e identifiquen los problemas en cada una de ellas. Luego, escriban por los menos tres recomendaciones para cada caso.

1. Juan Miguel leyó un anuncio en Internet que ofrecía un trabajo de telemercado en la ciudad de Miami. Solicitó el puesto y lo llamaron a una entrevista. El día de la entrevista, Juan Miguel se puso los pantalones cortos que había comprado para la ocasión, zapatos de tenis, una camisa blanca y un par de aretes. Llegó a la entrevista puntualmente, esperó unos minutos hasta que alguien lo invitó a pasar a su oficina. Cuando entró a la oficina del entrevistador, éste lo miró con sorpresa. Nunca lo llamaron para ofrecerle el trabajo. Juan Miguel se pregunta por qué.

2. Consuelo es la secretaria personal del presidente de una gran compañía de productos tecnológicos. Su jefe siempre se reúne con personas importantes con quienes la compañía hace negocios. Por su trabajo, él comparte todo tipo de información con ella. Para no poner en riesgo a la compañía, Consuelo debe mantener esta información confidencial. Hace una semana, sin darse cuenta (*not realizing*), ella contestó unas preguntas de uno de sus amigos que era vendedor de otra compañía. De esa manera le dio información vital a su amigo. Consuelo pensó que su amigo vendedor no usaría la información para beneficiar a su propia compañía. En realidad, él no solamente usó la información sino que también provocó el fracaso (*failure*) de un proyecto importante para la compañía donde trabaja Consuelo. Ahora ella piensa que su jefe la va a despedir (*fire*) si descubre que ella es la responsable del fracaso.

A conversar

② **9-38 Consejos.** En el papel de Juan Miguel o de Consuelo, explíquenle al/a la consejero/a (su compañero/a) lo siguiente. El/La consejero/a va a hacerle preguntas y darle algunos consejos. Luego, cambien de papel.

1. Narre la experiencia que vive/vivió y diga cuáles son las complicaciones o consecuencias de sus acciones.
2. Hable de cómo se siente después de lo que ocurrió.
3. Tome notas de las mejores sugerencias que el/la consejero/a le dé.

Después de conversar

G **9-39 Reflexiones.** Conversen sobre lo siguiente.

1. ¿Fue útil la conversación con el/la consejero/a? ¿Por qué?
2. ¿Qué sugerencias le parecieron mejores? ¿Qué recomendación o recomendaciones es/son la(s) más difícil(es) de seguir? ¿Por qué?

 ## Leer

In *Lección 9*, you will practice identifying categories in the text and making inferences based on visuals, headlines, and subheadings.

Guía de prelectura

First, look at the photo and read the title and subhead of the article in **9-42**. Then, using the cues provided by the visuals and the headline and subheading, and relying on your knowledge of the topic, answer the following questions:

1. What ideas do you expect to find in this text?
   a. The gap between men and women at work has disappeared in Chile.
   b. The work world in Chile is still a man's world.
   c. Women make the same salary as men in equal jobs.

2. On what did you base your answers to question 1? Circle the corresponding letter.
   a. The headline and subheading only
   b. The photos in the text
   c. My personal knowledge of the topic

3. After reading the headline and subheading, can you guess some of the content of the text? Use your previously learned skills to anticipate the main topic of the text.

   The text will probably discuss the following ideas. Mark with an X all that may apply.
   a. _____ In the last decades, Chilean women have entered the work place in larger numbers.
   b. _____ Chilean women are discriminated against in the work place.
   c. _____ Women in Chile enjoy the same working conditions as men.
   d. _____ Although working women in Chile have made progress regarding their labor rights, they still have not been granted the same treatment at work that men enjoy.

Antes de leer

9-40 Preparación. En general, la mujer en muchas partes del mundo no comenzó a trabajar fuera de casa hasta el siglo XX. Marque con una X las posibles razones de este fenómeno, según usted. Si tiene otra opción, agréguela.

1. _____ La mujeres antes del siglo XX tenían poca educación.
2. _____ Las mujeres decidieron trabajar fuera de casa porque no querían cuidar a sus hijos.
3. _____ Las economías de algunos países mejoraron y se presentaron más ofertas de trabajo para las mujeres.
4. _____ Los hombres se retiraron de sus trabajos para ayudar a las mujeres.
5. _____ Con más educación, las mujeres comenzaron a tener más confianza (*confidence*) en sí mismas.
6. _____ Por los cambios sociales, los jefes empezaron a valorar la capacidad de la mujer y las contribuciones que ésta podía hacer en el lugar de trabajo.
7. _____ ¿?

9-41 ¿Trabajos femeninos o masculinos? Primera fase. Algunas personas piensan que hay trabajos que las mujeres pueden hacer mejor que los hombres y viceversa. De la siguiente lista, indique cuáles áreas de trabajo se consideran en general más apropiadas para las mujeres (**M**) y cuáles para los hombres (**H**).

1. _____ educación
2. _____ enfermería
3. _____ gerencia (*management*)
4. _____ telemercado
5. _____ relaciones públicas
6. _____ economía
7. _____ medicina
8. _____ psicología
9. _____ mecánica
10. _____ limpieza (*cleaning*)

Segunda fase. Comparen sus respuestas y respondan a estas preguntas.

1. Según ustedes, ¿hay realmente trabajos más apropiados para las mujeres que para los hombres? ¿Cuáles?
2. ¿Se basan las diferencias en la calidad de trabajo que hacen las personas de ese género (*gender*) o en otra cosa? Si su respuesta es afirmativa, explíquenla.

A leer

9-42 Primera mirada. Lea el siguiente artículo y haga lo que se indica.

¿Es justo el mundo laboral chileno?

Varias razones explican la creciente incorporación de la mujer chilena al mundo laboral. La bonanza financiera de los años 90 favoreció la creación de nuevos negocios y empresas, y un aumento de las ofertas de trabajo. Aunque la presencia femenina en la economía nacional es evidente, las chilenas aún no logran los niveles de participación de las argentinas y las colombianas.

Las estadísticas indican que la fuerza laboral femenina chilena aumentó de un 34% en 2002 a un 36% en 2004. No obstante, Colombia y Argentina superan a Chile con una tasa de un 45%. Según datos del Ministerio del Trabajo, entre febrero y abril de 2004, las empresarias chilenas aumentaron en un 50% y las mujeres que trabajan para otros en un 47%.

Según Fernanda Villegas, asesora laboral del Servicio Nacional de la Mujer (SERNAM), la mayor presencia femenina en el mundo laboral responde a un cambio generacional. Juan Pablo Swett, gerente del portal Trabajando.com, piensa que el incremento laboral femenino se debe a la mayor confianza de los jefes en la capacidad de la mujer.

Algunos sociólogos opinan que la tendencia al aumento de la presencia femenina en el mundo laboral es el resultado de cambios socioculturales, por eso, debería continuar, independientemente de las variaciones económicas. Sin embargo, algunos estudios muestran que la incorporación de la mujer al trabajo funciona por ciclos, es decir, cuando mejora la economía, la mujer participa en el desarrollo económico del país, pero deja de hacerlo cuando hay crisis. Afortunadamente, existen otros indicadores que prometen una participación más estable de la mujer en la economía: el continuo mejoramiento del nivel educativo femenino y la creación de pequeñas empresas dirigidas por mujeres.

Tipos y condiciones de trabajo para las mujeres

Las investigaciones indican que las mujeres chilenas en general trabajan en recursos humanos, mercadeo y relaciones públicas, áreas en que pueden hacer un mejor trabajo que el hombre.

Según expertos del Ministerio del Trabajo, aunque las mujeres pueden realizar ciertos trabajos desde casa, como el teletrabajo, las madres de familia que trabajan fuera de casa no siempre cuentan con las condiciones para hacerlo. Muchas de ellas no tienen acceso a guarderías para el cuidado de sus hijos, ni el apoyo del hombre en la casa. Además, afirma Alexandra Ruedas, del Ministerio del Trabajo, existen algunos mitos que las mujeres chilenas deben enfrentar. Muchos creen que las mujeres tienen menos años de estudio que los hombres. Pero las estadísticas indican que en promedio la mujer chilena tiene 11,7 años de estudios, mientras que el hombre estudia un promedio de 10,5 años.

A pesar de su mayor escolaridad, las chilenas ganan menos que los hombres en trabajos y especialidades iguales. Aunque estas diferencias están desapareciendo lentamente, algunas empresas prefieren contratar a un hombre y no a una mujer, especialmente durante los años de maternidad.

Sin duda, la entrada de la mujer en el mundo del trabajo marcó un momento histórico importante. Los avances que ésta ha hecho también son significativos, pero aún queda mucho camino por andar.

Indique cuáles de las siguientes afirmaciones son inferencias (I) basadas en el contenido del artículo. Si la afirmación es una inferencia (I), indique la(s) línea(s) donde está la información en que ésta se basa.

1. _____ El progreso de la economía es una de las causas del aumento de la presencia de la mujer en el trabajo.
2. _____ En comparación con Argentina, en Chile hay menos mujeres que trabajan.
3. _____ En el año 2002, hubo un incremento de la fuerza laboral femenina.
4. _____ En Colombia y Argentina el 45% de los trabajadores son mujeres.

5. _____ En 2004, era mayor el número de mujeres que participaban en el desarrollo económico de Chile.

6. _____ Los porcentajes indican que posiblemente más mujeres trabajan para sí mismas en casa.

7. _____ Se piensa que el aumento de trabajadoras en Chile responde a cambios sociales y culturales.

8. _____ Las mujeres tienen más capacidad que los hombres para vender y relacionarse con los clientes.

9. _____ Para las chilenas con hijos no es fácil trabajar fuera de casa.

10. _____ Las chilenas sufren de discriminación en el trabajo.

9-43 Segunda mirada. Las siguientes palabras aparecen en el artículo. Agrúpelas según el campo (*field*) con que se asocian.

tasa	teletrabajo	estadísticas	sociólogo
bonanza	tendencia	relaciones públicas	crisis
desarrollo	creación	empresarias	datos
aumento	asesora laboral	gerente	recursos humanos

1. Números o porcentaje: _____

2. Trabajos/profesiones: _____

3. Áreas de trabajo: _____

4. Condiciones económicas: _____

Después de leer

9-44 Lluvia de ideas. El Ministerio de la Mujer de Chile pide la colaboración de las empresas para mejorar la situación laboral de las mujeres. El gerente de su compañía solicita que los jefes de personal identifiquen por lo menos **dos** problemas de las trabajadoras y den **tres** recomendaciones para cada problema. Respóndanle usando el documento que aparece a continuación. Usen los mandatos.

Para: Gerencia General

De: Jefes de Personal: _____ (nombres)

Estimado Sr. Gerente:

En respuesta a su petición sobre los problemas de las trabajadoras en nuestra compañía, los jefes de personal exponemos lo siguiente:

En nuestra opinión, las trabajadoras de nuestra empresa enfrentan estos problemas que requieren una pronta solución:

1. _____
2. _____

Para ayudar a resolverlos, sugerimos lo siguiente:

Para solucionar el primer problema, _____
_____

Para solucionar el segundo problema, _____
_____

Esperamos trabajar juntos con usted en beneficio de nuestras colegas.

Atentamente,

Jefes de Personal

Escribir

In today's world, getting the job you want may be difficult because of the job market. Therefore, answering a want ad takes as much skill as giving a good interview.

The following are some basic tips that may prove useful when answering a want ad in any language. Pay attention to . . .

a. the academic requirements of the job: Does it require a high school diploma or a college degree?
b. the worker profile the employer has in mind: Is experience required or not? If required, what kind and how much experience is required? What personality criteria will you need to meet to be considered for the job?
c. job-specific skills: Should you be a specialist in a field? What skills or dexterities should you possess? Should you be good at answering questions, speaking and/or writing in another language?, etc.

Antes de escribir

9-45 Preparación. Usted es un/a exitoso/a profesional chileno/a que hace un par de meses se divorció. Ahora debe cuidar a un hijo de cuatro años y a una hija de seis. Como necesita ayuda, usted escribió un anuncio en Internet para solicitar los servicios de una niñera (*nanny*). En preparación para la actividad 9-47, lea el siguiente mensaje electrónico que una persona interesada le escribió en respuesta a su anuncio en Internet.

De: sofia.morales@entel.chile

Para: rruiz@ct.chile

Ref.: Cuidado de sus hijos

Estimado/a señor/a Ruiz:

Mi nombre es Sofía Morales. Soy secretaria de profesión, pero por el momento estoy desempleada. Aunque no tengo mucha experiencia como niñera, pienso que puedo hacer un buen trabajo porque me fascinan los niños. Si me permite, me gustaría hacerle algunas preguntas preliminares para saber más sobre sus hijos.

Primero, con respecto al temperamento y gustos de los niños: ¿Son sociables? ¿Se adaptan fácilmente a personas desconocidas? ¿Lloran mucho cuando usted no está? ¿Qué se debe hacer para mantenerlos tranquilos y felices?

Segundo, en relación con los hábitos de ellos: ¿Se despiertan y se levantan temprano? ¿Duermen la siesta? ¿Se acuestan antes que usted regrese de su trabajo? ¿Cómo se divierten durante el día?

Tercero, con respecto a la comida: ¿Qué desayunan o almuerzan? ¿Debo prepararles el desayuno y el almuerzo? ¿Hay algo que deben o no deben comer o beber?

Finalmente, ¿a qué hora vuelve usted a casa? Yo debo regresar a mi casa antes de las 8:00 de la noche.

Tengo referencias que le puedo propocionar cuando usted las necesite.

Estaré encantada de conocer a sus hijos. Estoy segura de que si usted me da el trabajo, los niños y yo vamos a llevarnos muy bien.

Atentamente,

Sofía Morales

9-46 ¡Las prioridades deciden! A usted le gusta la candidata que le escribió. Puesto que necesita pronto su servicio escríbale una carta inmediatemente.

1. Para la introducción de su carta, puede agradecer así: "Muchas gracias por responder al anuncio de niñera que puse en Internet". Ahora, escriba otra manera de agradecerle a la persona que respondió a su anuncio.

_____

2. Para contestar las preguntas de la candidata, lea con cuidado la lista de preguntas que recibió y responda a cada una de ellas. Recuerde que en general, los mandatos van a ser muy útiles para indicarle a la candidata lo que debe hacer. Por ejemplo, "Mándeme sus referencias por correo".

3. Para terminar su carta, informe a la candidata sobre la posible fecha y hora de la entrevista y cuándo va a saber la decisión final que usted tomó. Por ejemplo, "Por favor, llámeme por teléfono el lunes por la mañana para hablar sobre fecha y hora de la entrevista".

A escribir

9-47 Manos a la obra. Respóndale —con la mayor cantidad de detalles posible— el mensaje electrónico a su futura niñera. Use la información de la actividad **9-46.**

Después de escribir

9-48 Revisión. Ahora lea su mensaje electrónico, pensando en su lectora. Verifique lo siguiente:

■ El contenido: ¿Respondió usted a todas las preguntas de la candidata? ¿Le dio los detalles necesarios?

■ La organización: ¿Tiene su correo electrónico una organización clara, es decir, una introducción, un cuerpo y un cierre?

■ La forma de su mensaje:
  a. ¿Revisó la gramática: el vocabulario correcto, algunas expresiones de cortesía y de despedida, la concordancia, el tiempo (presente, pasado), el uso de los mandatos, etc.?
  b. ¿Usó la puntuación y la ortografía correctas?

Finalmente, comparta su mensaje electrónico con un/a compañero/a. Esto puede darle la perspectiva de un lector potencial.

ENFOQUE CULTURAL

TEMAS: LA ECONOMÍA

Para pensar

Generalmente, ¿es fácil conseguir trabajo después de graduarse de la universidad? ¿Hay mucho desempleo en los Estados Unidos? ¿Ganan mucho dinero los profesionales jóvenes y con poca experiencia? ¿Existen aún diferencias notables entre las oportunidades y la remuneración que perciben los hombres y las mujeres por un trabajo similar?

Muchos niños y jóvenes de las clases más pobres trabajan desde pequeños limpiando zapatos, vendiendo periódicos o dulces en la calle, y aun como empleados domésticos.

Hay países hispanos con problemas económicos y pocas posibilidades de empleo en el sector privado y en el público.

Los sueldos bajos traen una serie de consecuencias sociales: los jóvenes tienen que permanecer en la casa de sus padres y deben conseguir dos y hasta tres empleos para sobrevivir.

Para contestar

2 Los trabajos. Respondan a las siguientes preguntas.

1. Mencionen algunos trabajos que los jóvenes de las clases más pobres tienen en algunos países hispanos.
2. ¿Cuáles son algunas consecuencias de una economía en crisis?

G Riqueza cultural. En grupos de tres, identifiquen lo siguiente y compartan luego esta información con la clase.

a. Las zonas de los Estados Unidos que tienen un mayor desarrollo económico
b. Dos países hispanos que muestran desarrollo en algunas áreas de la economía

Cerca de Santiago, se encuentran las grandes industrias del vino con sus viñedos. Concha y Toro, Santa Rita y Macul exportan sus vinos a muchos países del mundo. La fruta constituye también una de las industrias más prósperas de Chile. Éstas se exportan a varios continentes en todas las estaciones del año.

Para pensar

¿Sabe usted dónde está Chile? ¿Sabe usted qué productos chilenos se consumen mucho en los Estados Unidos? ¿Conoce usted a alguna persona chilena famosa?

Chile está en el suroeste de América del Sur y tiene una larga costa en el Océano Pacífico. La capital de Chile es Santiago.

La economía chilena ha mejorado mucho en los últimos años. La producción agrícola, mineral e industrial es muy importante y ha contribuido a mejorar la economía del país. Varias compañías que se nacionalizaron en los años 70 ahora son privadas.

Viña del Mar es el principal balneario en el centro del país. En esta ciudad se lleva a cabo el famoso Festival Internacional de la Canción.

Algunos de los lugares favoritos para ir a esquiar en la nieve, especialmente de junio a octubre, son Portillo, Farellones, La Parva y Valle Nevado.

Valparaíso es el principal puerto de Chile. La ciudad de Valparaíso es un lugar turístico y cultural muy interesante. Allí se encuentra la casa museo del poeta Pablo Neruda, ganador del Premio Nobel de Literatura en 1971.

Expresiones chilenas:

pololo/a	María, te presento a mi pololo.	*María, this is my boyfriend.*
planchado/sin chaucha	Está planchado/sin chaucha.	*He is broke.*
tinca	Me tinca que hizo algo malo.	*I have the feeling that he/she did something wrong.*
el descueve	Mi jefe es el descueve.	*My boss is far out.*

Para contestar

En el mapa

1. Diga qué ciudades chilenas están cerca de la frontera con Perú.
2. ¿Qué países están cerca de Chile?
3. Mencione una característica geográfica de Chile.

Ahora diga...

1. si le gustaría visitar Santiago y por qué.
2. qué lugar visitaría en Valparaíso.

¿Qué dice Ud. si...

1. tiene una fuerte impresión de que su amigo fue a una entrevista y le ofrecieron el trabajo.
2. tiene planes de ir al cine con la persona a quien ama.
3. se da cuenta de que no tiene dinero.
4. piensa que la nueva gerente de su compañía es excepcional.

Para investigar en Internet

Busque en la página de un periódico chileno qué trabajos se ofrecen, qué sueldos pagan y cuáles son los requisitos necesarios para obtenerlos, etc. Compare los puestos que ofrecen estos avisos en Chile con los puestos que se ofrecen en avisos semejantes en los periódicos de los Estados Unidos. Comente las semejanzas y diferencias con sus compañeros/as de clase.

¡Prepárese!

9-49 Misterios y pistas. ¿Qué relaciones hay entre las palabras clave de las pistas del Misterio 4? ¿Con qué las asocia? ¿Qué cree que simbolizan? ¿Cómo se pueden relacionar estas cosas con el misterio, "Un lugar estratégico"?

1. La **fuente** de la **civilización**
2. La **flor** de la **civilización**
3. El **manantial** del **romance**
4. El **barco** de la **vida**

Con un/a compañero/a, indique lo siguiente:

	RELACIÓN CON	SÍMBOLO DE
fuente		
civilización		
flor		
manantial		
romance		
barco		
vida		

Manolo quiere que el concurso tenga un tono más personal.

Aunque cuestiona su amistad, Carlos quizás perdone a Katie.

Katie y Efraín forman una alianza.

Katie y Efraín comparten sus pistas.

Tito le pregunta a Sabrina si ella está celosa.

Sabrina quiere ganar y dice que va a ganar.

¡Responda!

9-50 ¿Qué deben hacer? Carlos está decepcionado de Katie; Efraín quiere formar una alianza con Katie; Sabrina quiere ganar el concurso. ¿Qué les puede decir a los participantes para ayudarlos en sus planes? Use los mandatos formales para darles instrucciones y consejos sobre lo que ocurre en este episodio.

MODELO: Carlos   No perdone a Katie porque ella lo decepcionó.

PARTICIPANTE	SU CONSEJO
Carlos	_____
Katie	_____
Efraín	_____
Sabrina	_____

La música de Violeta Parra se reconoce por altó contenido social y es representativa de la Nueva Canción, una forma artística musical de Latinoamérica en la cual el autor expresa sus opiniones políticas y la importancia de la cultura autóctona.

¡Prepárese!

9-51 El simbolismo. Lea esta lista de palabras que se usan en "Gracias a la vida" y exprese lo que pueden simbolizar, según su experiencia personal.

PALABRA	PUEDE SIMBOLIZAR...
luceros	_____
el abecedario	_____
el oído	_____
la risa	_____
el llanto	_____

¡Escuche!

9-52 La canción. Lea parte de la letra de "Gracias a la vida". Después de escuchar la canción conteste las preguntas.

Gracias a la vida que me ha dado tanto
me dio dos luceros que cuando los abro
perfecto distingo lo negro del blanco
y en el alto cielo su fondo estrellado
y en las multitudes el hombre que yo amo.
[...]
me ha dado el oído que en todo su ancho
graba noche y día grillos y canarios
[...]
me ha dado el sonido y el abecedario
con él las palabras que pienso y declaro
[...]

me ha dado la marcha de mis pies cansados
con ellos anduve ciudades y charcos
[...]
me dio el corazón que agita su marco
cuando miro el fruto del cerebro humano,
cuando miro al bueno tan lejos del malo,
[...]
me ha dado la risa y me ha dado el llanto,
así yo distingo dicha de quebranto
los dos materiales que forman mi canto
y el canto de ustedes que es el mismo canto
y que el canto de todos que es mi propio canto.

1. En su opinión, ¿cuáles son los temas de "Gracias a la vida"?
2. ¿Cuáles son algunos de los mensajes de la canción?
3. ¿A quién cree que se dirige la cantautora?
4. ¿Qué palabras puede usar para describir esta canción?

¡Responda!

9-53 El pasado. La autora de "Gracias a la vida" recuerda cosas y actividades importantes de su vida. Piense en las cosas y actividades de su niñez o del lugar donde vivía antes de estudiar en la universidad que eran importantes para usted. Escriba una breve composición sobre este tema, usando los tiempos pasados para contar lo que hacía y cómo era su vida entonces.

MODELO: Cuando yo era niño/a...

VOCABULARIO

Profesiones, oficios y ocupaciones

el/la abogado/a	lawyer
el actor/la actriz	actor/actress
el ama de casa	housewife, homemaker
el/la arquitecto/a	architect
el/la bibliotecario/a	librarian
el/la bombero/a	firefighter
el/la cajero/a	cashier
el/la chofer	driver
el/la científico/a	scientist
el/la contador/a	accountant
el/la ejecutivo/a	executive
el/la electricista	electrician
el/la empleado/a	employee
el/la enfermero/a	nurse
el/la gerente (de ventas)	(sales) manager
el hombre/la mujer de negocios	businessman/woman
el/la ingeniero/a	engineer
el/la intérprete	interpreter
el/la jefe/jefa	boss
el/la juez	judge
el/la locutor/a	radio announcer
el/la médico/a	medical doctor
el/la obrero/a	worker
el/la peluquero/a	hairdresser
el/la periodista	journalist
el/la plomero/a	plumber
el policía/la (mujer) policía	policeman, policewoman
el/la (p)sicólogo/a	psychologist
el/la técnico/a	technician
el/la vendedor/a	salesman, saleswoman

Lugares

el banco	bank
la compañía/empresa	company
el consultorio	doctor's office
la peluquería	beauty salon, barbershop

Trabajo

el anuncio	ad (advertisement)
el/la cliente/a	client
el currículum	résumé
la entrevista	interview
la experiencia	experience
el incendio	fire
la llamada	call
el puesto	position
la oportunidad	opportunity
la solicitud	application
el sueldo	salary
la vacante	opening
las ventas	sales

Verbos

apagar	to extinguish, to turn off
atender (ie)	to answer, to attend
comenzar (ie)	to begin
comunicar(se)	to communicate
cortar	to cut
dejar	to leave
enviar	to send
esperar	to wait for
indicar	to indicate
llenar	to fill (out)
mandar	to send
mejorar	to improve
ofrecer (zc)	to offer
solicitar	to apply (for)

Palabras y expresiones útiles

actualmente	at the present time
¡Cómo no!	Of course!
lo importante	the important thing
por cierto	by the way
por correo	by mail
propio/a	own
en realidad/realmente	in fact, really
la señal	signal
sin embargo	nevertheless

10

LA COMIDA Y LA NUTRICIÓN

Objetivos comunicativos

- Discussing food, shopping, and planning menus
- Expressing wishes and hope
- Making requests and expressing opinions
- Expressing doubt
- Giving advice

Contenido

A primera vista

Explicación y expansión

Mosaicos

Enfoque cultural

Vocabulario

En el supermercado

Frutas y verduras

el ajo · los pimientos verdes · las zanahorias
los pepinos · las espinacas · el maíz, el elote, el choclo
las cebollas · los plátanos/las bananas · las peras
las manzanas · las toronjas/los pomelos · las uvas
los aguacates · las cerezas · las fresas

Productos lácteos

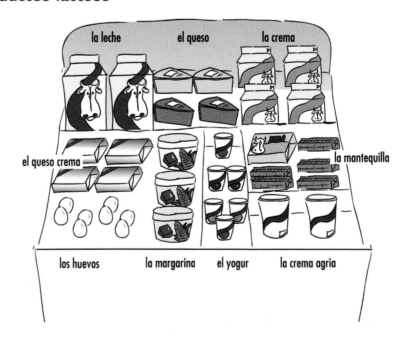

la leche · el queso · la crema
el queso crema · la mantequilla
los huevos · la margarina · el yogur · la crema agria

Pescado y Mariscos

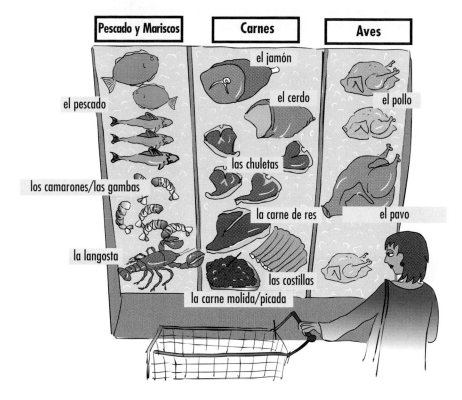

| Pescado y Mariscos | Carnes | Aves |

el jamón

el pescado

el cerdo

el pollo

las chuletas

los camarones/las gambas

la carne de res

el pavo

la langosta

las costillas

la carne molida/picada

Los condimentos

la sal

la pimienta

la mostaza

la vainilla

la harina

el/la azúcar

el vinagre   el aceite

el aderezo

el pan

las galletas

los churros

el pan dulce

la manteca   la salsa de tomate   la mayonesa

los refrescos   el vino tinto   el vino blanco

¿Qué dice usted?

10-1 Asociaciones. Después de asociar cada explicación con la palabra adecuada, comenten entre ustedes si les gustan o no estos alimentos.

1. _____ Se toma mucho en el verano, cuando hace calor.
2. _____ Se pone en la ensalada.
3. _____ Se usan para hacer vino.
4. _____ Se come en el desayuno con huevos fritos.
5. _____ Se prepara para el Día de Acción de Gracias.
6. _____ Se usa para preparar la ensalada de atún o de pollo.

a. el jamón
b. las uvas
c. la mayonesa
d. el helado
e. el aderezo
f. el pavo

10-2 Dietas diferentes. Primera fase. Completen la tabla con comidas adecuadas para estas dietas. Luego, discutan entre ustedes por qué se debe o no se debe comer cada cosa.

DIETA	SE DEBE COMER	NO SE DEBE COMER
vegetariana		
para diabéticos		
para engordar (*gain weight*)		
para bajar de peso (*lose weight*)		

EN DIRECTO

To give some general advice:
Deben + *infinitive* (comer/beber/ etc...)
Para bajar de peso, recomendamos + *noun* (las verduras, el agua, etc.)
Para obtener calcio/proteínas/fibra es bueno + *infinitive* (comer/beber/ etc.)

Segunda fase. Completen las siguientes ideas con sus recomendaciones para cada una de estas personas. Digan por qué.

1. Pedro, que es vegetariano, debe comer...
2. Mi padre, que es diabético,...
3. Luisa está muy delgada y...
4. Joaquín y Fabricio quieren bajar de peso. Por lo tanto...

10-3 ¿Qué necesitamos? Ustedes son estudiantes de intercambio en Ecuador. Le quieren preparar una cena a la familia con la que viven, pero no tienen todos los ingredientes necesarios. ¿Qué necesitan y cuánto cuestan estos ingredientes?

MODELO: E1: Vamos a preparar hamburguesas. Necesitamos un kilo de carne molida.
E2: Eso cuesta tres dólares el kilo.

10-4 Los estudiantes y la comida. Primera fase. En pequeños grupos, hablen de las comidas típicas de los estudiantes de su universidad. ¿Qué comen? ¿Cuándo comen?

Segunda fase. Hagan una lista de recomendaciones para una dieta estudiantil más saludable (*healthy*) y compártanla con el resto de la clase. Piensen en el desayuno, el almuerzo y la cena.

La mesa

el tenedor
el plato
el vaso
la servilleta
el cuchillo
la botella
la cuchara
la bandeja
la taza
la copa
la cucharita
el mantel

¿Qué dice usted?

10-5 Entrenamiento de un/a camarero/a. Usted y su compañero/a son camareros/as en un restaurante y uno/a de ustedes es nuevo/a en el puesto. Dígale a su nuevo/a compañero/a dónde debe poner cada cosa de acuerdo con el dibujo. Después cambien de papel.

MODELO: E1: Ponga el cuchillo a la derecha del plato.
E2: Muy bien. ¿Y dónde pongo la copa?
E1: _____.

CULTURA

La comida de los países hispanoamericanos es muy variada. En Ecuador, al igual que en Perú, el ceviche de pescado o de camarón es muy popular. Como plato principal, se sirve la fritada, un combinado de diversas carnes con plátano (*plantain*) maduro, plátano tostado y maíz. Y entre los postres, además de la pastelería, es muy sabroso el dulce de higos (*fig jelly*).

¿Dónde se compra?

En el área del Caribe, se consumen muchas frutas tropicales, como los plátanos, los mangos, las piñas y las papayas. En Estados Unidos, durante el invierno, se importan muchas frutas de Chile y otros países del hemisferio sur. Ecuador cultiva mucha fruta —sobre todo piña, limón, melón, papaya y maracuyá— y la exporta a los países europeos y a Estados Unidos.

En Bolivia, como en todos los países hispanos, hay buenas **pastelerías** donde se venden los **dulces** típicos de la región.

El pescado y los mariscos son muy importantes en la dieta de algunos países hispanoamericanos como Chile, Perú y Ecuador. En la provincia de Esmeraldas, en Ecuador, uno de los platos típicos es el encocado, pescado que se cocina con leche de coco.

La **artesanía** de Paraguay —especialmente los tejidos y los cestos— es muy apreciada en todo el mundo.

¿Qué dice usted?

10-6 La compra y los preparativos. Primero preparen un menú y luego una lista de lo que tienen que comprar para una cena. Después háganle preguntas a otra pareja para obtener la siguiente información:

1. menú
2. ingredientes
3. número de invitados
4. costo de la cena
5. división del trabajo
6. limpieza

10-7 Una cena. Usted estuvo muy ocupado/a ayer porque tuvo invitados a cenar. Dígale a su compañero/a todas las cosas que hizo. Su compañero/a le va a preguntar dónde hizo la compra, a quién invitó, qué sirvió, y si lo pasaron bien (*had fun*). Después cambien de papel.

EMPANADAS
salteñas bolivianas

MASA

6 tazas de harina	6 cucharadas de manteca
2 yemas de huevo	$\frac{1}{2}$ taza de leche
1 cucharada de azúcar	$1\frac{1}{2}$ tazas de agua tibia
1 cucharadita de sal	

Prepare la masa el día anterior. Mezcle todos los ingredientes para la masa. Amase bastante y envuelva la masa en una servilleta húmeda. Déjela en el refrigerador toda la noche.

RELLENO

3 cucharadas de manteca	1 taza de cebolla blanca picada
1 taza de cebolla verde picada	$1\frac{1}{2}$ cucharada de gelatina sin sabor disuelta en $\frac{1}{2}$ taza de agua
$\frac{1}{2}$ taza de ají colorado	sal y azúcar al gusto
comino y orégano al gusto	1 libra de carne de res picada
1 taza de arvejas cocinadas	1 taza de papas a medio cocinar en cubitos
$\frac{1}{2}$ taza de pasas	2 huevos duros, cortados
6 aceitunas negras, cortadas y sin pepa	

Prepare el relleno también el día anterior. Fría la cebolla en la manteca y agregue el ají, la sal, el azúcar, el comino y el orégano. Añada la carne y cocínela ligeramente. Retire el relleno del fuego y deje que se enfríe un poco. Añada la gelatina, las arvejas y la papa. Deje el relleno en el refrigerador toda la noche.

Para hacer las empanadas, haga unos círculos con la masa de 7 a 10 centímetros de diámetro y $\frac{1}{4}$ centímetro de grosor. Ponga encima de cada círculo un poco del relleno y añádale las pasas, el huevo duro y las aceitunas. Doble y haga pequeños pliegues en el borde de la masa para que no se salga el relleno. Pase un poco de leche o de huevo batido por el borde. Ponga las empanadas sobre moldes de horno enharinados. Póngales un poco de leche o huevo por encima a cada una para que tomen color.

Hornear a 400 grados por 20 a 30 minutos.

10-8 Mi receta favorita. Escojan una receta simple. Escriban los ingredientes y después explíquenle a otra pareja cómo se prepara el plato. Las siguientes palabras pueden facilitarles la explicación: **batir** (*to beat*), **hervir** (**ie**) (*to boil*), **freír** (**i**) (*to fry*), **cortar** (*to cut*).

AUDIO **10-9 Una cena perfecta.** You will listen to a married couple talking about their plans for dinner tonight. Before you listen, make a list of four ingredients you would need to prepare a salad and an entrée.

ensalada _____

plato principal _____

Now, pay attention to the general idea of what is said. Then, as you listen mark the appropriate ending to each statement.

1. Rodolfo es...
   _____ un buen cocinero.
   _____ muy perezoso.
   _____ el esposo de Manuela.
2. Manuela va a...
   _____ cocinar ceviche.
   _____ poner la mesa.
   _____ llamar a los invitados.
3. Rodolfo va a comprar...
   _____ pescado y maíz.
   _____ limón y camarones.
   _____ espinacas y aguacates.
4. Manuela tiene...
   _____ todos los ingredientes.
   _____ muchos vegetales y frutas.
   _____ casi todos los ingredientes.

Antes de seguir...

The indicative and the subjunctive

In previous lessons, you used the indicative mood to state facts (what is happening, what regularly happens, or what has happened) and to talk about what you are certain will occur. Thus, in the sentence *Yo sé que Pepe siempre come en ese restaurante*, the speaker is stating the facts as he or she knows them to be true: Pepe always eats at that restaurant. The indicative is used to talk about actions, events, or states the speaker sees as real.

In this chapter, you will learn about the subjunctive, a verbal mood used for anticipated or hypothetical actions, events, or states. You already know and have used two forms of the subjunctive when you practiced the formal commands in *Lección 9*. With a command, you are trying to impose your will on someone else since you are expressing what you want that person to do: *Venga temprano* is equivalent to saying *Quiero que venga temprano*. Note that the arrival has not happened yet, in fact, it may not happen at all; therefore, it is an unrealized action and the subjunctive is needed.

In this chapter, you will learn about the use of the subjunctive to talk about what you want, hope, or doubt will happen.

1. The present subjunctive

SR. MENA: ¿Qué traigo del supermercado?

SRA. MENA: Necesito que traigas un kilo de camarones frescos y también lechuga y tomate para la ensalada.

SR. MENA: ¿Eso es todo?

SRA. MENA: Sí, y espero que vuelvas rápido y que me puedas ayudar. Tengo mil cosas que hacer.

■ To form the present subjunctive, use the **yo** form of the present indicative, drop the final **-o,** and add the subjunctive ending. Notice that as with **usted/ustedes** commands, **-ar** verbs change the **-a** to **-e,** while **-er** and **-ir** verbs change the **e** and the **i** to **a.**

	HABLAR	COMER	VIVIR
yo	hable	coma	viva
tú	hables	comas	vivas
Ud., él, ella	hable	coma	viva
nosotros/as	hablemos	comamos	vivamos
vosotros/as	habléis	comáis	viváis
Uds., ellos/as	hablen	coman	vivan

■ The present subjunctive of the following verbs with irregular indicative **yo** forms is as follows:

conocer:	conozca, conozcas...	salir:	salga, salgas...
decir:	diga, digas...	tener:	tenga, tengas...
hacer:	haga, hagas...	traer:	traiga, traigas...
oír:	oiga, oigas...	venir:	venga, vengas...
poner:	ponga, pongas...	ver:	vea, veas...

■ The present subjunctive of **hay** is **haya**. The following verbs also have irregular subjunctive forms:

ir:	**vaya, vayas...**	saber:	**sepa, sepas...**
ser:	**sea, seas...**		

■ Stem-changing **-ar** and **-er** verbs follow the same pattern as the present indicative.

pensar: piense, pienses, piense, pensemos, penséis, piensen
volver: vuelva, vuelvas, vuelva, volvamos, volváis, vuelvan

■ Stem-changing **-ir** verbs follow the same pattern as the present indicative but have an additional change in the **nosotros** and **vosotros** forms.

preferir: prefiera, prefieras, prefiera, prefiramos, prefiráis, prefieran
dormir: duerma, duermas, duerma, durmamos, durmáis, duerman

■ Verbs ending in **-car, -gar, -ger, -zar,** and **-guir** have spelling changes.

sacar: saque, saques, saque, saquemos, saquéis, saquen
jugar: juegue, juegues, juegue, juguemos, juguéis, jueguen
recoger: recoja, recojas, recoja, recojamos, recojáis, recojan
almorzar: almuerce, almuerces, almuerce, almorcemos, almorcéis, almuercen
seguir: siga, sigas, siga, sigamos, sigáis, sigan

LENGUA

Remember that you have seen these same orthographic changes in the formal commands:
Saque los platos.
No jueguen ahora.

¿Qué dice usted?

10-10 En la cocina. Escoja la forma verbal correcta para completar lo que le dice un chef a su nuevo asistente.

1. Yo sé que tú _____ (quieres, quieras) ser un buen cocinero.
2. El secreto de la buena cocina _____ (es, sea) usar ingredientes de primera calidad.
3. Debes saber que nosotros _____ (compramos, compremos) vegetales frescos todos los días.
4. Quiero que tú _____ (estás, estés) aquí temprano para lavar y preparar los vegetales.
5. Los primeros días quiero que _____ (miras, mires) cómo cortan los vegetales para aprender a hacerlo bien.
6. Aquí traen los mariscos y el pescado fresco por la mañana, y quiero que _____ (llegas, llegues) antes de las 10 para recibir el pescado y enseñarte a reconocerlo.

Ⓖ **10-11 Excursión a las islas Galápagos. Primera fase.** Su clase está planeando una excursión a las islas Galápagos, en Ecuador. Primero, busquen en Internet la siguiente información sobre estas islas y coméntenla entre ustedes.

1. localización
2. clima
3. lugares de interés
4. tipo de alojamiento (*accomodation*)
5. tipo de transporte para llegar allí

Segunda fase. Ahora escriban una lista de todas las cosas que hay que hacer para preparar la excursión.

MODELO: E1: Hay que reservar los pasajes.
 E2: Sí, y necesitamos comprar unas mochilas.

Tercera fase. Por último, decidan qué quieren ustedes que haga cada persona de su grupo y compártanlo con la clase.

MODELO: reservar los pasajes
 Queremos que Juan reserve los pasajes

2. Subjunctive to express wishes and hope

■ Notice in the examples below that there are two clauses, each with a different subject. When the verb of the main clause expresses a wish or hope, use a subjunctive verb form in the dependent clause.

MAIN CLAUSE	DEPENDENT CLAUSE
La mamá **quiere**	que Alfredo **ponga** la mesa.
The mother wants	*Alfredo to set the table.*
Yo **espero**	que él **termine** temprano.
I hope	*he finishes early.*

■ When there is only one subject, use the infinitive instead of the subjunctive.

Los niños **necesitan almorzar** temprano para ir al gimnasio.	*The children need to have lunch early to go to the gym.*
El mayor **quiere prepararse** un sándwich.	*The older one wants to make himself a sandwich.*
El menor **desea tomar** leche con galletas.	*The younger one wants to have milk and cookies.*

■ With the verb **decir**, use the subjunctive in the dependent clause when expressing a wish or an order. Use the indicative when reporting information.

Dice que los niños **duermen.** (reporting information)	*She says (that) the children are sleeping.*
Dice que los niños **duerman.** (expressing an order)	*She says (that) the children should sleep.*

■ Some common verbs that express want and hope are **desear, esperar, necesitar, preferir,** and **querer.**

> Quieren/Desean que **compres** mariscos.
> *They want you to buy seafood.*

■ Verbs which express an intention to influence the actions of others (**aconsejar, pedir, permitir, prohibir, recomendar**) also require the subjunctive. With these verbs, Spanish speakers often use an indirect object.

> **Les** permite que **salgan** esta noche.
> *She allows them to go out tonight.*

■ The expression **ojalá** (**que**) (*I/we hope*), which comes from Arabic, originally meaning *May Allah grant that . . .*, is always followed by the subjunctive.

> Ojalá (que) ellos **vengan** temprano.
> *I hope they will come early.*
>
> Ojalá (que) **puedas** ir al supermercado.
> *I hope you can go to the supermarket.*

■ You may also try to impose your will or express your influence, wishes, and hope through some impersonal expressions such as **es necesario, es importante, es bueno,** and **es mejor.**

> Es necesario que ellos **vengan** temprano.
> *It is necessary that they come early.*
>
> Es mejor que **comas** pescado.
> *It is better that you eat fish.*

■ If you are not addressing or speaking about someone in particular, use the infinitive.

> Es mejor **comer** pescado.
> *It is better to eat fish.*

¿Qué dice usted?

2 **10-12 Comentarios y deseos.** El Club de Español va a dar una fiesta mañana. Marque los comentarios o deseos de los estudiantes.

1. _____ Esperamos que la fiesta empiece puntualmente.
2. _____ Ojalá que no sirvan comida.
3. _____ Esperamos que pongan música ecuatoriana.
4. _____ Queremos que también inviten a los estudiantes de francés.
5. _____ Ojalá que la fiesta termine temprano.
6. _____ Deseamos que los profesores traigan mucha comida.

2 **10-13 Una fiesta de aniversario. Primera fase.** Los hijos de los señores Sánchez están muy ocupados preparando la fiesta de aniversario de sus padres, quienes cumplen cincuenta años de casados. ¿Qué quiere, necesita o espera la persona responsable de la fiesta que hagan estas personas?

Pedro, Carlos y Mirta   Ana   César

Lola   Jorge y Roberto   Hilda y Ramiro

2 **Segunda fase.** Aparte de la decoración y la comida, ¿qué es importante, necesario o imprescindible que los hijos hagan para hacer felices a sus padres? Escriban una lista de cuatro cosas más como mínimo.

2 **10-14 Unos invitados para el fin de semana.** Prepare una lista de las cosas que usted necesita hacer y otra lista con lo que espera que hagan sus invitados. Después, compare sus listas con las de un/a compañero/a.

MODELO: E1: Necesito limpiar la sala el viernes.
              E2: Yo también necesito limpiarla./Yo no, la sala está limpia. Yo necesito comprar leche y jugo.
              E1: Espero que mis invitados lleguen temprano.
              E2: Y yo espero que a mis invitados les gusten los platos que voy a servir.

LO QUE USTED NECESITA HACER	LO QUE ESPERA QUE HAGAN SUS INVITADOS
_____	_____
_____	_____
_____	_____
_____	_____

10-15 Un trabajo complicado. Primera fase. Usted trabaja en un supermercado. Marque las actividades que se prohíben, las que se permiten y las que se recomiendan durante las horas de trabajo.

	SE PROHÍBE	SE PERMITE	SE RECOMIENDA
1. fumar			
2. comer frutas			
3. hablar por teléfono			
4. descansar 15 minutos			
5. ayudar a los clientes a encontrar los productos			
6. usar el baño			

② **Segunda fase.** Ustedes descubrieron que ambos/as trabajan en supermercados. Por eso, cada uno/a de ustedes tiene curiosidad por saber cuáles son las obligaciones y condiciones de trabajo del/de la otro/a. Háganse preguntas usando los verbos **pedir, prohibir, permitir, decir, recomendar.**

MODELO: E1: ¿Qué te prohíbe tu jefe en el trabajo?
E2: Me prohíbe que hable por teléfono con mis amigos.
E1: ¿Qué te recomiendan tus compañeros de trabajo?
E2: Me recomiendan que sea amable con los clientes.

1. llevar un uniforme limpio
2. cambiar las verduras que no están frescas
3. usar el celular mientras trabajo
4. llegar temprano al trabajo
5. revisar las fechas de la leche y los quesos
6. atender a los clientes en la caja
7. saber dónde están los diferentes productos
8. ...

Ⓖ **10-16 Consejos y sugerencias.** Usted está organizando un nuevo restaurante de comida boliviana y ecuatoriana, y tiene algunos problemas en ciertas áreas. Explíqueles a dos de sus compañeros/as cuáles son los problemas. Ellos/as deben decirle qué debe hacer.

MODELO: cocineros
E1: Los cocineros que tengo no son nativos de esos países.
E2: Es importante que pongas anuncios en los periódicos para conseguir cocineros nativos.
E3: Y también es bueno que algunos camareros sean de Ecuador o de Bolivia.

1. productos de comida
2. cervezas y otras bebidas
3. decoración del lugar
4. música ambiental
5. ingredientes para las empanadas salteñas
6. publicidad

SITUACIONES

Role A. You are unable to go to the market this week because you are sick (*enfermo/a*). Call a friend to explain your predicament, and ask him/her to go for you. Answer his/her questions and a) say what you need him/her to buy for you (chicken, some vegetables, fruit, bread, and so on), b) give him advice about the shops where he/she can get those items, c) explain that you will pay him/her when he/she comes to your house, and d) thank him/her.

Role B. When a friend of yours calls to ask for a favor, a) say that you will be happy to do his/her shopping, and b) ask what he/she needs. After writing down the list, say that it is important that he/she rest and that you will be at his/her house around 11:00 a.m.

3. Subjunctive with verbs and expressions of doubt

■ When the verb in the main clause expresses doubt or uncertainty, use a subjunctive verb form in the dependent clause.

Dudo que **vendan** pescado fresco.	*I doubt (that) they sell fresh fish.*

■ When the verbs **creer** and **pensar** are used in the negative and doubt is implied, the subjunctive is used. In questions with these verbs, the subjunctive may be used to express uncertainty or to anticipate a negative response. If the question simply seeks information, use the indicative.

SUBJUNCTIVE

Hace sol; no creo que **llueva** hoy.	*It is sunny out; I do not think it will rain.*
¿Crees que **haga** frío en La Paz?	*Do you think it will be cold in La Paz?* (I am not sure.)

INDICATIVE

¿Crees que **hace** frío en La Paz?	*Do you think it is/will be cold in La Paz?* (Should I wear a coat?)

■ Use the subjunctive with impersonal expressions that denote doubt or uncertainty, such as **es dudoso que, es difícil que, es probable que,** and **es posible que.**

Es dudoso que **encontremos** frutas tropicales allí.	*It is doubtful that we will find tropical fruits there.*
Es posible que **vendan** uvas.	*It is possible that they sell grapes.*

- Use the indicative with impersonal expressions that denote certainty: **es cierto/verdad que, es seguro que,** and **es obvio que.**

> Es verdad/cierto que el vino **es** muy bueno.   *It is true that the wine is very good.*

- Since the expressions **tal vez** and **quizá(s)** convey uncertainty, the subjunctive is normally used.

> Tal vez
Quizá(s) } ella **pruebe** el postre.   *Perhaps she will try the dessert.*

¿Qué dice usted?

10-17 ¿Están de acuerdo? Primera fase. Lean las siguientes opiniones y marquen si están de acuerdo o no con ellas.

	Sí	No
1. Yo creo que el aceite de oliva es bueno para la salud.	_____	_____
2. Yo dudo que el yogur con frutas tenga muchas calorías.	_____	_____
3. Creo que el agua que se bebe en las ciudades de este país es muy buena.	_____	_____
4. Es posible que los dulces tengan más calorías que el queso.	_____	_____
5. Es obvio que el pescado es mejor que la carne para la salud.	_____	_____
6. No creo que la comida afecte nuestra personalidad.	_____	_____

Segunda fase. Ahora intercambien opiniones basándose en lo que marcaron en la **Primera fase.**

MODELO: E1: Yo creo que el aceite de oliva es bueno para la salud, y debemos usarlo en ensaladas y para cocinar.

            E2: Tal vez/Quizá(s) sea mejor que otros aceites, pero debemos usar poco.

10-18 Opiniones. Intercambien opiniones sobre los siguientes temas. Después, comparen sus opiniones con las de otros/as compañeros/as y compartan el resultado con la clase. Pueden usar algunas de estas expresiones si lo desean.

caloría	grasa
proteína	vitamina
sano/a	peligroso/a (*dangerous*)

MODELO: la carne de cerdo

            E1: Creo que una porción de carne de cerdo tiene menos grasa que un bistec.

            E2: Estoy de acuerdo, pero dudo que tenga menos grasa que el pescado.

1. las bebidas alcohólicas
2. el pescado y los camarones
3. las frutas y las verduras
4. la vida sedentaria

EN DIRECTO

To report agreement:

Todos creemos/pensamos que...

Nosotros estamos de acuerdo con que...

To report different opinions:

No hay consenso entre nosotros/ellos. Unos piensan que..., otros creen que...

2 **10-19 Una cena con alguien famoso. Primera fase.** Ustedes ganaron un concurso, y el premio es una cena con la persona que ustedes admiran más. Escojan a la persona admirada y después hagan una lista de tres cosas que esperan que pasen y tres cosas que dudan que pasen en la cena. Expliquen por qué.

MODELO: Persona admirada: Marc Anthony
          E1: Esperamos que Marc Anthony pague la cena porque él tiene mucho dinero.
          E2: Dudo que Marc Anthony cante durante la cena porque no va a querer que lo reconozcan.

Segunda fase. Reúnanse con otra pareja y explíquenle a quién escogieron ustedes y por qué. Infórmenle sobre sus esperanzas (*hopes*) y dudas con respecto a la situación. Comenten si están de acuerdo o no con lo que dicen sus compañeros/as.

SITUACIONES

You have to give a class presentation about food from Ecuador, Bolivia or Paraguay. Go to your local market, find the section where Hispanic foods are sold or search for information on the Internet. During the next class meeting, interview a classmate about the following topics. Then exchange roles.

- Three items of produce or products typical of the country

- Prices of these produce items or products if bought in the United States

- The recipe of a dish in which the items are used, including ingredients and manner of preparation

- Your main source of information

EN DIRECTO

To show interest in someone else's work:
¿Cómo va tu presentación/ proyecto/trabajo?
¿Cómo vas con…?
¡Genial!

Escuchar

Recording detail

Sometimes you need to recognize specific information from a list of various possibilities. For example, if you have a list of all the groceries that you usually buy, but somebody tells you specifically what to buy, you write a check mark only next to those you are being told to buy and disregard the others.

Antes de escuchar

10-20 ¡Un lío! (*A mess*). In **10-21**, you will listen to a list of groceries that Andrea, Carolina, Roberto, and Darío bought. Before you listen, write down a list of the groceries you regularly buy, and those you buy on special occasions.

regularmente _____

en ocasiones especiales _____

A escuchar

AUDIO **10-21.** Now, listen to the list of groceries that Andrea, Carolina, Roberto and Darío bought. As you listen, mark A, C, R or D next to each product to identify who bought what.

_____ aderezo	_____ cerdo	_____ pepinos
_____ aguacates	_____ espinacas	_____ pimienta
_____ ajos	_____ jamón	_____ pimientos verdes
_____ camarones	_____ langosta	_____ pollo
_____ carne molida	_____ maíz	_____ sal
_____ cebollas	_____ papas	_____ zanahorias

Después de escuchar

2 **10-22 ¿Y usted?** With a classmate, share your answers to the following questions.

1. ¿Cuál es su plato favorito?
2. ¿Qué productos compra usted para preparar su plato favorito?
3. ¿Con quién comparte generalmente su plato favorito y por qué?

Antes de escuchar

10-23 Productos típicos. In **10-24**, you will listen to a conversation between Isabel and Raimundo regarding the origin of various products. Before you listen, write down the Spanish names of four fruits and four vegetables you like.

Frutas: _____

Vegetales: _____

A escuchar

AUDIO **10-24.** Now, listen to the conversation between Isabel y Raimundo. As you listen, mark all products that are originally from America (**A**) and those that are not (**NA**).

_____ aguacate	_____ chocolate	_____ papa
_____ arroz	_____ maíz	_____ té
_____ café	_____ naranja	_____ tomate

Después de escuchar

10-25 ¿Y usted? With a classmate, share your answers to the following questions.

1. ¿Cuáles son las frutas y vegetales típicos de América que le gustan? ¿Cuáles no le gustan?
2. ¿Puede usted conseguir esos productos siempre en su ciudad? ¿Dónde los compra? ¿Son caros o baratos?
3. ¿Cuándo come usted estos productos? ¿Cómo los come: crudos, cocinados, fritos, en ensaladas, en sopas, etc.?

Conversar

Antes de conversar

10-26 ¿Más o menos saludable? Primera fase. Clasifiquen los siguientes productos o alimentos en la columna correspondiente, según su opinión.

los camarones	las papas	el pollo
las espinacas	el vino	el queso
el jamón	la fruta	la carne de res
las legumbres	el helado	las bebidas con gas
la cerveza	el pan blanco	las bebidas alcohólicas

MÁS SALUDABLES:	MENOS SALUDABLES:

G **Segunda fase.** Escriban en la tabla los productos o alimentos de la **Primera fase** que en general producen los siguientes efectos.

ENGORDAN	AYUDAN A ADELGAZAR	DAN ENERGÍA	AUMENTAN EL COLESTEROL

A conversar

G **10-27 ¿Qué hábitos de comida tienes?** Averigüen las preferencias de comida de los miembros del grupo en las siguientes categorías. Después, sumen los números en las columnas para saber qué comida les gusta más y cuál les gusta menos.

MODELO: los mariscos
  E1: ¿Te gustan los mariscos?
  E2: Me encantan. ¿Y a ti?
  E1: A mí no me gustan.

ALIMENTO	ENCANTAR	GUSTAR MUCHO	GUSTAR	NO GUSTAR
la fruta				
las verduras				
la carne				
los mariscos				
los productos lácteos				
los dulces				

Después de conversar

G **10-28 Reflexiones.** Comparen los resultados de **10-27** para determinar las categorías de alimentos que se consumen más en la clase. Luego, respondan a estas preguntas.

1. ¿Qué tipos de comida se comen más en su clase?
2. En general, ¿ustedes se alimentan bien o mal? ¿Por qué?
3. ¿Deben ustedes mejorar su dieta? ¿Qué es importante que hagan?

Antes de conversar

10-29 ¡A pasarlo bien! Determinen si las siguientes son preocupaciones de los organizadores (**O**) de una fiesta, de los invitados (**I**) o de ambos (**A**).

1. _____ el grado de formalidad de la fiesta
2. _____ hacer la lista de invitados
3. _____ la ropa que se va a llevar
4. _____ la música que se va a tocar

5. _____ la comida que se va a servir
6. _____ el horario de la fiesta
7. _____ la limpieza y la decoración
8. _____ el transporte
9. _____ el permiso o la prohibición de bebidas alcohólicas
10. _____ dar disculpas por no poder ir

A conversar

Ⓖ **10-30 Mil decisiones.** Éste es un momento especial del año y ustedes van a dar una fiesta diferente de otras. Va a ser una fiesta con comida nutritiva y saludable. Preparen un plan y traten de convencer al resto de la clase sobre su plan con buenas ideas y material visual si es necesario.

1. el tipo de fiesta que van a dar (formal o informal), el lugar, la fecha y la hora
2. los invitados. ¿A quiénes van a invitar? ¿Cuántas personas son?
3. la comida, las bebidas, etc. ¿Qué comida se va a servir? ¿Es necesario que haya algo para los vegetarianos? ¿Y para las personas que no beben alcohol?
4. las actividades, la música. ¿Cómo van a divertirse? ¿Es importante que haya juegos para las personas que no bailan?

Después de conversar

Ⓖ **10-31 Nuestra votación.** Ahora discutan cuál es el plan presentado por los grupos durante la actividad **10-30** que ustedes van a escoger. Explíquenle a la clase por qué.

Leer

In *Lección 10*, you will review some previous strategies and will discover new meanings by identifying words that are related semantically (in meaning) or linguistically (in grammatical form). This strategy may also help you expand your vocabulary.

Guía de prelectura

Use the cues provided by the visuals, the headline, and the subheading in activity **10-34,** and your personal knowledge to answer the following questions:

1. What information will you likely find in this article?
   a. A brand new diet born in the Mediterranean countries
      Yes   No
   b. A diet that the Mediterranean peoples have followed for centuries
      Yes   No
   c. A balanced diet based on the foods grown or produced in the Mediterranean countries
      Yes   No
   d. The effect of food and life style on the lives of Mediterranean peoples
      Yes   No

EN DIRECTO
To influence someone's decision:
Es mejor/menos dañino (*harmful*) que... + subjuntivo
¿No te/le(s) parece más saludable que + subjuntivo...?
¿Qué te/le(s) parece si + indicativo...?

EN DIRECTO
To explain the reason behind a decision:
Votamos por el plan... porque...
Nos gustó/convenció el plan... por el valor nutritivo de la comida/el costo/la variedad de..., etc.
Nuestra decisión se basa en lo siguiente: ...

2. What helped you answer question 1? Circle the corresponding letter.
   a. The headline, subheading and photo
   b. Only the visuals in the text
   c. My personal knowledge of diets

3. Now, can you hypothesize about some content of the text? Anticipate the main ideas of the text. Mark with a circle all that may apply.
   a. Health quality and longevity are dependent on people's eating habits and life style.
   b. Certain produce grown in the Mediterranean countries helps people maintain a balanced diet.
   c. Diets that are rich in carbohydrates, fruit, white meats, and grains are healthful.
   d. Certain produce and foods help prevent, among others, some heart-related diseases that kill millions in other parts of the world.
   e. A healthy life is more than the food people eat. It is also a lifestyle.

Antes de leer

G **10-32 Preparación.** Considerando el clima de cada región, indiquen si los siguientes alimentos se consumen más (**+**) o igual (**=**) en el Mediterráneo o en su país.

	MEDITERRÁNEO	NUESTRO PAÍS
1. el aceite de oliva	_____	_____
2. las frutas	_____	_____
3. el pan	_____	_____
4. las carnes blancas	_____	_____
5. los frutos secos	_____	_____
6. el vino	_____	_____
7. las verduras	_____	_____
8. el pescado	_____	_____

2 **10-33 Hábitos y comidas saludables.** ¿Qué alimentos y actividades son saludables para el organismo humano? Marquen los que correspondan, según ustedes.

1. _____ el pan y las pastas
2. _____ caminar al aire libre
3. _____ las legumbres
4. _____ la leche sin grasa
5. _____ beber alcohol
6. _____ las verduras
7. _____ la crema de leche
8. _____ tomar vino en la cena
9. _____ las carnes rojas
10. _____ los pescados y mariscos

A leer

10-34 Primera mirada. Lea el siguiente artículo sobre una dieta y, luego, siga las instrucciones.

La dieta mediterránea: ¿una nueva moda o un nuevo modo de vivir?

Los europeos que viven en las costas del mediterráneo tienen una calidad de vida mejor que en muchos otros países del mundo, viven más años y tienen mejor salud. La explicación de este fenómeno, según los expertos, está en la dieta mediterránea.

La dieta del Mediterráneo se basa en alimentos ricos en hidratos de carbono como el pan y la pasta, el aceite de oliva, moderadas cantidades de vino durante las comidas, verduras, vegetales, frutas, frutos secos y legumbres, que le dan al organismo humano fibra y antioxidantes. Además, se consumen menos carnes rojas y grasas animales y mayor cantidad de carnes blancas y pescado, productos lácteos y huevos, de donde se obtienen las proteínas.

¿Por qué se la considera una dieta saludable?

Varios estudios realizados en Grecia sabrayaron la eficacia de esta dieta. Los científicos observaron que los habitantes del Mediterráneo sufrían menos de enfermedades cardiovasculares, arteriosclerosis y enfermedades degenerativas. Por eso, tenían una expectativa de vida superior a la de las personas de otras regiones del globo.

Así entre 1958 y 1964, se estudiaron los hábitos dietéticos de siete países, cuatro no mediterráneos: Estados Unidos, Japón, Finlandia y Holanda, y tres mediterráneos: Yugoslavia, Italia y Grecia.

¿En qué consiste la dieta mediterránea?

Los expertos observaron que la dieta de los países del Mediterráneo tenía ciertas características comunes: gran consumo de pescado y carnes blancas, cereales y legumbres, frutas y verduras, poca carne roja, consumo moderado de vino con el almuerzo o la cena, además del uso del aceite de oliva para cocinar. Todo lo anterior coincidía con una baja incidencia de enfermedades coronarias y menos colesterol entre los habitantes de estos países en comparación con los de otros.

Una dieta y un estilo de vida

Aunque el clima, los cultivos y la comida varían de región a región en el mundo, es posible construir una pirámide de alimentos que incluya los nutrientes necesarios para una buena alimentación.

Los estudios y los expertos concluyen que para mantener una buena nutrición y una vida sana nuestra dieta debe incluir lo siguiente:

- muchas verduras y cereales, pan y papas
- fruta fresca
- legumbres al menos dos veces a la semana
- alimentos frescos de temporada
- aceite de oliva
- leche, yogures y quesos bajos en grasa para obtener calcio
- pescado tres o cuatro veces por semana
- carne sin grasa dos o tres veces por semana y carnes rojas una vez al mes
- poca sal, pero condimentos como el ajo, la cebolla, el vinagre, el limón o las hierbas aromáticas
- unos dos litros de agua al día
- pocos dulces
- poco o nada de alcohol, excepto el vino a la hora de las comidas
- caminar y hacer ejercicio al aire libre
- dormir unas siete u ocho horas

Según el contenido del artículo, ¿son las siguientes afirmaciones ciertas (**C**) o falsas (**F**)? Si la afirmación es falsa, dé la información correcta.

1. _____ El artículo afirma que la alimentación mediterránea es más sana para el cuerpo humano que la de otros lugares del mundo.
2. _____ La dieta mediterránea prolonga la vida las personas.
3. _____ Los seguidores de esta dieta deben eliminar los hidratos de carbono.
4. _____ Para mantenerse sana, la gente del mediterráneo evita las proteínas.
5. _____ Las carnes rojas se consumen en grandes cantidades.
6. _____ Los estudiosos afirman que esta dieta previene (*prevents*) algunas enfermedades.
7. _____ Esta dieta ayuda a controlar mejor el colesterol.
8. _____ Solamente en el mediterráneo se puede seguir esta dieta.
9. _____ Los expertos sugieren que para ser sanas, las personas sólo deben preocuparse de su alimentación.
10. _____ Según los científicos, una dieta equilibrada y la actividad física ayudan a tener buena salud y vivir más años.

10-35 Segunda mirada. Busque en el artículo palabras que se asocien con lo siguiente.

1. hidratos de carbono: _____
2. fibras y antioxidantes: _____
3. proteínas: _____
4. grasa: _____
5. algunos países mediterráneos: _____
6. actividades que afectan positivamente la salud: _____

10-36 Una raíz (*root*) común. Busque en el artículo los sustantivos o adjetivos asociados con los siguientes verbos. Escríbalos en la línea correspondiente.

VERBOS	SUSTANTIVOS
1. explicar:	
2. nacer:	
3. consumir:	
4. incidir:	
5. enfermarse:	
6. habitar:	
7. alimentar:	
8. nutrir:	
	ADJETIVOS
9. moderar:	
10. degenerar:	

Después de leer

10-37 Aplicación. Una nutricionista norteamericana le pide ayuda para preparar un panfleto (*flyer*) en español. Su objetivo es convencer a la comunidad hispana de que mejore su dieta para vivir más y mejor. Ayúdela en las áreas donde tiene duda. Marque la alternativa correcta.

¿Alguna vez pensó que su dieta puede acortar su vida?

Coma bien y viva sin (1) _____ (enfermedades/enfermos). Su (2) _____ (alimento/alimentación) puede (3) _____ (influir, influencia) positiva o negativamente en su salud. Imite a los (4) _____ (habitados/habitantes) de los países mediterráneos. Consuma hidratos de carbono y vino con (5) _____ (moderadas/moderación). Cocine legumbres y coma frutas y carnes blancas en cantidades ilimitadas. No olvide que las enfermedades (6) _____ (degeneradas/degenerativas) ocurren por falta de proteínas, hidratos de carbono, calcio, etcétera. Cuide su salud y la de su familia con una buena (7) _____ (nutritiva/nutrición).

Escribir

We are often confronted with situations, conflicts, and dilemmas in which our input or advice is needed or required. At work or at home, we must tell others what to do; with friends, we may act as confidants and, as such, give them advice. Overall, advice and guidance constitute social, communicative tasks that we accomplish with or for others.

In Spanish, giving advice or telling others what to do requires the following:

■ special attention to the degree of intimacy or familiarity with the person you are addressing: is he/she a friend or a stranger? Are you giving directions or advice to someone younger or older than you? Is the person your superior at work or someone under your supervision? etc.

■ the use of expressions that signal the degree of familiarity or intimacy with the person to whom you are talking or writing. In Spanish this is indicated, among other ways, with the personal pronouns **tú** and **usted**.

In *Lección 10* you will have the opportunity to correspond with someone and give guidance and advice.

Antes de escribir

10-38 Análisis. Primera fase. Usted acaba de recibir esta carta de uno de sus buenos amigos. Léala y siga las instrucciones.

Querido/a amigo/a,

Te pido disculpas por no escribirte antes, pero te explico las razones a continuación. Desde hace tiempo, siempre me siento fatigado. Aunque estoy trabajando sólo seis horas por día, a las 3:00 de la tarde ya quiero irme a casa a descansar. Como no tengo apetito, cocino poco. Generalmente preparo algo rápido y fácil: una sopa enlatada o huevos fritos con tocino. De vez en cuando cocino una hamburguesa y, a veces, cuando me canso de la carne, tomo una buena porción de helados con galletas. ¡Ah, claro, mis amigos siempre me encuentran en los cafés de la universidad bebiendo un expreso o un capuchino! Necesito la cafeína para tener energía y hacer mi trabajo. El único problema es que el café me llena de energía y entusiasmo de día, pero no puedo dormir de noche. Las mañanas son una verdadera tortura. Generalmente me levanto tarde, falto a clases a veces y no me alcanza el tiempo para hacer mi trabajo.

Creo que debo buscar ayuda. Quisiera ver un médico, pero no tengo dinero ahora. ¿Qué te parece? Estoy pobre y enfermo.

Bueno, escríbeme para saber de ti. Te contestaré tan pronto pueda. Cuídate mucho.

Un fuerte abrazo,

Tomás

Segunda fase. Answer the following questions, based on the letter in **Primera fase.**

1. Mark with an X the likely purpose(s) of the letter:
   a. To restart communication with someone close after some period of silence
   b. To apologize and explain something
   c. To tell a friend how things are going
   d. To arouse compassion

2. Based on its purpose(s), is the letter effective?
   _____ Yes   _____ No

3. Mark some possible reasons for your response to question 2.
   a. Tomás describes in detail what he does on a daily basis.
   b. Tomás provides his friend with credible reasons for his silence.
   c. Tomás explains the cause for not writing and acknowledges he needs help.
   d. The tone of Tomás's letter is intimate.

4. Write down some expressions in the letter that signal the degree of familiarity or intimacy Tomás has with the person to whom he is writing.

10-39 Preparación. Primera fase. En la actividad **10-40**, usted va a responder la carta de Tomás. Pero antes, escriba tres problemas de su amigo en la primera columna y en la otra, algunas ideas para ayudarlo a resolver cada problema.

PROBLEMAS DE TOMÁS:	ALGUNAS POSIBLES SOLUCIONES:
1.	1.
2.	2.
3.	3.

Segunda fase. Ahora…

1. escriba algunas formas gramaticales que se usan para dar sugerencias. ¿Son formas personales o impersonales?

2. escriba algunas ideas (deseos, peticiones, sugerencias) que usted va a incluir en el párrafo de cierre (*closing*).

   MODELO: Espero que sigas mis consejos.

A escribir

10-40 Manos a la obra. Respóndale a la carta a su amigo. Use la información que preparó en la actividad **10-39**. No se olvide de usar un tono amistoso en su carta.

Después de escribir

10-41 Revisión. Antes de darle la carta a su compañero/a editor/a, léala y verifique lo siguiente, pensando en Tomás:

- El contenido. ¿Le demostró interés o preocupación por su situación a Tomás? ¿Le indicó los problemas más serios, en su opinión? ¿Le dio algunas posibles soluciones?

- La organización. ¿Tiene la carta una introducción, un cuerpo, un párrafo de cierre y una despedida?

- La gramática. ¿Usó el vocabulario correcto, algunas expresiones de cohesión, la concordancia, el tiempo (presente, pasado), las formas para recomendar, etc.?

- La puntuación y la ortografía. ¿Usó comas, puntos, etc. donde eran necesarios?

Finalmente, comparta su carta con su compañero/a.

ENFOQUE CULTURAL

TEMAS: LOS MERCADOS AL AIRE LIBRE Y LOS MERCADOS (O LAS FERIAS) ARTESANALES

Para pensar

¿Dónde se puede comprar artesanía en los Estados Unidos? ¿Hay algún lugar cerca de donde usted vive? ¿Qué se puede comprar ahí? ¿Cómo son los precios? Generalmente, ¿qué tipo de artesanía se vende: de cerámica, metal, madera, cuero?

En estos mercados se pueden encontrar artículos de lana y alpaca como suéteres, ponchos, sombreros, guantes, alfombras. Uno de los mercados más conocidos es el mercado de Otavalo en Ecuador.

Los mercados artesanales son muy comunes en muchos países hispanos, especialmente en aquellos con una población indígena grande, como Bolivia, Ecuador, Paraguay.

Para contestar

2 Los mercados. Respondan a las siguientes preguntas.

1. ¿Han visitado alguna vez un mercado artesanal o un mercado al aire libre en los Estados Unidos? ¿Y en el extranjero?
2. ¿Qué productos pueden comprar en un mercado artesanal? ¿Y en un mercado al aire libre?
3. Imagínense que ustedes van a ir al Ecuador. Digan a qué famoso mercado les gustaría ir y qué quisieran comprar.

G Riqueza cultural. En grupos de tres, comenten:

a. Las ventajas y desventajas de comprar productos en un mercado artesanal en vez de una tienda.
b. Las ventajas y desventajas de comprar verduras y frutas en un mercado al aire libre en vez de supermercados.

Luego, presenten a la clase sus conclusiones.

También en los mercados al aire libre se puede comprar todo tipo de frutas frescas, verduras, hierbas, etc.

Para pensar

¿Sabe usted dónde están Ecuador, Bolivia y Paraguay? ¿Sabe usted qué famoso archipiélago está frente a las costas del Ecuador? ¿Sabe usted cómo se llama el lago que comparten Bolivia y Perú? ¿Alguna vez oyó el arpa paraguaya?

Bolivia y Paraguay son los dos países de América del Sur que no tienen salida al mar.

Frente a las costas del Ecuador está el Archipiélago de las Islas Galápagos. Ahí se encuentran especies únicas como la famosa tortuga gigante, llamada galápago.

Expresiones ecuatorianas:

un cuaje de risa	Me dio **un cuaje de risa.**	*I laughed a lot.*
buena nota	Ella es una **buena nota.**	*She's a nice person.*
creer ocho veces	Sí, sí, te **creo ocho veces.**	*Yeah, sure, I believe you (said with disbelief).*

386

Bolivia comparte con Perú el lago Titicaca, el lago navegable más alto del mundo. Bolivia tien una gran riqueza minera. Es uno de los más grandes productores mundiales de estaño (tin), cobre y plata.

Muchos misioneros jesuitas fueron al Paraguay durante la época de la colonia. Ellos les enseñaron español a los indígenas, pero también aprendieron su lengua, el guaraní.

Expresiones bolivianas:

gallo tuerto	Es tan desconfiado/a como **gallo tuerto.**	*He/she distrusts everybody.*
samba canuta	Te voy a dar una **samba canuta.**	*I am going to spank you.*

Expresiones paraguayas:

caigue	No seas **caigue.**	*Do not be lazy.*
salame	Es un **salame.**	*He is a fool.*

Para contestar

En el mapa

1. Diga cuáles son las ciudades capitales del Ecuador, Bolivia y Paraguay.
2. ¿Qué países están al sur/norte de Bolivia? ¿Y de Ecuador?
3. Mencione una diferencia geográfica muy importante entre Ecuador y Bolivia y Ecuador y Paraguay.

Ahora diga...

1. si le gustaría visitar las Islas Galápagos y por qué.
2. qué lugar de Bolivia o Paraguay le gustaría visitar.

¿Qué dice usted si...

1. usted cree que su hermano/a no está diciendo la verdad.
2. su compañero/a no quiere ayudarlo a arreglar su departamento/casa.
3. alguien lo/la hace reír mucho.

Paraguay tiene una rica tradición folclórica expresada en su música (la polka y la guaranía), sus hermosos tejidos (weavings) y su comida variada.

Para investigar en Internet

Busque información acerca de los mercados artesanales en Bolivia, Ecuador, Paraguay. Diga dónde están, qué tipo de productos venden y, si es posible, traiga a clase una ilustración de los productos que ofrecen. Vaya a www.prenhall.com/mosaicos.

¡Prepárese!

10-42 Opiniones. En este episodio hay sorpresas y cambios. Efraín se muestra atraído por Katie, Katie piensa todavía en Carlos y Sabrina revela que ella y Katie están trabajando juntas. En su opinión, ¿quién es honesto y quién no? ¿Es posible saberlo con seguridad? Indique sus opiniones.

En mi opinión...

1. ... Katie es / no es honesta porque _____.
2. ... Efraín es / no es honesto porque _____.
3. ... Sabrina es / no es honesta porque _____.
4. ... Carlos es / no es honesto porque _____.

¿Tienen las mismas opiniones sus compañeros de clase? ¿Por qué?

Ángela y Manolo no están seguros de quién va a ganar el concurso.

Katie y Efraín están en Xochimilco para buscar la solución al cuarto Misterio.

Katie entendió las pistas porque leyó sobre la historia de Xochimilco.

Parece que a Efraín le gusta mucho Katie.

¡Katie y Efraín solucionaron el misterio!

Sabrina dice que ella y Katie están concentradas para ganar.

¡Responda!

10-43 Más opiniones. Complete las oraciones siguientes de una manera lógica con la forma correcta de un verbo en el presente de subjuntivo o de indicativo.

1. Le recomiendo a Katie que...
2. Ojalá que Katie y Sabrina...
3. Efraín espera que Katie...
4. Es bueno que Carlos y Katie...
5. Es verdad que el concurso...
6. El público cree que Carlos...
7. Yo dudo que Efraín...
8. Es importante que el concurso...
9. ...

Esta canción es un ejemplo de la música taquirari, original de Bolivia y una combinación de tradiciones musicales indígenas y españolas. Aunque un tema típico de taquirari es el amor, "Sol de primavera" es una canción instrumental.

¡Prepárese!

10-44 Preferencias. ¿Qué tipo de música prefieren sus compañeros y Ud.? Hable con otros cinco estudiantes para averiguar sus preferencias. Luego compare su información con la del resto de la clase.

MÚSICA	NOMBRE	LE GUSTA PORQUE...
instrumental	_____	_____
clásica	_____	_____
rock	_____	_____
ska	_____	_____
latina	_____	_____
otra	_____	_____

¡Escuche!

10-45 Asociaciones. Lea las siguientes oraciones Luego, escuche la canción y llene los espacios en blanco, según su opinión.

1. "Sol de primavera" me hace pensar en _____.
2. La canción me hace sentir _____.
3. Cuando escucho esta canción tengo deseos de _____.
4. Una buena ocasión para escuchar esta canción o este estilo de música es _____.
5. La guitarra y la quena (una flauta andina) son _____.

¡Responda!

10-46 Temas. Escriba por lo menos cinco temas posibles para "Sol de primavera" y compártalos con un/a compañero/a. Túrnense usando el presente de subjuntivo para dar sus opiniones sobre los diferentes temas. Pueden usar los verbos y expresiones de la lista.

MODELO: E1: Un tema posible es el amor.
          E2: Yo dudo que el tema **sea** el amor.

dudar   negar   no creer   no estar seguro/a de   tal vez   quizás

VOCABULARIO

Comida

el aceite	oil
el aderezo	salad dressing
el aguacate	avocado
el ajo	garlic
las aves	poultry, foul
el/la azúcar	sugar
el camarón	shrimp
la carne	meat
molida/picada	ground beef
de res	beef/steak
la cebolla	onion
el cerdo	pork
la cereza	cherry
la chuleta	chop
la costilla	rib
la crema	cream
el dulce	candy/sweets
las espinacas	spinach
la fresa	strawberry
la galleta	cookie
la gelatina	gelatin
la harina	flour
la langosta	lobster
el limón	lemon
el maíz/elote	corn
la mantequilla	butter
la manzana	apple
la margarina	margarine
los mariscos	shellfish
la masa	dough
la mayonesa	mayonnaise
la mostaza	mustard
la pastelería	pastry shop
el pavo	turkey
el pepino	cucumber
la pera	pear
la pimienta	pepper
el pimiento verde	green pepper
la piña	pineapple
el plátano/la banana	banana
la receta	recipe
la sal	salt
la salsa de tomate	tomato sauce
la toronja/el pomelo	grapefruit
la uva	grape
la vainilla	vanilla
la verdura	vegetable
el vinagre	vinegar
el vino (tinto)	(red) wine
el yogur	yogurt
la zanahoria	carrot

En la mesa

la bandeja	tray
la botella	bottle
la copa	(stemmed) glass
la cuchara	spoon
la cucharita	teaspoon
el cuchillo	knife
el mantel	tablecloth
el plato	plate, dish
la servilleta	napkin
la taza	cup
el tenedor	fork
el vaso	glass

Verbos

aconsejar	to advise
añadir	to add
batir	to beat
dudar	to doubt
esperar	to hope, to expect
freír (i)	to fry
hervir (ie, i)	to boil
permitir	to permit, to allow
prohibir	to prohibit, to forbid
recomendar	to recommend

Descripciones

agrio/a	sour
lácteo/a	dairy (product), milky
sano/a	healthy

Palabras y expresiones útiles

la artesanía	handicraft
ojalá	I/we hope
quizá(s)/tal vez	maybe

*For impersonal expressions requiring the subjunctive and the indicative see pages 368, 371 and 372.

11

LA SALUD Y LOS MÉDICOS

Objetivos comunicativos

- Talking about the body
- Describing health conditions and medical treatments
- Expressing emotions, opinions, and attitudes
- Expressing expectations and wishes
- Giving informal orders and instructions
- Expressing goals and purposes

Contenido

Las partes del cuerpo

el pelo/cabello
la cara
la boca
el hombro
la espalda
el pecho
la cintura
la muñeca
la cadera
la rodilla
el tobillo

la frente
la oreja
el brazo
el codo
los dedos
la mano
el pie
la pierna

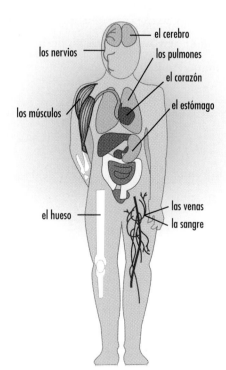

el cerebro
los nervios
los pulmones
los músculos
el corazón
el estómago
el hueso
las venas
la sangre

la cabeza
la ceja
las pestañas
la mejilla
el ojo
la nariz
los labios
los dientes
el cuello

La salud

AUDIO **¿Qué les pasa a estas personas?**

Tiene **catarro. Estornuda** y tiene mucha **tos.**

Se torció el tobillo.

Se cayó y **se fracturó** el brazo.

¿Qué dice usted?

11-1 Asociación. Primera fase. Decidan en qué parte del cuerpo se ponen estos accesorios y esta ropa.

1. los calcetines _____
2. el anillo _____
3. los guantes _____
4. el cinturón _____
5. el collar _____
6. los aretes _____
7. el reloj _____
8. el sombrero _____

   a. la muñeca
   b. el dedo
   c. la cintura
   d. las orejas
   e. el cuello
   f. la cabeza
   g. los pies
   h. las manos

Segunda fase. Digan qué accesorios de la lista no tienen ustedes y mencionen tres que consideren absolutamente indispensables en su vida. ¿Por qué? Comparen sus respuestas.

11-2 ¿Para qué sirve/n? Asocien la explicación de la derecha con la parte del cuerpo correspondiente. Después, ustedes deben decir para qué sirven estas partes del cuerpo.

MODELO: los dedos
              Hay cinco en cada mano.
              Sirven para tocar el piano.

1. las manos _____
2. la sangre _____
3. los pulmones _____
4. los brazos _____
5. los ojos _____
6. las piernas _____
7. los dientes _____
8. el cerebro _____

   a. Unen las manos con el cuerpo.
   b. Permiten que las personas vean.
   c. Toman el oxígeno del aire y lo pasan a la sangre.
   d. Es un líquido rojo que circula por el cuerpo.
   e. Unen el cuerpo con los pies.
   f. Se deben lavar después de comer.
   g. Están al final de los brazos.
   h. Le da órdenes al cuerpo.

Jorgito está enfermo

AUDIO SRA. VILLA: Jorgito, **tienes muy mala cara.** ¿Estás **enfermo?**

JORGITO: **Me siento** muy mal y **tengo dolor de garganta.** Anoche tosí mucho.

SRA. VILLA: (Le pone el termómetro.) Tienes una **fiebre** de 39 grados. Te voy a dar una **aspirina** y enseguida llamo al Dr. Bosque.

DOCTOR: Vamos a ver, Jorgito. Cuéntame cómo te sientes.

JORGITO: Ahora **me duele** la cabeza y también me duelen los **oídos.**

DOCTOR: Vamos a **examinarte** los **oídos** y la garganta. Abre bien la boca y di "Ah". Tienes una **infección.** No es **seria,** pero es necesario que **te cuides.**

JORGITO: Doctor, no quiero que me ponga una **inyección.**

DOCTOR: ¡No, qué va! Te voy a **recetar** unas **pastillas.** Debes tomarlas **cada cuatro horas.**

JORGITO: Está bien, doctor.

DOCTOR: **Además,** tienes **gripe.** Debes descansar y beber mucho líquido. Aquí está la **receta,** señora.

SRA. VILLA: Gracias, doctor.

¿Qué dice usted?

11-3 La enfermedad de Jorgito. Completen la tabla con la información correcta.

Síntomas:	
Recomendaciones:	
Nombre del médico:	

11-4 Usted es el/la doctor/a. ¿Qué recomienda en estos casos? Primero, escoja la mejor recomendación. Luego compare sus repuestas con las de su compañero/a, y juntos piensen en otras dos sugerencias para el mismo problema.

1. Su paciente tiene una infección en los ojos. Le recomiendo que...
   a. nade en la piscina.
   b. tome antibióticos.
   c. lea mucho.
   d. ...

2. Su paciente tiene fiebre y le duele el cuerpo. Le aconsejo que...
   a. descanse y tome aspirinas.
   b. coma mucho y camine.
   c. vaya a su trabajo.
   d. ...

3. A su paciente le duelen mucho una rodilla y un pie. Le pido que...
   a. corra todos los días.
   b. tome clases de baile.
   c. descanse y no camine.
   d. ...

4. A su paciente le duele la garganta y tiene tos. Le digo que es importante que...
   a. hable poco y no salga.
   b. vaya a esquiar.
   c. cante en el concierto.
   d. ...

11-5 En el consultorio. Usted tiene un catarro terrible y va a ver a su médico/a. Dígale cómo se siente y pregúntele qué debe hacer. El/La médico/a debe hacerle alguna recomendación y contestar sus preguntas.

MODELO: E1: Me siento.../Tengo...
E2: Creo que...
E1: ¿Es/No es bueno comer muchas frutas y verduras?
E2: Es excelente comer frutas y verduras porque tienen muchas vitaminas.

RECOMENDACIONES

1. tomar vitaminas, especialmente vitamina C
2. comer carne frecuentemente
3. beber ocho vasos de agua todos los días
4. hacer ejercicio cada día
5. ...

11-6 ¿A quién debo llamar? Primera fase. Explíquele a su compañero/a sus síntomas o lo que usted necesita. Su compañero/a le va a decir a quién debe llamar de acuerdo con los anuncios de abajo.

MODELO: necesitar un examen médico para un nuevo trabajo
     E1: Necesito un examen médico para un nuevo trabajo.
     E2: Debes llamar a la Dra. Corona López.

Dr. Fco. Javier Amador Cumplido
Cirugía y enfermedades de los ojos
86-43-57
Consultorio 204

Dra. Silvia Corona López
Medicina Interna
86-51-49

Clínica de Asma y Alergias
Dr. Rubén Shturman
Amsterdam 219-A
2º piso
294-3866
584-0153

DR. RAÚL ELGUEZÁBAL R.
Medicina Familiar y Cirugía
86-34-73 EU.
428-4846
Consultorio 309

Dr. Héctor Molina Oviedo
Psiquiatra
86-51-49
Consultorio 402

Dr. Jaime A. Rodríguez Peláez
Pediatra
Niños y Adolescentes
86-17-15

Dra. Gabriela Jacobo de Alcaraz
Cirujano Dentista
86-48-44
Consultorio 314

1. dolerle la cabeza cuando lee o mira televisión
2. sentirse triste y deprimido/a
3. estar enfermo/a y tener fiebre
4. buscar un médico para un sobrino de cinco años
5. no poder respirar bien y tener la piel (*skin*) irritada
6. dolerle los dientes cuando come
7. no poder dormir
8. ...

Segunda fase. Escojan dos de los problemas mencionados. Uno/a de ustedes es el/la enfermo/a y otro/a el/la médico/a elegido/a. El/La enfermo/a debe explicar los síntomas y detalles de su enfermedad. El/La médico/a debe hacer recomendaciones y sugerencias al/a la enfermo/a. Después cambien de papel.

Médicos, farmacias y hospitales

*Una enfermera le toma **la tensión arterial** a una paciente en un hospital.*

*En muchos países hispanos, los médicos recién graduados tienen que trabajar en zonas rurales o muy pobres, como una forma de servicio social, antes de establecer su propio **consultorio** o trabajar en un hospital.*

*En varios países hispanos la restricción sobre la venta de medicinas es similar a la de los Estados Unidos. Los antibióticos y somníferos, por ejemplo, ya no se venden sin receta. Sin embargo, en otros países, hay menos restricciones sobre las medicinas, y se pueden obtener muchas de ellas sin receta médica. En casos que no son graves, los clientes siguen los consejos del **farmacéutico**, estableciéndose de esta forma una relación personal entre ellos. Los farmacéuticos también ponen inyecciones y toman la tensión arterial.*

¿Qué dice usted?

11-7 Una emergencia. Primera fase. Usted y su amigo/a están de viaje en la República Dominicana, y su amigo/a tiene un problema de salud. En un cibercafé de Santo Domingo, han encontrado la información en la página 400 sobre médicos y farmacias de turno. Decidan cuál es el número más apropiado para llamar, basándose en el problema médico de su amigo/a.

Segunda fase. Haga la llamada, describa la enfermedad y pida la dirección de la consulta o la farmacia. Después el/la farmacéutico/a o el/la médico/a le debe hacer preguntas y sugerir el remedio adecuado.

11-8 **Me duele mucho.** You will listen to a young man talking to his father about how he feels after twisting his ankle. Before you listen, list two symptoms you think he has.

_____

_____

Now, pay attention to the general idea of what is said. Then, as you listen circle the letter that indicates the appropriate ending to each statement.

1. Esteban tiene...
   a. una infección en el tobillo.
   b. mucho dolor.
   c. fiebre.

2. El padre de Esteban quiere...
   a. que Esteban descanse y se cuide.
   b. llevar a Esteban al hospital.
   c. que Esteban tome una aspirina.

3. El padre de Esteban le dice que...
   a. lo ayuda a caminar para llevarlo al hospital.
   b. decida si prefiere descansar o ir al hospital.
   c. el médico puede verlo esa tarde.

4. Esteban decide...
   a. no escuchar a su padre.
   b. jugar al fútbol al día siguiente.
   c. ir al hospital con su padre.

1. The subjunctive with expressions of emotion

■ When the verb of the main clause expresses emotion (e.g., fear, happiness, sorrow), use a subjunctive verb form in the dependent clause.

Sentimos mucho que el niño **tenga** fiebre.	*We are very sorry (that) the child has a fever.*
Me alegro de que **estés** con él.	*I am glad (that) you are with him.*

■ Some common verbs that express emotion are **alegrarse (de), sentir, gustar, encantar, molestar,** and **temer** (*to fear*).

■ Impersonal expressions and other expressions that show emotion are also followed by the subjunctive.

Es triste que el niño **esté** enfermo.	*It is sad that the child is sick.*
¡Qué lástima que no **pueda** ir a la fiesta!	*What a shame that he cannot go to the party!*

¿Qué dice usted?

11-9 Un amigo enfermo. Asocie cada comentario sobre la enfermedad de su amigo con la reacción adecuada.

1. Pedro está muy enfermo. _____
2. Sus padres llegan hoy para estar con él. _____
3. Creo que el doctor Pérez lo va a operar. _____
4. Dicen que es una operación seria. _____
5. No va a poder participar en el campeonato. _____

a. Me alegro de que vengan.
b. Siento mucho que esté tan mal.
c. ¡Qué bueno que sea ése el médico!
d. Es una lástima que no pueda jugar.
e. Ojalá que no tenga complicaciones.

② **11-10 Una visita a un/a amigo/a.** Han operado a su amigo/a de la rodilla. Usted va a visitarlo/la a la clínica. A continuación está lo que su amigo/a le dice. Usted debe escoger entre las expresiones de **En directo** para responderle.

1. Me duele bastante la rodilla.
2. Tengo fiebre y dolor de cabeza.
3. Tengo dolor de estómago porque las medicinas son muy fuertes.
4. Tengo náuseas por los efectos de la anestesia.
5. Detesto estar acostado tanto tiempo.
6. La comida del hospital es buenísima.
7. Las enfermeras vienen a verme cada media hora.
8. La cirujana que me operó es muy simpática.

> **EN DIRECTO**
>
> **To express empathy:**
> Siento que...
> Me alegro de que...
> Temo que...
> Espero que...
> No me gusta que...
> ¡Qué agradable que...

11-11 Reacciones. María Luisa y Rafael trabajan en un hospital. Su compañero/a le va a decir lo que ellos piensan hacer la semana próxima. Reaccione usando las expresiones de **En directo.** Después cambien de papel.

PERSONAS	LUNES	MIÉRCOLES	VIERNES	DOMINGO
María Luisa	empezar una dieta	ir al gimnasio	hacer ejercicio en su casa	caminar 2 Km.
Rafael	trabajar en el hospital todo el día	salir del hospital temprano para ir al cine	quedarse en su casa	reunirse con sus amigos

11-12 ¿Qué me molesta? Primera fase. Haga una lista de los hábitos de otras personas que le molestan. Compare su lista con la de su compañero/a.

MODELO: Me molesta que mis amigos lleguen tarde.

Segunda fase. En pequeños grupos, comparen sus listas y escojan los seis hábitos que les molestan más a todos en el grupo. Digan por qué. Compartan sus resultados con el resto de la clase.

SITUACIONES

1. **Role 1.** Recently you decided to change your lifestyle and to join an aerobics class (*clase de ejercicios aeróbicos*). You are also following a healthful diet and feel much better. You run into a friend whom you have not seen for some time. Answer your friend's questions. Convince him/her to join you in your exercise class.

   Role 2. You run into a friend whom you have not seen for some time. Tell him/her a) that he/she looks (*verse*) great, and b) ask what he/she is doing. After listening to his/her explanation, a) inquire how many times a week he/she goes to the gym, b) at what time, c) how much the classes cost, and d) what he/she eats and drinks. He/She will try to persuade you to join the program.

2. One of you is a doctor and the other is a patient. The patient should describe all his/her symptoms and his/her lifestyle (*vida activa, vida sedentaria*). While the patient is talking, the doctor should ask pertinent questions and approve or disapprove of his/her lifestyle. As a final step, the doctor should give some advice or prescribe some medication for the patient.

2. Informal commands

Consejos para una vida sana

Respira por la nariz; no respires por la boca.
Relájate para evitar el estrés.
Empieza un programa de ejercicios.
Cuídate, y no te canses mucho los primeros días.
Come muchas frutas y verduras.
No comas mucha grasa.

- Use informal commands with those whom you address as **tú**. To form the affirmative **tú** command, use the present indicative **tú** form without the final **-s.**

	PRESENT INDICATIVE	AFFIRMATIVE *TÚ* COMMAND
llamar:	llamas	**llama**
leer:	lees	**lee**
escribir:	escribes	**escribe**

- For the negative **tú** command, use the **tú** subjunctive form.

  No llames.
  No leas.
  No escribas.

- Placement of object and reflexive pronouns with **tú** commands is the same as with **usted** commands.

AFFIRMATIVE COMMAND	NEGATIVE *TÚ* COMMAND
Bébela.	No **la** bebas.
Háblale.	No **le** hables.
Siéntate.	No **te** sientes.

- The plural of **tú** commands in Spanish-speaking America is the **ustedes** command.

  Escribe (tú).   **Escriban** (ustedes).

- Some **-er** and **-ir** verbs have shortened affirmative **tú** commands, but their negative command takes the subjunctive form like other verbs.

	AFFIRMATIVE	NEGATIVE
poner:	**pon**	**no pongas**
salir:	**sal**	**no salgas**
tener:	**ten**	**no tengas**
venir:	**ven**	**no vengas**
hacer:	**haz**	**no hagas**
decir:	**di**	**no digas**
ir:	**ve**	**no vayas**
ser:	**sé**	**no seas**

¿Qué dice usted?

11-13 Consejos. Escoja los consejos más adecuados para cada situación.

1. Su compañero se torció el tobillo y le duele mucho.
   a. Mira más programas de televisión.
   b. Llama al médico.
   c. Ve al cine con tu novio/a.
   d. Camina una hora esta tarde.
   e. Practica en el laboratorio.
   f. Quédate en cama.

2. Su hermana está embarazada (*pregnant*).
   a. No comas hamburguesas.
   b. No hagas ejercicios fuertes.
   c. No bebas té.
   d. No fumes.
   e. No bebas vino ni cerveza.
   f. No consumas cafeína.

3. Su amiga tiene mucho catarro.
   a. Ve al cine por la noche.
   b. Bebe mucho líquido.
   c. Escucha los casetes de español.
   d. No tomes aspirinas.
   e. Camina por el campo.
   f. Toma sopa de pollo.

4. A su mamá le duele el estómago.
   a. Evita (*avoid*) la grasa.
   b. Toma muchos helados.
   c. No comas mucho.
   d. Compra papas fritas.
   e. Acuéstate y descansa.
   f. Si no te sientes mejor, llama al médico.

5. Su amigo quiere preparar unas empanadas salteñas.
   a. Corta las papas en cuadritos.
   b. Compra más tomates y lechuga.
   c. Hierve los huevos durante un minuto.
   d. Prepara la masa el día anterior.
   e. No le pongas carne al relleno.
   f. Ponle pasas y aceitunas.

6. Su primo quiere visitar Cuba este verano.
   a. Lleva un abrigo de invierno.
   b. Prueba las frutas tropicales.
   c. Camina por la parte antigua de La Habana.
   d. Visita la playa de Varadero.
   e. Practica español antes de ir.
   f. Compra varios mapas.

11-14 Una cura de reposo. Su amigo/a estuvo muy enfermo, y su médico le recomendó pasar dos semanas de descanso total en Puerto Rico. Usted está de acuerdo con el médico, y le dice a su amigo/a lo que debe hacer allí. Después cambien de papel.

MODELO: visitar el parque nacional de El Yunque / no pensar en los negocios
          Visita el parque nacional de El Yunque. / No pienses en los negocios.

1. disfrutar de las playas de Isla Verde
2. respirar aire puro y descansar
3. no llamar a tu oficina
4. caminar por la parte histórica de San Juan
5. probar una comida típica, como el mofongo
6. salir por las noches y aprender a bailar la bomba y la plena

---

A INVESTIGAR

Haga una investigación sobre una de estas tres ciudades: Santo Domingo, La Habana o San Juan. Averigüe lo siguiente:

■ Ubicación y tamaño
■ Tres lugares de interés
■ Dos platos típicos
■ El nombre y la dirección de un hospital
■ Un dato que le parezca interesante

Escriba un breve párrafo para informar a la clase.

G **11-15 Una vida sana.** Ustedes están preocupados por el estilo de vida de uno/a de sus amigos/as. En grupos, lean lo que hace en un día típico e identifiquen los problemas que tiene. Después, hagan una lista de cinco actividades que él/ella debe hacer y cinco que no debe hacer para cambiar su estilo de vida. Comparen su lista con las de otros grupos.

> Se levanta tarde todos los días. Tan pronto se levanta, se sienta a comer su desayuno favorito: tres huevos fritos con tostadas y dos tazas de café cubano con bastante azúcar. Luego lee el periódico en su dormitorio, mira televisión unas cuatro horas y habla con amigos por teléfono. Como no le gusta cocinar, llama por teléfono al restaurante de la esquina y pide el almuerzo. Generalmente come hamburguesas o bistec con papas fritas y toma una o dos cervezas. Por la tarde, duerme una siesta larga, se levanta y prepara su bebida favorita: un Cuba Libre. Por la noche, les escribe cartas a sus amigos, ve las noticias, se sienta en el balcón de su casa a mirar a la gente que pasa por la calle y se acuesta a las 10:00 de la noche.

G **11-16 En la consulta de un/a fisioterapista (*physical therapist*).** En grupos, túrnense para representar a un/a fisioterapista y a sus pacientes. Cada integrante del grupo debe darle una orden a otro/a estudiante. Este/a estudiante debe hacer lo que le indicaron. Además de los verbos que conocen, los siguientes verbos pueden ser útiles para sus órdenes: **estirar** (*to stretch*), **doblar** (*to bend*), **cruzar** (*to cross*).

MODELO: Levántate rápidamente, camina un poco y siéntate enseguida.

2 **11-17 El correo sentimental.** Ustedes están a cargo del correo sentimental de un periódico y tienen que contestar las cartas que se reciben. ¿Qué consejos le van a dar a "Un enamorado"?

Querida Violeta:

Estoy desesperado y no sé con quién debo hablar ni qué debo hacer. Soy estudiante universitario y estoy en el último año de mi carrera. Hace poco conocí a una muchacha muy bonita y simpática en una de mis clases. Yo me enamoré de ella y empezamos a salir. Ella me decía que me quería mucho y que debíamos casarnos después de terminar los estudios. Yo también la quería mucho, pero un día le dije que era mejor esperar un poco antes de tomar una decisión tan seria como el matrimonio. Ella lo comprendió y me dijo que estaba de acuerdo conmigo.

Poco después empecé a notar que cada vez que venía a mi apartamento, faltaban cosas. Un día fue un cuchillo, otro día fue un tenedor, más adelante fue mi cámara, la semana pasada desaparecieron unos antibióticos del baño, etc. La otra noche fuimos a un restaurante a comer y vi que ponía dos cucharitas en su bolsa y que tomaba unas pastillas blancas muy pequeñas.

¿Qué debo hacer? Ella es una muchacha de una familia muy decente y no necesita estas cosas. Me siento culpable, pues no sé si esto es la consecuencia de nuestra conversación sobre el matrimonio o si es una enfermedad psicológica. Estoy totalmente confundido. Aconséjeme, por favor.

Un enamorado

Tomás

SITUACIONES

1. **Role A.** Your friend is not feeling well, and you go to his/her apartment to offer help. Ask how he/she is feeling. Then tell him/her to a) have some chicken soup, b) go to bed, and c) call the doctor. Offer to go out to get some chicken soup and help with house chores.

   Role B. You are not feeling well and a friend has come to help you. Explain a) that you have a sore throat and fever, and b) that you coughed a lot last night. After listening to your friend's advice and thanking him/her, say a) that you are not hungry now, b) that you already called your doctor and left a message (*mensaje*), and c) that you are going to rest while you wait for the doctor's call.

2. **Role A.** Call a friend and tell him/her the bad news that your mutual friend Roberto broke an ankle and he is at the hospital. Answer your friend's questions by saying a) that Roberto is doing fine and b) that you are planning to visit him this afternoon. Then ask your friend if he/she would like to come along, and agree to pick him/her up at five.

   Role B. A friend calls to tell you about Roberto's accident. Ask him/her a) how Roberto is, and b) say that you would like to see him. Then ask your friend if he/she is planning to visit him at the hospital. Use the expressions in the *En directo* box to express your reaction.

3. *Por* and *para* (review)

In previous lessons, you have used **por** in expressions such as **por favor, por ejemplo,** and **por ciento.** You have also used **por** and **para** to express the following meanings:

POR	PARA
MOVEMENT	
■ through or by a place	■ toward a destination
Caminaron **por** el hospital.	Caminaron **para** el hospital.
They walked through the hospital.	*They walked toward the hospital.*
TIME	
■ duration of an event	■ action deadline
Estuvo con el médico **por** una hora.	Necesita el antibiótico **para** el martes.
He was with the doctor for an hour.	*He needs the antibiotic by Tuesday.*
ACTION	
■ reason or motive of an action	■ for whom something is intended or done
Ana fue al consultorio **por** el dolor de garganta.	Compró el antibiótico **para** Ana.
Ana went to the doctor's office because of a sore throat.	*He bought the antibiotic for Ana.*

4. Other uses of *por* and *para*

Use **por** to:

■ indicate exchange or substitution

Irma pagó $120 **por** la medicina.	*Irma paid $120 for the medicine.*
Cambió estas pastillas **por** ésas.	*She changed these pills for those.*

■ express unit or rate

Yo camino 5 kilómetros **por** hora.	*I walk 5 kilometers per hour.*
El interés es (el) diez **por** ciento.	*The interest is ten per cent.*

■ express means of transportation

Lo mandaron **por** avión.	*They sent it by plane.*
Prefieren ir **por** tren.	*They'd rather go by train.*

■ express the object of an errand

Fue **por** las aspirinas.	*He went for the aspirins.*
Pasamos **por** ti a las 5:00.	*We'll come by for you at 5:00.*

Use **para** to...

■ express judgment or point of view.

Para nosotros, esta es la mejor farmacia.	*For us, this is the best drugstore.*
Es un caso difícil **para** un médico joven.	*It is a difficult case for a young doctor.*

■ indicate intention or purpose, when followed by an infinitive.

Fueron **para** comprar aspirinas.	*They went to buy aspirin.*
Salió **para** ayudar a los enfermos.	*He left to help the sick people.*

¿Qué dice usted?

11-18 ¿Por o para? Casi todas las oraciones siguientes pueden completarse con **por** o **para**, pero sólo una de estas preposiciones refleja lo que quiere decir la persona. Trace un círculo alrededor de la preposición que debe usarse.

1. Toward a destination
   Salimos **por/para** el consultorio del médico a las nueve de la mañana.
2. Through
   Fuimos **por/para** el túnel para llegar más rápido.
3. Reason or motive of an action
   Ana fue a ver al médico **por/para** su dolor de garganta.
4. For whom something is intended or done
   El médico escribió la receta de un antibiótico **por/para** Ana.
5. The object of an errand
   Yo fui a la farmacia **por/para** el antibiótico.
6. Indicate exchange or substitution
   Pagué veinte pesos **por/para** el antibiótico.

11-19 ¿Por dónde y para dónde van? Túrnense para hacer y contestar preguntas según los siguientes dibujos.

MODELO: E1: ¿Por dónde va el alumno?
E2: Va por el pasillo.
E1: ¿Para dónde va?
E2: Va para su clase de español.

1.

2.

3.

4.

11-20 En el laboratorio. Túrnense para averiguar cuándo van a estar listos los resultados de los análisis (*tests*) de unos pacientes. Consulten la tabla para obtener la información correcta.

MODELO: Alfredo Benítez   un análisis   2:00 de la tarde
E1: ¿Cuándo va a estar listo el análisis del Sr. Benítez?
E2: Va a estar listo para las dos (de la tarde).

PACIENTE	ANÁLISIS	RESULTADOS
Hilda Corvalán	1	11:00 de la mañana
Alfonso González	2	esta tarde
Jorge Pérez Robles	3	3:15 de la tarde
Aleida Miranda	1	mañana por la mañana
César Gómez Villegas	4	martes
Irene Santa Cruz	1	...

11-21 ¿Par...   ...eron? Túrnense y pregúntense para qué fueron las personas a estos lug... ...eben usar su imaginación para contestar y dar detalles adicionales.

MODELO: Pablo fue al supermercado.
E1: ¿Para qué fue al supermercado?
E2: Fue para comprar leche y huevos.
Quiere hacer un postre.

1. Jorge fue al hospital.
2. Ignacio fue a la farmacia.
3. Sara y Gloria fueron al gimnasio.
4. La Sra. Méndez fue al centro comercial.
5. Alejandro y Martín fueron a Cuba el 24 de diciembre.
6. Carlos fue a ver al psicólogo.

11-22 La graduación de un nuevo médico. Complete estos párrafos sobre la graduación de Fernando con **por** o **para,** según el contexto.

El 14 de junio es la graduación de Fernando en la Facultad de Medicina de la Universidad Católica Madre y Maestra de Santiago de los Caballeros. Sus padres, los señores Rovira, viven en Puerto Plata, pero van a ir (1) _____ la graduación y quieren llevarle un regalo a Fernando. El lunes pasado fueron a una tienda y pagaron $100 (2) _____ un regalo muy bonito (3) _____ Fernando. Graciela, su hermana gemela, vive en Miami y no puede ir (4) _____ su trabajo. Ella también le compró un regalo y se lo envió (5) _____ avión porque quiere que llegue (6) _____ el día de la graduación.

El día 14 (7) _____ la mañana, los padres de Fernando salieron (8) _____ la universidad. Estaba lloviendo, y (9) _____ eso salieron temprano. Normalmente, ellos pueden estar en la universidad en una hora más o menos, pero (10) _____ la lluvia, el viaje duró casi dos horas. (11) _____ ellos, que son mayores, el viaje fue un poco largo, pero al final pudieron pasar ese día con su hijo.

SITUACIONES

Role A. You are stressed out and need to rest. Following doctor's orders you are planning to rent a furnished apartment at the beach. You found one in the classified ads. Call the landlord and tell him/her a) when you will need the apartment, and b) for how long. Ask how much the rent is and inquire about the size of the rooms and other facilities. Answer his/her question(s) and then make an appointment to see it.

Role B. You are a landlord who is renting an apartment at the beach. A prospective renter calls you. Answer his/her questions and ask him/her how many people will be staying at the apartment. Agree on a date and time to show the property.

5. Relative pronouns

- The relative pronouns **que** and **quien(es)** combine two clauses into one sentence.

Los médicos trabajan en ese hospital.	*The doctors work at that hospital.*
Los médicos son excelentes.	*The doctors are excellent.*
Los médicos **que** trabajan en ese hospital son excelentes.	*The doctors who work at that hospital are excellent.*

- **Que** is the most commonly used relative pronoun. It introduces a dependent clause, and it may refer to persons or things.

Las vitaminas **que** yo tomo son muy caras.	*The vitamins that I take are very expensive.*
Ése es el médico **que** me receta las vitaminas.	*That is the doctor who prescribes the vitamins.*

- **Quien(es)** refers only to persons and may replace **que** in a clause set off by commas.

Los Márquez, **quienes/que** viven en la ciudad, prefieren el campo.	*The Márquezes, who live in the city, prefer the country.*

- Use **quien(es)** after a preposition (**a, con, de, por, para,** etc.) when referring to people.

Allí está el enfermero **con quien** hablé esta mañana.	*There is the nurse with whom I spoke this morning.*
Ésos son los señores **a quienes** les debes dar la receta.	*Those are the gentlemen to whom you should give the prescription.*

¿Qué dice usted?

11-23 Una telenovela dominicana. Joaquín está enfermo hoy, y por eso empezó a mirar una telenovela en uno de los canales de la televisión. Le gustó tanto que le mandó un correo electrónico a un amigo, contándole detalles de la telenovela. Complete el correo electrónico de Joaquín con **que** o **quien**.

Mi corazón es una telenovela dominicana (1) _____ tiene mucho público. El actor principal es Agustín Montalvo. Él es el actor de (2) _____ todos hablan. La crítica cree que este año va a ganar el premio Talía, (3) _____ es el equivalente del Óscar norteamericano. El 90 por ciento de las chicas dicen que Agustín es el actor con (4) _____ les gustaría salir. En la telenovela, Agustín hace el papel del médico (5) _____ quiere salvar la vida de Silvina del Bosque, la actriz principal, (6) _____ tuvo un accidente terrible y está inconsciente. Agustín es el hombre (7) _____ ella quiere, pero Agustín está enamorado de Esmeralda del Valle, una mujer a (8) _____ sólo le interesa el dinero de Agustín. La telenovela es muy melodramática y siempre hay problemas (9) _____ mantienen el interés del público.

11-24 Un accidente. Completen esta conversación con el nombre de una persona y los pronombres **que** o **quien.**

E1: ¿Qué haces aquí en el hospital? ¿A quién viniste a ver?

E2: A _____, el/la chico/a con _____ estoy saliendo.

E1: ¿Y cómo está?

E2: Bastante bien, gracias a Dios. Tuvimos un accidente bastante serio con el carro _____ su padre le regaló.

E1: ¡Qué horror! ¿Y llamaste a alguien?

E2: No tuve tiempo. Enseguida llegó la policía. Bueno, te hablo después. Allí viene la doctora _____ nos atendió, y quiero hacerle unas preguntas.

11-25 Mi médico/a o dentista. Descríbale su médico/a o dentista a su compañero/a. Mencione por lo menos tres características.

MODELO: Mi médico/a es... Es un/a médico/a que...

SITUACIONES

Role A. A close relative of yours (husband, wife, son, daughter) has recently had surgery (*una operación*), and you need some information in order to fill out an insurance form. You call the hospital and ask a) the name of the doctor who performed surgery on your relative, b) the amount of time that the surgery took, c) the prescriptions that the doctor gave him/her, d) the number of days that he/she will have to stay at the hospital.

Role B. You work answering the phone at a local hospital. A relative of one of the patients calls to find out some information he/she needs in order to fill out an insurance form. Identify yourself and answer his/her questions.

Escuchar

Summarizing information

Sometimes when you listen to a conversation, a news report, or a lecture you need to summarize what was said for someone who was not present. To that end, you will give the general information of what was said and, when asked for or needed, will include some details to make your summary clearer. Needless to say, note taking is of paramount importance when summarizing. Therefore, jot down key information (ideas, words, concepts, data, etc.) in the order in which it appears in a listening text (a conversation, a lecture, etc.). Those notes will serve as the basis for your summary.

Antes de escuchar

11-26 ¿Cómo está Sebastián? In activity **11-27**, you will listen to a conversation between two friends regarding Sebastian's health. Before you listen, write down the Spanish names for three health professionals, three symptoms patients might experience, and three different types of treatments they might receive.

profesionales de la salud _____
síntomas   _____
tratamientos   _____

A escuchar

AUDIO **11-27.** Now, read the following statements. Then, listen to the conversation between two friends regarding Sebastian's health. Finally, circle the statement that better summarizes what you have heard.

1. Los padres y amigos de Sebastián están preocupados porque Sebastián está enfermo y no va a poder celebrar su cumpleaños la próxima semana.
2. Sebastián está en el hospital con una infección intestinal. Antes de ir, él tenía dolor de estómago, náuseas y fiebre. Ahora toma antibióticos y tiene una dieta especial.
3. Sebastián vive solo. Por eso, siempre come en un restaurante, y la semana pasada comió algo que no estaba fresco. Ahora, sus padres han venido a cuidarlo y a prepararle comida especial.
4. El Dr. Méndez es un excelente médico y dice que Sebastián va a salir del hospital pronto, pero tiene que empezar una dieta y cuidarse mucho.

Después de escuchar

11-28 ¿Y usted? Share your answers to the following questions:

1. ¿Tiene usted una dieta sana? ¿Qué come típicamente para el almuerzo o la cena?
2. ¿Come usted en restaurantes frecuentemente? ¿Por qué?
3. ¿Qué cree usted que debe hacer para mantener o mejorar su salud?

Antes de escuchar

11-29 Consejos de la nutricionista. In 11-30, you will listen to a conversation between a nutritionist and a group of college students. Before you listen, write down a list of four suggestions you think the nutritionist will make and two questions the students will probably ask her.

consejos. _____

_____

posibles preguntas _____

_____

A escuchar

 11-30 Consejos de la nutricionista. Now, read the following statements and, then, listen to the advice a nutritionist gives a group of college students. Finally, circle the statement that best summarizes what you have heard.

1. La nutricionista les recomienda a los estudiantes que vean al médico una vez por mes.
2. La nutricionista les aconseja que hagan mucho ejercicio y coman comida con poca sal.
3. La nutricionista les sugiere que coman comida rápida y beban alcohol sólo los fines de semana.
4. La nutricionista aconseja la moderación en la comida, bebida y ejercicios para mantener una vida saludable.

Después de escuchar

11-31 ¿Y usted? With a classmate, share your answers to the following questions.

1. ¿Cuál es su rutina diaria con respecto a su comida y actividades?
2. ¿Qué hace usted para mantener una vida saludable?
3. ¿Qué aspecto de su vida piensa usted que puede cambiar para mejorar su estado físico?

Conversar

Antes de conversar

11-32 ¿Quiere vivir más? Primera fase. Marque los hábitos o condiciones que, según usted, ayudan a prolongar la vida de las personas.

1. _____ hacer ejercicio físico regularmente
2. _____ trabajar poco
3. _____ tener mucho estrés
4. _____ comer regularmente carne roja
5. _____ ser vegetariano/a
6. _____ consumir carne blanca
7. _____ beber vino con el almuerzo o la cena
8. _____ pasar muchas horas inactivo
9. _____ usar la medicina alternativa
10. _____ usar muchos condimentos
11. _____ ponerle mucha sal a la comida

G **Segunda fase.** Primero, comparen sus respuestas a las preguntas de la **Primera fase** y, luego, escriban un cuestionario para determinar si las personas hacen o no lo necesario para vivir más años. Consideren las siguientes áreas en su cuestionario.

TEMAS	EJEMPLOS
1. actividades/hábitos	¿Se mantiene usted activo/a?
2. comida	¿Consume verduras regularmente?
3. bebidas	¿Bebe alcohol? ¿Con qué frecuencia?

A conversar

11-33 ¿Te cuidas para vivir más? Usen el cuestionario de la actividad **11-32, Segunda fase** para entrevistarse entre ustedes. Tomen notas de la información adicional importante que mencione su compañero/a durante la conversación. Esto los/las puede ayudar a determinar si cada uno de ustedes realmente se cuida o no para vivir más.

Después de conversar

11-34 Para reflexionar. Use la información que le dio su compañero/a en **11-33** y converse con él/ella sobre lo siguiente:

1. Mencione las actividades de su compañero/a que, según usted, van a contribuir a una vida más larga. Felicítelo/la (*Congratulate him/her*).
2. También indique los buenos hábitos de alimentación (comida, bebida) de su compañero/a que prolongarán la vida de él/ella.
3. Si es necesario, dele consejos o recomendaciones para mejorar sus hábitos.

Antes de conversar

11-35 Las enfermedades del siglo XXI. Primera fase. Marquen los tipos de enfermedades que probablemente se asocian con este siglo.

1. _____ cardiovasculares
2. _____ respiratorias
3. _____ mentales
4. _____ nerviosas

Segunda fase. Escriban por lo menos dos ejemplos de enfermedades específicas en cada grupo.

1. cardiovasculares _____
2. respiratorias _____
3. mentales _____
4. nerviosas _____

EN DIRECTO

To congratulate or praise someone:

Felicitaciones por + [*verb, noun*].

Te felicito. Te alimentas muy bien.

¡Qué bien, [*name*]! Vas a vivir muchos años.

To express happiness or satisfaction at someone's success:

Me alegro de que + [*subjunctive*].

¡Qué fabuloso que + [*subjunctive*]!

A conversar

11-36 ¿Qué es bueno hacer? Averigüen si alguien que ustedes conocen (familiar, amigo o conocido) sufre de alguna de las enfermedades mencionadas en actividad **11-35**. Luego, den una recomendación general y otra específica para los pacientes con estas enfermedades.

ENFERMEDAD ESPECÍFICA	PACIENTE	RECOMENDACIÓN GENERAL	RECOMENDACIÓN ESPECÍFICA
Cardiovascular: _____			
Respiratoria: _____			
Mental: _____			
Nerviosa: _____			

Después de conversar

11-37 ¿Qué debemos saber y hacer? Preparen una breve presentación de una enfermedad del siglo XXI que a ustedes les interese para compartir con la clase. Hagan lo siguiente:

1. Den el nombre de la enfermedad e indiquen los órganos o partes del cuerpo afectados.
2. Indiquen los síntomas básicos de la enfermedad.
3. Mencionen algunos tratamientos médicos.
4. Den dos recomendaciones generales y dos específicas para los pacientes.

Para que su presentación sea más clara e interesante, usen material visual, como fotos, videos, afiches, etc.

 Leer

> **EN DIRECTO**
>
> **To make a general recommendation:**
> Es importante/bueno/ conveniente/aconsejable + [*infinitive*].
>
> **To make a recommendation to someone specific:**
> Es importante que + [*name*(s)] + [*subjunctive*].

Identifying what information is relevant in a text and disregarding what is irrelevant are time-saving strategies. They help you become not only a more fluent reader, but also a more focused one. By filtering information (identifying what's important and letting go of what is not), you also become a more accurate reader. The following cues may help you identify what is important:

- Read the title and subtitle of the text.

- Brainstorm its possible content by using your knowledge of the topic or theme.

- Take notes of key information or ideas that, in your view, the text should include.

Guía de prelectura

Look at the visuals, the title, and the subheads in activity **11-40** and then answer the following questions. Use the cues provided by the headline and subheading and your personal knowledge to answer. Do not worry if your attempts to anticipate the content of the text are incorrect. You will be able to correct your responses later.

1. What key information (concepts, ideas, etc.) will this article likely contain?
   a. Diseases unknown to man appear because of the opening of new economic markets around the world.
   b. Diseases that experts thought had disappeared emerge again due to environmental changes around the world.
   c. Infectious, killer diseases that travel across the oceans are on the rise.
   d. Poor, developing nations export their diseases as their citizens migrate to developed countries.

2. How did you figure out the answers to question 1? Circle the corresponding letter.
   a. The title, subtitle, and photo
   b. The visuals in the text
   c. Knowledge of the topic
   d. Some research I did before reading the article

3. Now, can you hypothesize about the probable content of the text? The article will probably present the following content. Circle all that apply:
   a. The names of some of the diseases more commonly associated with globalization.
   b. Key geographical areas around the world where some infectious diseases were born.
   c. Explanation for the emergence of some diseases that were previously eliminated.
   d. Some measures the governments are taking to prevent the spread of such infectious disease.
   e. An analysis of how globalization is responsible for the spread of certain diseases.

Antes de leer

11-38 Preparación. Primera fase. ¿Cuáles de las siguientes enfermedades se consideran enfermedades tropicales? Márquenlas.

1. _____ la gripe
2. _____ la tuberculosis
3. _____ el dengue
4. _____ el virus del Nilo
5. _____ la fiebre del pollo (*SARS*)
6. _____ la malaria
7. _____ la viruela (*smallpox*)
8. _____ la neumonía

Segunda fase. Determinen lo siguiente:

1. ¿Cuál(es) de las enfermedades de la **Primera fase** ya está(n) presentes en su país?
2. ¿Cuál(es) de las enfermedades de la **Primera fase** es/son contagiosa(s)?

11-39 ¿Cuáles son las causas y síntomas? Hagan una breve investigación para averiguar las causas y síntomas de **dos** de estas enfermedades: la malaria, la fiebre del pollo, la tuberculosis, el dengue. Luego, compartan la información con la clase. El siguiente plan les puede ser útil.

1. lugar de origen y causa de la enfermedad
2. síntomas
3. posibles tratamientos

A leer

11-40 Primera mirada. Lea el siguiente artículo y, luego, siga las instrucciones.

Las enfermedades y la globalización

Enfermedades tropicales como el dengue, la viruela, la malaria, la tuberculosis, la enfermedad del sueño que, según muchos, ya no existían, reaparecen y se extienden por todo el mundo. Las causas de su reaparición son evidentes: cambios en el medio ambiente y el constante movimiento de personas entre los continentes. Los turistas y los trabajadores migratorios transportan estos virus e infecciones. De la misma manera, los cambios climáticos facilitan la adaptación de los virus a nuevos ambientes y los hacen resistentes.

Desafíos y prevención

Un claro ejemplo del nivel de adaptabilidad de estas enfermedades infecciosas es la tuberculosis. Los científicos pensaban que ésta estaba controlada en los países desarrollados. Sin embargo, los hechos nos muestran que esta enfermedad ha evolucionado de tal manera que en países desarrollados como Alemania, Italia o España, por ejemplo, hay pacientes con tuberculosis porque las bacterias no reaccionan a los medicamentos tradicionales. Se piensa que alrededor de un 32% de la población del mundo sufre y morirá de esta enfermedad.

La Organización Mundial de la Salud (OMS) expresa gran preocupación por la malaria. Según los expertos, el mosquito que la provoca puede sobrevivir largos viajes interocéanicos. Por eso, hay personas enfermas de malaria en muchas partes del mundo. Sin duda, la malaria es peligrosa si no se detecta a tiempo. Sus síntomas son semejantes a los de la gripe; por lo tanto un médico sin experiencia en este tipo de enfermedades la puede confundir con la gripe y tratarla con medicamentos inadecuados.

El virus del Nilo constituye otra de las enfermedades turistas. Esta enfermedad mató por lo menos a 125 norteamericanos en el año 2002 y alarmó a varios países europeos.

Sorpresa y medidas

A fines del siglo XX, gracias a una campaña mundial contra la viruela, casi toda la población mundial fue inmunizada contra esta enfermedad. Sin embargo, en la actualidad, la viruela de los monos, una variedad típica de la selva de algunos países africanos, ya se reproduce en otros lugares del globo, como los Estados Unidos. En este país se están volviendo a fabricar vacunas contra esta enfermedad que no se producían desde hacía años.

El dengue es indudablemente la enfermedad más extendida en los últimos años. Los expertos afirman que es posible que dos quintas partes de la población del mundo contraigan esta mortal fiebre endémica. Geográficamente, el dengue nació en el suroeste asiático, pero rápidamente pasó al Caribe y Centro y Sudamérica. En los últimos años, se han detectado casos incluso en España.

Las migraciones en masa, causadas por las guerras, y la falta de fondos en los ministerios de salud han provocado el retorno de la enfermedad del sueño en África. Los estudios indican que más de 100.000 individuos están infectados en el África subsahariana. Este fenómeno se repite en países como Sudán y Uganda.

La lista de enfermedades que surgen de nuevo por la movilidad de la población del mundo actual es larga, pero los fondos mundiales para realizar investigaciones sobre las enfermedades que causan el 90 por ciento de las muertes en el mundo son mínimos y limitados. Sin duda, la globalización ha resuelto algunos problemas, pero ha creado otros.

De las siguientes afirmaciones, indique cuáles representan ideas principales (**P**) del artículo y cuáles son ideas secundarias (**S**).

1. _____ La reaparición de algunas enfermedades es causada por la interconexión de los mercados del mundo.
2. _____ La gran movilidad de las personas por razones económicas causa la reaparición de enfermedades tropicales que en algún momento desaparecieron.
3. _____ Los cambios de clima, provocados por los cambios en el medio ambiente (*environment*), ayudan a que algunos virus sean más resistentes.
4. _____ Las enfermedades turistas mataron a norteamericanos y europeos.
5. _____ Algunas enfermedades que nacieron en un punto específico del mundo se expanden a otros continentes.
6. _____ Los países desarrollados como los Estados Unidos están fabricando vacunas para combatir algunas enfermedades contagiosas.

11-41 Segunda mirada. Según el contenido del artículo, subraye las expresiones que se relacionan con estos temas:

1. Enfermedades tropicales: las infecciones, la viruela, el virus del Nilo, la tuberculosis, la enfermedad del sueño
2. Desafíos de las enfermedades para los expertos: la infección, la adaptabilidad, el desarrollo, la evolución, la resistencia
3. Medidas que los gobiernos toman para enfrentar estas enfermedades: campañas, inmunización, reproducción, vacunas, prevención

Después de leer

11-42 Ampliación. Primera fase. Busque en el artículo la palabra que se asocia con los verbos de la lista. Luego clasifíquela en la columna apropiada. Subraye la terminación de la palabra. ¿Qué género tiene, femenino o masculino?

VERBO	SUSTANTIVO	GÉNERO
1. enfermarse		
2. reaparecer		
3. mover		
4. adaptar		
5. prevenir		
6. migrar		
7. retornar		
8. globalizar		

Segunda fase. Complete el siguiente texto con un verbo o sustantivo de la **Primera fase.**

La interconexión del mundo actual

Muchos piensan que los efectos de la (1) _____ siempre son positivos. Sin embargo, hay un gran número de personas en todo el mundo que cree lo contrario. Según ellos, es triste ver que muchas de las (2) _____ que ya se creían eliminadas (3) _____ con mucha fuerza y amenazan matar a millones de víctimas inocentes en todos los continentes. Piensan que los países desarrollados y más ricos pueden tomar medidas para (4) _____ la propagación de estas enfermedades mortales. No obstante, la realidad indica que el (5) _____ masivo de inmigrantes entre los continentes inevitablemente facilita el (6) _____ de éstas.

Escribir

In our daily lives, we regularly share information by summarizing what we hear, see, or read. The focus of a good summary is on the main issues or facts upon which the story, event, or experience is based. When we summarize, we progressively reduce the original text by eliminating secondary ideas, redundancies, repetitions, etc.

A good written summary has, among others, the following features:

a. It presents the main ideas or characteristics of the object being summarized
b. It sums up all the parts of what is being recapitulated
c. It has a cohesive and coherent organization

Therefore, to write a good summary, keep in mind the following:

a. Read a text or observe carefully. Identify the theme of your summary, the time frame when what you are summarizing exists or takes place, the reasons for its existence or why it happened, who is responsible for its existence or occurrence, what the consequences are (when applicable), etc.
b. Collect all the relevant information and organize it. Distinguish main ideas or information from secondary ones. Underline them.
c. Find a method or system that will help you remember. Taking notes, diagramming, outlining may work for you.
d. Be brief; that is, avoid details.

Antes de escribir

11-43 Preparación. Primera fase. El siguiente es un resumen de un evento histórico relacionado con la salud. Léalo y, luego, siga las instrucciones.

> Según algunos, el año 1526 marca un evento trágico para los indígenas de América. Ocurre la primera epidemia de viruela que mata a miles de indios en los Andes. Esta nueva enfermedad contagiosa que llegó con los europeos al continente americano encontró a los nativos sin defensas para enfrentarla.
>
> Sin embargo, la historia nos indica que fueron los indígenas del Caribe los primeros contagiados por las enfermedades europeas. Se piensa que el 9 de diciembre de 1493, la influenza tocó las puertas de América cuando 1.500 hombres y animales domésticos desembarcaron en Santo Domingo. Al día siguiente de su llegada, los pasajeros del barco Isabela empezaron a presentar síntomas evidentes de influeza: alta fiebre e intenso dolor en el cuerpo al punto de la postración. Éstos contagiaron a los indígenas, quienes murieron por miles.
>
> Aunque varias enfermedades cruzaron los océanos para llegar a América, la que causó mayor desolación y muerte entre la población indígena fue la viruela. Nuevamente, los indios de Santo Domingo fueron las primeras víctimas en 1518 y 1519. Según los datos históricos, sólo un millón de ellos lograron sobrevivir la mortal epidemia.

Segunda fase. Answer the following questions, based on the summary in the **Primera fase.**

1. Circle the theme of the summary:
   a. Indigenous people of America infected the helpless conquistadors with their infectious diseases.
   b. Conquistadors brought unknown, contagious diseases that killed large numbers of indigenous people in America.
   c. Animals brought by conquistadors killed only American Indians with whom they came into contact.

2. Is there a time frame for this historical event?   Yes   No

3. If yes, indicate a time frame when the event happened.
   a. The beginning of the sixteenth century
   b. The end of the fifteenth and the beginning of the sixteenth centuries

4. Mark some possible reasons that explain this event.
   a. The Spaniards wanted to kill as many Indians as possible to take over their land.
   b. The animals the conquistadors brought along spread the infectious disease among the ship crew who, in turn, passed it on to the American Indians with whom they came into contact.
   c. The American Indians' immune systems were defenseless and unprepared to fight these diseases.

5. Identify the consequences of this event.
   a. Everyone infected survived.
   b. Probably some of the Spaniards survived, but many American Indians died.
   c. Everyone died.

11-44 Antes de resumir. Primera fase. En la actividad **11-45,** usted va a resumir un texto sobre un tema de salud de su elección. Pero antes, lea la siguiente lista de posibles temas y seleccione uno que le interese. Escriba algunas ideas que lo/la ayuden a enfocar su atención en el tema que escogió.

1. la viruela
2. la fiebre del pollo
3. la enfermedad del sueño
4. el dengue
5. la malaria
6. la hepatitis

ENFERMEDAD	LUGAR DE ORIGEN	CAUSAS	SÍNTOMAS BÁSICOS
• _____	• _____	• _____	• _____
		• _____	• _____
		• _____	• _____

Segunda fase. Ahora haga lo siguiente.

1. Lea el/los artículo(s) del tema que seleccionó.
2. Identifique el tema del texto, el tiempo en que se sitúa o existe, las razones de su existencia, el/los responsable(s), las consecuencias, etc.
3. Separe la información (ideas, conceptos, datos, etc.) más importante de la secundaria y tome notas.
4. Haga una lista de palabras que le van a ser útiles para darle cohesión a su texto.

A escribir

11-45 Manos a la obra. Escriba el resumen del texto que leyó en **11-44, Segunda fase.** Use la información que preparó en la actividad **11-44, Segunda fase.** No olvide que su resumen debe ser breve y conciso.

Después de escribir

11-46 Revisión. Antes de darle el resumen a su compañero/a editor/a, léalo y verifique lo siguiente, pensando en su lector.

- El contenido. En su resumen, ¿se concentró en el tema central del artículo? ¿Incluyó toda la información importante? ¿Puso el evento/la experiencia/el fenómeno dentro de un marco de tiempo? ¿Dio las razones que lo explican?

- La organización. ¿Tiene su resumen un orden y organización claros?

- La gramática. ¿Usó el vocabulario correcto, algunas expresiones de cohesión, la concordancia, el tiempo (presente, pasado) y modos (indicativo, subjuntivo), etc.?

- La puntuación y ortografía. ¿Usó comas, puntos, etc. donde eran necesarios?

Finalmente, comparta su resumen con su compañero/a.

ENFOQUE CULTURAL

TEMAS: LAS FARMACIAS Y LA MEDICINA NO TRADICIONAL

Para pensar

Cuando usted necesita una operación o tiene un accidente, ¿adónde va? ¿Tiene que pagar o no? Cuando usted está enfermo/a y necesita medicinas, ¿adónde va a comprarlas? ¿Qué necesita para comprarlas?

En la mayor parte de los países hispanos existen hospitales y centros de salud financiados por el gobierno donde las personas pueden ir sin tener que pagar absolutamente nada por los servicios o medicinas que reciben.

En muchos países, especialmente en los caribeños, algunas personas van a ver a los curanderos, quienes, según la creencia popular, tienen poderes especiales para curar todo tipo de enfermedad.

En el mundo hispano, las farmacias están en locales separados y venden todo tipo de remedios y artículos de belleza. Al igual que en los Estados Unidos, en muchos lugares se necesita tener receta médica para comprar antibióticos. Muchas veces los clientes de la farmacia le preguntan al/a la farmacéutico/a qué remedio o antibiótico deben comprar para curar o tratar su enfermedad.

Para contestar

2 **El sistema de salud.** Respondan a las siguientes preguntas.

1. ¿Qué saben ustedes del sistema de salud público y privado en algunos países hispanos?
2. ¿Cómo son las farmacias en los países hispanos? ¿Qué venden?
3. Además de las medicinas tradicionales, ¿qué otro tipo de medicinas toman algunas personas en los países hispanos? Nombren dos o tres medicinas y digan para qué sirven.

G **Riqueza cultural.** En grupos de tres, discutan las ventajas y desventajas de consultar a un curandero (especialista en yerbas medicinales) o algún otro especialista en medicina alternativa como un acupunturista o un reflexólogo. Luego, presenten a la clase sus conclusiones.

Muchas personas prefieren curarse con yerbas medicinales. Por ejemplo, para el dolor de estómago se recomienda tomar un té de manzanilla (camomille), o un té de ruda (rue). Otra yerba medicinal muy conocida es la uña de gato (cat's claw), que se considera buena para el tratamiento del cáncer.

Para pensar

¿Sabe usted dónde quedan Cuba, Puerto Rico y la República Dominicana?
¿Sabe usted que Santo Domingo es la ciudad más antigua de las Américas?
¿Conoce usted a algún deportista o artista famoso de estos países?

Cuba, La República Dominicana y Puerto Rico se encuentran en el Mar Caribe.

En La Habana existen edificios de gran belleza y valor histórico, como el Castillo del Morro y la Fortaleza de la Cabaña.

La industria del tabaco es muy importante en Cuba. Se dice que el mejor tabaco del mundo se cultiva en Vuelta Abajo, en Pinar del Río, en el oeste de Cuba.

El Viejo San Juan es una hermosa zona de Puerto Rico donde hay tiendas de diferentes tipos, hermosas plazas, cafés al aire libre, museos, galerías de arte e interesantes edificios que datan de los siglos XVI y XVII. Al lado del Viejo San Juan está el San Juan moderno.

Expresiones cubanas:

la guagua	Ahí viene la **guagua**.	*The bus is coming.*
despeluzar	La quiere **despeluzar**.	*He wants to take all her money.*
fula	No tiene **fulas**.	*He does not have dollars.*

En el bosque tropical El Yunque se puede caminar por diferentes senderos, explorar hermosas caídas de agua y admirar diferentes especies de aves y una gran variedad de plantas, como las orquídeas y los helechos.

Santo Domingo, la capital, tiene una hermosa zona colonial con edificios que datan del siglo XVI. Entre ellos están la Catedral Primada de América, el Alcázar de Colón, las ruinas de San Francisco, el Museo de las Casas Reales y muchos más.

Expresiones puertorriqueñas:

macacoa	Yo no compro la lotería porque tengo una **macacoa** terrible.	*I do not buy the lottery because I have horrible bad luck.*
revolú	Se formó el **revolú**.	*Things got messy.*
bendito	¡Ay, **bendito**!	*Oh, my!*

Expresiones dominicanas:

varado	Me tiene **varado/a**.	*He/she keeps me from succeeding.*
aceitado	Está **aceitado/a**.	*He/she is ready to comply.*
se aflojó	Ya **se aflojó**.	*He/she chickened out.*

Para contestar

En el mapa

1. Diga dónde están Cuba, Puerto Rico y la República Dominicana y cuáles son sus capitales.
2. ¿Qué países están cerca de la República Dominicana?

Ahora diga...

1. si le gustaría visitar La Habana, San Juan o Santo Domingo y por qué.
2. qué lugar de San Juan o de La Habana le interesaría visitar.

¿Qué dice usted si...

1. su amigo/a tiene miedo de hacer lo que pensaba hacer.
2. su amigo/a tiene mala suerte.
3. alguien le quiere quitar su dinero.

En la República Dominicana hay muchos lagos y hermosos parques nacionales. Uno de los más conocidos es el Lago Enriquillo. En el centro de este lago se encuentra el Parque Nacional Isla Cabritos.

Para investigar en Internet

Busque información *www.prenhall.com/mosaicos* acerca de la medicina no tradicional en Cuba, Puerto Rico o la República Dominicana. Diga quiénes la practican, qué remedios, yerbas o productos usan, y qué personas recurren a ellos.

¡Prepárese!

11-47 Por y Para. Llene los espacios en blanco con **por** o **para.**

1. Ángela y Manolo trabajan _____ muchas horas en el concurso cada día.
2. Carlos perdona a Katie _____ llevarse mejor con ella.
3. Carlos mira el papel en la mochila de Katie _____ saber qué pista tiene ella.
4. _____ sus acciones, Katie piensa que Carlos y Efraín tienen una alianza.
5. _____ Efraín, la relación entre Katie y Carlos no es importante.
6. Efraín opina que la confianza es importante _____ tener éxito en el amor.

A Ángela no le gustan las acciones de Katie aunque ella está ganando.

Parece que Carlos ha perdonado a Katie.

Carlos mira el papel que está en la mochila de Katie.

Efraín admite que tiene una alianza con Carlos.

A Tito le interesa la relación entre Carlos y Katie, pero a Efraín no le importa.

Según Efraín, la falta de confianza no es buena para el amor.

¡Responda!

11-48 Asociaciones. Imagínese que es uno de los concursantes. Haga una asociación de palabras entre el Misterio 5 y las cuatro pistas. Después compare su lista con la de un/a compañero/a.

Misterio 5
Un lugar sagrado: _____

Pistas

1. Cerro sagrado: _____
2. Enseñanza militar: _____
3. Residencia presidencial: _____
4. Manantial y acueducto: _____

11-49 Soluciones. Al comparar su lista con la de su compañero/a, ¿qué ideas tienen para tratar de solucionar este misterio?

_____
_____
_____

En el Caribe el pregonero iba de casa en casa vendiendo muchos productos, especialmente frutas y vegetales. En esta canción Tito Nieves, cantante puertorriqueño conocido como el Pavarotti de la salsa, canta sobre el trabajo y los productos típicos del pregonero.

¡Prepárese!

11-50 Los productos. Lea la lista de productos que vende el pregonero y trate de rellenar los espacios en blanco mientras escucha la canción.

quenepa	piña	guayaba	caña	tamarindo	guineitos
mango	naranja	coco	pomarrosas	toronja	

Ay, casera,
llevo la _____ fresca,
la _____ madura,
llevo la _____ dulce
Y el _____ seco, cáscara dura.
...

De Ponce le traigo la _____,
de Mayagüez el _____,
para rebajar la _____,
refresco de _____.

Venga y cómpreme caserita
porque yo soy pregonero

del río traigo _____,
del cañaveral caña dulce,
de mi bella playa coco seco
para ponerla dura la _____
para la desilusión corazones
de mi guineal _____

Salsa

el medio

izquierda (left)   derecha (right)

1. Both feet in middle
2. Right foot forward; left foot in middle
3. Step in place with left foot, then move right foot back to middle
4. Both feet in middle
5. Left foot back; right foot in middle
6. Step in place with right foot, then move left foot back to middle
7. Both feet in middle

¡Escuche!

11-51 ¡Vamos a bailar salsa! "El pregonero" es un ejemplo de música **salsa**, un estilo musical bailable muy popular en las islas hispánicas del Caribe. Su ritmo es muy alegre y vivo; sus temas pueden ser serios o muy alegres. No importa el tema; a todos les gusta bailar salsa. Mire el diagrama de abajo y trate de seguir los pasos de salsa con sus compañeros de clase mientras escuchan la canción.

¡Responda!

11-52 El pregonero y la casera. La casera usa mandatos informales para hablar con el pregonero mientras él usa mandatos formales. Complete el diálogo.

PREGONERO: ¡(1) _____ (Comprar) frutas y vegetales! ¡(2) _____ (Mirar) lo que tengo aquí!

CASERA: (3) _____ (Venir) acá; (4) _____ (enseñarme) las frutas más frescas que tienes.

PREGONERO: Tengo naranjas y piñas dulces. Tengo cocos buenísimos y también guíneos.

CASERA: (5) _____ (Darme) una piña, tres naranjas y dos cocos, por favor. ¿Cuánto es?

PREGONERO: (6) _____ (Pagarme) dos dólares, por favor.

CASERA: ¿Tienes cambio?

PREGONERO: Sí, señora.

CASERA: Está bien. Gracias.

LAS VACACIONES Y LOS VIAJES

VOCABULARIO

AUDIO **El cuerpo humano**

la boca	*mouth*
el brazo	*arm*
el cabello	*hair*
la cabeza	*head*
la cadera	*hip*
la cara	*face*
la ceja	*eyebrow*
el cerebro	*brain*
la cintura	*waist*
el codo	*elbow*
el corazón	*heart*
el cuello	*neck*
el dedo	*finger*
el diente	*tooth*
la espalda	*back*
el estómago	*stomach*
la frente	*forehead*
la garganta	*throat*
el hombro	*shoulder*
el hueso	*bone*
el labio	*lip*
la mano	*hand*
la mejilla	*cheek*
la muñeca	*wrist*
el músculo	*muscle*
la nariz	*nose*
el nervio	*nerve*
el oído	*(inner) ear*
la oreja	*(outer) ear*
el pecho	*chest*
la pestaña	*eyelash*
el pie	*foot*
la pierna	*leg*
el pulmón	*lung*
la rodilla	*knee*
la sangre	*blood*
el tobillo	*ankle*
la vena	*vein*

Tratamientos médicos

la aspirina	*aspirin*
la inyección	*injection*
la pastilla	*pill*
la receta	*prescription*
el termómetro	*thermometer*

La salud

el catarro	*cold*
la enfermedad	*illness*
el/la farmacéutico/a	*pharmacist*
la fiebre	*fever*
la gripe	*flu*
la infección	*infection*
el síntoma	*symptom*
la tensión (arterial)	*(blood) pressure*
la tos	*cough*

Verbos

alegrarse (de)	*to be glad (about)*
caer(se)	*to fall*
cuidar(se)	*to take care of*
doler (ue)	*to hurt*
enfermarse	*to become sick*
estornudar	*to sneeze*
examinar	*to examine*
fracturar(se)	*to fracture, break*
fumar	*to smoke*
molestar	*to bother, be bothered by*
recetar	*to prescribe*
respirar	*to breathe*
sentir (ie, i)	*to be sorry*
sentirse (ie, i)	*to feel*
temer	*to fear*
torcer(se) (ue)	*to twist*
toser	*to cough*

Descripciones

deprimido/a	*depressed*
enfermo/a	*sick*
serio/a	*serious*

Palabras y expresiones útiles

cada... horas	*every . . . hours*
el consultorio	*doctor's office*
¿Qué te/le(s) pasa?	*What's wrong (with you)?*
tener dolor de...	*to have a(n) . . . ache*
tener mala cara	*to look terrible*

Objetivos comunicativos

- Making travel arrangements
- Asking about and discussing itineraries
- Describing and getting hotel accommodations

- Expressing denial and uncertainty
- Expressing possession (emphatically)
- Talking about the future

Contenido

A primera vista

- Los medios de transporte
- Las reservaciones y el hotel

Explicación y expansión

- Affirmative and negative expressions
- Indicative and subjunctive in adjective clauses
- Stressed possessive adjectives

- Possessive pronouns
- The future tense

Mosaicos

- Escuchar: Reporting what was said
- Conversar: Finding out people's plans and reporting them; giving advice

- Leer: Summarizing a text
- Escribir: Stating facts and giving advice

Enfoque cultural

- Temas: La música y el baile
- Vistas: Panamá y Costa Rica
  Para investigar en Internet

- Fortunas: Episodio 12
- Notas: "Ligia Elena", *Rubén Blades*

Vocabulario

Los medios de transporte

AUDIO

Mucha gente usa el transporte público. Los **autobuses** son populares en las ciudades y también para **viajar** largas distancias. Son la solución para las personas que no tienen **carro,** o a quienes simplemente no les gusta **manejar** en las **carreteras** y **autopistas.** El **metro** es otra forma de transporte eficiente en los centros urbanos, como Madrid, Barcelona, Santiago, Buenos Aires, Caracas y la Ciudad de México.

AVE, el **tren** español de alta velocidad entre Madrid y otras grandes ciudades españolas, viaja a unos 300 kilómetros por hora. La RENFE (Red Nacional de Ferrocarriles Españoles) es tan importante en España, un país relativamente pequeño, como las **líneas aéreas** en los Estados Unidos.

Un **crucero** es otra forma de **viajar.** En **barcos** modernos con una capacidad de 400 hasta más de 2.000 **pasajeros,** se puede hacer de todo. En las **escalas** en los diferentes puertos hay excursiones organizadas y oportunidades para ir de compras. De noche, la diversión continúa en la discoteca, el casino y el teatro. Un crucero es un medio de transporte y un lugar para pasar las vacaciones.

En un avión

el/la auxiliar de vuelo

un asiento de pasillo

primera clase

clase turista

la ventanilla

El **avión** es la solución, aunque más cara, para viajar rápidamente de un lugar a otro, especialmente en zonas donde es difícil construir carreteras por la geografía o el clima, como en las selvas y en las montañas.

En el aeropuerto

Los pasajeros **hacen cola** frente al mostrador de la **aerolínea** para **facturar** el **equipaje,** pedir un **asiento** y conseguir la **tarjeta de embarque.**

el inspector de aduana

la aduana

el mostrador

SALA DE ESPERA

VUELO: 190

DESTINO: SAN JOSÉ

SALIDA: 9:30

la maleta

el equipaje

el maletín

En el mostrador de la línea aérea

AUDIO EMPLEADA: Buenos días. Su **pasaporte** y su **boleto,** por favor.

VIAJERO: Aquí están. Y si es posible, prefiero un asiento cerca de una **salida de emergencia.**

EMPLEADA: Muy bien. ¿**Ventanilla** o pasillo?

VIAJERO: Pasillo, por favor. Señorita, ¿usted sabe si se venden **cheques de viajero** aquí en el **aeropuerto?**

EMPLEADA: Sí, hay una oficina de American Express enfrente a la derecha.

VIAJERO: Gracias. ¿Me acreditó los kilómetros a mi programa de viajero frecuente?

EMPLEADA: Sí, y su **pasaje** es **de ida y vuelta,** así que va a tener bastantes kilómetros. Su asiento a San José es el 10F. Aquí tiene su tarjeta de embarque. La puerta de salida es la 80. ¡Que tenga un buen viaje!

El avión para San José sale a las tres y media por la puerta 1A. ¿A qué hora sale el **vuelo** para Panamá?

SALIDA DEPARTURE DESTINATION	ABORDAR BOARDING	SALA LOUNGE	PUERTA GATE	DESTINO DESTINATION
3:30	3:00	B	1A	SAN JOSÉ
3:50	3:20	B	4	MANAGUA
4:10	3:40	B	6	GUATEMALA
4:25	3:55	B	10	PANAMÁ
4:45	4:15	B	8	LIMÓN
5:10	4:40	B	5	MÉXICO D.F.
6:00	5:30	D	5	KINGSTON

¿Qué dice usted?

12-1 Asociaciones. Primera fase. Asocie cada palabra con su descripción. Luego, compare sus respuestas con las de un/a compañero/a.

1. _____ tren de alta velocidad
2. _____ viaje en un barco grande
3. _____ persona que sirve la comida en un vuelo
4. _____ transporte subterráneo
5. _____ inspección al llegar a otro país
6. _____ documento de identificación necesario para viajar al extranjero
7. _____ pasaje para ir de Quito a San José y volver a Quito
8. _____ se viaja en un asiento cómodo y se come bien

a. el/la auxiliar de vuelo
b. pasaporte
c. primera clase
d. AVE
e. metro
f. aduana
g. boleto de ida y vuelta
h. crucero

2 **Segunda fase.** Hablen de su último viaje. Especifiquen:

- medio de transporte
- tipo de boleto
- comodidad (primera clase, turista, etc.)
- necesidad de pasaporte, pasar por aduana, etc.

2 **12-2 Solicitud del cliente.** Usted es un/a agente de viajes y su compañero/a es su cliente/a. Hágale preguntas a su cliente/a para llenar el siguiente formulario (*form*) y después hágale algunas recomendaciones para el viaje.

NOMBRE: _____
Nº de pasaporte: _____
Fecha/s de viaje: _____
Medio de transporte: _____
Destino: _____

2 **12-3 En una agencia de viajes. Primera fase.** Busquen en Internet la siguiente información para planear un viaje turístico a Costa Rica:

- itinerario posible
- hoteles
- medios de transporte
- actividades y visitas
- precios de las distintas opciones

Segunda fase. Ahora túrnense para hacer el papel de agente de viaje y cliente/a. El/La cliente/a debe decirle al/a la agente de viajes que quiere viajar a Costa Rica. El/La agente debe recomendarle un viaje de acuerdo con los datos que obtuvo en la *Primera fase*.

Viajando en coche

el capó · el espejo retrovisor · el limpiaparabrisas · el maletero · el motor · la rueda · el radiador · la guandera · la placa · parachoques · las llantas · el volante

¿Qué dice usted?

12-4 ¿Qué es? Busquen en el dibujo la palabra que corresponda a las siguientes descripciones. Después, den una descripción de las otras partes del coche indicadas en el dibujo para ver si otra pareja sabe qué son.

1. Es para poner el equipaje. _____
2. Permite ver bien cuando llueve. _____
3. Son negras y llevan aire por dentro. _____
4. Controla la dirección del coche. _____
5. Hay que ponerle agua si no queremos que se caliente el motor.

12-5 Mi auto favorito. Primero, averigüen qué medio de transporte usa cada uno de ustedes con más frecuencia. Después, pregúntense cuál es el auto favorito de cada uno y por qué. Cada uno debe dar cuatro razones para explicar por qué le gusta más.

Las reservaciones y el hotel

AUDIO

[Map of Panama City showing streets and landmarks including: Ave. Roosevelt, Ave. 3 Norte, Ave. 2 Norte, Ave. 1 Norte, Ave. Perú, C. La Boca, Calle Balboa, Ave. Central, Ave. Cuba, Ave. Justo Arosemena, Hotel Gran Canal, Ave. de Los Mártires, Oficina de Migración, Museo Antropológico, CHORRILLO, Ave. A, Ave. Ancón, Code B, Ave. Central, Ave. B, Plaza 5 de Mayo, Terminal de Buses a Chiriquí, Alcaldía de Panamá, Ave. de los Postos, Plaza Santa Ana, STA. ANA, Centro Turístico Mi Pueblito, Palacio Presidencial, AMADOR, Iglesia Catedral Metropolitana, San Felipe (Casco Viejo), Museo de Historia del Canal de Panamá, Plaza de las Bóvedas]

EMPLEADO: Buenas tardes. ¿En qué le puedo servir?

SRA. LOAIZA: Buenas tardes. Tenemos dos **habitaciones** reservadas a nuestro nombre, señores Loaiza.

EMPLEADO: Sí, señora. Tengo **una doble** y **una sencilla.**

SRA. LOAIZA: Muy bien. Una es para nosotros y otra para nuestro hijo. Quisiera dejar algunos cheques de viajero en un lugar seguro. ¿Podría usted...?

EMPLEADO: ¿Por qué no los deja en la **caja fuerte** de su habitación.

SRA. LOAIZA: Muy bien.

EMPLEADO: Bueno, aquí tiene las **llaves.** Enseguida les subirán las **maletas.** Sus habitaciones están en el segundo piso.

(*Más tarde.*)

SR. LOAIZA: Por favor, ¿nos puede indicar cómo llegar a la Plaza 5 de Mayo?

CONSERJE: Sí, cómo no. Mire, sigan derecho por esta calle hasta la próxima **esquina.** Allí, **doblen a la izquierda** y caminen una cuadra hasta la plaza que está **a la derecha.** No se pueden **perder.**

SR. LOAIZA: Muchísimas gracias.

¿Qué dice usted?

12-6 Estamos perdidos. Use el plano que aparece en la página 446 y pregúntele a su compañero/a cómo ir a ciertos lugares. Su compañero/a le debe explicar cómo llegar.

USTED ESTÁ EN:

la Plaza 5 de Mayo
la Avenida Ancón y la Avenida A
el Museo de Historia del Canal de Panamá

USTED DESEA IR:

al Palacio Presidencial
al Casco Viejo
al Centro Turístico Mi Pueblito

12-7 El hotel. Primera fase. Busquen en www.prenhall.com/mosaicos la siguiente información sobre el hotel de Costa Rica Selva Bananito Lodge y compártanla entre ustedes.

1. localización
2. instrucciones para llegar
3. servicios que ofrece el hotel
4. atracciones más interesantes en su opinión

Segunda fase. Usted sabe que el hotel *Selva Bananito Lodge* acepta guías voluntarios para los turistas que hablan inglés. Hable con el/la jefe/a de personal —otro/a compañero/a— para ofrecer sus servicios y obtener la siguiente información sobre el trabajo.

1. obligaciones y horarios
2. beneficios que reciben (comidas, alojamiento, etc.)
3. número de semanas o meses que dura el trabajo
4. fecha en que comienza el trabajo
5. forma más conveniente de llegar al hotel

El correo y la correspondencia

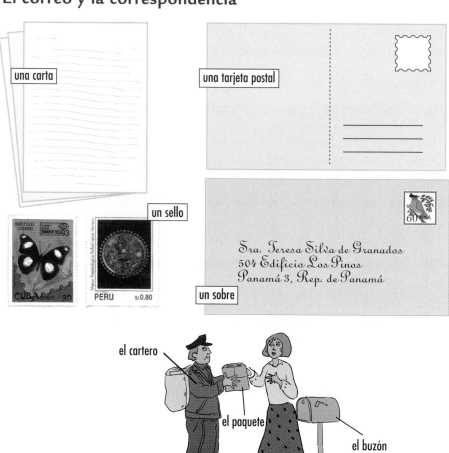

una carta

una tarjeta postal

un sello

un sobre

Sra. Teresa Silva de Granados
504 Edificio Los Pinos
Panamá 3, Rep. de Panamá

el cartero

el paquete

el buzón

¿Qué dice usted?

12-8 La correspondencia. Primera fase. Completen las oraciones con la palabra adecuada y escriban la letra correspondiente.

1. _____ El lugar donde se recoge la correspondencia y se compran sellos es el...
2. _____ La persona que reparte cartas y tarjetas es el...
3. _____ El depósito donde ponemos las cartas que queremos enviar es el...
4. _____ Para mandar una carta la ponemos dentro de un...

a. cartero
b. correo
c. sello
d. sobre
e. paquete
f. buzón

5. _____ Si queremos mandar un regalo de una ciudad a otra, tenemos que preparar un...
6. _____ No se puede mandar una carta sin escribir la dirección y ponerle un...

Segunda fase. Respondan a las siguientes preguntas.

1. ¿Cuándo fue la última vez que usted fue al correo?
2. ¿Para qué fue? ¿Para comprar sellos o un sobre o para enviar un paquete?
3. ¿Es el correo electrónico un medio de comunicación más eficaz que el correo postal? ¿Por qué?

12-9 Un correo electrónico nostálgico. Primera fase. Envíele un mensaje electrónico o una postal a su compañero/a favorito/a. Cuéntele algunos aspectos especiales de sus últimas vacaciones:

- lugar(es) que visitó
- personas que conoció
- experiencias interesantes o divertidas que vivió
- otras experiencias que recuerda con nostalgia

Su compañero/a le responderá por escrito, reaccionará a sus comentarios y le hará preguntas para obtener más detalles.

AUDIO 12-10 Antes de viajar. You will listen to a young man who is checking in at the airport. Before you listen, list two questions you think the airline employee might ask him and the answers that you think the young man might provide.

_____

_____

Now, pay attention to the general idea of what is said. Then, as you listen mark the appropriate ending to each statement.

1. El viajero va a facturar...
   a. tres maletas
   b. un maletín de mano
   c. dos maletas

2. El viajero prefiere un asiento...
   a. al lado de ventanilla
   b. en el pasillo
   c. en la parte posterior del avión

3. El agente le puede conseguir un asiento...
   a. de pasillo, el 28C
   b. en el centro, entre la ventanilla y el pasillo
   c. en la ventanilla en primera clase

4. La empleada le dice al pasajero que...
   a. tiene tiempo para llamar por teléfono
   b. puede llamar desde el avión
   c. no tiene que pasar por seguridad

1. Affirmative and negative expressions

AGENTE: Lo siento, ese **vuelo** está **lleno.** No hay ningún asiento disponible.

RICARDO: ¿Y el de la tarde?

AGENTE: Hay algunos asientos **vacíos,** pero el vuelo **hace escala** en San José.

MARISELA: ¿Y no hay otro vuelo directo?

AGENTE: No, es el único; pero, ¿por qué no reservan en el vuelo de la tarde y los pongo en la **lista de espera** para el otro?

RICARDO: Está bien. Siempre hay alguien que **cancela.**

AFFIRMATIVE		NEGATIVE	
todo	*everything*	nada	*nothing*
algo	*something, anything*		
todos	*everybody, all*	nadie	*no one, nobody*
alguien	*someone, anyone*		
algún, alguno/a (-os, -as)	*some, any, several*	ningún, ninguno/a	*no, not any, none*
o... o	*either . . . or*	ni... ni	*neither . . . nor*
siempre	*always*	nunca	*never, (not) ever*
una vez	*once*		
alguna vez	*sometime, ever*	jamás	*never, (not) ever*
algunas veces	*sometimes*		
a veces	*at times*		
también	*also, too*	tampoco	*neither, not*

- Negative words may precede or follow the verb. If they follow the verb, use the word **no** before the verb.

  Nadie vive aquí.   *No one/Nobody lives here.*
  No vive **nadie** aquí.

- **Alguno** and **ninguno** shorten to **algún** and **ningún** before masculine singular nouns.

  ¿Ves **algún** coche?   *Do you see any cars?*
  No veo **ningún** coche.   *I do not see any car.*

- Use the personal **a** when **alguno/a/os/as** and **ninguno/a** refer to persons and are the direct object of the verb. Use it also with **alguien** and **nadie** since they always refer to people. Notice that in the negative only the singular forms **ninguno** and **ninguna** are used.

  ¿Conoces **a alguno** de los chicos?   *Do you know any of the boys?*
  No, no conozco **a ninguno**.   *No, I do not know any.*
  ¿Conoces **alguno** de los libros?   *Do you know any of the books?*
  No, **no** conozco **ninguno**.   *No, I do not know any.*

> ## LENGUA
>
> In Spanish, **ningunos/as** is used only with plural nouns that do not have a singular form; for example, **víveres** (*food, provisions*): **No trajeron ningunos víveres.**

¿Qué dice usted?

12-11 Nada de nada. Asocie cada pregunta con sus probables respuestas.

1. _____ ¿Visitó usted Costa Rica alguna vez?
2. _____ ¿Conoce a alguien en Panamá?
3. _____ ¿Baila alguno de los bailes típicos de la región?
4. _____ ¿Alguien sabe dónde está el volcán Irazú?
5. _____ ¿Hay muchos estudiantes que viajaron a Panamá?
6. _____ ¿Conoce alguna canción de Rubén Blades?

    a. No, ninguna.
    b. No, ninguno.
    c. Nadie lo sabe.
    d. No, a nadie.
    e. No, nunca.
    f. Sólo fueron algunos.

12-12 ¿Con qué frecuencia? Complete la siguiente tabla, indicando la frecuencia con que usted participa en las siguientes actividades, y diga por qué las hace. Después pregúntele a su compañero/a y anote la información obtenida.

MODELO: viajar a California
        E1: Yo viajo a California dos veces al año para visitar a mis padres. ¿Y tú?
        E2: Yo no viajo nunca porque mis padres viven en mi ciudad./Yo los llamo por teléfono todos los días porque los quiero mucho.

ACTIVIDAD	YO	RAZÓN	MI COMPAÑERO/A	RAZÓN
ver programas sobre la naturaleza				
practicar el ciclismo				
comer en restaurantes hispanos				
dormir la siesta				
ir de vacaciones al Caribe				
viajar en tren				
usar el transporte público				

12-13 Un restaurante malo. Usted está de viaje con un/a compañero/a y quiere ir a un restaurante que está cerca del hotel. Su compañero/a, que ya conoce el restaurante, va a contestar sus preguntas negativamente.

MODELO:　　servir platos típicos
　　　　　　　　E1: ¿Sirven platos típicos?
　　　　　　　　E2: No, no sirven ningún plato típico.

1. preparar platos de dieta
2. tener ensaladas buenas
3. servir pescado fresco
4. tener vinos de la región
5. aceptar tarjetas de crédito
6. ...

12-14 ¡La negatividad es contagiosa! Después de pasar el día con un amigo/a muy negativo/a, usted se siente influenciado/a y contesta a todo negativamente.

MODELO:　　llamar a alguien
　　　　　　　　E1: ¿Vas a llamar a alguien?
　　　　　　　　E2: No, no voy a llamar a nadie.

1. visitar Panamá alguna vez
2. ver alguna película esta noche
3. leer o escuchar música
4. salir con algún amigo
5. mandarle a alguien un correo electrónico
6. ...

12-15 Planeando un viaje. Primera fase. Ustedes quieren hacer ecoturismo en Costa Rica. Primero comenten qué van o no van a hacer antes de llegar a su destino.

MODELO:　　comprar el pasaje dos semanas antes
　　　　　　　　E1: Yo quiero comprar el pasaje dos semanas antes.
　　　　　　　　E2: Yo también./Pues yo no. Es más barato comprarlo un mes
　　　　　　　　　　antes.
　　　　　　　　no llevar cheques de viajero
　　　　　　　　E1: Yo no voy a llevar cheques de viajero.
　　　　　　　　E2: Yo tampoco./Yo voy a llevar algunos y también mi tarjeta de
　　　　　　　　　　crédito.

1. buscar información sobre Costa Rica
2. comprar zapatos cómodos para caminar
3. pedir un asiento de pasillo
4. no llevar mucha ropa
5. facturar el equipaje
6. no gastar mucho dinero
7. ...
8. ...

Segunda fase. Conversen sobre todo lo que van a hacer después de llegar a su destino. Después, reúnanse con otra pareja y explíquenle tres de sus planes. Sus compañeros/as deben hacerles preguntas para averiguar detalles adicionales.

SITUACIONES

1. **Role A:** You are a flight attendant in business class. Ask one of your passengers if he/she would like to a) drink something, b) eat, and c) watch the film. Then a) answer his/her questions on the time of landing, b) tell him/her there are no magazines in Spanish, and c) offer him/her a blanket and pillow.

   Role B: You are a passenger in business class. Answer the flight attendant's questions negatively. Then a) ask him/her at what time the flight is scheduled to arrive in Panama, b) ask for a magazine in Spanish, and c) thank him/her.

2. One of you is a passenger, the other is a customs officer. The customs officer asks you, the passenger, if you are carrying a) any plants or seeds (*semillas*), b) fruit, and c) more than $10,000. Answer the questions in the negative. The customs officer will then ask you to open your luggage so that he/she can check it.

2. Indicative and subjunctive in adjective clauses

■ An adjective clause is a dependent clause that is used as an adjective.

ADJECTIVE

Vamos a ir a un hotel muy **moderno.**

ADJECTIVE CLAUSE

Vamos a ir a un hotel **que es muy moderno.**

■ Use the indicative in an adjective clause that refers to a person, place, or thing (antecedent) that exists or is known.

> Hay un hotel que **queda** cerca de la estación.
> *There is a hotel that is near the station.*

> Quiero viajar en el tren que **sale** por la mañana.
> *I want to travel on the train that leaves in the morning.*
> (You know there is such a train.)

■ Use the subjunctive in an adjective clause that refers to a person, place, or thing that does not exist or whose existence is unknown or in question.

> No hay ningún hotel que **quede** cerca de la estación.
> *There is not any hotel that is near the station.*

> Quiero viajar en un tren que **salga** por la mañana.
> *I want to travel on a train that leaves in the morning.*
> (Any train, as long as it leaves in the morning.)

■ When the antecedent is a specific person and functions as a direct object, use the indicative and the personal **a.** If the antecedent is not a specific person, use the subjunctive and do not use the personal **a.**

> Busco **a** la/una auxiliar que **va** en ese vuelo.
> *I am looking for the/a flight attendant that goes on that flight.*
> (A specific flight attendant that I know is on that flight.)

> Busco una auxiliar que **vaya** en ese vuelo.
> *I am looking for a flight attendant that goes on that flight.*
> (Any flight attendant as long as she goes on that flight.)

■ In questions, you may use the indicative or the subjunctive according to the degree of certainty you have about the matter.

¿Hay alguien aquí que **sale** en ese vuelo?
Is there anyone here leaving on that flight?
(I do not know, but assume there may be.)

¿Hay alguien aquí que **salga** en ese vuelo?
Is there anyone here leaving on that flight?
(I do not know, but I doubt it.)

¿Qué dice usted?

12-16 ¿Cuál es la respuesta correcta? Marque la forma verbal (indicativo o subjuntivo) para completar correctamente cada grupo de oraciones.

1. Hay un vuelo que _____ por la mañana.   a. sale
2. No hay ningún vuelo que _____ por la noche.   b. salga

3. Me interesa un hotel (*any hotel*) que _____ cerca del centro.   a. queda
4. Hay un hotel que no es muy caro y _____ en el centro.   b. quede

5. Busco al empleado que _____ inglés.   a. habla
6. Busco un empleado (*any employee*) que _____ inglés.   b. hable

12-17 ¡Ni idea! Usted no tiene ni idea sobre algunos aspectos de la vida de sus compañeros/as de la clase de español. Túrnense para hacerse preguntas. Si la respuesta es afirmativa, deben decir quién es esa persona y dar información adicional.

MODELO: usar vaqueros cuando viaja
        E1: ¿Hay alguien que use vaqueros cuando viaja?
        E2: Sí, hay alguien que siempre usa vaqueros cuando viaja.
        E1: ¿Quién es?
        E2: Es Marta. Sé que le gustan los vaqueros y siempre se los pone.
        E1: ¿Hay alguien que sea costarricense?
        E2: No, no hay nadie que sea costarricense.

1. tenerles fobia a los aviones
2. usar mucho su diccionario en los viajes
3. conocer una de las siete maravillas del mundo
4. saber pilotear un avión
5. ir a esquiar en sus vacaciones de invierno
6. viajar a Panamá este año

12-18 Emergencia. Dos empleados de la aerolínea costarricense Travelair se enfermaron, y hay mucho trabajo inconcluso en el aeropuerto. Túrnense para hacer los papeles de gerente y de ayudante de la aerolínea. El/La gerente necesita que se hagan ciertas cosas; su ayudante debe informarle si hay o no alguien que pueda hacerlas. Si no hay nadie, el/la gerente debe ofrecer soluciones.

MODELO: programar la computadora
E1: Necesito a alguien que programe la computadora para los itinerarios.
E2: Hay un empleado/alguien en el aeropuerto que puede hacerlo. *o* No hay nadie en el aeropuerto que la pueda programar.
E1: Es indispensable buscar/que busquemos a alguien que lo haga.

1. hablar inglés, japonés y español en el vuelo a Tamarindo
2. recibir el vuelo que viene de Puerto Jiménez
3. darles esta información a los pasajeros del vuelo 562
4. llevar a los pasajeros a inmigración
5. poder trabajar este fin de semana
6. ...

12-19 Un lugar para descansar. Primera fase. Túrnense para hacerse preguntas sobre un lugar de descanso. Deben contestar según la información de la tabla.

MODELO: hotel / tener piscina para niños
E1: ¿Hay un hotel que tenga piscina para niños?
E2: Sí, hay un hotel que tiene piscina para niños. *o* No, no hay ningún hotel que tenga piscina para niños.

HAY	NO HAY
tiendas / vender ropa para esquiar	autobús / llegar por la mañana
cines / dar películas españolas	cafetería / servir comida vegetariana
lugares / aceptar cheques de viajero	lugares / aceptar cheques personales

Segunda fase. Ahora ustedes deben describir cómo desean que sea su lugar ideal de descanso, explicando su localización, ambiente y atracciones. Después, intercambien ideas con otra pareja.

12-20 Agencia *Viaje ahora*. Usted piensa viajar al extranjero, pero no conoce ninguna buena agencia de viajes. Dígale a su compañero/a adónde quiere ir y pídale información sobre una agencia. Su compañero/a le va a dar información basándose en el anuncio de la agencia Viaje Ahora. Usted debe hacerle por lo menos tres preguntas adicionales.

TURISMO
Viaje ahora
Servicio de viajes
Le planeamos su viaje a cualquier parte de Panamá y del extranjero.
Boletos de avión, de barco; alquiler de autos; reservaciones de hoteles; excursiones
20 años sirviendo al público
TELÉFONOS: 270-2040   270-3230
Calle 50 #134

SITUACIONES

Role A. You want to visit Panama. Call your travel agent to find out: a) the cost of the trip, b) the flight schedule, and c) if you need a visa. Once you have the answers, explain to your travel agent the class of hotel you would like to stay in (area, approximate price range, etc.)

Role B. You are a travel agent. Answer your customer's questions and give him/her a) the prices of economy- and business-class tickets, b) the departure time. Ask for his/her nationality to know whether he/she needs a visa. Regarding hotels, give him/her information on two different rates and explain what each rate offers. You must also tell him/her what he/she should visit in Panama (the Canal, the old part of the city, the San Blas Islands, Darién, etc.).

3. Stressed possessive adjectives

SINGULAR		PLURAL		
MASCULINE	FEMININE	MASCULINE	FEMININE	
mío	mía	míos	mías	*my, (of) mine*
tuyo	tuya	tuyos	tuyas	*your (familiar), (of) yours*
suyo	suya	suyos	suyas	*your (formal), his, her, its, their, (of) yours, his, hers, theirs*
nuestro	nuestra	nuestros	nuestras	*our, (of) ours*
vuestro	vuestra	vuestros	vuestras	*your (familiar), (of) yours*

■ Stressed possessive adjectives follow the noun they modify and agree with it in gender and number. An article or demonstrative adjective usually precedes the noun. Use stressed possessives for emphasis.

El cuarto **mío** es grandísimo.	*My room is very big.*
La maleta **mía** está en la recepción.	*My suitcase is at the front desk.*
Esos primos **míos** llegan hoy.	*Those cousins of mine arrive today.*
Las llaves **mías** están en la puerta.	*My keys are in the door.*

4. Possessive pronouns

SINGULAR		PLURAL	
MASCULINE	FEMININE	MASCULINE	FEMININE
el ⎰ mío tuyo suyo nuestro vuestro	la ⎰ mía tuya suya nuestra vuestra	los ⎰ míos tuyos suyos nuestros vuestros	las ⎰ mías tuyas suyas nuestras vuestras

■ Possessive pronouns have the same form as stressed possessive adjectives.

■ The definite article precedes the possessive pronoun, and they both agree in gender and number with the noun to which they refer.

¿Tienes la mochila suya?	*Do you have his backpack?*
Sí, tengo **la suya.**	*Yes, I have his.*

■ After the verb **ser,** the article is usually omitted.

Esa maleta es **mía.**	*That suitcase is mine.*

■ To be clearer and more specific, the following structures may be used to replace any corresponding form of **el/la suyo/a.**

la de usted	*yours* (singular)
la de él	*his*
la de ella	*hers*

la mochila suya → **la suya** *or*

la de ustedes	*yours* (plural)
la de ellos	*theirs* (masculine, plural)
la de ellas	*theirs* (feminine, plural)

¿Qué dice usted?

12-21 ¿De quién(es) son estas cosas? Escoja la repuesta correcta para cada una de las preguntas y escriba la letra correspondiente en la columna de la izquierda.

1. ¿Es ésta tu mochila? _____   a. Sí, es la mía.   b. Sí, es la tuya.
2. ¿Son éstas las llaves de Pedro? _____   a. Sí, son las suyas.   b. Sí, son las mías.
3. ¿Es éste el maletín de Alicia? _____   a. No, es la tuya.   b. No, no es el suyo.
4. ¿Es éste su asiento? _____   a. Sí, es la mía.   b. Sí, es el mío.
5. ¿Son éstos los boletos nuestros? _____   a. Sí, son los suyos.   b. Sí, son las suyas.

12-22 Las posesiones. Es el fin del año escolar, y usted y su compañero/a están poniendo sus cosas y las de otro/a compañero/a en dos coches. Háganse preguntas para averiguar de quién es cada cosa.

MODELO: esta lámpara
　　　　　　E1: ¿De quién es esta lámpara?
　　　　　　E2: Es suya. Va en su coche. *o* Es mía. Va en mi coche.

1. esos casetes
2. esta maleta
3. este maletín
4. estos discos

5. las revistas
6. el radio
7. la bicicleta
8. esta mochila

12-23 Preparándose para un viaje. Ustedes van a hacer un viaje en auto, y deben tomar varias decisiones antes de salir. Háganse preguntas para decidir lo que van a hacer, y den una razón.

MODELO: usar mi coche/tu coche
　　　　　　E1: ¿Vamos a usar mi coche o el tuyo?
　　　　　　E2: Prefiero usar el tuyo/mío porque es mejor/más nuevo.

1. hablar con mi agente/tu agente
2. llevar tus maletas/las de mi hermano
3. usar mis mapas/tus mapas

4. llevar tu cámara/mi cámara
5. llevar tu celular/el de mi madre
6. …

12-24 Unas vacaciones en un crucero. Usted y un/a amigo/a tomaron un crucero durante las vacaciones. Su compañero/a tomó otro crucero. Intercambien sus experiencias en las áreas siguientes.

MODELO: el barco
　　　　　　E1: Nuestro barco era nuevo y grandísimo.
　　　　　　E2: El nuestro era pequeño, pero muy cómodo. *o*
　　　　　　　　　El nuestro era muy grande también.

1. el camarote (*cabin*)
2. los compañeros de mesa
3. la comida

4. el/la guía
5. las excursiones
6. …

SITUACIONES

1. **Role A:** Yesterday you lost your wallet (black, new, with $20, some photos, and a credit card inside) in a San Jose hotel. Answer all the questions the employee at the Lost and Found desk asks you. Then show him/her an identification document and thank him/her.

   Role B: You work at the Lost and Found desk of a hotel in San José, and you are helping a customer who lost a wallet. Get the following information: a) the name of the person, b) the description of the wallet, c) the date it was lost, and d) a list of what was in the wallet. You must then ask him/her for some identification and return the wallet back to him/her.

2. Each of you has a condominium in an exclusive summer resort and wants to impress the other. Speak of your condominium, giving the most information possible.

EN DIRECTO

To boast about something:
No te lo puedes ni imaginar.
You could not even imagine.
¡Es increíble!
Lo que te diga es poco.
I cannot tell you enough.

5. The future tense

You have been using the present tense and **ir + a** + *infinitive* to express future plans. Spanish also has a future tense. Although you have these other ways to express a future action, event, or state, you should be able to recognize the future tense in reading and in listening.

■ The future tense is formed by adding the future endings **-é, -ás, -á, -emos, -éis**, and **-án** to the infinitive. These endings are the same for **-ar, -er,** and **-ir** verbs.

FUTURE TENSE			
	HABLAR	COMER	VIVIR
yo	hablaré	comeré	viviré
tú	hablarás	comerás	vivirás
Ud., él, ella	hablará	comerá	vivirá
nosotros/as	hablaremos	comeremos	viviremos
vosotros/as	hablaréis	comeréis	viviréis
Uds., ellos/as	hablarán	comerán	vivirán

■ A few verbs have irregular stems in the future tense and can be grouped into three categories. The first group drops the **e** from the infinitive ending.

IRREGULAR FUTURE—GROUP 1		
INFINITIVE	NEW STEM	FUTURE FORMS
poder	**podr-**	podré, podrás, podrá, podremos, podréis, podrán
querer	**querr-**	querré, querrás, querrá, querremos, querréis, querrán
saber	**sabr-**	sabré, sabrás, sabrá, sabremos, sabréis, sabrán

■ The second group replaces the **e** or **i** of the infinitive ending with a **d**.

IRREGULAR FUTURE—GROUP 2		
INFINITIVE	NEW STEM	FUTURE FORMS
poner	**pondr-**	pondré, pondrás, pondrá, pondremos, pondréis, pondrán
tener	**tendr-**	tendré, tendrás, tendrá, tendremos, tendréis, tendrán
salir	**saldr-**	saldré, saldrás, saldrá, saldremos, saldréis, saldrán
venir	**vendr-**	vendré, vendrás, vendrá, vendremos, vendréis, vendrán

■ The third group consists of two verbs (**decir, hacer**) that have completely different stems in the future tense.

IRREGULAR FUTURE—GROUP 3		
INFINITIVE	NEW STEM	FUTURE FORMS
decir	**dir-**	diré, dirás, dirá, diremos, diréis, dirán
hacer	**har-**	haré, harás, hará, haremos, haréis, harán

- In addition to referring to future actions, the Spanish future tense can also be used to express probability in the present.

Todavía no están en el hotel.	*They still are not at the hotel.*
El vuelo **estará** atrasado, ¿no?	*The flight is probably/must be late, right?*
Dice que va a ver la telenovela, así que **serán** las nueve.	*He says he is going to watch the soap opera, so it must be nine.*

- The future of **hay** is **habrá**.

Habrá muchos pasajeros en el vuelo.	*There will be many passengers on the flight.*

¿Qué dice usted?

12-25 ¿Qué lugares de Panamá van a visitar los miembros de esta familia?
Complete las oraciones de la izquierda con la forma correcta del verbo.

1. La abuela _____ a una prima que vive en Panamá.　　a. visitaré
2. La madre y su hija _____ la Catedral Metropolitana.　　b. visitarás
3. Mi padre y yo _____ el Canal.　　c. visitará
4. Tú _____ las Islas San Blas.　　d. visitaremos
5. Yo _____ el Casco Viejo.　　e. visitarán

12-26 Intercambio: Un viaje a Panamá. Ramiro va a la Ciudad de Panamá a visitar a su familia. Háganse preguntas y contesten de acuerdo con la agenda que Ramiro preparó.

MODELO:　E1: ¿Qué hará Ramiro el miércoles por la noche?
　　　　　E2: Cenará con unos amigos.
　　　　　E1: ¿Cuándo irá al cine con los primos?
　　　　　E2: Irá al cine con los primos el martes.

LUNES	MARTES	MIÉRCOLES	JUEVES	VIERNES
salir para Panamá	visitar el Casco Viejo	salir de compras	visitar las Islas San Blas	preparar las maletas
comer con los tíos	conocer a otros familiares	ir a un museo	comprar artesanías	almorzar con su tío
acostarse temprano	ir al cine con los primos	cenar con unos amigos	ir a un concierto	ir a una discoteca

12-27 Un crucero inolvidable. Los Almagro viven en Miami, y van a tomar un crucero que atravesará el Canal de Panamá y llegará hasta Acapulco. De allí regresarán a Miami en avión. Primero, digan qué harán los miembros de la familia, usando los verbos entre paréntesis. Después, pongan las acciones en orden cronológico y comparen sus respuestas con las de otros/as compañeros/as.

_____ Los Almagro _____ (llegar) a Acapulco.

_____ El crucero _____ (hacer) escala en Cozumel, y los pasajeros _____ (disfrutar) de un día en la playa.

_____ La señora de Almagro _____ (ir) a la agencia de viajes para comprar los pasajes.

_____ Por la mañana del primer día en Acapulco, la familia _____ (ir) al mercado para comprar artesanías.

_____ En el aeropuerto, los agentes de aduana _____ (revisar) el equipaje, y la familia Almagro _____ (regresar) a su casa.

_____ Sus hijos _____ (pasar) la tarde en la playa porque saben que es el último día de sus vacaciones.

_____ Los señores Almagro y sus hijos Mauro y Gloria _____ (tomar) el barco en Miami.

_____ De allí, el crucero _____ (seguir) a Panamá y _____ (cruzar) el Canal.

12-28 ¿Por qué lo harán? Cada uno tiene diferentes motivos para hacer lo que hace. Piensen en dos motivos probables para cada una de las situaciones siguientes.

MODELO: Los Rivas van a Europa todos los años.
            E1: Tendrán mucho dinero, ¿no?
            E2: Tendrán familiares allá.

1. Pedro siempre viaja con poco equipaje.
2. Los Pérez nunca están los fines de semana en la ciudad.
3. Rosa no contesta el teléfono hace dos días.
4. Pilar no llama a sus parientes cuando viene a la ciudad.
5. Los Gómez están en el aeropuerto.
6. El vuelo va a salir una hora más tarde.
7. Pedro siempre saca muy buenas notas en sus clases.
8. El señor López toma el tren para ir a trabajar.

12-29 Planes futuros. Hablen del futuro en relación con los siguientes puntos y luego compartan sus planes con otra pareja.

MODELO: su graduación
            E1: Dentro de 2 años terminaremos la universidad.
            E2: No, yo no terminaré todavía. Tendré que estudiar un semestre más.

1. sus estudios
2. su vivienda
3. sus amistades

4. su vida profesional
5. sus planes de viaje
6. …

12-30 El horóscopo. Escriban su nombre en un papel. Luego, pongan el papel en una caja o en otro lugar designado por su profesor/a. Mezclen bien los papeles. Luego, cada estudiante debe sacar un papel al azar (_at random_). Después, preparen el horóscopo de esa persona para leerlo en la próxima clase. Los demás estudiantes tratarán de averiguar de quién es el horóscopo.

SITUACIONES

One of you is about to spend a few days' holiday in your favorite place. The other is very curious and will ask questions to find out: a) where, how, with whom, and for how long the other one is going, and b) where he/she will be staying.

Escuchar

Reporting What was Said

When you report what somebody said, most of the time you do not remember the exact words that were used. Instead, you retell what was said, using the third person. For example, in Spanish you may say, "Pedro dice que este verano él va a ir a Puerto Rico," or "Ellos dicen que ese carro es suyo."

Antes de escuchar

12-31 Un viaje. In activity **12-32** you will listen to a conversation between a travel agent and a client, Silvana, who wants to buy a vacation package to Latin America. Before you listen, write down the information you think Silvana will need before choosing the right package.

_____

_____

_____

A escuchar

 12-32 Read the report statements below. Then, listen to the conversation between Silvana and the travel agent about the two different vacation packages she had inquired about. As you listen, circle the statements that best report what was said.

1. Silvana habla con el agente de viajes y le pregunta las diferentes posibilidades que tiene para viajar a México y a Panamá.
2. Silvana dice que prefiere ir a Panamá porque siempre quiso conocer ese país.
3. El agente de viajes le dice a Silvana que el viaje a México es por más tiempo y un poco más caro que el viaje a Panamá.
4. El agente de viajes le dice a Silvana que le enviará los pasajes y la información sobre los hoteles por correo regular ese mismo día.

Después de escuchar

12-33 ¿Y usted? With a classmate, share your answers to the following questions.

1. ¿Alguna vez viajó usted a México, Panamá o algún otro país hispano? ¿Qué lugares visitó?
2. ¿Por qué cree usted que debe ser interesante cruzar el Canal de Panamá?
3. ¿Qué otro país hispano quisiera conocer? ¿Por qué?

Antes de escuchar

12-34 Buscando un hotel. In activity **12-35** you will listen to a conversation between Mr. Hernández, who is looking for a good hotel in San José, Costa Rica, and a travel agent. Before you listen, write down a list of four questions you think Mr. Hernández will ask.

_____

_____

A escuchar

 12-35 Read the report statements below. Then, listen to the conversation between Mr. Hernández and the travel agent. As you listen, circle the statements that best report what was said.

1. El Sr. Hernández dice que quiere un hotel económico que esté cerca del centro de la ciudad.
2. La agente le dice que tiene varias posibilidades y le describe tres hoteles para que él escoja.
3. El Sr. Hernández dice que él prefiere que sus hijos y esposa estén cómodos aunque (*even though*) él tenga que tomar un taxi o manejar mucho.
4. La agente le dice al cliente que la elección que ha hecho no es buena porque el hotel es muy caro y está muy lejos del centro de la ciudad.

Después de escuchar

 12-36 ¿Y usted? With a classmate, share your answers to the following questions.

1. Cuando usted busca un hotel, ¿es importante que el hotel sea económico o que sea de lujo?
2. ¿Qué servicios o comodidades prefiere usted que ofrezca un hotel?
3. ¿Cuál es su hotel favorito? ¿Por qué?

Conversar

Antes de conversar

12-37 Viaje de trabajo. Primera fase. Algunos profesionales viajan a otros países para hacer negocios o investigaciones relacionadas con su profesión. Primero seleccionen a **uno** de los siguientes profesionales:

1. bióloga que hará investigación en Costa Rica sobre reservas forestales
2. etnólogo que realizará una investigación sobre los indígenas panameños
3. gerente de una compañía estadounidense que piensa hacer negocios en Costa Rica
4. publicista norteamericano que desea promocionar productos de su país en Costa Rica y Panamá

Ahora preparen un plan de trabajo básico para la persona que escogieron en el país que visitará. Cubran los siguientes puntos:

1. explicación del plan de trabajo
2. cuándo y cómo lo va realizar
3. con quién(es) se va a reunir

Segunda fase. Basándose en el plan del/de la profesional que escogieron en la **Primera fase,** completen la tabla con las posibles necesidades de este/a profesional.

PROFESIONAL	NECESIDADES
_____ bióloga	alojamiento: _____
_____ etnólogo	transporte: _____
_____ gerente	actividades de tiempo libre: _____
_____ publicista	_____

A conversar

2 **12-38 Planes.** Usted es el/la profesional de la actividad **12-37.** Hoy debe ponerse en contacto con un/a ejecutivo/a o profesional en el país que visitará. Llámelo/la por teléfono para informarle sobre sus planes. Dele la siguiente información:

1. la fecha y hora de llegada a la ciudad de destino
2. la aerolínea y el número de vuelo en que viajará
3. las actividades profesionales que hará durante su estancia
4. algunas actividades de tiempo libre que le gustaría hacer; pídale información si es necesario

Después de conversar

12-39 ¡A informar a los superiores! Usted es el ejecutivo que recibió la llamada. Escríbale un correo electrónico a su jefe/a para informarle sobre los planes de la persona con quien usted conversó. Dele la siguiente información:

1. la fecha de llegada de esta persona
2. las actividades de negocio o profesionales durante su estancia
3. algunas actividades de tiempo libre que usted le recomendó

Antes de conversar

G **12-40 ¿Quién lo merece (deserves)?** Después de estudiar español juntos por un año, ustedes deben separarse de sus compañeros con quienes compartieron muchas experiencias en el salón de clase. Por eso, decidieron premiar (reward) a una persona del grupo con unas vacaciones inolvidables. Hagan lo siguiente:

a. Escojan a una persona de la clase, quien, en su opinión, merece unas vacaciones inolvidables. Den tres razones para justificar su elección.

b. Luego, indiquen...

- una ciudad hispana adonde ustedes quieren que él/ella vaya.

- el medio de transporte en que viajará.

- la cantidad de dinero (moneda nacional del país) que ustedes le darán a esta persona y algunas recomendaciones de cómo gastarlo.

c. Den un mínimo de cinco sugerencias de actividades a realizar (qué comprar, adónde ir, qué comer o beber, qué ver, etc.).

A conversar

 12-41 Nuestro/a candidato/a y nuestro plan. Informen detalladamente a la clase sobre lo siguiente:

a. la persona a quien escogieron y las razones de su elección.
b. la ciudad hispana adonde ustedes quieren que él/ella vaya, el transporte que usará, la cantidad de dinero que ustedes le darán y algunas sugerencias de cómo gastarlo.
c. cinco actividades que ustedes le sugieren a esta persona para hacer. Finalmente, la clase votará por el mejor plan de vacaciones.

Después de conversar

12-42 ¡Qué viaje tan inolvidable! Usted es el/la estudiante que recibió el premio. Después de pasar la primera semana de sus vacaciones inolvidables, quiere compartir con sus compañeros/as sus impresiones, experiencias y aventuras en el lugar adonde viajó. Escríbales una carta para contarles los detalles de su viaje. También incluya algunos planes detallados para los días de vacaciones que le quedan.

Leer

In this chapter, however, you will practice summarizing a newspaper article whose content is not presented in a chronological order. Therefore, summarizing a text of this nature requires a different approach. You need to discern what pieces of information are important to represent the text as a whole. The following considerations may help you summarize a text like this:

- First, read the title or headline and subtitles or subheadings, when appropriate.

- Using your knowledge of the topic, anticipate some potential content of the text.

- Underline the main ideas in each paragraph.

- Look for the content relationship between and among paragraphs. This will help you see how individual pieces (each paragraph) fit in the whole (text).

- Take notes of key information and ideas.

Guía de prelectura

Use the cues provided by the visuals, the headline, and subheading in activity **12-44** and your personal knowledge to answer these questions. Try making educated guesses about the content of the text. You will be able to verify your answers later.

1. What key information will this article probably tackle?
   a. Bad weather conditions may scare flyers.
   b. Many people prefer means of transportation other than airplanes.
   c. Fear may negatively affect frequent business flyers.
   d. Panic of flying is treatable.

2. How did you figure out the answers to question 1? Circle the appropriate letter.
   a. The headline, subheading, and visuals
   b. Your personal travel experience

3. Now, can you hypothesize about the probable content of the text? Anticipate some of the secondary ideas.

   The article will probably include this content. Circle all that apply.
   a. Some data to convince aerophobic people that the fear of flying is groundless
   b. Examples of drawbacks caused by the fear of flying
   c. Airline losses caused by the fear of traveling by plane
   d. Classes aerophobic people can take to cope with their problem
   e. Step-by-step methods to combat aerophobia
   f. Alternative means of transportation for aerophobic people

Antes de leer

12-43 Preparación. Primera fase. Marque con una *X* las oraciones que reflejan su opinión sobre los viajes.

1. _____ Prefiero viajar por tierra porque los autobuses y los carros son más seguros.
2. _____ Me encantan los viajes por avión porque son más rápidos.
3. _____ Cuando viajo por avión, me pongo nervioso/a porque pienso que el avión tendrá un accidente.
4. _____ Al subir al avión, pienso que podemos chocar (*crash*) en el aire.
5. _____ Es mejor beber alcohol para relajarse durante un viaje en avión.
6. _____ El estar encerrado en el avión me produce asfixia (*suffocation*).
7. _____ No como en el avión porque pienso que voy a atragantarme (*choke*).
8. _____ Creo que soy aviofóbico/a; es decir, tengo pánico de viajar por avión.

Segunda fase. Ahora comparen sus respuestas y respondan a las siguientes preguntas.

1. ¿Es alguno de ustedes aviofóbico/a?
2. ¿Necesitan ustedes relajarse durante un vuelo? ¿Cómo lo hacen?
3. ¿Creen ustedes que la fobia a viajar en avión se puede curar? ¿Cómo?

A leer

12-44 Primera mirada. Lea el artículo y siga las indicaciones.

El cielo puede esperar

CÓMO PERDER EL MIEDO AL AVIÓN

Hay más probabilidades de que ganes la lotería dos semanas seguidas que de que se caiga un aeroplano. Según las estadísticas, en Estados Unidos, por cada víctima de accidente aéreo, mueren 210 conductores de autos, hay 110 asesinatos, 65 caídas fatales, 15 asfixiados por atragantarse y cuatro que mueren simplemente por caerles objetos encima cuando caminan por la calle.

Sin embargo, el avión es el medio de transporte que despierta mayor pánico entre los viajeros: uno de cuatro españoles experimenta esa alergia al vuelo; algunos superan sus problemas a base de coraje, tranquilizantes o alcohol, pero ésta no es una buena solución, como afirma Enrique Gil Ángel, siquiatra y profesor del cursillo *Miedo a volar.*

Para los profesionales que deben viajar frecuentemente en avión, el asunto puede convertirse en algo muy serio: oportunidades de negocio perdidas, puestos de trabajo a los que no se puede aspirar sólo por el miedo a volar... Sacrificarse y viajar por aire a pesar de la fobia tampoco sirve de nada: el ejecutivo que llega a una reunión de trabajo con estrés, ansiedad y falta de concentración por culpa del calvario de un viaje por aire no responde satisfactoriamente y, en muchos casos, llega a la conclusión de que es mejor no hacerlo.

En España, desde hace cinco años, la empresa Grupo Especial Directivos de Iberia ofrece el seminario *Cómo perder el miedo al avión.* El cursillo propone que el miedo a volar puede superarse con información directa sobre la seguridad aérea, apoyo psicológico específico y experiencia real de vuelo en un ambiente adecuado.

Los aviofóbicos tienen dos miedos:
- Miedo técnico: piensan que el avión puede caerse, porque no son capaces de asimilar que vuele un artefacto como ése.
- Miedo psicológico: angustia ante la expectativa de estar encerrados en el aire.

Durante el seminario, Javier del Campo desmonta las teorías catastrofistas de los asistentes con argumentos técnicos y explica exhaustivamente las severas pruebas de seguridad que pasan los aparatos y las frecuentes revisiones periódicas a que obliga la ley. "Todo está previsto en la aviación; por ejemplo, poca gente sabe que para probar la resistencia de los cristales se lanzan pollos con un cañón de artillería, de manera que chocan a unos 300 kilómetros por hora contra el avión, que es la velocidad a la que puede impactar un ave en vuelo real."

Del Campo asegura que después de asistir al cursillo, los participantes no tienen la más mínima duda sobre la seguridad en los aviones: sólo les queda "la parte irracional del problema".

De esta materia se encarga el doctor Gil Nagel, quien trata cada caso individualmente, enseña técnicas de autocontrol, y vigila las reacciones emocionales de los asistentes para liberarlos del problema. Nagel utiliza también terapia de grupo y un método denominado *desensibilización sistemática,* que consiste en enfrentar al paciente con la causa de su miedo.

Tanto el comandante del Campo como el doctor Nagel coinciden en que las personas con aviofobia generalmente son algo más inteligentes que la persona media, tratan siempre de tenerlo todo bajo control y son muy creativas.

Marque la afirmación que resume mejor el contenido del artículo.

1. _____ Por razones lógicas, algunas personas sienten un miedo horrible de viajar en avión; según los científicos, este pánico, que afecta solamente a la víctima que la sufre, no tiene cura. Así lo demostraron, los intentos que hicieron los psiquíatras y expertos en aviación en España.

2. _____ La fobia de muchas personas a viajar por avión no es racional ni fundamentada. En la mayoría de los casos, las víctimas de la aviofobia no poseen información técnica sobre el control de calidad que realizan las compañías que construyen los aviones. Los problemas psicológicos, económicos y laborales causados por este miedo extremo se pueden evitar con información científica y tratamiento, como lo demuestran algunos tratamientos realizados en España.

3. _____ El pánico de algunas personas a volar se basa en la gran cantidad de accidentes de aviación. Aunque los técnicos y científicos digan lo contrario, las estadísticas de accidentes indican que la mayor cantidad de muertes ocurren en la industria de la aviación. Algunos expertos en aeronáutica y psicólogos españoles han tratado de ayudar a los aviofóbicos con cursos especialmente diseñados para ellos, pero no han tenido ningún éxito.

12-45 Segunda mirada. Basándose en la información del artículo, ordene las siguientes causas de muerte de 1 a 5 (5, más significativa; 1, menos significativa), según el número de víctimas que ocasionan.

_____ accidentes automovilísticos   _____ caídas mortales

_____ asfixias   _____ asesinatos

_____ accidentes de aviación

12-46 Una mirada más. Busque en el artículo la siguiente información.

1. Tres maneras tradicionales que los viajeros utilizan para controlar el miedo al avión antes de tomar el cursillo: _____

2. Tres efectos psicológicos que sufren los aviofóbicos: _____

3. Las estrategias que se utilizan en el cursillo para ayudar a superar…

   a. el miedo técnico: _____

   _____

   _____

   b. el miedo psicológico: _____

   _____

   _____

Después de leer

12-47 Ampliación. Primera fase. ¿Qué palabras del artículo están asociadas por su significado con las siguientes?

1. aéreo: _____
2. muertos: _____
3. miedo: _____
4. chocar: _____

Segunda fase. Complete el siguiente texto con un verbo o sustantivo de la **Primera fase**.

La persona que es (1) _____ del pánico a volar, o (2) _____, cree que cuando viaja en un (3) _____, éste va a sufrir un (4) _____ fatal y va a morir. Sin embargo, las estadísticas indican que es más probable que una persona muera en un (5) _____ que en un choque de aviones, por ejemplo. Usando información real, los expertos tratan de curar el miedo infundado del (6) _____.

Escribir

In academic life, you are often faced with tasks that require presenting factual information. Facts are considered objective, neutral, impartial measures or representations of reality. Therefore, to maintain objectivity, you should provide reliable data such as statistics, opinions and statements made by experts, etc.

Facts also serve as the basis to support a personal view on an issue. A psychologist, for example, may recommend a class instead of medication to an aerophobic person based on the fact that certain fears are better cured by confronting them.

Therefore, to take an objective position on a particular issue or problem.

- inform yourself by reading and/or consulting sources
- make statements based on the information you collected
- acknowledge the sources as you present facts

Antes de escribir

12-48 Preparación. Su amigo, Sebastián, ganó en un concurso un pasaje de ida y vuelta a San José, Costa Rica. Quiere devolver el premio porque les tiene pánico a los aviones y le escribió a usted para pedirle consejo. Para escribirle una carta objetiva y ayudarlo a superar su enfermedad, haga lo siguiente:

a. Lea uno o dos artículo(s) sobre el tema y subraye las ideas, los conceptos, los datos concretos.
b. Tome nota de los datos objetivos más relevantes sobre la aviación que puedan ayudar a su amigo. Puede usar la información de "El cielo puede esperar", otro texto o el conocimiento de los expertos.
c. Haga una lista de palabras que le van a ser útiles para darle cohesión a su texto.
d. Seleccione algunos ejemplos que lo/la puedan ayudar a demostrar su posición o razonamiento (*reasoning*) sobre la aviofobia.
e. Finalmente, escriba algunas formas lingüísticas que lo/la ayudarán a expresar información concreta y dar sugerencias a su amigo.

A escribir

12-49 Manos a la obra. Contéstele a Sebastián. Incluya los datos objetivos y concretos que preparó en la actividad **12-48**. Además, recuerde darle buenos consejos para que su amigo olvide su fobia de volar.

Después de escribir

12-50 Revisión. Antes de enviar su carta, léala y verifique lo siguiente, pensando en su lector/a.

- El contenido: ¿Se concentró en las fobias en su carta? ¿Hizo afirmaciones basadas en datos concretos o en la opinión de los expertos?

- La organización: ¿Está su carta bien organizada? ¿Sigue un orden claro?

- La gramática. ¿Usó conceptos relevantes al tema, expresiones de cohesión, la concordancia correcta, el tiempo (presente, pasado, futuro) y modos (indicativo, subjuntivo, etc.) apropiados?

- La puntuación y ortografía. ¿Utilizó las comas, puntos, etc. necesarios? Finalmente, comparta su carta con su compañero/a editor/a.

TEMAS: LA MÚSICA Y EL BAILE

Para pensar

¿Cuál es su música favorita? ¿Qué tipo de música puede usted escuchar en la radio? ¿Hay algún tipo de música que sea típicamente estadounidense? ¿Cuál es?

La música hispana contemporánea es muy variada y refleja la variedad étnica de los diferentes países.

En los países con una población indígena significativa (México, Guatemala, Perú, Bolivia, Ecuador), se escucha mucha música indígena. Ésta puede ser triste y melancólica, o rápida y alegre. Un ejemplo de música indígena es el huayno peruano.

En todos los países hispanos se escucha y se baila música de origen africano, que se caracteriza por ser rápida, alegre y vibrante. La cumbia, el merengue, la salsa y la rumba son ejemplos de esta música tan popular.

Para contestar

2 **La música hispana.** Respondan a las siguientes preguntas.

1. ¿Por qué se dice que la música hispana contemporánea es muy variada? Expliquen.
2. Cada país tiene su música típica. Mencione la música típica de Chile, Venezuela y Panamá.
3. ¿Cuáles son algunos cantantes hispanos famosos?

G **Riqueza cultural.** En grupos de tres, comparen los diferentes tipos de música que ustedes escuchan generalmente con algunos de los ritmos hispanos mencionados arriba.

Hay muchísimos cantantes famosos en el mundo hispano. Por ejemplo, Celia Cruz (de Cuba), llamada la reina de la salsa, Thalía (de México), Enrique Iglesias (de España), José Luis Rodríguez (de Venezuela), Rubén Blades (de Panamá), Gloria Estefan de Cuba y los Estados Unidos.

Para pensar

¿Sabe usted dónde queda Panamá? ¿Tiene usted idea de cuándo se construyó el Canal de Panamá y cuál es su importancia? ¿Sabe usted dónde está Costa Rica? ¿Conoce usted algún político, cantante, deportista o persona famosa de estos países?

Panamá y Costa Rica se encuentran en la América Central y tienen costas en el Océano Pacífico y en el Mar Caribe.

Hay muchos lugares de interés que se pueden visitar en el Casco Viejo de la Ciudad de Panamá, como el Museo de Arte Colonial Religioso. Pero también siempre hay algo que hacer para divertirse, como ir a un festival de jazz, a las exposiciones de arte, a las competencias deportivas, etc.

Cerca de la Ciudad de Panamá se encuentra el famoso Canal de Panamá que conecta el Océano Pacífico con el Mar Caribe.

El folclore panameño es muy rico e interesante. Al norte de Panamá, todos los años se celebra la Fiesta de la Pollera, en la cual se pueden apreciar bailes regionales tradicionales como la Danza de los Toros y la Danza de los Diablos.

Expresiones panameñas:

desorejado/a	Es una **desorejada.**	*She is tone deaf.*
embolatar	Él la **embolató y no** se casó con ella.	*He lied and made false promises and did not marry her.*
pachocha	¡Apúrense! ¡Ustedes tienen una **pachocha!**	*Hurry up! You are so slow!*

La marimba y la guitarra son importantes instrumentos en la música de los "ticos" —nombre con el que se conoce a los costarricenses—. La guitarra se usa especialmente en danzas típicas como el punto guanacasteco, el baile nacional.

Costa Rica es un país ideal para hacer ecoturismo y para practicar una serie de deportes como windsurfing, ciclismo o tabla hawaiana.

Expresiones costarricenses:

upe	¡Upe!	*(Type of greeting)*
chunche	Pásame ese **chunche.**	*Give me that thing.*
maje	El es un **maje.**	*He is a fool.*
paltó	No tengo **paltó.**	*I do not have a jacket.*
fajarse	**Me fajé,** pero terminé el trabajo.	*I put a lot of effort, but finished the job.*

Para contestar

En el mapa

1. Diga dónde está Panamá y cuál es su capital. ¿Y Costa Rica?
2. ¿Qué países están cerca de Panamá? ¿Y de Costa Rica?
3. Mencione una semejanza geográfica entre Panamá y Costa Rica.

Ahora diga…

1. si le gustaría visitar Panamá o Costa Rica, y por qué.
2. qué lugar de Panamá le interesaría visitar.
3. si le gustaría visitar Sarchi, y por qué.

¿Qué dice usted si…

1. su amigo no sabe ni puede cantar.
2. su compañero siempre llega tarde a todas partes.
3. usted estudió mucho.

No muy lejos de San José está el pueblito de Sarchí, famoso por sus hermosas carretas pintadas de brillantes colores y carteras de cuero.

Para investigar en Internet

Busque información acerca de dos conjuntos panameños de música popular y dos conjuntos de música folclórica de algún otro país latinoamericano. Para cada conjunto, diga cómo se llama, qué tipo de música toca, qué instrumentos usa, etc. Traiga esta información a clase para hacer una presentación de lo que averiguó, y diga qué conjunto le gusta más y por qué. Si puede, traiga una grabación del conjunto y toque la música en clase.

¡Prepárese!

2 **12-51 Predicciones.** Ahora que ha visto once episodios de *Fortunas*, haga predicciones sobre lo que pasará en el Episodio 12. Recuerde que en este episodio los participantes están tratando de solucionar el quinto misterio y ganar la segunda fortuna. Use el tiempo futuro y escriba oraciones completas para los sujetos de la lista siguiente. Intercambie sus predicciones con las de un/a compañero/a.

1. Katie...
2. Efraín...
3. Sabrina...
4. Carlos...
5. La segunda fortuna...
6. Los cuatro participantes...
7. El público...
8. ...

Ángela y Manolo comentan el engaño y la falta de integridad de los participantes.

Carlos y Efraín formaron una alianza.

Carlos y Efraín solucionan el quinto misterio y ganan la segunda fortuna.

Efraín se entera de que él y Carlos tienen que compartir el misterio y la fortuna con Katie.

Katie formó alianzas con Carlos y con Sabrina, pero todavía está en primer lugar.

Sabrina está muy enfadada por las acciones de Katie.

12-52 Resultados. Lea las predicciones que le dio su compañero/a. Sus predicciones para el Episodio 12 ¿eran correctas? ¿Y las suyas?

¡Responda!

12-53 Los participantes. ¿Quién quiere que gane el concurso? ¿Por qué? Imagínese que es el/la ganador/a y escriba un breve informe que explique lo que va a hacer después de ganar *Fortunas*. Su informe debe tener por lo menos cinco oraciones completas. Use el tiempo futuro y/o la estructura *ir + a + infinitivo*.

Rubén Blades, de Panamá, es conocido no sólo por su música sino también por su talento como actor y su activismo social. Frecuentemente comenta temas sociales en sus canciones y *Ligia Elena* no es una excepción ya que trata del tema de un amor prohibido por diferencias raciales y socioeconómicas.

¡Prepárese!

12-54 La canción. Túrnense para formular y contestar negativamente las siguientes preguntas sobre el tema, la letra y el artista de "Ligia Elena."

1. ¿Conoces alguna canción de Rubén Blades?
2. ¿Sabes la letra de "Ligia Elena"?
3. ¿Alguna vez fuiste a un concierto de música latina?
4. ¿Alguien te compró un disco compacto de este artista?
5. ¿Escuchas música con temas sociales?
6. ¿A todos los estudiantes les gusta la canción?

¡Escuche!

12-55 Reacciones y opiniones. Mientras escucha "Ligia Elena" complete la siguiente tabla con adjetivos u otras palabras o expresiones que reflejen sus reacciones y opiniones sobre la canción. Parte de la letra está incluida aquí.

ELEMENTOS	ES.../SON...
El ritmo	
La letra	
El tema	
La vocalización	
Los instrumentos	

LIGIA ELENA

Ligia Elena la cándida niña de la sociedad
se ha fugado con un trompetista de la vecindad.
El padre la busca afanosamente,
lo está comentando toda la gente
y la madre angustiada pregunta ¿en dónde estará?

De nada sirvieron regaños ni viajes ni monjas,
ni las promesas de amor que le hicieran los niños de bien.
Fue tan buena la nota que dio aquel humilde trompeta
que entre acordes de cariño eterno se fue ella con él.

Pudo más el amor que el dinero, señor.
¡Qué buena la nota que dio aquel trompeta!
Eso del racismo, *brother,* no está en na'.
Deja que la agarre nos jura el papá.

Ligia Elena está llena de felicidad.

¡Responda!

12-56 ¿Qué hará Rubén Blades? Imagínese que es reportero/a para Univisión, el canal hispano, y que va a entrevistar a Rubén Blades sobre su carrera. Use el tiempo futuro para hacerle cinco preguntas sobre sus planes.

12-57 Entrevista. Intercambie sus preguntas con un/a compañero/a y túrnese con él/ella para hacer los papeles de reportero/a y de Rubén Blades. Después hagan sus entrevistas frente a la clase.

VOCABULARIO

AUDIO ## Medios de transporte

el auto(móvil)/coche/carro	*car*
el autobús/bus	*bus*
el avión	*plane*
el barco	*ship/boat*
el metro	*subway*
el tren	*train*

En el aeropuerto

la aduana	*customs*
la aerolínea	*airline*
el mostrador	*counter*
la puerta (de salida)	*gate*
el vuelo	*flight*

En un avión

el asiento	*seat*
de pasillo/ventanilla	*aisle/window seat*
la ventanilla	*window*

El correo

el buzón	*mailbox*
la carta	*letter*
el paquete	*package*
el sello	*stamp*
el sobre	*envelope*
la tarjeta postal	*post card*

Personas

el/la agente de viajes	*travel agent*
el/la auxiliar de vuelo	*flight attendant*
el/la cartero/a	*letter carrier*
el/la conserje	*concierge*
el/la empleado/a	*employee*
el/la pasajero/a	*passenger*

Partes de un coche

la batería/el acumulador	*battery*
el capó	*hood*
el espejo retrovisor	*rearview mirror*
la guantera	*glove compartment*
el limpiaparabrisas	*windshield wiper*
la llanta	*tire*
el maletero	*trunk*
el parabrisas	*windshield*
el parachoques	*bumper*
la placa	*plates*
el radiador	*radiator*
la rueda	*wheel*
el volante	*steering wheel*

Viajes

la agencia de viajes	*travel agency*
la autopista	*freeway*
el boleto/pasaje	*ticket*
la carretera	*highway*
el cheque de viajero	*traveler's check*
el crucero	*cruise*
el destino	*destination*
el equipaje	*luggage*
la hora de llegada/salida	*arrival/departure time*
la lista de espera	*waiting list*
la maleta	*suitcase*
el maletín	*briefcase*
el pasaporte	*passport*
la tarjeta de embarque	*boarding pass*
la velocidad	*speed*

En el hotel

la caja fuerte	*safe box*
la habitación doble/sencilla	*double/single room*
la llave	*key*
la recepción	*front desk*

Lugares

la cuadra	*city block*
la esquina	*corner*

Descripciones

lleno/a	*full*
vacío/a	*empty*

Verbos

cancelar	*to cancel*
doblar	*to turn*
facturar	*to check in (luggage)*
manejar	*to drive*
perderse (ie)	*to get lost*
reservar	*to make a reservation*
revisar	*to inspect*
viajar	*to travel*
volar (ue)	*to fly*

Palabras y expresiones útiles

a la izquierda/derecha	*to the left/right*
de ida y vuelta	*round trip*
hacer cola	*to stand in line*
hacer escala	*to make a stopover*
seguir (i) derecho	*to go straight ahead*
una vez	*once*

*For a list of affirmative and negative expressions, see pages 450–451. For a list of stressed possessive adjectives and pronouns, see pages 456–457.

EXPANSIÓN GRAMATICAL

This special grammatical supplement includes structures considered optional for the introductory level by instructors emphasizing proficiency, except for the *vosotros* command forms. The *vosotros* forms are included in this section for the instructors who use them to address their students. The other functions and structures presented here are normally beyond the level of performance of first-year students, therefore most instructors would present them for recognition only.

The explanation and activities in this section use the same format as grammatical material throughout *Mosaicos* in order to facilitate their incorporation into the core lessons of the program or their addition as another chapter in the book.

Objetivos comunicativos

Giving informal orders or commands to two or more people (in Spain)
Expressing an indirect wish so that a third party do something
Suggesting that someone and the speaker do something
Reacting to a past occurrence or event
Hypothesizing about an occurrence or event in the past
Expressing contrary-to-fact conditions in the past
Emphasizing a fact resulting from the action of someone or something

Estructuras

▦ *Vosotros* commands

▦ Indirect commands

▦ The Spanish equivalents of English *let's*

▦ The present perfect subjunctive

▦ The conditional perfect and the pluperfect subjunctive

▦ *If*-clauses (using the perfect tense)

▦ The passive voice

1. *Vosotros* commands

	AFFIRMATIVE	NEGATIVE
hablar	hablad	no habléis
comer	comed	no comáis
escribir	escribid	no escribáis

- To use the affirmative **vosotros** command, change the final **-r** of the infinitive to **-d.**

- Use the **vosotros** form of the present subjunctive for the **vosotros** negative command.

- For the affirmative **vosotros** command of reflexive verbs, drop the final **-d** and add the pronoun **os: levantad + os = levantaos.** The verb **irse** is an exception: **idos.**

¿Qué dice usted?

EG-1 Buenos consejos. Usted quiere que sus mejores amigos cambien sus hábitos y vivan una vida más sana. Dígales qué deben hacer.

MODELO: caminar dos kilómetros todos los días
Caminad dos kilómetros todos los días.

1. comer muchas frutas y vegetales
2. empezar un programa de ejercicios
3. no respirar por la boca
4. no cansarse mucho los primeros días
5. relajarse para evitar el estrés
6. dormir no menos de ocho horas

Ⓖ EG-2 Órdenes en grupo. Cada uno/a de ustedes va a hacer el papel de profesor/a de educación física y le va a dar una orden a los otros estudiantes del grupo. Los estudiantes deben hacer lo que el/la profesor/a les indica.

MODELO: *Levantad los brazos y las piernas.*

SITUACIONES

You and your partner have rented a cabin in the mountains for a month. Some of your friends are going to use the cabin part of the time and you would like to give them some rules to make sure they leave everything in order. Write the rules and then compare them with those of another couple.

2. Indirect commands

You have used commands directly to tell others to do something: **Salga/Salgan ahora.** Now you are going to use indirect commands to say what someone else should do: **Que salga Berta.** Note that this indirect command is equivalent to saying **Quiero que Berta salga,** but without expressing the main verb **quiero.**

- The word **que** introduces the indirect command. The subject, if stated, normally follows the verb.

> **Que cocine** Roberto.   *Let Roberto cook.*
> **Que descanse** María.   *Let María rest.*

■ Reflexive and object pronouns always precede the verb.

Que **se siente** a la mesa.	*Let him sit at the table.*
Que **le sirvan** la cena.	*Let them serve him dinner.*
Que **se la sirvan** ahora.	*Let them serve it to him now.*

EG-3 Una clase de cocina. Un chef muy conocido ha accedido a dar una clase de cocina con el fin de recaudar (*raise*) dinero para una obra social. Usted y su compañero/a forman parte del comité que organiza la clase. Su compañero/a tiene la lista de las personas que desean ayudar y usted tiene la lista de las tareas pendientes. Háganse preguntas y contéstense con la información que cada uno/a tiene.

MODELO: *Eduardo, Alicia y Pedro preparar los anuncios, comprar los refrescos*
E1: *¿Quién va a preparar los anuncios?*
E2: *Que los preparen Alicia y Pedro. ¿Y qué va a hacer Eduardo?*
E1: *Que compre los refrescos.*

Personas

Beatriz
Alberto y Rubén
Miguel
Elena y Amanda
Ana María
Emilio
Un camarero

Tareas

traer los platos
tener los ingredientes listos
buscar las sillas
copiar las recetas
servir el vino
recibir a las personas
ayudar al chef

EG-4 Una fiesta hispana. Primera fase. Para celebrar el final de curso ustedes han decidido organizar una fiesta en el departamento de español. Hagan una lista de todo lo que necesitan y otra lista de todas las personas que van a invitar, además de sus compañeros/as de clase.

Segunda fase. Decidan qué otras personas de la clase pueden encargarse de cada sección y por qué. Su compañero/a, que está de acuerdo con usted, le dará algunas ideas.

MODELO: E1: *Que se encargue Juan de comprar las invitaciones porque tiene que ir al supermercado esta tarde.*
E2: *Sí, pero que las escriban María y Pedro que escriben mejor.*

Role A. You are a new manager for the Student Union who wants to improve the food and the service at the cafeteria. In a meeting with the cafeteria manager, say a) that it is important that students receive a better service, b) inform the manager of the type of food you would like to find in the cafeteria and of the ways in which the service could be improved, and c) say that you hope the prices will not increase **(subir)** this semester.

Role B. You are the cafeteria manager. Agree with the Student Union manager and tell him/her a) that you have a good team and you want everyone to do a good job, b) that you will be happy to meet with a student committee and have students suggest **(sugerir)** menus, and c) that you will do your best **(hacer lo posible)** to convince your team to incorporate your suggestions.

EN DIRECTO

To negotiate politely:
Esperamos que...
Es mejor que ...
Proponemos que...

To show agreement:
¡Claro!
¡Por supuesto!
¡Cómo no!
¡Desde luego!

3. The Spanish equivalents of English *let's*

In Spanish, you may suggest that two or more people, including yourself, do something together in the following ways.

■ **Vamos + a +** *infinitive* is commonly used in Spanish to express English *let's + verb*.

> **Vamos a llamar** al doctor.   *Let's call the doctor.*

■ Use **vamos** by itself to mean *let's go*. The negative *let's not go* is **no vayamos**.

> **Vamos** al hospital.   *Let's go to the hospital.*
> **No vayamos** al hospital.   *Let's not go to the hospital.*

■ Another equivalent for *let's + verb* is the **nosotros** form of the present subjunctive.

> **Hablemos** con el médico.   *Let's talk to the doctor.*
> **No hablemos** con la enfermera.   *Let's not talk to the nurse.*

■ The final **-s** of reflexive affirmative commands is dropped when the pronoun **nos** is attached. Note the additional written accent.

> **Levantemos + nos**   →   **Levantémonos.**
> **Sirvamos + nos**   →   **Sirvámonos.**

■ Placement of object and reflexive pronouns is the same as with **usted(es)** commands.

> **Comprémosla.**   *Let's buy it.*
> **No la compremos.**   *Let's not buy it.*

¿Qué dice usted?

EG-5 ¿Qué debemos hacer? Usted está estudiando con un/a compañero/a y cuidando al mismo tiempo a su hermanito. El niño les dice que se siente mal. Cada uno/a de ustedes debe escoger tres de las siguientes opciones y decirle a su compañero/a lo que deben o no deben hacer.

MODELO: llevarlo a su cuarto   llamar a tus padres
                E1: *Llevémoslo a su cuarto.*   E2: *Llamemos a tus padres.*

1. darle agua
2. llevarlo al parque
3. comprarle juguetes
4. ponerle el termómetro
5. llamar al médico
6. preguntarle qué le duele
7. prepararle una hamburguesa
8. explicarle los síntomas al doctor
9. ponerle la televisión
10. acostarlo

EG-6 Resoluciones. Usted y su compañero/a deciden llevar una vida más sana. Túrnense para decir lo que piensan hacer. Su compañero/a va a decirle si está de acuerdo o no con su sugerencia.

MODELO: comer más verduras
                E1: *Vamos a comer más verduras.*
                E2: *Sí, comamos más verduras./No,(no comamos más verduras,)*
                     comamos más frutas.

1. tomar vitaminas y minerales
2. caminar tres kilómetros diariamente
3. beber ocho vasos de agua todos los días
4. acostarse más temprano
5. dormir ocho horas todas las noches
6. ...

EG-7 Los preparativos para un beneficio. En pequeños grupos, decidan qué actividades van a hacer para recaudar (*collect*) fondos a beneficio de un hospital. Deben mencionar cinco actividades.

MODELO: Organicemos un partido del equipo de basquetbol.

SITUACIONES

You and your partner are planning to visit a classmate who is in the hospital. Decide a) when you will visit him/her, b) what you are going to take him/her, and c) what you can do for your classmate after he/she leaves the hospital. Then, exchange this information with another pair of students.

4. The present perfect subjunctive

Use the present perfect subjunctive to react to a past occurrence, event or condition. The present perfect subjunctive is formed with the present subjunctive of the verb **haber** + *past participle*.

PRESENT SUBJUNCTIVE OF *HABER* + *PAST PARTICIPLE*		
yo	haya	
yú	hayas	
Ud., él/ella	haya	hablado
nosotros/as	hayamos	comido
vosotros/as	hayáis	vivido
Uds., ellos/as	hayan	

Note that the dependent clause using the present perfect subjunctive describes what has happened before the time expressed or implied in the main clause, which is the present. Its English equivalent is normally *has/have* + *past participle*, but it may vary according to the context.

Your friend tells you:	Your reaction to this past event:
Mis hijos volvieron de sus vacaciones.	Me alegro de que **hayan llegado**. *I'm glad they arrived early.*

Your secretary informs you:	Your reaction to this past news:
El gerente de ventas no vino a trabajar ayer.	Es posible que **haya estado** enfermo. *It's possible that he may have been sick.*

¿Qué dice usted?

2 EG-8 ¿Qué espera usted? Escoja la oración que complete lógicamente las siguientes Situaciones. Compare sus respuestas con las de su compañero/a.

1. Su computadora no estaba funcionando bien y usted se la dio a un técnico para que la reparara. Usted espera que...
   a. la haya vendido.
   b. haya destruido sus programas.
   c. haya encontrado el problema.

2. Su amigo acaba de regresar de Puerto Rico, donde fue a pasar sus vacaciones. Usted le dice: "Espero que...
   a. hayas visitado el Viejo San Juan".
   b. te hayas aburrido mucho".
   c. hayas perdido todo tu dinero".

3. Uno de sus compañeros ha estado muy grave en el hospital, pero ya está en la casa. Usted le habla y le dice: "Siento mucho que...
   a. hayas vendido la casa".
   b. hayas estado tan mal".
   c. hayas salido del hospital".

4. Usted llama por teléfono a un amigo para invitarlo a cenar, pero nadie contesta el teléfono. Es probable que su amigo...
   a. haya cenado ya.
   b. haya salido de su casa.
   c. haya cambiado su teléfono.

5. Uno de sus parientes dijo una mentira (*lie*). Como es natural, a usted le molesta mucho que no...
   a. haya dicho la verdad.
   b. haya dicho nada.
   c. haya hablado con sus parientes.

EG-9 Un viaje. Uno de sus amigos pasó un semestre en Los Ángeles. Túrnese con su compañero/a para decirle lo que esperan que haya hecho en su visita.

MODELO: ir a Beverly Hills / visitar la Biblioteca Huntington
   E1: *Espero que hayas ido a Beverly Hills.*
   E2: *Y yo espero que hayas visitado la Biblioteca Huntington.*

1. ver las Torres de Watts
2. ir a los Estudios Universal
3. caminar por la calle Olvera
4. comer comida mexicana
5. manejar hasta el observatorio del Monte Wilson
6. asistir al Desfile de las Rosas

EG-10 Los adelantos científicos. Usted y su compañero/a trabajan con otros científicos en un laboratorio de ingeniería genética. Háganse preguntas para saber qué han o no han logrado en sus investigaciones.

MODELO: aislar el nuevo virus / es posible que
   E1: *¿Han aislado el nuevo virus?*
   E2: *Es posible que lo hayamos / hayan aislado.*

1. cambiar la estructura de la célula / dudar
2. no hacer implantes nuevos / es una lástima
3. duplicar órganos / no creer que
4. regular el ritmo del corazón / esperar
5. reactivar los músculos atrofiados / es probable que
6. modificar los genes / es importante que

SITUACIONES

You and your classmate graduated years ago and are remembering the times when you were at the university. You have found a group photo of your Spanish class. Talk about each of your classmates saying a) what you know they have done in their lives, b) what you hope they have done, and c) what you doubt they have done. Use your imagination and the expressions in the box to sound more natural.

5. The conditional perfect and the pluperfect subjunctive

In this section you will study two new verb tenses: the conditional perfect and the pluperfect subjunctive. Use this tense to hypothesize about an occurrence or event in the past.

■ Use the conditional of **haber** + *past participle* to form the conditional perfect.

CONDITIONAL PERFECT		
yo	habría	
tú	habrías	
Ud., él, ella	habría	hablado
nosotros/as	habríamos	comido
vosotros/as	habríais	vivido
Uds., ellos/as	habrían	

■ The conditional perfect usually corresponds to English *would have + past participle.*

Sé que le **habría gustado** esta casa.   *I know you/he/she would have liked this house.*

■ Use the past subjunctive of **haber** + *past participle* to form the pluperfect subjunctive.

PLUPERFECT SUBJUNCTIVE		
yo	hubiera	
tú	hubieras	
Ud., él, ella	hubiera	hablado
nosotros/as	hubiéramos	comido
vosotros/as	hubierais	vivido
Uds., ellos/as	hubieran	

■ The pluperfect subjunctive corresponds to English *might have, would have,* or *had + past participle.* It is used in constructions where the subjunctive is normally required.

Dudaba que **hubiera venido** temprano.   *I doubted that he had/would have come early.*

Esperaba que **hubieran comido** en casa.   *I was hoping that they would have eaten at home.*

Ojalá que **hubieran visto** ese letrero.   *I wish they had seen that sign.*

¿Qué dice usted?

EG-11 ¿Qué habría hecho en estas Situaciones? Primera fase. Digan qué habría hecho cada uno/a de ustedes en las siguientes situaciones. Después escojan la respuesta que les parezca mejor para cada situación.

MODELO: Usted recibió una invitación para una recepción en la Casa Blanca.
E1: *Se lo habría dicho a todos mis compañeros.*
E2: *Habría leído la invitación varias veces porque habría pensado que era una broma.*

1. En el aeropuerto le dijeron que podía viajar en primera clase todo el año sin pagar.
2. Le pidieron sugerencias para mejorar la situación de los vuelos y los aeropuertos.
3. La NASA lo/la llamó para ver si le interesaba vivir tres meses en una estación espacial.
4. Le dijeron que organizara la fiesta de fin de curso de su clase.
5. Le pidieron que revisara los programas en su universidad y sugiriera los cambios necesarios.

Segunda fase. Comparen las respuestas que escogieron con las de otra pareja y decidan cuál es la mejor. Después compartan sus respuestas con el resto de la clase.

EG-12 Nuestras esperanzas. Usted y su compañero/a esperaban que el nuevo gobierno hiciera muchas cosas en beneficio de la sociedad. Se lograron algunas cosas, pero otras no. Túrnense para decir qué esperaban que el nuevo gobierno y su gabinete hubieran hecho y si lo han hecho o no.

MODELO:　subir el sueldo mínimo / mejorar el sistema de educación
　　　　　　E1: *Esperaba que hubieran subido el sueldo mínimo y (no) lo hanhecho.*
　　　　　　E2: *Y yo esperaba que hubieran mejorado el sistema de educación (no) lo han hecho.*

1. bajar los impuestos (*taxes*)
2. mejorar el transporte público
3. terminar con la corrupción
4. construir viviendas (*housing*) para familias pobres
5. ofrecer mejores planes de salud
6. proteger el medio ambiente
7. ...
8. ...

SITUACIONES

Role A. You had an argument **(pelea)** with your significant other. Explain to your best friend what happened and ask him/her what he/she would have done in your place. Then tell him/her what you intend to do.

Role B. Your best friend explains to you that he/she had an argument with his/her significant other. Ask questions to obtain some details. Then a) tell him/her what you would have done in the same situation, b) ask him/her what he/she intends to do and c) give him/her your advice.

6. *If*-clauses (using the perfect tenses)

The conditional perfect and pluperfect subjunctive are used in contrary-to-fact if-statements which refer to actions, events, experiences related to the past.

Si **hubieras venido**, te **habría gustado** la conferencia.	*If you had come (which you did not), you would have liked the lecture.*

¿Qué dice usted?

EG-13 La vida sería diferente. Con su compañero/a, diga cuáles habrían sido las consecuencias si...

MODELO: no se hubieran inventado los aviones
            E1: *Habríamos viajado en barco, en tren o en autobús.*
            E2: *Habríamos contaminado menos la atmósfera.*

1. no se hubiera inventado la bomba atómica
2. no se hubieran deforestado los bosques
3. los ingleses hubieran descubierto América
4. las mujeres hubieran tenido siempre las mismas oportunidades que los hombres
5. no se hubieran creado las vacunas (*vaccination*)
6. los jóvenes hubieran gobernado el mundo

EG-14 Unas excusas. ¿Qué excusas darían ustedes en las siguientes Situaciones?

MODELO: Un amigo le pidió que participara en un experimento.
            E1: *Si mis padres me lo hubieran permitido, habría participado.*
            E2: *Si hubiera tenido tiempo, habría participado.*

1. Una organización quería que usted donara botellas y papeles para reciclar.
2. Le pidieron su coche para llevar unas ratas al laboratorio.
3. Lo/La necesitaban de voluntario/a para probar una vacuna contra el catarro.
4. Un/a compañero/a quería venderle su computadora portátil.
5. Una compañía necesitaba probar unos paracaídas y buscaba personas interesadas en las pruebas.
6. Alquilaban un robot para que hiciera las tareas domésticas.

EG-15 Volver a vivir. Piense en una experiencia negativa que usted haya tenido. Cuéntele a su compañero/a qué le pasó y dígale qué habría hecho si hubiera sabido en ese momento lo que sabe hoy. Después, su compañero/a debe hacer lo mismo.

SITUACIONES

Role A. You attended a conference/lecture about the city of the future. Tell your classmate a) where and when the conference/lecture took place, b) that he/she would have found it very interesting, and c) the things that he/she would have learned if he/she had attended.

Role B. Your classmate has attended a conference/lecture about the city of the future. Ask him/her questions to find out more about the things he/she learned.

7. The passive voice

The passive voice emphasizes a fact resulting from the action of someone or something.

■ The passive voice in Spanish is formed with the verb **ser** + *past participle;* the passive voice is most commonly used in the preterit, though at times you may see it used in other tenses.

La planta nuclear **fue construida** en 1980.

The nuclear plant was built in 1980.

■ Use the preposition **por** when indicating who or what performs the action.

El bosque **fue destruido.** (Who or what did it is not expressed.)

The forest was destroyed.

El bosque **fue destruido por** el fuego. (The fire id it.)

The forest was destroyed by the fire.

■ The past participle functions as an adjective and therefore agrees in gender and number with the subject.

Los árboles fueron **destruidos** por la lluvia ácida.

The trees were destroyed by the acid rain.

La cura fue **descubierta** el año pasado.

The cure was discovered last year.

■ You'll most often find the passive voice in written Spanish, especially in newspapers and formal writing. However, in conversation, Spanish speakers normally use two different constructions that you have already studied—a third person plural verb or a **se** construction.

Vendieron el laboratorio.

They sold the laboratory.

Se vendió el edificio.

The building was sold.

¿Qué dice usted?

EG-16 La comunicación oral. Túrnese con su compañero/a para decir lo que pasó en una reunión del presidente y los ministros. ¿Cómo lo dirían los periódicos? ¿Cómo lo dirían ustedes en una conversación?

MODELO: ministros / recibir / el presidente
  E1: *Los ministros fueron recibidos por el presidente.*
  E2: *El presidente recibió a los ministros.*

1. la agenda / preparar / el secretario
2. la agenda / aprobar / todos
3. el proyecto para disminuir la contaminación / escribir / el Sr. Sosa
4. el proyecto / presentar / la Ministra de Salud
5. unos comentarios / leer / el presidente
6. las preguntas / contestar / el ministro

EG-17 Dos reporteros. Túrnese con su compañero/a para decir cómo escribirían las siguientes noticias para un periódico.

MODELO: la lluvia ácida dañó las cosechas
Las cosechas fueron dañadas por la lluvia ácida.

1. La zona del Amazonas se conoce como el "pulmón" del planeta.
2. Los campesinos deforestaron la selva.
3. Los campesinos cultivaron la tierra.
4. Estos grupos cortaron muchos árboles.
5. La invasión de los seres humanos exterminó muchas especies de animales.
6. El gobierno plantará mil árboles para mejorar la situación.

SITUACIONES

You and your classmate are TV newscasters. You must write and give a piece of news to your viewers on a great discovery. Inform them that a) some very secret plans have been discovered by the CIA, b) that important security measures have been taken, c) that politicians are now deliberating on how to respond to a possible threat **(peligro)** to the population, d) that public transport has been interrupted in major cities, e) that the situation is under control and f) that nobody should be afraid.

Composition correction codes

As part of the process of developing good writing skills in Spanish, you will be exchanging compositions with a classmate. The following correction codes can be very helpful as you critique each other's work.

Code   Interpretation

C   Conjugation of a verb, or an error in some derived verb form, for example **la puerta estaba *abrida.**

Cog   False cognate, for example **sopa** for **jabón**, or **ropa** for **soga.**

D   Dictionary error, for example **banco** for **orilla**, or even **morderse las uñas** for **comerse las uñas.**

F   Form (often a "regularized" adjective, such as **una niña muy *jóvena**).

G   Incorrect gender assignment to a noun, for example **la programa** for **el programa.**

Mode   Mode confusion (if subjunctive, change to indicative and vice versa).

Nag   Noun agreements (gender, number) with adjectives and other noun-centered forms such as pronouns, demonstratives, possessives.

NE   **No existe.** Use this code to signal a made-up word or expression that does not exist in Spanish, for example ***en facto** for **en realidad.**

Prim   Preterite/imperfect confusion (if preterite, change to imperfect and vice versa).

R   Rewrite successfully completed.

Ref   Reflexive. Use this code to signal that a reflexive verb/construction is needed.

Sag   Subject-verb agreement error, for example ***Juan querías salir.**

S/E   **Ser/estar** confusion (if **ser**, change to **estar** and vice versa).

Sp   Spelling error. Use this code to signal errors in spelling. Note that written accent marks are considered part of a word's spelling in Spanish.

T   Tense. Use this code to signal any non-Prim (see above) tense error.

X   Any basic grammatical error not covered by some other symbol, but which the student should reasonably know, such as **después de *yendo** for **después de ir.**

Wo   Word order error, for example, ***es no grande** for **no es grande.**

+   Use this code to signal any especially nice touch in the student's writing.

?   Use this code to signal that the reader could not make any sense of the word, clause, sentence, or paragraph.

Adapted from Higgs, 1979

Word formation in Spanish

Recognizing certain patterns in Spanish word formation can be a big help in deciphering meaning. Use the following information about word formation to help you as you read.

- **Prefixes.** Spanish and English share a number of prefixes that shade the meaning of the word to which they are attached: **inter-** (between, among); **intro/a-** (within); **ex-** (former, toward the outside); **en-/em-** (the state of becoming); **in-/a-** (not, without), among others.

inter-	interdisciplinario, interacción
intro/a-	introvertido, introspección
ex-	ex-esposo, exponer *(expose)*
en-/em-	enrojecer *(to turn red)*, empobrecer *(to become poor)*
in-/a-	inmoral, incompleto, amoral, asexual

- **Suffixes.** Suffixes and, in general, word endings will help you identify various aspects of words such as part of speech, gender, meaning, degree, etc. Common Spanish suffixes are **-ría, -za, -miento, -dad/tad, -ura, -oso/a, -izo/a, -(c)ito/a,** and **-mente.**

-ría	place where something is made and/or bought: **panadería, zapatería** *(shoe store)*, **librería.**
-za	feminine, abstract noun: **pobreza** *(poverty)*, **riqueza** *(wealth, richness).*
-miento	masculine, abstract noun: **empobrecimiento** *(impoverishment)*, **entrenamiento** *(training).*
-dad/tad	feminine noun: **ciudad** *(city)*, **libertad** *(liberty, freedom)*
-ura	feminine noun: **verdura, locura** *(craziness).*
-oso/a	adjective meaning having the characteristics of the noun to which it's attached: **montañoso, lluvioso** *(rainy).*
-izo/a	adjective meaning having the characteristics of the noun to which it's attached: **rojizo** *(reddish)*, **enfermizo** *(sickly).*
-(c)ito/a	diminutive form of noun or adjective: **Juanito, mesita** *(little table)*, **Carmencita.**
-mente	attached to the feminine form of adjective to form an adverb: **rápidamente, felizmente** *(happily).*

- **Compounds.** Compounds are made up of two words (e.g., *mailman*), each of which has meaning in and of itself: **tocadiscos** *(record player)* from **tocar** and **disco; sacacorchos** *(cork screw)* from **sacar** and **corcho.** Your knowledge of the root words will help you recognize the compound; and likewise, learning compounds can help you to learn the root words. What do you think **sacar** means?

- **Spanish-English associations.** Learning to associate aspects of word formation in Spanish with aspects of word formation in English can be very helpful. Look at the associations below.

SPANISH	ENGLISH
es/ex + consonant	s + consonant
esclerosis, extraño	*sclerosis, strange*
gu-	w-
guerra, Guillermo	*war, William*
-tad/dad	-ty
libertad, calidad	*liberty, quality*
-sión/-ción	-sion/-tion
tensión, emoción	*tension, emotion*

Stress and written accents in Spanish

In Spanish, normal word stress falls on the second-to-last syllable of words ending in a vowel, **-n,** or **-s,** and on the last syllable of words ending in other consonants.

hablo	clase	amiga	libros
escuchan	comer	universidad	venir

When a word does not follow this pattern, a written accent is used to signal where the word is stressed. Below are examples of words that do not follow the pattern.

1. Words accented on the third-to-last syllable:

física	sábado	simpático
catástrofe	gramática	matemáticas

2. Words that are accented on the last syllable despite ending in a vowel, **-n** or **-s.**

hablé	comí	están	estás
alemán	Belén	inglés	conversación

3. Words that are accented on the second-to-last syllable despite ending in a consonant other than **-n** or **-s.**

lápiz	útil	débil	mártir
Félix	cárcel	módem	fácil

Diphthongs

The combination of an unstressed **i** or **u** with another vowel forms a single syllable which is called a diphthong. When the diphthong is in the accented syllable of a word and a written accent is required, it is written over the other vowel, not over the **i** or **u.**

Dios	adiós	bien	también
seis	dieciséis	continuo	continuó

When a stressed **i** or **u** appears with another vowel, two syllables are formed, and a written accent mark is used over the **i** or **u**.

cafetería	país	Raúl	frío
continúa	río	leíste	economía

Interrogative and monosyllabic words

Some words in Spanish follow normal stress patterns but use written accents for other reasons. For example, interrogative and exclamatory words always use a written accent on the stressed vowel: **¿Dónde viven ellos?, ¿Cuántas clases tienes?, ¡Qué bueno!** Many one-syllable (monosyllabic) words carry a written accent to distinguish them from other words with the same spelling but different meanings.

dé	*give* (formal command)	de	*of*
él	*he*	el	*the*
más	*more*	mas	*but*
mí	*me*	mi	*my*
sé	*I know, be* (formal command)	se	*him/herself, (to)him/her/them*
sí	*yes*	si	*if*
té	*tea*	te	*(to) you*
tú	*you*	tu	*your*

Verb Charts

REGULAR VERBS: SIMPLE TENSES

Infinitive Present Participle Past Participle	Indicative						Subjunctive		Imperative
	Present	Imperfect	Preterit	Future	Conditional		Present	Imperfect	

Infinitive Present Participle Past Participle	Present	Imperfect	Preterit	Future	Conditional	Present	Imperfect	Imperative
hablar hablando hablado	hablo hablas habla hablamos habláis hablan	hablaba hablabas hablaba hablábamos hablabais hablaban	hablé hablaste habló hablamos hablasteis hablaron	hablaré hablarás hablará hablaremos hablaréis hablarán	hablaría hablarías hablaría hablaríamos hablaríais hablarían	hable hables hable hablemos habléis hablen	hablara hablaras hablara habláramos hablarais hablaran	habla tú, no hables hable usted hablemos hablen Uds.
comer comiendo comido	como comes come comemos coméis comen	comía comías comía comíamos comíais comían	comí comiste comió comimos comisteis comieron	comeré comerás comerá comeremos comeréis comerán	comería comerías comería comeríamos comeríais comerían	coma comas coma comamos comáis coman	comiera comieras comiera comiéramos comierais comieran	come tú, no comas coma usted comamos coman Uds.
vivir viviendo vivido	vivo vives vive vivimos vivís viven	vivía vivías vivía vivíamos vivíais vivían	viví viviste vivió vivimos vivisteis vivieron	viviré vivirás vivirá viviremos viviréis vivirán	viviría vivirías viviría viviríamos viviríais vivirían	viva vivas viva vivamos viváis vivan	viviera vivieras viviera viviéramos vivierais vivieran	vive tú, no vivas viva usted vivamos vivan Uds.

Vosotros Commands

hablar	hablad, no habléis	comer	comed, no comáis	vivir	vivid, no viváis

REGULAR VERBS: PERFECT TENSES

	Indicative										Subjunctive			
	Present Perfect		**Past Perfect**		**Preterit Perfect**		**Future Perfect**		**Conditional Perfect**		**Present Perfect**		**Past Perfect**	
he	hablado	había	hablado	hube	hablado	habré	hablado	habría	hablado	haya	hablado	hubiera	hablado
has	comido	habías	comido	hubiste	comido	habrás	comido	habrías	comido	hayas	comido	hubieras	comido
ha	vivido	había	vivido	hubo	vivido	habrá	vivido	habría	vivido	haya	vivido	hubiera	vivido
hemos		habíamos		hubimos		habremos		habríamos		hayamos		hubiéramos	
habéis		habíais		hubisteis		habréis		habríais		hayáis		hubierais	
han		habían		hubieron		habrán		habrían		hayan		hubieran	

IRREGULAR VERBS

Infinitive / Present Participle / Past Participle	Indicative					Subjunctive		Imperative
	Present	**Imperfect**	**Preterit**	**Future**	**Conditional**	**Present**	**Imperfect**	
andar	ando	andaba	anduve	andaré	andaría	ande	anduviera	anda tú,
andando	andas	andabas	anduviste	andarás	andarías	andes	anduvieras	no andes
andado	anda	andaba	anduvo	andará	andaría	ande	anduviera	ande usted
	andamos	andábamos	anduvimos	andaremos	andaríamos	andemos	anduviéramos	andemos
	andáis	andabais	anduvisteis	andaréis	andaríais	andéis	anduvierais	anden Uds.
	andan	andaban	anduvieron	andarán	andarían	anden	anduvieran	
caer	caigo	caía	caí	caeré	caería	caiga	cayera	cae tú,
cayendo	caes	caías	caíste	caerás	caerías	caigas	cayeras	no caigas
caído	cae	caía	cayó	caerá	caería	caiga	cayera	caiga usted
	caemos	caíamos	caímos	caeremos	caeríamos	caigamos	cayéramos	caigamos
	caéis	caíais	caísteis	caeréis	caeríais	caigáis	cayerais	caigan Uds.
	caen	caían	cayeron	caerán	caerían	caigan	cayeran	
dar	doy	daba	di	daré	daría	dé	diera	da tú, no des
dando	das	dabas	diste	darás	darías	des	dieras	
dado	da	daba	dio	dará	daría	dé	diera	dé usted
	damos	dábamos	dimos	daremos	daríamos	demos	diéramos	demos
	dais	dabais	disteis	daréis	daríais	deis	dierais	den Uds.
	dan	daban	dieron	darán	darían	den	dieran	

IRREGULAR VERBS (CONTINUED)

Infinitive Present Participle Past Participle	Indicative						Subjunctive		Imperative
	Present	Imperfect	Preterit	Future	Conditional	Present	Present	Imperfect	
decir diciendo dicho	digo dices dice decimos decís dicen	decía decías decía decíamos decíais decían	dije dijiste dijo dijimos dijisteis dijeron	diré dirás dirá diremos diréis dirán	diría dirías diría diríamos diríais dirían	diga digas diga digamos digáis digan	dijera dijeras dijera dijéramos dijerais dijeran	di tú, no digas diga usted digamos decid vosotros, no digáis digan Uds.
estar estando estado	estoy estás está estamos estáis están	estaba estabas estaba estábamos estabais estaban	estuve estuviste estuvo estuvimos estuvisteis estuvieron	estaré estarás estará estaremos estaréis estarán	estaría estarías estaría estaríamos estaríais estarían	esté estés esté estemos estéis estén	estuviera estuvieras estuviera estuviéramos estuvierais estuvieran	está tú, no estés esté usted estemos estad vosotros, no estéis estén Uds.
haber habiendo habido	he has ha hemos habéis han	había habías había habíamos habíais habían	hube hubiste hubo hubimos hubisteis hubieron	habré habrás habrá habremos habréis habrán	habría habrías habría habríamos habríais habrían	haya hayas haya hayamos hayáis hayan	hubiera hubieras hubiera hubiéramos hubierais hubieran	
hacer haciendo hecho	hago haces hace hacemos hacéis hacen	hacía hacías hacía hacíamos hacíais hacían	hice hiciste hizo hicimos hicisteis hicieron	haré harás hará haremos haréis harán	haría harías haría haríamos haríais harían	haga hagas haga hagamos hagáis hagan	hiciera hicieras hiciera hiciéramos hicierais hicieran	haz tú, no hagas haga usted hagamos haced vosotros, no hagáis hagan Uds.
ir yendo ido	voy vas va vamos vais van	iba ibas iba íbamos ibais iban	fui fuiste fue fuimos fuisteis fueron	iré irás irá iremos iréis irán	iría irías iría iríamos iríais irían	vaya vayas vaya vayamos vayáis vayan	fuera fueras fuera fuéramos fuerais fueran	ve tú, no vayas vaya usted vamos, no vayamos id vosotros, no vayáis vayan Uds.

IRREGULAR VERBS (CONTINUED)

Infinitive Present Participle Past Participle	Indicative					Subjunctive		Imperative
	Present	Imperfect	Preterit	Future	Conditional	Present	Imperfect	
oír oyendo oído	oigo oyes oye oímos oís oyen	oía oías oía oíamos oíais oían	oí oíste oyó oímos oísteis oyeron	oiré oirás oirá oiremos oiréis oirán	oiría oirías oiría oiríamos oiríais oirían	oiga oigas oiga oigamos oigáis oigan	oyera oyeras oyera oyéramos oyerais oyeran	oye tú, no oigas oiga usted oigamos oigan Uds.
poder pudiendo podido	puedo puedes puede podemos podéis pueden	podía podías podía podíamos podíais podían	pude pudiste pudo pudimos pudisteis pudieron	podré podrás podrá podremos podréis podrán	podría podrías podría podríamos podríais podrían	pueda puedas pueda podamos podáis puedan	pudiera pudieras pudiera pudiéramos pudierais pudieran	
poner poniendo puesto	pongo pones pone ponemos ponéis ponen	ponía ponías ponía poníamos poníais ponían	puse pusiste puso pusimos pusisteis pusieron	pondré pondrás pondrá pondremos pondréis pondrán	pondría pondrías pondría pondríamos pondríais pondrían	ponga pongas ponga pongamos pongáis pongan	pusiera pusieras pusiera pusiéramos pusierais pusieran	pon tú, no pongas ponga usted pongamos pongan Uds.
querer queriendo querido	quiero quieres quiere queremos queréis quieren	quería querías quería queríamos queríais querían	quise quisiste quiso quisimos quisisteis quisieron	querré querrás querrá querremos querréis querrán	querría querrías querría querríamos querríais querrían	quiera quieras quiera queramos queráis quieran	quisiera quisieras quisiera quisiéramos quisierais quisieran	quiere tú, no quieras quiera usted queramos quieran Uds.
saber sabiendo sabido	sé sabes sabe sabemos sabéis saben	sabía sabías sabía sabíamos sabíais sabían	supe supiste supo supimos supisteis supieron	sabré sabrás sabrá sabremos sabréis sabrán	sabría sabrías sabría sabríamos sabríais sabrían	sepa sepas sepa sepamos sepáis sepan	supiera supieras supiera supiéramos supierais supieran	sabe tú, no sepas sepa usted sepamos sepan Uds.
salir saliendo salido	salgo sales sale salimos salís salen	salía salías salía salíamos salíais salían	salí saliste salió salimos salisteis salieron	saldré saldrás saldrá saldremos saldréis saldrán	saldría saldrías saldría saldríamos saldríais saldrían	salga salgas salga salgamos salgáis salgan	saliera salieras saliera saliéramos salierais salieran	sal tú, no salgas salga usted salgamos salgan Uds.

IRREGULAR VERBS (CONTINUED)

Infinitive Present Participle Past Participle	Indicative					Subjunctive		Imperative
	Present	Imperfect	Preterit	Future	Conditional	Present	Imperfect	
ser siendo sido	soy eres es somos sois son	era eras era éramos erais eran	fui fuiste fue fuimos fuisteis fueron	seré serás será seremos seréis serán	sería serías sería seríamos seríais serían	sea seas sea seamos seáis sean	fuera fueras fuera fuéramos fuerais fueran	sé tú, no seas sea usted seamos sed vosotros, no seáis sean Uds.
tener teniendo tenido	tengo tienes tiene tenemos tenéis tienen	tenía tenías tenía teníamos teníais tenían	tuve tuviste tuvo tuvimos tuvisteis tuvieron	tendré tendrás tendrá tendremos tendréis tendrán	tendría tendrías tendría tendríamos tendríais tendrían	tenga tengas tenga tengamos tengáis tengan	tuviera tuvieras tuviera tuviéramos tuvierais tuvieran	ten tú, no tengas tenga usted tengamos tened vosotros, no tengáis tengan Uds.
traer trayendo traído	traigo traes trae traemos traéis traen	traía traías traía traíamos traíais traían	traje trajiste trajo trajimos trajisteis trajeron	traeré traerás traerá traeremos traeréis traerán	traería traerías traería traeríamos traeríais traerían	traiga traigas traiga traigamos traigáis traigan	trajera trajeras trajera trajéramos trajerais trajeran	trae tú, no traigas traiga usted traigamos traed vosotros, no traigáis traigan Uds.
venir viniendo venido	vengo vienes viene venimos venís vienen	venía venías venía veníamos veníais venían	vine viniste vino vinimos vinisteis vinieron	vendré vendrás vendrá vendremos vendréis vendrán	vendría vendrías vendría vendríamos vendríais vendrían	venga vengas venga vengamos vengáis vengan	viniera vinieras viniera viniéramos vinierais vinieran	ven tú, no vengas venga usted vengamos venid vosotros, no vengáis vengan Uds.
ver viendo visto	veo ves ve vemos véis ven	veía veías veía veíamos veíais veían	vi viste vio vimos visteis vieron	veré verás verá veremos veréis verán	vería verías vería veríamos veríais verían	vea veas vea veamos veáis vean	viera vieras viera viéramos vierais vieran	ve tú, no veas vea usted veamos ved vosotros, no veáis vean Uds.

STEM-CHANGING AND ORTHOGRAPHIC-CHANGING VERBS

Infinitive Present Participle Past Participle	Indicative					Subjunctive		Imperative
	Present	Imperfect	Preterit	Future	Conditional	Present	Imperfect	
dormir (ue, u) durmiendo dormido	duermo duermes duerme dormimos dormís duermen	dormía dormías dormía dormíamos dormíais dormían	dormí dormiste durmió dormimos dormisteis durmieron	dormiré dormirás dormirá dormiremos dormiréis dormirán	dormiría dormirías dormiría dormiríamos dormiríais dormirían	duerma duermas duerma durmamos durmáis duerman	durmiera durmieras durmiera durmiéramos durmierais durmieran	duerme tú, no duermas duerma usted durmamos dormid vosotros, no durmáis duerman Uds.
incluir (y) incluyendo incluido	incluyo incluyes incluye incluimos incluís incluyen	incluía incluías incluía incluíamos incluíais incluían	incluí incluiste incluyó incluimos incluisteis incluyeron	incluiré incluirás incluirá incluiremos incluiréis incluirán	incluiría incluirías incluiría incluiríamos incluiríais incluirían	incluya incluyas incluya incluyamos incluyáis incluyan	incluyera incluyeras incluyera incluyéramos incluyerais incluyeran	incluye tú, no incluyas incluya usted incluyamos incluid vosotros, no incluyáis incluyan Uds.
pedir (i, i) pidiendo pedido	pido pides pide pedimos pedís piden	pedía pedías pedía pedíamos pedíais pedían	pedí pediste pidió pedimos pedisteis pidieron	pediré pedirás pedirá pediremos pediréis pedirán	pediría pedirías pediría pediríamos pediríais pedirían	pida pidas pida pidamos pidáis pidan	pidiera pidieras pidiera pidiéramos pidierais pidieran	pide tú, no pidas pida usted pidamos pedid vosotros, no pidáis pidan Uds.
pensar (ie) pensando pensado	pienso piensas piensa pensamos pensáis piensan	pensaba pensabas pensaba pensábamos pensabais pensaban	pensé pensaste pensó pensamos pensasteis pensaron	pensaré pensarás pensará pensaremos pensaréis pensarán	pensaría pensarías pensaría pensaríamos pensaríais pensarían	piense pienses piense pensemos penséis piensen	pensara pensaras pensara pensáramos pensarais pensaran	piensa tú, no pienses piense usted pensemos pensad vosotros, no penséis piensen Uds.

STEM-CHANGING AND ORTHOGRAPHIC-CHANGING VERBS (CONTINUED)

Infinitive / Present Participle / Past Participle	Indicative					Subjunctive		Imperative
	Present	Imperfect	Preterit	Future	Conditional	Present	Imperfect	
producir (zc) produciendo producido	produzco produces produce producimos producís producen	producía producías producía producíamos producíais producían	produje produjiste produjo produjimos produjisteis produjeron	produciré producirás producirá produciremos produciréis producirán	produciría producirías produciría produciríamos produciríais producirían	produzca produzcas produzca produzcamos produzcáis produzcan	produjera produjeras produjera produjéramos produjerais produjeran	produce tú, no produzcas produzca usted produzcamos pruducid vosotros, no produzcáis produzcan Uds.
reír (i, i) riendo reído	río ríes ríe reímos reís ríen	reía reías reía reíamos reíais reían	reí reíste rio reímos reísteis rieron	reiré reirás reirá reiremos reiréis reirán	reiría reirías reiría reiríamos reiríais reirían	ría rías ría riamos riáis rían	riera rieras riera riéramos rierais rieran	ríe tú, no rías ría usted riamos reíd vosotros, no riáis rían Uds.
seguir (i, i) (ga) siguiendo seguido	sigo sigues sigue seguimos seguís siguen	seguía seguías seguía seguíamos seguíais seguían	seguí seguiste siguió seguimos seguisteis siguieron	seguiré seguirás seguirá seguiremos seguiréis seguirán	seguiría seguirías seguiría seguiríamos seguiríais seguirían	siga sigas siga sigamos sigáis sigan	siguiera siguieras siguiera siguiéramos siguierais siguieran	sigue tú, no sigas siga usted sigamos seguid vosotros, no sigáis sigan Uds.
sentir (ie, i) sintiendo sentido	siento sientes siente sentimos sentís sienten	sentía sentías sentía sentíamos sentíais sentían	sentí sentiste sintió sentimos sentisteis sintieron	sentiré sentirás sentirá sentiremos sentiréis sentirán	sentiría sentirías sentiría sentiríamos sentiríais sentirían	sienta sientas sienta sintamos sintáis sientan	sintiera sintieras sintiera sintiéramos sintierais sintieran	siente tú, no sientas sienta usted sintamos sentid vosotros, no sintáis sientan Uds.
volver (ue) volviendo vuelto	vuelvo vuelves vuelve volvemos volvéis vuelven	volvía volvías volvía volvíamos volvíais volvían	volví volviste volvió volvimos volvisteis volvieron	volveré volverás volverá volveremos volveréis volverán	volvería volverías volvería volveríamos volveríais volverían	vuelva vuelvas vuelva volvamos volváis vuelvan	volviera volvieras volviera volviéramos volvierais volvieran	vuelve tú, no vuelvas vuelva usted volvamos volved vosotros, no volváis vuelvan Uds.

APÉNDICE 3

SPANISH TO ENGLISH VOCABULARY

This vocabulary includes all words presented in the text, except for proper nouns spelled the same in English and Spanish, diminutives with a literal meaning, typical expressions of the Hispanic countries presented in the **Enfoque cultural,** and cardinal numbers (found on pages 14 and 15). Other cognates and words easily recognized because of the context are not included either.

The number following each entry corresponds to the **lección** in which the word was first introduced. Numbers in italics followed by *r* signal that the item was presented for recognition rather than as active vocabulary.

A

a   *at, to* P
abajo   *below* 4r
el/la abogado/a   *lawyer* 9
el abrigo   *coat* 6
la abuela   *grandmother* 4
el abuelo   *grandfather* 4
aburrido/a   *boring* 1
aburrirse   *to be bored* 7r
acceder   *to agree* 10r
el acceso   *access* 9r
el accidente   *accident* 9r
la acción   *action* 8r
el aceite   *oil* 10
la aceituna   *olive* 10r
aceptar   *to accept* 8r
aclarar   *to clarify* 8r
acompañar   *to accompany* 8
aconsejable   *advisable* 12r
aconsejar   *to give advice* 5r, 10
acostar(se)   *to go to bed, to lie down* 7
acostar (ue)   *to put to bed* 7
acostumbrado/a   *used to* 10r
la actitud   *attitude* 5r
la actividad   *activity* 1r
el actor/la actriz   *actor/actress* 3r; 9
la actualidad   *present time* 4r
actualmente   *at the present time* 9
acuático/a   *adj. water* 7r
adecuado/a   *appropriate* 4r
adelante   *forward* 9r; más adelante *later on* 11r
adelgazar   (c) *to lose weight* 10r
adepto/a   *follower* 7r
el aderezo   *salad dressing* 10
adicional   *additional* 4r

administrativo/a   *administrative* 5r
el/la adolescente   *adolescent* 4r
¿Adónde?   *Where (to)?* 3
adornado/a   *decorated* 8r
la aduana   *customs* 12
adulto/a   *adult* 3r
la aerolínea   *airline* 12
afeitar(se)   *to shave* 7
el/la aficionado/a   *fan* 7
afirmativamente   *in the affirmative* 5r
las afueras   *outskirts* 5
la agencia de viajes   *travel agency* 12
la agenda   *agenda* 3r
el/la agente   *agent* 5r
el/la agente de viajes   *travel agent* 12
agradable   *nice* 2
agrícola   *agricultural* 9r
agrio/a   *sour* 10
el agua   *water* 3
el aguacate   *avocado* 10
ahí   *there* 1r
el/la ahijado/a   *godchild* 4
ahora   *now* 2
ahorrar   *to save* 6r
el aire acondicionado   *air conditioning* 5
al aire libre   *outdoors* 3
el ají   *pepper* 10r
el ajiaco   *type of soup* 4r
el ajo   *garlic* 10
al   *to the (contraction of a + el)* 3
la alarma   *alarm* 5r
alcohólico/a   *alcoholic* 10r
alegrarse (de)   *to be glad (about)* 11
alegre   *happy, glad* 2
la alegría   *joy* 8
el alfabeto   *alphabet* Pr
la alfombra   *carpet, rug* 5

el alga   *seaweed* 10r
algo   *something* 1
el algodón   *cotton* 6
algunos/as   *any, some* 5r
la alimentación   *diet* 10r
alimentar   *to feed* 10r
el alimento   *food* 5r
allá   *over there* 5
allí   *there* 1r, 3r, 5
el almacén   *department store* 6
la almohada   *pillow* 5
almorzar (ue)   *to have lunch* 4
¿Aló?   *Hello* 3
el almuerzo   *lunch* Pr, 3
el alojamiento   *lodging* 12r
alquilar   *to rent* 3
el alquiler   *rent* 5r
el altar   *altar* 8r
alto/a   *tall* 2
el/la alumno/a   *student* 1
el ama de casa   *housewife, homemaker* 9
el/la amante   *lover* 8r
amazónico/a   *Amazonian* 6r
ambicioso/a   *ambitious* Pr
ambiental   *environmental* 8r
americano/a   *American* 3r
el/la amigo/a   *friend* P
la ampliación   *enlargement, expansion* 1r
amueblado/a   *furnished* 5r
añadir   *to add* 6r, 10
ancho/a   *wide* 6
andino/a   *Andean* 6r
la angustia   *anguish* 12r
el anillo   *ring* 6
el anisado   *anisette (licor)* 3r
el aniversario   *anniversary* Pr

anotar *to jot down 6r*
el año *year P*
el antepasado *ancestor 8*
anterioridad: con anterioridad *in advance 8r*
antes *adv. in advance, before 1r; 8*
el antibiótico *antibiotic 11r*
antiguo/a *former, old 8*
antipático/a *unpleasant 2*
la antropología *anthropology 1*
anual *annual 7r*
el anuncio *ad (advertisement) 9*
apagar *to extinguish, to turn off 9*
el apartado postal (de correos) *P.O. box 9r*
el apartamento *apartment 1r, 5*
el apetito *appetite 10r*
aplaudir *to applaud 7*
el apoyo *support 9r*
aprender *to learn 1r*
apropiado/a *appropriate 4r*
aprovechar *to take advantage 7*
aquí *here 5*
el árbitro *umpire, referee 7*
el árbol *tree 4r, 7*
la arena *sand 7r*
arenoso/a *sandy 7r*
el arete *earring 6*
argentino/a *Argentinean 2*
el argumento *argument 12r*
el armario *closet, armoire 5*
la arqueología *archaeology 8r*
arqueológico/a *archaelogical 8r*
el/la arquitecto/a *architect 9*
arquitectura *architecture 1*
arreglar *to fix, to repair 9r*
arriba *above 5r*
arrogante *arrogant Pr*
el arroz *rice 3*
artesanal *adj. handicrafts 10r*
la artesanía *handicraft 10*
la arveja *pea 10r*
el ascensor *elevator 5r*
el aserrín *sawdust 8r*
el asesinato *assassination, murder 12r*
la asfixia *asphyxia 12r*
así *this way 6*
el asiento *seat 12*
la asistencia *attendance 7r*
el aspecto *appearance 8r*
la aspiradora *vacuum cleaner 5*
la aspirina *aspirin 11*
el/la astronauta *astronaut 9r*
la atención *attention, service 3r*
atender (ie) *to answer, to attend 9*
aterrorizar (c) *to terrorize 9r*
el/la atleta *athlete 7r*
atlético/a *athletic Pr*
la atmósfera *atmosphere 7*

el atractivo *attraction 8r; adj. attractive Pr*
atrasado/a *late 12r*
aun *even 9r*
aún *still 9r*
la ausencia *absence 9r*
auténtico/a *authentic 8r*
el auto(móvil)/coche/carro *car 12*
el autobús/bus *bus 12*
la autopista *freeway 12*
el/la autor/a *author 5r*
la autoridad *authority 7r*
autoritario/a *authoritarian 9r*
el/la auxiliar de vuelo *flight attendant 12*
el avance *advance 9r*
la avenida *avenue Pr*
las aves *poultry, foul 10*
el avión *plane 12*
la ayuda *help 4r*
ayudar *to help 5*
azar: el azar *at random 12r*
el/la azúcar *sugar 10*
el azulejo *tile 5r*

B

bailar *to dance 1*
el baile *dance 1r*
la bajada *slope 7r*
bajar *to get off, to come down 7r; bajar de peso to lose weight 3r*
bajo/a *short (in stature) 2*
el balboa *monetary unit of Panamá 1r*
el balcón *balcony 5r*
el baloncesto/basquetbol *basketball 7*
la bañadera *tub 5*
bañar(se) *to take a bath, to bathe 4*
el banco *bank 9*
la banda *band 8r*
la bandeja *tray 10*
el baño *bathroom 5*
el banquete *banquet Pr*
el bar *bar 4r*
barato/a *inexpensive, cheap 6*
la barbacoa *barbecue 5*
el barco *ship/boat 12*
barrer *to sweep 5*
el barrio *neighborhood 5*
básicamente *basically 4r*
bastante bien *a lot 10r*
la basura *garbage, trash 5*
la bata *robe 6*
el bate *bat 7*
la batería/el acumulador *battery 12*
batir *to beat 10*
el bautizo *baptism, christening 4*

beber *to drink 3*
la bebida *drink 3*
el béisbol *baseball 7*
el beneficio *benefit 5r*
la biblioteca *library 1*
el/la bibliotecario/a *librarian 9*
los bienes *goods 9r; bienes raíces real estate 5r*
bilingüe *bilingual 2*
el billete *ticket 3r*
la billetera *wallet 6*
la biología *biology 1r*
el bistec *steak 3*
la blusa *blouse 6*
la boca *mouth 11*
la boda *wedding 8*
el boleto/pasaje *ticket 12*
el bolígrafo *ballpoint pen P*
el bolívar *monetary unit of Venezuela 1r*
el boliviano *monetary unit of Bolivia 1r*
los bolos *bowling 7*
la bolsa *purse 6*
el/la bombero/a *firefighter 9*
bonito/a *pretty 2*
el borde *edge 10r*
el borrador *eraser P*
el bosque *forest 5r; bosque tropical rain forest 5r*
la bota *boot 6*
el bote *boat 10r*
la botella *bottle 10*
brasileño/a *Brazilian 7r*
el brazo *arm 11*
buena suerte *good luck 1*
la bufanda *scarf 6*
busca: en busca de *in search of 9r*
buscar *to look for 1*
la butaca *armchair 5*
el buzón *mailbox 12*

C

el cabello *hair 11*
la cabeza *head 11*
cada *adj. each, every 1r; each 7*
cada... horas *every . . . hours 11*
la cadera *hip 11*
caer bien *to like 6r*
caer(se) *to fall 11*
café *brown eyes 2*
el café *coffee 1r; plus café after dinner drink 3r*
el café *coffee house 1; coffee 3*
la cafetería *cafeteria 1*
la caída *drop 6r*
la caja *cash register 9r; box 12r*
la caja fuerte *safe box 12*

el/la cajero/a *cashier* 9
el calcetín *sock* 6
el calcio *calcium 10r*
la calculadora *calculator* P
el cálculo *calculus 1r*
la calefacción *heating* 5
la calidad *quality 5r*
caliente *hot* 3
callado/a *quiet* 2
la calle *street* P
el calor: hacer calor *to be hot (weather) 4r*
la caloría *calorie 10r*
el calzoncillo *boxer shorts* 6
la cama *bed* 5
el camarón *shrimp* 10
el camarote *cabin (on boat) 12r*
cambiar *to change, to exchange* 6
el camello *camel 8r*
el/la caminante *walker 3r*
caminar *to walk* 1
la caminata *walk 10r*
el camino *road, way* 8
el camión *truck 9r*
la camisa *shirt* 6
la camiseta *T-shirt* 6
el camisón *nightgown* 6
el campamento *camp 6r*
la campaña *campaign 9r*
el campeón/la campeona *champion* 7
el campeonato *championship* 7
el campo *field* 7
el canal *channel 7r; canal 12r*
cancelar *to cancel* 12
el cáncer *cancer 3r*
la cancha *court, golf course* 7
la canción *song* 3
cansado/a *tired* 2
el/la cantante *singer 3r*
cantar *to sing* 3
la cantidad *quantity, amount 4r*
cantonés/cantonesa *Cantonese 3r*
la capital *capital 1r*
el capitán/la capitana *captain 7r*
el capó *hood* 12
la cara *face* 11
el carácter *character 8r*
caribeño/a *from the Caribbean 6r*
el cariño *affection, love 5r*
el carnaval *carnival, Mardi Gras* 8
la carne *meat* 10
caro/a *expensive* 6
la carrera *career 1r; race* 7
la carreta *cart, wagon* 8
la carretera *highway* 12
la carroza *float* 8
la carta *menu 3r; letter* 12
el/la cartero/a *letter carrier* 12
la casa *house, home* 1
casado/a *married* 2

casarse *to get married 4r, 4,*
casero/a *adj. house 11r*
el casillero *pigeonhole 5r*
el caso *case 9r*
el catarro *cold* 11
católico/a *Catholic 8r*
la causa *cause 12r*
la cebolla *onion 5r, 10*
la ceja *eyebrow* 11
la celebración *celebration* 8
celebrar *to celebrate* 3
el celular *cellular phone 10r*
el cementerio *cemetery* 8
la cena *dinner, supper* 3
cenar *to have dinner* 3
centrar(se) *to center 10r*
el centro *downtown, center 1r, 5; centro comercial shopping center 5r, 6*
cerca (de) *near (close to)* 5
el cerdo *pork* 10
el cerebro *brain* 11
la ceremonia *ceremony 6r*
la cereza *cherry* 10
la cerveza *beer* 3
el césped *lawn* 5
el/la cesto/a *basket, hoop* 7
el cesto *wastepaper basket* P
[S.L.1]el ceviche *raw fish dish* 3
el champaña *champagne 4r*
la chaqueta *jacket* 6
el cheque de viajero *traveler's check 12; el cheque check 6r*
la chica *girl* P
el chico *boy* P
chileno/a *Chilean* 2
la chimenea *fireplace* 5
chocar (qu) *to crash 12r*
el chocolate *chocolate 3r*
el/la chofer *driver* 9
la chuleta *chop* 10
el churro *deep fried batter 10r*
el ciclismo *cycling* 7
el/la ciclista *cyclist* 7
el cielo *sky 12r*
ciencias *sciences 1; las ciencias políticas political science* 1
el/la científico/a *scientist* 9
cierto *adv. true, certain 1r*
la cima *summit, top 8r*
el cine *movies* 3
la cintura *waist* 11
el cinturón *belt* 6
la circunstancia *circumstance 5r*
el/la cirujano/a *surgeon 11r*
la ciudad *city 1r, 3*
la civilización *civilization 4r*
¡Claro! *of course* 5
el/la cliente/a *client 6r, 9*
la clínica *clinic, hospital 11r*

la cocina *kitchen* 5
cocinado/a *cooked 10r*
cocinar *to cook* 5
el coco *coconut 4r*
el codo *elbow* 11
el cognado *cognate Pr*
la coherencia *coherence 4r*
la colección *collection 4r*
el collar *necklace* 6
colombiano/a *Colombian* 2
el colón *monetary unit of Costa Rica and El Salvador 1r*
de color entero *solid color* 6
el colorido *color 8r; colorful 8r*
la columna *column 4r*
el comedor *dining room* 5
comentar *to comment, to discuss 6r*
comenzar (ie) *to begin* 8, 9
comer *to eat 1r, 3*
cómico/a *comic, funny Pr*
la comida *dinner, supper* 3
el comienzo *beginning* 8
el comino *cumin 10r*
la comisión *commission 7r*
como *adv. as, like 1r*
¿Cómo es? *What is he/she/it like?* P
la cómoda *dresser* 5
cómodo/a *comfortable 3r*
¡Cómo no! *Of course!* 9
¿Cómo se llama usted? *What's your name? (formal)* P
¿Cómo te llamas? *What's your name? (familiar)* P
¿Cómo te va? *How is it going?* 1
el/la compañero/a *partner, classmate Pr, 1*
la compañía/empresa *company* 9
la comparación *comparison 8r*
comparar *to compare 4r*
la comparsa *costumed group* 8
la compensación *compensation 5r*
la competencia *competition 1r*
competir (i) *to compete* 7
complicado/a *complex 10r*
el comportamiento *behavior 9r*
composición *composition 1r*
comprar *to buy* 1
la computadora *computer* P
comunicar(se) (qu) *to communicate 3r, 9*
la comunidad *community 4r*
con *with* 1
el concierto *concert Pr*
la concordancia *agreement 4r*
el concurso *contest 1r*
la condición *condition 10r*
el condimento *condiment 10r*
el condominio *condominium 1r*
la conferencia *lecture 1r*
congelar(se) *to freeze* 7

el congreso *congress, convention 5r*
el conjunto *set, group 12r;*
    adj. joint 9r
conmigo *with me 7*
conocer (zc) *to know, to meet 5*
el/la consejero/a *counselor,*
    adviser 9r
el consejo *advice 11r*
el/la conserje *concierge 12*
conservado/a *kept, preserved 5r*
considerablemente *considerably 7r*
la construcción *construction 5r*
el consultorio *doctor's office 9, 11*
la contabilidad *accounting 1r*
el/la contador/a *accountant 9*
el contagio *contagion, spreading of a*
    disease 11r
la contaminación *contamination 8r*
contaminado/a *polluted,*
    contaminated 7
contener (g, ie) *to contain 10r*
el contenido *n. contents 4r;*
    contenido adj. controlled 11r
contento/a *happy, glad 2*
contestar *to answer 6*
contigo *with you (familiar) 7*
continuación: a continuación
    below 10r
contra *against 7r*
contrario/a *opposite, contrary 7*
el contraste *contrast 4r*
el contrato *contract 9r*
la conversación *conversation Pr*
conversador/a *talkative 2*
conversar *to talk, to converse 1*
la copa *drink 3r; (stemmed) glass 10*
la copia *copy 6r*
copiar *to copy 1r*
el coraje *courage 12r*
el corazón *heart 11*
la corbata *tie 6*
el córdoba *monetary unit of*
    Nicaragua 1r
correcto/a *correct 4r*
correr *to run 3*
correspondiente *corresponding 7r*
la corrida (de toros) *bullfight 1r, 8*
cortar *to cut 5r, 9*
la cortesía *courtesy Pr*
la cortina *curtain 5*
corto/a *short (in length) 2*
la cosa *thing 1r*
el cosmético *cosmetic 6r*
cosmopolita *cosmopolitan 6r*
costar (ue) *to cost 4*
la costilla *rib 10*
la costumbre *custom 8*
crear *to create 4r*
creativo/a *creative Pr*
creer *to believe 5*

la crema *cream 10*
el crimen *crime 8r*
criollo/a *adj. Spanish American 3r*
el crucero *cruise 6r, 12*
el cuaderno *notebook P*
la cuadra *city block 12*
el cuadro *picture 5*
de cuadros *plaid 6*
cuando *adv. when 1r*
¿Cuánto cuesta? *How much is it? 1*
cuarto *quarter P*
el cuarto/dormitorio *bedroom 5*
cubano/a *Cuban 2*
el cubo: en cubitos *in cubes 10r*
la cucharada *spoon(full) 10r*
la cucharadita *teaspoon 10r*
la cuchara *spoon 10*
la cucharita *teaspoon 10*
el cuchillo *knife 10*
la cueca *typical Chilean music 12r*
el cuello *neck 11*
la cuenta: cuenta corriente *checking*
    account 9r
de cuero *leather 6*
cuidar(se) *to take care of 5r, 11*
la cumbia *Colombian music and*
    dance 4r
el cumpleaños *birthday Pr, 3*
el/la curandero/a *quack doctor 11r*
la curiosidad *curiosity 1r*
curioso/a *curious 5r*
el currículum *résumé 9*
el cursillo *short course of studies 12r*
el curso *course 1r*

D

dar *to give, to hand 6*
de *of, from 2*
debajo (de) *under P*
deber *ought to, should 3*
débil *weak 2*
decir (g, i) *to say, tell 4*
el dedo *finger 11*
la defensa *defense 11r*
dejar *to leave (behind) 5r; to leave 9*
delante de *in front of 9r*
delgado/a *thin 2*
la delincuencia *delinquency 8r*
del *of the (contraction of de + el)*
    1r, 2
el demostrativo *demonstrative 5r*
el/la dentista *dentist 11r*
dentro *inside, in 4r*
el departamento *department 1r*
el/la dependiente/a *salesperson 1*
el/la deportista *sportsman/woman 7r*
deportivo/a *adj. sport 1r*
deprimido/a *depressed 11*

la derecha *right 4r*
[S.L.2]desayunar *to have breakfast 4*
el desayuno *breakfast 3*
descansar *to rest 3*
el descanso *rest 7r*
desconocido/a *unknown 9r*
describir *describe 1r*
la descripción *description Pr*
el descuento *discount 6r*
desde luego *of course 7r*
desear *to wish, to want 2*
desempleado/a *unemployed 9r*
desfile de moda *fashion show 6r*
el desfile *parade 8*
el desierto *desert 3r*
desorganizado/a *disorganized 9r*
despacio *slowly Pr*
la despedida *farewell Pr*
despejado/a *clear 7*
el despertador *alarm clock 7r*
despertar(se) (ie) *to wake up 7*
después *after, later 1r; then 4r*
el destino *destination 3r, 12*
detener (g, ie) *to stop 7r*
el deterioro *damage 7r*
determinado/a *specific 6r*
detrás (de) *behind P*
el día *day P*
el/la diabético/a *diabetic 10r*
el diablo *devil 8r*
el diálogo *dialog 5r*
el diámetro *diameter 10r*
el dibujo *drawing 4r*
el diccionario *dictionary 1*
el diente *tooth 11*
la diferencia *difference 3r*
diferente *different 1r*
difícil *difficult 1*
difunto/a, muerto/a *dead 8*
dinámico/a *dynamic Pr*
el dinero *money 3r, 6*
Dios *God 8r*
la dirección *address P; direction 12r*
el directorio *directory 5r*
la discoteca *dance club 1*
discutir *to argue 7*
el/la diseñador/a *designer 5r*
diseñar *to design 9r*
el diseño *design 1r*
el disfraz *costume 8r*
disfrazarse *to wear a costume 8*
la distancia *distance 12r*
disuelto/a *dissolved 10r*
la diversión *entertainment 3r*
diverso *diverse, different 5r*
divertido/a *funny, amusing 2*
divertirse (ie, i) *to have a good*
    time 8; to have a good time/fun 3r
doblar *to fold 5; to bend 11r;*
    to turn 12

doble   *double 5r*
el/la doctor/a   *doctor Pr*
doler (ue)   *to hurt 11*
doméstico/a   *domestic 4r*
el/la dominicano/a   *Dominican 2, 11r*
dónde   *interrog. where 1r*
¿Dónde está...?   *Where is . . . ? P*
[S.L.3]dormir (ue)   *to sleep 4;* dormir la siesta *to take a nap 4*
dormirse (ue)   *to fall asleep 7*
la droga   *drug 8*
la ducha   *shower 5*
dudar   *to doubt 10*
el dulce   *candy/sweets 10*
durante   *during 1r*
durar   *to last 7*
duro/a   *hard 10r*
el/la camarero/a   *waiter/waitress 3*

E

ecológico/a   *ecological 7r*
la economía   *economics 1; economy 2r; inexpensive* [S.L.4]*5r*
ecuatoriano/a   *Ecuadorian 10r*
el edificio   *building 1r, 5*
educado/a   *educated 5r*
el efecto   *effect 10r*
eficiente   *efficient Pr*
el/la ejecutivo/a   *executive 9*
el ejemplo   *example 1r*
el ejercicio   *exercise 4r*
él   *he P*
el/la electricista   *electrician 9*
eléctrico/a   *electric 3r*
electrónico/a   *electronic 3r*
elegante   *elegant Pr*
eliminar   *to eliminate 10r*
ella   *she P*
ellos/ellas   *they 1*
embarazada   *pregnant 11r*
la emergencia   *emergency 9r*
emocionado/a   *excited 7*
la empanada   *small meat pie 10r;* empanadas salteñas *typical Bolivian meat pies 10r*
empezar (ie, c)   *to begin, start 3r; to begin, to start 4*
el/la empleado/a   *employee 9, 12*
en   *in P*
en efectivo   *cash 6*
en punto   *sharp P*
en realidad/realmente   *in fact, really 9*
enamorarse   *to fall in love 11r*
encantado/a   *delighted P*
encantar   *to delight, to love 6*
el encanto   *charm 1r*
encerrado/a   *locked up 12r*

encerrar (ie)   *to lock up 8*
el encierro (de los toros)   *penning (of bulls) 8r*
encima   *on top 10r*
encontrar (ue)   *to find 6*
la energía   *energy 1r*
enfermarse   *to become sick 11*
la enfermedad   *illness 11*
el/la enfermero/a   *nurse 9*
enfermo/a   *adj. sick 3r; sick 11*
enfrente (de)   *in front of P*
enfriar   *to cool down 10r*
engordar   *to gain weight 10r*
enharinado/a   *lightly covered with flour 10r*
enlatado/a   *canned 10r*
enojado/a   *angry 2*
la ensalada   *salad 3*
enseguida   *immediately 6*
entender (ie)   *to understand 4*
entonces   *then 8*
el entorno   *surroundings*[S.L.5] *7r*
la entrada   *appetizer 3r; ticket for admission 3r, 8; entrance 5r*
entrar   *to go in, to enter 6*
entre   *between, among P*
entregar   *to deliver 5r*
el/la entrenador/a   *coach 7*
el entrenamiento   *training 10r*
el entretenimiento   *entertainment 3r*
la entrevista   *interview 9*
el/la entrevistador/a   *interviewer 9r*
entrevistar   *to interview 4r*
el entusiasmo   *enthusiasm 10r*
enviar   *to send 9*
el episodio   *episode 4r*
el equipaje   *luggage 12*
el equipo   *team 7*
eres   *you are (familiar) P*
es   *you are (formal), he/she is P*
la escala   *stopping point 12r*
el escaparate   *shop window 6r*
la escasez   *lack, scarcity 7r*
la escena   *scene 8r*
escoger (j)   *to choose 1r*
escolar   *adj. school 4r*
escribir   *to write 3*
el escritorio   *desk P*
escuchar   *to listen Pr; to listen (to) 1*
la escuela   *school 1r*
ese/a   *that (adjective) P*
espacial   *adj. space 9r*
el espacio   *space 7r*
espacioso/a   *spacious 5r*
la espalda   *back 11*
español/a   *adj. Spanish 1r, 2*
el español   *n. Spanish Pr, 1*
la especia   *spice 5r*
especial   *special 3r; en especial especially 8r*

la especialidad   *specialty 1r*
la especie   *species 3r*
especificar (qu)   *to specify, to point out 4r*
el espectáculo   *show 3r*
el/la espectador/a   *spectator 7r*
el espejo   *mirror 5; el espejo retrovisor rearview mirror 12*
la esperanza   *hope 10r*
esperar   *to wait for 9; to hope, to expect 10*
las espinacas   *spinach 10*
el espíritu   *spirit, disposition 7r*
la esposa   *wife 4*
el esposo   *husband 4*
el esquí   *skiing, ski 7*
esquiar   *to ski 7*
la esquina   *corner 11r, 12*
está   *he/she is, you are (formal) P*
establecer(se) (zc)   *to establish, to settle 11r*
el estadio   *stadium 3r*
el estado   *state 1r; condition 7r*
estándar   [S.L.6]*standard 10r*
estar   *to be Pr, 1*
estar a cargo   *to be in charge 9r*
estar de acuerdo   *to agree 7*
estar de moda   *to be fashionable 6*
estar en forma   *to keep fit 4r*
estás   *you are (familiar) P*
este/a   *this 1*
el este   *east 1r*
el estéreo   *stereo 5r*
el estilo   *style 5r*
estirar   *to stretch 11r*
esto   *this 4r*
el estómago   *stomach 3r, 11*
estornudar   *to sneeze 11*
la estrategia   *strategy 7r*
estrecho/a   *narrow, tight 6*
el estrés   *stress 12r*
la estructura   *structure 4r*
el/la estudiante   *student P*
estudiantil   *adj student 1r*
estudiar   *to study 1*
el estudio   *study 1r; studying 9r*
estudioso/a   *studious 1*
la estufa   *stove 5*
la etapa   *stage 4r*
el evento   *event 1r*
la evidencia   *evidence 12r*
el examen   *test, examination 1*
examinar   *to examine 11*
excelente   *excellent 1*
excepcional   *exceptional 5r*
la excursión   *excursion 3r*
exhaustivamente   *exhaustingly 12r*
la experiencia   *experience 1r, 9*
el/la experto/a   *expert 7r*
la explicación   *explanation 9r*

la exportación *export 9r*
expresar *to express 10r*
extender(se) (ie) *to extend,*
  to expand 2r
la extinción *extinction 5r*
extranjero/a *adj. foreign 1r*
extrovertido/a *extroverted Pr*

F

fabuloso/a *fabulous, great 3*
fácil *easy 1*
fácilmente *easily 9r*
facturar *to check in (luggage) 12*
la falda *skirt 6*
falso/a *false 1r*
la familia *family Pr*
famoso/a *famous 1r*
fanático/a *fanatic 4r*
fantástico/a *fantastic 3r*
el/la farmacéutico/a *pharmacist 11*
fascinante *fascinating 4r*
la fase *phase 1r*
el fastidio *annoyance 4r*
la fatiga *fatigue 10r*
fatigado/a *fatigued, tired 10r*
la fecha *date P*
felicitar *to congratulate 7r*
feliz *happy 2*
feo/a *ugly 2*
la feria *fair 1r*
la ferretería *hardware shop 6r*
la festividad *festivity 8r*
festivo *festive 8r*
la fibra *fiber 10r*
la fiebre *fever 11*
fielmente *faithfully 7r*
la fiesta *party Pr, 3*
la filosofía *philosophy 1r*
el fin *end 7*
fin de semana *objective 9r[S.L.7]*
el fin de semana *weekend 1*
el final *end 5r*
finalista *finalist 7r*
financiado/a *financed 11r*
la firma *signature 1r*
la física *physics Pr*
físicamente *physically 7r*
el/la fisioterapista *physiotherapist*
  11r
la flor *flower 5r, 7*
la fobia *phobia 12r*
los fondos *money 9r; fund 11r*
la formación *formation 7r*
la fortaleza *fortress 3r*
la fortuna *fortune 1r*
la foto(grafía) *photo 4*
la fotocopiadora *photocopier 9r*
fracturar(se) *to fracture, break 11*

la frase *phrase 8r*
la frecuencia *frequency 1r*
el fregadero *kitchen sink 5*
freír (i) *to fry 10*
la frente *forehead 11*
la fresa *strawberry 10*
fresco/a *cool 7, fresh 10r*
los frijoles *beans 3r*
frío/a *cold 3*
frito/a *fried 3*
la fruta *fruit 3*
la fuente *fountain 1r; source 8r*
fuerte *strong 2*
fumar *to smoke 11*
el fútbol *soccer 7*
el/la futbolista *football player 7r*

G

la gabardina *raincoat 7r*
las gafas de sol *sunglasses 6*
la galleta *cookie 10*
la gamba *shrimp (in Spain) 10r*
el/la ganador/a *winner 7r*
ganar *to win 7*
el garaje *garage 5*
la garganta *throat 11*
la gasolina *gasoline 12r*
gastar *to spend 6*
la gelatina *gelatin 10*
gemelo/a *twin 4*
genealógico/a *genealogical 4r*
generoso/a *generous Pr*
el género *type 4r*
la gente *people 8*
la geografía *geography 1*
el/la gerente (de ventas) *(sales)*
  manager 9
gigante *adj. giant 5r*
el gimnasio *gymnasium 1*
gordo/a *fat 2*
la gorra *cap 6*
la grabadora *tape recorder, cassette*
  player P
el grado *degree 7r; grade 8r*
la graduación *graduation Pr*
gráfico/a *graphic 1r*
gramatical *grammatical 4r*
gran *great 1r*
grande *big 1*
el grano *grain 10r*
la grasa *fat 10r*
la gripe *flu 11*
grueso/a *coarse 7r*
el grupo *group 1r*
el guajolote *turkey 10r*
el guante *glove 6*
la guantera *glove compartment 12*
guapo/a *good-looking, handsome 2*

el guaraní *monetary unit of Paraguay*
  1r; language spoken in Paraguay
  10r
guatemalteco/a *Guatemalan 2*
la guayabera *loose-fitting men's*
  shirt 6r
el/la guía *guide 3r*
la guitarra *guitar 3*
gustar *to be pleasing to, to like 6;*
  le gusta(n) *you (formal) like 2;*
  me gusta(n) *I like 2*
te gusta(n) *you (familiar) like 2; Me*
  gustaría... *I would like . . . 6*
el gusto *liking, taste 6r*

H

había *there was, there were 8*
la habitación *room 5r*
la habitación doble/sencilla
  double/single room 12
el hábito *habit 6r*
hablar *to speak 1*
Hace calor. *It's hot. 7*
hacer (g) *to do, make 1r, 4*
hacer cola *to stand in line 12*
hacer el papel *play the part 6r*
hacer escala *to make a*
  stopover 12
hacer la cama *to make the bed 4*
hacer la maleta *to pack 12r*
hacer preguntas *to ask questions 4r*
hacerse *to become 4r*
hacia *towards, near 8r*
la hamburguesa *hamburger 1r, 3*
la hamburguesería *hamburger*
  place 3r
la harina *flour 10*
hay *there is, there are P*
el helado *ice cream 3*
el hemisferio *hemisphere 10r*
la hermana *sister 4*
el hermano *brother 4*
hervir (ie, i) *to boil 10*
el hielo *ice 7*
la hierba/yerba *herb 3r*
la hija *daughter 4*
el hijo *son 4*
hijo/a único/a *only child 4*
hiperactivo/a *hyperactive 1r*
hípico/a *adj. horse 7r*
hispano/a *Hispanic 1r*
la historia *history 1*
el hombre *man 4r*
el hombre/la mujer de negocios
  businessman/woman 9
el hombro *shoulder 11*
hondureño/a *Honduran 5r*
la hora *hour, time P*

hora americana/inglesa *precise time* Pr
la hora de llegada/salida *arrival/ departure time* 12
hora de salida *dismissal time* 4r
el horario *schedule* Pr
hornear *to bake* 10r
el hospital *hospital* 1r
hoy *today* P
hoy en día *nowadays* 4r, 8
el hueso *bone* 11
el huevo *egg* 3
huevo duro *hard-boiled egg* 10r
humanidades *humanities* 1
húmedo/a *humid, damp* 10r

I

de ida y vuelta *round trip* 12
idealista *adj. idealistic* Pr
la identificación *identification* Pr
la iglesia *church* 1r, 8
igual *adj. the same* 1r; **al igual que** *like, same as* 1r
igualmente *likewise* P
el imperio *empire* 3r
el impermeable *raincoat* 6
importante *important* Pr; **lo importante** *the important thing* 9
impresionante *impressive* 1r
el impuesto *tax* 12r
impulsivo/a *impulsive* Pr
Inapropiado/a *inappropriate* 9r
el/la inca *Inca* 3r
el incendio *fire* 9
incentivar *to encourage, to incite* 7r
inconcluso/a *unfinished* 12r
indeciso/a *undecided* 5r
independencia *independence* 3r
independiente *independent* Pr
indicado/a *indicated, recommended* 8r
indicar *to indicate* 9
inesperado *unexpected* 8r
la infección *infection* 11
infeccioso/a *infectious* 11r
la influencia *influence* 5r
influenciar *to influence* 10r
informal *informal* Pr
informática *computer science* 1
el/la ingeniero/a *engineer* 9
el inglés *English* 1r
ingresar *to be admitted* 1r
el ingreso *income* 9r
el inodoro *toilet* 5
inquieto/a *restless* 7r
el instituto *institute* 9r
el instrumento *instrument* 3r
el/la integrante *member* 11r

inteligente *intelligent* Pr
el/la interesado/a *interested (person), applicant* 9r
interesante *interesting* Pr
interesar *to interest* 6
el/la intérprete *interpreter* 9
íntimo/a *intimate, close* 1r
introducir (zc) *to introduce* 7r
introvertido/a *introvert* Pr
inventar *to invent* 7r
la invitación *invitation* 8
invitar *to invite* 3r, 8
la inyección *injection* 11
ir de compras *to go shopping* 6
ir(se) *to go away, to leave* 7
irónico/a *ironic* 9r
ir *to go* Pr, 3; **ir de compras** *to go shopping* 3r
la isla *island* 6r
el itinerario *itinerary* 12r
la izquierda *left* 4r
a la izquierda/derecha *to the [S.L.8]left/right* 12
el jabón *soap* 5r

J

Januká *Hanukka* 3r
el jardín *backyard, garden* 5
el/la jefe/jefa *boss* 9
el jesuita *Jesuit* 10r
Jesús *Jesus* 8r
el joropo *typical Venezuelan music* 12r
joven *young* 2
el/la joven *young man/woman* 3
la joya *jewel, jewelry* 5r
la joyería *jewelry* 3r
el juego/partido *game* 7
el/la juez *judge* 9
el/la jugador/a *player* 7
jugar (ue) *to play (game, sport)* 4
jugar a los bolos *to bowl* 7
el jugo *juice* 3
el juguete *toy* 6r
la jungla *jungle* 5r
juntos/as *together* 4

L

el labio *lip* 11
el laboratorio *laboratory* 1; **el laboratorio de lenguas** *language lab* 1
lácteo/a *dairy (product), milky* 10
al lado (de) *next to* P
el lago *lake* 7

la lámpara *lamp* 5
la lana *wool* 6
la langosta *lobster* 10
lanzar (c) *to throw* 7r
el lápiz *pencil* P
largo/a *long* 2
[S.L.9]latinoamericano/a *Latin-American* 7r
el lavabo *washbowl, bathroom sink* 5
la lavadora *washer* 5
la lavandería *laundry room* 5r
el lavaplatos *dishwasher* 5
lavar(se) *to wash (oneself)* 4
lavar(se) los dientes *to brush one's teeth* 7
la leche *milk* 3
la lechuga *lettuce* 3
leer *to read* 3
la legumbre *legume, vegetable* 10r
lejos (de) *far (from)* 5
el lempira *monetary unit of Honduras* 5r
los lentes de contacto *contact lenses* 2
el león *lion* 3r
la letra *letter* 9r
levantar *to raise* 7
levantarse *to get up* 4
la libra *pound* 10r
libre *free* 1r
la librería *bookstore* 1
el libro *book* P
el limón *lemon* 10
el limpiaparabrisas *windshield wiper* 12
limpiar *to clean* 5
limpio/a *clean* 5
la lista de espera *waiting list* 12
listo/a *smart, ready* 2
la literatura *literature* 1
la llamada *call* 9
llamar *to call* 3r
la llanta *tire* 12
la llave *key* 12
la llegada *arrival* 8r
me llamo... *my name is . . .* P
llegar *to arrive* 1
llenar *to fill (out)* 9
lleno/a *full* 12
llevar *to wear, to take* 6
llevarse mal *to not get along* 2r
llover (ue) *to rain* 7
la lluvia *rain* 7
la localización *location* 5r
loco/a *crazy* 6r
el/la locutor/a *radio announcer* 9
el logro *accomplishment* 8r
la loma *hill* 5r
la longitud *length* 7r

lo *pron. you, him, it;* **lo** + *adj. the* 1r; **lo que** *what, that which* 1r
la lotería *lottery* 5r
luego *then* 1r; *after* 6r
el lugar *place* Pr; **tener lugar** *to take place* 8r
lujoso/a *luxurious* 6r
luna de miel *honeymoon* 7r
de lunares *polka-dotted* 6

M

la madera *wood* 5r
la madrastra *stepmother* 4
la madre *mother* 4
el/la madrileño/a *person from Madrid* 1r
la madrina *godmother* 4
la madrugada *early morning, dawn* 1r
magnífico/a *great* 6
el maíz/elote *corn* 10
la maleta *suitcase* 12
el maletero *trunk* 12
el maletín *briefcase* 12
malo/a *bad* 1
la mamá *mom* 1r, 4
la mañana *morning* P
mañana *tomorrow* P
mandar *to send* 5r, 9
el mandato *order, command* 9r
manejar *to drive* 12
la manera *way* 4r
el mango *mango* 10r
la mano *hand* Pr, 11; **manos a la obra** *let's get to work* 1r
la manta *blanket* 5
el mantel *tablecloth* 10
mantener (g, ie) *maintain* 8
la mantequilla *butter* 10
el manual *manual* 5r
la manzana *apple* 10
la manzanilla *camomile* 11r
el mapa *map* 1
maquillar(se) *to put on makeup* 7
máquina de escribir *typewriter* 9r; **la máquina fotográfica** *camera* 6r
maravilloso/a *marvelous* 8
la marca *brand name* 6r
la margarina *margarine* 10
el mariachi *Mexican band* 8r
la marinera *typical Peruvian music* 12r
los mariscos *shellfish* 10
el mar *sea* 1r, 3
más o menos *more or less* P
más... que *more . . . than, . . . -er than (e.g., shorter than)* 8
la masa *dough* 10

las matemáticas *mathematics* Pr
el material *material* 8r
materno/a *adj. mother,* 4r
el matrimonio *marriage, wedding* 4r
máximo/a *maximum* 7r
la mayonesa *mayonnaise* 10
el/la mayor *greater* 4r; **la mayor parte** *most* 1r
la mayoría *the majority* 5r
mayor *older* 2
el/la mayor *the oldest* 4
el médano *slope* 7r
media *half* P
la media *average* 12r; *adj. middle* 4r
la media hermana *half sister* 4
mediano/a *average, medium (height)* 2
las medias *stockings, socks* 6
la medicina *medication* 11r
medicina *medicine* 1
[S.L.10]**el/la médico/a** *medical doctor* 9
el medio *means* 2r
el medio hermano *half brother* 4
la megatienda *superstore* 6r
la mejilla *cheek* 11
mejor *best* 7
mejorar *to improve* 9
la melodía *melody* 8
el/la menor *the youngest* 4
menos *minus, to (for telling time)* P
menos... que *less than, fewer than* 8
el mensaje *message* 4r
el menú *menu* 3r
el mercado *market* 6r; **el mercado al aire libre** *open-air market* 6
el merengue *typical music of the Dominican Republic* 11r
el mes *month* P
la mesa *table* P
la mesa de noche *night stand* 5
el método *method* 1r
el metro *subway* 6r, 12; *meter* 6r
mexicano/a *Mexican* 2
mi *my* P
el micrófono *microphone* 9r
el (horno) microondas *microwave oven* 5
el microscopio *microscope* 9r
mientras *while* 8
el milagro *miracle* 8r
el milenio *millennium* 7r
la milla *mile* 3r
minero/a *adj. mining* 9r
mirar *to look (at)* 1
el/la misionero/a *missionary* 10r
lo mismo *the same thing* 7r
el misterio *mystery* 1r
la mochila *backpack* P
el/la modelo *model* 3r

moderno/a *modern* Pr
molestar *to bother, be bothered by* 11
molida/picada *ground beef* 10
monetario/a *monetary* 5r
el monstruo *monster* 9r
montar *to ride* 1
montar en bicicleta *to ride a bicycle* 1
moreno/a *brunet, brunette* 2
el/la moro/a *Moor* 1r
la mostaza *mustard* 10
el mostrador *counter* 12
mostrar (ue) *to show* 6
el motivo *motive* 8r
la moto(cicleta) *motorcycle* 4r
mover (ue) *to move* 8
la movilidad *mobility* 8r
mucho/a *much, a lot* 1r; *much, a lot* 2
mucho gusto *pleased/nice to meet you* P
la mueblería *furniture store* 5r
la muestra *sample* 3r
mundial *worldwide* 7
la muñeca *wrist* 11
el músculo *muscle* 11
el museo *museum* 1r
la música *music* 1r, 3; **música ambiental** *background music* 4r
el/la músico/a *musician* 9r

N

la nación *nation* 3r
nadar *to swim* 3
la naranja *orange* 3
la nariz *nose* 11
la narración *narration* 6r
la natación *swimming* 7r
nativo/a *native* 1r
la naturaleza *nature* 7r
la náusea *nausea* 11r
navegable *navigable* 10r
la navidad *Christmas* 3r
necesitar *to need* 1
negativo/a *negative* 4r
el nervio *nerve* 11
nervioso/a *nervous* 2
nevar (ie) *to snow* 7
nicaragüense *Nicaraguan* 2
la nieta *granddaughter* 4
el nieto *grandson* 4
la nieve *snow* 7
la niñera *nanny* 9r
ninguno/a *not any, none* 7r
el/la niño/a *child* 1r, 4
no (ni)... ni *neither . . . nor* 2
no sé *I don't know* Pr

nocturno/a *adj. night 8r*
el nombre *name Pr*
nominado/a *nominated 8r*
el norte *north 1r*
norteamericano/a *American 1*
nosotros/nosotras *we 1*
la nota *note, grade 1*
notablemente *notably 9r*
la noticia *news 4*
la novia *fiancée, girlfriend 4*
el novio *fiancé, boyfriend 4*
nublado/a *cloudy 7*
nuestro/a(s) *our 1r*
nuevo/a *new 1r, 2; nuevo sol
monetary unit of Peru 1r*
el número *number P*
la nutrición *nutrition 10r*

O

el objetivo *objective 1r*
obra de teatro *play 3r*
el/la obrero/a *worker 9*
obtener (g, ie) *to obtain, to get 3r*
ocupado/a *busy 4*
la oferta *offer 6r*
la oficina *office 1*
ofrecer (zc) *to offer 9*
el oído *(inner) ear 11*
oír (g) *to hear 4*
ojalá *I/we hope 10*
los ojos *eyes 2*
ojos azules *blue eyes 2; ojos verdes
green eyes 2*
la ola *wave 7r*
oliva: de oliva *olive 10r*
la operación *operation 11r*
operar *to operate 11r*
la opinión *opinion 1r*
la oportunidad *opportunity 9*
optimista *adj. optimistic Pr*
la oración *sentence 4r*
el orden *order 4r; el orden público
law and order 9r; la orden order,
command 9r*
ordenado/a *tidy 5*
el ordenador *computer 1r*
ordenar *to tidy up 5*
la oreja *(outer) ear 11*
el/la organizador/a *organizer 10r*
el oro *gold 3r*
la orquesta *orchestra 8*
la ortografía *orthography 4r*
otavaleño/a *from Otavalo,
Ecuador 10r*
otro/a *other, another 1r, 3; otra vez
again Pr, 7r; de vez en cuando now
and then 10r*
oxígeno *oxygen 11r*

P

el/la paciente *patient Pr, 9r*
[S.L.11]el padrastro *stepfather 4*
el padre *father 3r, 4*
los padres *parents 4*
el padrino *godfather 4*
pagar *to pay 6*
la página *page Pr*
el pago *payment 6r*
el país *country 1r; country, nation 3*
la palabra *word Pr*
el palacio *palace 1r*
los palos *golf clubs 7*
el pan *bread 3*
la panadería *bakery 6r*
el pánico *panic 12r*
los pantalones *pants 6*
los pantalones cortos *shorts 6*
las pantimedias *pantyhose 6*
el pañuelo *handkerchief 6*
el papá *dad 4*
la papa *potato 3*
papas chorreadas *Colombian typical
dish 4r; las papas fritas French
fries 3*
la papaya *papaya 10r*
el papel *paper 1r; cambiar de papel
switch roles Pr; hacer el papel play
the part 6r*
el paquete *package 12*
el par *pair 7r; sin par without
equal 1r*
para *for, to 1*
el parabrisas *windshield 12*
el parachoques *bumper 12*
el paraguas *umbrella 6*
paraguayo/a *Paraguayan 10r*
parecer (zc) *to seem 1r, 6*
el parentesco *kinship 4r*
los parientes *relatives 4*
el parque *park 1r*
el párrafo *paragraph 4r*
la participación *participation 8r*
el/la participante *participant 8r*
participar *to participate 1r, 7*
particular: en particular *especially 3r*
el partido *game Pr*
la pasa *raisin 10r*
el pasaje *ticket 3r; passage 9r*
el/la pasajero/a *passenger 12*
el pasaporte *passport 12*
pasar *to go through 4r; to spend
(time) 4; pour 5r; to happen 6r; to
come in 9r; pasarlo bien to have
fun 3r; pasar lista to call roll
Pr; ¿Qué pasa? What's going on? 9r*
[S.L.12]pasar la aspiradora *to
vacuum 5*

pasear *to take a walk, to stroll 4*
el paseo *walk 4r*
de pasillo/ventanilla *aisle/window
seat 12*
pasivo/a *passive Pr*
el pastel *pie, cake 8r*
la pastelería *pastry shop 10*
la pastilla *pill 11*
patinar *to skate 7*
el pavo *turkey 10*
el pecho *chest 11*
pedir (i) *to ask for 4*
peinar(se) *to comb 4*
la pelea *argument 4r*
la película *film 3*
el peligro *danger 5r*
peligroso/a *dangerous 10r*
pelirrojo/a *redhead 2*
el pelo *hair 2*
pelo castaño *brown hair 2*
pelo negro *black hair 2*
la pelota *ball 7*
la peluquería *beauty salon,
barbershop 9[S.L.13]*
el/la peluquero/a *hairdresser 9*
[S.L.14]la península *peninsula 7r*
pensar (ie) *to think 1r, 4*
pensar + inf. *to plan to + [verb] 4*
[S.L.15]peor *worse, worst 8*
la pepa *seed 10r*
el pepino *cucumber 10*
pequeño/a *small 1*
la pera *pear 10*
perder (ie) *to lose 7*
perderse (ie) *to get lost 12*
perdido/a *lost 12r*
perezoso/a *lazy 2*
perfeccionista *perfectionist Pr*
el periódico *newspaper 3*
el/la periodista *journalist,
newspaperman/woman 7r, 9*
permitir *to permit, to allow 10*
pero *but 1, 2*
el/la perro/a *dog 4r, 5*
perseguir *to chase 8r*
el personaje *character 8r;
person 9r*
la perspectiva *perspective 9r*
peruano/a *Peruvian 2*
el pescado *fish 3*
pesimista *pessimist Pr*
el peso *weight 3r*
la pestaña *eyelash 11*
el petróleo *petroleum, oil 6r*
el/la pianista *pianist 8r*
picado/a *chopped, ground 10r*
la piedra *stone 6r*
el pie *foot 10r, 11; a pie on
foot 10r*
la piel *skin 11r*

la pierna   *leg* 3r, 11
la pieza   *piece, object* 5r
pilotear   *to pilot, to fly* 12r
el/la piloto   *pilot* 9r
la pimienta   *pepper* 10
el pimiento verde   *green pepper* 10
la piña   *pineapple* 10
la piñata   *pottery filled with candies* 8r
pintado/a   *painted* 12r
el pintor   *painter* 5r
la piscina   *swimming pool* 5
el piso   *floor* 5
la pista   *clue* 1r; *slope, court, track* 7
el/la piyama   *pajama* 6r
la pizarra   *chalkboard* P
la pizzería   *pizza place* 4r
la placa   *plates* 12
el placer   *pleasure* 8r
planchar   *to iron* 5
planear   *to plan* 12r
el planeta   *planet* 5r
el plano/a   *plan* 5r; *level* 10r
la planta baja   *first floor* 5
plástico/a   *plastic* 9r
la plata   *silver* 10r
el plátano/la banana   *banana* 10
el plato   *dish, plate* 5, 10
la playa   *beach* 1
la plaza (de toros)   *bullring* 8
el pliegue   *fold* 10r
el/la plomero/a   *plumber* 9
poblado/a   *inhabited* 8r
pobre   *poor* 2
poder (ue)   *to be able to, can* 4
el poema   *poem* 1r
el/la poeta   *poet* 9r
la polémica   *polemic* 7r
el policía/la (mujer) policía   *policeman, policewoman* 9
el poliéster   *polyester* 6
el/la político/a   *politician* 2r; *political adj.* 1r
la pollera   *typical Panamanian dress* 12r
el pollo   *chicken* 3
el polo   *pole* 5r
poner (g)   *to put, to turn on* 4
poner la mesa   *to set the table* 4
ponerse   *to put on* 6
popularidad   *popularity* 7r
popular   *popular* Pr
por   *by,* 1r; por eso *that's why* 1r; por ejemplo *for instance* 1r; por lo menos *at least* 1r; por lo tanto *therefore* 10r
por cierto   *by the way* 9
por correo   *by mail* 9r, 9
por lo menos   *at least* 1r

[S.L.16]
la porción   *portion* 10r
portugués/a   *Portuguese* 1r
las Posadas   *Hispanic festivities* 8r
positivo/a   *positive* 5r
el postre   *dessert* 3r
la práctica   *practice* 1r; *adj. practical* 9r
practicar   *to practice* 1
el precio   *price* 6
precioso/a   *precious* 6r; *beautiful* 6
precisamente   *precisely* 7r
la precisión   *precision* 4r
predilecto/a   *favorite* 7r
preferir (ie)   *to prefer* 1r, 4
la pregunta   *question* Pr
el premio   *award, prize* 6r
preocupar(se)   *to worry* 10r
la preparación   *preparation* 1r
preparar   *to prepare* 5
el preparativo   *preparation* 5r, 8
presente   *present, here* Pr
prestar   *to lend* 6r
primario/a   *elementary* 5r
primero/a   *first* 1r
el/la primo/a   *cousin* 4
el príncipe   *prince* 5r
privado/a   *private* Pr
privilegiado/a   *exceptional* 7r
probablemente   *probably* 3r
probarse (ue)   *to try on* 6
el problema   *problem* Pr
la procesión   *procession* 8
el/la profesor/a   *professor* P
el programa   *program* 1r
programar   *to program* 12r
la prohibición   *prohibition* 7r
prohibir   *to prohibit, to forbid* 10
prolongado/a   *lengthy* 10r
la promesa   *promise* 7r
el pronombre   *pronoun* 1r
propio/a   *own* 9
la provincia   *province* 8r
la (p)sicología   *psychology* 1
el/la (p)sicólogo/a   *psychologist* 9
el/la psiquiatra   *psychiatrist* 9r
la publicidad   *advertisement* 9r
público/a   *public* 1r
el pueblo   *town* 8
el puente   *bridge* 9r
la puerta   *door* P
la puerta (de salida)   *gate* 12
puertorriqueño/a   *Puerto Rican* 2
pues   *(interj.) well* 3r
el puesto   *position* 9
el pulmón   *lung* 11
la pulsera   *bracelet* 6
la puntuación   *punctuation* 6r
puntual   *punctual* 7r
el pupitre   *student's desk* P

Q

que   *that* 1r, 2; lo que *what* 1r
quedar   *to fit, to be left over* 6
la quema   *burning* 8r
querer (ie)   *to want* 1r, 4
¿de quién?   *whose?* 2
¿En qué puedo servirle(s)?   *How may I help you?* 6
¿Quién es...?   *Who is . . . ?* P
¡Qué lástima!   *What a pity!* 1
¡Qué pena!   *What a pity!* 8
¿Qué te/le(s) pasa?   *What's wrong (with you)?* 11
¿Qué tiempo hace?   *What's the weather like?* 7
la química   *chemistry* 1r
químico/a   *chemical* 9r
Quisiera...   *I would like . . .* 6
quitar   *to take away, to remove* 7
quitar(se)   *to take off* 7
quizá(s)/tal vez   *maybe* 10

R

el radiador   *radiator* 12r, 12
el/la radio   *radio* 5
el ramadán   *Ramadan* 3r
rápido/a   *fast* 3
la raqueta   *racket* 7
el rato   *time* 3r
la razón   *reason* 4r
de rayas   *striped* 6
realizar (c)   *to carry out* 4r; *to take place* 5r
realmente   *really* 4r
la rebaja   *sale* 6
rebajado/a   *marked down* 6
rebelde   *rebellious* Pr
la recepción   *reception* 6r; *front desk* 12
el/la recepcionista   *receptionist* 9r
el receso   *recess* Pr
la receta   *recipe* 10; *prescription* 11
recetar   *to prescribe* 11
el recibo   *receipt* 9r
recién   *adv. recently* 11r
recoger (j)   *to pick up* 5
recomendar   *to recommend* 10
recordar (ue)   *to remember* 8
el recuerdo   *memory* 8r
el recurso   *resource* 6r
la red World Wide Web   7r, 7
la referencia   *reference* 4r
referir(se) (ie, i)   *to refer* 5r
el refresco   *soda* 3
el refrigerador   *refrigerator* 5
regalar   *to give (a present)* 6
el regalo   *present* 6

regar (ie)   to water 5
regatear   to bargain 6r
la región   region 1r
regresar   to come back 5
la reja   iron grill 5r
la relación   relationship 4r
religioso/a   adj. religious Pr
el relleno   filling 10r
el reloj   clock P
el remedio   remedy 11r
la reparación   reparation, repair 7r
repente: de repente   suddenly 8r
el/la reportero/a   reporter 7r
el reposo   rest 11r
el/la representante   representative 5r
representar   to represent 7
de res   beef/steak 10
la reserva   reserve 3r
reservado/a   reserved 12r
reservar   to make a reservation 8r, 12
el/la residente   resident 5r
resolver (ue)   to solve 6r
respecto: con respecto a   in relation
    to 4r
respetar   to respect 8
respirar   to breathe 11
responsable   responsible Pr
el resto   rest 4r
el resultado   result, outcome 4r
en resumen   to summarize 4r
la reunión   meeting, gathering 3
reunirse   to get together 8
revisar   to inspect 12
la revisión   revision, inspection 1r
la revista   magazine 1r, 3
el rey/la reina   king/queen 8
rico/a   rich, wealthy 2
el riesgo   risk, danger 9r
la riqueza   wealth 1r
el robot   robot 3r
la roca   rock 7r
la rodilla   knee 11
la ropa   clothing 5r; ropa interior
    underwear 6r
rubio/a   blond 2
la rueda   wheel 12
el ruido   noise 8
las ruinas   ruins 3r

S

la sábana   sheet 5
saber   to know 5
sacar (qu)   to get, to take (out) 1
sacar fotos   to take photos 12r
el saco   blazer 6
la sal   salt 4r, 10
la sala   living room 5
salir (g)   to leave 3r, 4

la salsa de tomate   tomato sauce 10
la salud   health 7r
saludable   healthy 10r
el saludo   greeting Pr
salvadoreño/a   Salvadoran 5r
la sandalia   sandal 6
la sangre   blood 11
sano/a   healthy 10r, 10
la sardana   typical Catalonian
    dance 1r
el secador   hairdryer 9r
la secadora   dryer 5
secar   to dry 5; secarse to dry
    oneself 4
la sección   section 3r
seco/a   dry 5
secundario/a   secondary 1r
la seda   silk 6
sedentario/a   sedentary 10r
seguido/a   followed 8r
seguidor/a   follower 10r
seguir (i)   to follow, to go on 4
seguir derecho   to go straight
    ahead 12
segundo/a   second 1r
la seguridad   safety, security 5r, 8
el seguro   insurance 6r; adj. sure 5r;
    n. safe 12r
la selección   selection 7r
el sello   stamp 12
la selva   jungle 6r
la semana   week P
Semana Santa   Holy Week 1r
semejante   similar 4r
la semejanza   similarity 4r
la semilla   seed 8r
el/la senador/a   senator 1r
la señal   signal 9
el señor   lord 8r
señor (Sr.)   Mr. P
señora (Sra.)   Mrs. P
señorita (Srta.)   Miss P
sentar(se) (ie)   to sit down 7
sentimental   sentimental Pr
el sentimiento   feeling 5r
sentir (ie, i)   to feel 5; to be sorry 11
sentirse (ie, i)   to feel 11
ser   to be Pr, 2
la serie   series 4r
serio/a   serious Pr, 11
la servilleta   napkin 10
servir (i)   to serve 3r, 4
severo/a   severe, serious 12r
el sexo   sex 8
si   if 1r, 3
sí   yes P
el siglo   century 1r
el significado   meaning 7r
siguiente   adj. following 1r
la silla   chair P

simbolizar   to symbolize 8r
el símbolo   symbol 8r
simpático/a   nice, charming 2
simplemente   simply 4r
simultáneamente   simultaneously 9r
sin   without 7
sin embargo   nevertheless 9
sincero/a   sincere Pr
el síntoma   symptom 11
la sirena   siren 9r
la situación   situation, location 4r
sobre   on, above P
el sobre   envelope 12
la sobrina   niece 4
el sobrino   nephew 4
la sociología   sociology 1
el sodio   sodium 10r
el sofá   sofa 5
el sol   sun 7
solicitar   to apply (for) 9
la solicitud   application 9
sólo   adv. only 1r
solo/a   adj. one 6r
soltero/a   single 2
la solución   solution 6r
el sombrero   hat 6
el somnífero   sleeping pill 11r
son   they, you (plural) are P
la sopa   soup 3
el sostén   bra 6
soy   I am P
su   his, her, their, your (formal) 1
suave   soft 8
subir   to go up 8r; to increase 10r;
    subir de peso gain weight 3r
sucio/a   dirty 5
la sudadera   jogging suit, sweatshirt 6
el sueldo   salary 9
el suéter   sweater 6
la sugerencia   suggestion 3r
sumar   to add 1r
la superación   improvement 9r;
    overcoming 2r
superar   to surpass 9r; to
    overcome 12r
el supermercado   supermarket 6r
el sur   south 1r
el sureste   southeast 7r
el/la surfista   surfer 7r
suroeste   southwest 2r
el sustantivo   noun 10r
suyo (-a, -os, -as)   (of) yours, his,
    hers, theirs 5r

T

la tabla   chart 4r; cutting board 5r
el talento   talent 8r
la talla   size 6

el tamaño   *size 4r*
también   *also 1*
tampoco   *adv. neither, nor,
   either 5r*
tan... como   *as . . . as 8*
tan pronto   *as soon as 11r*
tanto/a como   *as much as 8*
tantos/as como   *as many as 8*
tarde   *late 1r, 4*
la tarea   *assignment, homework
   Pr, 1*
la tarjeta de crédito   *credit card 6*
la tarjeta de embarque   *boarding
   pass 12*
la tarjeta postal   *post card 12*
la taza   *cup 10*
el teatro   *theater 3r, 8*
el techo   *roof 8r*
la técnica   *technique 12r*
el/la técnico/a   *adj. technical 9r;
   technician 9*
la tecnología   *technology 8r*
el tejido   *weaving 8r*
la tela   *fabric 6r*
telefónico/a   *adj. telephone 9r*
el teléfono   *telephone Pr, 3*
la telenovela   *soap opera 11r*
la telepatía   *telepathy 3r*
el televisor   *television set P*
temer   *to fear 11*
el temperamento   *temperament 9r*
temprano   *early 4*
tender (ie)   *to hang (clothes); to make
   (a bed) 5*
el tenedor   *fork 10*
tener (g, ie)   *to have Pr, 4;* tener que
   + inf. to have to + verb 1r; tener
   lugar *to take place 8r*
tener deseos de + inf.   *to feel like, to
   want 8*
tener dolor de...   *to have a(n) . . .
   ache 11*
tener mala cara   *to look terrible 11*
Tengo... años.   *I am . . . years old. 2*
tengo/tienes   *I/you have 1*
el/la tenista   *tennis player 7*
el tenis   *tennis Pr, 7*
la tensión (arterial)   *(blood)
   pressure 11*
el tequila   *Mexican liqueur 8r*
el termómetro   *thermometer 11*
la terraza   *terrace 1r, 5*
la tía   *aunt 4*
tibio/a   *lukewarm 10r*
el tiempo   *time Pr;* tiempo libre *free
   time 1r, 3*
la tienda   *store 6*
tiene   *he/she has, you (formal)
   have 2*

tímido/a   *timid Pr*
el tío   *uncle 4*
típico/a   *typical 1r, 3*
el tipo   *type, style, 3r; kind 10r*
el título   *title 4r*
la tiza   *chalk P*
la toalla   *towel 5*
el tobillo   *ankle 11*
tocar   *to touch 3;* tocar un
   instrumento *to play an
   instrument 3*
tolerante   *tolerant 1r*
tomar   *to take, to drink 1*
tomar apuntes   *to take notes 1*
tomar el sol   *to sunbathe 3*
tomar notas   *take notes 1r*
el tomate   *tomato 3*
tonto/a   *silly, foolish 2*
torcer(se) (ue)   *to twist 11*
el torneo   *tournament 7r, 7*
la toronja/el pomelo   *grapefruit 10*
la tortura   *torture 10r*
la tos   *cough 11*
toser   *to cough 11*
la tostada   *toast 3*
trabajador/a   *hardworking 2*
trabajar   *to work 1*
la tradición   *tradition 8*
tradicional   *traditional Pr*
traducir (zc)   *to translate 7*
traer (g)   *to bring 4*
el tráfico   *traffic 12r*
el traje   *suit 6*
el traje de baño   *bathing suit 6*
el traje pantalón   *pantsuit 6*
tranquilizante   *tranquilizer 12r*
tranquilo/a   *calm, tranquil Pr, 2*
transparente   *transparent 9r*
el transporte   *transportation 5r*
el tren   *train 11r, 12*
triste   *sad 2*
el triunfo   *victory 7r*
el trofeo   *trophy 7r*
tropical   *tropical 10r*
tu   *your (familiar) P*
tú   *you (familiar) P*
el túnel   *tunnel 3r*
la túnica   *tunic 8r*
turístico/a   *adj. tourist 7r*
el turno   *turn, shift 11r*

U

la ubicación   *location 5r*
la úlcera   *ulcer 11r*
último/a   *last 8*
un/una   *a, an P*
un poco   *a little 4*

una vez   *once 12*
la unidad   *unity 5r*
unido/a   *united 1r*
el uniforme   *uniform 3r*
la unión   *union 7r*
la universidad   *university 1*
universitario/a   *adj. university 1r*
urbano/a   *urban 12r*
urgente   *urgent 1r*
urgentemente   *urgently 9r*
uruguayo/a   *Uruguayan 7r*
usar   *to use 2*
usted   *you (formal) P;* ustedes *you
   (plural) 1*
la uva   *grape 10*

V

las vacaciones   *vacation 1r, 3*
la vacante   *opening 9*
vacío/a   *empty 12*
la vainilla   *vanilla 10*
valer   *to be worth 6*
valiente   *brave Pr*
valioso/a   *valuable 2r*
el valle   *valley 9r*
el vallenato   *typical Colombian
   music 4r*
el valor   *value, price 3r*
el vaquero   *cowboy 7r*
los vaqueros/jeans   *jeans 6*
variable   *variable, changeable 9r*
la variante   *variant 7r*
varios/as   *various, several 1r*
el vaso   *glass 3r, 10*
el vecindario   *neighborhood 5r*
el/la vecino/a   *neighbor 5r*
el vegetal/la verdura   *vegetable 3*
la vela   *candle 4r*
la velocidad   *speed 12*
la vena   *vein 11*
el/la vendedor/a   *salesman,
   saleswoman 6r, 9*
vender   *to sell 6*
venezolano/a   *Venezuelan 2*
venir (g, ie)   *to come 4*
la ventana   *window P*
la ventanilla   *window 12*
las ventas   *sales 9*
el verbo   *verb 1r*
¿Verdad?   *Right? 1*
la verdura   *vegetable 10*
verificar (qu)   *to verify 4r*
versátil   *versatile 7r*
ver   *to see 1r, 3*
el vestido   *dress 6*
vestir(se) (i)   *to dress, to get
   dressed 4*

el **vestuario** *dressing room* 7r
viajar *to travel* 12
el **video** *video* 1r
la **videocasetera** *VCR* P
viejo/a *old* 2
el **viento** *wind* 7
el **vinagre** *vinegar* 10
el **viñedo** *vineyard* 9r
el **vino** *wine* 3; el **vino tinto** *red wine* 10
la **violencia** *violence* 8
el/la **violinista** *violinist* 8r
la **virgen** *virgin* 8r
virtual *virtual* 3r
la **visa** *visa* 3r

la **visita** *guest* 5r
visitar *to visit* 1r, 4
la **vista** *view* 5r
la **vitalidad** *vitality* 1r
la **vitamina** *vitamin* 10r
vivir *to live* 1r, 3
vivo/a *alive, living* 4r
el **vocabulario** *vocabulary* Pr
el **volante** *steering wheel* 12
volar (ue) *to fly* 5r, 12
el **voleibol** *volleyball* 7
la **voluntad** *will, will power* 2r
volver (ue) *to return* 4
votar *to vote* 12r
el **vuelo** *flight* 3r, 12

Y

y *and* P
ya *already* 3r; **ya que** *since* 8r;
ya sea *whether* 9r
la **yema** *egg yolk* 10r
el **yogur** *yogurt* 10
yo *I* P

Z

la **zanahoria** *carrot* 10
la **zapatilla** *slipper* 6
el **zapato** *shoe* 6

ENGLISH TO SPANISH VOCABULARY [S.L.2]

A

a, an   un/una
above   arriba
absence   la ausencia
to accept   aceptar
access   el acceso
accident   el accidente
accompany   acompañar
accomplishment   el logro
according   según
accountant   el/la contador/a
accounting   la contabilidad
to act   actuar
action   la acción
activity   la actividad
actor/actress   el actor/la actriz
ad (advertisement)   el anuncio
to add   sumar, añadir
additional   adicional
address, direction   la dirección
administrative   administrativo/a
adolescent   el/la adolescente
adult   adulto/a
advance   el avance
advantage   la ventaja
advertisement   la publicidad
advice   el consejo
advisable   aconsejable
affection, love   el cariño
after, later, then   después
again   de vez en cuando [S.L.3]
against   contra
agenda   la agenda
agent   el/la agente
to agree   estar de acuerdo
to agree, access   acceder
agreement   la concordancia
agricultural   agrícola
air conditioned   climatizado/a
air conditioning   el aire
   acondicionado
airline   la aerolínea
aisle/window seat   de
   pasillo/ventanilla
alarm   la alarma
alarm clock   el despertador
alcoholic   alcohólico/a
alive, living   vivo/a
alone   solo/a

alphabet   el alfabeto
already   ya
also   también
altar   el altar
Amazonian   amazónico/a
ambitious   ambicioso/a
American   americano/a,
   norteamericano/a
ancestor   el antepasado
and   y
Andean   andino/a
angry   enojado/a
anguish   la angustia
anisette (licor)   el anisado
ankle   el tobillo
anniversary   el aniversario
annoyance   el fastidio
annual   anual
to answer   contestar
to answer, attend   atender (ie)
anthropology   la antropología
antibiotic   el antibiótico
any, some   algunos/as
apartment   el apartamento
appearance   el aspecto
appetite   el apetito
appetizer, ticket for admission,
   entrance   la entrada
to applaud   aplaudir
apple   la manzana
application   la solicitud
to apply (for)   solicitar
appropriate   adecuado/a, apropiado/a
approval   la aprobación
archaeological   arqueológico/a
archaeology   la arqueología
architect   el/la arquitecto/a
architecture   arquitectura
area   el área
Argentinean   argentino/a
to argue   discutir
argument   el argumento, la pelea
arm   el brazo
armchair   la butaca
arrival   la llegada
arrival/departure time   la hora de
   llegada/salida
to arrive   llegar
arrogant   arrogante
as, like   adv. como

as . . . as   tan... como
as many as   tantos/as como
as much . . . as   tanto/a como
as soon as   tan pronto
ask for   pedir (i)
asphyxia   la asfixia
aspirin   la aspirina
assassination, murder   el asesinato
assignment, homework   la tarea
astronaut   el/la astronauta
at   a
at least   por lo menos
at random   azar, el azar
at the present time   actualmente,
   en la actualidad
athlete   el/la atleta
athletic   atlético/a
atmosphere   la atmósfera
attendance   la asistencia
attention, service   la atención
attitude   la actitud
attractive   atractivo [S.L.4]
aunt   la tía
authentic   auténtico/a
author   el/la autor/a
authoritarian   autoritario/a
authority   la autoridad
avenue   la avenida
average   el promedio
average, medium height   mediano/a
average, middle   adj. la media
avocado   el aguacate
award, prize   el premio

B

back   la espalda
backpack   la mochila
backyard, garden   el jardín
bad   malo/a
to bake   hornear
bakery   la panadería
balcony   el balcón
ball   la pelota
ballpoint pen   el bolígrafo
banana   el plátano/la banana
band   la banda
bank   el banco
banquet   el banquete

baptism, christening el bautizo
bar el bar
barbecue la barbacoa
to bargain regatear
baseball el béisbol
basically básicamente
basket, hoop el/la cesto/a
basketball el baloncesto/basquetbol
bat el bate
bathing suit el traje de baño
bathroom el baño
battery la batería/el acumulador
to be estar, ser; be able to, can
   poder (ue); be admitted ingresar;
   be bored aburrirse; be born nacer
   (zc); be enough bastar; be
   fashionable estar de moda; be glad
   (about) alegrarse (de); be hot
   (weather) hacer calor; be in love
   estar enamorado/a; be pleasing to,
   like gustar; be successful tener
   éxito; be worth valer; be in charge
   estar a cargo; be fit estar en forma
beach la playa
beans los frijoles
to beat batir
beauty salon, barbershop la
   peluquería
to become sick enfermarse
bed la cama
bedroom el cuarto/dormitorio
beef/steak de res
beer la cerveza
before antes
begin, start comenzar (ie), empezar
   (ie, c)
beginning el comienzo
behavior el comportamiento
behind detrás (de)
to believe creer
below abajo, continuación: a
   continuación
belt el cinturón
benefit el beneficio
best mejor
between, among entre
big grande
bilingual bilingüe
biology la biología
biosphere la biosfera
bird el pájaro
birth la natalidad
birthday el cumpleaños
[S.L.5] blanket la manta
blazer el saco
blind ciego/a
(city) block la cuadra
blond rubio/a
blood la sangre
blouse la blusa

[S.L.6] board of directors la directiva
boarding pass la tarjeta de
   embarque
boat el bote
to boil hervir (ie, i)
bone el hueso
book el libro
bookstore la librería
boot la bota
boring aburrido/a
boss el/la jefe/jefa
to bother, be bothered by molestar
bottle la botella
bowl jugar a los bolos
bowling los bolos
boxer shorts el calzoncillo
boy el chico
bra el sostén
bracelet la pulsera
brain el cerebro
branch (business) la sucursal
brand name la marca
brave valiente
Brazilian brasileño/a
bread el pan
to break romper
to break down descomponer
breakfast el desayuno
to breathe respirar
bridge el puente
briefcase el maletín
to bring traer (g)
brother el hermano
[S.L.7] brunet, brunette moreno/a
to brush one's teeth lavar(se) los
   dientes
to build construir (y)
building el edificio
bullfight la corrida (de toros)
bullring la plaza (de toros)
bumper el parachoques
burning la quema
bus el autobús/bus
businessman/woman el hombre/la
   mujer de negocios
busy ocupado/a
but pero
butter la mantequilla
buy comprar
by por; that's why por eso; for
   instance por ejemplo; at least
   por lo menos; therefore por lo
   tanto

C

[S.L.8]cabin (on boat) el camarote
cabin, cockpit la cabina
cafeteria la cafetería

cage la jaula
calcium el calcio
calculator la calculadora
calculus el cálculo
to call la llamada, llamar
calm, tranquil tranquilo/a
calorie la caloría
camel el camello
camomile la manzanilla
camp el campamento
campaign la campaña
to cancel cancelar
cancer el cáncer
candle la vela
candy/sweets el dulce
canned enlatado/a
Cantonese cantonés/cantonesa
cap la gorra
capital la capital
captain el capitán/la capitana
car el auto(móvil)/coche/carro
cardboard (de) cartón
career, race la carrera
Caribbean caribeño/a
carnival, Mardi Gras el carnaval
carpet, rug la alfombra
carrot la zanahoria
to carry out, take place realizar (c)
cart, wagon la carreta
case el caso
cash register, box la caja
cash en efectivo
cashier el/la cajero/a
to catch atrapar
Catholic católico/a
cause la causa
celebrate celebrar
celebration la celebración
cellular phone el celular
cemetery el cementerio
to center centrar(se)
center el centro; shopping center
   centro comercial
century el siglo
ceremony la ceremonia
chair la silla
chalk la tiza
chalkboard la pizarra
champagne el champaña
champion el campeón/la campeona
championship el campeonato
change, exchange cambiar
channel, canal el canal
character el carácter
character, person el personaje
charm el encanto
chart, cutting board la tabla
to chase perseguir
to check in (luggage) facturar
check el cheque

checking account   la cuenta: cuenta corriente
cheek   la mejilla
chemical   químico/a
chemistry   la química
cherry   la cereza
chest   el pecho
chicken   el pollo
child   el/la niño/a
Chilean   chileno/a
chocolate   el chocolate
choose   escoger (j)
chop   la chuleta
chopped, ground   picado/a
Christmas   la navidad
church   la iglesia
circumstance   la circunstancia
city   la ciudad
[S.L.9] civilization   la civilización
to clarify   aclarar
to clean   limpiar; clean   limpio/a
clear   despejado/a
client   el/la cliente, el/la cliente/a
clinic, hospital   la clínica
clock   el reloj
closet, armoire   el armario
clothing   la ropa; underwear   ropa interior [S.L.10]
cloudy   nublado/a
clue   la pista
coach   el/la entrenador/a
coarse   grueso/a
coat   el abrigo
coconut   el coco
coffee, coffee house   el café; after-dinner drink   plus café
cognate   el cognado
coherence   la coherencia
cold   el catarro, frío/a
collection   la colección
Colombian   colombiano/a
Colombian music and dance   la cumbia
Colombian typical dish   papas chorreadas
color, colorful   colorido
column   la columna
to comb   peinar(se)
to come   venir (g, ie)
to come back   regresar
to come from   proceder (de)
comfortable   cómodo/a
comic, funny   cómico/a
to comment, discuss   comentar
commerce   el comercio
commission   la comisión
communicate   comunicar(se) (qu)
community   la comunidad
company   la compañía/empresa
to compare   comparar

comparison   la comparación
compensation   la compensación
to compete   competir (i)
competition   la competencia
complex   complicado/a
composition   composición
computer   la computadora, el ordenador
computer science   informática
concert   el concierto
concierge   el/la conserje
condiment   el condimento
condition   la condición
condominium   el condominio
to congratulate   felicitar
congress, convention   el congreso
considerably   considerablemente
construction   la construcción
contact lenses   los lentes de contacto
contagion, spreading of a disease   el contagio
to contain   contener (g, ie)
contamination   la contaminación
contents,   contenido; controlled   el contenido
contest   el concurso
to continue   continuar
contract   el contrato, el contraste [S.L.11]
conversation   la conversación
to cook   cocinar
cooked   cocinado/a
cookie   la galleta
cool   fresco/a
to cool down   enfriar
to copy   copiar; copy   la copia
corn   el maíz/elote
corner   la esquina
correct   correcto/a
corresponding   correspondiente
cosmetic   el cosmético
cosmopolitan   cosmopolita
cost   costar (ue)
costume   el disfraz
costumed group   la comparsa
cotton   el algodón
cough   la tos, toser
counselor, adviser   el/la consejero/a
counter   el mostrador
country, nation   el país
courage   el coraje
course   el curso
court, golf course   la cancha
courtesy   la cortesía
cousin   el/la primo/a
to cover   cubrir
cowboy   el vaquero
crash   chocar (qu)
crazy   loco/a

cream   la crema
to create   crear
creative   creativo/a
credit card   la tarjeta de crédito
crime   el crimen
crisis   la crisis
crowd   la multitud
cruise   el crucero
Cuban   cubano/a
cucumber   el pepino
cultivation   el cultivo
cumin   el comino
cup   la taza
curiosity   la curiosidad
curious   curioso/a
curtain   la cortina
custom   la costumbre
customs   la aduana
to cut   cortar
cycling   el ciclismo
cyclist   el/la ciclista

D

dad   el papá
dairy (product), milky   lácteo/a
damage   el deterioro
to dance   bailar; dance   el baile
dance club   la discoteca
dancer   el/la bailarín/bailarina
danger   el peligro
dangerous   peligroso/a
data   los datos
date   la fecha
daughter   la hija
day   el día
dead   difunto/a, muerto/a
deaf   sordo/a
decorated   adornado/a
decuple, tenfold   el décuplo
deep-fried batter   el churro
defense   la defensa
deforestation   la deforestación
degree, grade   el grado
to delight, love   encantar
delighted   encantado/a
delinquency   la delincuencia
to deliver   entregar
demonstrative   el demostrativo
dense   denso/a
dentist   el/la dentista
department   el departamento
department store   el almacén
depressed   deprimido/a
to describe   describir
description   la descripción
desert   el desierto
to design   diseñar, el diseño
designer   el/la diseñador/a

desk el escritorio
dessert el postre
destination el destino
devil el diablo
diabetic el/la diabético/a
dialog el diálogo
diameter el diámetro
dictionary el diccionario
to die morir (ue)
diet la alimentación
difference la diferencia
different diferente
difficult difícil
dining room el comedor
dinner, supper la cena, la comida
directory el directorio
dirty sucio/a
discount el descuento
discrimination la discriminación
dish, plate el plato
dishwasher el lavaplatos
dismissal time hora de salida
disorganized desorganizado/a
dissolved disuelto/a
distance la distancia
diverse, different diverso
divorce divorciarse, el divorcio
divorced divorciado/a
to do, make hacer (g); pack hacer la maleta; ask questions hacer preguntas; become hacerse; play the part hacer el papel
doctor el/la doctor/a
doctor's office el consultorio
dog el perro, el/la perro/a
domestic doméstico/a
Dominican dominicano/a, el/la dominicano/a
door la puerta
double doble
double/single room la habitación doble/sencilla
doubt dudar
dough la masa
dove la paloma
downtown, center el centro
drawing el dibujo
dress el vestido
to dress, get dressed vestir(se) (i)
dresser la cómoda
dressing room el vestuario
to drink beber; drink la bebida
drive, manage, handle manejar
driver el/la chofer
drop la caída
drug la droga
drug traffic el narcotráfico
to dry (oneself) secar(se); dry seco/a
dryer la secadora

due to debido a
during durante
dynamic dinámico/a

E

each, every, each adj. cada
ear el oído, la oreja
early temprano
early morning, dawn la madrugada [S.L.12]
earring el arete
easily fácilmente
east el este
easy fácil
to eat comer
ecological ecológico/a
economics, economy, inexpensive la economía
Ecuadorian ecuatoriano/a
edge el borde
educated educado/a
effect el efecto
efficiency la eficiencia
efficient eficiente
egg el huevo
egg yolk la yema
elbow el codo
electric eléctrico/a
electrician el/la electricista
electronic electrónico/a
elegant elegante
elementary primario/a
elevator el ascensor
to eliminate eliminar
e-mail el correo electrónico
to embrace abrazar(se) (c)
emergency la emergencia
emigrant el/la emigrante
to emigrate emigrar
empire el imperio
employee el/la empleado/a
empty vacío/a
to encourage, incite incentivar
end el fin, el final
energetic enérgico/a
energy la energía
engineer el/la ingeniero/a
English el inglés
enlargement, expansion la ampliación
entertainment el entretenimiento, la diversión
enthusiasm el entusiasmo
envelope el sobre
environmental ambiental, el medio ambiente
episode el episodio
equality la igualdad

eraser el borrador
especially particular: en particular
to establish, settle establecer(se) (zc)
even aun
event el evento
every . . . hours cada... horas
evidence la evidencia
to examine examinar
example el ejemplo
excellent excelente
exceptional excepcional, privilegiado/a
excited emocionado/a
excursion la excursión
executive el/la ejecutivo/a
exercise el ejercicio
exhaustingly exhaustivamente
expensive caro/a
experience la experiencia
experiment el experimento
expert el/la experto/a
explanation la explicación
export la exportación
to express expresar
to extend, expand extender(se) (ie)
extinction la extinción
to extinguish, turn off, turn off the lights apagar
extrovert extrovertido/a
eyebrow la ceja
eyelash la pestaña
eyes los ojos; blue eyes ojos azules; brown eyes café; green eyes ojos verdes, ojos (de color)

F

fabric la tela
fabulous, great fabuloso/a
face la cara
factory la fábrica
fair la feria
faithfully fielmente
to fall caer(se); fall asleep dormirse (ue); fall in love enamorarse
false falso/a
family la familia
famous famoso/a
fan el/la aficionado/a
fanatic fanático/a
fantastic fantástico/a
far (from) lejos (de)
farewell la despedida
fascinating fascinante
fashion show desfile de moda, desfile de modas
fast rápido/a
fat gordo/a, la grasa
father el padre

fatigue la fatiga
fatigued, tired fatigado/a
favorite predilecto/a
fear temer
feed alimentar
to feel sentirse (ie, i); **feel, be sorry** sentir (ie, i)
to feel like, want tener deseos de + inf.
feeling el sentimiento
festive festivo
festivity la festividad
fever la fiebre
fiancé, boyfriend el novio
fiancée, girlfriend la novia
[S.L.13] fiber la fibra
field el campo
to fight pelear
figure la cifra
to fill (out) llenar
filling el relleno
film la película
finalist finalista
financed financiado/a
financial financiero
to find encontrar (ue)
finger el dedo
to finish acabar
fire el incendio
firefighter el/la bombero/a
fireplace la chimenea
first primero/a
first floor la planta baja
fish el pescado
fishing la pesca
to fit, be left over quedar
to fix, repair arreglar
flight el vuelo
flight attendant el/la auxiliar de vuelo
float la carroza
floor el piso
flour la harina
flower la flor
flu la gripe
to fly volar (ue)
flying volador
fold el pliegue
to fold, bend, turn doblar
to follow, go on seguir (i)
followed seguido/a
follower adepto/a, seguidor/a
following *adj.* siguiente
food el alimento
foot el pie; **on foot** a pie
football player el/la futbolista
for para
forehead la frente
foreign *adj.* extranjero/a
forest el bosque; **rain forest** bosque tropical

to forget olvidar
fork el tenedor
formation la formación
former, old antiguo/a
formula la fórmula
fortress la fortaleza
fortune la fortuna
forward adelante; **later on** más adelante [S.L.14]
fountain, source la fuente
fracture, break fracturar(se)
free libre; **free time** tiempo libre
freeway la autopista
to freeze congelar(se)
French fries las papas fritas
frequency la frecuencia
fresh fresco/a
fried frito/a
friend el/la amigo/a
front desk la recepción
fruit la fruta
to fry freír (i)
full lleno/a
full, busy nutrido/a
funny, amusing divertido/a
furnished amueblado/a
furniture store la mueblería

G

to gain weight engordar
game el juego/partido, el partido
garage el garaje
garbage, trash la basura
garlic el ajo
gasoline la gasolina
gate la puerta (de salida)
gelatin la gelatina
genealogical genealógico/a
generous generoso/a
genetic genético/a
geography la geografía
gesture el ademán
to get along well llevarse bien; **get lost** perderse (ie); **get married** casarse; **get off, come down** bajar; **lose weight** bajar de peso; **get together** reunirse; **get up** levantarse; **get, take (out)** sacar
ghetto el gueto
giant gigante *adj.*
girl la chica
to give (a present) regalar; **give advice** aconsejar; **give, hand** dar
glass el vaso
glass, drink la copa
glove el guante
glove compartment la guantera

to go ir; **go shopping** ir de compras;
go away, leave ir(se); **go bed, lie down** acostar(se); **go in, enter** entrar; **go shopping** ir de compras; **go straight ahead** seguir (i) derecho; **go through; spend (time); pour, happen, come in have fun [S.L.15]**pasar, pasarlo bien; **call roll** pasar lista; **What's going on?** ¿Qué pasa?; **go up, increase** subir; **gain weight** subir de peso
God Dios
godchild el/la ahijado/a
godfather el padrino
godmother la madrina
gold el oro
golf clubs los palos
good luck buena suerte
good-looking, handsome guapo/a
[S.L.16]goods los bienes; **real estate** bienes raíces
[S.L.17]government el gobierno
gradually gradualmente, paulatinamente
to graduate graduarse
graduation la graduación
grain el grano
grammatical gramatical
granddaughter la nieta
grandfather el abuelo
grandmother la abuela
grandson el nieto
grape la uva
grapefruit la toronja/el pomelo
graphic gráfico/a
great gran, magnífico/a
greater el/la mayor
[S.L.18]green pepper el pimiento verde [S.L.19]
to greet saludar(se)
greeting el saludo
ground beef molida/picada
group el grupo
growth el crecimiento
Guatemalan guatemalteco/a
guest la visita
guide el/la guía
guitar la guitarra
guitar player el/la guitarrista
gymnasium el gimnasio

H

habit el hábito
hair el cabello, el pelo; **black hair** pelo negro; **brown hair** pelo castaño
hairdresser el/la peluquero/a

hairdryer   el secador
half   la mitad, media
half brother   el medio hermano
half sister   la media hermana
hamburger   la hamburguesa
hamburger place   la hamburguesería
hand   la mano; **let's get to work**
   manos a la obra
handicraft   la artesanía; **handicrafts**
   adj. artesanal
handkerchief   el pañuelo
to hang (clothes), make (a bed)
   tender (ie)
Hanukka   Januká
happy   feliz
happy, glad   alegre, contento/a
hard   duro/a
hard-boiled egg   huevo duro,
hardware shop   la ferretería
hardworking   trabajador/a
hat   el sombrero
to hate   odiar
to have (auxiliary verb)   haber, tener
   (g, ie); **have a good time, have a**
   good time/fun divertirse (ie, i);
   have a(n) . . . ache tener dolor
   de...; **have breakfast** desayunar;
   have dinner cenar; **have just + past**
   participle acabar de + inf.; **have**
   lunch almorzar (ue); **have**
   tener (g, ie); **+ inf. have + verb**
   tener que; [S.L.20]**take place**
   tener lugar
[S.L.21] **he**   él
he/she has, you (formal) have   tiene
he/she is, you are (formal)   está
head   la cabeza
health   la salud; **healthy** saludable,
   sano/a
to hear   oír (g)
heart   el corazón
heating   la calefacción
height   estatura
Hello?   ¿Aló?
to help   ayudar; **help** la ayuda
hemisphere   el hemisferio
herb   la hierba/yerba
here   aquí
highway   la carretera
hill   la loma
hip   la cadera
to hire   contratar
his, her, their, your (formal)   su
   [S.L.22]
Hispanic   hispano/a
Hispanic festivities   las Posadas
history   la historia
hole   el agujero
Holy Week   Semana Santa
home   el hogar

Honduran   hondureño/a
honesty   la honestidad
honeymoon   luna de miel
hood   el capó
hope   la esperanza
horse   *adj.* hípico/a
hospital   el hospital
hot   caliente
hour, time   la hora
house, home,   *adj.* casero/a
   [S.L.23]la casa
housewife, homemaker   el ama de
   casa
How is it going?   ¿Cómo te va?
How may I help you?   ¿En qué puedo
   servirle(s)?
How much is it?   ¿Cuánto cuesta?
human being   el ser humano
humanities   humanidades
humid, damp   húmedo/a
to hurt   doler (ue)
husband   el esposo
hyperactive   hiperactivo/a

I

I am . . . years old   Tengo... años
I am   soy
I don't know   no sé [S.L.24]
I   yo
I/we hope   ojalá
I/you have   tengo/tienes
ice   el hielo
ice cream   el helado
idealistic   *adj.* idealista
identification   la identificación
if   si
illiteracy   el analfabetismo; **illiterate**
   analfabeto/a
illness   la enfermedad
immediately   enseguida
immigrant   el/la inmigrante
implant   el implante
important   importante
impressive   impresionante
to improve   mejorar
improvement, overcoming   la
   superación
impulsive   impulsivo/a
in   en
in advance   anterioridad: con
   anterioridad
in advance, before   *adv.* antes
in cubes   el cubo: en cubitos
in fact, really   en realidad/realmente
in front of   delante de, enfrente (de)
in relation   respecto: con respecto a
in search of   busca: en busca de
in the affirmative   afirmativamente

inappropriate   inapropiado/a
Inca   el/la inca
income   el ingreso
incorrect   incorrecto/a
independence   independencia;
   independent independiente
to indicate   indicar
indicated, recommended   indicado/a
inexpensive, cheap   barato/a
infection   la infección
infectious   infeccioso/a
to influence   influenciar, la influencia
informal   informal
inhabitant   el/la habitante
inhabited   poblado/a
injection   la inyección
inside, in   dentro
to inspect   revisar
institute   el instituto
instrument   el instrumento
insurance,   sure (*adj.*), safe (*n.*) el
   seguro
intelligent   inteligente
intention   la intención
to interest   interesar; **interested**
   (person), applicant el/la
   interesado/a; **interesting**
   interesante
interpreter   el/la intérprete
[S.L.25]**interview**   entrevistar, la
   entrevista; **interviewer** el/la
   entrevistador/a
intimate, close   íntimo/a
to introduce   introducir (zc)
introvert   introvertido/a
to invent   inventar; **investigate**
   investigar (gu)
invitation   la invitación
to invite   invitar
to iron   planchar
iron grill   la reja
ironic   irónico/a
island   la isla
It's hot   Hace calor
itinerary   el itinerario

J

jacket   la chaqueta
jeans   los vaqueros/jeans
Jesuit   el jesuita
Jesus   Jesús
jewel, jewelry   la joya; **jewelry** la
   joyería
jogging suit, sweatshirt   la sudadera
to jot down   anotar
journalist, newspaperman/woman
   el/la periodista
joy   la alegría

judge el/la juez
juice el jugo
to jump saltar
jungle la selva, la jungla

K

kept, preserved conservado/a
key la llave
king/queen el rey/la reina
kinship el parentesco
to kiss besar
kitchen la cocina
kitchen sink el fregadero
knee la rodilla
knife el cuchillo
to know saber
to know, meet conocer (zc)

L

laboratory el laboratorio
lack, scarcity la escasez
lake el lago
lamp la lámpara
to land aterrizar (c)
land, soil la tierra
language el idioma
language lab el laboratorio de lenguas
language spoken in Paraguay el guaraní
to last durar; **last, final** último/a
late tarde, atrasado/a
Latin-American latinoamericano/a
laundry room la lavandería
law la ley
lawn el césped
lawyer el/la abogado/a
layer la capa
lazy perezoso/a
lead el plomo
to learn aprender
leather de cuero
to leave (behind), leave dejar, salir (g)
lecture la conferencia
left la izquierda
leg la pierna
legume, vegetable la legumbre
lemon el limón
to lend prestar
length la longitud
lengthy prolongado/a
less than, fewer than menos que
letter la letra [S.L.26]
letter carrier el/la cartero/a
lettuce la lechuga
level el nivel

librarian el/la bibliotecario/a
library la biblioteca
life la vida
light ligero/a
lightly covered with flour enharinado/a
to like caer bien; **you (familiar) like** te gusta(n); **you (formal) like** le gusta(n); **I like** me gusta(n); **I would like . . .** Me gustaría..., Quisiera...
likewise igualmente
liking, taste el gusto
lion el león
lip el labio
to listen, listen (to) escuchar
literature la literatura
little un poco
to live vivir
living room la sala
lobster la langosta
location la localización, la ubicación
to lock up encerrar (ie); **locked up** encerrado/a
lodging el alojamiento
long largo/a
to look (at) mirar
to look for buscar
to look terrible tener mala cara
loose-fitting men's shirt la guayabera
lord el señor
to lose perder (ie)
to lose weight adelgazar (c)
loss la pérdida
lost perdido/a
lot bastante bien
lottery la lotería
to love amar
lover el/la amante
luggage el equipaje
lukewarm tibio/a
lunch el almuerzo
lung el pulmón
luxurious lujoso/a

M

machine máquina; **camera** la máquina fotográfica; **typewriter** máquina de escribir
of Madrid madrileño/a
[S.L.27] magazine la revista
mail por correo
mailbox el buzón
to maintain mantener (g, ie)
the majority la mayoría
to make a reservation reservar
to make a stopover hacer escala

to make the bed hacer la cama
man el hombre
manager el/la gerente (de ventas)
mango el mango
manual el manual
map el mapa
margarine la margarina
marked down rebajado/a
market el mercado
marriage, wedding el matrimonio
married casado/a
marvelous maravilloso/a
masterpiece obra maestra
material el material
mathematics las matemáticas
maximum máximo/a
maybe quizá(s)/tal vez
mayonnaise la mayonesa
meaning el significado
means el medio
meat la carne
medical doctor el/la médico/a
medication, medicine la medicina
meeting, gathering la reunión
melody la melodía
member el/la integrante
memory el recuerdo
menu el menú; **menu, letter** la carta
message el mensaje
method el método
Mexican mexicano/a
Mexican band el mariachi
Mexican liqueur el tequila
microphone el micrófono
microscope el microscopio
microwave oven el (horno) microondas
mile la milla
milk la leche
millennium el milenio
mining *adj.* la minería, minero/a
ministry el ministerio
minus (for telling time) menos
miracle el milagro
mirror el espejo
Miss señorita (Srta.)
missionary el/la misionero/a
mobility la movilidad
model el/la modelo
modern moderno/a
mom la mamá
monetary monetario/a; **monetary unit of Bolivia** el boliviano; **monetary unit of Costa Rica and El Salvador** el colón; **monetary unit of Honduras** el lempira; **monetary unit of Nicaragua** el córdoba; **monetary unit of Panamá** el balboa; **monetary unit of Paraguay;**

monetary unit of Peru nuevo sol;
[S.L.28]**monetary unit of Venezuela**
el bolívar
money el dinero
money, funds los fondos
monster el monstruo
month el mes
Moor el/la moro/a
**more . . . than, . . . -er than (e.g.,
shorter than)** más... que
more or less más o menos
morning la mañana
most la mayor parte
mother la madre; **mother** adj.
materno/a
motive el motivo
motorcycle la moto(cicleta)
mouse el ratón
mouth la boca
to move mover (ue); **move** la
mudanza
movies el cine
Mr. señor (Sr.)
Mrs. señora (Sra.)
much, a lot mucho/a
muscle el músculo
museum el museo
music la música; **background music**
música ambiental
musician el/la músico/a
mustard la mostaza
my mi
my name is . . . me llamo...
mystery el misterio

N

name el nombre
nanny la niñera
napkin la servilleta
narration la narración; **narrator**
el/la narrador/a
narrow, tight estrecho/a
nation la nación
native nativo/a
nature la naturaleza
nausea la náusea
navigable navegable
near (close to) cerca (de)
neck el cuello
necklace el collar
to need hacer falta, necesitar
negative negativo/a
neighbor el/la vecino/a
neighborhood el barrio, el vecindario
neither . . . nor no (ni)... ni
neither, nor, either adv. tampoco
nephew el sobrino
nerve el nervio

nervous nervioso/a
nevertheless sin embargo
new nuevo/a;
[S.L.29] **news** la noticia
newspaper el periódico
next al lado (de)
Nicaraguan nicaragüense
nice agradable; **nice, charming**
simpático/a
niece la sobrina
night adj. nocturno/a
night stand la mesa de noche
nightgown el camisón
noise el ruido
nominated nominado/a
north el norte
nose la nariz
not any, none ninguno/a
not even ni siquiera
to not get along llevarse mal
notable, noteworthy notable; **notably**
notablemente
note, grade la nota
notebook el cuaderno
noun el sustantivo
novel la novela
novelist el/la novelista
now ahora
now and then otra vez [S.L.30]
nowadays hoy en día
number el número
nurse el/la enfermero/a
nutrition la nutrición

O

objective el objetivo, fin de
to obtain, get obtener (g, ie)
of, from de
of course desde luego, ¡Cómo no!,
¡Claro!
of the del (contraction of de + el)
offer la oferta, ofrecer (zc)
office la oficina
oil el aceite
old mayor, viejo/a; **oldest** el/la
mayor
olive la aceituna, oliva: de oliva
on top encima
on, above sobre
once una vez
one adj. solo/a [S.L.31]
onion la cebolla
only adv. sólo
only child hijo/a único/a
open-air market el mercado al aire
libre
opening la vacante
operate operar

operation la operación
opinion la opinión
opportunity la oportunidad
opposite, contrary contrario/a
optimistic adj. optimista
optional optativo/a
orange la naranja
orchestra la orquesta
order el orden; **law and order** el
orden público; **order, command** la
orden, el mandato
organizer el/la organizador/a
orthography la ortografía
of Otavalo, Ecuador otavaleño/a
other, another otro/a; **again**
otra vez
ought to, should deber
our nuestro/a(s)
outdoors al aire libre
outskirts las afueras
outstanding, distinguished destacado/a
over there allá
own propio/a
oxygen oxígeno

P

P.O. box el apartado postal (de
correos)
pacemaker el marcapasos
package el paquete
page la página
painted pintado/a
painter el pintor, el/la pintor/a
painting la pintura
pair el par; **without equal** sin par
pajama el/la piyama
palace el palacio
panic el pánico
pants los pantalones
pantsuit el traje pantalón
pantyhose las pantimedias
papaya la papaya
paper el papel; **switch roles**
cambiar de papel; **play the part**
hacer el papel
parachute el paracaídas
parade el desfile
paragraph el párrafo
Paraguayan paraguayo/a
parents los padres
park el parque
part el repuesto
participant el/la participante;
participate participar; **participation**
la participación
partner, classmate el/la compañero/a
party la fiesta
passenger el/la pasajero/a

passive   pasivo/a
passport   el pasaporte
pastime   el pasatiempo
pastry shop   la pastelería
patient   *n.* el/la paciente
to pay   pagar
payment   el pago
pea   la arveja
pear   la pera
peasant   el/la campesino/a
pencil   el lápiz
peninsula   la península
penning (of bulls)   el encierro (de los toros)
people   la gente
pepper   la pimienta, el ají
percentage   el porcentaje
perfectionist   perfeccionista
to permit, allow   permitir
[S.L.32]perspective   la perspectiva
Peruvian   peruano/a
pessimist   pesimista
petroleum, oil   el petróleo
pharmacist   el/la farmacéutico/a
phase   la fase
philosophy   la filosofía
phobia   la fobia
photo   la foto (grafía)
photocopier   la fotocopiadora
phrase   la frase
physically   físicamente
physics   la física
physiotherapist   el/la fisioterapista
pianist   el/la pianista
to pick up   recoger (j)
picture   el cuadro
pie, cake   el pastel
piece, object   la pieza
pigeonhole   el casillero
pill   la pastilla
pillow   la almohada
pilot   el/la piloto; **to pilot, fly** pilotear
pin   el alfiler
pineapple   la piña
pizza place   la pizzería
place   el lugar; **to take place** tener lugar
plaid   de cuadros
to plan   planear; **plan + verb** pensar + inf.
plan, level   el plano/a
plane   el avión
planet   el planeta
plastic   plástico/a
plates   la placa
play (an instrument)   tocar (un instrumento)
play (game, sport)   jugar (ue)
player   el/la jugador/a

plea   el ruego, la súplica
pleased/nice meet you   mucho gusto
pleasure   el placer
plumber   el/la plomero/a
poem   el poema
poet   el/la poeta
pole   el polo
polemic   la polémica
policeman, policewoman   el policía/la (mujer) policía
political science   las ciencias políticas
politician, political (*adj.*) el/la político/a
politics   la política
polka-dotted   de lunares
polluted, contaminated   contaminado/a
polyester   el poliéster
poor   pobre
popular   popular; **popularity** popularidad
population   la población
pork   el cerdo
portable   portátil
portion   la porción
Portuguese   portugués/a
position   el puesto
positive   positivo/a
post card   la tarjeta postal
potato   la papa
pottery [S.L.33]filled with candies   la piñata
poultry, foul   las aves
pound   la libra
to practice   practicar; **practice, practical** *adj.* la práctica
precious, beautiful   precioso/a
precise time   hora americana/inglesa
precisely   precisamente
precision   la precisión
to prefer   preferir (ie)
pregnant   embarazada
preparation   el preparativo, la preparación
to prepare   preparar
to prescribe   recetar
present time   la actualidad
present, current   actual; **present, here** presente
present, gift   el regalo
preservation   la conservación
to press   apretar (ie)
pressure   la tensión (arterial)
pretty   bonito/a
price   el precio
prince   el príncipe
private   privado/a
probably   probablemente

problem   el problema
procession   la procesión
productivity   la productividad
professor   el/la profesor/a
profile   el perfil
to program   programar; **program** el programa,
to prohibit, forbid   prohibir
prohibition   la prohibición
promise   la promesa
pronoun   el pronombre
protection   la protección
province   la provincia
psychiatrist   el/la psiquiatra
psychologist   el/la (p)sicólogo/a
psychology   la (p)sicología
public   público/a
Puerto Rican   puertorriqueño/a
punctual   puntual
punctuation   la puntuación
purse   la bolsa
to put to bed   acostar (ue); **put on makeup** maquillar(se); **put on** ponerse; **put, turn on** poner (g)

Q

quack doctor   el/la curandero/a
quality   la calidad
quantity, amount   la cantidad
quarter   cuarto
question   la pregunta
quiet   callado/a

R

racket   la raqueta
radiator   el radiador
radio   el/la radio
radio announcer   el/la locutor/a
rail   el riel
rain   la lluvia, llover (ue)
raincoat   el impermeable, la gabardina
rain forest   el bosque tropical
to raise   levantar
raisin   la pasa
Ramadan   el ramadán
rate, interest   la tasa
raw fish dish   el ceviche
to read   leer
ready   dispuesto/a
really   realmente
rearview mirror   el espejo retrovisor
reason   la razón

rebellious   rebelde
receipt   el recibo
recently   *adv.* recién
reception   la recepción; **receptionist**
  el/la recepcionista
recess   el receso
recipe, prescription   la receta
to recommend   recomendar
recycle   reciclar
redhead   pelirrojo/a
to refer   referir(se) (ie, i)
reference   la referencia
refrigerator   el refrigerador
region   la región
relationship   la relación
relatives   los parientes
released   liberado/a
religious   *adj.* religioso/a
remedy   el remedio
to remember   recordar (ue)
to rent   alquilar, el alquiler
reparation, repair   la reparación
reporter   el/la reportero/a
to represent   representar;
  representative el/la
  representante
reproduction   la reproducción
reserve   la reserva
reserved   reservado/a
resident   el/la residente
resource   el recurso
to respect   respetar
responsible   responsable
to rest   descansar; **rest** el descanso, el
  reposo, el resto
restless   inquieto/a
result, outcome   el resultado
résumé   el currículum
to return   volver (ue)
revision, inspection   la revisión
rib   la costilla
rice   el arroz
rich, wealthy   rico/a
to ride   montar; **ride a bicycle**
  montar en bicicleta right (legal) el
  derecho, (direction) la derecha;
  Right? ¿Verdad?
ring   el anillo
risk, danger   el riesgo
river basin   la cuenca
road, way   el camino
robe   la bata
robot   el robot
rock   la roca
rocket   el cohete
roof   el techo
room   la habitación
round trip   de ida y vuelta
ruins   las ruinas
to run   correr

S

to take photos   sacar (qu) fotos
sad   triste
safe and sound   sano/a y salvo/a
safe box   la caja fuerte
safety, security   la seguridad
salad   la ensalada
salad dressing   el aderezo
salary   el sueldo
sale   la rebaja
sales   las ventas
salesman, saleswoman   el/la
  vendedor/a
salesperson   el/la dependiente/a
salt   la sal
Salvadoran   salvadoreño/a
salvation   la salvación
same   *adj.* igual; **same thing** lo
  mismo; **like, same as** al igual que
sample   la muestra
sand   la arena
sandal   la sandalia
sandy   arenoso/a
to save   ahorrar
sawdust   el aserrín
to say, tell   decir (g, i)
scarf   la bufanda
scene   la escena
schedule   el horario
school   *n.* la escuela, *adj.* escolar
sciences   ciencias
scientist   el/la científico/a
sculptor   el/la escultor/a
sea   el mar
seat   el asiento
seaweed   el alga
second   segundo/a
secondary   secundario/a
section   la sección
sedentary   sedentario/a
to see   ver
seed   la pepa, la semilla
to seem   parecer (zc)
selection   la selección
to sell   vender
senator   el/la senador/a
to send   enviar, mandar
sentence   la oración
sentimental   sentimental
separation   la separación
series   la serie
serious   serio/a
seriousness   la gravedad
to serve   servir (i)
to set the table   poner la mesa
set, group,   el conjunto; **joint** *adj.*
  conjunto
severe, serious   severo/a
sex   el sexo

sharp   en punto
to shave   afeitar(se)
she   ella
sheet   la sábana
shellfish   los mariscos
ship/boat   el barco
shirt   la camisa
shoe   el zapato
shop window   el escaparate
shopping center   el centro comercial
short (in length)   corto/a; **short (in
  stature)** bajo/a
short course of studies   el cursillo
shorts   los pantalones cortos
shoulder   el hombro
to show   mostrar (ue); **show** el
  espectáculo
shower   la ducha
shrimp   el camarón; **shrimp (in Spain)**
  la gamba
sick   *adj.* enfermo/a
sign   el letrero
signal   la señal
signature   la firma
silk   la seda
silly, foolish   tonto/a
silver   la plata
similar   semejante
similarity   la semejanza
simply   simplemente
simultaneously   simultáneamente
since   desde, ya que
sincere   sincero/a
to sing   cantar
singer   el/la cantante
single   soltero/a
siren   la sirena
sister   la hermana
to sit down   sentar(se) (ie)
situation, location   la situación
size   el tamaño, la talla
to skate   patinar
to ski   esquiar
skiing, ski   el esquí
skin   la piel
skirt   la falda
sky   el cielo
to sleep   dormir (ue)
sleeping pill   el somnífero
slipper   la zapatilla
slope   el médano, la bajada
slope, court, track   la pista
slowly   despacio
small meat pie   la empanada; **typical
  Bolivian meat pies** empanadas
  salteñas
[S.L.34]small   pequeño/a
smart, ready   listo/a
to smoke   fumar
to sneeze   estornudar

to snow nevar (ie); **snow** la nieve
soap el jabón
soap opera la telenovela
soccer el fútbol
society la sociedad
sociology la sociología
sock el calcetín
soda el refresco
sodium el sodio
sofa el sofá
soft suave
solid color de color entero
solution la solución
to solve resolver (ue)
something algo
son el hijo
song la canción
sorrounding el entorno
soup la sopa
sour agrio/a
south el sur
southeast el sureste
southwest suroeste
space el espacio, *adj.* espacial
spaceship la nave espacial
space shuttle el transbordador espacial
spacious espacioso/a
Spanish el español, *adj.* español/a
Spanish American *adj.* criollo/a
Spanish speaker el/la hispanohablante
sparrow la golondrina
to speak hablar
special especial; **especially** en especial
specialty la especialidad
species la especie
specific determinado/a
to specify, point out especificar (qu)
spectator el/la espectador/a
speed la velocidad
to spend gastar
spice la especia
spinach las espinacas
spirit, disposition el espíritu
spoon la cuchara
spoon(full) la cucharada
sport *adj.* deportivo/a
sportsman/woman el/la deportista
square cuadrado/a
stadium el estadio
stage la etapa
stamp el sello
to stand in line hacer cola
standard estándar [S.L.35]
state, condition el estado
statistic la estadística
steak el bistec
steering wheel el volante

to step on pisar
stepfather el padrastro
stepmother la madrastra
stereo el estéreo
still, yet aún, todavía
stockings, socks las medias
stomach el estómago
stone la piedra
to stop detener (g, ie)
stopping point la escala
store la tienda
story el cuento
stove la estufa
strategy la estrategia
strawberry la fresa
street la calle
stress el estrés
to stretch estirar
striped de rayas
strong fuerte
structure la estructura
student el/la alumno/a, el/la estudiante, *adj.* estudiantil
student's desk el pupitre
studious estudioso/a
to study estudiar; **study, studying** el estudio
style el estilo
subway, meter el metro
suddenly de repente
sugar el/la azúcar
suggestion la sugerencia
suit el traje
suitcase la maleta
summary el resumen; **to summarize** en resumen
summit, top la cima
sun el sol
to sunbathe tomar el sol
sunglasses las gafas de sol
supermarket el supermercado
superstore la megatienda
support el apoyo
surfer el/la surfista
surgeon el/la cirujano/a
to surpass, overcome superar
sweater el suéter
sweep barrer
to swim nadar; **swimming** la natación
swimming pool la piscina
symbol el símbolo; **to symbolize** simbolizar
symptom el síntoma

T

table la mesa
tablecloth el mantel

to take a bath, bathe bañar(se); **take a nap** dormir la siesta; **take a walk, stroll** pasear; **take advantage** aprovechar; **take away, remove** quitar; **take care of** cuidar(se); **take notes** tomar apuntes; **take notes** tomar notas; **take off** despegar, quitar(se); **take, drink** tomar
talent el talento
to talk, converse conversar; **talkative** conversador/a
tall alto/a
tape recorder, cassette player la grabadora
tax el impuesto
team el equipo
to tear romper
teaspoon la cucharadita, la cucharita
technical *adj.* el/la técnico/a; **technician** el/la técnico/a
technique la técnica
technology la tecnología
telepathy la telepatía
telephone el teléfono, el teléfono, *adj.* telefónico/a
television set el televisor
to tell, count contar (ue)
temperament el temperamento
tennis el tenis
tennis player el/la tenista
terrace la terraza
territory el territorio
to terrorize aterrorizar (c)
test, examination el examen
that (*adj.*) ese/a, que
thaw el deshielo
the (contraction of *a + el*) al; **the** lo; **the important thing** lo importante; [S.L.36] [S.L.37] [S.L.38]
[S.L.39]**theater** el teatro
then entonces; **then, after** luego
there ahí, allí
there is, there are hay; **there was, there were** había
thermometer el termómetro
they ellos/ellas; **they, you (plural) are** son
thin delgado/a
thing la cosa
to think pensar (ie)
this este/a, esto
this way así
threaten, menace amenazar (c)
throat la garganta
through a través de
throw lanzar (c)

ticket, passage   el billete, el boleto/ pasaje; ticket for admission   la entrada
tidy   ordenado/a
to tidy up   ordenar
tie   la corbata
tile   el azulejo
time   el rato, el tiempo; free time   tiempo libre
timid   tímido/a
tire   la llanta
tired   cansado/a
title   el título
toast   la tostada
today   hoy
together   juntos/as
toilet   el inodoro
tolerant   tolerante
tomato   el tomate
tomato sauce   la salsa de tomate
tomorrow   mañana
tooth   el diente
torture   la tortura
to touch   tocar
tourist   adj. turístico/a
tournament   el torneo
toward, near   hacia
towel   la toalla
town   el pueblo
toy   el juguete
tradition   la tradición; traditional   tradicional
traffic   el tráfico
train   el tren
training   el entrenamiento
tranquilizer   tranquilizante
to translate   traducir (zc)
transparent   transparente
transportation   el transporte
to travel   viajar; travel agency   la agencia de viajes; travel agent   el/la agente de viajes; traveler's check   el cheque de viajero
tray   la bandeja
tree   el árbol
trophy   el trofeo
tropical   tropical
truck   el camión
true, certain   adv. cierto
trunk   el maletero
trust   la confianza
trustworthy   fiable
to try on   probarse (ue)
T-shirt   la camiseta
tub   la bañadera
tunic   la túnica
tunnel   el túnel
turkey   el guajolote, el pavo
turn, shift   el turno
twin   gemelo/a

to twist   torcer(se) (ue)
type   el género; type, style, kind   el tipo
type of soup   el ajiaco
typical   típico/a, típico/a; typical Catalonian dance   la sardana; typical Chilean music   la cueca; typical Colombian music   el vallenato; typical music of the Dominican Republic   el merengue; typical Panamanian dress   la pollera; typical Peruvian music   la marinera; typical Venezuelan music   el joropo

U

[S.L.40]U
ugly   feo/a
ulcer   la úlcera
umbrella   el paraguas
umpire, referee   el árbitro
uncle   el tío
undecided   indeciso/a
under   debajo (de)
to understand   entender (ie)
unemployed   desempleado/a
unexpected   inesperado
unfinished   inconcluso/a
uniform   el uniforme
union   la unión
united   unido/a
unity   la unidad
university   la universidad, adj. universitario/a
unknown   desconocido/a
unpleasant   antipático/a
urban   urbano/a
urgent   urgente; urgently   urgentemente
Uruguayan   uruguayo/a
to use   usar
used to, accustomed   acostumbrado/a

V

vacation   las vacaciones
to vacuum   pasar la aspiradora; vacuum cleaner   la aspiradora
valley   el valle
valuable   valioso/a
value, price   el valor
vanilla   la vainilla
variable, changeable   variable
variant   la variante
various, several   varios/as
VCR   la videocasetera

vegetable   el vegetal, la verdura
vegetation   la vegetación
vein   la vena
Venezuelan   venezolano/a
verb   el verbo
to verify   verificar (qu)
versatile   versátil
victory   el triunfo
video   el video
view   la vista
vinegar   el vinagre
vineyard   el viñedo
violence   la violencia
violinist   el/la violinista
virgin   la virgen
virtual   virtual
visa   la visa
to visit   visitar
vitality   la vitalidad
vitamin   la vitamina
vocabulary   el vocabulario
voice   la voz
volleyball   el voleibol
volunteer   el/la voluntario/a
to vote   votar

W

waist   la cintura
to wait for, hope, expect   esperar
waiter/waitress   el/la camarero/a
waiting list   la lista de espera
to wake up   despertar(se) (ie)
to walk   caminar; walk   el paseo, la caminata
walker   el/la caminante
wallet   la billetera
to want   querer (ie)
warming   el calentamiento
to wash (oneself)   lavar(se)
washbowl, bathroom sink   el lavabo
washer   la lavadora
wastepaper basket   el cesto
to water   regar (ie); water   el agua, adj. acuático/a
wave   la ola
way   la manera, por cierto
we   nosotros/nosotras
weak   débil
wealth   la riqueza
to wear, take   llevar
to wear a costume   disfrazarse
weaving   el tejido
[S.L.41]wedding   la boda
week   la semana
weekend   el fin de semana
weight   el peso
well   (interj.) pues
what, that which   lo que

What a pity! ¡Qué lástima!, ¡Qué pena!

What is he/she/it like? ¿Cómo es?

What's the weather like? ¿Qué tiempo hace?

What's wrong (with you)? ¿Qué te/le(s) pasa?

What's your name? (familiar) ¿Cómo te llamas?

What's your name? (formal) ¿Cómo se llama usted?

wheat el trigo

wheel la rueda

when *adv.* cuando

where (*interrog.*) dónde

Where (to)? ¿Adónde?

Where is . . . ? ¿Dónde está...?

whether ya sea

while mientras

Who is . . . ? ¿Quién es...?

whose? ¿de quién?

wide ancho/a

widow la viuda

widower el viudo

wife la esposa

will, will power la voluntad

to win ganar

wind el viento

window la ventana, la ventanilla

windshield el parabrisas

windshield wiper el limpiaparabrisas

wine el vino; **red wine** el vino tinto

winner el/la ganador/a

to wish, want desear

with con; **with me** conmigo; **with you (familiar)** contigo

without sin

wood la madera

wool la lana

word la palabra

to work trabajar; **work** la obra; **play** obra de teatro

worker el/la obrero/a

World Wide Web la red

worldwide mundial

to worry preocupar(se)

worse, worst peor

wrist la muñeca

to write escribir

writer el/la escritor/a

Y

year el año

yes sí

yogurt el yogur

you (familiar) tú; **you (formal)** usted; **you (plural)** ustedes; **you, him, it** lo; [S.L.42] [S.L.43] **you are (familiar)** eres, estás; **you are (formal), he/she is** es

young joven; **young man/woman** el/la joven; **youngest** el/la menor

your (familiar) tu

yours, his, hers, theirs suyo(-a, -os, -as)

CREDITS

TEXT CREDITS

p. 48: "Un buen repaso a la Universidad de Salamanca" reprinted with permission from Alberto López Nájera; **p. 79:** ® All Rights Reserved by World Editors, Inc.; **p. 457:** "El cielo puede esperar" from Quo magazine N° 8. Reprinted with permission from Quo—H F Revistas.

PHOTO CREDITS

p. 2 © Robert Frerck/Odyssey/Chicago; p. 5 (top) Ian O'Leary; p. 5 (center) Copyright © 2004 by Robert Frerck and Odyssey Productions, Inc. p. 22 © Robert Frerck/Odyssey/Chicago; p. 24 (top) Robert Frerck; p. 24 (center) © Robert Fried / robertfriedphotography.com; p. 28 Robert Frerck; p. 51 PETER MENZEL PHOTOGRAPY; p. 51 (top) © Robert Frerck/Odyssey/Chicago; p. 51 (center) Jeremy Horner; p. 52 (top) John Morrison; p. 52 (center) Charles Graham; p. 53 (top) John Wood; p. 53 (center/left) Joanna B. Pinneo; p. 58 Courtesy of the Library of Congress; p. 60 (top) © Jimmy Dorantes/Latin Focus.com; p. 61 (bottom) EyeWire Collection; p. 65 Ryan McVay; p. 65 CHABRUKEN; p. 79 © World Editors; p. 85 (center/right) Robert Brenner; p. 85 (middle) Tony Freeman; p. 85 (center/left) Getty Images, Inc.; p. 86 John Neubauer; p. 86 (top) Andrea Booher; p. 86 Jeff Greenberg; p. 87 (bottom) Angelo Cavalli; p. 92 Tony Freeman; p. 94 (center) Nik Wheeler; p. 94 (bottom) Robert Frerck; p. 95 © Bob Daemmrich/PhotoEdit; p. 98 (top/left) © Latin Focus.com; p. 98 (top/right) © Latin Focus.com; p. 98 (center) Ian O'Leary © Dorling Kindersley; p. 101 Kevin Schafer; p. 116 Bill Pogue; p. 121 (top) Myrleen Ferguson Cate; p. 121 (center) Russell, Nicolas; p. 121 (bottom) Reuters/Silva Izquierdo; p. 122 (bottom) Robert Frerck; p. 123 (top/right) William Albert Allard/NGS Image Collection; p. 123 (top/left) Ernesto Rios; p. 128 Myrleen Ferguson; p. 130 (top) N. Frank; p. 130 (center) K. McGlynn; p. 152 Mary Kate Denny; p. 153 Bruce Ayres; p. 157 (top) Tony Freeman; p. 157 (center/left) Robert Harbison; p. 157 (center/right) Tony Freeman; p. 157 (bottom) Rachel Epstein; p. 159 (top/right) Peter Menzel;

p. 159 (top/left); David Ashby © Dorling Kindersley; p. 164 Anna Elias; p. 166 (top) © Chip and Rosa Maria de la Cueva Peterson; p. 197 (top/left) Mahaux Photography; p. 197 (top/right) Philippe Colombi; p. 197 (bottom right) Rob Lewine; p. 198 (bottom left) Nik Wheeler; p. 199 (top left) Rob Crandall; p. 199 (top right) [Photographer's Name]/NGS Image Collection; p. 204 © David Allen/CORBIS; p. 209 Ulrike Welsch; p. 210 David J. Sams/Texas Inprint; p. 235 (top) Rob Crandall; p. 235 (center) Beryl Goldberg; p. 235 (bottom) Silva, Juan; p. 236 (bottom left) Rob Crandall; p. 237 (top) Syndicated Features/Topham Picture Point; p. 237 (top center) Yann Arthus-Betrand; p. 244 (top) Marcos Brindicci/Reuters; p. 244 (center) Bill Bachmann; p. 244 (bottom) Reuters/Sam Mircovich; p. 269 (top left) CARL SCHNEIDER; p. 269 (top right) David Young-Wolff; p. 269 (center left) Tony Freeman; p. 269 (center right) Carrie Beecroft; p. 271 L. Mangino; p. 273 (top) Claudia Daut/Reuters; p. 273 (center left) Chad Ehlers; p. 273 (center/right) © Latin Focus.com; p. 273 (bottom) © Ricardo Barbato/Latin Focus.com; p. 274 (center/right) Daniel Rivademar; p. 274 (center left) © Russell Gordon/Odyssey/ Chicago; p. 275 (top left) Jos? Fust? Raga; p. 275 George Haling; p. 275 (top right) Mula–Eshet; p. 275 (center) © Wolfgang Kaehler www.wkaehlerphoto.com; p. 313 Betrahd Demee; p. 280 A. Ramey; p. 282 (top) Owen Franken; p. 282 (center) © Robert Frerck/Odyssey/Chicago; p. 282 (bottom) Joe Viesti; p. 283 (top) Jeremy Horner; p. 283 (center) © Robert Frerck/Odyssey/Chicago; p. 283 (bottom) Larry Mangino; p. 287 Pascal Le Segretain; p. 306 (top) © Robert Frerck/Odyssey/Chicago; p. 306 (center) Charles Lenars; p. 306 (bottom) Terrance Klassen; p. 311 (top) Garry Adams; p. 311 (center) Nik Wheeler; p. 311 (bottom) Copyright © 2004 by Robert Frerck and Odyssey Productions, Inc.; p. 312 (center left) David R. Frazier; p. 312 (center right) Ken Welsh; p. 312 (bottom) Will & Deni McIntyre; p. 313 (top right) Steve Vidler; p. 313 (center) Patricia Jordan; p. 313 (bottom) © Robert Frerck/Odyssey/Chicago; p. 318 Kaluzny/Thatcher; p. 320 (top)

Michael Newman; p. 320 (bottom) Ed Lallo; p. 321 (top left) © Robert Frerck/Odyssey/Chicago; p. 321 (top right) Bob Daemmrich; p. 321 (center left) Rob Crandall; p. 321 Elena Rooraid; p. 345 Gordon, Larry Dale; p. 349 (top right) Tony Freeman; p. 349 (center left) Tony Freeman; p. 349 (center right) Lawrence Migdale; p. 349 (bottom right) Mark Harvey; p. 350 (bottom right) © Fernando Pastene/Latin Focus.com; p. 351 (top right) Lea; p. 351 (center left) Walter Bibikow; p. 356 Charles Sleicher; p. 362 (top left) © Robert Frerck/ Odyssey/Chicago; p. 362 (top right) © Robert Frerck/Odyssey/Chicago; p. 362 (bottom left) Jeremy Horner; p. 379 JENNY MILLS; p. 385 Bill Cardoni; p. 385 (top right) © Robert Frerck/Odyssey/Chicago; p. 385 (center right) © Jeremy Horner/CORBIS; p. 386 Aldo Brando; p. 387 (top left) © Hubert Stadler/CORBIS; p. 387 (top right) © Ken Laffal; p. 387 (center right) Jeremy Horner; p. 392 Jose' L. Pelaez; p. 398 Amy Etra; p. 399 (top right) Paul Smith; p. 399 (bottom right) David R. Frazier; p. 423 (center right) Beryl Goldberg; p. 423 (bottom right) Adalberto Rios; p. 424 Jose' Fuste Raga; p. 424 (bottom right) Angelo Cavalli; p. 425 (top right) Joe Viesti; p. 425 (bottom left) Joe Viesti; p. 425 (bottom right) Kevin O'Hara; p. 430 Tom McCarthy; p. 432 (top) Claudia Dhimitri; p. 432 (center) John F. Mason; p. 432 (bottom) Michele Burgess; p. 461 (top right) David Young-Wolff; p. 461 (center left) Mary Altier; p. 461 (center) Pedro Coll; p. 461 (bottom right) © Steve Starr/Corbis; p. 462 Ken Welsh; p. 462 Sarah Stone; p. 462 J.G. Fuller; p. 463 Wolfgang Kaehler; p. 463 HIRB; p. 463 Ken Gillham

Cover image

Antonio Gaudi y Cornet. Mosaics in Park Guell, Barcelona. Mosaics made from ceramic pieces set into concrete stand by the stairway in Gaudi's Park Guell, Barcelona, Spain. Date created: 1900–1914. Photographer: Charles Lenars.

D.F. Repro.duction authorized by the Instituto Nacional de Bellas Artes y Literatura.CNAC/MNAM/Dist. Reunion des Musees Nationaux/Art Resource, NY

INDEX OF LANGUAGE FUNCTIONS

INDEX